D1612228

16.95

Toyota
Celica
FWD
Automotive
Repair
Manual

by Larry Warren
and John H Haynes
Member of the Guild of Motoring Writers

Models covered:
All Toyota Celica front wheel drive models
1986 through 1993
Does not include all-wheel drive information

(1Y6 - 92020)
(2038)

ABCDE
FGHIJ
KL

Haynes Publishing Group
Sparkford Nr Yeovil
Somerset BA22 7JJ England

Haynes North America, Inc
861 Lawrence Drive
Newbury Park
California 91320 USA

Acknowledgements

We are grateful for the help and cooperation of the Toyota Motor Corporation for their assistance with technical information, certain illustrations and vehicle photos. The Champion Spark Plug Company supplied the illustrations of various spark plug conditions. Technical writers who contributed to this project include Alan Ahlstrand, J.J. Haynes and Doug Nelson.

© **Haynes North America, Inc.   1992, 1995**
With permission from J.H. Haynes & Co. Ltd.

A book in the Haynes Automotive Repair Manual Series

Printed in the U.S.A.

ISBN 1 56392 210 X

Library of Congress Catalog Card Number 95-82333

Contents

1992 Toyota Celica convertible

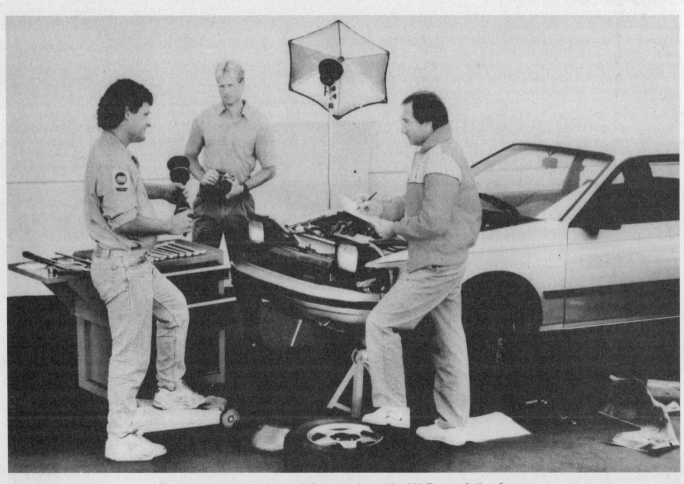

Haynes mechanic, author and photographer with 1987 Toyota Celica Coupe

About this manual

Its purpose

The purpose of this manual is to help you get the best value from your vehicle. It can do so in several ways. It can help you decide what work must be done, even if you choose to have it done by a dealer service department or a repair shop; it provides information and procedures for routine maintenance and servicing; and it offers diagnostic and repair procedures to follow when trouble occurs.

We hope you use the manual to tackle the work yourself. For many simpler jobs, doing it yourself may be quicker than arranging an appointment to get the vehicle into a shop and making the trips to leave it and pick it up. More importantly, a lot of money can be saved by avoiding the expense the shop must pass on to you to cover its labor and overhead costs. An added benefit is the sense of satisfaction and accomplishment that you feel after doing the job yourself.

Using the manual

The manual is divided into Chapters. Each Chapter is divided into numbered Sections, which are headed in bold type between horizontal lines. Each Section consists of consecutively numbered paragraphs.

At the beginning of each numbered Section you will be referred to any illustrations which apply to the procedures in that Section. The reference numbers used in illustration captions pinpoint the pertinent Section and the Step within that Section. That is, illustration 3.2 means the illustration refers to Section 3 and Step (or paragraph) 2 within that Section.

Procedures, once described in the text, are not normally repeated. When it's necessary to refer to another Chapter, the reference will be given as Chapter and Section number. Cross references given without use of the word "Chapter" apply to Sections and/or paragraphs in the same Chapter. For example, "see Section 8" means in the same Chapter.

References to the left or right side of the vehicle assume you are sitting in the driver's seat, facing forward.

Even though we have prepared this manual with extreme care, neither the publisher nor the author can accept responsibility for any errors in, or omissions from, the information given.

NOTE

A Note provides information necessary to properly complete a procedure or information which will make the procedure easier to understand.

CAUTION

A Caution provides a special procedure or special steps which must be taken while completing the procedure where the Caution is found. Not heeding a Caution can result in damage to the assembly being worked on.

WARNING

A Warning provides a special procedure or special steps which must be taken while completing the procedure where the Warning is found. Not heeding a Warning can result in personal injury.

Introduction to the Toyota Celica

Toyota Celica models are available in two-door sedan and liftback body styles.

The transversely mounted inline four-cylinder engines used in these models are equipped with electronic fuel injection.

The engine drives the front wheels through either a five-speed manual or a three- or four-speed automatic transaxle via independent driveaxles.

Independent suspension, featuring coil spring/strut damper units, is used on all four wheels. The power-assisted rack and pinion steering unit is mounted behind the engine.

The brakes are disc at the front with either drum or discs at the rear, depending on model, with power assist standard.

Vehicle identification numbers

Modifications are a continuing and unpublicized process in vehicle manufacturing. Since spare parts manuals and lists are compiled on a numerical basis, the individual vehicle numbers are essential to correctly identify the component required.

Vehicle Identification Number (VIN)

This very important identification number is stamped on the firewall in the engine compartment and on a plate attached to the dashboard inside the windshield on the driver's side of the vehicle **(see illustration)**. The VIN also appears on the Vehicle Certificate of Title and Registration. It contains information such as where and when the vehicle was manufactured, the model year and the body style.

Manufacturer's plate

The manufacturer's plate is attached to the firewall in the engine compartment **(see illustration)**. The plate contains the name of the manufacturer, the month and year of production, the Gross Vehicle Weight Rating (GVWR), the Gross Axle Weight Rating (GAWR) and the certification statement.

Engine numbers

The engine code numbers can be found in a variety of locations, depending on engine type **(see illustrations)**.

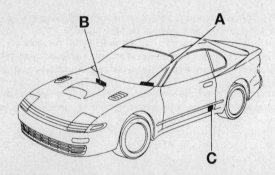

Important ID numbers and other information can be found in several locations on the vehicle

A   *Vehicle Identification Number (visible through the driver's side of the windshield)*
B   *Manufacturer's plate*
C   *Certification regulation label*

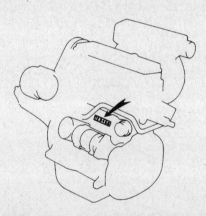

Location of the engine identification number - 2S-E engine

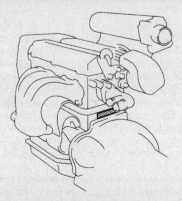

Location of the engine identification number - 3S-FE, 3S-GE, 3S-GTE and 5S-FE engines

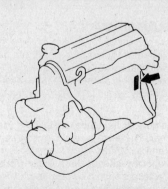

Location of the engine identification number - 4A-FE engine

Buying parts

Replacement parts are available from many sources, which generally fall into one of two categories - authorized dealer parts departments and independent retail auto parts stores. Our advice concerning these parts is as follows:

Retail auto parts stores: Good auto parts stores will stock frequently needed components which wear out relatively fast, such as clutch components, exhaust systems, brake parts, tune-up parts, etc. These stores often supply new or reconditioned parts on an exchange basis, which can save a considerable amount of money. Discount auto parts stores are often very good places to buy materials and parts needed for general vehicle maintenance such as oil, grease, filters, spark plugs, belts, touch-up paint, bulbs, etc. They also usually sell tools and general accessories, have convenient hours, charge lower prices and can often be found not far from home.

Authorized dealer parts department: This is the best source for parts which are unique to the vehicle and not generally available elsewhere (such as major engine parts, transmission parts, trim pieces, etc.).

Warranty information: If the vehicle is still covered under warranty, be sure that any replacement parts purchased - regardless of the source - do not invalidate the warranty!

To be sure of obtaining the correct parts, have engine and chassis numbers available and, if possible, take the old parts along for positive identification.

Maintenance techniques, tools and working facilities

Maintenance techniques

There are a number of techniques involved in maintenance and repair that will be referred to throughout this manual. Application of these techniques will enable the home mechanic to be more efficient, better organized and capable of performing the various tasks properly, which will ensure that the repair job is thorough and complete.

Fasteners

Fasteners are nuts, bolts, studs and screws used to hold two or more parts together. There are a few things to keep in mind when working with fasteners. Almost all of them use a locking device of some type, either a lockwasher, locknut, locking tab or thread adhesive. All threaded fasteners should be clean and straight, with undamaged threads and undamaged corners on the hex head where the wrench fits. Develop the habit of replacing all damaged nuts and bolts with new ones. Special locknuts with nylon or fiber inserts can only be used once. If they are removed, they lose their locking ability and must be replaced with new ones.

Rusted nuts and bolts should be treated with a penetrating fluid to ease removal and prevent breakage. Some mechanics use turpentine in a spout-type oil can, which works quite well. After applying the rust penetrant, let it work for a few minutes before trying to loosen the nut or bolt. Badly rusted fasteners may have to be chiseled or sawed off or removed with a special nut breaker, available at tool stores.

If a bolt or stud breaks off in an assembly, it can be drilled and removed with a special tool commonly available for this purpose. Most automotive machine shops can perform this task, as well as other repair procedures, such as the repair of threaded holes that have been stripped out.

Flat washers and lockwashers, when removed from an assembly, should always be replaced exactly as removed. Replace any damaged washers with new ones. Never use a lockwasher on any soft metal surface (such as aluminum), thin sheet metal or plastic.

Fastener sizes

For a number of reasons, automobile manufacturers are making wider and wider use of metric fasteners. Therefore, it is important to be able to tell the difference between standard (sometimes called U.S. or SAE) and metric hardware, since they cannot be interchanged.

All bolts, whether standard or metric, are sized according to diameter, thread pitch and length. For example, a standard 1/2 - 13 x 1 bolt is 1/2 inch in diameter, has 13 threads per inch and is 1 inch long. An M12 - 1.75 x 25 metric bolt is 12 mm in diameter, has a thread pitch of 1.75 mm (the distance between threads) and is 25 mm long. The two bolts are nearly identical, and easily confused, but they are not interchangeable.

In addition to the differences in diameter, thread pitch and length, metric and standard bolts can also be distinguished by examining the bolt heads. To begin with, the distance across the flats on a standard bolt head is measured in inches, while the same dimension on a metric bolt is sized in millimeters (the same is true for nuts). As a result, a standard wrench should not be used on a metric bolt and a metric wrench should not be used on a standard bolt. Also, most standard bolts have slashes radiating out from the center of the head to denote the grade or strength of the bolt, which is an indication of the amount of torque that can be applied to it. The greater the number of slashes, the greater the strength of the bolt. Grades 0 through 5 are commonly used on automobiles. Metric bolts have a property class (grade) number, rather than a slash, molded into their heads to indicate bolt strength. In this case, the higher the number, the stronger the bolt. Property class numbers 8.8, 9.8 and 10.9 are commonly used on automobiles.

Strength markings can also be used to distinguish standard hex nuts from metric hex nuts. Many standard nuts have dots stamped into one side, while metric nuts are marked with a number. The greater the number of dots, or the higher the number, the greater the strength of the nut.

Metric studs are also marked on their ends according to property class (grade). Larger studs are numbered (the same as metric bolts), while smaller studs carry a geometric code to denote grade.

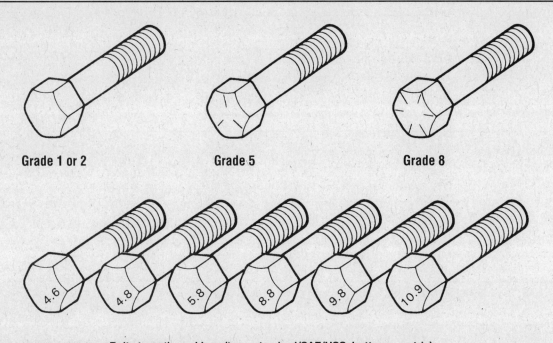

Bolt strength markings (top - standard/SAE/USS; bottom - metric)

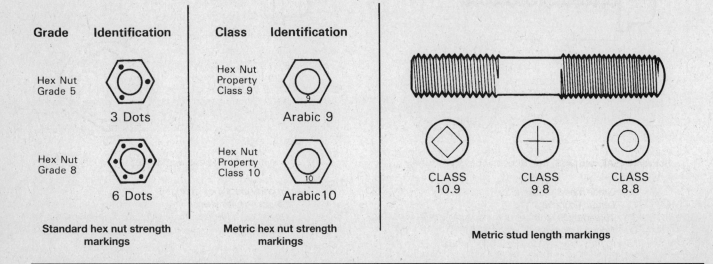

Standard hex nut strength markings

Metric hex nut strength markings

Metric stud length markings

It should be noted that many fasteners, especially Grades 0 through 2, have no distinguishing marks on them. When such is the case, the only way to determine whether it is standard or metric is to measure the thread pitch or compare it to a known fastener of the same size.

Standard fasteners are often referred to as SAE, as opposed to metric. However, it should be noted that SAE technically refers to a non-metric fine thread fastener only. Coarse thread non#metric fasteners are referred to as USS sizes.

Since fasteners of the same size (both standard and metric) may have different strength ratings, be sure to reinstall any bolts, studs or nuts removed from your vehicle in their original locations. Also, when replacing a fastener with a new one, make sure that the new one has a strength rating equal to or greater than the original.

Tightening sequences and procedures

Most threaded fasteners should be tightened to a specific torque value (torque is the twisting force applied to a threaded component such as a nut or bolt). Overtightening the fastener can weaken it and cause it to break, while undertightening can cause it to eventually come loose. Bolts, screws and studs, depending on the material they are made of and their thread diameters, have specific torque values, many of which are noted in the Specifications at the beginning of each Chapter. Be sure to follow the torque recommendations closely. For fasteners not assigned a specific torque, a general torque value chart is presented here as a guide. These torque values are for dry (unlubricated) fasteners threaded into steel or cast iron (not aluminum). As was previously mentioned, the size and grade of a fastener determine

Metric thread sizes	Ft-lbs	Nm
M-6	6 to 9	9 to 12
M-8	14 to 21	19 to 28
M-10	28 to 40	38 to 54
M-12	50 to 71	68 to 96
M-14	80 to 140	109 to 154

Pipe thread sizes		
1/8	5 to 8	7 to 10
1/4	12 to 18	17 to 24
3/8	22 to 33	30 to 44
1/2	25 to 35	34 to 47

U.S. thread sizes		
1/4 - 20	6 to 9	9 to 12
5/16 - 18	12 to 18	17 to 24
5/16 - 24	14 to 20	19 to 27
3/8 - 16	22 to 32	30 to 43
3/8 - 24	27 to 38	37 to 51
7/16 - 14	40 to 55	55 to 74
7/16 - 20	40 to 60	55 to 81
1/2 - 13	55 to 80	75 to 108

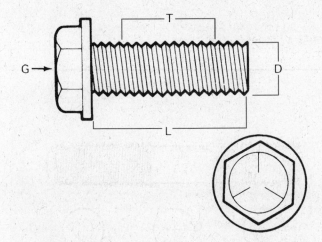

Standard (SAE and USS) bolt dimensions/grade marks

G   Grade marks (bolt length)
L   Length (in inches)
T   Thread pitch (number of threads per inch)
D   Nominal diameter (in inches)

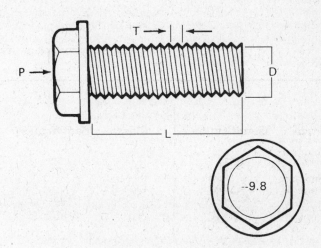

Metric bolt dimensions/grade marks

P   Property class (bolt strength)
L   Length (in millimeters)
T   Thread pitch (distance between threads in millimeters)
D   Diameter

the amount of torque that can safely be applied to it. The figures listed here are approximate for Grade 2 and Grade 3 fasteners. Higher grades can tolerate higher torque values.

Fasteners laid out in a pattern, such as cylinder head bolts, oil pan bolts, differential cover bolts, etc., must be loosened or tightened in sequence to avoid warping the component. This sequence will normally be shown in the appropriate Chapter. If a specific pattern is not given, the following procedures can be used to prevent warping.

Initially, the bolts or nuts should be assembled finger-tight only. Next, they should be tightened one full turn each, in a criss-cross or diagonal pattern. After each one has been tightened one full turn, return to the first one and tighten them all one-half turn, following the same pattern. Finally, tighten each of them one-quarter turn at a time until each fastener has been tightened to the proper torque. To loosen and remove the fasteners, the procedure would be reversed.

Component disassembly

Component disassembly should be done with care and purpose to help ensure that the parts go back together properly. Always keep track of the sequence in which parts are removed. Make note of special characteristics or marks on parts that can be installed more than one way, such as a grooved thrust washer on a shaft. It is a good idea to lay the disassembled parts out on a clean surface in the order that they were removed. It may also be helpful to make sketches or take instant photos of components before removal.

When removing fasteners from a component, keep track of their locations. Sometimes threading a bolt back in a part, or putting the washers and nut back on a stud, can prevent mix-ups later. If nuts and bolts cannot be returned to their original locations, they should be kept in a compartmented box or a series of small boxes. A cupcake or muffin tin is ideal for this purpose, since each cavity can hold the bolts and nuts from a particular area (i.e. oil pan bolts, valve cover bolts, engine mount bolts, etc.). A pan of this type is especially helpful when working on assemblies with very small parts, such as the carburetor, alternator, valve train or interior dash and trim pieces. The cavities can be marked with paint or tape to identify the contents.

Whenever wiring looms, harnesses or connectors are separated, it is a good idea to identify the two halves with numbered pieces of masking tape so they can be easily reconnected.

Gasket sealing surfaces

Throughout any vehicle, gaskets are used to seal the mating surfaces between two parts and keep lubricants, fluids, vacuum or pressure contained in an assembly.

Many times these gaskets are coated with a liquid or paste-type gasket sealing compound before assembly. Age, heat and pressure can sometimes cause the two parts to stick together so tightly that they are very difficult to separate. Often, the assembly can be loosened by striking it with a soft-face hammer near the mating surfaces. A regular hammer can be used if a block of wood is placed between the hammer and the part. Do not hammer on cast parts or parts that could be easily damaged. With any particularly stubborn part, always recheck to make sure that every fastener has been removed.

Avoid using a screwdriver or bar to pry apart an assembly, as they can easily mar the gasket sealing surfaces of the parts, which must remain smooth. If prying is absolutely necessary, use an old broom handle, but keep in mind that extra clean up will be necessary if the wood splinters.

After the parts are separated, the old gasket must be carefully scraped off and the gasket surfaces cleaned. Stubborn gasket material can be soaked with rust penetrant or treated with a special chemical to soften it so it can be easily scraped off. A scraper can be fashioned from a piece of copper tubing by flattening and sharpening one end. Copper is recommended because it is usually softer than the surfaces to be scraped, which reduces the chance of gouging the part. Some gaskets can be removed with a wire brush, but regardless of the method used, the mating surfaces must be left clean and smooth. If for some reason the gasket surface is gouged, then a gasket sealer thick enough to fill scratches will have to be used during reassembly of the components. For most applications, a non-drying (or semi-drying) gasket sealer should be used.

Hose removal tips

Warning: *If the vehicle is equipped with air conditioning, do not disconnect any of the A/C hoses without first having the system depressurized by a dealer service department or a service station.*

Hose removal precautions closely parallel gasket removal precautions. Avoid scratching or gouging the surface that the hose mates against or the connection may leak. This is especially true for radiator hoses. Because of various chemical reactions, the rubber in hoses can bond itself to the metal spigot that the hose fits over. To remove a hose, first loosen the hose clamps that secure it to the spigot. Then, with slip-joint pliers, grab the hose at the clamp and rotate it around the spigot. Work it back and forth until it is completely free, then pull it off. Silicone or other lubricants will ease removal if they can be applied between the hose and the outside of the spigot. Apply the same lubricant to the inside of the hose and the outside of the spigot to simplify installation.

As a last resort (and if the hose is to be replaced with a new one anyway), the rubber can be slit with a knife and the hose peeled from the spigot. If this must be done, be careful that the metal connection is not damaged.

If a hose clamp is broken or damaged, do not reuse it. Wire-type clamps usually weaken with age, so it is a good idea to replace them with screw-type clamps whenever a hose is removed.

Tools

A selection of good tools is a basic requirement for anyone who plans to maintain and repair his or her own vehicle. For the owner who has few tools, the initial investment might seem high, but when compared to the spiraling costs of professional auto maintenance and repair, it is a wise one.

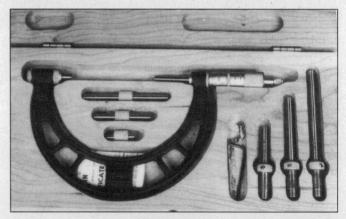

Micrometer set

Dial indicator set

Dial caliper

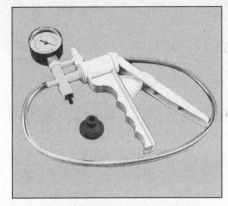

Hand-operated vacuum pump

Timing light

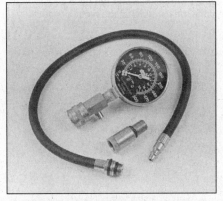

Compression gauge with spark plug hole adapter

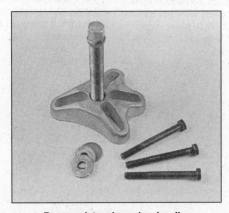

Damper/steering wheel puller

General purpose puller

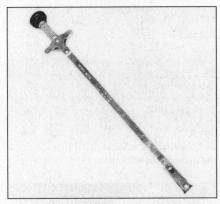

Hydraulic lifter removal tool

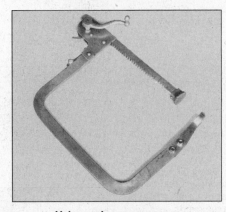

Valve spring compressor

Valve spring compressor

Ridge reamer

Piston ring groove cleaning tool

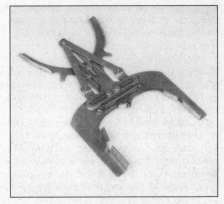

Ring removal/installation tool

Ring compressor

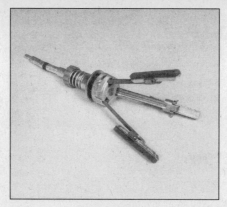

Cylinder hone

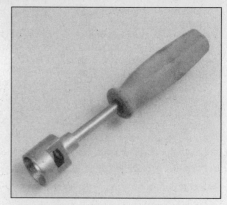

Brake hold-down spring tool

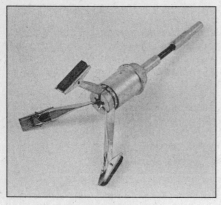

Brake cylinder hone

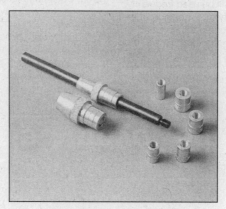

Clutch plate alignment tool

Tap and die set

To help the owner decide which tools are needed to perform the tasks detailed in this manual, the following tool lists are offered: Maintenance and minor repair, Repair/overhaul and Special.

The newcomer to practical mechanics should start off with the maintenance and minor repair tool kit, which is adequate for the simpler jobs performed on a vehicle. Then, as confidence and experience grow, the owner can tackle more difficult tasks, buying additional tools as they are needed. Eventually the basic kit will be expanded into the repair and overhaul tool set. Over a period of time, the experienced do-it-yourselfer will assemble a tool set complete enough for most repair and overhaul procedures and will add tools from the special category when it is felt that the expense is justified by the frequency of use.

Maintenance and minor repair tool kit

The tools in this list should be considered the minimum required for performance of routine maintenance, servicing and minor repair work. We recommend the purchase of combination wrenches (box-end and open-end combined in one wrench). While more expensive than open end wrenches, they offer the advantages of both types of wrench.

Combination wrench set (1/4-inch to 1 inch or 6 mm to 19 mm)
Adjustable wrench, 8 inch
Spark plug wrench with rubber insert
Spark plug gap adjusting tool
Feeler gauge set
Brake bleeder wrench
Standard screwdriver (5/16-inch x 6 inch)
Phillips screwdriver (No. 2 x 6 inch)
Combination pliers - 6 inch
Hacksaw and assortment of blades
Tire pressure gauge
Grease gun
Oil can
Fine emery cloth
Wire brush
Battery post and cable cleaning tool
Oil filter wrench

Funnel (medium size)
Safety goggles
Jackstands (2)
Drain pan

Note: *If basic tune-ups are going to be part of routine maintenance, it will be necessary to purchase a good quality stroboscopic timing light and combination tachometer/dwell meter. Although they are included in the list of special tools, it is mentioned here because they are absolutely necessary for tuning most vehicles properly.*

Repair and overhaul tool set

These tools are essential for anyone who plans to perform major repairs and are in addition to those in the maintenance and minor repair tool kit. Included is a comprehensive set of sockets which, though expensive, are invaluable because of their versatility, especially when various extensions and drives are available. We recommend the 1/2-inch drive over the 3/8-inch drive. Although the larger drive is bulky and more expensive, it has the capacity of accepting a very wide range of large sockets. Ideally, however, the mechanic should have a 3/8-inch drive set and a 1/2-inch drive set.

Socket set(s)
Reversible ratchet
Extension - 10 inch
Universal joint
Torque wrench (same size drive as sockets)
Ball peen hammer - 8 ounce
Soft-face hammer (plastic/rubber)
Standard screwdriver (1/4-inch x 6 inch)
Standard screwdriver (stubby - 5/16-inch)
Phillips screwdriver (No. 3 x 8 inch)
Phillips screwdriver (stubby - No. 2)
Pliers - vise grip
Pliers - lineman's
Pliers - needle nose
Pliers - snap-ring (internal and external)

Cold chisel - 1/2-inch
Scribe
Scraper (made from flattened copper tubing)
Centerpunch
Pin punches (1/16, 1/8, 3/16-inch)
Steel rule/straightedge - 12 inch
Allen wrench set (1/8 to 3/8-inch or 4 mm to 10 mm)
A selection of files
Wire brush (large)
Jackstands (second set)
Jack (scissor or hydraulic type)

Note: Another tool which is often useful is an electric drill with a chuck capacity of 3/8-inch and a set of good quality drill bits

Special tools

The tools in this list include those which are not used regularly, are expensive to buy, or which need to be used in accordance with their manufacturer's instructions. Unless these tools will be used frequently, it is not very economical to purchase many of them. A consideration would be to split the cost and use between yourself and a friend or friends. In addition, most of these tools can be obtained from a tool rental shop on a temporary basis.

This list primarily contains only those tools and instruments widely available to the public, and not those special tools produced by the vehicle manufacturer for distribution to dealer service departments. Occasionally, references to the manufacturer's special tools are included in the text of this manual. Generally, an alternative method of doing the job without the special tool is offered. However, sometimes there is no alternative to their use. Where this is the case, and the tool cannot be purchased or borrowed, the work should be turned over to the dealer service department or an automotive repair shop.

Valve spring compressor
Piston ring groove cleaning tool
Piston ring compressor
Piston ring installation tool
Cylinder compression gauge
Cylinder ridge reamer
Cylinder surfacing hone
Cylinder bore gauge
Micrometers and/or dial calipers
Hydraulic lifter removal tool
Balljoint separator
Universal-type puller
Impact screwdriver
Dial indicator set
Stroboscopic timing light (inductive pick-up)
Hand operated vacuum/pressure pump
Tachometer/dwell meter
Universal electrical multimeter
Cable hoist
Brake spring removal and installation tools
Floor jack

Buying tools

For the do-it-yourselfer who is just starting to get involved in vehicle maintenance and repair, there are a number of options available when purchasing tools. If maintenance and minor repair is the extent of the work to be done, the purchase of individual tools is satisfactory. If, on the other hand, extensive work is planned, it would be a good idea to purchase a modest tool set from one of the large retail chain stores. A set can usually be bought at a substantial savings over the individual tool prices, and they often come with a tool box. As additional tools are needed, add-on sets, individual tools and a larger tool box can be purchased to expand the tool selection. Building a tool set gradually allows the cost of the tools to be spread over a longer period of time and gives the mechanic the freedom to choose only those tools that will actually be used.

Tool stores will often be the only source of some of the special tools that are needed, but regardless of where tools are bought, try to avoid cheap ones, especially when buying screwdrivers and sockets, because they won't last very long. The expense involved in replacing cheap tools will eventually be greater than the initial cost of quality tools.

Care and maintenance of tools

Good tools are expensive, so it makes sense to treat them with respect. Keep them clean and in usable condition and store them properly when not in use. Always wipe off any dirt, grease or metal chips before putting them away. Never leave tools lying around in the work area. Upon completion of a job, always check closely under the hood for tools that may have been left there so they won't get lost during a test drive.

Some tools, such as screwdrivers, pliers, wrenches and sockets, can be hung on a panel mounted on the garage or workshop wall, while others should be kept in a tool box or tray. Measuring instruments, gauges, meters, etc. must be carefully stored where they cannot be damaged by weather or impact from other tools.

When tools are used with care and stored properly, they will last a very long time. Even with the best of care, though, tools will wear out if used frequently. When a tool is damaged or worn out, replace it. Subsequent jobs will be safer and more enjoyable if you do.

Working facilities

Not to be overlooked when discussing tools is the workshop. If anything more than routine maintenance is to be carried out, some sort of suitable work area is essential.

It is understood, and appreciated, that many home mechanics do not have a good workshop or garage available, and end up removing an engine or doing major repairs outside. It is recommended, however, that the overhaul or repair be completed under the cover of a roof.

A clean, flat workbench or table of comfortable working height is an absolute necessity. The workbench should be equipped with a vise that has a jaw opening of at least four inches.

As mentioned previously, some clean, dry storage space is also required for tools, as well as the lubricants, fluids, cleaning solvents, etc. which soon become necessary.

Sometimes waste oil and fluids, drained from the engine or cooling system during normal maintenance or repairs, present a disposal problem. To avoid pouring them on the ground or into a sewage system, pour the used fluids into large containers, seal them with caps and take them to an authorized disposal site or recycling center. Plastic jugs, such as old antifreeze containers, are ideal for this purpose.

Always keep a supply of old newspapers and clean rags available. Old towels are excellent for mopping up spills. Many mechanics use rolls of paper towels for most work because they are readily available and disposable. To help keep the area under the vehicle clean, a large cardboard box can be cut open and flattened to protect the garage or shop floor.

Whenever working over a painted surface, such as when leaning over a fender to service something under the hood, always cover it with an old blanket or bedspread to protect the finish. Vinyl covered pads, made especially for this purpose, are available at auto parts stores.

Jacking and towing

Jacking

Warning: *The jack supplied with the vehicle should only be used for changing a tire or placing jackstands under the frame. Never work under the vehicle or start the engine while this jack is being used as the only means of support.*

The vehicle should be on level ground. Place the shift lever in Park, if you have an automatic, or Reverse if you have a manual transaxle. Block the wheel diagonally opposite the wheel being changed. Set the parking brake.

Remove the spare tire and jack from stowage. Remove the wheel cover and trim ring (if so equipped) with the tapered end of the lug nut wrench by inserting and twisting the handle and then prying against the back of the wheel cover. On aluminum wheels, tap the back side of the wheel hub cover after removing the wheel (do not attempt to pull off the wheel hub cover by hand). Loosen, but do not remove, the lug nuts (one-half turn is sufficient).

Place the scissors-type jack under the side of the vehicle and adjust the jack height until it fits between the notches in the vertical rocker panel flange nearest the wheel to be changed. There is a front and rear jacking point on each side of the vehicle **(see illustration)**.

Turn the jack handle clockwise until the tire clears the ground. Remove the lug nuts and pull the wheel off. Replace it with the spare.

Install the lug nuts with the beveled edges facing in. Tighten them snugly. Don't attempt to tighten them completely until the vehicle is lowered or it could slip off the jack. Turn the jack handle counterclockwise to lower the vehicle. Remove the jack and tighten the lug nuts in a criss-cross pattern.

Install the cover (and trim ring, if used) and be sure it's snapped into place all the way around.

Stow the tire, jack and wrench. Unblock the wheels.

Towing

As a general rule, the vehicle should be towed with the front (drive) wheels off the ground. If they can't be raised, place them on a dolly. The ignition key must be in the ACC position, since the steering lock mechanism isn't strong enough to hold the front wheels straight while towing.

Vehicles equipped with an automatic transaxle can be towed from the front only with all four wheels on the ground, provided that speeds don't exceed 30 mph and the distance is not over 50 miles. Before towing, check the transmission fluid level (see Chapter 1). If the level is below the HOT line on the dipstick, add fluid or use a towing dolly. Release the parking brake, put the transaxle in Neutral and place the ignition key in the ACC position. **Caution:** *Never tow a vehicle with an automatic transaxle from the rear with the front wheels on the ground.*

When towing a vehicle equipped with a manual transaxle with all four wheels on the ground, be sure to place the shift lever in neutral and release the parking brake.

Equipment specifically designed for towing should be used. It should be attached to the main structural members of the vehicle, not the bumpers or brackets.

Safety is a major consideration when towing and all applicable state and local laws must be obeyed. A safety chain system must be used at all times. Remember that power steering and power brakes will not work with the engine off.

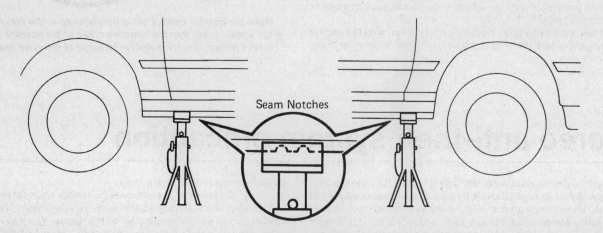

Seam Notches

The jack fits over the rocker panel flange, between the two notches (there are two jacking points on each side of the vehicle)

Booster battery (jump) starting

Observe these precautions when using a booster battery to start a vehicle:

a) Before connecting the booster battery, make sure the ignition switch is in the Off position.
b) Turn off the lights, heater and other electrical loads.
c) Your eyes should be shielded. Safety goggles are a good idea.
d) Make sure the booster battery is the same voltage as the dead one in the vehicle.
e) The two vehicles MUST NOT TOUCH each other!
f) Make sure the transaxle is in Neutral (manual) or Park (automatic).
g) If the booster battery is not a maintenance-free type, remove the vent caps and lay a cloth over the vent holes.

Connect the red jumper cable to the positive (+) terminals of each battery **(see illustration)**.

Connect one end of the black jumper cable to the negative (-) terminal of the booster battery. The other end of this cable should be connected to a good ground on the vehicle to be started, such as a bolt or bracket on the body.

Start the engine using the booster battery, then, with the engine running at idle speed, disconnect the jumper cables in the reverse order of connection.

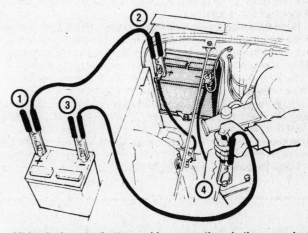

Make the booster battery cable connections in the numerical order shown (note that the negative cable of the booster battery is NOT attached to the negative terminal of the dead battery)

Stereo anti-theft system precaution

Stereo systems displaying "ANTI-THEFT SYSTEM" on the cassette tape slot cover have a built-in theft deterrent system designed to render the stereo inoperative should the stereo be stolen. If the power source to the stereo is cut, the anti-theft system will activate. Even if the power source is immediately reconnected, the stereo will not function. If your vehicle is equipped with this anti-theft system, do not disconnect the cable from the negative terminal of the battery, remove the stereo or disconnect related components unless you have the individual ID (code) number for the stereo.

If you discover that the system is inoperative after disconnecting and reconnecting the power source, enter the ID number. If the wrong number is entered, "Err" will appear on the display. You may make up to nine errors - a tenth error will activate the system and "HELP" will appear on the display. If this occurs, contact your local Toyota dealer service department.

Automotive chemicals and lubricants

A number of automotive chemicals and lubricants are available for use during vehicle maintenance and repair. They include a wide variety of products ranging from cleaning solvents and degreasers to lubricants and protective sprays for rubber, plastic and vinyl.

Cleaners

Carburetor cleaner and choke cleaner is a strong solvent for gum, varnish and carbon. Most carburetor cleaners leave a dry-type lubricant film which will not harden or gum up. Because of this film it is not recommended for use on electrical components

Brake system cleaner is used to remove grease and brake fluid from the brake system, where clean surfaces are absolutely necessary. It leaves no residue and often eliminates brake squeal caused by contaminants.

Electrical cleaner removes oxidation, corrosion and carbon deposits from electrical contacts, restoring full current flow. It can also be used to clean spark plugs, carburetor jets, voltage regulators and other parts where an oil-free surface is desired.

Demoisturants remove water and moisture from electrical components such as alternators, voltage regulators, electrical connectors and fuse blocks. They are non-conductive, non-corrosive and non-flammable.

Degreasers are heavy-duty solvents used to remove grease from the outside of the engine and from chassis components. They can be sprayed or brushed on and, depending on the type, are rinsed off either with water or solvent.

Lubricants

Motor oil is the lubricant formulated for use in engines. It normally contains a wide variety of additives to prevent corrosion and reduce foaming and wear. Motor oil comes in various weights (viscosity ratings) from 5 to 80. The recommended weight of the oil depends on the season, temperature and the demands on the engine. Light oil is used in cold climates and under light load conditions. Heavy oil is used in hot climates and where high loads are encountered. Multi-viscosity oils are designed to have characteristics of both light and heavy oils and are available in a number of weights from 5W-20 to 20W-50.

Gear oil is designed to be used in differentials, manual transmissions and other areas where high-temperature lubrication is required.

Chassis and wheel bearing grease is a heavy grease used where increased loads and friction are encountered, such as for wheel bearings, balljoints, tie-rod ends and universal joints.

High-temperature wheel bearing grease is designed to withstand the extreme temperatures encountered by wheel bearings in disc brake equipped vehicles. It usually contains molybdenum disulfide (moly), which is a dry-type lubricant.

White grease is a heavy grease for metal-to-metal applications where water is a problem. White grease stays soft under both low and high temperatures (usually from -100 to +190-degrees F), and will not wash off or dilute in the presence of water.

Assembly lube is a special extreme pressure lubricant, usually containing moly, used to lubricate high-load parts (such as main and rod bearings and cam lobes) for initial start-up of a new engine. The assembly lube lubricates the parts without being squeezed out or washed away until the engine oiling system begins to function.

Silicone lubricants are used to protect rubber, plastic, vinyl and nylon parts.

Graphite lubricants are used where oils cannot be used due to contamination problems, such as in locks. The dry graphite will lubricate metal parts while remaining uncontaminated by dirt, water, oil or acids. It is electrically conductive and will not foul electrical contacts in locks such as the ignition switch.

Moly penetrants loosen and lubricate frozen, rusted and corroded fasteners and prevent future rusting or freezing.

Heat-sink grease is a special electrically non-conductive grease that is used for mounting electronic ignition modules where it is essential that heat is transferred away from the module.

Sealants

RTV sealant is one of the most widely used gasket compounds. Made from silicone, RTV is air curing, it seals, bonds, waterproofs, fills surface irregularities, remains flexible, doesn't shrink, is relatively easy to remove, and is used as a supplementary sealer with almost all low and medium temperature gaskets.

Anaerobic sealant is much like RTV in that it can be used either to seal gaskets or to form gaskets by itself. It remains flexible, is solvent resistant and fills surface imperfections. The difference between an anaerobic sealant and an RTV-type sealant is in the curing. RTV cures when exposed to air, while an anaerobic sealant cures only in the absence of air. This means that an anaerobic sealant cures only after the assembly of parts, sealing them together.

Thread and pipe sealant is used for sealing hydraulic and pneumatic fittings and vacuum lines. It is usually made from a Teflon compound, and comes in a spray, a paint-on liquid and as a wrap-around tape.

Chemicals

Anti-seize compound prevents seizing, galling, cold welding, rust and corrosion in fasteners. High-temperature ant-seize, usually made with copper and graphite lubricants, is used for exhaust system and exhaust manifold bolts.

Anaerobic locking compounds are used to keep fasteners from vibrating or working loose and cure only after installation, in the absence of air. Medium strength locking compound is used for small nuts, bolts and screws that may be removed later. High-strength locking compound is for large nuts, bolts and studs which aren't removed on a regular basis.

Oil additives range from viscosity index improvers to chemical treatments that claim to reduce internal engine friction. It should be noted that most oil manufacturers caution against using additives with their oils.

Gas additives perform several functions, depending on their chemical makeup. They usually contain solvents that help dissolve gum and varnish that build up on carburetor, fuel injection and intake parts. They also serve to break down carbon deposits that form on the inside surfaces of the combustion chambers. Some additives contain upper cylinder lubricants for valves and piston rings, and others contain chemicals to remove condensation from the gas tank.

Miscellaneous

Brake fluid is specially formulated hydraulic fluid that can withstand the heat and pressure encountered in brake systems. Care must be taken so this fluid does not come in contact with painted surfaces or plastics. An opened container should always be resealed to prevent contamination by water or dirt.

Weatherstrip adhesive is used to bond weatherstripping around doors, windows and trunk lids. It is sometimes used to attach trim pieces.

Undercoating is a petroleum-based, tar-like substance that is designed to protect metal surfaces on the underside of the vehicle from corrosion. It also acts as a sound-deadening agent by insulating the bottom of the vehicle.

Waxes and polishes are used to help protect painted and plated surfaces from the weather. Different types of paint may require the use of different types of wax and polish. Some polishes utilize a chemical or abrasive cleaner to help remove the top layer of oxidized (dull) paint on older vehicles. In recent years many non-wax polishes that contain a wide variety of chemicals such as polymers and silicones have been introduced. These non-wax polishes are usually easier to apply and last longer than conventional waxes and polishes.

Safety first

Regardless of how enthusiastic you may be about getting on with the job at hand, take the time to ensure that your safety is not jeopardized. A moment's lack of attention can result in an accident, as can failure to observe certain simple safety precautions. The possibility of an accident will always exist, and the following points should not be considered a comprehensive list of all dangers. Rather, they are intended to make you aware of the risks and to encourage a safety conscious approach to all work you carry out on your vehicle.

Essential DOs and DON'Ts

DON'T rely on a jack when working under the vehicle. Always use approved jackstands to support the weight of the vehicle and place them under the recommended lift or support points.

DON'T attempt to loosen extremely tight fasteners (i.e. wheel lug nuts) while the vehicle is on a jack - it may fall.

DON'T start the engine without first making sure that the transmission is in Neutral (or Park where applicable) and the parking brake is set.

DON'T remove the radiator cap from a hot cooling system - let it cool or cover it with a cloth and release the pressure gradually.

DON'T attempt to drain the engine oil until you are sure it has cooled to the point that it will not burn you.

DON'T touch any part of the engine or exhaust system until it has cooled sufficiently to avoid burns.

DON'T siphon toxic liquids such as gasoline, antifreeze and brake fluid by mouth, or allow them to remain on your skin.

DON'T inhale brake lining dust - it is potentially hazardous (see Asbestos below)

DON'T allow spilled oil or grease to remain on the floor - wipe it up before someone slips on it.

DON'T use loose fitting wrenches or other tools which may slip and cause injury.

DON'T push on wrenches when loosening or tightening nuts or bolts. Always try to pull the wrench toward you. If the situation calls for pushing the wrench away, push with an open hand to avoid scraped knuckles if the wrench should slip.

DON'T attempt to lift a heavy component alone - get someone to help you.

DON'T rush or take unsafe shortcuts to finish a job.

DON'T allow children or animals in or around the vehicle while you are working on it.

DO wear eye protection when using power tools such as a drill, sander, bench grinder, etc. and when working under a vehicle.

DO keep loose clothing and long hair well out of the way of moving parts.

DO make sure that any hoist used has a safe working load rating adequate for the job.

DO get someone to check on you periodically when working alone on a vehicle.

DO carry out work in a logical sequence and make sure that everything is correctly assembled and tightened.

DO keep chemicals and fluids tightly capped and out of the reach of children and pets.

DO remember that your vehicle's safety affects that of yourself and others. If in doubt on any point, get professional advice.

Asbestos

Certain friction, insulating, sealing, and other products - such as brake linings, brake bands, clutch linings, torque converters, gaskets, etc. - contain asbestos. Extreme care must be taken to avoid inhalation of dust from such products, since it is hazardous to health. If in doubt, assume that they do contain asbestos.

Fire

Remember at all times that gasoline is highly flammable. Never smoke or have any kind of open flame around when working on a vehicle. But the risk does not end there. A spark caused by an electrical short circuit, by two metal surfaces contacting each other, or even by static electricity built up in your body under certain conditions, can ignite gasoline vapors, which in a confined space are highly explosive. Do not, under any circumstances, use gasoline for cleaning parts. Use an approved safety solvent.

Always disconnect the battery ground (-) cable at the battery before working on any part of the fuel system or electrical system. Never risk spilling fuel on a hot engine or exhaust component.It is strongly recommended that a fire extinguisher suitable for use on fuel and electrical fires be kept handy in the garage or workshop at all times. Never try to extinguish a fuel or electrical fire with water.

Fumes

Certain fumes are highly toxic and can quickly cause unconsciousness and even death if inhaled to any extent. Gasoline vapor falls into this category, as do the vapors from some cleaning solvents. Any draining or pouring of such volatile fluids should be done in a well ventilated area.

When using cleaning fluids and solvents, read the instructions on the container carefully. Never use materials from unmarked containers.

Never run the engine in an enclosed space, such as a garage. Exhaust fumes contain carbon monoxide, which is extremely poisonous. If you need to run the engine, always do so in the open air, or at least have the rear of the vehicle outside the work area.

If you are fortunate enough to have the use of an inspection pit, never drain or pour gasoline and never run the engine while the vehicle is over the pit. The fumes, being heavier than air, will concentrate in the pit with possibly lethal results.

The battery

Never create a spark or allow a bare light bulb near a battery. They normally give off a certain amount of hydrogen gas, which is highly explosive.

Always disconnect the battery ground (-) cable at the battery before working on the fuel or electrical systems.

If possible, loosen the filler caps or cover when charging the battery from an external source (this does not apply to sealed or maintenance-free batteries). Do not charge at an excessive rate or the battery may burst.

Take care when adding water to a non maintenance-free battery and when carrying a battery. The electrolyte, even when diluted, is very corrosive and should not be allowed to contact clothing or skin.

Always wear eye protection when cleaning the battery to prevent the caustic deposits from entering your eyes.

Household current

When using an electric power tool, inspection light, etc., which operates on household current, always make sure that the tool is correctly connected to its plug and that, where necessary, it is properly grounded. Do not use such items in damp conditions and, again, do not create a spark or apply excessive heat in the vicinity of fuel or fuel vapor.

Secondary ignition system voltage

A severe electric shock can result from touching certain parts of the ignition system (such as the spark plug wires) when the engine is running or being cranked, particularly if components are damp or the insulation is defective. In the case of an electronic ignition system, the secondary system voltage is much higher and could prove fatal.

Conversion factors

Length (distance)
Inches (in)	X	25.4	= Millimetres (mm)	X 0.0394	= Inches (in)
Feet (ft)	X	0.305	= Metres (m)	X 3.281	= Feet (ft)
Miles	X	1.609	= Kilometres (km)	X 0.621	= Miles

Volume (capacity)
Cubic inches (cu in; in³)	X	16.387	= Cubic centimetres (cc; cm³)	X 0.061	= Cubic inches (cu in; in³)
Imperial pints (Imp pt)	X	0.568	= Litres (l)	X 1.76	= Imperial pints (Imp pt)
Imperial quarts (Imp qt)	X	1.137	= Litres (l)	X 0.88	= Imperial quarts (Imp qt)
Imperial quarts (Imp qt)	X	1.201	= US quarts (US qt)	X 0.833	= Imperial quarts (Imp qt)
US quarts (US qt)	X	0.946	= Litres (l)	X 1.057	= US quarts (US qt)
Imperial gallons (Imp gal)	X	4.546	= Litres (l)	X 0.22	= Imperial gallons (Imp gal)
Imperial gallons (Imp gal)	X	1.201	= US gallons (US gal)	X 0.833	= Imperial gallons (Imp gal)
US gallons (US gal)	X	3.785	= Litres (l)	X 0.264	= US gallons (US gal)

Mass (weight)
Ounces (oz)	X	28.35	= Grams (g)	X 0.035	Ounces (oz)
Pounds (lb)	X	0.454	= Kilograms (kg)	X 2.205	= Pounds (lb)

Force
Ounces-force (ozf; oz)	X	0.278	= Newtons (N)	X 3.6	= Ounces-force (ozf; oz)
Pounds-force (lbf; lb)	X	4.448	= Newtons (N)	X 0.225	= Pounds-force (lbf; lb)
Newtons (N)	X	0.1	= Kilograms-force (kgf; kg)	X 9.81	= Newtons (N)

Pressure
Pounds-force per square inch (psi; lbf/in²; lb/in²)	X	0.070	= Kilograms-force per square centimetre (kgf/cm²; kg/cm²)	X 14.223	= Pounds-force per square inch (psi; lbf/in²; lb/in²)
Pounds-force per square inch (psi; lbf/in²; lb/in²)	X	0.068	= Atmospheres (atm)	X 14.696	= Pounds-force per square inch (psi; lbf/in²; lb/in²)
Pounds-force per square inch (psi; lbf/in²; lb/in²)	X	0.069	= Bars	X 14.5	= Pounds-force per square inch (psi; lbf/in²; lb/in²)
Pounds-force per square inch (psi; lbf/in²; lb/in²)	X	6.895	= Kilopascals (kPa)	X 0.145	= Pounds-force per square inch (psi; lbf/in²; lb/in²)
Kilopascals (kPa)	X	0.01	= Kilograms-force per square centimetre (kgf/cm²; kg/cm²)	X 98.1	= Kilopascals (kPa)

Torque (moment of force)
Pounds-force inches (lbf in; lb in)	X	1.152	= Kilograms-force centimetre (kgf cm; kg cm)	X 0.868	= Pounds-force inches (lbf in; lb in)
Pounds-force inches (lbf in; lb in)	X	0.113	= Newton metres (Nm)	X 8.85	= Pounds-force inches (lbf in; lb in)
Pounds-force inches (lbf in; lb in)	X	0.083	= Pounds-force feet (lbf ft; lb ft)	X 12	= Pounds-force inches (lbf in; lb in)
Pounds-force feet (lbf ft; lb ft)	X	0.138	= Kilograms-force metres (kgf m; kg m)	X 7.233	= Pounds-force feet (lbf ft; lb ft)
Pounds-force feet (lbf ft; lb ft)	X	1.356	= Newton metres (Nm)	X 0.738	= Pounds-force feet (lbf ft; lb ft)
Newton metres (Nm)	X	0.102	= Kilograms-force metres (kgf m; kg m)	X 9.804	= Newton metres (Nm)

Power
Horsepower (hp)	X	745.7	= Watts (W)	X 0.0013	= Horsepower (hp)

Velocity (speed)
Miles per hour (miles/hr; mph)	X	1.609	= Kilometres per hour (km/hr; kph)	X 0.621	= Miles per hour (miles/hr; mph)

Fuel consumption*
Miles per gallon, Imperial (mpg)	X	0.354	= Kilometres per litre (km/l)	X 2.825	= Miles per gallon, Imperial (mpg)
Miles per gallon, US (mpg)	X	0.425	= Kilometres per litre (km/l)	X 2.352	= Miles per gallon, US (mpg)

Temperature

Degrees Fahrenheit = ($^{\circ}$C x 1.8) + 32

Degrees Celsius (Degrees Centigrade; °C) = (°F - 32) x 0.56

*It is common practice to convert from miles per gallon (mpg) to litres/100 kilometres (l/100km), where mpg (Imperial) x l/100 km = 282 and mpg (US) x l/100 km = 235

Troubleshooting

Contents

This section provides an easy reference guide to the more common problems which may occur during the operation of your vehicle. These problems and their possible causes are grouped under headings denoting various components or systems, such as Engine, Cooling system, etc. They also refer you to the chapter and/or section which deals with the problem.

Remember that successful troubleshooting is not a mysterious black art practiced only by professional mechanics. It is simply the result of the right knowledge combined with an intelligent, systematic approach to the problem. Always work by a process of elimination, starting with the simplest solution and working through to the most complex - and never overlook the obvious. Anyone can run the gas tank dry or leave the lights on overnight, so don't assume that you are exempt from such oversights.

Finally, always establish a clear idea of why a problem has occurred and take steps to ensure that it doesn't happen again. If the electrical system fails because of a poor connection, check the other connections in the system to make sure that they don't fail as well. If a particular fuse continues to blow, find out why - don't just replace one fuse after another. Remember, failure of a small component can often be indicative of potential failure or incorrect functioning of a more important component or system.

Engine

1 Engine will not rotate when attempting to start

1   Battery terminal connections loose or corroded (Chapter 1).
2   Battery discharged or faulty (Chapter 1).
3   Automatic transmission not completely engaged in Park (Chapter 7) or clutch not completely depressed (Chapter 8).
4   Broken, loose or disconnected wiring in the starting circuit (Chapters 5 and 12).
5   Starter motor pinion jammed in flywheel ring gear (Chapter 5).
6   Starter solenoid faulty (Chapter 5).
7   Starter motor faulty (Chapter 5).
8   Ignition switch faulty (Chapter 12).
9   Starter pinion or flywheel teeth worn or broken (Chapter 5).

2 Engine rotates but will not start

1   Fuel tank empty.
2   Battery discharged (engine rotates slowly) (Chapter 5).
3   Battery terminal connections loose or corroded (Chapter 1).
4   Leaking fuel injector(s), faulty cold start valve, fuel pump, pressure regulator, etc. (Chapter 4).
5   Fuel not reaching fuel rail (Chapter 4).
6   Ignition components damp or damaged (Chapter 5).
7   Worn, faulty or incorrectly gapped spark plugs (Chapter 1).
8   Broken, loose or disconnected wiring in the starting circuit (Chapter 5).
9   Loose distributor is changing ignition timing (Chapter 5).
10   Broken, loose or disconnected wires at the ignition coil or faulty coil (Chapter 5).

3 Engine hard tko start when cold

1   Battery discharged or low (Chapter 1).
2   Malfunctioning fuel system (Chapter 4).
3   Faulty cold start injector (Chapter 4).
4   Injector(s) leaking (Chapter 4).
5   Distributor rotor carbon tracked (Chapter 5).

4 Engine hard to start when hot

1   Air filter clogged (Chapter 1).
2   Fuel not reaching the fuel injection system (Chapter 4).
3   Corroded battery connections, especially ground (Chapter 1).

5 Starter motor noisy or excessively rough in engagement

1   Pinion or flywheel gear teeth worn or broken (Chapter 5).
2   Starter motor mounting bolts loose or missing (Chapter 5).

6 Engine starts but stops immediately

1   Loose or faulty electrical connections at distributor, coil or alternator (Chapter 5).
2   Insufficient fuel reaching the fuel injector(s) (Chapters 1 and 4).
3   Vacuum leak at the gasket between the intake manifold/plenum and throttle body (Chapters 1 and 4).

7 Oil puddle under engine

1   Oil pan gasket and/or oil pan drain bolt washer leaking (Chapter 2).
2   Oil pressure sending unit leaking (Chapter 2).
3   Cylinder head covers leaking (Chapter 2).
4   Engine oil seals leaking (Chapter 2).
5   Oil pump housing leaking (Chapter 2).

8 Engine lopes while idling or idles erratically

1   Vacuum leakage (Chapters 2 and 4).
2   Leaking EGR valve (Chapter 6).
3   Air filter clogged (Chapter 1).
4   Fuel pump not delivering sufficient fuel to the fuel injection system (Chapter 4).
5   Leaking head gasket (Chapter 2).
6   Timing belt and/or pulleys worn (Chapter 2).
7   Camshaft lobes worn (Chapter 2).

9 Engine misses at idle speed

1   Spark plugs worn or not gapped properly (Chapter 1).
2   Faulty spark plug wires (Chapter 1).
3   Vacuum leaks (Chapter 1).
4   Incorrect ignition timing (Chapter 1).
5   Uneven or low compression (Chapter 2).

10 Engine misses throughout driving speed range

1   Fuel filter clogged and/or impurities in the fuel system (Chapter 1).
2   Low fuel output at the injector(s) (Chapter 4).
3   Faulty or incorrectly gapped spark plugs (Chapter 1).
4   Incorrect ignition timing (Chapter 5).
5   Cracked distributor cap, disconnected distributor wires or damaged distributor components (Chapters 1 and 5).
6   Leaking spark plug wires (Chapters 1 or 5).
7   Faulty emission system components (Chapter 6).
8   Low or uneven cylinder compression pressures (Chapter 2).
9   Weak or faulty ignition system (Chapter 5).
10   Vacuum leak in fuel injection system, intake manifold, air control valve or vacuum hoses (Chapter 4).

11 Engine stumbles on acceleration

1 Spark plugs fouled (Chapter 1).
2 Fuel injection system needs faulty (Chapter 4).
3 Fuel filter clogged (Chapters 1 and 4).
4 Incorrect ignition timing (Chapter 5).
5 Intake manifold air leak (Chapters 2 and 4).

12 Engine surges while holding accelerator steady

1 Intake air leak (Chapter 4).
2 Fuel pump faulty (Chapter 4).
3 Loose fuel injector wire harness connectors (Chapter 4).
4 Defective ECU or information sensor (Chapter 6).

13 Engine stalls

1 Idle speed incorrect (Chapter 1).
2 Fuel filter clogged and/or water and impurities in the fuel system (Chapters 1 and 4).
3 Distributor components damp or damaged (Chapter 5).
4 Faulty emissions system components (Chapter 6).
5 Faulty or incorrectly gapped spark plugs (Chapter 1).
6 Faulty spark plug wires (Chapter 1).
7 Vacuum leak in the fuel injection system, intake manifold or vacuum hoses (Chapters 2 and 4).
8 Valve clearances incorrectly set (Chapter 1).

14 Engine lacks power

1 Incorrect ignition timing (Chapter 5).
2 Excessive play in distributor shaft (Chapter 5).
3 Worn rotor, distributor cap or wires (Chapters 1 and 5).
4 Faulty or incorrectly gapped spark plugs (Chapter 1).
5 Fuel injection system out of adjustment or excessively worn (Chapter 4).
6 Faulty coil (Chapter 5).
7 Brakes binding (Chapter 9).
8 Automatic transaxle fluid level incorrect (Chapter 1).
9 Clutch slipping (Chapter 8).
10 Fuel filter clogged and/or impurities in the fuel system (Chapters 1 and 4).
11 Emission control system not functioning properly (Chapter 6).
12 Low or uneven cylinder compression pressures (Chapter 2).
13 Obstructed exhaust system (Chapter 4).

15 Engine backfires

1 Emission control system not functioning properly (Chapter 6).
2 Ignition timing incorrect (Chapter 5).
3 Faulty secondary ignition system (cracked spark plug insulator, faulty plug wires, distributor cap and/or rotor) (Chapters 1 and 5).
4 Fuel injection system in need of adjustment or worn excessively (Chapter 4).
5 Vacuum leak at fuel injector(s), intake manifold, air control valve or vacuum hoses (Chapters 2 and 4).
6 Valve clearances incorrectly set and/or valves sticking (Chapter 1).

16 Pinging or knocking engine sounds during acceleration or uphill

1 Incorrect grade of fuel.

2 Ignition timing incorrect (Chapter 5).
3 Fuel injection system faulty (Chapter 4).
4 Improper or damaged spark plugs or wires (Chapter 1).
5 Worn or damaged distributor components (Chapter 5).
6 EGR valve not functioning (Chapter 6).
7 Vacuum leak (Chapters 2 and 4).

17 Engine runs with oil pressure light on

1 Low oil level (Chapter 1).
2 Idle rpm below specification (Chapter 1).
3 Short in wiring circuit (Chapter 12).
4 Faulty oil pressure sender (Chapter 2).
5 Worn engine bearings and/or oil pump (Chapter 2).

18 Engine diesels (continues to run) after switching off

1 Idle speed too high (Chapter 1).
2 Excessive engine operating temperature (Chapter 3).
3 Ignition timing in need of adjustment (Chapter 5).

Engine electrical system

19 Battery will not hold a charge

1 Alternator drivebelt defective or not adjusted properly (Chapter 1).
2 Battery electrolyte level low (Chapter 1).
3 Battery terminals loose or corroded (Chapter 1).
4 Alternator not charging properly (Chapter 5).
5 Loose, broken or faulty wiring in the charging circuit (Chapter 5).
6 Short in vehicle wiring (Chapter 12).
7 Internally defective battery (Chapters 1 and 5).

20 Alternator light fails to go out

1 Faulty alternator or charging circuit (Chapter 5).
2 Alternator drivebelt defective or out of adjustment (Chapter 1).
3 Alternator voltage regulator inoperative (Chapter 5).

21 Alternator light fails to come on when key is turned on

1 Warning light bulb defective (Chapter 12).
2 Fault in the printed circuit, dash wiring or bulb holder (Chapter 12).

Fuel system

22 Excessive fuel consumption

1 Dirty or clogged air filter element (Chapter 1).
2 Incorrectly set ignition timing (Chapter 5).
3 Emissions system not functioning properly (Chapter 6).
4 Fuel injection internal parts excessively worn or damaged (Chapter 4).
5 Low tire pressure or incorrect tire size (Chapter 1).

23 Fuel leakage and/or fuel odor

1 Leaking fuel feed or return line (Chapters 1 and 4).

2   Tank overfilled.
3   Evaporative canister filter clogged (Chapters 1 and 6).
4   Fuel injector internal parts excessively worn (Chapter 4).

Cooling system

24   Overheating

1   Insufficient coolant in system (Chapter 1).
2   Water pump drivebelt defective or out of adjustment (Chapter 1).
3   Radiator core blocked or grille restricted (Chapter 3).
4   Thermostat faulty (Chapter 3).
5   Electric coolant fan blades broken or cracked (Chapter 3).
6   Radiator cap not maintaining proper pressure (Chapter 3).
7   Ignition timing incorrect (Chapter 5).

25   Overcooling

1   Faulty thermostat (Chapter 3).
2   Inaccurate temperature gauge sending unit (Chapter 3)

26   External coolant leakage

1   Deteriorated/damaged hoses; loose clamps (Chapters 1 and 3).
2   Water pump defective (Chapter 3).
3   Leakage from radiator core or coolant reservoir bottle (Chapter 3).
4   Engine drain or water jacket core plugs leaking (Chapter 2).

27   Internal coolant leakage

1   Leaking cylinder head gasket (Chapter 2).
2   Cracked cylinder bore or cylinder head (Chapter 2).

28   Coolant loss

1   Too much coolant in system (Chapter 1).
2   Coolant boiling away because of overheating (Chapter 3).
3   Internal or external leakage (Chapter 3).
4   Faulty radiator cap (Chapter 3).

29   Poor coolant circulation

1   Inoperative water pump (Chapter 3).
2   Restriction in cooling system (Chapters 1 and 3).
3   Water pump drivebelt defective/out of adjustment (Chapter 1).
4   Thermostat sticking (Chapter 3).

Clutch

30   Pedal travels to floor - no pressure or very little resistance

1   Master or release cylinder faulty (Chapter 8).
2   Hose/pipe burst or leaking (Chapter 8).
3   Connections leaking (Chapter 8).
4   No fluid in reservoir (Chapter 8).
5   If fluid level in reservoir rises as pedal is depressed, master cylinder center valve seal is faulty (Chapter 8).

6   If there is fluid on dust seal at master cylinder, piston primary seal is leaking (Chapter 8).
7   Broken release bearing or fork (Chapter 8).

31   Fluid in area of master cylinder dust cover and on pedal

Rear seal failure in master cylinder (Chapter 8).

32   Fluid on release cylinder

Release cylinder plunger seal faulty (Chapter 8).

33   Pedal feels spongy when depressed

Air in system (Chapter 8).

34   Unable to select gears

1   Faulty transaxle (Chapter 7).
2   Faulty clutch disc (Chapter 8).
3   Release lever and bearing not assembled properly (Chapter 8).
4   Faulty pressure plate (Chapter 8).
5   Pressure plate-to-flywheel bolts loose (Chapter 8).

35   Clutch slips (engine speed increases with no increase in vehicle speed)

1   Clutch plate worn (Chapter 8).
2   Clutch plate is oil soaked by leaking rear main seal (Chapter 8).
3   Clutch plate not seated. It may take 30 or 40 normal starts for a new one to seat.
4   Warped pressure plate or flywheel (Chapter 8).
5   Weak diaphragm spring (Chapter 8).
6   Clutch plate overheated. Allow to cool.

36   Grabbing (chattering) as clutch is engaged

1   Oil on clutch plate lining, burned or glazed facings (Chapter 8).
2   Worn or loose engine or transaxle mounts (Chapters 2 and 7).
3   Worn splines on clutch plate hub (Chapter 8).
4   Warped pressure plate or flywheel (Chapter 8).
5   Burned or smeared resin on flywheel or pressure plate (Chapter 8).

37   Transaxle rattling (clicking)

1   Release lever loose (Chapter 8).
2   Clutch plate damper spring failure (Chapter 8).
3   Low engine idle speed (Chapter 1).

38   Noise in clutch area

1   Fork shaft improperly installed (Chapter 8).
2   Faulty bearing (Chapter 8).

39   Clutch pedal stays on floor

1   Clutch master cylinder piston binding in bore (Chapter 8).
2   Broken release bearing or fork (Chapter 8).

40 High pedal effort

1 Piston binding in bore (Chapter 8).
2 Pressure plate faulty (Chapter 8).
3 Incorrect size master or release cylinder (Chapter 8).

Manual transaxle

41 Knocking noise at low speeds

1 Worn driveaxle constant velocity (CV) joints (Chapter 8).
2 Worn side gear shaft counterbore in differential case (Chapter 7A).*

42 Noise most pronounced when turning

Differential gear noise (Chapter 7A).*

43 Clunk on acceleration or deceleration

1 Loose engine or transaxle mounts (Chapters 2 and 7A).
2 Worn differential pinion shaft in case.*
3 Worn side gear shaft counterbore in differential case (Chapter 7A).*
4 Worn or damaged driveaxle inboard CV joints (Chapter 8).

44 Clicking noise in turns

Worn or damaged outboard CV joint (Chapter 8).

45 Vibration

1 Rough wheel bearing (Chapters 1 and 10).
2 Damaged driveaxle (Chapter 8).
3 Out of round tires (Chapter 1).
4 Tire out of balance (Chapters 1 and 10).
5 Worn CV joint (Chapter 8).

46 Noisy in neutral with engine running

1 Damaged input gear bearing (Chapter 7A).*
2 Damaged clutch release bearing (Chapter 8).

47 Noisy in one particular gear

1 Damaged or worn constant mesh gears (Chapter 7A).*
2 Damaged or worn synchronizers (Chapter 7A).*
3 Bent reverse fork (Chapter 7A).*
4 Damaged fourth speed gear or output gear (Chapter 7A).*
5 Worn or damaged reverse idler gear or idler bushing (Chapter 7A).*

48 Noisy in all gears

1 Insufficient lubricant (Chapter 7A).
2 Damaged or worn bearings (Chapter 7A).*
3 Worn or damaged input gear shaft and/or output gear shaft (Chapter 7A).*

49 Slips out of gear

1 Worn or improperly adjusted linkage (Chapter 7A).
2 Transaxle loose on engine (Chapter 7A).
3 Shift linkage does not work freely, binds (Chapter 7A).
4 Input gear bearing retainer broken or loose (Chapter 7A).*
5 Dirt between clutch cover and engine housing (Chapter 7A).
6 Worn shift fork (Chapter 7A).*

50 Leaks lubricant

1 Side gear shaft seals worn (Chapter 7).
2 Excessive amount of lubricant in transaxle (Chapters 1 and 7A).
3 Loose or broken input gear shaft bearing retainer (Chapter 7A).*
4 Input gear bearing retainer O-ring and/or lip seal damaged (Chapter 7A).*

51 Locked in gear

Lock pin or interlock pin missing (Chapter 7A).*

* Although the corrective action necessary to remedy the symptoms described is beyond the scope of the home mechanic, the above information should be helpful in isolating the cause of the condition so that the owner can communicate clearly with a professional mechanic.

Automatic transaxle

Note: Due to the complexity of the automatic transaxle, it is difficult for the home mechanic to properly diagnose and service this component. For problems other than the following, the vehicle should be taken to a dealer or transmission shop.

52 Fluid leakage

1 Automatic transmission fluid is a deep red color. Fluid leaks should not be confused with engine oil, which can easily be blown onto the transaxle by air flow.
2 To pinpoint a leak, first remove all built-up dirt and grime from the transaxle housing with degreasing agents and/or steam cleaning. Then drive the vehicle at low speeds so air flow will not blow the leak far from its source. Raise the vehicle and determine where the leak is coming from. Common areas of leakage are:
   a) Pan (Chapters 1 and 7)
   b) Dipstick tube (Chapters 1 and 7)
   c) Transaxle oil lines (Chapter 7)
   d) Speed sensor (Chapter 7)

53 Transaxle fluid brown or has a burned smell

Transaxle fluid burned (Chapter 1).

54 General shift mechanism problems

1 Chapter 7, Part B, deals with checking and adjusting the shift linkage on automatic transaxles. Common problems which may be attributed to poorly adjusted linkage are:
   a) Engine starting in gears other than Park or Neutral.
   b) Indicator on shifter pointing to a gear other than the one actually being used.

c)   Vehicle moves when in Park.

2   Refer to Chapter 7B for the shift linkage adjustment procedure.

55   Transaxle will not downshift with accelerator pedal pressed to the floor

Throttle valve cable out of adjustment (Chapter 7B).

56   Engine will start in gears other than Park or Neutral

Neutral start switch malfunctioning (Chapter 7B).

57   Transaxle slips, shifts roughly, is noisy or has no drive in forward or reverse gears

There are many probable causes for the above problems, but the home mechanic should be concerned with only one possibility - fluid level. Before taking the vehicle to a repair shop, check the level and condition of the fluid as described in Chapter 1. Correct the fluid level as necessary or change the fluid and filter if needed. If the problem persists, have a professional diagnose the cause.

Driveaxles

58   Clicking noise in turns

Worn or damaged outboard CV joint (Chapter 8).

59   Shudder or vibration during acceleration

1   Excessive toe-in (Chapter 10).
2   Incorrect spring heights (Chapter 10).
3   Worn or damaged inboard or outboard CV joints (Chapter 8).
4   Sticking inboard CV joint assembly (Chapter 8).

60   Vibration at highway speeds

1   Out of balance front wheels and/or tires (Chapters 1 and 10).
2   Out of round front tires (Chapters 1 and 10).
3   Worn CV joint(s) (Chapter 8).

Brakes

Note: *Before assuming that a brake problem exists, make sure that:*
    a)   The tires are in good condition and properly inflated (Chapter 1).
    b)   The front end alignment is correct (Chapter 10).
    c)   The vehicle is not loaded with weight in an unequal manner.

61   Vehicle pulls to one side during braking

1   Incorrect tire pressures (Chapter 1).
2   Front end out of line (have the front end aligned).
3   Front, or rear, tires not matched to one another.
4   Restricted brake lines or hoses (Chapter 9).
5   Malfunctioning drum brake or caliper assembly (Chapter 9).
6   Loose suspension parts (Chapter 10).
7   Loose calipers (Chapter 9).
8   Excessive wear of brake shoe or pad material or disc/drum on one side.

62   Noise (high-pitched squeal when the brakes are applied)

Front and/or rear disc brake pads worn out. The noise comes from the wear sensor rubbing against the disc (does not apply to all vehicles). Replace pads with new ones immediately (Chapter 9).

63   Brake roughness or chatter (pedal pulsates)

1   Excessive lateral runout (Chapter 9).
2   Uneven pad wear (Chapter 9).
3   Defective disc (Chapter 9).

64   Excessive brake pedal effort required to stop vehicle

1   Malfunctioning power brake booster (Chapter 9).
2   Partial system failure (Chapter 9).
3   Excessively worn pads or shoes (Chapter 9).
4   Piston in caliper or wheel cylinder stuck or sluggish (Chapter 9).
5   Brake pads or shoes contaminated with oil or grease (Chapter 9).
6   New pads or shoes installed and not yet seated. It will take a while for the new material to seat against the disc or drum.

65   Excessive brake pedal travel

1   Partial brake system failure (Chapter 9).
2   Insufficient fluid in master cylinder (Chapters 1 and 9).
3   Air trapped in system (Chapters 1 and 9).

66   Dragging brakes

1   Incorrect adjustment of brake light switch (Chapter 9).
2   Master cylinder pistons not returning correctly (Chapter 9).
3   Restricted brakes lines or hoses (Chapters 1 and 9).
4   Incorrect parking brake adjustment (Chapter 9).

67   Grabbing or uneven braking action

1   Malfunction of proportioning valve (Chapter 9).
2   Malfunction of power brake booster unit (Chapter 9).
3   Binding brake pedal mechanism (Chapter 9).

68   Brake pedal feels spongy when depressed

1   Air in hydraulic lines (Chapter 9).
2   Master cylinder mounting bolts loose (Chapter 9).
3   Master cylinder defective (Chapter 9).

69   Brake pedal travels to the floor with little resistance

1   Little or no fluid in the master cylinder reservoir caused by leaking caliper piston(s) (Chapter 9).
2   Loose, damaged or disconnected brake lines (Chapter 9).

70   Parking brake does not hold

Parking brake linkage improperly adjusted (Chapters 1 and 9).

Suspension and steering systems

Note: *Before attempting to diagnose the suspension and steering systems, perform the following preliminary checks:*

a) Tires for wrong pressure and uneven wear.
b) Steering universal joints from the column to the rack and pinion for loose connectors or wear.
c) Front and rear suspension and the rack and pinion assembly for loose or damaged parts.
d) Out-of-round or out-of-balance tires, bent rims and loose and/or rough wheel bearings.

71 Vehicle pulls to one side

1 Mismatched or uneven tires (Chapter 10).
2 Broken or sagging springs (Chapter 10).
3 Wheel alignment (Chapter 10).
4 Front brake dragging (Chapter 9).

72 Abnormal or excessive tire wear

1 Wheel alignment (Chapter 10).
2 Sagging or broken springs (Chapter 10).
3 Tire out of balance (Chapter 10).
4 Worn strut damper (Chapter 10).
5 Overloaded vehicle.
6 Tires not rotated regularly.

73 Wheel makes a thumping noise

1 Blister or bump on tire (Chapter 10).
2 Improper strut damper action (Chapter 10).

74 Shimmy, shake or vibration

1 Tire or wheel out-of-balance or out-of-round (Chapter 10).
2 Loose or worn wheel bearings (Chapters 1, 8 and 10).
3 Worn tie-rod ends (Chapter 10).
4 Worn lower balljoints (Chapters 1 and 10).
5 Excessive wheel runout (Chapter 10).
6 Blister or bump on tire (Chapter 10).

75 Hard steering

1 Lack of lubrication at balljoints, tie-rod ends and rack and pinion assembly (Chapter 10).
2 Front wheel alignment (Chapter 10).
3 Low tire pressure(s) (Chapters 1 and 10).

76 Poor returnability of steering to center

1 Lack of lubrication at balljoints and tie-rod ends (Chapter 10).
2 Binding in balljoints (Chapter 10).
3 Binding in steering column (Chapter 10).
4 Lack of lubricant in steering gear assembly (Chapter 10).
5 Front wheel alignment (Chapter 10).

77 Abnormal noise at the front end

1 Lack of lubrication at balljoints and tie-rod ends (Chapters 1 and 10).

2 Damaged strut mounting (Chapter 10).
3 Worn control arm bushings or tie-rod ends (Chapter 10).
4 Loose stabilizer bar (Chapter 10).
5 Loose wheel nuts (Chapters 1 and 10).
6 Loose suspension bolts (Chapter 10)

.78 Wander or poor steering stability

1 Mismatched or uneven tires (Chapter 10).
2 Lack of lubrication at balljoints and tie-rod ends (Chapters 1 and 10).
3 Worn strut assemblies (Chapter 10).
4 Loose stabilizer bar (Chapter 10).
5 Broken or sagging springs (Chapter 10).
6 Wheels out of alignment (Chapter 10).

79 Erratic steering when braking

1 Wheel bearings worn (Chapter 10).
2 Broken or sagging springs (Chapter 10).
3 Leaking wheel cylinder or caliper (Chapter 10).
4 Warped rotors or drums (Chapter 10).

80 Excessive pitching and/or rolling around corners or during braking

1 Loose stabilizer bar (Chapter 10).
2 Worn strut dampers or mountings (Chapter 10).
3 Broken or sagging springs (Chapter 10).
4 Overloaded vehicle.

81 Suspension bottoms

1 Overloaded vehicle.
2 Worn strut dampers (Chapter 10).
3 Incorrect, broken or sagging springs (Chapter 10).

82 Cupped tires

1 Front wheel or rear wheel alignment (Chapter 10).
2 Worn strut dampers (Chapter 10).
3 Wheel bearings worn (Chapter 10).
4 Excessive tire or wheel runout (Chapter 10).
5 Worn balljoints (Chapter 10).

83 Excessive tire wear on outside edge

1 Inflation pressures incorrect (Chapter 1).
2 Excessive speed in turns.
3 Front end alignment incorrect (excessive toe-in). Have professionally aligned.
4 Suspension arm bent or twisted (Chapter 10).

84 Excessive tire wear on inside edge

1 Inflation pressures incorrect (Chapter 1).
2 Front end alignment incorrect (toe-out). Have professionally aligned.
3 Loose or damaged steering components (Chapter 10).

85   Tire tread worn in one place

1   Tires out of balance.
2   Damaged or buckled wheel. Inspect and replace if necessary.
3   Defective tire (Chapter 1).

86   Excessive play or looseness in steering system

1   Wheel bearing(s) worn (Chapter 10).

2   Tie-rod end loose (Chapter 10).
3   Steering gear loose (Chapter 10).
4   Worn or loose steering intermediate shaft (Chapter 10).

87   Rattling or clicking noise in steering gear

1   Steering gear loose (Chapter 10).
2   Steering gear defective.k

Chapter 1   Tune-up and routine maintenance

Contents

Specifications

Recommended lubricants and fluids

Engine oil type	API grade SG or SG/CD multigrade and fuel efficient oil
Viscosity	See accompanying chart
Fuel	Unleaded gasoline, 87 octane or higher
Automatic transaxle fluid type	DEXRON II automatic transmission fluid
Automatic transaxle differential fluid type	DEXRON II automatic transmission fluid
Manual transaxle lubricant type	DEXRON II automatic transmission fluid
1989 and earlier	DEXRON II automatic transmission fluid
1990 and later	API GL-5 75W90 gear oil

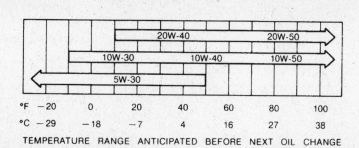

RECOMMENDED ENGINE OIL VISCOSITY

TEMPERATURE RANGE ANTICIPATED BEFORE NEXT OIL CHANGE

Recommended lubricants and fluids (continued)

Brake fluid type... DOT 3 brake fluid
Clutch fluid type.. DOT 3 brake fluid
Power steering system fluid .... DEXRON II automatic transmission fluid

Capacities

Engine oil (including filter)
  1989 and earlier
    2S-E engine .... 4.2 qts
    3S-GE engine .... 4.1 qts
    3S-FE engine .... 4.3 qts
  1990 and later
    4A-FE engine .... 3.4 qts
    5S-FE engine
      Without oil cooler .... 4.2 qts
      With oil cooler .... 4.5 qts
Coolant
  1989 and earlier.. 7 qts
  1990 and later .... 6 qts
Transaxle
  Automatic
    1989 and earlier
      Dry fill... 5 qts
      Drain and refill (filter replacement).................................... 4 qts
      Differential .... 1.7 qts
    1990 and later
      Dry fill... 8.2 qts
      Drain and refill (filter replacement).................................... 3 qts
  Manual.. 2.6 qts

Ignition system

Spark plug type and gap
  1986
    2S-E engine
      Type.. Champion RC12YC or equivalent
      Gap... 0.044 inch
    3S-GE engine
      Type.. Champion RN11YCA or equivalent
      Gap... 0.044 inch
  1987
    3S-FE engine
      Type.. Champion RC12YC or equivalent
      Gap... 0.044 inch
    3S-GE engine
      Type.. Champion RC9YCN4 or equivalent
      Gap... 0.044 inch
  1988
    3S-FE engine
      Type.. Champion RC12YC or equivalent
      Gap... 0.044 inch
    3S-GE engine
      Type.. Champion RC9YCN4 or equivalent
      Gap... 0.044 inch
  1989
    3S-FE engine
      Type.. Champion RC9YCN4 or equivalent
      Gap... 0.044 inch
    3S-GE engine
      Type.. Champion RC9YCN4 or equivalent
      Gap... 0.044 inch
  1990
    4A-FE engine
      Type.. Champion RC9YCN4 or equivalent
      Gap... 0.032 inch
    5S-FE engine
      Type.. Champion RC12YC or equivalent
      Gap... 0.044 inch
  1991
    4A-FE engine
      Type.. NGK BCPR5EY or equivalent
      Gap`.. 0.032 inch

5S-FE engine
    Type... NGK BKR5YPA11 or equivalent
    Gap... 0.044 inch
1992 and later
  4A-FE engine
    Type... NGK BCPR5EY or equivalent
    Gap... 0.032 inch
  5S-FE engine
    Type... NGK BKR6EP-11 or equivalent
    Gap... 0.044 inch
Spark plug wire resistance .... Less than 25000 ohms
Engine firing order 1-3-4-2

0764H

4A-FE

Idle speed

1986
  2-SE engine.. 700 rpm
  3S-GE engine.. 750 rpm
1987 through 1989
  3S-FE engine.. 700 to 750
  3S-GE engine.. 750 rpm
1990 and 1991
  4A-FE engine.. 800 rpm
  5S-FE engine
    US models .... 700 to 750 rpm
    Canadian models
      Manual transaxle .... 800 to 850 rpm
      Automatic transaxle................................ 750 to 800 rpm
1992
  4A-FE engine.. 800 rpm
  5S-FE engine
    US models .... 700 to 750 rpm
    Canadian models....................................... 750 to 800 rpm

0763H

3S-FE, 3S-GE and 5S-FE

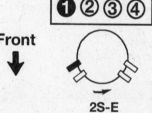

Front

2S-E

Cylinder location and distributor rotation

Valve clearances (engine cold)

1989 and earlier
  Intake valve
    3S-FE engine .... 0.007 to 0.011 inch
    3S-GE engine .... 0.006 to 0.010 inch
  Exhaust valve
    3S-FE engine .... 0.011 to 0.015 inch
    3S-GE engine .... 0.008 to 0.012 inch

1990 and later
  Intake valve
    4A-FE engine .... 0.006 to 0.010 inch
    5S-FE engine .... 0.007 to 0.011 inch
  Exhaust valve
    4A-FE engine .... 0.008 to 0.012 inch
    5S-FE engine .... 0.011 to 0.015 inch

Cooling system

Thermostat rating
  Starts to open... 190-degrees F
  Fully open.. 212-degrees F
Accessory drivebelt tension (with Burroughs or Nippondenso
tension gauge) - used belt
  1989 and earlier
    Power steering pump................................. 80 to 100 lbs
    Alternator .... 125 to 150 lbs
    Air conditioning compressor...................... 115 to 145 lbs
  1990 and later
    Power steering pump................................. 80 to 100 lbs
    Alternator .... 115 to 140 lbs
    Air conditioning compressor...................... 95 to 115 lbs

Clutch

Clutch pedal freeplay... 7/32 to 5/8 inch
Pedal height
  1989 and earlier... 6.0 to 6.5 inch
  1990 and later .... 6.5 to 7.0 inch
Pushrod play at pedal top .... 3/64 to 13/64 inch

Brakes

Disc brake pad lining thickness (minimum)...	1/16 inch
Drum brake shoe lining thickness (minimum).................................	1/16 inch
Parking brake adjustment..	4 to 7 clicks

Suspension and steering

Steering wheel freeplay limit..	1-3/16 inch
Balljoint allowable movement	0 inch

Torque specifications

Ft-lbs (unless otherwise indicated)

Automatic transaxle	
Pan bolts	48 in-lbs
Filter bolt	84 in-lbs
Drain plug	36
Manual transaxle drain and filler plugs...	36
Wheel lug nuts...	76
Chassis and body	
1989 and earlier	
Front seat mounting bolt	27
Engine mounting center crossmember-to-body bolt	29
1990 and later	
Front seat mounting bolt	27
Engine mounting center crossmember-to-body bolt	38
Front suspension lower crossmember-to-body bolt	112
Spark plugs...	13

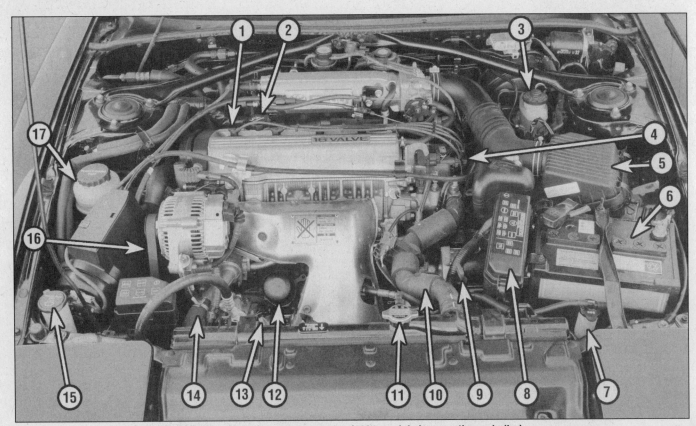

Engine compartment components (1991 model shown, others similar)

1	Spark plugs (Section 24)	10	Upper radiator hose (Section 14)
2	Oil filler cap (Section 4)	11	Radiator cap (Section 26)
3	Brake fluid reservoir (Section 4)	12	Engine oil filter (Section 8)
4	Distributor (Section 25)	13	Engine oil dipstick (Section 4)
5	Air cleaner assembly (Section 17)	14	Lower radiator hose (Section 14)
6	Battery (Section 11)	15	Windshield and rear washer fluid
7	Coolant reservoir (Section 4)		reservoir (Section 4)
8	Fuse block (Chapter 12)	16	Drivebelt (Section 12)
9	Automatic transaxle dipstick (Section 19)	17	Power steering fluid reservoir (Section 6)

Engine compartment underside components (1987 model shown, others similar)

1   Lower radiator hose (Section 14)
2   Radiator drain (Section 26)
3   Suspension strut and spring (Section 21)
4   Front disc brake (Section 16)
5   Suspension balljoint (Section 21)
6   Suspension crossmember bolt (Section 31)
7   Automatic transaxle differential drain plug (Section 29)

8   Automatic transaxle drain plug (Section 29)
9   Muffler (Section 28)
10 Exhaust system hanger (Section 28)
11 Engine oil pan drain plug (Section 8)
12 Driveaxle boot (Section 22)
13 Drivebelt (Section 12)

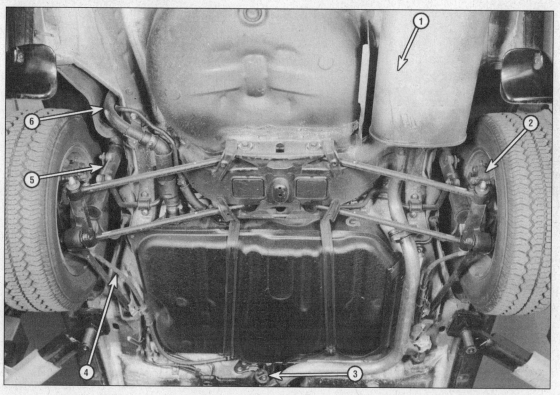

Typical rear underside components (1992 model shown, others similar)

1   Muffler (Section 28)
2   Rear brake (Section 16)
3   Exhaust system hanger (Section 28)

4   Parking brake cable (Section 16)
5   Suspension strut and spring (Section 21)
6   Gas tank filler hose (Section 18)

1 Toyota Celica
maintenance schedule

The maintenance intervals in this manual are provided with the assumption that you, not the dealer, will be doing the work. These are the minimum maintenance intervals recommended by the factory for Celicas that are driven daily. If you wish to keep your vehicle in peak condition at all times, you may wish to perform some of these procedures even more often. Because frequent maintenance enhances the efficiency, performance and resale value of your car, we encourage you to do so. If you drive in dusty areas, tow a trailer, idle or drive at low speeds for extended periods or drive for short distances (less than four miles) in below freezing temperatures, shorter intervals are also recommended.

When your vehicle is new, it should be serviced by a factory authorized dealer service department to protect the factory warranty. In many cases, the initial maintenance check is done at no cost to the owner.

Every 250 miles or weekly, whichever comes first

Check the engine oil level (Section 4)
Check the engine coolant level (Section 4)
Check the windshield washer fluid level (Section 4)
Check the brake and clutch fluid levels (Section 4)
Check the tires and tire pressures (Section 5)

Every 3000 miles or 3 months, whichever comes first

All items listed above plus:
Check the power steering fluid level (Section 6)
Check the automatic transaxle fluid level (Section 7)
Change the engine oil and oil filter (Section 8)

Every 6000 miles or 6 months, whichever comes first

Inspect and replace if necessary the windshield wiper blades (Section 9)
Check the clutch pedal for proper freeplay (Section 10)
Check and service the battery (Section 11)
Check and adjust if necessary the engine drivebelts (Section 12)
Inspect and replace if necessary all underhood hoses (Section 13)
Check the cooling system (Section 14)
Rotate the tires (Section 15)

Every 15,000 miles or 12 months, whichever comes first

All items listed above plus:
Inspect the brake system (Section 16)*
Replace the air filter (Section 17)
Inspect the fuel system (Section 18)
Check the automatic transaxle differential lubricant level (Section 19)*
Check the manual transaxle lubricant level (Section 20)*
Inspect the suspension and steeringcomponents (Section 21)*
Check the driveaxle boots (Section 22)

Every 30,000 miles or 24 months, whichever comes first

All items listed above plus:
Replace the fuel filter (Section 23)
Check and replace if necessary the spark plugs (Section 24)
Inspect and replace if necessary the spark plug wires, distributor cap and rotor (Section 25)
Service the cooling system (drain, flush and refill) (Section 26)
Inspect the evaporative emissions control system (Section 27)
Inspect the exhaust system (Section 28)
Change the automatic transaxle fluid and filter and differential oil (Section 29) **
Change the manual transaxle lubricant (Section 30)
Check and tighten critical chassis and body fasteners (Section 31)

Every 60,000 miles or 48 months, whichever comes first

Inspect and if necessary adjust the valve clearance (DOHC models only) (Section 32)
Replace the timing belt (Chapter 2A) ***
Replace the fuel tank cap gasket (Section 33)
Check and adjust if necessary the engine idle speed (Section 34)
Check and replace if necessary the PCV valve (Section 35)

* This item is affected by "severe" operating conditions as described below. If your vehicle is operated under "severe" conditions, perform all maintenance indicated with an asterisk (*) at 3000 mile/3 month intervals. Severe conditions are indicated if you mainly operate your vehicle under one or more of the following conditions:

Operating in dusty areas
Towing a trailer
Idling for extended periods and/or low speed operation
Operating when outside temperatures remain below freezing and when most trips are less than 4 miles
** If operated under one or more of the following conditions, change the automatic transaxle fluid and differential lubricant every 15,000 miles:
In heavy city traffic where the outside temperature regularly reaches 90-degrees F (32-degrees C) or higher
In hilly or mountainous terrain
Frequent trailer pulling

*** Replace the timing belt at 60,000 miles only if operated under severe conditions.

4.2 The engine oil dipstick (arrow) is located on the front side of the engine, behind the radiator

2   Introduction

This chapter is designed to help the home mechanic maintain the Toyota Celica front wheel drive models for peak performance, economy, safety and long life.

On the following pages is a master maintenance schedule, followed by sections dealing specifically with each item on the schedule. Visual checks, adjustments, component replacement and other helpful items are included. Refer to the accompanying illustrations of the engine compartment and the underside of the vehicle for the location of various components.

Servicing your Celica in accordance with the mileage/time maintenance schedule and the following Sections will provide it with a planned maintenance program that should result in a long and reliable service life. This is a comprehensive plan, so maintaining some items but not others at the specified service intervals will not produce the same results.

As you service your Celica, you will discover that many of the procedures can - and should - be grouped together because of the nature of the particular procedure you're performing or because of the close proximity of two otherwise unrelated components to one another.

For example, if the vehicle is raised for any reason, you should inspect the exhaust, suspension, steering and fuel systems while you're under the vehicle. When you're rotating the tires, it makes good sense to check the brakes and wheel bearings since the wheels are already removed.

Finally, let's suppose you have to borrow or rent a torque wrench. Even if you only need to tighten the spark plugs, you might as well check the torque of as many critical fasteners as time allows.

The first step of this maintenance program is to prepare yourself before the actual work begins. Read through all sections pertinent to the procedures you're planning to do, then make a list of and gather together all the parts and tools you will need to do the job. If it looks as if you might run into problems during a particular segment of some procedure, seek advice from your local parts man or dealer service department.

3   Tune-up general information

The term tune-up is used in this manual to represent a combination of individual operations rather than one specific procedure.

If, from the time the vehicle is new, the routine maintenance schedule is followed closely and frequent checks are made of fluid levels and high wear items, as suggested throughout this manual, the engine will be kept in relatively good running condition and the need for

additional work will be minimized.

More likely than not, however, there will be times when the engine is running poorly due to lack of regular maintenance. This is even more likely if a used vehicle, which has not received regular and frequent maintenance checks, is purchased. In such cases, an engine tune-up will be needed outside of the regular routine maintenance intervals.

The first step in any tune-up or engine diagnosis to help correct a poor running engine would be a cylinder compression check. A check of the engine compression (Chapter 2 Part B) will give valuable information regarding the overall performance of many internal components and should be used as a basis for tune-up and repair procedures. If, for instance, a compression check indicates serious internal engine wear, a conventional tune-up will not help the running condition of the engine and would be a waste of time and money.

The following series of operations are those most often needed to bring a generally poor running engine back into a proper state of tune.

Minor tune-up

Clean, inspect and test the battery (Section 11)
Check all engine related fluids (Section 4)
Check and adjust the drivebelts (Section 12)
Replace the spark plugs (Section 24)
Inspect the distributor cap and rotor (Section 25)
Inspect the spark plug and coil wires (Section 25)
Check and adjust the idle speed (Section 34)
Check the air filter (Section 17)
Check the cooling system (Section 14)
Check all underhood hoses (Section 13)

Major tune-up

All items listed under Minor tune-up, plus . . .
Check the ignition system (Section 25)
Check the charging system (Chapter 5)
Check the fuel system (Section 18)
Replace the air filter (Section 17)
Replace the distributor cap and rotor (Section 25)
Replace the spark plug wires (Section 25)

4   Fluid level checks (every 250 miles or weekly)

1   Fluids are an essential part of the lubrication, cooling, brake, clutch and other systems. Because these fluids gradually become depleted and/or contaminated during normal operation of the vehicle, they must be periodically replenished. See *Recommended lubricants and fluids* and *capacities* at the beginning of this Chapter before adding fluid to any of the following components. **Note:** *The vehicle must be on level ground before fluid levels can be checked.*

Engine oil

Refer to illustrations 4.2, 4.4 and 4.6
2   The engine oil level is checked with a dipstick located at the front side of the engine **(see illustration)**. The dipstick extends through a metal tube from which it protrudes down into the engine oil pan.
3   The oil level should be checked before the vehicle has been driven, or about 15 minutes after the engine has been shut off. If the oil is checked immediately after driving the vehicle, some of the oil will remain in the upper engine components, producing an inaccurate reading on the dipstick.
4   Pull the dipstick from the tube and wipe all the oil from the end with a clean rag or paper towel. Insert the clean dipstick all the way back into its metal tube and pull it out again. Observe the oil at the end of the dipstick. At its highest point, the level should be between the L and F marks **(see illustration)**.
5   It takes one quart of oil to raise the level from the L mark to the F mark on the dipstick. Do not allow the level to drop below the L mark or oil starvation may cause engine damage. Conversely, overfilling the engine (adding oil above the F mark) may cause oil fouled spark plugs, oil leaks or oil seal failures.
6   Remove the threaded cap from the camshaft cover to add oil

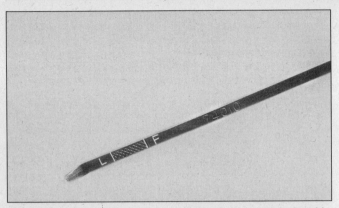

4.4 The oil level should be at or near the F mark - if it isn't, add enough oil to bring the level to near the F mark (it takes one full quart to raise the level from the L to the F mark)

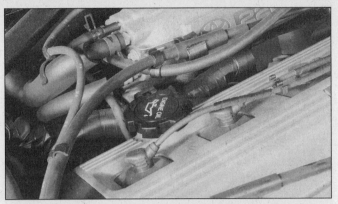

4.6 The threaded oil filler cap is located on the camshaft cover - always make sure the area around the opening is clean before unscrewing the cap to prevent dirt from contaminating the engine

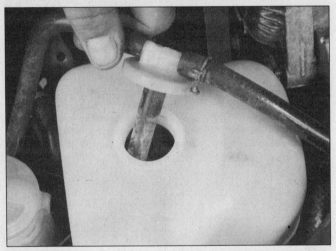

4.8a The coolant reservoir is located in the right front corner of the engine compartment on 1989 and earlier models - remove the cap to add coolant

4.8b On 1990 and later models, the coolant reservoir is located next to the battery - make sure the level is between Low and Full marks on the filler neck

(see illustration). Use a funnel to prevent spills. After adding the oil, install the filler cap hand tight. Start the engine and look carefully for any small leaks around the oil filter or drain plug. Stop the engine and check the oil level again after it has had sufficient time to drain from the upper block and cylinder head galleys.

7   Checking the oil level is an important preventive maintenance step. A continually dropping oil level indicates oil leakage through damaged seals, from loose connections, or past worn rings or valve guides. If the oil looks milky in color or has water droplets in it, a cylinder head gasket may be blown. The engine should be checked immediately. The condition of the oil should also be checked. Each time you check the oil level, slide your thumb and index finger up the dipstick before wiping off the oil. If you see small dirt or metal particles clinging to the dipstick, the oil should be changed (Section 8).

Engine coolant

Refer to illustrations 4.8a and 4.8b

Warning: *Do not aiiow antifreeze to come in contact with your skin or painted surfaces of the vehicle. Flush contaminated areas immediatiy with plenty of water. Don't store new coolant or leave old coolant lying around where it's accessible to children or pets – they're attracted by its sweet smell. Ingestion of even a small amount of coolant can be fatal! Wipe up garage floor and drip pan spills immediately. Keep antifreeze containers covered and repair cooling system leaks as soon as they'r noticed.*

8   All vehicles covered by this manual are equipped with a pressurized coolant recovery system. A white coolant reservoir located in the front corner of the engine compartment is connected by a hose to the base of the coolant filler cap (see illustrations). If the coolant heats up during engine operation, coolant can escape through a pressurized filler cap, then through a connecting hose into the reservoir. As the engine cools, the coolant is automatically drawn back into the cooling system to maintain the correct level.

9   The coolant level should be checked regularly. It must be between the Full and Low lines on the tank. The level will vary with the temperature of the engine. When the engine is cold, the coolant level should be at or slightly above the Low mark on the tank. Once the engine has warmed up, the level should be at or near the Full mark. If it isn't, allow the fluid in the tank to cool, then remove the cap from the reservoir and add coolant to bring the level up to the Full line. Use only ethylene/glycol type coolant and water in the mixture ratio recommended by your owner's manual. Do not use supplemental inhibitorsor additives. If only a small amount of coolant is required to bring the system up to the proper level, water can be used. However, repeated additions of water will dilute the recommended antifreeze and water solution. In order to maintain the proper ratio of antifreeze and water, it is advisable to top up the coolant level with the correct mixture. Refer to your owner's manual for the recommended ratio.

10   If the coolant level drops within a short time after replenishment, there may be a leak in the system. Inspect the radiator, hoses, engine coolant filler cap, drain plugs, air bleeder plugs and water pump. If no leak is evident, have the radiator cap pressure tested by your dealer.

Warning: *Never remove the radiator cap or the coolant recovery reservoir cap when the engine is running or has just been shut down, because the cooling system is hot. Escaping steam and scalding liquid could cause serious injury.*

11   If it is necessary to open the radiator cap, wait until the system has cooled completely, then wrap a thick cloth around the cap and

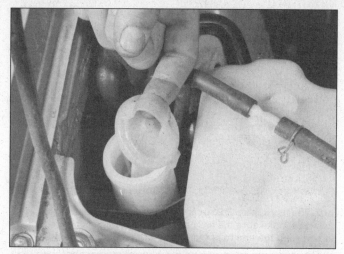

4.14 The windshield washer fluid reservoir tank is located in the right front corner of the engine compartment - fluid can be added after flipping up the cap

turn it to the first stop. If any steam escapes, wait until the system has cooled further, then remove the cap.

12   When checking the coolant level, always note its condition. It should be relatively clear. If it is brown or rust colored, the system should be drained, flushed and refilled. Even if the coolant appears to be normal, the corrosion inhibitors wear out with use, so it must be replaced at the specified intervals.

13   Do not allow antifreeze to come in contact with your skin or painted surfaces of the vehicle. Flush contacted areas immediately with plenty of water.

Windshield washer fluid

Refer to illustration 4.14

14   Fluid for the windshield washer system is stored in a plastic reservoir which is located at the right front corner of the engine compartment **(see illustration)**. In milder climates, plain water can be used to top up the reservoir, but the reservoir should be kept no more than two-thirds full to allow for expansion should the water freeze. In colder climates, the use of a specially designed windshield washer fluid, available at your dealer and any auto parts store, will help lower the freezing point of the fluid. Mix the solution with water in accordance with the manufacturer's directions on the container. Do not use regular antifreeze. It will damage the vehicle's paint.

Battery electrolyte

Refer to illustration 4.15

15   On models not equipped with a sealed battery, check the electrolyte level of all six battery cells. It must be between the upper and lower levels **(see illustration)**. If the level is low, unscrew the filler/vent cap and add distilled water. Install and securely retighten the cap. **Caution:** *Overfilling the cells may cause electrolyte to spill over during periods of heavy charging, causing corrosion or damage.*

Brake and clutch fluid

Refer to illustration 4.17

16   The brake master cylinder is mounted on the front of the power booster unit in the engine compartment. The clutch cylinder used on manual transaxles is located next to the master cylinder.

17   To check the fluid level of the brake master cylinder reservoir, simply look at the MAX and MIN marks on the reservoir **(see illustration)**. To check the fluid level of the clutch master cylinder reservoir, note whether the fluid level is even with the maximum level line. The level should be within the specified distance from the maximum fill line for both reservoirs.

18   If the level is low for either reservoir, wipe the top of the reservoir cover with a clean rag to prevent contamination of the brake or clutch system before lifting the cover.

19   Add only the specified brake fluid to the brake or clutch reservoir

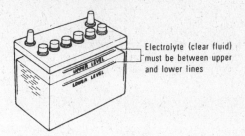

Electrolyte (clear fluid) must be between upper and lower lines

4.15 On non-sealed batteries, keep the electrolyte level of all the cells in the battery between the Upper and Lower levels - use only distilled water to replenish a cell and never overfill it or electrolyte may squirt out of the battery during periods of heavy charging

4.17 The brake fluid level should be kept between the MIN and MAX marks on the translucent plastic reservoir - lift up the cap to add fluid

(refer to *Recommended lubricants and fluids* at the front of this chapter or to your owner's manual). Mixing different types of brake fluid can damage the system. Fill the brake master cylinder reservoir only to the dotted line - this brings the fluid to the correct level when you put the cover back on. **Warning:** *Use caution when filling either reservoir- brake fluid can harm your eyes and damage painted surfaces. Do not use brake fluid that has been opened for more than one year or has been left open. Brake fluid absorbs moisture from the air. Excess moisture can cause a dangerous loss of braking.*

20   While the reservoir cap is removed, inspect the master cylinder reservoir for contamination. If deposits, dirt particles or water droplets are present, the system should be drained and refilled (see Chapter 8 for clutch reservoir or Chapter 9 for brake reservoir).

21   After filling the reservoir to the proper level, make sure the lid is properly seated to prevent fluid leakage and/or system pressure loss.

22   The brake fluid in the master cylinder will drop slightly as the brake pads at each wheel wear down during normal operation. If the master cylinder requires repeated replenishing to keep it at the proper level, this is an indication of leakage in the brake system, which should be corrected immediately. Check all brake lines and connections, along with the wheel cylinders and booster (see Section 16 for more information).

23   If, upon checking the master cylinder fluid level, you discover one or both reservoirs empty or nearly empty, the brake system should be bled (see Chapter 9).

---

5   Tire and tire pressure checks (every 250 miles or weekly)

Refer to illustrations 5.2, 5.3, 5.4a, 5.4b and 5.8

1   Periodic inspection of the tires may spare you from the inconvenience of being stranded with a flat tire. It can also provide you with vital information regarding possible problems in the steering and sus-

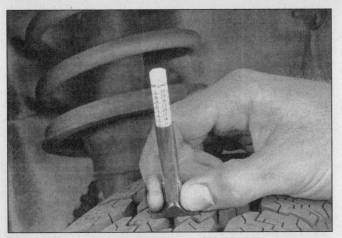

5.2 A tire tread depth indicator should be used to monitor tire wear - they are available at auto parts stores and service stations and cost very little

pension systems before major damage occurs.

2   Normal tread wear can be monitored with a simple, inexpensive device known as a tread depth indicator **(see illustration)**. When the tread depth reaches the specified minimum, replace the tire(s).

3   Note any abnormal tread wear **(see illustration)**. Tread pattern ir regularities such as cupping, flat spots and more wear on one side than the other are indications of front end alignment and/or balanceproblems. If any of these conditions are noted, take the vehicle to a tire shop or service station to correct the problem.

4   ¨Look closely for cuts, punctures and embedded nails or tacks. Sometimes a tire will hold its air pressure for a short time or leak down very slowly even after a nail has embedded itself into the tread. If a slow leak persists, check the valve stem core to make sure it is tight **(see illustration)**. Examine the tread for an object that may have embedded itself into the tire or for a "plug" that may have begun to leak (radial tire punctures are repaired with a plug that is installed in a

puncture). If a puncture is suspected, it can be easily verified by spraying a solution of soapy water onto the puncture area **(see illustration)**. The soapy solution will bubble if there is a leak. Unless the puncture is inordinately large, a tire shop or gas station can usually repair the punctured tire.

5   Carefully inspect the inner sidewall of each tire for evidence of brake fluid leakage. If you see any, inspect the brakes immediately.

6   Correct tire air pressure adds miles to the lifespan of the tires, improves mileage and enhances overall ride quality. Tire pressure cannot be accurately estimated by looking at a tire, particularly if it is a radial. A tire pressure gauge is therefore essential. Keep an accurate gauge in the glovebox. The pressure gauges fitted to the nozzles of air hoses at gas stations are often inaccurate.

7   Always check tire pressure when the tires are cold. "Cold," in this case, means the vehicle has not been driven over a mile in the three hours preceding a tire pressure check. A pressure rise of four to eight pounds is not uncommon once the tires are warm.

8   Unscrew the valve cap protruding from the wheel or hubcap and push the gauge firmly onto the valve **(see illustration)**. Note the reading on the gauge and compare this figure to the recommended tire pressure shown on the tire placard on the left door. Be sure to reinstall the valve cap to keep dirt and moisture out of the valve stem mechanism. Check all four tires and, if necessary, add enough air to bring them up to the recommended pressure levels.

9   Don't forget to keep the spare tire inflated to the specified pressure (consult your owner's manual). Note that the air pressure specified for the compact spare is significantly higher than the pressure of the regular tires.

6   Power steering fluid level check (every 3000 miles or 3 months)

All models

1   Unlike manual steering, the power steering system relies on fluid which may, over a period of time, require replenishing.

Condition	Probable cause	Corrective action	Condition	Probable cause	Corrective action
Shoulder wear	• Underinflation (both sides wear) • Incorrect wheel camber (one side wear) • Hard cornering • Lack of rotation	• Measure and adjust pressure. • Repair or replace axle and suspension parts. • Reduce speed. • Rotate tires.	Feathered edge Toe wear	• Incorrect toe	• Adjust toe-in.
Center wear	• Overinflation • Lack of rotation	• Measure and adjust pressure. • Rotate tires.	Uneven wear	• Incorrect camber or caster • Malfunctioning suspension • Unbalanced wheel • Out-of-round brake drum • Lack of rotation	• Repair or replace axle and suspension parts. • Repair or replace suspension parts. • Balance or replace. • Turn or replace. • Rotate tires.

5.3 This chart will help you determine the condition of your tires, the probable cause(s) of abnormal wear and the corrective action necessary

5.4a If a tire loses air on a steady basis, check the valve core first to make sure it's snug (special inexpensive wrenches are commonly available at auto parts stores)

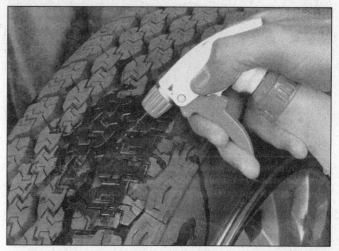

5.4b If the valve core is tight, raise the corner of the vehicle with the low tire and spray a soapy water solution onto the tread as the tire is turned slowly - slow leaks will cause small bubbles to appear

1

5.8 To extend the life of your tires, check the air pressure at least once a week with an accurate gauge (don't forget the spare!)

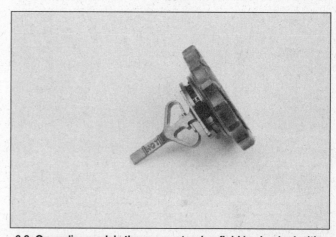

6.6 On earlier models the power steering fluid is checked with a dipstick which is part of the cap - the fluid level varies with temperature, so the fluid can be checked hot or cold

1989 and earlier models

Refer to illustration 6.6

4   Use a clean rag to wipe off the reservoir cap and the area around the cap. This will help prevent any foreign matter from entering the reservoir during the check.

5   Twist off the cap and check the temperature of the fluid at the end of the dipstick with your finger.

6   Wipe off the fluid with a clean rag, reinsert it, then withdraw it and read the fluid level. The level should be at the HOT mark if the fluid was hot to the touch. It should be at the COLD mark if the fluid was cool to the touch. Note that the marks (HOT and COLD) are on opposite sides of the dipstick **(see illustration)**. At no time should the fluid level drop below the upper mark for each heat range.

1990 and later models

Refer to illustration 6.7

7   On these models the reservoir is translucent plastic and the fluid level can be checked visually **(see illustration)**.

All models

8   If additional fluid is required, pour the specified type directly into the reservoir, using a funnel to prevent spills.

9   If the reservoir requires frequent fluid additions, all power steering hoses, hose connections, the power steering pump and the rack and pinion assembly should be carefully checked for leaks.

6.7 On later models, the power steering fluid reservoir is translucent so the fluid level can be checked without removing the cap

2   The fluid reservoir for the power steering pump is located on the inner fender panel near the front of the engine.

3   For the check, the front wheels should be pointed straight ahead and the engine should be off.

7.4a The automatic transaxle dipstick is located in a tube which extends back from behind the radiator to the transaxle

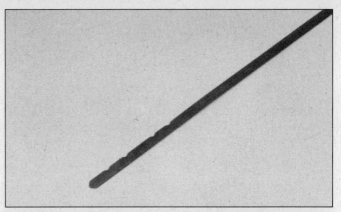

7.4b If the automatic transaxle fluid is cold, the level should be between the two lower notches; if it's at operating temperature, the level should be between the two upper notches

7   Automatic transaxle fluid level check (every 3000 miles or 3 months)

Refer to illustrations 7.4a and 7.4b

1   The level of the automatic transaxle fluid should be carefully maintained. Low fluid level can lead to slipping or loss of drive, while overfilling can cause foaming, loss of fluid and transaxle damage.

2   The transaxle fluid level should only be checked when the transaxle is hot (at its normal operating temperature). If the vehicle has just been driven over 10 miles (15 miles in a frigid climate), and the fluid temperature is 160 to 175-degrees F, the transaxle is hot. **Caution:** *If the vehicle has just been driven for a long time at high speed or in city traffic in hot weather, or if it has been pulling a trailer, an accurate fluid level reading cannot be obtained. Allow the fluid to cool down for about 30 minutes.*

3   If the vehicle has not just been driven, park the vehicle on level ground, set the parking brake and start the engine. While the engine is idling, depress the brake pedal and move the selector lever through all the gear ranges, beginning and ending in Park.

4   With the engine still idling, remove the dipstick from its tube **(see illustration)**. Check the level of the fluid on the dipstick **(see illustration)** and note its condition.

5   Wipe the fluid from the dipstick with a clean rag and reinsert it back into the filler tube until the cap seats.

6   Pull the dipstick out again and note the fluid level. If the transaxle is cold, the level should be in the COLD or COOL range on the dipstick. If it is hot, the fluid level should be in the HOT range. If the level is at the low side of either range, add the specified automatic transmission fluid through the dipstick tube with a funnel.

7   Add just enough of the recommended fluid to fill the transaxle to the proper level. It takes about one pint to raise the level from the low mark to the high mark when the fluid is hot, so add the fluid a little at a time and keep checking the level until it is correct.

8   The condition of the fluid should also be checked along with the level. If the fluid at the end of the dipstick is black or a dark reddish brown color, or if it emits a burned smell, the fluid should be changed (see Section 29). If you are in doubt about the condition of the fluid, purchase some new fluid and compare the two for color and smell.

8   Engine oil and oil filter change (every 3000 miles or 3 months)

Refer to illustrations 8.2, 8.7, 8.13, and 8.15

1   Frequent oil changes are the best preventive maintenance the home mechanic can give the engine, because aging oil becomes diluted and contaminated, which leads to premature engine wear.

2   Make sure that you have all the necessary tools before you begin

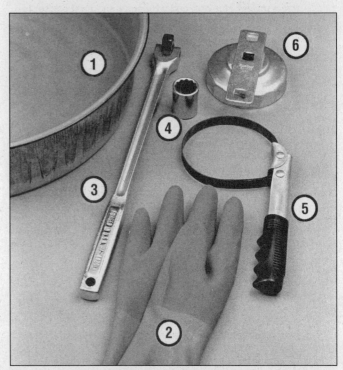

8.2 These tools are required when changing the engine oil and filter

1   **Drain pan** - It should be fairly shallow in depth, but wide in order to prevent spills

2   **Rubber gloves** - When removing the drain plug and filter, it is inevitable that you will get oil on your hands (the gloves will prevent burns)

3   **Breaker bar**- Sometimes the oil drain plug is pretty tight and a long breaker bar is needed to loosen it

4   **Socket** – To be used with the breaker bar or a ratchet (must be the correct size to fit the drain plug)

5   **Filter wrench** - This is a metal band-type wrench, which requires clearance around the filter to be effective

6   **Filter wrench** - This type fits on the bottom of the filter and can be turned with a ratchet or beaker bar (different size wrenches are available for different types of filters)

this procedure **(see illustration)**. You should also have plenty of rags or newspapers handy for mopping up any spills.

3   Access to the underside of the vehicle is greatly improved if the vehicle can be lifted on a hoist, driven onto ramps or supported by jackstands. **Warning:** *Do not work under a vehicle which is supported only by a bumper, hydraulic or scissors-type jack.*

8.7 Use a proper size box-end wrench or six-point socket to remove the oil drain plug and avoid rounding it off

8.13 Since the oil filter is mounted in the upside down position, pack rags around it before removal it to minimize the mess - since it's usually on very tight, you'll need a special wrench for removal - DO NOT use the wrench to tighten the new filter

4   If this is your first oil change, get under the vehicle and familiarize yourself with the location of the oil drain plug. The engine and exhaust components will be warm during the actual work, so try to anticipate any potential problems before the engine and accessories are hot.

5   Park the vehicle on a level spot. Start the engine and allow it to reach its normal operating temperature (the needle on the temperature gauge should be at least above the bottom mark). Warm oil and sludge will flow out more easily. Turn off the engine when it's warmed up. Remove the filler cap in the rear cam cover.

6   Raise the vehicle and support it on jackstands. **Warning:** *To avoid personal injury, never get beneath the vehicle when it is supported by only by a jack. The jack provided with your vehicle is designed solely for raising the vehicle to remove and replace the wheels. Always use jackstands to support the vehicle when it becomes necessary to place your body underneath the vehicle.*

7   Being careful not to touch the hot exhaust components, place the drain pan under the drain plug in the bottom of the pan and remove the plug **(see illustration)**. You may want to wear gloves while unscrewing the plug the final few turns if the engine is really hot.

8   Allow the old oil to drain into the pan. It may be necessary to move the pan farther under the engine as the oil flow slows to a trickle. Inspect the old oil for the presence of metal shavings and chips.

9   After all the oil has drained, wipe off the drain plug with a clean rag. Even minute metal particles clinging to the plug would immediately contaminate the new oil.

10   Clean the area around the drain plug opening, reinstall the plug and tighten it securely, but do not strip the threads.

11   Move the drain pan into position under the oil filter.

12   Remove all tools, rags, etc. from under the vehicle, being careful not to spill the oil in the drain pan, then lower the vehicle.

13   Loosen the oil filter **(see illustration)** by turning it counterclockwise with the filter wrench. Any standard filter wrench will work. Sometimes the oil filter is screwed on so tightly that it cannot be loosened. If this situation occurs, punch a metal bar or long screwdriver directly through the side of the canister and use it as a T-bar to turn the filter. Be prepared for oil to spurt out of the canister as it is punctured. Once the filter is loose, use your hands to unscrew it from the block. Just as the filter is detached from the block, immediately tilt the open end up to prevent the oil inside the filter from spilling out. **Warning:** *The engine exhaust manifold may still be hot, so be careful.*

14   With a clean rag, wipe off the mounting surface on the block. If a residue of old oil is allowed to remain, it will smoke when the block is heated up. It will also prevent the new filter from seating properly. Also make sure that the none of the old gasket remains stuck to the mounting surface. It can be removed with a scraper if necessary.

15   Compare the old filter with the new one to make sure they are the same type. Smear some engine oil on the rubber gasket of the new filter and screw it into place **(see illustration)**. Because overtightening the filter will damage the gasket, do not use a filter wrench to tighten

8.15 Lubricate the oil filter gasket with clean engine oil before installing the filter on the engine

the filter. Tighten it by hand until the gasket contacts the seating surface. Then seat the filter by giving it an additional 3/4-turn.

16   Add new oil to the engine through the oil filler cap in the valve cover. Use a spout or funnel to prevent oil from spilling onto the top of the engine. Pour three quarts of fresh oil into the engine. Wait a few minutes to allow the oil to drain into the pan, then check the level on the oil dipstick (see Section 4 if necessary). If the oil level is at or near the F mark, install the filler cap hand tight, start the engine and allow the new oil to circulate.

17   Allow the engine to run for about a minute. While the engine is running, look under the vehicle and check for leaks at the oil pan drain plug and around the oil filter. If either is leaking, stop the engine and tighten the plug or filter slightly.

18   Wait a few minutes to allow the oil to trickle down into the pan, then recheck the level on the dipstick and, if necessary, add enough oil to bring the level to the F mark.

19   During the first few trips after an oil change, make it a point to check frequently for leaks and proper oil level.

20   The old oil drained from the engine cannot be reused in its present state and should be discarded. Oil reclamation centers, auto repair shops and gas stations will normally accept the oil, which can be refined and used again. After the oil has cooled, it can be drained into a suitable container (capped plastic jugs, topped bottles, milk cartons, etc.) for transport to one of these disposal sites.

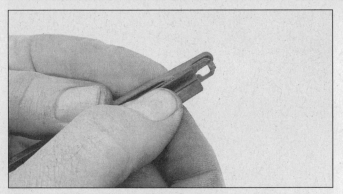

9.5a To remove the old wiper blade element, pull the top end of the element down until you can see the replacement hole in the frame . . .

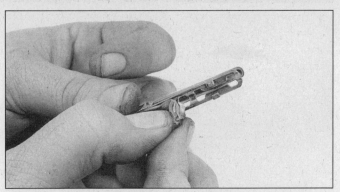

9.5b . . . then pull the element tab out of the hole (note the relationship to the frame) and slide the element from the frame

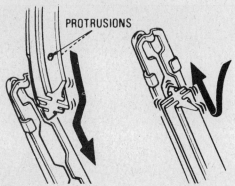

9.7 To install a new element, insert the end of the blade with the small protrusions into the replacement hole and work the rubber along the slot in the blade frame - once all the rubber is in the frame slot, allow it to expand and fill in the end

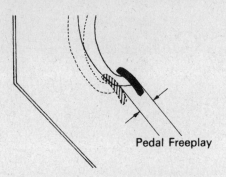

10.1 To check clutch pedal freeplay, measure the distance between the natural resting place of the pedal and the point at which you encounter resistance

9   Windshield wiper blade inspection and replacement (every 6000 miles or 6 months)

Refer to illustrations 9.5a, 9.5b and 9.7

1   The windshield wiper and blade assembly should be inspected periodically for damage, loose components and cracked or worn blade elements.

2   Road film can build up on the wiper blades and affect their efficiency, so they should be washed regularly with a mild detergent solution.

3   The action of the wiping mechanism can loosen bolts, nuts and fasteners, so they should be checked and tightened, as necessary, at the same time the wiper blades are checked.

4   If the wiper blade elements are cracked, worn or warped, or no longer clean adequately, they should be replaced with new ones.

5   Lift the arm assembly away from the glass for clearance and pull the top end of the rubber blade element in **(see illustrations)** until the rubber blade is free of the end slot and you can see the replacement hole.

6   Remove the rubber blade from the frame and discard it.

7   To install a new rubber wiper element, insert the end with the small protrusions **(see illustration)** into the replacement hole and work the rubber along the slot in the blade frame.

8   Once all the rubber is in the frame slot, allow it to expand and fill in the end.

10   Clutch pedal freeplay check and adjustment (every 6000 miles or 6 months)

Refer to illustrations 10.1 and 10.2

1   Press down lightly on the clutch pedal and, with a small steel

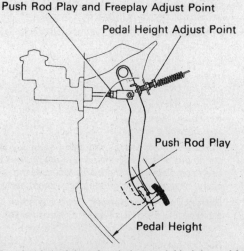

10.2 The clutch pedal pushrod play, pedal height and freeplay adjustments are made by loosening the locknut and turning the threaded adjuster

ruler, measure the distance that it moves freely before the clutch resistance is felt **(see illustration)**. The freeplay should be within the specified limits. If it isn't, it must be adjusted.

2   Loosen the locknut on the pedal end of the clutch pushrod **(see illustrations)**.

3   Turn the pushrod until pedal freeplay and pushrod freeplay are correct.

4   Tighten the locknut.

5   After adjusting the pedal freeplay, check the pedal height.

6   If pedal height is incorrect, loosen the locknut and turn the stopper bolt until the height is correct. Tighten the locknut.

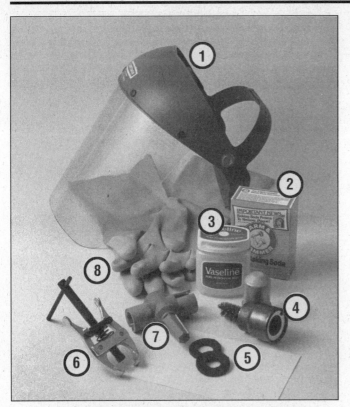

11.1 Tools and materials required for battery maintenance

1   ***Face shield/safety goggles*** - *When removing corrosion with a brush, the acidic particles can easily fly up into your eyes*

2   ***Baking soda*** - *A solution of baking soda and water can be used to neutralize corrosion*

3   ***Petroleum jelly*** - *A layer of this on the battery posts will help prevent corrosion*

4   ***Battery post/cable cleaner*** - *This wire brush cleaning tool will remove all traces of corrosion from the battery posts and cable clamps*

5   ***Treated felt washers*** - *Placing one of these on each post, directly under the cable clamps, will help prevent corrosion*

6   ***Puller*** - *Sometimes the cable clamps are very difficult to pull off the posts, even after the nut/bolt has been completely loosened. This tool pulls the clamp straight up and off the post without damage*

7   ***Battery post/cable cleaner*** - *Here is another cleaning tool which is a slightly different version of number 4 above, but it does the same thing*

8   ***Rubber gloves*** - *Another safety item to consider when servicing the battery; remember that's acid inside the battery*

11   Battery check, maintenance and charging (every 6000 miles or 6 months)

Refer to illustrations 11.1, 11.6a, 11.6b, 11.7a, 11.7b and 11.8
Warning: *Certain precautions must be followed when checking and servicing the battery. Hydrogen gas, which is highly flammable, is always present in the battery cells, so keep lighted tobacco and all other open flames and sparks away from the battery. The electrolyte inside the battery is actually dilute sulfuric acid, which will cause injury if splashed on your skin or in your eyes. It will also ruin clothes and painted surfaces. When removing the battery cables, always detach the negative cable first and hook it up last!*

11.6a Battery terminal corrosion usually appears as light, fluffy powder

11.6b Removing a cable from the battery post with a wrench - sometimes a special battery pliers is required for this procedure if corrosion has caused deterioration of the nut hex (always remove the ground cable first and hook it up last!)

Caution: *If the stereo in your vehicle is equiped with an anti-theft system, refer to the information on page 0-15 at the front of this manual befor detaching the cable.*

1   A routine preventive maintenance program for the battery in your vehicle is the only way to ensure quick and reliable starts. But before performing any battery maintenance, make sure that you have the proper equipment necessary to work safely around the battery **(see illustration)**.

2   There are also several precautions that should be taken whenever battery maintenance is performed. Before servicing the battery, always turn the engine and all accessories off and disconnect the cable from the negative terminal of the battery.

3   The battery produces hydrogen gas, which is both flammable and explosive. Never create a spark, smoke or light a match around the battery. Always charge the battery in a ventilated area.

4   Electrolyte contains poisonous and corrosive sulfuric acid. Do not allow it to get in your eyes, on your skin on your clothes. Never ingest it. Wear protective safety glasses when working near the battery. Keep children away from the battery.

5   Note the external condition of the battery. If the positive terminal and cable clamp on your vehicle's battery is equipped with a rubber protector, make sure that it's not torn or damaged. It should completely cover the terminal. Look for any corroded or loose connections, cracks in the case or cover or loose hold-down clamps. Also check the entire length of each cable for cracks and frayed conductors.

6   If corrosion, which looks like white, fluffy deposits **(see illustration)** is evident, particularly around the terminals, the battery should be removed for cleaning. Loosen the cable clamp bolts with a wrench, being careful to remove the ground cable first, and slide them off the terminals **(see illustration)**. Then disconnect the hold-down clamp bolt and nut, remove the clamp and lift the battery from the engine compartment.

11.7a When cleaning the cable clamps, all corrosion must be removed (the inside of the clamp is tapered to match the taper on the post, so don't remove too much material)

11.7b Regardless of the type of tool used to clean the battery posts, a clean, shiny surface should be the result

11.8 Make sure the battery hold-down nut (arrow) is tight

7   Clean the cable clamps thoroughly with a battery brush or a terminal cleaner and a solution of warm water and baking soda **(see illustration)**. Wash the terminals and the top of the battery case with the same solution but make sure that the solution doesn't get into the battery When cleaning the cables, terminals and battery top, wear safety goggles and rubber gloves to prevent any solution from coming in contact with your eyes or hands. Wear old clothes too - even diluted, sulfuric acid splashed onto clothes will burn holes in them. If the terminals have been extensively corroded, clean them up with a terminal cleaner **(see illustration)**. Thoroughly wash all cleaned areas with plain water.
8   Make sure that the battery tray is in good condition and the hold-down clamp bolt or nut is tight **(see illustration)**. If the battery is removed from the tray, make sure no parts remain in the bottom of the tray when the battery is reinstalled. When reinstalling the hold-down clamp bolt or nut, do not overtighten it.
9   Information on removing and installing the battery can be found in Chapter 5. Information on jump starting can be found at the front of this manual. For more detailed battery checking procedures, refer to the *Haynes Automotive Electrical Manual*.

Cleaning

10   Corrosion on the hold-down components, battery case and surrounding areas can be removed with a solution of water and baking soda. Thoroughly rinse all cleaned areas with plain water.
11   Any metal parts of the vehicle damaged by corrosion should be covered with a zinc-based primer, then painted.

Charging

Warning: *When batteries are being charged, hydrogen gas, which is very explosive and flammable, is produced. Do not smoke or allow*

open flames near a charging or a recently charged battery. Wear eye protection when near the battery during charging. Also, make sure the charger is unplugged before connecting or disconnecting the battery from the charger.
12   Slow-rate charging is the best way to restore a battery that's discharged to the point where it will not start the engine. It's also a good way to maintain the battery charge in a vehicle that's only driven a few miles between starts. Maintaining the battery charge is particularly important in the winter when the battery must work harder to start the engine and electrical accessories that drain the battery are in greater use.
13   It's best to use a one or two-amp battery charger (sometimes called a "trickle" charger). They are the safest and put the least strain on the battery. They are also the least expensive. For a faster charge, you can use a higher amperage charger, but don't use one rated more than 1/10th the amp/hour rating of the battery. Rapid boost charges that claim to restore the power of the battery in one to two hours are hardest on the battery and can damage batteries not in good condition. This type of charging should only be used in emergency situations.
14   The average time necessary to charge a battery should be listed in the instructions that come with the charger. As a general rule, a trickle charger will charge a battery in 12 to 16 hours.

---

12   Drivebelt check, adjustment and replacement (every 6000 miles or 6 months)

Refer to illustrations 12.3, 12.4, 12.5, 12.6 and 12.10

Check

1   The alternator and air conditioning compressor drivebelts, also referred to as V-ribbed belts or simply "fan" belts, are located at the right end of the engine. The good condition and proper adjustment of the alternator belt is critical to the operation of the engine. Because of their composition and the high stresses to which they are subjected, drivebelts stretch and deteriorate as they get older. They must therefore be periodically inspected.
2   The number of belts used on a particular vehicle depends on the accessories installed. One belt transmits power from the crankshaft to the alternator and air conditioning. If the vehicle is equipped with power steering, the pump is driven by it's own belt.
3   With the engine off, open the hood and locate the drivebelts at the left end of the engine. With a flashlight, check each belt for separation of the adhesive rubber on both sides of the core, core separation from the belt side, a severed core, separation of the ribs from the adhesive rubber, cracking or separation of the ribs, and torn or worn ribs or cracks in the inner ridges of the ribs **(see illustration)**. Also check for fraying and glazing, which gives the belt a shiny appearance. Both sides of the belt should be inspected, which means you will have to twist the belt to check the underside. Use your fingers to feel the belt where you can't see it. If any of the above conditions are evident, re-

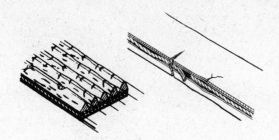

12.3 Check the V-ribbed belt for signs of wear like these – if the belt looks worn, replace it

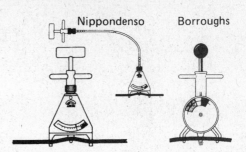

12.4 If you are able to borrow either a Nippondenso or Burroughs belt tension gauge, this is how it's installed on the belt - compare the reading on the scale with the specified drivebelt tension

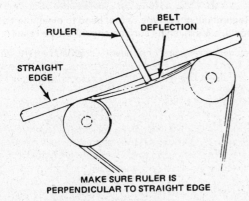

12.5 Measuring drivebelt deflection with a straightedge and ruler

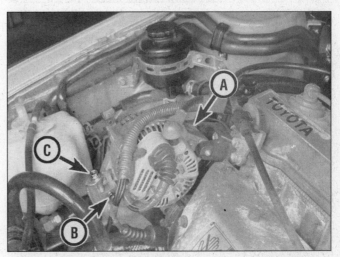

12.6 After loosening the pivot bolt (A) and locking bolt (B), a socket with an extension can be used to turn the adjusting bolt(C)

place the belt (go to Step 8).

4   To check the tension of each belt in accordance with factory specifications, install either a Nippondenso or Burroughs belt tension gauge on the belt (see illustration). Measure the tension in accordance with the manufacturer's instructions and compare your measurement to the specified drivebelt tension for either a used or new belt. **Note:** *A "used" belt is defined as any belt which has been operated more than five minutes on the engine; a "new" belt is one that has been used for less than five minutes.*

5   If you don't have either of the above tools, and cannot borrow one, the following rule of thumb method is recommended: Push firmly on the belt with your thumb at a distance halfway between the pulleys and note how far the belt can be pushed (deflected). Measure this deflection with a ruler (see illustration). The belt should deflect 1/4-inch if the distance from pulley center to pulley center is between 7 and 11 inches; the belt should deflect 1/2-inch if the distance from pulley center to pulley center is between 12 and 16 inches.

Adjustment

6   If the alternator/air conditioner compressor belt must be adjusted, loosen the alternator pivot bolt located on the front left corner of the block. Loosen the locking bolt and turn the adjusting bolt (see illustration). Measure the belt tension in accordance with one of the above methods. Repeat this step until the air conditioning compressor drivebelt is adjusted.

7   Adjust the power steering pump belt by loosening adjustment bolt that secures the pump to the slotted bracket and pivot the pump (away from the engine to tighten the belt, toward it to loosen it). Repeat the procedure until the drivebelt tension is correct and tighten the bolt.

Replacement

8   To replace a belt, follow the above procedures for drivebelt adjustment but slip the belt off the crankshaft pulley and remove it. If youare replacing the power steering pump belt, you will have to remove the air conditioning compressor belt first because of the way they are arranged on the crankshaft pulley. Because of this and be-

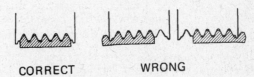

12.10 When installing a V-ribbed belt, make sure that it is centered - it must not overlap either edge of the pulley

cause belts tend to wear out more or less together, it is a good idea to replace both belts at the same time. Mark each belt and its appropriate pulley groove so the replacement belts can be installed in their proper positions.

9   Take the old belts to the parts store in order to make a direct comparison for length, width and design.

10   After replacing the drivebelt, make sure that it fits properly in the ribbed grooves in the pulleys (see illustration). It is essential that the belt be properly centered.

11   Adjust the belt(s) in accordance with the procedure outlined above.

13   Underhood hose check and replacement (every 6000 miles or 6 months)

Caution: *Replacement of air conditioning hoses must be left to a dealer service department or air conditioning shop that has the equipment to depressurize the system safely. Never remove air conditioning components or hoses until the system has been depressurized.*

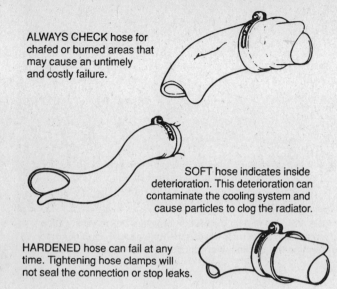

ALWAYS CHECK hose for chafed or burned areas that may cause an untimely and costly failure.

SOFT hose indicates inside deterioration. This deterioration can contaminate the cooling system and cause particles to clog the radiator.

HARDENED hose can fail at any time. Tightening hose clamps will not seal the connection or stop leaks.

SWOLLEN hose or oil soaked ends indicate danger and possible failure from oil or grease contamination. Squeeze the hose to locate cracks and breaks that cause leaks.

14.4 Hoses, like drivebelts, have a habit of failing at the worst possible time - to prevent the inconvenience of a blown radiator or heater hose, inspect them carefully as shown here

General

1   High temperatures in the engine compartment can cause the deterioration of the rubber and plastic hoses used for engine, accessory and emission systems operation. Periodic inspection should be made for cracks, loose clamps, material hardening and leaks.

2   Information specific to the cooling system hoses can be found in Section 14.

3   Some, but not all, hoses are secured to the fittings with clamps. Where clamps are used, check to be sure they haven't lost their tension, allowing the hose to leak. If clamps aren't used, make sure the hose has not expanded and/or hardened where it slips over the fitting, allowing it to leak.

Vacuum hoses

4   It's quite common for vacuum hoses, especially those in the emissions system, to be color coded or identified by colored stripes molded into them. Various systems require hoses with different wall thicknesses, collapse resistance and temperature resistance. When replacing hoses, be sure the new ones are made of the same material.

5   Often the only effective way to check a hose is to remove it completely from the vehicle. If more than one hose is removed, be sure to label the hoses and fittings to ensure correct installation.

6   When checking vacuum hoses, be sure to include any plastic T-fittings in the check. Inspect the fittings for cracks and the hose where it fits over the fitting for distortion, which could cause leakage.

7   A small piece of vacuum hose (1/4-inch inside diameter) can be used as a stethoscope to detect vacuum leaks. Hold one end of the hose to your ear and probe around vacuum hoses and fittings, listening for the "hissing" sound characteristic of a vacuum leak. **Warning:** *When probing with the vacuum hose stethoscope, be very careful not to come into contact with moving engine components such as the drivebelts, cooling fan, etc.*

Fuel hose

Warning: *There are certain precautions which must be taken when inspecting or servicing fuel system components. Work in a well ventilated area and do not allow open flames (cigarettes, appliance pilot lights, etc.) or bare light bulbs near the work area. Mop up any spills immediately and do not store fuel soaked rags where they could ignite.*

8   Check all rubber fuel lines for deterioration and chafing. Check especially for cracks in areas where the hose bends and just before fittings, such as where a hose attaches to the fuel filter.

9   High quality fuel line, usually identified by the word *Fluroelastomer* printed on the hose, should be used for fuel line replacement. Never, under any circumstances, use unreinforced vacuum line, clear plastic tubing or water hose for fuel lines.

10   Spring-type clamps are commonly used on fuel lines. These clamps often lose their tension over a period of time, and can be "sprung" during removal. Replace all spring-type clamps with screw clamps whenever a hose is replaced.

Metal lines

11   Sections of metal line are often used for fuel line between the fuel pump and fuel injection unit. Check carefully to be sure the line has not been bent or crimped and that cracks have not started in the line.

12   If a section of metal fuel line must be replaced, only seamless steel tubing should be used, since copper and aluminum tubing don't have the strength necessary to withstand normal engine vibration.

13   Check the metal brake lines where they enter the master cylinder and brake proportioning unit (if used) for cracks in the lines or loose fittings. Any sign of brake fluid leakage calls for an immediate thorough inspection of the brake system.

---

14   Cooling system check (every 6000 miles or 6 months)

Refer to illustration 14.4

1   Many major engine failures can be attributed to a faulty cooling system. If the vehicle is equipped with an automatic transaxle, the cooling system also cools the transaxle fluid and thus plays an important role in prolonging transaxle life.

2   The cooling system should be checked with the engine cold. Do this before the vehicle is driven for the day or after the engine has been shut off for at least three hours.

3   Remove the radiator cap by turning it to the left until it reaches a stop. If you hear a hissing sound (indicating there is still pressure in the system), wait until it stops. Now press down on the cap with the palm of your hand and continue turning to the left until the cap can be removed. Thoroughly clean the cap, inside and out, with clean water. Also clean the filler neck on the radiator. All traces of corrosion should be removed. The coolant inside the radiator should be relatively transparent. If it's rust colored, the system should be drained and refilled (see Section 26). If the coolant level isn't up to the top, add additional antifreeze/coolant mixture (see Section 4).

4   Carefully check the large upper and lower radiator hoses along with the smaller diameter heater hoses which run from the engine to the firewall. Inspect each hose along its entire length, replacing any hose which is cracked, swollen or shows signs of deterioration. Cracks may become more apparent if the hose is squeezed **(see illustration)**. Regardless of condition, it's a good idea to replace hoses with new ones every two years.

5   Make sure that all hose connections are tight. A leak in the cooling system will usually show up as white or rust colored deposits on the areas adjoining the leak. If wire-type clamps are used at the ends of the hoses, it may be a good idea to replace them with more secure screw-type clamps.

6   Use compressed air or a soft brush to remove bugs, leaves, etc. from the front of the radiator or air conditioning condenser. Be careful not to damage the delicate cooling fins or cut yourself on them.

7   Every other inspection, or at the first indication of cooling system problems, have the cap and system pressure tested. If you don't have a pressure tester, most gas stations and repair shops will do this for a minimal charge.

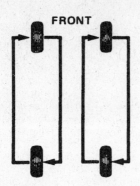

15.2 The recommended tire rotation pattern for these vehicles

15   Tire rotation (every 6000 miles or 6 months)

Refer to illustration 15.2

1   The tires should be rotated at the specified intervals and whenever uneven wear is noticed. Since the vehicle will be raised and the tires removed anyway, check the brakes (see Section 16) at this time.
2   Radial tires must be rotated in a specific pattern **(see illustration)**.
3   Refer to the information in *Jacking and towing* at the front of this manual for the proper procedures to follow when raising the vehicle and changing a tire. If the brakes are to be checked, do not apply the parking brake as stated. Make sure the tires are blocked to prevent the vehicle from rolling.
4   Preferably, the entire vehicle should be raised at the same time. This can be done on a hoist or by jacking up each corner and then lowering the vehicle onto jackstands placed under the frame rails. Always use four jackstands and make sure the vehicle is firmly supported.
5   After rotation, check and adjust the tire pressures as necessary and be sure to check the lug nut tightness.
6   For further information on the wheels and tires, refer to Chapter 10.

16   Brake check (every 15,000 miles or 12 months)

Note: *For detailed photographs of the brake system, refer to Chapter 9.*
1   In addition to the specified intervals, the brakes should be inspected every time the wheels are removed or whenever a defect is suspected. Any of the following symptoms could indicate a potential brake system defect: The vehicle pulls to one side when the brake pedal is depressed; the brakes make squealing or dragging noises when applied; brake travel is excessive; the pedal pulsates; brake fluid leaks, usually onto the inside of the tire or wheel.
2   The disc brake pads have built-in wear indicators which should make a high pitched squealing or scraping noise when they are worn to the replacement point. When you hear this noise, replace the pads immediately or expensive damage to the discs can result.
3   Loosen the wheel lug nuts.
4   Raise the vehicle and place it securely on jackstands.
5   Remove the wheels (see *Jacking and towing* at the front of this book, or your owner's manual, if necessary).

Disc brakes

Refer to illustration 16.6
6   There are two pads - an outer and an inner - in each caliper. The pads are visible through small inspection holes in each caliper **(see illustration)** .
7   Check the pad thickness by looking at each end of the caliper and through the inspection hole in the caliper body. If the lining material is less than the thickness listed in this Chapter's Specifications, replace the pads. **Note:** *Keep in mind that the lining material is riveted or bonded to a metal backing plate and the metal portion is not in-*

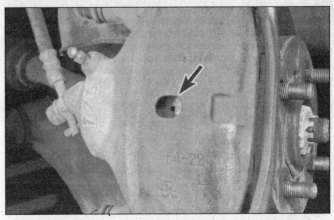

16.6 You will find an inspection hole like this in each caliper - placing a steel ruler across the hole should enable you to determine the thickness of remaining pad material for both inner and outer pads

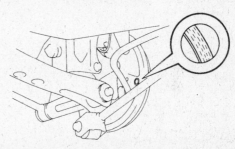

16.13 A quick check of the remaining drum brake shoe lining material can be made by removing the rubber plug in the backing plate and looking through the inspection hole

cluded in this measurement.
8   If it is difficult to determine the exact thickness of the remaining pad material by the above method, or if you are at all concerned about the condition of the pads, remove the caliper(s), then remove the pads from the calipers for further inspection (refer to Chapter 9).
9   Once the pads are removed from the calipers, clean them with brake cleaner and remeasure them with a small steel pocket ruler or a vernier caliper.
10   Measure the disc thickness with a micrometer to make sure that it still has service life remaining. If any disc is thinner than the specified minimum thickness, replace it (refer to Chapter 9). Even if the disc has service life remaining, check its condition. Look for scoring, gouging and burned spots. If these conditions exist, remove the disc and have it resurfaced (see Chapter 9).
11   Before installing the wheels, check all brake lines and hoses for damage, wear, deformation, cracks, corrosion, leakage, bends and twists, particularly in the vicinity of the rubber hoses at the calipers. Check the clamps for tightness and the connections for leakage. Make sure that all hoses and lines are clear of sharp edges, moving parts and the exhaust system. If any of the above conditions are noted, repair, reroute or replace the lines and/or fittings as necessary (see Chapter 9).
12   Some models are equipped with disc brakes on the rear wheels which incorporate drum-type parking brakes into the rear discs. The inspection procedure for these parking brakes is the same as for the rear drum brakes described below.

Rear drum brakes

Refer to illustrations 16.13, 16.16 and 16.18
13   To check the brake shoe lining thickness without removing the brake drums, remove the rubber plug from the backing plate and use a flashlight to inspect the linings **(see illustration)**. For a more thorough brake inspection, follow the procedure below.
14   Refer to Chapter 9 and remove the rear brake drums.

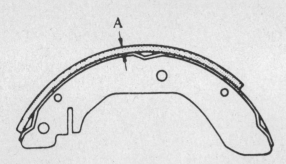

16.16 If the lining is bonded to the brake shoe, measure the lining thickness from the outer surface to the metal shoe, as shown here; if the lining is riveted to the shoe, measure from the lining outer surface to the rivet head

16.18 Carefully peel back the wheel cylinder boot and check for leaking fluid indicating that the cylinder must be replaced or rebuilt

17.1   Push down on the four clips to detach them

15   **Warning:** *Brake dust produced by lining wear and deposited on brake components contains asbestos, which is hazardous to your health. DO NOT blow it out with compressed air and DO NOT inhale it! DO NOT use gasoline or solvents to remove the dust. Brake system cleaner should be used to flush the dust into a drain pan. After the brake components are wiped clean with a damp rag, dispose of the contaminated rag(s) and solvent in a covered and labelled container. Try to use non-asbestos replacement parts whenever possible.*

16   Note the thickness of the lining material on the rear brake shoes **(see illustration)** and look for signs of contamination by brake fluid and grease. If the lining material is within 1/16-inch of the recessed rivets or metal shoes, replace the brake shoes with new ones. The shoes should also be replaced if they are cracked, glazed (shiny lining surfaces) or contaminated with brake fluid or grease. See Chapter 9 for the replacement procedure.

17   Check the shoe return and hold-down springs and the adjusting mechanism to make sure they're installed correctly and in good condition. Deteriorated or distorted springs, if not replaced, could allow the linings to drag and wear prematurely.

18   Check the wheel cylinders for leakage by carefully peeling back the rubber boots **(see illustration)**. If brake fluid is noted behind the boots, the wheel cylinders must be replaced (see Chapter 9).

19   Check the drums for cracks, score marks, deep scratches and hard spots, which will appear as small discolored areas. If imperfections cannot be removed with emery cloth, the drums must be resurfaced by an automotive machine shop (see Chapter 9 for more detailed information).

20   Refer to Chapter 9 and install the brake drums.

21   Install the wheels and snug the wheel lug nuts finger tight.

22   Remove the jackstands and lower the vehicle.

23   Tighten the wheel lug nuts to the torque listed.

Brake booster check

24   Sit in the driver's seat and perform the following sequence of tests.

25   With the engine stopped, depress the brake pedal several times-the travel distance should not change.

26   With the brake fully depressed, start the engine - the pedal should move down a little when the engine starts.

27   Depress the brake, stop the engine and hold the pedal in for about 30 seconds - the pedal should neither sink nor rise.

28   Restart the engine, run it for about a minute and turn it off. Then firmly depress the brake several times - the pedal travel should decrease with each application.

29   If your brakes do not operate as described above when the preceding tests are performed, the brake booster is either in need of repair or has failed. Refer to Chapter 9 for the removal procedure.

Parking brake

30   Slowly pull up on the parking brake and count the number of clicks you hear until the handle is up as far as it will go. The adjustment is correct if you hear the specified number of clicks. If you hear more or fewer clicks, it's time to adjust the parking brake (refer to Chapter 9).

31   An alternative method of checking the parking brake is to park the vehicle on a steep hill with the parking brake set and the transmission in Neutral. If the parking brake cannot prevent the vehicle from rolling, it is in need of adjustment (see Chapter 9).

---

17   Air filter replacement (every 15,000 miles or 12 months)

Refer to illustrations 17.1 and 17.2

1   The air filter is located inside a housing at the left (drivers) side of the engine compartment. To remove the air filter, release the four spring clips that keep the two halves of the air cleaner housing together **(see illustration)**.

2   Lift the cover up and remove the air filter element **(see illustration)**.

3   Inspect the outer surface of the filter element. If it is dirty, replace it. If it is only moderately dusty, it can be reused by blowing it clean from the back to the front surface with compressed air. Because it is a pleated paper type filter, it cannot be washed or oiled. If it cannot be cleaned satisfactorily with compressed air, discard and replace it. **Caution:** *Never drive the vehicle with the air cleaner removed. Excessive engine wear could result and backfiring could even cause a fire under the hood.*

4   Installation is the reverse of removal.

17.2 Raise the air cleaner cover and lift the element out of the housing

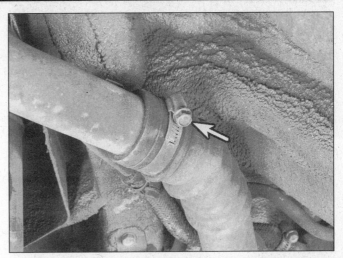

18.5 Inspect filler hose for cracks and make sure the clamp (arrow) is tight

1

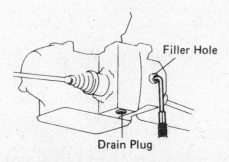

19.3 Use a pump to fill the differential

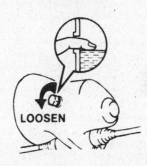

20.1 Use your finger as a pipstick to check the manual transaxle lubricant level

18 Fuel system check (every 15,000 miles or 12 months)

Refer to illustration 18.5

Warning: *Certain precautions should be observed when inspecting or servicing the fuel system components. Work in a well ventilated area and do not allow open flames (cigarettes, appliance pilot lights, etc.) near the work area. Mop up spills immediately and do not store fuel soaked rags where they could ignite. It is a good idea to keep a dry chemical (Class B) fire extinguisher near the work area any time the fuel system is being serviced.*

1   If you smell gasoline while driving or after the vehicle has been sitting in the sun, inspect the fuel system immediately.

2   Remove the gas filler cap and inspect if for damage and corrosion. The gasket should have an unbroken sealing imprint. If the gasket is damaged or corroded, remove it and install a new one (Section 33).

3   Inspect the fuel feed and return lines for cracks. Make sure that the threaded flare nut type connectors which secure the metal fuel lines to the fuel injection system and the banjo bolts which secure the banjo fittings to the in-line fuel filter are tight.

4   Since some components of the fuel system - the fuel tank and part of the fuel feed and return lines, for example - are underneath the vehicle, they can be inspected more easily with the vehicle raised on a hoist. If that's not possible, raise the vehicle and suport it securely on jackstands.

5   With the vehicle raised and safely supported, inspect the gas tank and filler neck for punctures, cracks and other damage. The connection between the filler neck and the tank is particularly critical. Sometimes a rubber filler neck will leak because of loose clamps or deteriorated rubber **(see illustration)**. These are problems a home mechanic can usually rectify. **Warning:** *Do not, under any circumstances, try to repair a fuel tank (except rubber components). A welding torch or any open flame can easily cause fuel vapors inside the tank to explode.*

6   Carefully check all rubber hoses and metal lines leading away from the fuel tank. Check for loose connections, deteriorated hoses, crimped lines and other damage. Carefully inspect the lines from the tank to the fuel injection system. Repair or replace damaged sections as necessary (see Chapter 4).

19 Automatic transaxle differential lubricant level check (1989 and earlier models only) (every 15,000 miles or 12 months)

Refer to illustration 19.3

1   The automatic transaxle differential has a separate lubricant supply with a check/fill plug which must be removed to check the level. If the vehicle is raised to gain access to the plug, be sure to support it safely on jackstands - DO NOT crawl under the vehicle when it's supported only by the jack.

2   Remove the check/fill plug from the front of the differential.

3   Use your little finger as a dipstick to make sure the lubricant level is even with the bottom of the plug hole. If not, use a syringe or a gear oil pump to add the recommended lubricant (see this Chapter's Specifications) until it just starts to run out of the opening **(see illustration)**.

4   Install the plug and tighten it securely.

20 Manual transaxle lubricant level check (every 15,000 miles or 12 months)

Refer to illustration 20.1

1   The manual transaxle does not have a dipstick. To check the fluid level, raise the vehicle and support it securely on jackstands. On the lower front side of the transaxle housing, you will see a plug **(see illustration)**. Remove it. If the lubricant level is correct, it should be up to the lower edge of the hole.

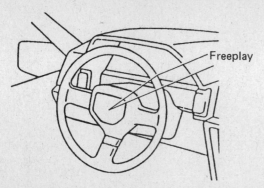

21.1 Steering wheel freeplay is the amount of travel between an initial steering input and the point at which the front wheels begin to turn (indicated by a slight resistance)

21.7 To check a balljoint for wear, raise the vehicle, and support it on jackstands, place a 7-inch thick block of wood under the tire, block the wheel with chocks and lower the jack until there is about half a load on the coil spring - then move the lower arm up and down with a prybar to make sure there is no play in the balljoint (if there is, replace it)

21.8 Push on the balljoint boot to check for damage

2   If the transaxle needs more lubricant (if the level is not up to the hole), use a syringe or a gear oil pump to add more. Stop filling the transaxle when the lubricant begins to run out the hole.
3   Install the plug and tighten it securely. Drive the vehicle a short distance, then check for leaks.

22.2 Flex the driveaxle boots by hand to check for cracks and/or leaking grease

---

21   Steering and suspension check (every 15,000 miles or 12 months)

Refer to illustrations 21.1, 21.7 and 21.8
Note: *For detailed illustrations of the steering and suspension components, refer to Chapter 10.*

With the wheels on the ground

1   With the vehicle stopped and the front wheels pointed straight ahead, rock the steering wheel gently back and forth. If freeplay **(see illustration)** is excessive , a front wheel bearing, main shaft yoke, intermediate shaft yoke, lower arm balljoint or steering system joint is worn or the steering gear is out of adjustment or broken. Refer to Chapter 10 for the appropriate repair procedure.
2   Other symptoms, such as excessive vehicle body movement over rough roads, swaying (leaning) around corners and binding as the steering wheel is turned, may indicate faulty steering and/or suspension components.
3   Check the shock absorbers by pushing down and releasing the vehicle several times at each corner. If the vehicle does not come back to a level position within one or two bounces, the shocks/struts are worn and must be replaced. When bouncing the vehicle up and down, listen for squeaks and noises from the suspension components. Additional information on suspension components can be found in Chapter 10.

Under the vehicle

4   Raise the vehicle with a floor jack and support it securely on jackstands. See *Jacking and towing* at the front of this book for the proper jacking points.
5   Check the tires for irregular wear patterns and proper inflation. See Section 5 in this Chapter for information regarding tire wear and Chapter 10 for the wheel bearing replacement procedures.
6   Inspect the universal joint between the steering shaft and the steering gear housing. Check the steering gear housing for grease leakage or oozing. Make sure that the dust seals and boots are not damaged and that the boot clamps are not loose. Check the steering linkage for looseness or damage. Check the tie-rod ends for excessive play. Look for loose bolts, broken or disconnected parts and deteriorated rubber bushings on all suspension and steering components. While an assistant turns the steering wheel from side to side, check the steering components for free movement, chafing and binding. If the steering components do not seem to be reacting with the movement of the steering wheel, try to determine where the slack is located.
7   Check the balljoints for wear by placing a 7-inch thick wooden block under each tire. Lower the jack until there is about half a load on the coil spring. Make sure that the front wheels are in a straight forward position and block the wheel with chocks. Move each lower arm up and down with a pry bar **(see illustration)** to ensure that its balljoint

23.3a Using a backup wrench, remove the banjo bolt at the top and . . .

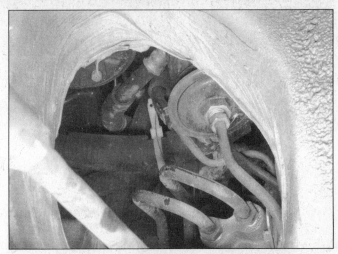

23.3b . . . loosen the fitting at the bottom of the filter

has no play. If any balljoint does have play, replace it. See Chapter 10 for the front balljoint replacement procedure.

8   Inspect the balljoint boots for damage and leaking grease **(see illustration)**. Replace the balljoints with new ones if they are damaged (see Chapter 10).

22   Driveaxle boot check (every 15,000 miles or 12 months)

Refer to illustration 22.2

1   The driveaxle boots are very important because they prevent dirt, water and foreign material from entering and damaging the constant velocity (CV) joints. Oil and grease can cause the boot material to deteriorate prematurely, so it's a good idea to wash the boots with soap and water.

2   Inspect the boots for tears and cracks as well as loose clamps **(see illustration)**. If there is any evidence of cracks or leaking lubricant, they must be replaced as described in Chapter 8.

23   Fuel filter replacement (every 30,000 miles or 24 months)

Refer to illustrations 23.3a and 23.3b

Warning: *Gasoline is extremely flammable, so take extra precautions when you work on any part of the fuel system. Don't smoke or allow open flames or bare light bulbs near the work area, and don't work in a garage where a natural-type appliance (such as a water heater or clothes dryer) with a pilot light is present. If you spill any fuel on your skin, rinse it off immediately with soap and water. When your perform any kind of work on the fuel system, wear safety glasses and have a Class B type fire extinguisher on hand.*

1   Before detaching any part of the fuel system, be sure to relieve the fuel line and tank pressure by removing the fuel tank cap and disconnecting the battery. Cover the fitting being disconnected with a rag to absorb any fuel that may spray out. **Caution:** *If the stereo in your vehicle is equipped with an anti-theft system, refer to the information on page 0-15 at the front of this manual before detaching the cable.*

2   Remove the air cleaner assembly (see Chapter 4) and evaporative canister (see Chapter 6).

3   Using a backup wrench to steady the filter, remove the threaded banjo bolt at the top and loosen the fitting at the bottom of the fuel filter (use a flare nut wrench if possible **(see illustrations)**

4   Remove both bracket bolts from the firewall and remove the old filter and the filter support bracket assembly.

5   Note that the inlet and outlet pipes are clearly labelled on their respective ends of the filter and that the flanged end of the filter faces down. Make sure the new filter is installed so that it's facing the proper direction as noted above. When correctly installed, the filter should be installed so that the outlet pipe faces up and the inlet pipe faces down.

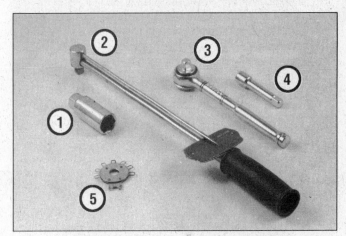

24.1 Tools required for changing spark plugs

1   *Spark plug socket - This will have special padding inside to protect the spark plug porcelain insulator*
2   *Torque wrench - Although not mandatory, use of this tool is the best way to ensure that the plugs are tightened properly*
3   *Ratchet - Standard hand tool to fit the plug socket*
4   *Extension - Depending on model and accessories, you may need special extensions and universal joints to reach one or more of the plugs*
5   *Spark plug gap gauge - This gauge for checking the gap comes in a variety of styles. Make sure the gap for your engine is included*

6   Using the new crush washers provided by the filter manufacturer, install the inlet and outlet banjo fittings and tighten them securely.

7   The remainder of installation is the reverse of the removal procedure.

24   Spark plug check and replacement (every 30,000 miles or 24 months)

Refer to illustrations 24.1, 24.4a, 24.4b, 24.6, 24.8a, 24.8b and 24.10

1   Spark plug replacement requires a spark plug socket which fits onto a ratchet wrench. This socket is lined with a rubber grommet to protect the porcelain insulator of the spark plug and to hold the plug while you insert it into the spark plug hole. You will also need a wire-type feeler gauge to check and adjust the spark plug gap and a torque wrench to tighten the new plugs to the specified torque **(see illustration)**.

24.4a Spark plug manufacturers recommend using a wire-type gauge when checking the gap - if the wire does not slide between the electrodes with a slight drag, adjustment is required

24.4b To change the gap, bend the side electrode only, as indicated by the arrows, and be very careful not to crack or chip the porcelain insulator surrounding the center electrode

2 If you are replacing the plugs, purchase the new plugs, adjust them to the proper gap and then replace each plug one at a time. **Note:** *When buying new spark plugs, it's essential that you obtain the correct plugs for your specific vehicle. This information can be found in the Specifications Section at the beginning of this Chapter, on the Vehicle Emissions Control Information (VECI) label located on the underside of the hood or in the owner's manual. If these sources specify different plugs, purchase the spark plug type specified on the VECI label because that information is provided specifically for your engine.*

3 Inspect each of the new plugs for defects. If there are any signs of cracks in the porcelain insulator of a plug, don't use it.

4 Check the electrode gaps of the new plugs. Check the gap by inserting the wire gauge of the proper thickness between the electrodes at the tip of the plug **(see illustration)**. The gap between the electrodes should be identical to that listed in this Chapter's Specifications or on the VECI label. If the gap is incorrect, use the notched adjuster on the feeler gauge body to bend the curved side electrode slightly **(see illustration)**.

5 If the side electrode is not exactly over the center electrode, use the notched adjuster to align them. **Caution:** *If the gap of a new plug must be adjusted, bend only the base of the ground electrode – do not touch the tip.*

Removal

6 To prevent the possibility of mixing up spark plug wires, work on one spark plug at a time. Remove the wire and boot from one spark plug. Grasp the boot - not the cable - as shown, give it a half twisting motion and pull straight up **(see illustration)**.

7 If compressed air is available, blow any dirt or foreign material away from the spark plug area before proceeding (a common bicycle pump will also work).

8 Remove the spark plug **(see illustrations)**.

9 Whether you are replacing the plugs at this time or intend to reuse the old plugs, compare each old spark plug with those shown in the accompanying photos to determine the overall running condition of the engine.

Installation

10 It's often difficult to insert spark plugs into their holes without cross-threading them. To avoid this possibility, fit a short piece of 3/16-inch ID rubber hose over the end of the spark plug **(see illustration)**. The flexible hose acts as a universal joint to help align the plug with the plug hole. Should the plug begin to cross-thread, the hose will slip on the spark plug, preventing thread damage. Tighten the plug to the torque listed in this Chapter's Specifications.

24.6 When removing the spark plug wires, pull only on the boot and use a twisting/pulling motion

24.8a Use a socket wrench with a long extension to unscrew the spark plug

24.8b Lift the spark plug out of the valve cover

For a COLOR version of this spark plug diagnosis page, please see the inside rear cover of this manual

CARBON DEPOSITS
Symptoms: Dry sooty deposits indicate a rich mixture or weak ignition. Causes misfiring, hard starting and hesitation.

Recommendation: Check for a clogged air cleaner, high float level, sticky choke and worn ignition points. Use a spark plug with a longer core nose for greater anti-fouling protection.

OIL DEPOSITS
Symptoms: Oily coating caused by poor oil control. Oil is leaking past worn valve guides or piston rings into the combustion chamber. Causes hard starting, misfiring and hesition.

Recommendation: Correct the mechanical condition with necessary repairs and install new plugs.

TOO HOT
Symptoms: Blistered, white insulator, eroded electrode and absence of deposits. Results in shortened plug life.

Recommendation: Check for the correct plug heat range, over-advanced ignition timing, lean fuel mixture, intake manifold vacuum leaks and sticking valves. Check the coolant level and make sure the radiator is not clogged.

PREIGNITION
Symptoms: Melted electrodes. Insulators are white, but may be dirty due to misfiring or flying debris in the combustion chamber. Can lead to engine damage.

Recommendation: Check for the correct plug heat range, over-advanced ignition timing, lean fuel mixture, clogged cooling system and lack of lubrication.

HIGH SPEED GLAZING
Symptoms: Insulator has yellowish, glazed appearance. Indicates that combustion chamber temperatures have risen suddenly during hard acceleration. Normal deposits melt to form a conductive coating. Causes misfiring at high speeds.

Recommendation: Install new plugs. Consider using a colder plug if driving habits warrant.

GAP BRIDGING
Symptoms: Combustion deposits lodge between the electrodes. Heavy deposits accumulate and bridge the electrode gap. The plug ceases to fire, resulting in a dead cylinder.

Recommendation: Locate the faulty plug and remove the deposits from between the electrodes.

NORMAL
Symptoms: Brown to grayish-tan color and slight electrode wear. Correct heat range for engine and operating conditions.

Recommendation: When new spark plugs are installed, replace with plugs of the same heat range.

ASH DEPOSITS
Symptoms: Light brown deposits encrusted on the side or center electrodes or both. Derived from oil and/or fuel additives. Excessive amounts may mask the spark, causing misfiring and hesitation during acceleration.

Recommendation: If excessive deposits accumulate over a short time or low mileage, install new valve guide seals to prevent seepage of oil into the combustion chambers. Also try changing gasoline brands.

WORN
Symptoms: Rounded electrodes with a small amount of deposits on the firing end. Normal color. Causes hard starting in damp or cold weather and poor fuel economy.

Recommendation: Replace with new plugs of the same heat range.

DETONATION
Symptoms: Insulators may be cracked or chipped. Improper gap setting techniques can also result in a fractured insulator tip. Can lead to piston damage.

Recommendation: Make sure the fuel anti-knock values meet engine requirements. Use care when setting the gaps on new plugs. Avoid lugging the engine.

SPLASHED DEPOSITS
Symptoms: After long periods of misfiring, deposits can loosen when normal combustion temperature is restored by an overdue tune-up. At high speeds, deposits flake off the piston and are thrown against the hot insulator, causing misfiring.

Recommendation: Replace the plugs with new ones or clean and reinstall the originals.

MECHANICAL DAMAGE
Symptoms: May be caused by a foreign object in the combustion chamber or the piston striking an incorrect reach (too long) plug. Causes a dead cylinder and could result in piston damage.

Recommendation: Remove the foreign object from the engine and/or install the correct reach plug.

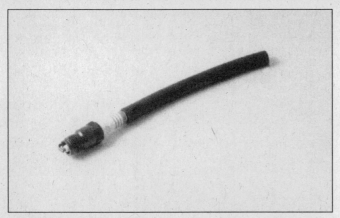

24.10   A length of 3/8-inch ID rubber hose will save time and prevent damaged threads when installing the spark plugs

11   Attach the plug wire to the new spark plug, again using a twisting motion on the boot until it is firmly seated on the end of the spark plug.
12   Follow the above procedure for the remaining spark plugs, replacing them one at a time to prevent mixing up the spark plug wires.

---

25   Spark plug wire, distributor cap and rotor check and replacement (every 30,000 miles or 24 months)

Refer to illustrations 25.11, 25.12 and 25.13
1   The spark plug wires should be checked whenever new spark plugs are installed.
2   Begin this procedure by making a visual check of the spark plug wires while the engine is running. In a darkened garage (make sure there is ventilation) start the engine and observe each plug wire. Be careful not to come into contact with any moving engine parts. If there is a break in the wire, you will see arcing or a small spark at the damaged area. If arcing is noticed, make a note to obtain new wires, then allow the engine to cool and check the distributor cap and rotor.
3   The spark plug wires should be inspected one at a time to prevent mixing up the order, which is essential for proper engine operation. Each original plug wire should be numbered to help identify its location. If the number is illegible, a piece of tape can be marked with the correct number and wrapped around the plug wire.
4   Disconnect the plug wire from the spark plug. A removal tool can be used for this purpose or you can grasp the rubber boot, twist the boot half a turn and pull the boot free. Do not pull on the wire itself.
5   Check inside the boot for corrosion, which will look like a white crusty powder.
6   Push the wire and boot back onto the end of the spark plug. It should fit tightly onto the end of the plug. If it doesn't, remove the wire and use pliers to carefully crimp the metal connector inside the wire boot until the fit is snug.
7   Using a clean rag, wipe the entire length of the wire to remove built-up dirt and grease. Once the wire is clean, check for burns, cracks and other damage. Do not bend the wire sharply, because the conductor might break.
8   Disconnect the wire from the distributor. Again, pull only on the rubber boot. Check for corrosion and a tight fit. Replace the wire in the distributor.
9   Inspect the remaining spark plug wires, making sure that each one is securely fastened at the distributor and spark plug when the check is complete.
10   If new spark plug wires are required, purchase a set for your specific engine model. Pre-cut wire sets with the boots already installed are available. Remove and replace the wires one at a time to avoid mix-ups in the firing order.
11   Detach the distributor cap by removing the two cap retaining bolts. Look inside it for cracks, carbon tracks and worn, burned or loose contacts **(see illustration)**.
12   Pull the rotor off the distributor shaft and examine it for cracks

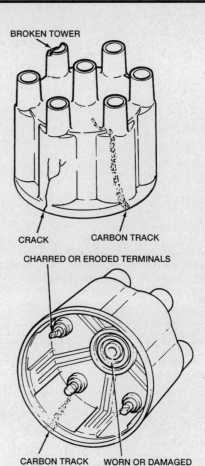

25.11 Shown here are some of the common defects to look for when inspecting the distributor cap (if in doubt about its condition, install a new one)

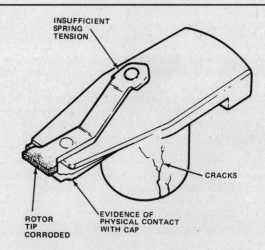

25.12 The ignition rotor should be checked for wear and corrosion as indicated here (if in doubt about its condition, buy a new one)

and carbon tracks **(see illustration)**. Replace the cap and rotor if any damage or defects are noted.
13   It is common practice to install a new cap and rotor whenever new spark plug wires are installed, but if you wish to continue using the old cap, check the resistance between the spark plug wires and

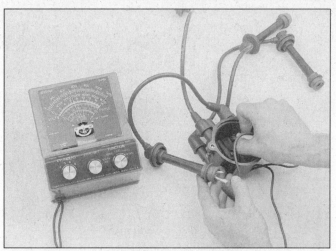

25.13 Measure the resistance value of the distributor cap and the spark plug wires - if it exceeds the specified maximum value, replace either the cap, or the wires, or both

26.4 On most models you will have to remove a cover for access to the radiator drain fitting located at the bottom of the radiator - before opening the valve, push a short section of 3/8-inch ID hose onto the plastic fitting (some models are already equipped with one) to prevent the coolant from splashing as it drains

26.5 The block drain plug (arrow) is located on the side of the engine block

the cap first **(see illustration)**. If the indicated resistance is more than the maximum value listed in this Chapter's Specifications, replace the cap and/or wires.

14   When installing a new cap, remove the wires from the old cap one at a time and attach them to the new cap in the exact same location – do not simultaneously remove all the wires from the old cap or firing order mix-ups may occur.

---

26   Cooling system servicing (draining, flushing and refilling) (every 30,000 miles or 24 months)

Warning: *Do not allow engine coolant (antifreeze) to come in contact with your skin or painted surfaces of the vehicle. Rinse off spills immediately with plenty of water. Antifreeze is highly toxic if ingested. Never leave antifreeze laying around in an open container or in puddles on the floor; children and pets are attracted by it's sweet smell and may drink it. Check with local authorities about disposing of used antifreeze. Many communities have collection centers which will see that antifreeze is disposed of safely.*

1   Periodically, the cooling system should be drained, flushed and refilled to replenish the antifreeze mixture and prevent formation of rust and corrosion, which can impair the performance of the cooling system and cause engine damage. When the cooling system is serviced, all hoses and the radiator cap should be checked and replaced if necessary.

Draining

Refer to illustrations 26.4 and 26.5

2   Apply the parking brake and block the wheels. If the vehicle has just been driven, wait several hours to allow the engine to cool down before beginning this procedure.

3   Once the engine is completely cool, remove the radiator cap.

4   Move a large container under the radiator drain to catch the coolant. Attach a 3/8-inch inner diameter hose to the drain fitting to direct the coolant into the container (some models are already equipped with a hose), then open the drain fitting (a pair of pliers may be required to turn it) **(see illustration)**.

5   After the coolant stops flowing out of the radiator, move the container under the engine block drain plug **(see illustration)**. Loosen the plug and allow the coolant in the block to drain.

6   While the coolant is draining, check the condition of the radiator hoses, heater hoses and clamps (refer to Section 13 if necessary).

7   Replace any damaged clamps or hoses (see Chapter 3).

Flushing

8   Once the system is completely drained, flush the radiator with fresh water from a garden hose until water runs clear at the drain. The flushing action of the water will remove sediments from the radiator but will not remove rust and scale from the engine and cooling tube surfaces.

9   These deposits can be removed by the chemical action of a cleaner. Follow the procedure outlined in the manufacturer's instructions. If the radiator is severely corroded, damaged or leaking, it should be removed (see Chapter 3) and taken to a radiator repair shop.

10   Remove the overflow hose from the coolant recovery reservoir. Drain the reservoir and flush it with clean water, then reconnect the hose.

Refilling

11   Close and tighten the radiator drain. Install and tighten the block drain plug.

12   Place the heater temperature control in the maximum heat position.

13   Slowly add new coolant (a 50/50 mixture of water and antifreeze) to the radiator until it's full. Add coolant to the reservoir up to the lower mark.

14   Leave the radiator cap off and run the engine in a well-ventilated area until the thermostat opens (coolant will begin flowing through the radiator and the upper radiator hose will become hot).

15   Turn the engine off and let it cool. Add more coolant mixture to bring the level back up to the lip on the radiator filler neck.

27.2 Check the evaporative canister for damage and the hose connections (arrows) for cracks and damage

29.7 Use an Allen wrench to remove the transaxle drain plug

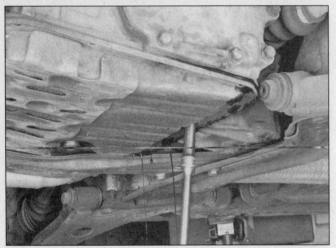

29.8a After loosening the front bolts, remove the rear transaxle bolts and . . .

16   Squeeze the upper radiator hose to expel air, then add more coolant mixture if necessary. Replace the radiator cap.

17   Start the engine, allow it to reach normal operating temperature and check for leaks.

27   Evaporative emissions control system check (every 30,000 miles or 24 months)

Refer to illustration 27.2

1   The function of the evaporative emissions control system is to draw fuel vapors from the gas tank and fuel system, store them in a charcoal canister and then burn them during normal engine operation.

2   The most common symptom of a fault in the evaporative emissions system is a strong fuel odor in the engine compartment. If a fuel odor is detected, inspect the charcoal canister, located at the front of the engine compartment. Check the canister and all hoses for damage and deterioration **(see illustration)**.

3   The evaporative emissions control system is explained in more detail in Chapter 6.

28   Exhaust system check (every 30,000 miles or 24 months)

1   With the engine cold (at least three hours after the vehicle has been driven), check the complete exhaust system from its starting point at the engine to the end of the tailpipe. This should be done on a hoist where unrestricted access is available.

2   Check the pipes and connections for evidence of leaks, severe corrosion or damage. Make sure that all brackets and hangers are in good condition and tight.

3   At the same time, inspect the underside of the body for holes, corrosion, open seams, etc. which may allow exhaust gases to enter the passenger compartment. Seal all body openings with silicone or body putty.

4   Rattles and other noises can often be traced to the exhaust system, especially the mounts and hangers. Try to move the pipes, muffler and catalytic converter. If the components can come in contact with the body or suspension parts, secure the exhaust system with new mounts.

5   Check the running condition of the engine by inspecting inside the end of the tailpipe. The exhaust deposits here are an indication of engine state-of-tune. If the pipe is black and sooty or coated with white deposits, the engine is in need of a tune-up, including a thorough fuel system inspection.

29   Automatic transaxle/differential fluid and filter change (every 30,000 miles or 24 months)

Refer to illustrations 29.7, 29.8a, 29.8b, 29.9, 29.11, 29.13a and 29.13b

1   At the specified time intervals, the automatic transaxle and differential fluid (1989 and earlier models) should be drained and replaced.

2   Before beginning work, purchase the specified transmission fluid (see *Recommended fluids and lubricants* at the front of this chapter).

3   Other tools necessary for this job include jackstands to support the vehicle in a raised position, a 10 mm Allen wrench, a drain pan capable of holding at least eight pints, newspapers and clean rags.

4   The fluid should be drained immediately after the vehicle has been driven. Hot fluid is more effective than cold fluid at removing built up sediment. **Warning:** *Fluid temperature can exceed 350-degrees F in a hot transaxle. Wear protective gloves.*

5   After the vehicle has been driven to warm up the fluid, raise it and place it on jackstands for access to the transaxle and differential drain plugs.

6   Move the necessary equipment under the vehicle, being careful not to touch any of the hot exhaust components.

7   Place the drain pan under the drain plug in the transaxle pan and remove the drain plug with the Allen wrench **(see illustration)**. Be sure the drain pan is in position, as fluid will come out with some force. Once the fluid is drained, reinstall the drain plug securely.

8   Remove the front transaxle pan bolts, then loosen the rear bolts and carefully pry the pan loose with a screwdriver and allow the remaining fluid to drain **(see illustrations)**. Once the fluid had drained,

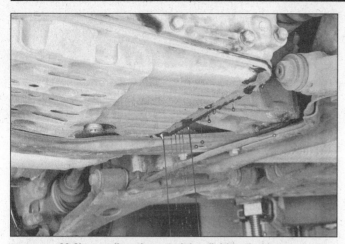

29.8b . . . allow the remaining fluid to drain out

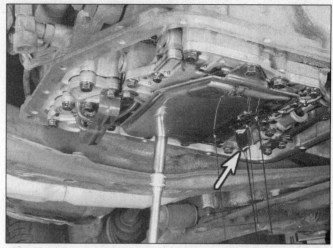

29.9 Remove the filter bolts and lower the filter (be careful, there will be some residual fluid) - note that here one of the pan magnets is stuck to the filter (arrow), be sure to clean any magnets and return them to the pan

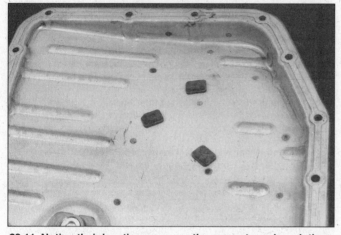

29.11 Noting their locations, remove the magnets and wash them and the pan in solvent before reinstalling them

remove the bolts and lower the pan.
9   Remove the filter retaining bolts, disconnect the clip (some models) and lower the filter from the transaxle (see illustration). Be careful when lowering the filter as it contains residual fluid.
10   Place the new filter in position, connect the clip (if equipped) and install the bolts. Tighten the bolts to the torque listed in the Specifications Section at the beginning of this Chapter.
11   Carefully clean the gasket surfaces of the fluid pan, removing all traces of old gasket material. Noting their location, remove the magnets, wash the pan in clean solvent and dry it with compressed air. Be sure to clean and reinstall the magnets (see illustration).
12   Install a new gasket, place the fluid pan in position and install the bolts in their original positions. Tighten the bolts to the torque listed in the Specifications Section at the beginning of this Chapter.
13   On 1989 and earlier models, find the differential drain plug. Place the drain pan underneath the plug, remove it with the Allen wrench and drain the fluid (see illustrations). When the differential fluid has drained, reinstall the plug securely.
14   Referring to Section 19, add new fluid to the differential until it begins to run out of the filler hole (see Recommended lubricants and fluids at the beginning of this Chapter for the specified fluid type and capacity). Caution: Do not overfill. The automatic transaxle and the differential are separate units.
15   Lower the vehicle.
16   With the engine off, add new fluid to the transaxle through the dipstick tube (see Recommended fluids and lubricants for the recommended fluid type and capacity). Use a funnel to prevent spills. It is best to add a little fluid at a time, continually checking the level with the dipstick (see Section 7). Allow the fluid time to drain into the pan.
17   Start the engine and shift the selector into all positions from P through L, then shift into P and apply the parking brake.

29.13a Use an Allen wrench to remove the differential drain plug

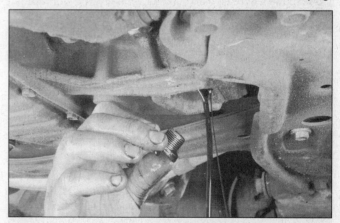

29.13b   Be careful when removing the plug because the fluid usually comes out with some force

18   With the engine idling, check the fluid level. Add fluid up to the Cool level on the dipstick.

---

30   Manual transaxle lubricant change (every 30,000 miles or 24 months)

---

1   Remove the drain plug(s) and drain the fluid.
2   Reinstall the drain plug(s) securely.

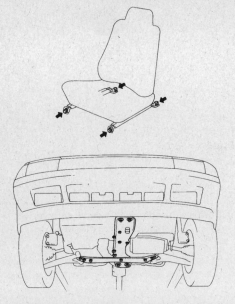

31.1 The mounting bolts and nuts for the front seats and front suspension and crossmember should be periodically checked and tightened

3   Add new fluid until it begins to run out of the filler hole (Section 20). See *Recommended lubricants and fluids* for the specified lubricant type.

31   Chassis and body fastener check (every 30,000 miles or 24 months)

Refer to illustration 31.1
1   Tighten the following parts to the torque values listed in this Chapter's Specifications: front seat mounting bolts and front suspension member-to-body mounting bolts and nuts (left and right sides) **(see illustration)**.

32   Valve clearance check and adjustment (DOHC engines only) (every 60,000 miles or 48 months)

Refer to illustrations 32.6a, 32.6b, 32.7, 32.9a, 32.9b and 32.10
Note: *The following procedure requires the use of a special valve lifter tool. It is impossible to perform this task without it.*
1   Disconnect the negative cable from the battery. **Caution:** *If the stereo in your vehicle is equiped with an anti-theft system, refer to the information on page 0-15 at the front of this manual befor detaching the cable.*
2   Disconnect the cruise control cable, air cleaner duct or other components which will interfere with valve cover removal.
3   Blow out the recessed area between the camshafts with compressed air, if available, to remove any debris that might fall into the cylinders, then remove the spark plugs (see Section 24).
4   Remove the valve cover (refer to Chapter 2).
5   Refer to Chapter 2 and position the number 1 piston at TDC on the compression stroke.
6   Measure the clearances of the indicated valves with a feeler gauge of the specified thickness **(see illustrations)**. Record the measurements which are out of specification. They will be used later to determine the required replacement shims.
7   Turn the crankshaft one complete revolution and realign the timing marks. Measure the remaining valves **(see illustration)**.
8   After all the valve clearances have been measured, turn the crankshaft pulley until the camshaft lobe above the first valve which you intend to adjust is pointing upward, away from the shim.
9   Position the notch in the valve lifter toward the spark plug. Then

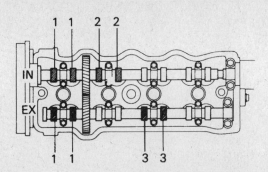

32.6a When the no. 1 piston is at TDC on the compression stroke, the valve clearances for the no. 1 and no. 3 exhaust valves and the no. 1 and no. 2 intake valves can be measured

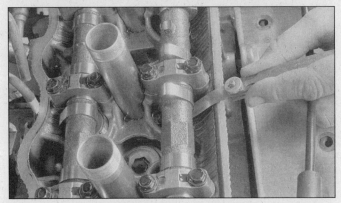

32.6b Measure the clearance for each valve with a feeler gauge of the specified thickness - if the clearance is correct, you should feel a slight drag on the gauge as you pull it out

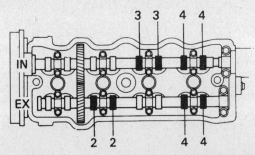

32.7 When the no. 4 piston is at TDC on the compression stroke, the valve clearances for the no. 2 and no. 4 exhaust valves and the no. 3 and no. 4 intake valves can be measured

press down the valve lifter with the special valve lifter tool **(see illustration)**. Place the special valve lifter tool in position as shown, with the longer jaw of the tool gripping the lower edge of the cast lifter bossand the upper, shorter jaw gripping the upper edge of the lifter itself. Press down the valve lifter by squeezing the handles of the valve lifter tool together and remove the adjusting shim with a small screwdriver or a pair of tweezers **(see illustration)**. Note that the wire hook on the end of one valve lifter tool handle can be used to clamp both handles together to keep the lifter depressed while the shim is removed.
10   Measure the thickness of the shim with a micrometer **(see illustration)**. To calculate the correct thickness of a replacement shim that will place the valve clearance within the specified value, use the following formula:

Intake side: $N = T + (A - 0.008\text{-inch})$
Exhaust side: $N = T + (A - 0.010\text{-inch})$
   T = thickness of the old shim
   A = valve clearance measured
   N = thickness of the new shim

32.9a Install the valve lifter tool as shown and squeeze the handles together to lower the valve lifter so the shim can be removed

32.9b Remove the shim with a small screwdriver, a pair of tweezers or a magnet

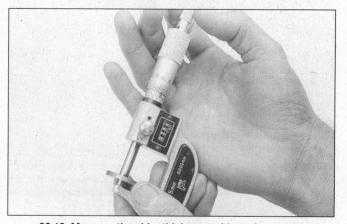

32.10 Measure the shim thickness with a micrometer

33.2 Use a small screwdriver to carefully pry out the old gasket - take care not to damage the cap

11　Select a shim with a thickness as close as possible to the valve clearance calculated. Shims, which are available in 17 sizes in increments of 0.0020-inch (0.050 mm), range in size from 0.0984-inch (2.500 mm) to 0.1299-inch (3.300 mm). **Note:** *Through careful analysis of the shim sizes needed to bring all the out-of-specification valve clearances within specification, it is often possible to simply move a shim that has to come out anyway to another valve lifter requiring a shim of that particular size, thereby reducing the number of new shims that must be purchased.*

12　Place the special valve lifter tool in position as shown in illustration 32.9a, with the longer jaw of the tool gripping the lower edge of the cast lifter boss and the upper, shorter jaw gripping the upper edge of the lifter itself, press down the valve lifter by squeezing the handles of the valve lifter tool together and install the new adjusting shim (note that the wire hook on the end of one valve lifter tool handle can be used to clamp the handles together to keep the lifter depressed while the shim is inserted). Measure the clearance with a feeler gauge to make sure that your calculations are correct.

13　Repeat this procedure until all the valves which are out of clearance have been corrected.

14　Installation of the spark plugs, valve cover, spark plug wires and boots, accelerator cable bracket, etc. is the reverse of removal.

33　Fuel tank cap gasket replacement (every 60,000 miles or 48 months)

Refer to illustration 33.2

1　Obtain a new gasket.

2　Remove the tank cap and carefully pry the old gasket out of the recess **(see illustration)**. Be very careful not to damage the sealing

surface inside the cap.

3　Work the new gasket into the cap recess.

4　Install the cap, then remove it and make sure the gasket seals all the way around.

34　Idle speed check and adjustment (every 60,000 miles or 48 months)

Refer to illustrations 34.3a, 34.3b, 34.7a, 34.7b and 34.8

1　Engine idle speed is the speed at which the engine operates when no accelerator pedal pressure is applied, as when stopped at a traffic light. This speed is critical to the performance of the engine itself, as well as many engine subsystems.

2　Set the parking brake firmly and block the wheels to prevent the vehicle from rolling. Put the transaxle in Neutral. Unplug the engine fan electrical connector(s). If the fan(s) should come on during the idle adjustment procedure, idle speed is affected.

3　Connect a hand held tachometer **(see illustrations)**. **Caution:** *Don't allow the tachometer to touch ground or damage to the igniter and/or the ignition coil.* **Note:** *Some tachometers may not be compatible with this ignition system. It is recommended that you consult the manufacturer.*

4　Start the engine and allow it to reach normal operating temperature.

5　Check, and adjust if necessary, the ignition timing (see Chapter 5).

6　Allow the engine to idle for two minutes.

7　On 2-SE engines, disconnect the vacuum hose from the idle speed control.On 1987 and later models, connect a jumper wire between the E1 and TE1 terminals of the check connector **(see illustra-**

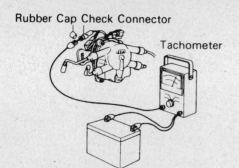

34.3a Typical tachometer connection details – 1986 2-SE engine

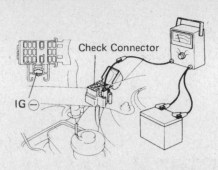

34.3b On later models the tachometer terminal is part of the check connector

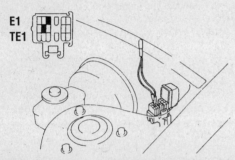

34.7a Connect a jumper wire between the check connector E1 and TE1 terminals before checking the idle speed on 1987 and later models

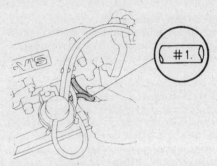

34.7b On 3S-GE engines, pinch the number 1 vacuum hose shut at the air intake chamber when checking the idle speed

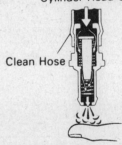

35.4   To check the PVC valve, first attach a clean section of hose to the cylinder head side of the valve and blow through it – air should pass through easily – then blow through the intake manifold side of the valve and varify that air passes through it

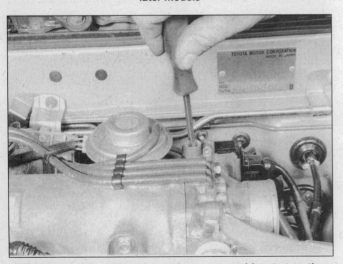

34.8 Pry out the rubber plug and use a screwdriver to turn the adjusting screw on the throttle body - note that the idle speed is quite sensitive to even the slightest turn of this screw

tion). On 3S-GE engines, pinch the number 1 vacuum hose at the air intake chamber shut **(see illustration)**.
8   Check the engine idle speed on the tachometer and compare it to those listed in the Specifications Section at the beginning of this Chapter or the Vehicle Emission Control Information label in the engine compartment. If there is a difference between the Specifications Section and the VECI label, always assume that the information on the label is correct.
8   If the idle speed is too low or too high, turn the idle speed adjusting screw **(see illustration)** until the specified idle speed is obtained.
9   Turn off the engine, disconnect the tachometer and reconnect any components which were disconnected.

35   Positive Crankcase Ventilation (PCV) valve and hose check and replacement (1990 and later models only)(every 60,000 miles or 48 months)

Refer to illustration 35.4
1   The PCV valve and hose is located in the valve cover.
2   Disconnect the hose, pull the PCV valve from the cover, then re-connect the hose.
3   With the engine idling at normal operating temperature, place your finger over the valve opening. If there's no vacuum at the valve, check for a plugged hose or valve. Replace any plugged or deterio rated hoses.
4   Turn off the engine. Remove the PCV valve from the hose. Blow through the valve from the valve cover (cylinder head) end. If air will not pass through the valve in this direction, replace it with a new one **(see illustration)**.
5   When purchasing a replacement PCV valve, make sure it's for your particular vehicle and engine size. Compare the old valve with the new one to make sure they're the same.

Chapter 2 Part A Engines

Contents

2A

Specifications

General

Engine type
    2S-E .... SOHC, two valves per cylinder
    3S-FE, 5S-FE, 3S-GE, 4A-FE .... DOHC, four valves per cylinder
Cylinder numbers (drivebelt end-to-transaxle end) 1-2-3-4
Firing order 1-3-4-2

4A-FE

0764H

3S-FE, 3S-GE and 5S-FE

0763H

Front ↓

2S-E

Cylinder location and distributor rotation

Warpage limits

Cylinder head-to-block surface
    2S-E, 3S-FE, 5S-FE and 4A-FE engines .... 0.002 inch
    3S-GE engine .... 0.008 inch
Intake and exhaust manifolds
    2S-E engine .... 0.012 inch
    3S-FE and 5S-FE engines .... 0.0031 inch
    3S-GE engine
        Intake manifold .... 0.012 inch
        Exhaust manifold .... 0.039 inch
    4A-FE engine
        Intake manifold .... 0.0079 inch
        Exhaust manifold .... 0.0118 inch
Camshaft housing surface (2S-E engine only) .... 0.0031 inch

Timing belt

Idler pulley spring tension

2S-E engine (at 51 mm)	16 to 19 lbs
3S-FE engine (at 51 mm)	13.2 to 15.4 lbs
3S-GE engine (at 51.9 mm)	16.6 lbs

5S-FE engine (at 51.9 mm)

1990	13.2 to 15.4 lbs
1991	10.6 to 11.1 lbs
1992 on	7.2 to 8.3 lbs

4A-FE engine

1990 (at 50.2 lbs)	7.9 to 8.8 lbs
1991 on (at 51.9 lbs)	7.9 to 8.8 lbs

Idler pulley spring free length

2S-E engine	2.01 inch
3S-FE and 1990 5S-FE engines	1.815 inch
1991 and later 5S-FE engine	1.811 inch
3S-GE engine	1.724 inch
4A-FE engine	1.512 inch

Camshaft

Thrust clearance (endplay)

2S-E engine

Standard	0.0031 to 0.0091 inch
Service limit	0.0138 inch

3S-FE and 5S-FE engines

Intake camshaft

Standard	0.0018 to 0.0039 inch
Service limit	0.0047 inch

Exhaust camshaft

Standard	0.0012 to 0.0033 inch
Service limit	0.0039 inch

3S-GE engine

1986

Standard	0.0039 to 0.0094 inch
Service limit	0.0118 inch

1987 through 1989

Standard	0.0012 to 0.0020 inch
Service limit	0.0118 inch

4A-FE engine

Intake camshaft

Standard	0.0012 to 0.0033 inch
Service limit	0.0043 inch

Exhaust camshaft

Standard	0.0014 to 0.0035 inch
Service limit	0.0043 inch

Journal diameter

2S-E engine

No.1	1.8291 to 1.8297 inch
No.2	1.8192 to 1.8199 inch
No.3	1.8094 to 1.8100 inch
No.4	1.7996 to 1.8002 inch
No.5	1.7897 to 1.7904 inch
No.6	1.7799 to 1.7805 inch
3S-FE, 5S-FE, 3S-GE engines (all journals)	1.0614 to 1.0620 inch

4A-FE engine

No. 1 exhaust	0.9822 to 0.9829 inch
All others	0.9035 to 0.9041 inch

Bearing oil clearance

2S-E engine

Standard	0.0010 to 0.0026 inch
Service limit	0.0039 inch

3S-FE and 5S-FE engines

Standard	0.0010 to 0.0024 inch
Service limit	0.0039 inch

3S-GE engine

Standard	0.0010 to 0.0024 inch
Service limit	0.0031 inch

4A-FE engine

Standard	0.0010 to 0.0026 inch
Service limit	0.0038 inch

Runout limit
  2S-E, 3S-FE, 5S-FE, 4A-FE engines .... 0.016 inch
  3S-GE engine .... 0.024 inch
Lobe height
  2S-E engine
    Standard .... 1.5325 to 1.5365 inch
    Service limit .... 1.5268 inch
  3S-FE engine
    Intake camshaft
      Standard .... 1.3744 to 1.3783 inch
      Service limit .... 1.3701 inch
    Exhaust camshaft
      Standard .... 1.4000 to 1.4039 inch
      Service limit .... 1.3957 inch
  5S-FE engine
    Intake camshaft
      1990 and 1991
      Standard .... 1.3902 to 1.3941 inch
      Service limit .... 1.3858 inch
      1992 on
      Standard .... 1.3744 to 1.3783 inch
      Service limit .... 1.3701 inch
    Exhaust camshaft
      Standard .... 1.4000 to 1.4039 inch
      Service limit .... 1.3957 inch
  3S-GE engine
    Standard .... 1.3980 to 1.4020 inch
    Service limit
      1986 .... 1.3976 inch
      1987 through 1989 .... 1.3937 inch
  4A-FE engine
    Intake camshaft
      Standard .... 1.3862 to 1.3902 inch
      Service limit .... 1.3705 inch
    Exhaust camshaft
      Standard .... 1.3744 to 1.3783 inch
      Service limit .... 1.3587 inch
Gear spring free length
  3S-FE and 5S-FE engines .... 0.886 to 0.902 inch
  4A-FE engine .... 0.669 to 0.693 inch
Gear backlash (3S-FE, 5S-FE and 4A-FE engines only)
  Standard .... 0.0008 to 0.0079 inch
  Service limit .... 0.0188 inch

Valve lifter (except 2S-E engine)

Diameter
  All except 1992 5S-FE .... 1.1014 to 1.1018 inch
  1992 5S-FE .... 1.2191 to 1.2195 inch
Bore diameter
  All except 1992 5S-FE .... 1.1024 to 1.1032 inch
  1992 5S-FE .... 1.2205 to 1.2213 inch
Oil clearance
  Standard
    All except 1992 and later 5S-FE .... 0.0005 to 0.0018 inch
    1992 and later 5S-FE .... 0.0009 to 0.0020 inch
  Service limit .... 0.0028 inch

Oil pump

Driven rotor-to-case clearance
  Except 4A-FE engine .... 0.0039 to 0.0063 inch
  4A-FE engine .... 0.0031 to 0.0079 inch
Rotor tip clearance
  Standard
    Except 4A-FE engine .... 0.0016 to 0.0063 inch
    4A-FE engine .... 0.0010 to 0.0033 inch
  Wear limit
    All except 4A-FE .... 0.0079 inch
    4A-FE .... 0.0138 inch

Torque specifications   **Ft-lbs** (unless otherwise indicated)

Intake manifold bolts	
2S-E engine	31
3S-FE, 5S-FE, 3S-GE and 4A-FE engines	14
Exhaust manifold bolts	
2S-E engine	31
3S-FE engine	
1987	29
1988 and 1989	31
3S-GE engine	32
5S-FE engine	
1990	31
1991 on	36
4A-FE engine	18
Crankshaft pulley-to-crankshaft bolt	
2S-E, 3S-FE, 5S-FE and 3S-GE engines	80
4A-FE engine	87
Flywheel/driveplate bolts	
2S-E and 3S-FE engines	
Flywheel	72
Driveplate	61
5S-FE engine	
Flywheel	
1990	72
1991-on	65
Driveplate	61
3S-GE engine	
Flywheel	
New bolt	65
Used bolt	69
Driveplate	61
4A-FE engine	
Flywheel	58
Driveplate	47
Idler pulley bolts	
2S-E, 3S-FE and 5S-FE engines	31
3S-GE engine	32
4A-FE engine	27
Cylinder head bolts	
2S-E, 3S-FE engines	47
3S-GE engine	40
5S-FE engine	
First turn	36
Second turn	Tighten 90-degrees
4A-FE engine	
1990	47
1991 on	44
Camshaft housing bolts (2S-E engine only)	9 to 13
Camshaft oil seal retainer bolts (2S-E engine only)	11
Camshaft bearing cap bolts	
All except 4A-FE engine	14
4A-FE engine	9
Camshaft pulley bolt(s)	
2S-E, 3S-FE and 5S-FE engines	40
3S-GE and 4A-FE engines	43
Oil pump bolts	
2S-E engine	82 in-lbs
3S-FE engine	
1987 and 1988	82 in-lbs
1989	69 in-lbs
5S-FE engine	82 in-lbs
3S-GE engine	69 in-lbs
4A-FE engine	16
Oil pump pulley nut	
2S-E engine	20
3S-FE, 5S-FE and 3S-GE engines	21
Oil pick-up (strainer) nuts/bolts	
2S-E engine	48 in-lbs
3S-FE engine	
1987 and 1988	48 in-lbs
1989	78 in-lbs

5S-FE engine
    1990 and 1991 .... 82 in-lbs
    1992 on .... 48 in-lbs
3S-GE engine
    1986
        Bolt .... 69 in-lbs
        Nut .... 48 in-lbs
    1987 through 1989 .... 48 in-lbs
4A-FE engine .... 82 in-lbs
Oil pan-to-block bolts
    2S-E, 3S-FE and 3S-GE engines .... 48 in-lbs
5S-FE engine
    1990 and 1991 .... 48 in-lbs
    1992 on .... 55 in-lbs
4A-FE engine .... 43 in-lbs
Rear crankshaft oil seal retainer bolts
    1986 .... 48 in-lbs
    1987 on .... 82 in-lbs

1   General information

This Part of Chapter 2 is devoted to in-vehicle repair procedures for all engines. All information concerning engine removal and installation and engine block and cylinder head overhaul can be found in Part B of this Chapter.

The following repair procedures are based on the assumption that the engine is installed in the vehicle. If the engine has been removed from the vehicle and mounted on a stand, many of the steps outlined in this Part of Chapter 2 will not apply.

The Specifications included in this Part of Chapter 2 apply only to the procedures contained in this Part. Part B of Chapter 2 contains the Specifications necessary for cylinder head and engine block rebuilding.

Five different four-cylinder gasoline engines were installed in the Celica during the years covered by this manual. The single overhead camshaft (SOHC), two valve-per-cylinder engine is designated the 2S-E by Toyota. The dual overhead camshaft (DOHC), four valve-per-cylinder engines are designated the 3S-FE, 3S-GE, 4A-FE and 5S-FE.

2   Repair operations possible with the engine in the vehicle

Many major repair operations can be accomplished without removing the engine from the vehicle.

Clean the engine compartment and the exterior of the engine with some type of degreaser before any work is done. It will make the job easier and help keep dirt out of the internal areas of the engine.

Depending on the components involved, it may be helpful to remove the hood to improve access to the engine as repairs are performed (refer to Chapter 11 if necessary). Cover the fenders to prevent damage to the paint. Special pads are available, but an old bedspread or blanket will also work.

If vacuum, exhaust, oil or coolant leaks develop, indicating a need for gasket or seal replacement, the repairs can generally be made with the engine in the vehicle. The intake and exhaust manifold gaskets, oil pan gasket, crankshaft oil seals and cylinder head gasket are all accessible with the engine in place.

Exterior engine components, such as the intake and exhaust manifolds, the oil pan, the oil pump, the water pump, the starter motor, the alternator, the distributor and the fuel system components can be removed for repair with the engine in place.

Since the cylinder head can be removed without pulling the engine, camshaft and valve component servicing can also be accomplished with the engine in the vehicle. Replacement of the timing belt and pulleys is also possible with the engine in the vehicle.

In extreme cases caused by a lack of necessary equipment, repair or replacement of piston rings, pistons, connecting rods and rod bearings is possible with the engine in the vehicle. However, this practice is not recommended because of the cleaning and preparation work that must be done to the components involved.

3   Top Dead Center (TDC) for number one piston - locating

Refer to illustration 3.8
Note: *The following procedure is based on the assumption that the distributor is correctly installed. If you are trying to locate TDC to install the distributor correctly, piston position must be determined by feeling for compression at the number one spark plug hole, then aligning the ignition timing marks as described in step 8.*

1   Top Dead Center (TDC) is the highest point in the cylinder that each piston reaches as it travels up-and-down when the crankshaft turns. Each piston reaches TDC on the compression stroke and again on the exhaust stroke, but TDC generally refers to piston position on the compression stroke.

2   Positioning the piston(s) at TDC is an essential part of many procedures such as camshaft and timing belt/pulley removal and distributor removal.

3   Before beginning this procedure, be sure to place the transmission in Neutral and apply the parking brake or block the rear wheels. Also, disable the ignition system by detaching the coil wire from the center terminal of the distributor cap and grounding it on the block with a jumper wire (or, on models with integrated ignition, disconnect the electrical connectors at the distributor). Remove the spark plugs (see Chapter 1).

4   In order to bring any piston to TDC, the crankshaft must be turned using one of the methods outlined below. When looking at the front of the engine, normal crankshaft rotation is clockwise.
  a) The preferred method is to turn the crankshaft with a socket and ratchet attached to the bolt threaded into the front of the crankshaft.
  b) A remote starter switch, which may save some time, can also be used. Follow the instructions included with the switch. Once the piston is close to TDC, use a socket and ratchet as described in the previous paragraph.
  c) If an assistant is available to turn the ignition switch to the Start position in short bursts, you can get the piston close to TDC without a remote starter switch. Make sure your assistant is out of the vehicle, away from the ignition switch, then use a socket and ratchet as described in Paragraph a) to complete the procedure.

5   Note the position of the terminal for the number one spark plug wire on the distributor cap. If the terminal isn't marked, follow the plug wire from the number one cylinder spark plug to the cap.

6   Use a felt-tip pen or chalk to make a mark on the distributor body directly under the terminal.

7   Detach the cap from the distributor and set it aside (see Chapter 1 if necessary).

8   Turn the crankshaft (see Paragraph 4 above) until the notch in the crankshaft pulley is aligned with the 0 on the timing plate (located at the front of the engine) **(see illustration)**.

9   Look at the distributor rotor - it should be pointing directly at the mark you made on the distributor body.

3.8   Align the crankshaft drivebelt pulley notch (arrow) with the 0 (zero) on the timing plate (3S-FE engine shown, others similar)

10   If the rotor is 180-degrees off, the number one piston is at TDC on the exhaust stroke.

11   To get the piston to TDC on the compression stroke, turn the crankshaft one complete turn (360-degrees) clockwise. The rotor should now be pointing at the mark on the distributor. When the rotor is pointing at the number one spark plug wire terminal in the distributor cap and the ignition timing marks are aligned, the number one piston is at TDC on the compression stroke. **Note:** *If it's impossible to align the ignition timing marks when the rotor is pointing at the mark on the distributor body, the timing belt may have jumped the teeth on the pulleys or may have been installed incorrectly.*

12   After the number one piston has been positioned at TDC on the compression stroke, TDC for any of the remaining pistons can be located by turning the crankshaft and following the firing order. Mark the remaining spark plug wire terminal locations on the distributor body just like you did for the number one terminal, then number the marks to correspond with the cylinder numbers. As you turn the crankshaft, the rotor will also turn. When it's pointing directly at one of the marks on the distributor, the piston for that particular cylinder is at TDC on the compression stroke.

---

4   Valve cover - removal and installation

---

1   Disconnect the negative cable from the battery.

All except 3S-GE engine

Refer to illustrations 4.4a through 4.4f, 4.6a, 4.6b, and 4.7

2   Detach the breather hose from the valve cover (if equipped).

3   If you're working on a 3S-FE, 5S-FE, or 4A-FE engine, remove the spark plug wires from the spark plugs.

4   Remove the mounting nuts and sealing washers, then detach the cover and gasket from the head. On the 3S-FE and 5S-FE engines, the spark plug tube nuts are used to hold the cover in place. On the 4A-FE

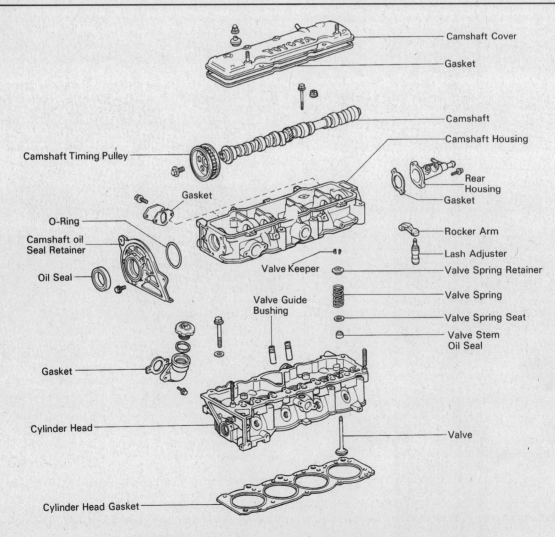

4.4a   2S-E (SOHC) engine cylinder head and related components - exploded view

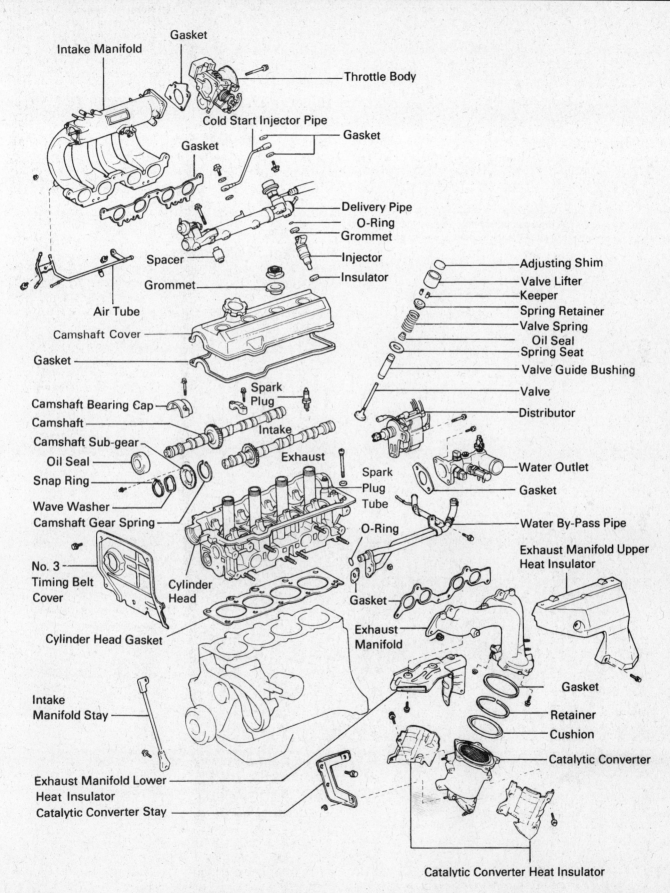

2A

4.4b   3S-FE (DOHC) engine cylinder head and related components - exploded view

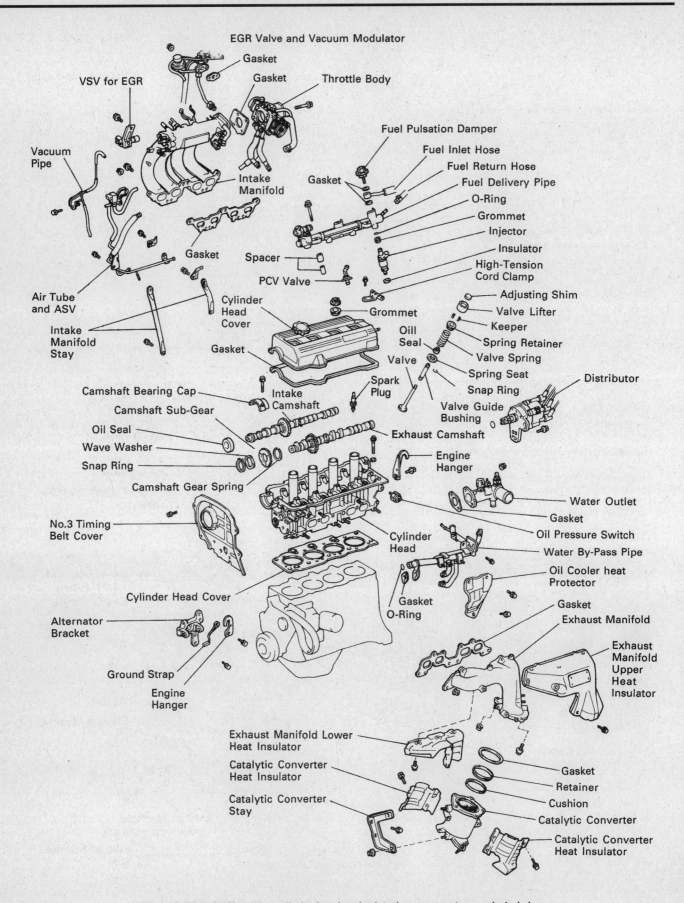

4.4c   5S-FE (DOHC) engine cylinder head and related components - exploded view

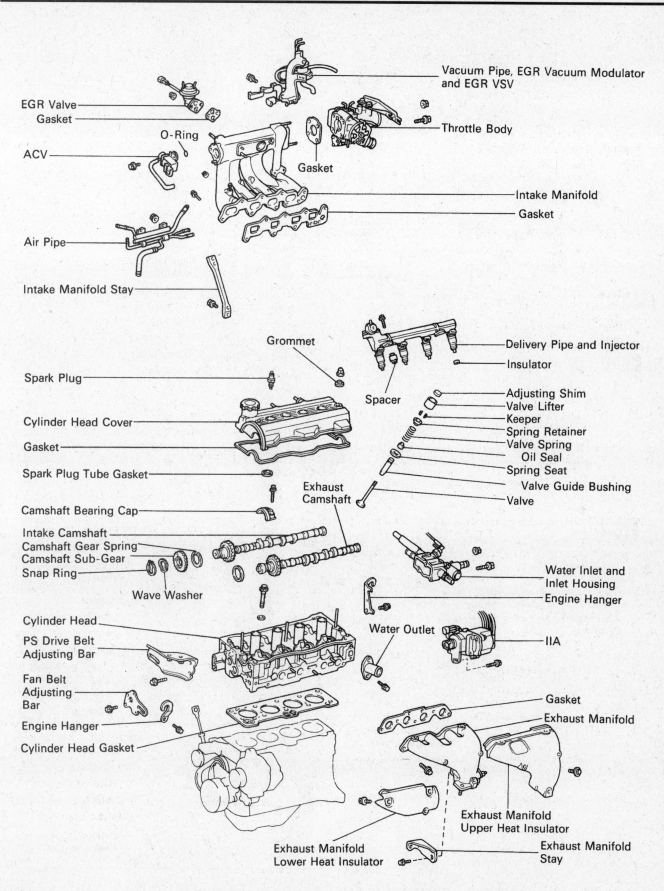

4.4d   4A-FE (DOHC) engine cylinder head and related components - exploded view

4.4e   On the 3S-FE and 5S-FE engines, the valve cover is held in place by the large spark plug tube nuts (arrows)

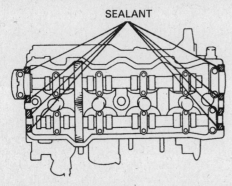

4.6a   On the 3S-FE and 5S-FE engines, apply sealant to the eight points indicated by the shaded areas before installing the valve cover

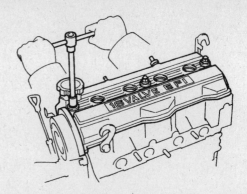

4.4f   On the 4A-FE engine, the valve cover is held in place by three acorn-type nuts

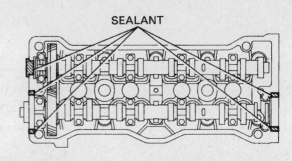

4.6b   On the 4A-FE engine, apply sealant to the five points indicated by the shaded areas before installing the valve cover

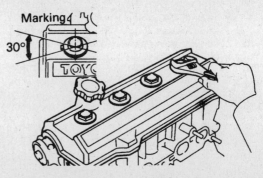

4.7   On the 3S-FE and 5S-FE engines, install the spark plug tube grommets with the index marks facing the timing belt end of the engine (3S-FE engine shown)

and 2S-E engines, acorn-type cap nuts are used **(see illustrations)**. If the cover is stuck to the head, bump the end with a block of wood and a hammer to jar it loose. If that doesn't work, try to slip a flexible putty knife between the head and cover to break the seal. **Caution:** *Don't pry at the cover or housing-to-head joint or damage to the sealing surfaces may occur, leading to oil leaks after the cover is reinstalled.*

5   The mating surfaces of the housing or cylinder head and cover must be clean when the cover is installed. Use a gasket scraper to remove all traces of sealant and old gasket material, then clean the mating surfaces with lacquer thinner or acetone. If there's residue or oil on the mating surfaces when the cover is installed, oil leaks may develop.

6   If you're working on a 3S-FE, 5S-FE, or 4A-FE engine, apply a thin, uniform layer of sealant (Toyota no. 08826-00080 or equivalent) to the gasket/seal joints **(see illustrations)**.

7   Position a new gasket and seals (if used) on the cylinder head, then install the valve cover, sealing washers and nuts. On 3S-FE and 5S-FE engines, install the spark plug tube grommets with the index marks facing the timing belt end of the engine **(see illustration)**.

8   Tighten the nuts in four steps until they're just snug; do not overtorque.

3S-GE engine

Refer to illustrations 4.10 and 4.12

9   Disconnect the spark plug wires from the spark plugs.

10   Remove the screws and detach the center cover, then remove the screws and lift off the valve covers **(see illustration)**. If the covers are stuck, bump them lightly with a soft-faced mallet.

11   Clean the mating surfaces of the cylinder head and cover (see Step 5).

12   Apply a thin, uniform layer of sealant (Toyota no. 08826-00080 or

equivalent) to the gasket/seal joints **(see illustration)**.

13   Install the cover gaskets and valve covers. Tighten the screws evenly in several passes until they're just snug; do not overtorque.

14   Install the center cover and tighten its screws evenly until they're just snug; do not overtorque.

All engines

15   Reinstall the remaining parts, run the engine and check for oil leaks.

---

5   Intake manifold - removal and installation

Refer to illustrations 5.4a, 5.4b, 5.5 and 5.8

1   Disconnect the negative cable from the battery.

2   Drain the cooling system (see Chapter 1).

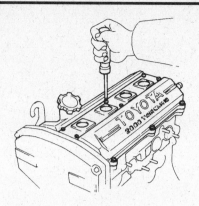

4.10 On the 3S-GE engine, remove the center cover, then the valve covers

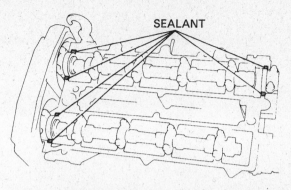

4.12 On the 3S-GE engine, apply sealant to the six points indicated by the shaded areas before installing the valve covers

5.4a The various hoses should be marked to ensure correct reinstallation

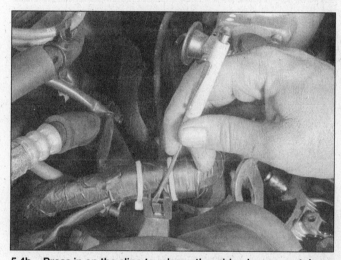

5.4b Press in on the clips to release the wiring harness retainers (3S-GE and 5S-FE engines)

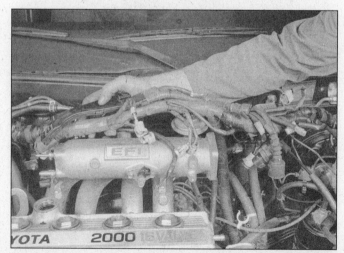

5.5 Lift the wiring harness over the intake manifold (3S-FE and 5S-FE engines)

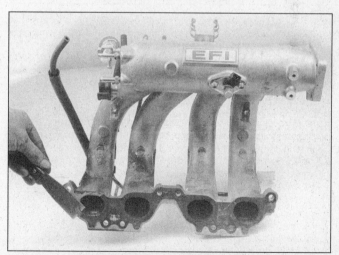

5.8 Remove all traces of old gasket material and sealant with a scraper - be careful not to gouge the manifold; it's made of aluminum

3   Remove the throttle body, fuel injectors and fuel rail (see Chapter 4).

4   Label and detach all wire harnesses, control cables and hoses still connected to the intake manifold **(see illustrations)**.

5   If you're working on a 3S-FE or 5S-FE engine, carefully lift the wire harness over the manifold **(see illustration)**.

6   Unbolt any braces still in place.

7   Remove the mounting nuts/bolts, then detach the manifold from the engine.

8   Use a scraper to remove all traces of old gasket material and sealant from the manifold and cylinder head **(see illustration)**, then clean the mating surfaces with lacquer thinner or acetone. If the gasket was leaking, have the manifold checked for warpage at an automotive machine shop and resurfaced if necessary.

9   Install a new gasket, then position the manifold on the head and

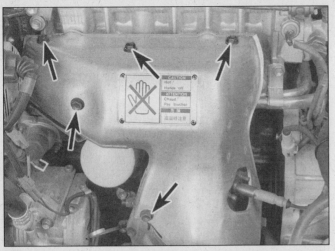

6.3   Remove the exhaust manifold heat insulator bolts (arrows) (3S-FE engine shown; others similar)

6.11   On 3S-FE and 3S-GE engines, be sure the marks on the exhaust manifold gasket face out - the arrow must point toward the rear (transaxle end) of the engine

install the nuts/bolts.

10   Tighten the nuts/bolts in three or four equal steps to the torque listed in this Chapter's Specifications. Work from the center out towards the ends to avoid warping the manifold.

11   Install the remaining parts in the reverse order of removal.

12   Before starting the engine, check the throttle linkage for smooth operation.

13   Run the engine and check for coolant and vacuum leaks.

14   Road test the vehicle and check for proper operation of all accessories, including the cruise control system.

6   Exhaust manifold - removal and installation

Refer to illustrations 6.3 and 6.11

Warning: *The engine must be completely cool before beginning this procedure.*

1   Disconnect the negative cable from the battery.

2   Unplug the oxygen sensor wire harness. If you're installing a new manifold, remove the sensor (see Chapter 6).

3   Remove the upper heat insulator from the manifold **(see illustration)**.

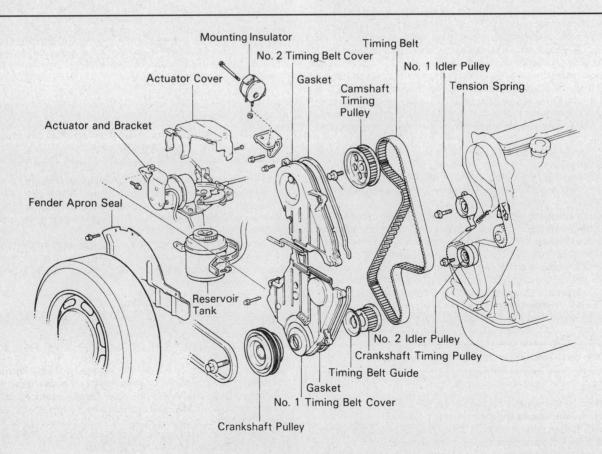

7.9a   2S-E engine timing belmt components - exploded view

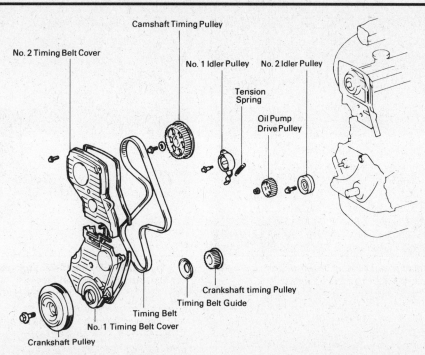

7.9b   3S-FE engine timing belt components - exploded view (5S-FE engine similar)

4   Apply penetrating oil to the exhaust manifold mounting nuts/bolts.
5   Remove the exhaust manifold brace.
6   Disconnect the exhaust pipe from the exhaust manifold (2S-E, 3S-GE and 4A-FE engines) or catalytic converter (all others) (see Chapter 4). On some models, it may be necessary to remove the front exhaust pipe from the vehicle. This may require removing the suspension crossmember, so be sure to observe all safety precautions.
7   Remove the nuts/bolts and detach the manifold and gasket. On 3S-FE and 5S-FE engines, the manifold is removed as an assembly with the catalytic converter.
8   If you're working on a 3S-FE or 5S-FE engine, disconnect the converter from the manifold if necessary (see Chapter 4).
9   Use a scraper to remove all traces of old gasket material and carbon deposits from the manifold and cylinder head mating surfaces. If the gasket was leaking, have the manifold checked for warpage at an automotive machine shop and resurfaced if necessary. **Caution:** *When scraping, be very careful not to gouge or scratch the delicate aluminum cylinder head.*
10   If you separated the catalytic converter from the manifold on a 3S-FE or 5S-FE engine, reassemble them with a new gasket (see Chapter 4).
11   Position a new exhaust manifold gasket over the cylinder head studs. **Note:** *On 3S-FE and 3S-GE engines, the marks on the gasket should face out (away from the head) and the arrow should point toward the rear (transaxle end) of the engine* **(see illustration).**
12   Install the manifold and thread the mounting nuts/bolts into place.
13   Working from the center out, tighten the nuts/bolts to the torque listed in this Chapter's Specifications in three or four equal steps.
14   Reinstall the remaining parts in the reverse order of removal.
15   Run the engine and check for exhaust leaks.

7   Timing belt - removal, inspection and installation

Removal

1   Disconnect the negative cable from the battery.
2   Block the rear wheels and set the parking brake.
3   Loosen the lug nuts on the right front wheel and raise the vehicle. Support the front of the vehicle securely on jackstands.
4   Remove the right front wheel and fender apron seal (see Chapter 11).

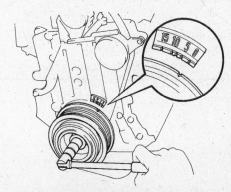

7.10a   On the 2S-E engine, align the crankshaft pulley groove with the zero mark . . .

5   Remove the spark plugs and drivebelts (see Chapter 1).
6   Remove the alternator and bracket (see Chapter 5).
7   Unbolt the power steering reservoir if it will obstruct removal of the timing belt. Remove the cruise control actuator (if equipped) and set them aside.
8   Support the engine and remove the right engine mount (see Section 18). **Note:** *If you're planning on removing the oil pan, in addition to the timing belt, support the engine with a hoist from above (see Chapter 2B - engine removal).*

2S-E, 3S-FE and 5S-FE engines
Refer to illustrations 7.9a, 7.9b, 7.10a, 7.10b, 7.11a, 7.11b, 7.12, 7.13, 7.14, 7.15a, 7.15b, 7.16, 7.17, 7.18a and 7.18b
9   Remove the upper (no. 2) timing belt cover and gaskets **(see illustrations)**.
10   If you're working on a 2S-E (SOHC) engine, turn the crankshaft clockwise until the groove in the crankshaft pulley is aligned with the zero mark on the lower timing belt cover **(see illustration)**. This is the number one position TDC. Check to be sure the center of the position hole in the camshaft pulley is aligned with the matchmark on the camshaft oil seal retainer **(see illustration)**. If the "E" mark is not up, rotate the crankshaft 360-degrees clockwise.
11   If you're working on a 3S-FE or 5S-FE engine, position the number one piston at TDC on the compression stroke (see Section 3).

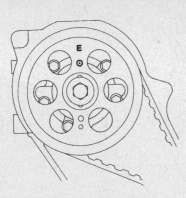

7.10b   . . . and the mark on the oil seal retainer should be visible through the inspection hole in the camshaft pulley (if the "E" mark is not up, rotate the crankshaft 360-degrees clockwise

7.11a   On 3S-FE and 5S-FE models, rotate the crankshaft until the hole in the camshaft pulley (arrow) is at the top . . .

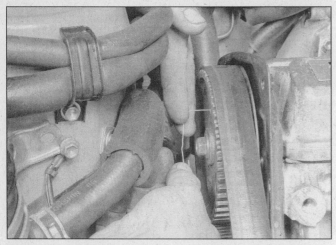

7.11b   . . . and insert a bent paper clip into the hole to make sure it's lined up with the notch at the top of the bearing cap

7.12   If you intend to reuse the timing belt, paint match marks on the pulley and belt (arrow)

7.13   Loosen the upper idler pulley set bolt (arrow) and unhook the spring to release the belt

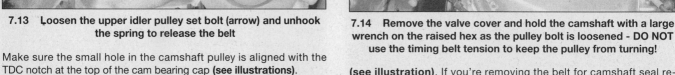

7.14   Remove the valve cover and hold the camshaft with a large wrench on the raised hex as the pulley bolt is loosened - DO NOT use the timing belt tension to keep the pulley from turning!

Make sure the small hole in the camshaft pulley is aligned with the TDC notch at the top of the cam bearing cap **(see illustrations)**.
12   If you plan to reuse the timing belt, paint match marks on the pulley and belt and an arrow indicating direction of travel on the belt **(see illustration)**.
13   Loosen the upper (no. 1) idler pulley set bolt and remove the spring to release the tension, then slip the timing belt off the pulley

(see illustration). If you're removing the belt for camshaft seal replacement or cylinder head or camshaft removal, it isn't necessary to detach the belt from the crankshaft pulley.
14   If the camshaft pulley is worn or damaged, remove the valve cover (see Section 4), hold the rear (intake) camshaft with a large wrench and remove the bolt, then detach the pulley **(see illustration)**.

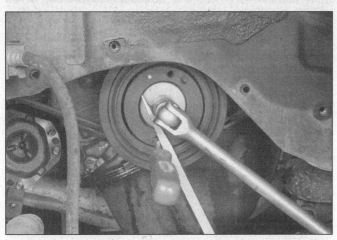

7.15a   Insert a Phillips screwdriver into one of the pulley holes, place a socket and breaker bar over the bolt head, wedge a screwdriver between the tools and loosen the crankshaft bolt - DO NOT use the timing belt tension to keep the pulley from turning!

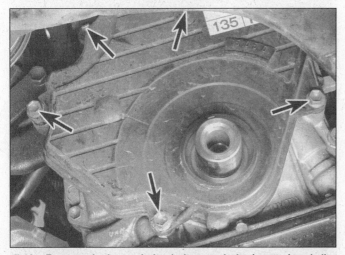

7.16   Remove the lower timing belt cover bolts (arrows) and slip the cover and gaskets off the engine (3S-FE shown, others similar)

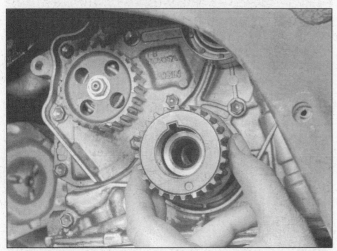

7.18a   The pulley should slide off the crankshaft quite easily

15   To proceed with timing belt removal, keep the crankshaft (accessory drivebelt) pulley from turning with a large Phillips screwdriver and a prybar **(see illustration)**, remove the bolt and detach the pulley by

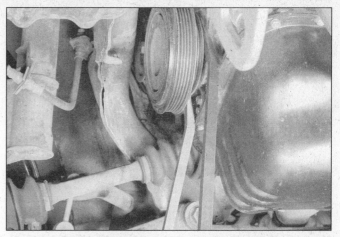

7.15b   Pry evenly on the pulley to remove it

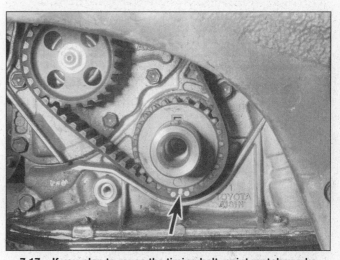

7.17   If you plan to reuse the timing belt, paint match marks (arrow) on the belt and pulleys

Shop Rag

7.18b   If the crankshaft pulley is stuck, protect the oil pump case with rags and pry the pulley off with two screwdrivers

prying evenly with two large screwdrivers **(see illustration)** or using a bolt-type vibration damper puller. Do not use a jaw-type gear puller! Sometimes the pulley can be removed by hand.
16   Remove the lower (no. 1) timing belt cover and gaskets **(see illustration)** and slip the belt guide off the crankshaft.
17   If you plan to reuse the timing belt, paint match marks on the pulley and belt **(see illustration)**.
18   Slip the timing belt off the pulley and remove it. If the pulley is worn or damaged, or if you need to get at the front crankshaft oil seal, remove the pulley from the crankshaft **(see illustrations)**. If you remove the inner belt guide, be careful to note how it's installed so you can reinstall it the same way (the cupped side faces away from the belt).

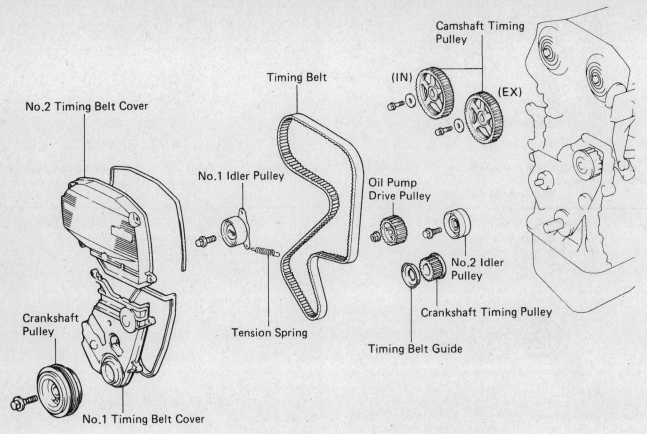

7.21a   3S-GE engine timing belt components - exploded view

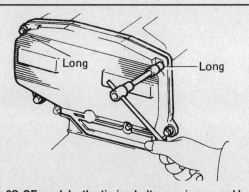

7.21b   On 3S-GE models, the timing belt cover is secured by six bolts - the upper two are longer

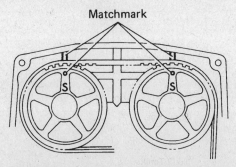

7.22a   On 3S-GE models, line up the mark on each pulley with the corresponding mark on the rear timing belt cover

3S-GE engine

Refer to illustrations 7.21a, 7.21b, 7.22a, 7.22b, 7.22c, 7.24, 7.25 and 7.27

19   Remove the radiator reservoir tank (see Chapter 3).
20   Remove the valve covers (see Section 4).
21   Remove the upper (No. 2) timing belt cover **(see illustrations)**.
22   Position the number one piston at TDC on the compression stroke (see Section 3). Make sure the matchmarks on the camshaft pulleys are aligned with the marks on the rear timing belt cover **(see illustration)**. Also check the camshaft alignment marks. The 3S-GE camshafts may be equipped with two or five knock pin holes (all replacement camshafts have five holes). On two-hole camshafts, the knock pins should align with the rear timing belt cover marks and the forward lobe on each camshaft should point away from the other camshaft **(see illustration)**. On five-hole camshafts, the notch in each camshaft should align with the drill mark in the bearing cap **(see illustration)**.

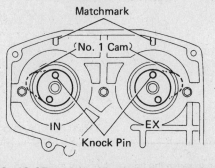

7.22b   On 3S-GE models with two-hole camshafts, make sure the knock pin on each camshaft is lined up with the mark on the rear timing belt cover and the forward cam lobes are turned away from each other

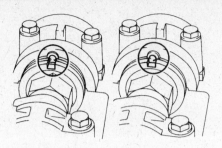

7.22c   On 3S-GE models with five-hole camshafts, make sure the groove in each camshaft is lined up with the drill mark on the front bearing cap

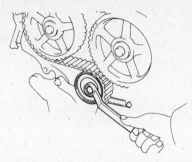

7.24   Move the idler pulley against spring tension to loosen the belt, then tighten its bolt to lock it temporarily

7.25   Remove the valve cover and hold each camshaft with a wrench on the raised hex as the pulley bolt is loosened - DO NOT use the timing belt tension to keep the pulley from turning!

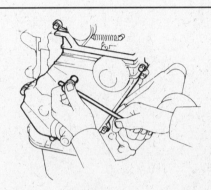

7.27   The 3S-GE lower timing belt cover is held by six bolts

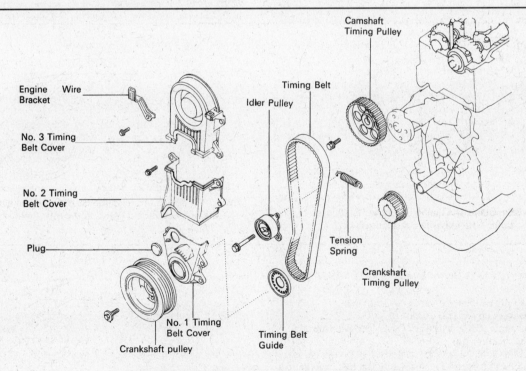

7.30   4A-FE engine timing belt components - exploded view

23   If you plan to reuse the timing belt, paint match marks on the pulleys and belt and an arrow indicating direction of travel on the belt **(see illustration 7.12).**

24   Loosen the upper (no. 1) idler pulley set bolt **(see illustration)** and push the pulley to the left (against spring tension) as far as it will go, then temporarily tighten it. Slip the timing belt off the pulleys. If you're removing the belt for camshaft seal replacement or camshaft or cylinder head removal, it isn't necessary to detach the belt from the crankshaft pulley.

25   If the camshaft pulleys are worn or damaged, remove the valve

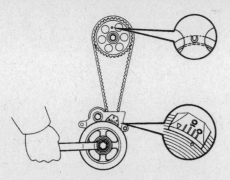

7.31   On 4A-FE models, the 0-degree mark must align with the crankshaft pulley notch and the camshaft pulley hole with the bearing cap mark at the same time

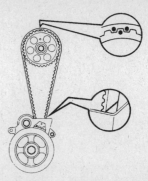

7.32   On 4A-FE models, paint match marks on the camshaft pulley and belt; also make a mark on the belt to indicate the edge of the lower cover - this will line up the belt correctly if you don't take the lower cover off

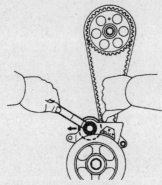

7.33   Remove the grommet from the lower belt cover, loosen the idler pulley bolt, push the idler pulley as far as possible to the left and tighten the bolt

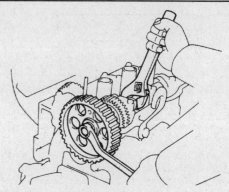

7.34   Hold the camshaft flat with a wrench if it's necessary to remove the pulley bolt - DO NOT use timing belt tension to hold the pulley!

cover, hold the camshaft with a large wrench and remove the bolt, then detach the pulley **(see illustration)**. Note: *The knock pins may come loose during pulley removal, so be prepared to catch them.*

26   To proceed with timing belt removal, keep the crankshaft (accessory drivebelt) pulley from turning with a large Phillips screwdriver and a prybar **(see illustration 7.15a)**, remove the bolt and detach the pulley with two screwdrivers or a bolt-type vibration damper puller **(see illustration 7.15b)**. Do not use a jaw-type gear puller! Sometimes the pulley can be removed by hand.

27   Remove the lower (no. 1) timing belt cover and gaskets **(see illustration)** and slip the belt guide off the crankshaft.

28   If you plan to reuse the timing belt, paint match marks on the pulley and belt **(see illustration 7.17)**.

29   Slip the timing belt off the pulley and remove it. If the pulley is worn or damaged, or if you need to get at the front crankshaft oil seal, remove the pulley from the crankshaft **(see illustrations 7.18a and 7.18b)**. If you remove the inner belt guide, be careful to note how it's installed so you can reinstall it the same way (the cupped side faces away from the belt).

4A-FE engine

Refer to illustrations 7.30, 7.31, 7.32, 7.33, and 7.34

30   Remove the upper (No. 3) and center (No. 2) timing belt covers **(see illustration)**.

31   Position the number one piston at TDC on the compression stroke (see Section 3). Make sure the alignment hole in the camshaft pulley is aligned with the mark on the camshaft bearing cap **(see illustration)**.

32   If you plan to reuse the timing belt, paint match marks on the pulley and belt, on the belt at the edge of the lower (No. 1) timing belt cover, and an arrow indicating direction of travel of the belt **(see illustration)**.

33   Loosen the idler pulley set bolt **(see illustration)** and push the

pulley to the left (against spring tension) as far as it will go, then temporarily tighten it. Slip the timing belt off the pulley. If you're removing the belt for camshaft seal replacement or camshaft or cylinder head removal, it isn't necessary to detach the belt from the crankshaft pulley.

34   If the camshaft pulley is worn or damaged, remove the valve cover, hold the front camshaft with a large wrench and remove the bolt, then detach the pulley **(see illustration)**.

35   To proceed with timing belt removal, keep the crankshaft (accessory drivebelt) pulley from turning with a large Phillips screwdriver and a prybar **(see illustration 7.15a)**, remove the bolt and detach the pulley with two screwdrivers or a bolt-type vibration damper puller **(see illustration 7.15b)**. Do not use a jaw-type gear puller! Sometimes the pulley can be removed by hand.

36   Remove the lower (no. 1) timing belt cover and gaskets **(see illustration 7.30)** and slip the belt guide off the crankshaft.

37   If you plan to reuse the timing belt, paint match marks on the pulley and belt **(see illustration 7.17)**.

38   Slip the timing belt off the pulley and remove it. If the pulley is worn or damaged, or if you need to get at the front crankshaft oil seal, remove the pulley from the crankshaft **(see illustrations 7.18a and 7.18b)**. If you remove the inner belt guide, be careful to note how it's installed so you can reinstall it the same way (the cupped side faces away from the belt).

Inspection

Refer to illustrations 7.39, 7.41, 7.42 and 7.43

Caution: *Do not bend, twist or turn the timing belt inside out. Do not allow it to come in contact with oil, coolant or fuel. Do not utilize timing belt tension to keep the camshaft or crankshaft from turning when installing the pulley bolt(s). Do not turn the crankshaft or camshaft more than a few degrees (necessary for tooth alignment) while the timing belt is removed.*

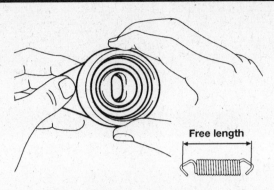

7.39   Check the idler pulley bearing for smooth operation and measure the free length of the tension spring for comparison to the Specifications

Free length

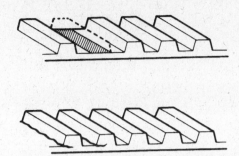

7.41   Check the timing belt for cracked and missing teeth

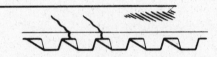

7.42   If the belt is cracked or worn, check the pulleys for nicks and burrs

7.43   Wear on one side of the belt indicates pulley misalignment problems

2A

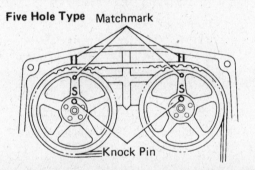

Five Hole Type   Matchmark

Knock Pin

7.47   On a 3S-GE engine with five-hole pulleys, align the marks as shown - the knock pins should be installed in whichever hole is aligned when all the marks (including the grooves and drilled marks shown in illustration 7.22c) are aligned

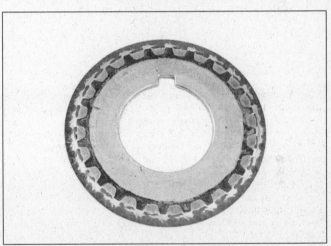

7.49   The belt guide should be installed with the tooth marks in contact with the timing belt and the cupped side out

39   Remove the idler pulleys and check the bearings for smooth operation and excessive play. Inspect the spring for damage and compare the free length to the Specifications **(see illustration)**.
40   If the timing belt broke during engine operation, the belt may have been contaminated or overtightened.
41   If the belt teeth are cracked or pulled off **(see illustration)**, the distributor, water pump, oil pump or camshaft(s) may have seized.
42   If there is noticeable wear or cracks in the belt, check to see if there are nicks or burrs on the pulleys **(see illustration)**.
43   If there is wear or damage on only one side of the belt, check the belt guide and the alignment of all pulleys **(see illustration)**.
44   Replace the timing belt with a new one if obvious wear or damage is noted or if it is the least bit questionable. Correct any problems which contributed to belt failure prior to belt installation. **Note:** *Professionals recommend replacing the belt whenever it is removed, since belt failure can lead to expensive engine damage.*

Installation

Refer to illustrations 7.47, 7.49, 7.50a, 7.50b and 7.54a through 7.54e
45   Remove all dirt and oil from the timing belt area at the front of the engine.
46   If they were removed, install the idler pulleys and tension spring. The upper (no. 1) idler (the only idler on 4A-FE engines) should be

pulled back against spring tension as far as possible and the bolt temporarily tightened, except on 3S-FE and 5S-FE engines. On 3S-FE and 5S-FE engines, the procedure is the same except that it isn't necessary to install the tension spring at this time.
47   If they were removed, install the camshaft and crankshaft sprockets and the crankshaft inner belt guide. Recheck the camshaft and crankshaft timing marks to be sure they are properly aligned (see Steps 10 through 12, 22 and 23, or 31 and 32, depending on engine). **Note:** *On 3S-GE engines with five camshaft knock pin holes, if you removed the knock pin, install the knock pin in whichever holes are aligned when the marks are aligned* **(see illustration)**. *If necessary, rotate the camshaft slightly to achieve proper alignment.*
48   Install the timing belt on the crankshaft, oil pump (except 4A-FE), water pump (except 4A-FE) and idler pulleys. If the original belt is being reinstalled, align the marks made during removal.
49   Slip the belt guide onto the crankshaft with the cupped side facing out **(see illustration)**.
50   Slip the timing belt over the camshaft pulley(s). Keep tension on the side nearest the front of the vehicle **(see illustration)**. If the original belt is being reinstalled, align the marks made during removal. On 3S-

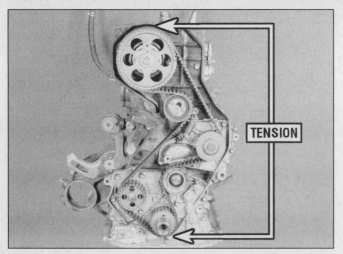

7.50a   There should be moderate tension on the side of the belt facing the front of the vehicle (3S-FE shown; others similar)

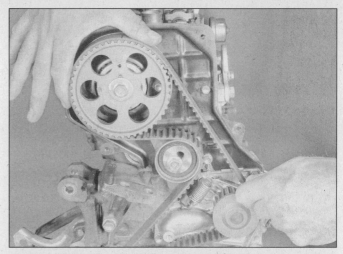

7.50b   On 3S-FE and 5S-FE engines, hold the belt in place and connect the tension spring

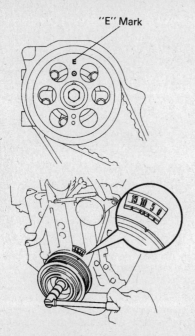

7.54a   Correct valve timing mark alignment - 2S-E engine

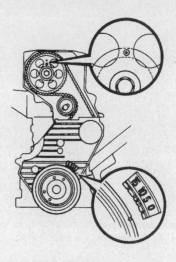

7.55b   On 3S-FE and 5S-FE engines, the marks should align as shown at Top Dead Center

FE and 5S-FE engines, install the tension spring **(see illustration)**.

51   Loosen the upper (no. 1) idler pulley bolt 1/2-turn, allowing the spring to apply pressure to the idler pulley.

52   Slowly turn the crankshaft clockwise two complete revolutions (720-degrees) by hand. **Caution:** *If you feel resistance while rotating the engine by hand, do not use force. The valves may be contacting the pistons due to incorrect valve timing.*

53   Tighten the idler pulley mounting bolt to the torque listed in this Chapter's Specifications.

54   Recheck the timing marks **(see illustrations)**. If the marks are not aligned exactly as shown, repeat the belt installation procedure. **Caution:** *DO NOT start the engine until you're absolutely certain that the timing belt is installed correctly. Serious and costly engine damage could occur if the belt is installed wrong.* **Note:** *On 3S-GE engines with five-hole timing pulleys, the timing can be adjusted in two-degree and five-degree increments by changing the pulley hole that aligns with the camshaft knock pin hole. Pull the pin(s) out with a magnet, then realign the holes as necessary* **(see illustration)**.

55   Reinstall the remaining parts in the reverse order of removal.

56   Run the engine and check for proper operation.

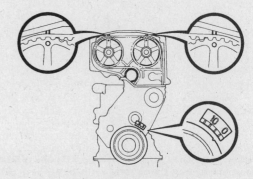

7.55c   On 3S-GE engines, the marks for both pulleys must align when the crankshaft marks align

8   Front crankshaft oil seal - replacement

Refer to illustrations 8.2 and 8.4

1   Remove the timing belt and crankshaft pulley (see Section 7).

2   Note how far the seal is seated in the bore, then carefully pry it

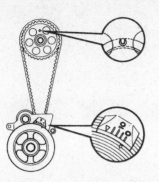

7.54d   On 4A-FE engines, the camshaft pulley hole and bearing cap mark must align when the crankshaft marks align

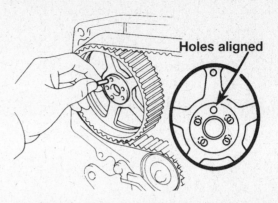

7.54e   On 3S-GE engines with five-hole pulleys, the timing can be adjusted by changing the pulley position on the camshaft; pull out the knock pin with a magnet and realign the pulley as needed

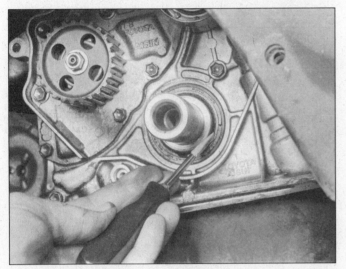

8.2   Wrap tape around the screwdriver tip and carefully work the crankshaft front oil seal out of the bore - DO NOT nick or scratch the crankshaft or oil seal bore!

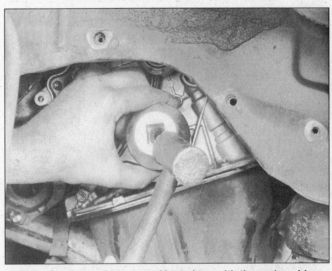

8.4   Gently tap the new seal into place with the spring side toward the engine

outside diameter of the seal, carefully drive the new seal into place with a hammer **(see illustration)**. Make sure it's installed squarely and driven in to the same depth as the original. If a socket isn't available, a short section of large diameter pipe will also work. Check the seal after installation to make sure the garter spring didn't pop out of place.

5   Reinstall the crankshaft pulley and timing belt (see Section 7).

6   Run the engine and check for oil leaks at the front seal.

9   Camshaft oil seal - replacement

1   Remove the timing belt and camshaft pulley(s) (see Section 7).

2S-E engine

Refer to illustrations 9.3 and 9.7

2   Remove the bolts and detach the camshaft oil seal retainer and O-ring from the head **(see illustration 4.4a)**.

3   Support the retainer on two blocks of wood and drive the old seal out from the back side **(see illustration)**.

4   Clean the retainer and cylinder head mating surfaces and the seal bore with lacquer thinner or acetone.

5   Coat the outer edge of the new seal with engine oil or multi-purpose grease.

6   Support the retainer as close to the seal bore as possible.

7   Using a socket with an outside diameter slightly smaller than the outside diameter of the seal, carefully drive the new seal into place

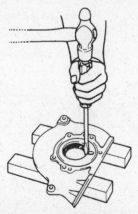

9.3   On 2S-E engines, remove the camshaft oil seal retainer from the head and drive the old seal out from the back side

out of the oil pump housing with a screwdriver or seal removal tool **(see illustration)**. Don't scratch the housing bore or damage the crankshaft in the process (if the crankshaft is damaged, the new seal will end up leaking).

3   Clean the bore in the housing and coat the outer edge of the new seal with engine oil or multi-purpose grease. Apply moly-base grease to the seal lip.

4   Using a socket with an outside diameter slightly smaller than the

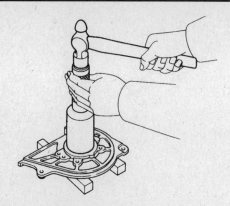

9.7   Tap the new seal into place with a large socket or piece of pipe and a hammer

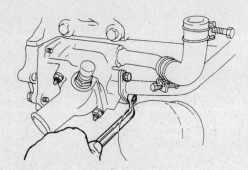

10.3   Disconnect the heater tube at the rear end housing (2S-E engine)

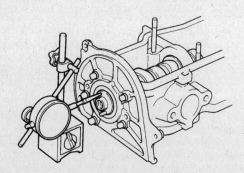

10.8   Mount a dial indicator as shown to measure camshaft endplay

with a hammer **(see illustration)**. Make sure it's installed squarely and check it after installation to make sure the garter spring didn't pop out of place. If a socket isn't available, a short section of large-diameter pipe will also work.

8   Clean the bolt threads and apply sealant (Toyota no. 08833-00070, Three Bond 1324 or equivalent) to the first three threads. Apply moly-base grease to the seal lip.

9   Install a new O-ring, then position the retainer on the head and install the bolts. Tighten the bolts in a criss-cross pattern to the torque listed in this Chapter's Specifications.

10   Proceed to Step 15.

All other engines

Refer to illustration 9.12

11   Unbolt the upper timing belt rear cover (if equipped).

9.12   On all except 2S-E engines, carefully pry the camshaft seal out of the bore - DO NOT nick or scratch the camshaft or seal bore (3S-FE shown; others similar)

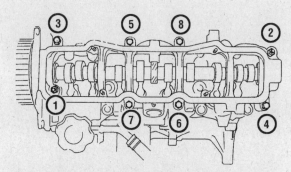

10.7   Camshaft housing bolt LOOSENING sequence (2S-E engine)

12   Note how far the seal is seated in the bore, then carefully pry it out with a small screwdriver **(see illustration)**. Don't scratch the bore or damage the camshaft in the process (if the camshaft is damaged, the new seal will end up leaking).

13   Clean the bore and coat the outer edge of the new seal with engine oil or multi-purpose grease. Apply moly-base grease to the seal lip.

14   Using a socket with an outside diameter slightly smaller than the outside diameter of the seal, carefully drive the new seal into place with a hammer. Make sure it's installed squarely and driven in to the same depth as the original. If a socket isn't available, a short section of pipe will also work.

All engines

15   Reinstall the camshaft pulley and timing belt (see Section 7).
16   Run the engine and check for oil leaks at the camshaft seal.

10   Camshaft, rocker arms and lash adjusters - removal, inspection and installation (2S-E engine only)

Removal

Refer to illustrations 10.3, 10.7 and 10.8

1   Remove the negative cable from the battery and detach the air cleaner inlet duct.

2   Drain the cooling system (see Chapter 1).

3   Label and disconnect all hoses wires, linkages, tubes and brackets attached to the camshaft housing **(see illustration)**.

4   Unbolt and remove the rear housing **(see illustration 4.4a)**.

5   Remove the timing belt and the camshaft pulley (see Section 7).

10.14a Check the cam lobes for pitting, wear and score marks - if scoring is excessive, as is the case here, replace the camshaft

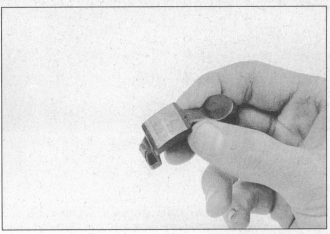

10.14b Check the rocker arm pads for wear and damage as well

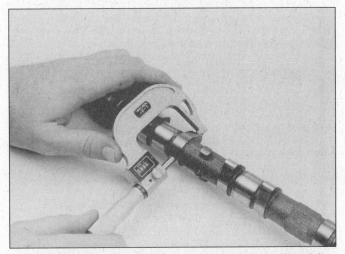

10.15 Measure the lobe heights on each camshaft - if any lobe height is less than the minimum listed in this Chapter's Specifications, replace that camshaft

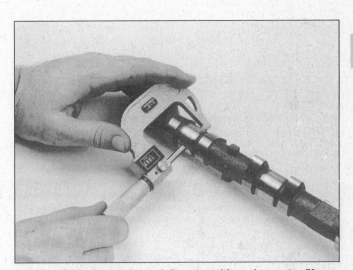

10.16 Measure each journal diameter with a micrometer (if any journal measures less than the specified limit, replace the camshaft)

6   Remove the valve cover (see Section 4).
7   Remove the camshaft housing by loosening each bolt a little at a time in the sequence shown **(see illustration)**.
8   With the camshaft still in the housing, use a dial indicator to check the endplay. Attach the gauge to the end of the housing and move the camshaft all the way to the rear. Next, use a screwdriver to pry it all the way forward. If the endplay exceeds the limit listed in this Chapter's Specifications, replace the camshaft and/or the housing **(see illustration)**.
9   Remove the camshaft from the housing after detaching the camshaft oil seal retainer **(see illustration 4.4a)**.
10   Use a small screwdriver to pry the O-ring out of the retainer.
11   While turning the camshaft, slowly pull it out, being careful not to damage the bearings in the housing.
12   Remove the rocker arms by lifting them off the lash adjusters.
13   The lash adjusters can then be withdrawn by pulling them out of the cylinder head **(see illustration 4.4a)**. Keep the rocker arms and lash adjusters in order during removal to ensure that they are reinstalled in their original locations.

Inspection

Refer to illustrations 10.14a, 10.14b, 10.15, 10.16, 10.18 and 10.20

14   Visually examine the camshaft journals and rocker arms. Check for score marks, pitting and evidence of overheating (blue, discolored areas) **(see illustrations)**. If wear is excessive or damage is evident,

the component will have to be replaced.
15   Using a micrometer, measure the cam lobe height and compare it to the Specifications. If the lobe height is less than the minimum allowable, the camshaft is worn and must be replaced **(see illustration)**.
16   Using a micrometer, measure the diameter of each journal and compare it to the Specifications **(see illustration)**. If the journals are worn or damaged, replace the camshaft.
17   Using an inside micrometer or a telescoping gauge, measure each housing bore. Subtract the journal diameter measurements from the housing bore measurements to determine the bearing oil clearance. Compare it to the Specifications. If the clearance is greater than the maximum, replace the camshaft and, if necessary, the housing.
18   Before being reinstalled, the lash adjusters must be bled. Immerse them, one at a time, in a container of light oil **(see illustration)**. Insert a pin punch into the plunger hole to depress the check valve and slide the plunger up-and-down several times while pushing down lightly on the check ball.
19   Replace the lash adjuster with a new one if the plunger stroke exceeds 0.020-inch (0.5 mm) after bleeding. Do not disassemble the lash adjusters.
20   Check the camshaft housing for warpage. Using a precision straightedge and feeler gauge, check the surface which contacts the cylinder head for warpage and compare it to the Specifications **(see illustration)**. If the warpage is greater than the maximum specified, replace the housing.

10.18   Place each lash adjuster in a container of light oil, insert an appropriate size tool into the plunger hole and slide the plunger up-and-down several times

10.22   Apply engine assembly lube or moly-base grease to the cam lobes and journals before installing the camshaft in the engine

Installation

Refer to illustrations 10.22, 10.24 and 10.25

21   Installation is basically the reverse of the removal procedure. However, keep the following points in mind.

22   Apply engine assembly lube or moly-base grease to the camshaft lobes and journals **(see illustration)**. Also apply the same lubricant to the rocker arms and lash adjusters.

23   Insert the camshaft into the housing, then install a new O-ring and the oil seal retainer. The retainer bolts must have anaerobic sealant (Toyota no. 08833-00070 or Three Bond no. 1324) on the first two or three threads.

24   Before attaching the camshaft housing to the cylinder head, clean the mating surfaces with lacquer thinner or acetone, then apply a bead of sealant (Toyota no. 08826-00080 or equivalent) as shown **(see illustration)**.

25   Install the housing bolts and tighten them in three steps, in the sequence shown **(see illustration)**, to the torque listed in this Chapter's Specifications.

---

11   Camshafts and valve lifters - removal, inspection and installation (all except 2S-E engine)

Removal

Refer to illustration 11.4

1   Remove the valve cover(s) as described in Section 4.

2   Remove the distributor (see Chapter 5).

3   Remove the timing belt and camshaft pulley(s) (see Section 7).

4   Measure the camshaft thrust clearance (endplay) with a dial indicator **(see illustration)**. If the clearance is greater than the maximum listed in this Chapter's Specifications, replace the camshaft and/or the cylinder head.

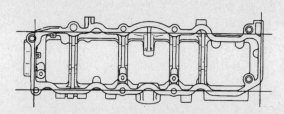

10.20   Using a straightedge and feeler gauges, check the camshaft housing surfaces for warpage and compare the results to the Specifications (2S-E engine)

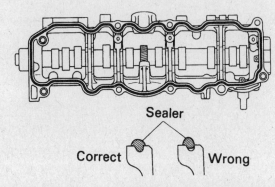

10.24   Apply a bead of sealant to the cylinder head side of the camshaft housing

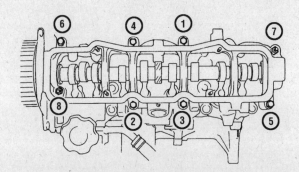

10.25   Camshaft housing bolt TIGHTENING sequence (2S-E engine)

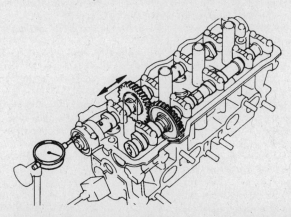

11.4   Position the dial indicator as shown, pry the camshaft back-and-forth with a screwdriver and note the endplay (3S-FE engine shown; others similar)

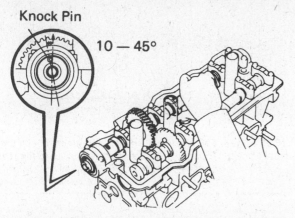

11.5 Turn the INTAKE camshaft until the knock pin is 10 to 45-degrees to the left of vertical (12 o'clock position)

11.6 Install a service bolt through the sub-gear, into the main gear (arrow)

2A

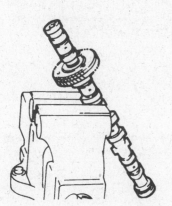

11.11a Grip the hex on the camshaft to hold it in the vise

11.11b Install a second service bolt in the unthreaded hole and rotate the sub-gear clockwise until the tension is released so the first bolt can be removed

11.12 Remove the sub-gear snap-ring with snap-ring pliers

3S-FE and 5S-FE exhaust camshaft

Refer to illustrations 11.5, 11.6, 11.11a, 11.11b and 11.12

Note: *Before beginning this procedure, obtain two 6 x 1.0 mm bolts 16 to 20 mm long. They will be referred to as service bolts in the text.*

5   Position the knock pin in the INTAKE camshaft at 10 to 45-degrees left of vertical **(see illustration)**. This will position the exhaust camshaft lobes so the camshaft will be pushed out evenly by the valve spring pressure.

6   Secure the exhaust camshaft sub-gear to the main gear with one of the service bolts **(see illustration)**.

7   Remove the rear exhaust camshaft bearing cap bolts and detach the bearing cap.

8   Loosen the number 1, 2 and 4 exhaust camshaft bearing cap bolts in 1/4-turn increments until the bolts can be removed by hand. Lift off the first, second and fourth bearing caps. **Caution:** *DO NOT remove the center (no. 3) bearing cap bolts at this point!*

9   Finally, loosen the number 3 bearing cap bolts in 1/4-turn increments until they can be removed by hand, then detach the center (no. 3) cap. **Caution:** *As the center bearing cap bolts are being loosened, make sure the camshaft is moving up evenly. If one end or the other stops moving and the cam gets cocked, start over by reinstalling the bearing caps and resetting the knock pin. DO NOT try to pry or force the camshaft out.*

10   Lift the camshaft out of the head.

11   Disassemble the exhaust camshaft. Mount it in a vise with the jaws gripping the large hex on the shaft **(see illustration)**. Install a second service bolt in the unthreaded hole in the camshaft sub-gear. Using a screwdriver positioned against the service bolt just installed, rotate the sub-gear clockwise and remove the first service bolt (see il-

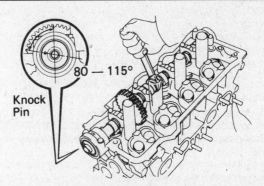

11.14 Turn the intake camshaft until the knock pin is 80 to 115-degrees to the left of vertical (12 o'clock position)

lustration).

12   Remove the sub-gear snap-ring **(see illustration)**.

13   The wave washer, sub-gear and camshaft gear spring can now be removed from the camshaft **(see illustration 4.4b)**.

3S-FE and 5 FS-FE intake camshaft

Refer to illustration 11.14

14   Position the knock pin in the intake camshaft at 80 to 115-degrees left of vertical **(see illustration)**.

15   Remove the front (timing belt end) intake camshaft bearing cap bolts and detach the bearing cap and oil seal. **Caution:** *Do not pry the cap off. If it doesn't come loose easily, leave it in place without bolts.*

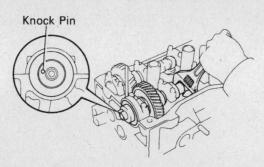

11.19 Turn the EXHAUST camshaft until the knock pin is slightly above the top surface of the cylinder head (4A-FE engine)

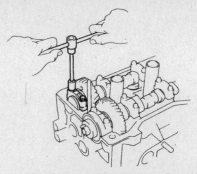

11.20   Loosen the two front bearing cap bolts in 1/4-turn increments (4A-FE engine)

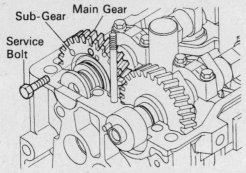

11.21   Install a service bolt through the sub-gear, into the main gear (4A-FE engine)

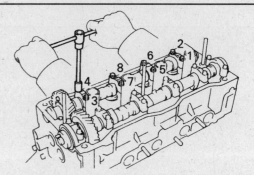

11.22   Intake camshaft bearing cap LOOSENING sequence (4A-FE engine)

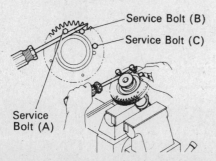

11.24   Install service bolts in holes A and B, pry against them to turn the sub-gear clockwise, and remove service bolt C (4A-FE engine)

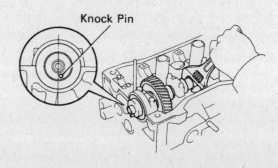

11.27   Turn the exhaust camshaft so the knock pin is slightly counterclockwise from the straight-down position (4A-FE engine)

16   Loosen the number 1, 3 and 4 intake camshaft bearing cap bolts in 1/4-turn increments until the bolts can be removed by hand. Lift off the first, third and fourth bearing caps. **Caution:** *DO NOT remove the center (no. 2) bearing cap bolts at this point!*

17   Finally, loosen the number 2 bearing cap bolts in 1/4-turn increments until they can be removed by hand, then detach the center (no. 2) cap. **Caution:** *As the center bearing cap bolts are being loosened, make sure the camshaft is moving up evenly. If one end or the other stops moving and the cam gets cocked, start over by reinstalling the bearing caps and resetting the knock pin. DO NOT try to pry or force the camshaft out.*

18   Lift the camshaft out of the head.

4A-FE intake camshaft

Refer to illustrations 11.19, 11.20, 11.21, 11.22 and 11.24

Note: *Before beginning this procedure, obtain three 6 x 1.0 mm bolts 16 to 20 mm long. They will be referred to as service bolts in the text.*

19   Position the knock pin on the EXHAUST camshaft slightly above the top surface of the cylinder head **(see illustration)**. This positions the intake camshaft so the lobes for no. 1 and no. 3 cylinders will push the

camshaft up evenly.

20   Remove the front (timing belt end) intake camshaft bearing cap bolts and detach the bearing cap and oil seal **(see illustration)**.

21   Secure the intake camshaft sub-gear to the main gear with one of the service bolts **(see illustration)**. **Caution:** *When removing the camshaft, make certain the torsional spring force of the sub-gear has been eliminated by the above operation.*

22   Uniformly loosen the intake camshaft bearing cap bolts in 1/4-turn increments in the sequence shown **(see illustration)** until the bolts can be removed by hand. Lift off the bearing caps and remove the camshaft. **Caution:** *As the center bearing cap bolts are being loosened, make sure the camshaft is moving up evenly. If one end or the other stops moving and the cam gets cocked, start over by reinstalling the bearing caps and resetting the knock pin. DO NOT try to pry or force the camshaft out.*

23   Lift the camshaft out of the head.

24   Disassemble the intake camshaft. Mount it in a vise as described in Step 11. Install two service bolts in the unthreaded holes in the camshaft sub-gear. Using a screwdriver positioned against the service bolts just installed, rotate the sub-gear clockwise and remove the

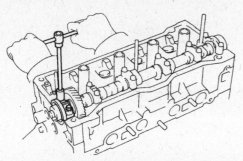

11.28 Loosen the front (timing belt end) bearing cap bolts in 1/4-turn increments, then remove the bearing cap - if the cap won't come loose easily, don't pry it off; leave it in place for the time being (4A-FE engine)

11.29 Exhaust camshaft bearing cap LOOSENING sequence (4A-FE engine)

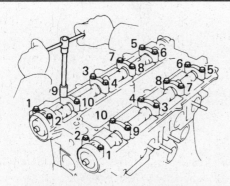

11.31 Camshaft bearing cap LOOSENING sequence (3S-GE engine)

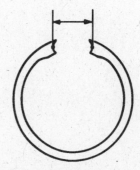

11.33 Measure the distance between the ends of the camshaft gear spring

2A

number three service bolt (the one installed in Step 21) **(see illustration)**.

25 Remove the sub-gear snap-ring **(see illustration 11.12)**.
26 The wave washer, sub-gear and camshaft gear spring can now be removed from the camshaft **(see illustration 4.4d)**.

4A-FE exhaust camshaft
Refer to illustrations 11.27, 11.28 and 11.29

27 Turn the exhaust camshaft so the knock pin is near the bottom as shown **(see illustration)**.
28 Loosen the front bearing bolts in 1/4-turn increments until the cap can be lifted out **(see illustration)**. If they won't come out easily, don't pry it. Leave it in position without bolts.
29 Loosen the remaining bearing cap bolts in 1/4-turn increments, following the sequence shown **(see illustration)**. **Caution:** *As the bearing cap bolts are being loosened, make sure the camshaft is moving up evenly. If one end or the other stops moving and the cam gets cocked, start over by reinstalling the bearing caps and resetting the knock pin. DO NOT try to pry or force the camshaft out.*
30 Remove the bearing caps and lift the camshaft out of the head.

3S-GE engine (both camshafts)
Refer to illustration 11.31

31 Loosen the camshaft bearing cap bolts in 1/4-turn increments, following the sequence shown **(see illustration)**.
32 Remove the bearing caps and lift the camshaft(s) out of the head. Lay the bearing caps in order on a clean surface.

Inspection
Refer to illustrations 11.33, 11.34, 11.35, 11.36a, 11.36b, 11.41a, 11.41b and 11.43

33 If you're working on a 3S-FE, 5S-FE or 4A-FE engine, measure the free length (distance between the ends) of the camshaft gear spring **(see illustration)** and compare it to the Specifications.
34 Carefully label, then remove the valve lifters and shims **(see illustration)**.

11.34 Wipe the oil off the valve shims and mark the intakes I and the exhausts E - a magnetic tool works well for removing lifters

35 Inspect each lifter for scuffing and score marks **(see illustration)**.
36 Measure the outside diameter of each lifter and the corresponding lifter bore inside diameter **(see illustrations)**. Subtract the lifter diameter from the lifter bore diameter to determine the oil clearance. Compare it to the Specifications. If the oil clearance is excessive, a new head and/or new lifters will be required.
37 Store the lifters in a clean box, separated from each other, so they won't be damaged. Make sure the shims stay with the lifters (don't mix them up).
38 Visually examine the cam lobes and bearing journals for score marks, pitting, galling and evidence of overheating (blue, discolored areas). Look for flaking away of the hardened surface layer of each lobe.

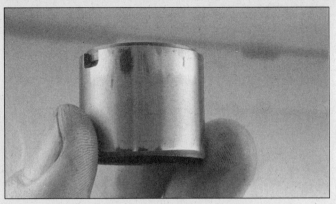

11.35   Wipe off the oil and inspect each lifter for wear and scuffing

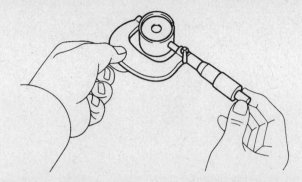

11.36a   Use a micrometer to measure lifter diameter

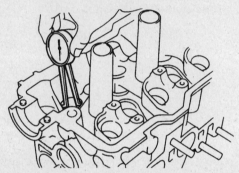

11.36b   Use a telescoping gauge to measure the lifter bores

11.41a   Lay a strip of Plastigage on each camshaft journal

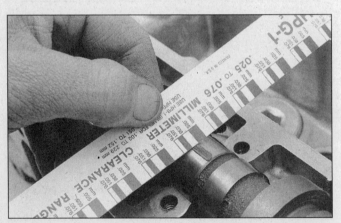

11.41b   Compare the width of the crushed Plastigage to the scale on the envelope to determine the oil clearance

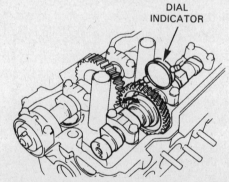

11.43   Position the dial indicator as shown here to measure gear backlash (freeplay) (3S-FE engine shown; others similar)

39   Using a micrometer, measure the height of each camshaft lobe **(see illustration 10.15)**. If the height for any one lobe is less than the specified minimum, replace the camshaft.

40   Using a micrometer, measure the diameter of each journal at several points **(see illustration 10.16)**. If the diameter of any one journal is less than specified, replace the camshaft.

41   Check the oil clearance for each camshaft journal as follows:

a)   Clean the bearing caps and the camshaft journals with lacquer thinner or acetone.

b)   Carefully lay the camshaft(s) in place in the head. Don't install the lifters and don't use any lubrication.

c)   Lay a strip of Plastigage on each journal **(see illustration)**.

d)   Install the bearing caps with the arrows pointing toward the front (timing belt end) of the engine.

e)   Tighten the bolts IN SEQUENCE **(see illustrations 11.49 and 11.59, 11.69 and 11.77 or 11.86)** to the torque listed in this Chapter's Specifications in 1/4-turn increments. **Note:** *Don't turn the camshaft while the Plastigage is in place.*

f)   Remove the bolts and detach the caps.

g)   Compare the width of the crushed Plastigage (at its widest point) to the scale on the Plastigage envelope **(see illustration)**.

h)   If the clearance is greater than specified, replace the camshaft and/or cylinder head.

i)   Scrape off the Plastigage with your fingernail or the edge of a credit card - don't scratch or nick the journals or bearing caps.

42   Temporarily install the camshafts without installing the lifters or exhaust camshaft sub-gear.

43   If you're working on a 3S-FE, 5S-FE or 4A-FE engine, measure the gear backlash (the free play between the gear teeth) with a dial indicator **(see illustration)** and compare it to the Specifications.

Installation

3S-FE and 5S-FE intake camshaft
Refer to illustrations 11.47, 11.48, 11.49, 11.56, 11.58 and 11.59

44   Apply moly-base grease or engine assembly lube to the lifters, then install them in their original locations. Make sure the valve adjust-

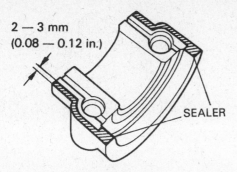

11.47 Apply sealant to the shaded areas of the front intake camshaft bearing cap (3S-FE and 5S-FE engines)

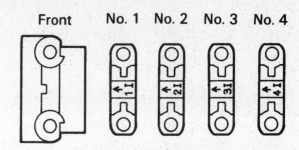

11.48 Intake camshaft bearing caps (3S-FE and 5S-FE engines) - the arrows point toward the timing belt end of the engine

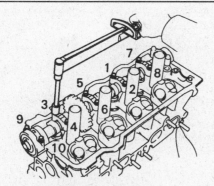

11.49 3S-FE and 5S-FE engine INTAKE camshaft bearing cap bolt tightening sequence

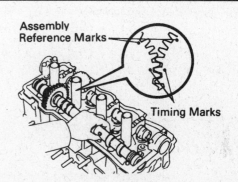

11.56 Align the camshaft gear timing marks as shown here (3S-FE and 5S-FE engines)

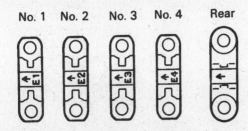

11.58 Exhaust camshaft bearing caps (3S-FE and 5S-FE engines) - the arrows point toward the timing belt end of the engine

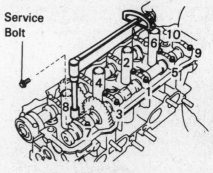

11.59 3S-FE and 5S-FE engine EXHAUST camshaft bearing cap bolt tightening sequence

2A (margin tab)

ment shims are in place in the lifters.

45 Apply moly-base grease or engine assembly lube to the camshaft lobes and bearing journals.

46 Position the intake camshaft in the cylinder head with the knock pin 80-degrees to the left of vertical (see illustration 11.14).

47 Apply a thin coat of sealant (Toyota no. 08826-00080 or equivalent) to the outer edge of the front bearing cap cylinder head mating surface (see illustration). Note: *The cap must be installed immediately or the sealant will dry prematurely.*

48 Install the bearing caps in numerical order with the arrows pointing toward the timing belt end of the engine (see illustration).

49 Tighten the bearing cap bolts in 1/4-turn increments until the torque listed in this Chapter's Specifications is reached. Follow the factory-recommended sequence (see illustration).

50 Refer to Section 9 and install a new camshaft oil seal.

3S-FE and 5S-FE exhaust camshaft

51 To reassemble the exhaust camshaft, install the cam gear spring, sub-gear and wave washer in the gear, then secure them with the snap-ring.

52 Reinstall the service bolt in the unthreaded hole, turn the sub-gear with a screwdriver and install the second service bolt in the

threaded hole. Tighten it to clamp the sub-gear to the camshaft gear, then remove the first bolt.

53 Apply moly-base grease or engine assembly lube to the lifters, then install them in their original locations. Make sure the valve adjustment shims are in place in the lifters.

54 Apply moly-base grease or engine assembly lube to the camshaft lobes and bearing journals.

55 Rotate the INTAKE camshaft until the knock pin is positioned 10-degrees to the left of vertical (see illustration 11.5).

56 Align the exhaust camshaft gear with the intake camshaft gear by matching up the timing marks on the gears (see illustration). Caution: *There are also assembly reference marks on each gear, above the timing marks - do not mistake them for the timing marks.*

57 Roll the exhaust camshaft down into position. Turn the intake camshaft back and forth a little until the exhaust camshaft sits in the bearings evenly.

58 Install the bearing caps in numerical order with the arrows pointing toward the timing belt end of the engine (see illustration).

59 Tighten the bearing cap bolts in 1/4-turn increments until the

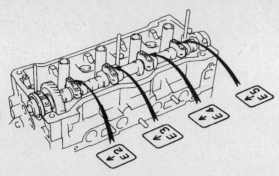

11.68   Exhaust camshaft bearing caps (4A-FE engine) - the arrows on the four rearward caps point toward the timing belt end of the engine

11.69   4A-FE engine EXHAUST camshaft bearing cap bolt tightening sequence

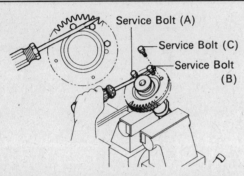

11.72   Pry against service bolts A and B to turn the sub-gear clockwise, then install service bolt C when the holes align (4A-FE engine)

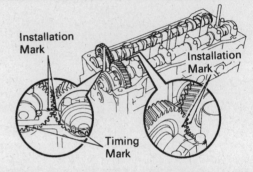

11.74   Align the camshaft gear installation marks as shown here (4A-FE engine)

torque listed in this Chapter's Specifications is reached. Follow the factory-recommended sequence **(see illustration)**.

60   Remove the service bolt from the camshaft gear.

61   Install the timing belt pulley on the intake camshaft and tighten the bolt to the torque listed in this Chapter's Specifications. Prevent the camshaft from turning by holding it with a wrench on the large hex **(see illustration 7.14)**.

4A-FE exhaust camshaft

Refer to illustrations 11.68 and 11.69

62   Apply moly-base grease or engine assembly lube to the lifters, then install them in their original locations. Make sure the valve adjustment shims are in place in the lifters.

63   Apply moly-base grease or engine assembly lube to the camshaft lobes and bearing journals.

64   Coat the thrust surface of the camshaft with multi-purpose grease.

65   Place the exhaust camshaft in the bearing saddles.

66   Turn the exhaust camshaft so the knock pin is near the bottom as shown **(see illustration 11.27)**.

67   Apply a thin coat of sealant (Toyota no. 08826-00080 or equivalent) to the front bearing cap mating surface on the cylinder head. **Note:** *The cap must be installed immediately or the sealant will dry prematurely.*

68   Install all five bearing caps in order. The four rear caps are numbered one through four, starting at the timing belt end of the engine. The arrows point toward the timing belt end **(see illustration)**.

69   Apply a light coat of engine oil to the threads and under the heads of the bearing cap bolts. Install the bolts and tighten them in 1/4-turn increments until the torque listed in this Chapter's Specifications is reached. Follow the factory-recommended sequence **(see illustration)**.

70   Refer to Section 9 and install a new camshaft oil seal.

4A-FE intake camshaft

Refer to illustrations 11.72, 11.74, 11.76, 11.77 and 11.80

71   To reassemble the intake camshaft, install the cam gear spring,

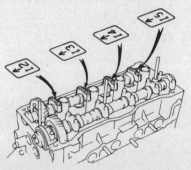

11.76   Intake camshaft bearing caps (4A-FE engine) - the arrows on the four rearward caps point toward the timing belt end of the engine

sub-gear and wave washer in the gear, then secure them with the snap-ring. Line up the ends of the snap-ring with the pins on the gears.

72   Reinstall two service bolts in the sub-gear **(see illustration)**. Turn the sub-gear with a screwdriver and install the third service bolt in the threaded hole. Tighten it to clamp the sub-gear to the camshaft gear, then remove the first two bolts.

73   Set the exhaust camshaft so the knock pin is slightly above the top surface of the cylinder head **(see illustration 11.19)**. Perform Steps 62 through 64.

74   Align the intake camshaft gear with the exhaust camshaft gear by matching up the installation marks on the gears **(see illustration)**. **Caution:** *There are also timing marks on each gear - do not mistake them for the installation marks.*

75   Roll the intake camshaft down into position. Turn the exhaust camshaft back and forth a little until the intake camshaft sits in the bearings evenly.

76   Install the four rear bearing caps in numerical order with the arrows pointing toward the timing belt end of the engine **(see illustration)**.

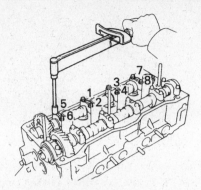

11.77 4A-FE engine INTAKE camshaft bearing cap bolt tightening sequence

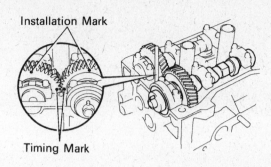

11.80 After installation, the camshaft timing marks should be positioned as shown here (4A-FE engine)

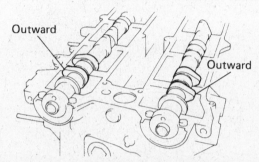

11.83 Install the camshafts with the front lobes (nearest the timing belt end) facing away from each other (3S-GE engine)

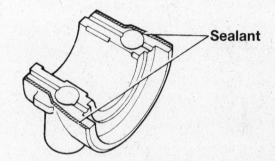

11.84 Apply sealant to the shaded areas of the front camshaft bearing caps (3S-GE engine)

77   Apply light coat of engine oil to the threads and under the heads of the camshaft bearing cap bolts. Tighten the bolts in 1/4-turn increments until the specified torque is reached. Follow the factory-recommended sequence **(see illustration)**.

78   Remove the service bolt from the camshaft gear.

79   Install the no. 1 bearing cap (closest to the timing belt end of the engine). If the cap doesn't fit properly, pry the camshaft to the rear with a large screwdriver. Tighten the bearing cap bolts evenly in 1/4-turn increments to the torque listed in this Chapter's Specifications.

80   Turn the exhaust camshaft clockwise so its knock pin is facing straight up. The timing marks on the two camshafts should line up **(see illustration)**. **Caution:** *If the marks don't line up properly, correct the problem before you continue.*

81   Install the timing belt pulley on the camshaft and tighten the bolt to the torque listed in this Chapter's Specifications. Prevent the camshaft from turning by holding it with a wrench on the large hex (see illustration 7.14).

3S-GE (both camshafts)

Refer to illustrations 11.83, 11.84, 11.85 and 11.86

82   Perform Steps 62 and 63.

83   Place the camshafts in the cylinder head with the No. 1 lobes facing away from each other **(see illustration)**.

84   Apply a thin coat of sealant (Toyota no. 08826-00080 or equivalent) to the outer edge of the front bearing cap-to-cylinder head mating surface **(see illustration)**. **Note:** *The cap must be installed immediately or the sealant will dry prematurely.*

85   Install the bearing caps in numerical order with the arrows pointing toward the timing belt end of the engine **(see illustration)**.

86   Apply a light coat of engine oil to the threads and under the heads of the camshaft bearing cap bolts. Tighten the bolts in 1/4-turn increments until the torque listed in this Chapter's Specifications is reached. Follow the factory-recommended sequence **(see illustration)**.

87   Refer to Section 9 and install new camshaft oil seals.

All engines

88   Install the timing belt (see Section 7).

89   Check valve clearances and adjust if necessary (see Chapter 1).

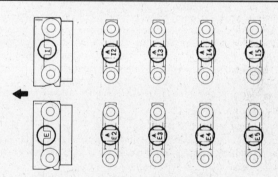

11.85 Install the bearing caps in order, on the correct camshaft and with their arrows pointing toward the timing belt end of the engine (3S-GE engine)

90   The remainder of installation is the reverse of the removal procedure.

12   Valve springs, retainers and seals - replacement (2S-E engine only)

Refer to illustrations 12.4 and 12.17

Note: *Broken valve springs and defective valve stem seals can be replaced without removing the cylinder head. Two special tools and a compressed air source are normally required to perform this operation, so read through this Section carefully and rent or buy the tools before beginning the job. If compressed air isn't available, a length of nylon rope can be used to keep the valves from falling into the cylinder during this procedure.*

1   Refer to Section 10 and remove the camshaft and camshaft housing.

2   Remove the spark plug from the cylinder which has the defective

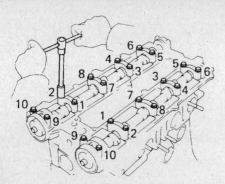

11.86   Camshaft bearing cap bolt tightening sequence (3S-GE engine)

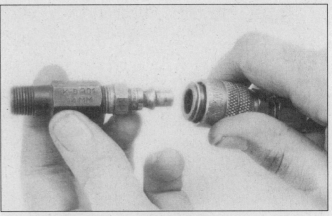

12.4   This is what the air hose adapter that threads into the spark plug hole looks like - they're commonly available from auto parts stores

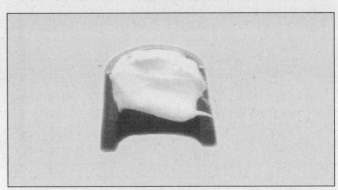

12.17   Apply a small dab of grease to each keeper before installation to hold them in place on the valve stem until the spring is released

component. If all of the valve stem seals are being replaced, all of the spark plugs should be removed.

3   Turn the crankshaft until the piston in the affected cylinder is at Top Dead Center (TDC) on the compression stroke (refer to Section 3 for instructions). If you're replacing all of the valve stem seals, begin with cylinder number one and work on the valves for one cylinder at a time. Move from cylinder-to-cylinder following the firing order sequence (see the Specifications).

4   Thread an adapter into the spark plug hole **(see illustration)** and connect an air hose from a compressed air source to it. Most auto parts stores can supply the air hose adapter. **Note:** *Many cylinder compression gauges utilize a screw-in fitting that may work with your air hose quick-disconnect fitting.*

5   Apply compressed air to the cylinder. **Warning:** *The piston may be forced down by compressed air, causing the crankshaft to turn suddenly. If the wrench used when positioning the number one piston at TDC is still attached to the bolt in the crankshaft nose, it could cause damage or injury when the crankshaft moves.*

6   The valves should be held in place by the air pressure. If the valve faces or seats are in poor condition, leaks may prevent air pressure from retaining the valves - refer to the alternative procedure below.

7   If you don't have access to compressed air, an alternative method can be used. Position the piston at a point just before TDC on the compression stroke, then feed a long piece of nylon rope through the spark plug hole until it fills the combustion chamber. Be sure to leave the end of the rope hanging out of the engine so it can be removed easily.

8   Use a large ratchet and socket to rotate the crankshaft in the normal direction of rotation (clockwise, viewed from the front) until slight resistance is felt.

9   Stuff shop rags into the cylinder head holes above and below the valves to prevent parts and tools from falling into the engine, then use a valve spring compressor to compress the spring. Remove the keepers with small needle-nose pliers or a magnet **(see illustration 4.4a)**. **Note:** *A couple of different types of tools are available for compressing the valve springs with the head in place. One type grips the lower spring coils and presses on the retainer as the knob is turned, while the other type utilizes a bolt or stud and nut for leverage. Both types work very well, although the lever type is usually less expensive.*

10   Remove the spring retainer and valve spring, then remove the stem oil seal. **Note:** *If air pressure fails to hold the valve in the closed position during this operation, the valve face and/or seat is probably damaged. If so, the cylinder head will have to be removed for additional repair operations.*

11   Wrap a rubber band or tape around the top of the valve stem so the valve won't fall into the combustion chamber, then release the air pressure. **Note:** *If a rope was used instead of air pressure, turn the crankshaft slightly in the direction opposite normal rotation.*

12   Inspect the valve stem for damage. Rotate the valve in the guide and check the end for eccentric movement, which would indicate that the valve is bent.

13   Move the valve up-and-down in the guide and make sure it doesn't bind. If the valve stem binds, either the valve is bent or the guide is

damaged. In either case, the head will have to be removed for repair.

14   Reapply air pressure to the cylinder to retain the valve in the closed position, then remove the tape or rubber band from the valve stem. If a rope was used instead of air pressure, rotate the crankshaft in the normal direction of rotation until slight resistance is felt.

15   Lubricate the valve stem with engine oil and install a new oil seal.

16   Install the spring in position over the valve. Be sure the closely wound coils are next to the head

17   Install the valve spring retainer. Compress the valve spring and carefully position the keepers in the groove. Apply a small dab of grease to the inside of each keeper to hold it in place if necessary **(see illustration)**.

18   Remove the pressure from the spring tool and make sure the keepers are seated.

19   Disconnect the air hose and remove the adapter from the spark plug hole. If a rope was used in place of air pressure, pull it out of the cylinder.

20   Refer to Section 10 and install the camshaft and housing.

21   Install the spark plug(s) and hook up the wire(s).

22   Start and run the engine, then check for oil leaks and unusual sounds coming from the valve cover area.

---

13   Cylinder head - removal and installation

Note: *The engine must be completely cool before beginning this procedure.*

Removal

Refer to illustrations 13.12, 13.13a, 13.13b, 13.13c and 13.14

1   Disconnect the negative cable from the battery.

2   Drain the coolant from the engine block and radiator (see Chapter1).

13.12   Remove the coolant tube bracket nut and the housing (arrows) (3S-FE and 5S-FE engines)

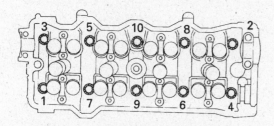

13.13b   Cylinder head bolt LOOSENING sequence (3S-FE and 5S-FE engine shown; 3S-GE uses the same sequence)

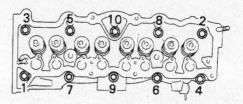

13.13a   Cylinder head bolt LOOSENING sequence (2S-E engine)

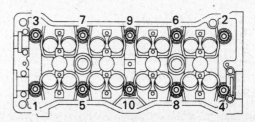

13.13c   Cylinder head bolt LOOSENING sequence (4A-FE engine)

13.14   If the head is stuck, pry only at the overhang, not between the mating surfaces

3   Drain the engine oil and remove the oil filter (see Chapter 1).
4   Remove the throttle body, the injectors and the fuel rails (see Chapter 4).
5   Remove the intake manifold (see Section 5).
6   Remove the exhaust manifold (see Section 6).
7   Remove the timing belt and upper idler pulley (see Section 7).
8   On 2S-E engines, remove the camshaft and housing (see Section 10).
9   On all except 2S-E engines, remove the camshafts and lifters (see Section 11). On 3S-FE, 5S-FE and 3S-GE engines, remove the rear (no. 3) timing belt cover (see illustration 4.4b).
10   Remove the alternator and distributor (see Chapter 5).
11   Unbolt the power steering pump and set it aside without disconnecting the hoses.
12   Check the cylinder head. Label and remove any remaining items, such as coolant fittings, tubes, cables, hoses or wires (see illustration). At this point the head should be ready for removal.
13   Using a breaker bar and the appropriate Allen-head driver or socket, loosen the cylinder head bolts in 1/4-turn increments until they can be removed by hand. Follow the recommended sequence (see illustrations) to avoid warping or cracking the head. Note: Most engines use Allen-head cylinder head bolts, but some may use bolts with 12-point heads, which require a twelve-point socket.
14   Lift the cylinder head off the engine block. If it's stuck, very carefully pry up at the transaxle end, beyond the gasket surface (see illustration).
15   Remove all external components from the head to allow for thorough cleaning and inspection. See Chapter 2, Part B, for cylinder head servicing procedures.

Installation
Refer to illustrations 13.17, 13.25a, 13.25b and 13.25c
16   The mating surfaces of the cylinder head and block must be perfectly clean when the head is installed.

13.17   Remove all traces of old gasket material - the cylinder head and block mating surfaces must be perfectly clean to ensure a good gasket seal

17   Use a gasket scraper to remove all traces of carbon and old gasket material (see illustration), then clean the mating surfaces with lacquer thinner or acetone. If there's oil on the mating surfaces when the head is installed, the gasket may not seal correctly and leaks could develop. When working on the block, stuff the cylinders with clean shop

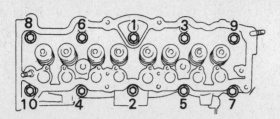

13.25a Cylinder head bolt TIGHTENING sequence (2S-E engine)

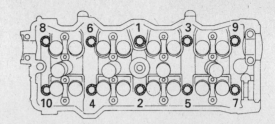

13.25b Cylinder head bolt TIGHTENING sequence (3S-FE and 5S-FE engine shown; 3S-GE uses the same sequence)

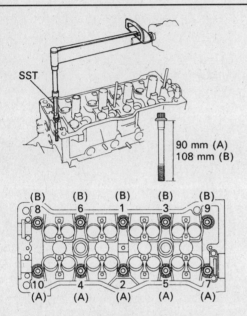

13.25c Cylinder head bolt TIGHTENING sequence (4A-FE engine) - the shorter bolts (A) go on the intake manifold side of the head; the long bolts (B) go on the exhaust side

14.7a Unbolt the rear crossmember and remove the engine mount nuts (arrows)

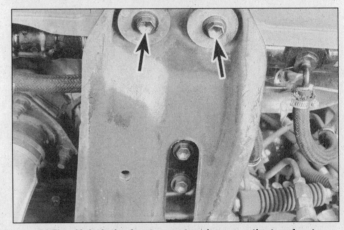

14.7b Unbolt the front mount and remove the two front crossmember bolts (arrows)

rags to keep out debris. Use a vacuum cleaner to remove material that falls into the cylinders.

18   Check the block and head mating surfaces for nicks, deep scratches and other damage. If damage is slight, it can be removed with a file; if it's excessive, machining may be the only alternative.

19   Use a tap of the correct size to chase the threads in the head bolt holes, then clean the holes with compressed air - make sure that nothing remains in the holes. **Warning:** *Wear eye protection when using compressed air!*

20   Mount each bolt in a vise and run a die down the threads to remove corrosion and restore the threads. Dirt, corrosion, sealant and damaged threads will affect torque readings.

21   Install the components that were removed from the head.

22   Position the new gasket over the dowel pins in the block.

23   Carefully set the head on the block without disturbing the gasket.

24   Before installing the head bolts, apply a small amount of clean engine oil to the threads.

25   Install the bolts in their original locations and tighten them finger tight. Following the recommended sequence, tighten the bolts in several steps to the torque listed in this Chapter's Specifications **(see illustrations)**.

26   The remaining installation steps are the reverse of removal.

27   On all except 2S-E engines, check and adjust the valves as necessary (see Chapter 1).

28   Refill the cooling system, install a new oil filter and add oil to the engine (see Chapter 1).

29   Run the engine and check for leaks. Set the ignition timing (see Chapter 5) and road test the vehicle.

14   Oil pan - removal and installation

Refer to illustrations 14.7a, 14.7b, 14.8, 14.9 and 14.14

1   Disconnect the negative cable from the battery.

2   Set the parking brake and block the rear wheels.

3   Raise the front of the vehicle and support it securely on jackstands.

4   Remove the splash shields under the engine, if equipped.

5   Drain the engine oil and remove the oil filter (see Chapter 1). Remove the oil dipstick.

6   Disconnect the front exhaust pipe from the engine and remove the clamp behind the engine to allow the pipe to hang down.

7   Unbolt the crossmember which connects the lower suspension mounts, then remove the crossmember under the oil pan **(see illustrations)**.

8   Remove the block-to-transaxle brace **(see illustration)**.

9   Remove the bolts and detach the oil pan. If it's stuck, pry it loose

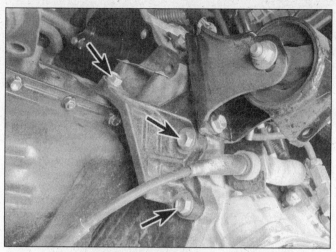

14.8 Unbolt the block-to-transaxle brace (arrows)

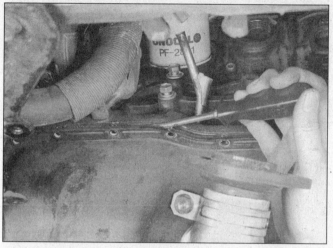

14.9 Carefully pry the oil pan away from the block - if the mating surfaces are damaged, oil leaks could develop

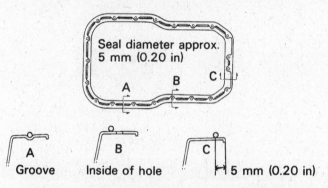

14.14 Apply a bead of sealant to the oil pan flange

2A

15.2 On 4A-FE engines, the oil dipstick tube is attached to the water pump with a bolt (arrow)

very carefully with a small screwdriver or putty knife **(see illustration)**. Don't damage the mating surfaces of the pan and block or oil leaks could develop.

10   Use a scraper to remove all traces of old gasket material and sealant from the block and oil pan. Clean the mating surfaces with lacquer thinner or acetone.

11   Make sure the threaded bolt holes in the block are clean.

12   Check the oil pan flange for distortion, particularly around the bolt holes. If necessary, place the pan on a block of wood and use a hammer to flatten and restore the gasket surface.

13   Inspect the oil pump pick-up tube assembly for cracks and a blocked strainer. If the pick-up was removed, install it now, using a new O-ring or gasket. Tighten the fasteners to the specified torque.

14   Apply a 5 mm wide bead of sealant (Toyota no. 08826-00080 or equivalent) to the oil pan flange **(see illustration)**. **Note:** *The oil pan must be installed within 3 minutes once the sealant has been applied.*

15   Carefully position the oil pan on the engine block and install the bolts. Working from the center out, tighten them to the torque listed in this Chapter's Specifications in three or four steps.

16   The remainder of installation is the reverse of removal. Be sure to add oil and install a new oil filter.

17   Run the engine and check for oil pressure and leaks.

15   Oil pump - removal, inspection and installation

Removal

Refer to illustrations 15.2, 15.3, 15.5a, 15.5b, 15.6a, 15.6b, 15.7, 15.8 and 15.11

1   Remove the oil pan (see Section 14).

2   If you're working on a 4A-FE engine, remove the dipstick. Unbolt the dipstick tube and pull the tube out of the engine **(see illustration)**.

15.3 The oil pick-up assembly and baffle plate are held in place with two nuts and two bolts (arrows)

3   Remove the nuts/bolts and detach the oil pick-up tube assembly and baffle plate **(see illustration)**.

4   Remove the timing belt, lower idler pulley and crankshaft pulley (see Section 7). **Note:** *Since the oil pan has been removed, the engine must be supported securely from above when removing the following components.*

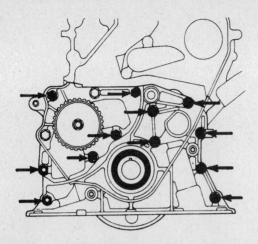

15.5a   Remove the oil pump case-to-block bolts (arrows) (all except 4A-FE engines)

15.5b   On 4A-FE engines, remove the oil pump bolts (arrows)

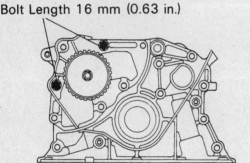

15.6a   Remove the oil pump body-to-oil pump case bolts (all except 4A-FE engines)

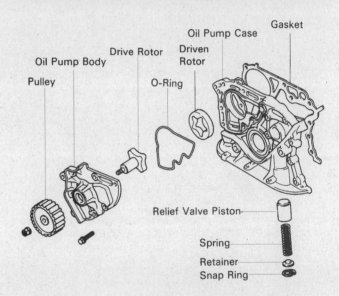

15.6b   Oil pump components - exploded view (all except 4A-FE engine)

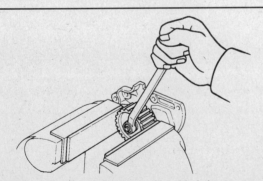

15.7   Clamp the pump pulley in a well padded vise to remove the pulley nut

5   Remove the bolts and detach the oil pump case from the engine **(see illustrations)**. You may have to pry carefully between the front main bearing cap and the pump case with a screwdriver.

All except 4A-FE engine

6   Remove the two remaining bolts **(see illustration)** and separate the pump body from the case. Lift out the driven rotor and remove the O-ring **(see illustration)**.

7   Clamp the pump pulley in a well padded vise **(see illustration)** and remove the pulley nut. Take off the pulley and remove the drive rotor **(see illustration 15.6b)**.

4A-FE engine

8   Remove five screws and lift off the pump cover **(see illustration)**.

9   Lift out the drive and driven rotors.

All engines

10   Use a scraper to remove all traces of sealant and old gasket material from the pump case and engine block, then clean the mating surfaces with lacquer thinner or acetone.

11   Remove the oil pressure relief valve snap-ring **(see illustration)**, retainer, spring and piston **(see illustration 15.6b or 15.8)**. Warning: *The spring is tightly compressed - be careful and wear eye protection.*

Inspection

Refer to illustrations 15.14a and 15.14b

12   Clean all components with solvent, then inspect them for wear and damage.

13   Check the oil pressure relief valve piston sliding surface and valve spring. If either the spring or the valve is damaged, they must be replaced as a set.

14   Check the driven rotor-to-case and drive rotor tip clearances with feeler gauges **(see illustrations)** and compare the results to the Specifications.

Installation

Refer to illustrations 15.15a, 15.15b and 15.18

15   Pry the old oil seal out with a screwdriver. Using a deep socket

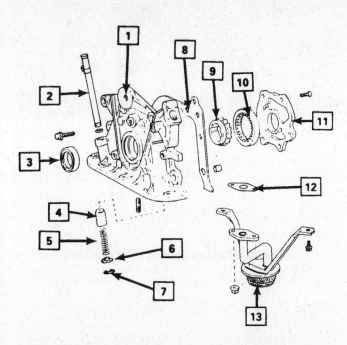

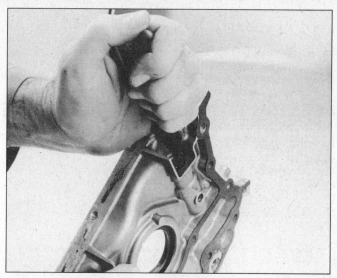

15.11   Remove the snap-ring to disassemble the oil pressure relief valve

15.8   Oil pump components - exploded view (4A-FE engine)

1	Oil pump	8	Gasket
2	Dipstick tube	9	Drive gear
3	Oil seal	10	Driven gear
4	Relief valve piston	11	Oil pump cover
5	Spring	12	Gasket
6	Retainer	13	Oil pick-up
7	Snap-ring		

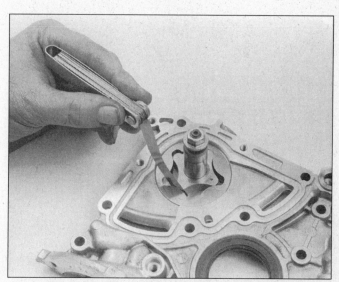

15.14b   . . . and the rotor tip clearance with feeler gauges

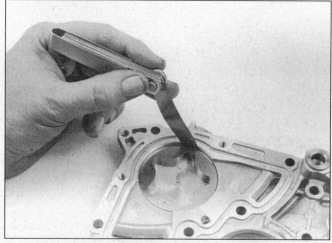

15.14a   Measure the driven rotor-to-case clearance . . .

and a hammer, carefully drive a new seal into place (**see illustrations**). Apply moly-base grease to the seal lip.

All except 4A-FE engine

16   Install a new crankshaft seal using the same procedure as outlined in the previous step. Apply moly-base grease to the seal lip.

17   Install a new O-ring.

18   Lubricate the driven rotor with clean engine oil and place it in the pump case with the mark facing out (**see illustration**).

19   Lubricate the shaft and install the drive rotor in the pump body, then reinstall the pulley and tighten the nut to the torque listed in this Chapter's Specifications.

20   Pack the pump cavity with petroleum jelly and attach the pump body to the case with the 16 mm long bolts (**see illustration 15.6a**).

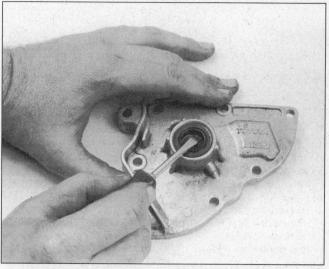

15.15a   Carefully pry the oil seal out of the pump body (3S-FE shown; others similar)

15.15b   Gently drive a new seal into place

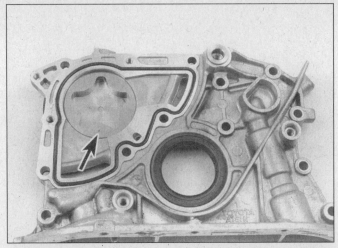

15.18   Oil pump case ready for pump body installation (all except
4A-FE engine) - note that the seal is in place, the O-ring is in place
and the mark on the driven rotor is facing out (arrow)

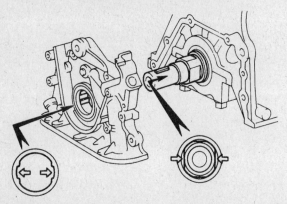

15.25   When installing the oil pump housing on the block, make
sure the splines on the drive gear are engaged with the flats on
the crankshaft

16.3   Mark the flywheel/driveplate and the crankshaft so they
can be reassembled in the same relative positions

16.5   On vehicles with spacer plates, note the position of the
locating pin (arrow)

4A-FE engine

21   Lubricate the rotors with clean engine oil and place them in the
pump case with the marks facing the cover.
22   Install the cover and tighten the screws to the torque listed in this
Chapter's Specifications.

All engines

Refer to illustration 15.25

23   Lubricate the oil pressure relief valve piston with clean engine oil
and reinstall the valve components in the pump case.
24   Place a new gasket on the engine block (the dowel pins should

hold it in place).
25   Position the pump against the block and install the mounting
bolts. If you're working on a 4A-FE engine, make sure the splines on
the drive gear are engaged with the flats on the crankshaft **(see illustration)**.
26   Tighten the bolts to the torque listed in this Chapter's Specifications in three or four steps. Follow a criss-cross pattern to avoid warping the case.
27   Using a new gasket or O-ring (whichever it came with), install the
oil pick-up tube assembly and baffle plate. Tighten the fasteners to the
torque listed in this Chapter's Specifications.
28   Reinstall the remaining parts in the reverse order of removal.
29   Add oil, start the engine and check for oil pressure and leaks.
30   Recheck the engine oil level.

16   Flywheel/driveplate - removal and installation

Refer to illustrations 16.3 and 16.5

1   Raise the vehicle and support it securely on jackstands, then refer to Chapter 7 and remove the transaxle. If it's leaking, now would be
a very good time to replace the front pump seal/O-ring (automatic
transaxle only).
2   Remove the pressure plate and clutch disc (Chapter 8) (manual
transaxle equipped vehicles). Now is a good time to check/replace the

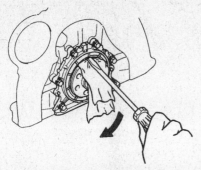

17.2   The quick (but not recommended) way to replace the rear crankshaft oil seal is to simply pry the old one out with a screwdriver, lubricate the crankshaft journal and the lip of the new seal with moly-base grease and push the new seal into place - the trouble is, the seal lip is stiff and can be easily damaged during installation if you're not careful

17.6   Drive the new seal into the retainer with a block of wood or a section of pipe, if you have one large enough - make sure that you don't cock the seal in the retainer bore

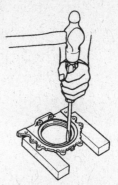

17.5   After removing the retainer assembly from the block, support it on a couple of wood blocks and drive out the old seal with a screwdriver and hammer

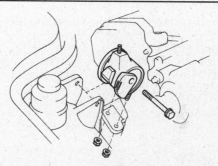

18.8a   To remove the right engine mount, remove the through bolt and the two nuts under the insulator (5S-FE engine shown)

clutch components and pilot bearing.

3   Use a center-punch or paint to make alignment marks on the flywheel/driveplate and crankshaft to ensure correct alignment during re-installation **(see illustration)**.

4   Remove the bolts that secure the flywheel/driveplate to the crankshaft. If the crankshaft turns, wedge a screwdriver in the ring gear teeth to jam the flywheel.

5   Remove the flywheel/driveplate from the crankshaft. Since the flywheel is fairly heavy, be sure to support it while removing the last bolt. Automatic transaxle equipped vehicles have spacers on both sides of the driveplate **(see illustration)**.

6   Clean the flywheel to remove grease and oil. Inspect the surface for cracks, rivet grooves, burned areas and score marks. Light scoring can be removed with emery cloth. Check for cracked and broken ring gear teeth. Lay the flywheel on a flat surface and use a straightedge to check for warpage.

7   Clean and inspect the mating surfaces of the flywheel/driveplate and the crankshaft. If the crankshaft rear seal is leaking, replace it before reinstalling the flywheel/driveplate.

8   Position the flywheel/driveplate against the crankshaft. Be sure to align the marks made during removal. Note that some engines have an alignment dowel or staggered bolt holes to ensure correct installation. Before installing the bolts, apply thread locking compound to the threads.

9   Wedge a screwdriver in the ring gear teeth to keep the flywheel/driveplate from turning as you tighten the bolts to the torque listed in this Chapter's Specifications. Follow a criss-cross pattern and

work up to the final torque in three or four steps.

10   The remainder of installation is the reverse of the removal procedure.

17   Rear crankshaft oil seal - replacement

Refer to illustrations 17.2, 17.5 and 17.6

1   The transaxle must be removed from the vehicle for this procedure (see Chapter 7).

2   The seal can be replaced without dropping the oil pan or removing the seal retainer. However, this method is not recommended because the lip of the seal is quite stiff and it's possible to cock the seal in the retainer bore or damage it during installation. If you want to take the chance, pry out the old seal with a screwdriver **(see illustration)**. Apply moly-base grease to the crankshaft seal journal and the lip of the new seal and carefully push the new seal into place. The lip is stiff so carefully work it onto the seal journal of the crankshaft with a smooth object like the end of an extension as you tap the seal into place. Don't rush it or you may damage the seal.

3   The following method is recommended but requires removal of the oil pan (see Section 14) and the seal retainer.

4   After the oil pan has been removed, remove the bolts, detach the seal retainer and peel off all the old gasket material.

5   Position the seal and retainer assembly on a couple of wood blocks on a workbench and drive the old seal out from the back side with a screwdriver **(see illustration)**.

6   Drive the new seal into the retainer with a block of wood **(see illustration)** or a section of pipe slightly smaller in diameter than the outside diameter of the seal.

7   Lubricate the crankshaft seal journal and the lip of the new seal with moly-base grease. Position a new gasket on the engine block.

8   Slowly and carefully push the seal onto the crankshaft. The seal lip is stiff, so work it onto the crankshaft with a smooth object such as the end of an extension as you push the retainer against the block.

9   Install and tighten the retainer bolts to the torque listed in this

18.8b   The right engine mount on some models has an additional stud (arrow) for a brace

18.10a   To access the rear engine mount (shown from below), the crossmembers must be removed

18.10b   Remove the mounting nuts (arrows)

Chapter's Specifications. The bottom sealing flange of the retainer must not extend below the bottom sealing flange (oil pan rail) of the block.
10   The remaining steps are the reverse of removal.

18   Engine mounts - check and replacement

Refer to illustrations 18.8a, 18.8b, 18.10a and 18.10b
1   Engine mounts seldom require attention, but broken or deteriorated mounts should be replaced immediately or the added strain placed on the driveline components may cause damage or wear.

Check
2   During the check, the engine must be raised slightly to remove the weight from the mounts.
3   Raise the vehicle and support it securely on jackstands, then position a jack under the engine oil pan. Place a large block of wood between the jack head and the oil pan, then carefully raise the engine just enough to take the weight off the mounts. **Warning:** *DO NOT place any part of your body under the engine when it's supported only by a jack!*
4   Check the mounts to see if the rubber is cracked, hardened or separated from the metal plates. Sometimes the rubber will split right down the center.
5   Check for relative movement between the mount plates and the engine or frame (use a large screwdriver or prybar to attempt to move the mounts). If movement is noted, lower the engine and tighten the mount fasteners.
6   Rubber preservative should be applied to the mounts to slow deterioration.

Replacement
7   Disconnect the negative battery cable from the battery, then raise the vehicle and support it securely on jackstands (if not already done). Support the engine as described in Step 3.
8   To remove the right engine mount, remove the nut and withdraw the through-bolt from the frame bracket **(see illustrations)**.
9   Remove the mount-to-bracket nuts and detach the mount.
10   To remove the rear engine mount, detach the crossmembers as described in Section 14, then remove the nuts from the side of the mount **(see illustrations)** and lower the mount from the bracket. **Warning:** *Do not remove the crossmembers if the upper mounts are disconnected!*
11   Installation is the reverse of removal. Use thread locking compound on the mount bolts/nuts and be sure to tighten them securely.
12   See Chapter 7 for transaxle mount replacement.

Chapter 2 Part B
General engine overhaul procedures

Contents

Specifications

General

Displacement
   2S-E, 3S-FE, 3S-GE .... 122 cubic inches (2.0 liters)
   5S-FE .... 134 cubic inches (2.2 liters)
   4A-FE .... 96.8 cubic inches (1.6 liters)
Cylinder compression pressure
   2S-E engine
      Standard .... 171 psi
      Minimum .... 128 psi
   3S-FE, 3S-GE, 5S-FE engines
      Standard .... 178 psi
      Minimum .... 142 psi
   4A-FE engine
      Standard .... 191 psi
      Minimum .... 142 psi
Oil pressure (engine warm)
   At 3000 rpm .... 36 to 71 psi
   At idle .... 4.3 psi minimum

Valves and related components

Minimum valve margin width
 Intake .... 0.020 inch
 Exhaust
  2S-E engine .... 0.039 inch
  All others .... 0.020 inch

Intake valve
 Stem diameter
  2S-E engine .... 0.3138 to 0.3144 inch
  3S-GE engine .... 0.2346 to 0.2352 inch
  3S-FE, 5S-FE and 4A-FE engines .... 0.2350 to 0.2356 inch
 Stem-to-guide clearance
  Standard .... 0.0010 to 0.0023 inch
  Service limit .... 0.0031 inch
 Length
  2S-E engine
   Standard .... 4.319 inches
   Minimum .... 4.299 inches
  3S-FE engine
   Standard .... 3.9606 inches
   Minimum .... 3.9410 inches
  3S-GE engine
   Standard .... 4.0492 inches
   Minimum .... 4.0216 inches
  5S-FE engine
   Standard
    1990 and 1991 .... 3.9606 inches
    1992 on .... 3.8425 inches
   Minimum
    1990 and 1991 .... 3.941 inches
    1992 on .... 3.823 inches
  4A-FE engine
   Standard .... 3.6004 inches
   Minimum .... 3.5807 inches

Exhaust valve
 Stem diameter
  2S-E engine .... 0.3136 to 0.3142 inch
  3S-FE engine .... 0.2348 to 0.2354 inch
  3S-GE engine .... 0.2344 to 0.2350 inch
  5S-FE and 4A-FE engines .... 0.2348 to 0.2354 inch
 Stem-to-guide clearance
  Standard .... 0.0012 to 0.0026 inch
  Service limit .... 0.0039 inch
 Length
  2S-E engine
   Standard .... 4.303 inches
   Minimum .... 4.283 inches
  3S-FE engine
   Standard .... 3.9547 inches
   Minimum .... 3.9370 inches
  3S-GE engine
   Standard .... 4.0118 inches
   Minimum .... 3.9842 inches
  5S-FE engine
   1990 and 1991
    Standard .... 3.9547 inches
    Minimum .... 3.937 inches
   1992 on
    Standard .... 3.8760 inches
    Minimum .... 3.858 inches
  4A-FE engine
   Standard .... 3.6181 inches
   Minimum .... 3.5984 inches

Valve spring
 Out-of-square limit .... 0.079 inch
 Free length
  2S-E engine .... 1.839 inches
  3S-FE engine .... 1.772 inches

3S-GE engine	1.6779 inches
5S-FE engine	
1990 and 1991	1.772 inches
1992 on	1.6520 to 1.6531 inches
4A-FE engine	1.774 inches
Pressure/length	
2S-E engine	68.0 lbs at 1.555 inches
3S-FE, 3S-GE and 5S-FE engines	36.8 to 42.5 lbs at 1.366 inches
4A-FE engine	32.2 to 34.8 lbs at 1.366 inches

Engine block

Cylinder head surface warpage limit	0.002 inch
Cylinder bore diameter	
2S-E engine	
Standard	3.3071 to 3.3083 inches
Service limit	3.3181 inches
3S-FE and 3S-GE engines	
Standard	3.3858 to 3.3870 inches
Service limit	3.3949 inches
5S-FE engine	
Standard	
Mark 1	3.4252 to 3.4256 inches
Mark 2	3.4256 to 3.4260 inches
Mark 3	3.4260 to 3.4264 inches
Service limit	3.4342 inches
4A-FE engine	
Standard	
Mark 1	3.1890 to 3.1894 inches
Mark 2	3.1894 to 3.1898 inches
Mark 3	3.1898 to 3.1902 inches
Service limit	3.1980 inches

Crankshaft and connecting rods

Connecting rod journal	
Diameter	
2S-E, 3S-FE and 3S-GE engines	1.8892 to 1.8898 inches
5S-FE engine	
1990	1.8892 to 1.8898 inches
1991-on	2.0466 to 2.0472 inches
4A-FE engine	1.5742 to 1.5748 inches
Taper and out-of-round limits	0.0008 inch
Bearing oil clearance	
Standard	
2S-E, 3S-FE, 3S-GE and 5S-FE engine	0.0009 to 0.0022 inch
4A-FE engine	0.0008 to 0.0020 inch
Service limit (all)	0.0031 inch
Connecting rod bolt minimum diameter	0.2992 inch
Connecting rod side clearance (endplay)	
Standard	
2S-E engine	0.0063 to 0.0083 inch
3S-FE, 3S-GE and 5S-FE engines	0.0063 to 0.0123 inch
4A-FE engine	0.0059 to 0.0098 inch
Service limit	
2S-E and 4A-FE engines	0.012 inch
3S-FE, 3S-GE and 5S-FE engines	0.014 inch
Main bearing journal	
Diameter	
2S-E engine	2.1648 to 2.1654 inches
3S-FE and 3S-GE engines	
Marked "0"	2.1652 to 2.1654 inches
Marked "1"	2.1650 to 2.1652 inches
Marked "2"	2.1648 to 2.1650 inches
5S-FE engine	2.1649 to 2.1655 inches
4A-FE engine	1.8891 to 1.8898 inches
Taper and out-of-round limits	0.0008 inch
Runout limit	0.0024 inch
Oil clearance (standard)	
1986 models	
No. 3 (center) main	0.0012 to 0.0022 inch
All others	0.0008 to 0.0019 inch
1987 and later models	

2B

3S-FE (1987 and 1988), all 3S-GE and 5S-FE engines	
No. 3 (center) main	0.0011 to 0.0019 inch
All others	0.0007 to 0.0015 inch
3S-FE engine (1989)	
No. 3 (center) main	0.0010 to 0.0017 inch
All others	0.0006 to 0.0013 inch
4A-FE engine	0.0006 to 0.0013 inch
Oil clearance (service limit)	
2S-E, 3S-FE, 3S-GE and 5S-FE engines	0.0031 inch
4A-FE engine	0.0039 inch
Crankshaft endplay	
Standard	0.0008 to 0.0087 inch
Service limit	0.0118 inch
Thrust washer thickness	0.0961 to 0.0980 inch

Pistons and rings

Piston diameter	
2S-E engine	3.3061 to 3.3073 inches
3S-FE engine	3.3836 to 3.3848 inches
3S-GE engine	3.3842 to 3.3846 inches
5S-FE engine	
1990 and 1991	
Mark 1	3.4217 to 3.4221 inches
Mark 2	3.4221 to 3.4225 inches
Mark 3	3.4225 to 3.4229 inches
1992 on	
Mark 1	3.4193 to 3.4197 inches
Mark 2	3.4197 to 3.4201 inches
Mark 3	3.4201 to 3.4205 inches
4A-FE engine	
Mark 1	3.1862 to 3.1866 inches
Mark 2	3.1866 to 3.1870 inches
Mark 3	3.1870 to 3.1874 inches
Piston-to-bore clearance	
2S-E engine	
Standard	0.0006 to 0.0014 inch
Service limit	0.0020 inch
3S-FE engine	
Standard	0.0018 to 0.0026 inch
Service limit	0.0033 inch
3S-GE engine	
Standard	0.0012 to 0.0020 inch
Service limit	0.0028 inch
5S-FE engine	
1990 and 1991	
Standard	0.0031 to 0.0039 inch
Service limit	0.0047 inch
1992 on	
Standard	0.0055 to 0.0063 inch
Service limit	0.0071 inch
4A-FE engine	
Standard	0.0024 to 0.0031 inch
Service limit	0.0039 inch

Piston ring end gap

2S-E engine	
No. 1 (top) 0.0110 to 0.0209 inch	
No. 2 (middle)	0.0083 to 0.0189 inch
Oil ring	0.0079 to 0.0323 inch
3S-FE engine	
Standard	
1987 models	
No. 1 (top)	0.0106 to 0.0193 inch
No. 2 (middle)	0.0106 to 0.0197 inch
Oil ring	0.0079 to 0.0311 inch
1988 models	
No. 1 (top)	0.0106 to 0.0205 inch
No. 2 (middle)	0.0106 to 0.0209 inch
Oil ring	0.0079 to 0.0323 inch
1989 models	
No. 1 (top)	0.0106 to 0.01971 inch

No. 2 (middle)	0.0106 to 0.0201 inch
Oil ring	0.0079 to 0.0217 inch
Service limit	
1987 models	
No. 1 (top)	0.0311 inch
No. 2 (middle)	0.0315 inch
Oil ring	0.0429 inch
1988 models	
No. 1 (top)	0.0323 inch
No. 2 (middle)	0.0327 inch
Oil ring	0.0441 inch
1989 models	
No. 1 (top)	0.0433 inch
No. 2 (middle)	0.0437 inch
Oil ring	0.0453 inch
3S-GE engine	
Standard	
No. 1 (top)	0.0130 to 0.0217 inch
No. 2 (middle)	0.0177 to 0.0276 inch
Oil ring	0.0079 to 0.0236 inch
Service limit	
No. 1 (top)	0.0335 inch
No. 2 (middle)	0.0394 inch
Oil ring	0.0354 inch
5S-FE engine	
Standard	
No. 1 (top)	0.0106 to 0.0197 inch
No. 2 (middle)	0.0138 to 0.0234 inch
Oil ring	0.0079 to 0.0217 inch
Service limit	
No. 1 (top)	0.0433 inch
No. 2 (middle)	0.0472 inch
Oil ring	0.0453 inch
4A-FE engine	
Standard	
No. 1 (top)	0.0098 to 0.0177 inch
No. 2 (middle)	0.0059 to 0.0157 inch
Oil ring	0.0039 to 0.0276 inch
Service limit	
No. 1 (top)	0.0413 inch
No. 2 (middle)	0.0394 inch
Oil ring	0.0512 inch
Piston ring side clearance	
2S-E and 3S-FE engines	0.0012 to 0.0028 inch
3S-GE engine	
1986	
Top ring	0.0008 to 0.0024 inch
Middle ring	0.0006 to 0.0022 inch
1987 on	
Top ring	0.0012 to 0.0028 inch
Middle ring	0.0008 to 0.0024 inch
5S-FE engine	
1990 and 1991 (top and middle ring)	0.0012 to 0.0028 inch
1992 on	
Top ring	0.0016 to 0.0031 inch
Middle ring	0.0012 to 0.0028 inch
4A-FE engine	
Top ring	0.0016 to 0.0032 inch
Middle ring	0.0012 to 0.0028 inch

Torque specifications*

	Ft-lbs
Main bearing cap bolts	
2S-E, 3S-FE, 3S-GE and 5S-FE engines	43
4A-FE engine	44
Connecting rod cap nuts	
2S-E engine	36
3S-FE engine	36
3S-GE engine	
1986	43
1987	47
1988 on	49

2B

5S-FE engine
    First turn 18
    Second turn .... tighten an additional 90-degrees
4A-FE engine 36
* **Note:** *Refer to Part A for additional torque specifications.*

General information

Included in this portion of Chapter 2 are the general overhaul procedures for the cylinder head and internal engine components.

The information ranges from advice concerning preparation for an overhaul and the purchase of replacement parts to detailed, step-by-step procedures covering removal and installation of internal engine components and the inspection of parts.

The following Sections have been written based on the assumption that the engine has been removed from the vehicle. For information concerning in-vehicle engine repair, as well as removal and installation of the external components necessary for the overhaul, see Part A of this Chapter and Section 7 of this Part.

The Specifications included in this Part are only those necessary for the inspection and overhaul procedures which follow. Refer to Part A for additional Specifications.

2 Engine overhaul - general information

Refer to illustrations 2.4a and 2.4b

It's not always easy to determine when, or if, an engine should be completely overhauled, as a number of factors must be considered.

High mileage is not necessarily an indication that an overhaul is needed, while low mileage doesn't preclude the need for an overhaul. Frequency of servicing is probably the most important consideration. An engine that's had regular and frequent oil and filter changes, as well as other required maintenance, will most likely give many thousands of miles of reliable service. Conversely, a neglected engine may require an overhaul very early in its life.

Excessive oil consumption is an indication that piston rings, valve seals and/or valve guides are in need of attention. Make sure that oil leaks aren't responsible before deciding that the rings and/or guides are bad. Perform a cylinder compression check to determine the extent of the work required (see Section 3).

Check the oil pressure with a gauge installed in place of the oil pressure sending unit **(see illustrations)** and compare it to the Specifications. If it's extremely low, the bearings and/or oil pump are probably worn out.

Loss of power, rough running, knocking or metallic engine noises, excessive valve train noise and high fuel consumption rates may also point to the need for an overhaul, especially if they're all present at the same time. If a complete tune-up doesn't remedy the situation, major mechanical work is the only solution.

An engine overhaul involves restoring the internal parts to the specifications of a new engine. During an overhaul, the piston rings are replaced and the cylinder walls are reconditioned (rebored and/or honed). If a rebore is done by an automotive machine shop, new oversize pistons will also be installed. The main bearings, connecting rod bearings and camshaft bearings are generally replaced with new ones and, if necessary, the crankshaft may be reground to restore the journals. Generally, the valves are serviced as well, since they're usually in less-than-perfect condition at this point. While the engine is being overhauled, other components, such as the distributor, starter and alternator, can be rebuilt as well. The end result should be a like new engine that will give many trouble free miles. **Note:** *Critical cooling system components such as the hoses, drivebelts, thermostat and water pump MUST be replaced with new parts when an engine is overhauled. The radiator should be checked carefully to ensure that it isn't clogged or leaking (see Chapter 3). Also, we don't recommend overhauling the oil pump - always install a new one when an engine is rebuilt.*

Before beginning the engine overhaul, read through the entire procedure to familiarize yourself with the scope and requirements of the job. Overhauling an engine isn't difficult, but it is time consuming. Plan on the vehicle being tied up for a minimum of two weeks, especially if parts must be taken to an automotive machine shop for repair or reconditioning. Check on availability of parts and make sure that any necessary special tools and equipment are obtained in advance. Most work can be done with typical hand tools, although a number of precision measuring tools are required for inspecting parts to determine if they must be replaced. Often an automotive machine shop will handle the inspection of parts and offer advice concerning reconditioning and replacement. **Note:** *Always wait until the engine has been completely disassembled and all components, especially the engine block, have been inspected before deciding what service and repair operations must be performed by an automotive machine shop. Since the block's condition will be the major factor to consider when determining whether to overhaul the original engine or buy a rebuilt one, never purchase parts or have machine work done on other components until the block has been thoroughly inspected. As a general rule, time is the primary cost of an overhaul, so it doesn't pay to install worn or substandard parts.*

As a final note, to ensure maximum life and minimum trouble from a rebuilt engine, everything must be assembled with care in a spotlessly clean environment.

3 Cylinder compression check

Refer to illustration 3.6

1   A compression check will tell you what mechanical condition the upper end (pistons, rings, valves, head gasket(s)) of your engine is in. Specifically, it can tell you if the compression is down due to leakage caused by worn piston rings, defective valves and seats or a blown head gasket. **Note:** *The engine must be at normal operating temperature and the battery must be fully charged for this check.*

2   Begin by cleaning the area around the spark plugs before you remove them (compressed air should be used, if available, otherwise a small brush or even a bicycle tire pump will work). The idea is to prevent dirt from getting into the cylinders as the compression check is being done.

3   Remove all of the spark plugs from the engine (Chapter 1).

4   Block the throttle wide open.

5   If the vehicle is equipped with a separate ignition coil, detach the coil wire from the center of the distributor cap and ground it on the engine block. Use a jumper wire with alligator clips on each end to ensure a good ground. If the vehicle is equipped with the IIA integral coil and distributor, disconnect the ignition primary wiring. On EFI-equipped models, the fuel pump circuit should also be disabled (see Chapter 4).

6   Install the compression gauge in the spark plug hole **(see illustration)**.

7   Crank the engine over at least seven compression strokes and watch the gauge. The compression should build up quickly in a healthy engine. Low compression on the first stroke, followed by gradually increasing pressure on successive strokes, indicates worn piston rings. A low compression reading on the first stroke, which doesn't build up during successive strokes, indicates leaking valves or a blown head gasket (a cracked head could also be the cause). Deposits on the undersides of the valve heads can also cause low compression.

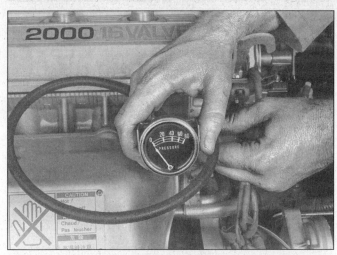

2.4a The oil pressure can be checked by removing the sending unit and installing a pressure gauge in the hole

2.4b On 3S-FE, 3S-GE and 5S-FE models, the oil pressure sending unit (arrow) is located on the left front corner of the cylinder head; on 2S-E engines, the sender is located in the left front corner of the engine block; on 4A-FE engines, it's on the front of the engine block near the oil filter

Record the highest gauge reading obtained.

8   Repeat the procedure for the remaining cylinders and compare the results to the Specifications.

9   Add some engine oil (about three squirts from a plunger-type oil can) to each cylinder, through the spark plug hole, and repeat the test.

10   If the compression increases after the oil is added, the piston rings are definitely worn. If the compression doesn't increase significantly, the leakage is occurring at the valves or head gasket. Leakage past the valves may be caused by burned valve seats and/or faces or warped, cracked or bent valves.

11   If two adjacent cylinders have equally low compression, there's a strong possibility that the head gasket between them is blown. The appearance of coolant in the combustion chambers or the crankcase would verify this condition.

12   If one cylinder is 20-percent lower than the others, and the engine has a slightly rough idle, a worn exhaust lobe on the camshaft could be the cause.

13   If the compression is unusually high, the combustion chambers are probably coated with carbon deposits. If that's the case, the cylinder head(s) should be removed and decarbonized.

14   If compression is way down or varies greatly between cylinders, it would be a good idea to have a leak-down test performed by an automotive repair shop. This test will pinpoint exactly where the leakage is occurring and how severe it is.

3.6 A compression gauge with a threaded fitting for the spark plug hole is preferred over the type that requires hand pressure to maintain the seal - be sure to open the throttle valve as far as possible during the compression check!

4   Engine removal - methods and precautions

If you've decided that an engine must be removed for overhaul or major repair work, several preliminary steps should be taken.

Locating a suitable place to work is extremely important. Adequate work space, along with storage space for the vehicle, will be needed. If a shop or garage isn't available, at the very least a flat, level, clean work surface made of concrete or asphalt is required.

Cleaning the engine compartment and engine before beginning the removal procedure will help keep tools clean and organized.

An engine hoist or A-frame will also be necessary. Make sure the equipment is rated in excess of the combined weight of the engine and transaxle. Safety is of primary importance, considering the potential hazards involved in lifting the engine out of the vehicle.

If the engine is being removed by a novice, a helper should be available. Advice and aid from someone more experienced would also be helpful. There are many instances when one person cannot simultaneously perform all of the operations required when lifting the engine out of the vehicle.

Plan the operation ahead of time. Arrange for or obtain all of the tools and equipment you'll need prior to beginning the job. Some of the equipment necessary to perform engine removal and installation safely and with relative ease are (in addition to an engine hoist) a heavy

duty floor jack, complete sets of wrenches and sockets as described in the front of this manual, wooden blocks and plenty of rags and cleaning solvent for mopping up spilled oil, coolant and gasoline. If the hoist must be rented, make sure that you arrange for it in advance and perform all of the operations possible without it beforehand. This will save you money and time.

Plan for the vehicle to be out of use for quite a while. A machine shop will be required to perform some of the work which the do-it-yourselfer can't accomplish without special equipment. These shops often have a busy schedule, so it would be a good idea to consult them before removing the engine in order to accurately estimate the amount of time required to rebuild or repair components that may need work.

Always be extremely careful when removing and installing the engine. Serious injury can result from careless actions. Plan ahead, take your time and a job of this nature, although major, can be accomplished successfully.

5   Engine - removal and installation

Refer to illustrations 5.5, 5.10, 5.15, 5.19, 5.20, 5.22a, 5.22b, 5.23a, 5.23b and 5.27

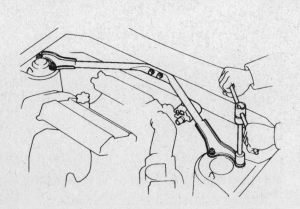

5.5   On 3S-GE and 5S-FE engines, remove the upper suspension brace

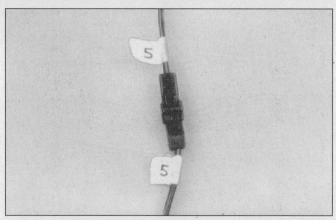

5.10   Label both ends of each wire before disconnecting it

5.15   Unbolt the air conditioning compressor and use wire or rope to tie it out of the way

5.19   Take up the slack in the hoist chain

Warning: *Gasoline is extremely flammable, so take extra precautions when disconnecting any part of the fuel system. Don't smoke or allow open flames or bare light bulbs in or near the work area and don't work in a garage where a natural gas appliance (such as a clothes dryer or water heater) is installed. If you spill gasoline on your skin, rinse it off immediately. Have a fire extinguisher rated for gasoline fires handy and know how to use it.*

Note: *Read through the entire Section before beginning this procedure. The engine and transaxle are removed as a unit and then separated outside the vehicle.*

Removal

1   Relieve the fuel system pressure (see Chapter 4).
2   Remove the battery (see Chapter 5).
3   Place protective covers on the fenders and cowl and remove the hood (see Chapter 11).
4   Remove the air cleaner assembly (see Chapter 4).
5   If you're working on a 3S-GE or 5S-FE engine, remove the suspension upper brace **(see illustration)**.
6   Remove the cruise control actuator and bracket.
7   If you're working on a 1990 or later model, remove the engine relay box and air conditioner relay box.
8   If you're working on a 1990 or later model, remove the evaporative emissions charcoal canister (see Chapter 6).
9   Raise the vehicle and support it securely on jackstands. Drain the cooling system and engine oil and remove the drivebelts (see Chapter 1).

10   Clearly label, then disconnect all vacuum lines, coolant and emissions hoses, wiring harness connectors, ground straps and fuel lines. Masking tape and/or a touch up paint applicator work well for marking items **(see illustration)**. Take instant photos or sketch the locations of components and brackets.
11   Remove the cooling fan(s), shroud(s) and radiator (see Chapter 3).
12   Release the residual fuel pressure in the tank by removing the gas cap, then undo the fuel lines connecting the engine to the chassis (see Chapter 4). Plug or cap all open fittings.
13   Disconnect the throttle linkage (and transaxle linkage speed control cable, when equipped) from the engine (see Chapter 4).
14   On power steering equipped vehicles, unbolt the power steering pump. If clearance allows, tie the pump aside without disconnecting the hoses. If necessary, remove the pump (see Chapter 10).
15   On air conditioning equipped vehicles, unbolt the compressor and set it aside **(see illustration)**. **Warning:** *Do not disconnect the refrigerant hoses.*
16   Remove the front exhaust pipe (see Chapter 4).
17   Remove the front suspension crossmember (see Chapter 10).
18   Remove the driveaxles and clutch release cylinder (if equipped) (see Chapter 8), wire harness, shift linkage and speedometer cable from the transaxle (see Chapter 7). It isn't necessary to disconnect the release cylinder hose.
19   Attach a lifting sling to the brackets on the engine. Position a hoist and connect the sling to it. Take up the slack until there is slight tension on the hoist **(see illustration)**.
20   If you're working on a 1989 or later model, remove the engine mounting center member **(see illustration)**.
21   Recheck to be sure nothing except the mounts are still connecting the engine/transaxle to the vehicle. Disconnect anything still remaining.

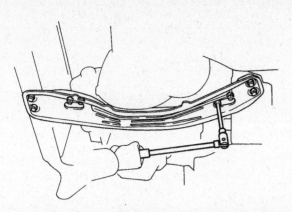

5.20   On 1989 and later models, remove the engine mounting center member

5.22a   If the transaxle mount through-bolt hits the fuel filter (arrow), unbolt the filter bracket and move it aside

5.22b   If you don't remove the rear transaxle mount on later models, it will catch on the steering rack (arrow) as you lift the engine

5.23a   Be sure the upper transaxle mount separates from the bracket (arrow)

22   Support the transaxle with a floor jack. Place a block of wood on the jack head to prevent damage to the transaxle. Remove the through-bolts from the engine and transaxle mounts (see illustration). On later models, unbolt the rear transaxle mount bracket from the transaxle (see Chapter 7) to prevent interference with the steering gear (see illustration). Warning: *Do not place any part of your body under the engine/transaxle when it's supported only by a hoist or other lifting device.*

23   Slowly lift the engine/transaxle out of the vehicle. It may be necessary to pry the mounts away from the frame brackets (see illustrations).

24   Move the engine/transaxle away from the vehicle and carefully lower the hoist until the transaxle is supported in a level position.

25   Remove the engine block-to-transaxle brace.

26   On automatic transaxle equipped models, detach the torque converter dust shield from the lower bellhousing. Remove the torque converter-to-driveplate fasteners (see Chapter 7) and push the converter back slightly into the bellhousing.

27   Remove the engine-to-transaxle bolts and separate the engine from the transaxle (see illustration). The torque converter should remain in the transaxle.

28   Place the engine on the floor or remove the flywheel or driveplate and mount the engine on an engine stand.

Installation

29   Check the engine/transaxle mounts. If they're worn or damaged, replace them.

30   On manual transaxle equipped models, inspect the clutch com-

5.23b   You may have to pry the mounts out of the frame brackets

ponents (see Chapter 8) and, on automatic transaxle models, inspect the converter seal and bushing.

31   On automatic transaxle equipped models, apply a dab of grease to the nose of the torque converter and to the seal lips.

5.27   Remove the transaxle-to-engine bolts and separate the engine from the transaxle

32   Carefully guide the transaxle into place, following the procedure outlined in Chapter 7. **Caution:** *Do not use the bolts to force the engine and transaxle into alignment. It may crack or damage major components. Install the torque converter-to-driveplate fasteners and tighten them to the torque listed in this Chapter's Specifications.*

33   Install the engine-to-transaxle bolts and tighten them securely.

34   Attach the hoist to the engine and carefully lower the engine/transaxle assembly into the engine compartment.

35   Install the mount bolts and tighten them securely.

36   Reinstall the remaining components and fasteners in the reverse order of removal.

37   Add coolant, oil, power steering and transmission fluids as needed (see Chapter 1).

38   Run the engine and check for proper operation and leaks. Shut off the engine and recheck the fluid levels.

6   Engine rebuilding alternatives

The do-it-yourselfer is faced with a number of options when performing an engine overhaul. The decision to replace the engine block, piston/connecting rod assemblies and crankshaft depends on a number of factors, with the number one consideration being the condition of the block. Other considerations are cost, access to machine shop facilities, parts availability, time required to complete the project and the extent of prior mechanical experience on the part of the do-it-yourselfer.

Some of the rebuilding alternatives include:

Individual parts - If the inspection procedures reveal that the engine block and most engine components are in reusable condition, purchasing individual parts may be the most economical alternative. The block, crankshaft and piston/connecting rod assemblies should all be inspected carefully. Even if the block shows little wear, the cylinder bores should be surface honed.

Short block - A short block consists of an engine block with a crankshaft and piston/connecting rod assemblies already installed. All new bearings are incorporated and all clearances will be correct. The existing camshaft, valve train components, cylinder head(s) and external parts can be bolted to the short block with little or no machine shop work necessary.

Long block - A long block consists of a short block plus an oil pump, oil pan, cylinder head, camshaft and valve train components, timing pulleys and belt. All components are installed with new bearings, seals and gaskets incorporated throughout. The installation of manifolds and external parts is all that's necessary.

Give careful thought to which alternative is best for you and discuss the situation with local automotive machine shops, auto parts dealers and experienced rebuilders before ordering or purchasing replacement parts.

7   Engine overhaul - disassembly sequence

Refer to illustration 7.5

1   It's much easier to disassemble and work on the engine if it's mounted on a portable engine stand. A stand can often be rented quite cheaply from an equipment rental yard. Before the engine is mounted on a stand, the flywheel/driveplate and rear oil seal retainer should be removed from the engine.

2   If a stand isn't available, it's possible to disassemble the engine with it blocked up on the floor. Be extra careful not to tip or drop the engine when working without a stand.

3   If you're going to obtain a rebuilt engine, all external components must come off first, to be transferred to the replacement engine, just as they will if you're doing a complete engine overhaul yourself. These include:

Alternator and brackets
Emissions control components
Distributor, spark plug wires and spark plugs
Thermostat and housing cover
Water pump
EFI components
Intake/exhaust manifolds
Oil filter
Engine mounts
Clutch and flywheel/driveplate
Engine rear plate

Note: *When removing the external components from the engine, pay close attention to details that may be helpful or important during installation. Note the installed position of gaskets, seals, spacers, pins, brackets, washers, bolts and other small items.*

4   If you're obtaining a short block, which consists of the engine block, crankshaft, pistons and connecting rods all assembled, then the cylinder head, oil pan and oil pump will have to be removed as well. See *Engine rebuilding alternatives* for additional information regarding the different possibilities to be considered.

5   If you're planning a complete overhaul, the engine must be disassembled and the internal components removed in the following order **(see illustration).**

Valve cover
Intake and exhaust manifolds
Timing belt covers
Timing belt and pulleys
Camshaft and rocker arms (2S-E engine)
Camshafts and lifters (all except 2S-E engine)
Cylinder head
Oil pan
Oil pump
Piston/connecting rod assemblies
Crankshaft rear oil seal retainer
Crankshaft and main bearings

6   Before beginning the disassembly and overhaul procedures, make sure the following items are available. Also, refer to *Engine overhaul - reassembly sequence* for a list of tools and materials needed for engine reassembly.

Common hand tools
Small cardboard boxes or plastic bags for storing parts
Gasket scraper
Ridge reamer
Vibration damper puller
Micrometers
Telescoping gauges
Dial indicator set
Valve spring compressor
Cylinder surfacing hone
Piston ring groove cleaning tool
Electric drill motor
Tap and die set
Wire brushes
Oil gallery brushes
Cleaning solvent

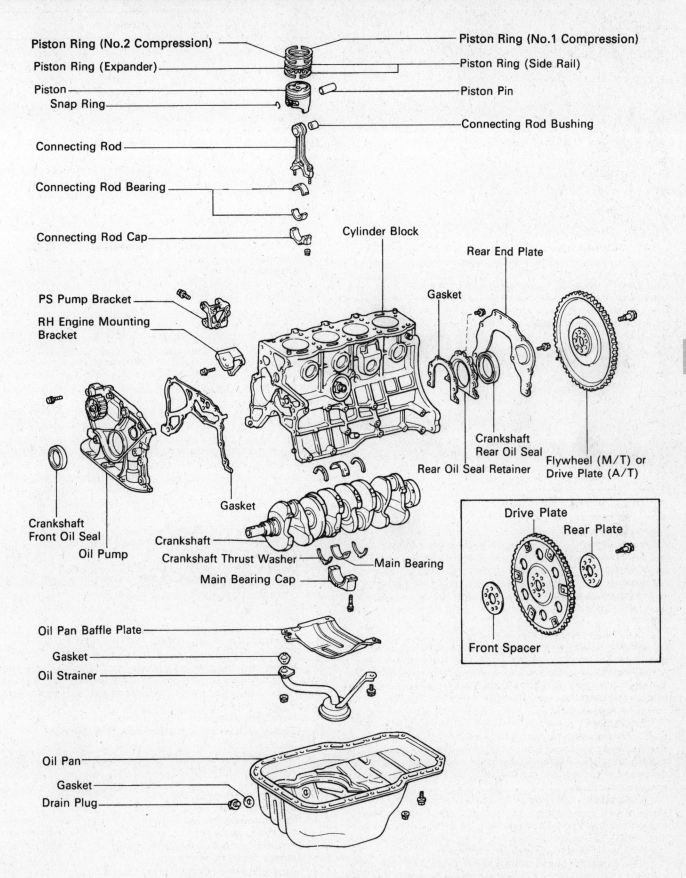

7.5 Engine lower end components (5S-FE engine shown; others similar)

Piston Ring (No.2 Compression)
Piston Ring (Expander)
Piston
Snap Ring
Connecting Rod
Connecting Rod Bearing
Connecting Rod Cap
Piston Ring (No.1 Compression)
Piston Ring (Side Rail)
Piston Pin
Connecting Rod Bushing

Cylinder Block
Rear End Plate
Gasket

PS Pump Bracket
RH Engine Mounting Bracket

Crankshaft Rear Oil Seal
Rear Oil Seal Retainer
Flywheel (M/T) or Drive Plate (A/T)

Crankshaft Front Oil Seal
Oil Pump
Gasket
Crankshaft
Crankshaft Thrust Washer
Main Bearing Cap
Main Bearing

Drive Plate
Rear Plate
Front Spacer

Oil Pan Baffle Plate
Gasket
Oil Strainer

Oil Pan
Gasket
Drain Plug

2B

8.2   A small plastic bag, with an appropriate label, can be used to store the valve train components so they can be kept together and reinstalled in the correct guide

8   Cylinder head - disassembly

Refer to illustrations 8.2 and 8.3

Note: *New and rebuilt cylinder heads are commonly available for most engines at dealerships and auto parts stores. Due to the fact that some specialized tools are necessary for the disassembly and inspection procedures, and replacement parts may not be readily available, it may be more practical and economical for the home mechanic to purchase a replacement head rather than taking the time to disassemble, inspect and recondition the original.*

1   Cylinder head disassembly involves removal of the intake and exhaust valves and related components. It's assumed that the lifters or rocker arms and camshaft(s) have already been removed (see Part A as needed).

2   Before the valves are removed, arrange to label and store them, along with their related components, so they can be kept separate and reinstalled in the same valve guides they are removed from **(see illustration)**.

3   Compress the springs on the first valve with a spring compressor and remove the keepers **(see illustration)**. Carefully release the valve spring compressor and remove the retainer, the spring and the spring seat (if used). **Caution:** *If you're working on any engine except a 2S-E, be very careful not to nick or otherwise damage the lifter bores when compressing the valve springs.*

4   Pull the valve out of the head, then remove the oil seal from the guide. If the valve binds in the guide (won't pull through), push it back into the head and deburr the area around the keeper groove with a fine file or whetstone.

5   Repeat the procedure for the remaining valves. Remember to keep all the parts for each valve together so they can be reinstalled in the same locations.

6   Once the valves and related components have been removed and stored in an organized manner, the head should be thoroughly cleaned and inspected. If a complete engine overhaul is being done, finish the engine disassembly procedures before beginning the cylinder head cleaning and inspection process.

9   Cylinder head - cleaning and inspection

Refer to illustrations 9.12, 9.14, 9.16, 9.17 and 9.18

1   Thorough cleaning of the cylinder head and related valve train components, followed by a detailed inspection, will enable you to decide how much valve service work must be done during the engine overhaul. **Note:** *If the engine was severely overheated, the cylinder head is probably warped (see Step 12).*

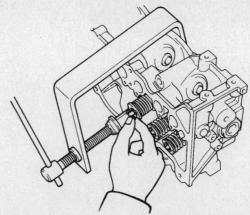

8.3   Compress the spring until the keepers can be removed

Cleaning

2   Scrape all traces of old gasket material and sealing compound off the head gasket, intake manifold and exhaust manifold sealing surfaces. Be very careful not to gouge the cylinder head. Special gasket removal solvents that soften gaskets and make removal much easier are available at auto parts stores.

3   Remove all built-up scale from the coolant passages.

4   Run a stiff wire brush through the various holes to remove deposits that may have formed in them.

5   Run an appropriate size tap into each of the threaded holes to remove corrosion and thread sealant that may be present. If compressed air is available, use it to clear the holes of debris produced by this operation. **Warning:** *Wear eye protection when using compressed air!*

6   Clean the exhaust and intake manifold stud threads with a wire brush.

7   Clean the cylinder head with solvent and dry it thoroughly. Compressed air will speed the drying process and ensure that all holes and recessed areas are clean. **Note:** *Decarbonizing chemicals are available and may prove very useful when cleaning cylinder heads and valve train components. They are very caustic and should be used with caution. Be sure to follow the instructions on the container.*

8   Clean the lifters and rocker arms (if used) with solvent and dry them thoroughly (don't mix them up during the cleaning process). Compressed air will speed the drying process and can be used to clean out the oil passages.

9   Clean all the valve springs, spring seats, keepers and retainers with solvent and dry them thoroughly. Do the components from one valve at a time to avoid mixing up the parts.

10   Scrape off any heavy deposits that may have formed on the valves, then use a motorized wire brush to remove deposits from the valve heads and stems. Again, make sure the valves don't get mixed up.

Inspection

Note: *Be sure to perform all of the following inspection procedures before concluding that machine shop work is required. Make a list of the items that need attention. The inspection procedures for the lifters and rocker arms, as well as the camshaft(s), can be found in Part A.*

Cylinder head

11   Inspect the head very carefully for cracks, evidence of coolant leakage and other damage. If cracks are found, check with an automotive machine shop concerning repair. If repair isn't possible, a new cylinder head should be obtained.

12   Using a straightedge and feeler gauge, check the head gasket mating surface for warpage **(see illustration)**. If the warpage exceeds the specified limit, it can be resurfaced at an automotive machine shop.

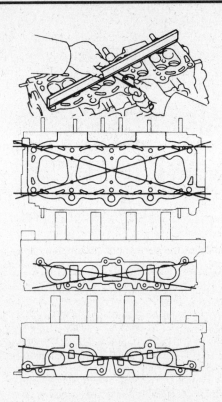

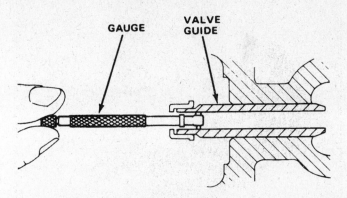

9.14   Use a small hole gauge to determine the inside diameter of the valve guides (the gauge is then measured with a micrometer)

9.12   Check the cylinder head gasket surfaces for warpage by trying to slip a feeler gauge under the precision straightedge (see the Specifications for the maximum warpage allowed and use a feeler gauge of that thickness)

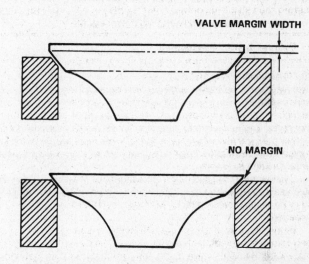

9.16   The margin width on each valve must be as specified (if no margin exists, the valve cannot be reused)

13   Examine the valve seats in each of the combustion chambers. If they're pitted, cracked or burned, the head will require valve service that's beyond the scope of the home mechanic.

14   Measure the valve guide inside diameter with a small hole gauge and micrometer **(see illustration)**, then measure the valve stem diameter and subtract it from the valve guide diameter to obtain the stem-to-guide clearance. Also, on the 2S-E engine, check the valve stem deflection crosswise (parallel to the rocker arm) with a dial indicator attached securely to the head. The valve must be in the guide and approximately 1/16-inch off the seat. The total valve stem movement indicated by the gauge needle must be noted. If it exceeds the specified stem-to-guide clearance limit, the valve guides should be replaced. After this is done, if there's still some doubt regarding the condition of the valve guides they should be checked by an automotive machine shop (the cost should be minimal).

Valves

15   Carefully inspect each valve face for uneven wear, deformation, cracks, pits and burned areas. Check the valve stem for scuffing and galling and the neck for cracks. Rotate the valve and check for any obvious indication that it's bent. Look for pits and excessive wear on the end of the stem. The presence of any of these conditions indicates the need for valve service by an automotive machine shop.

16   Measure the margin width on each valve **(see illustration)**. Any valve with a margin narrower than specified will have to be replaced with a new one.

Valve components

17   Check each valve spring for wear (on the ends) and pits. Measure the free length and compare it to the Specifications **(see illustration)**. Any springs that are shorter than specified have sagged and should not be reused. The tension of all springs should be checked with a special fixture before deciding that they're suitable for use in a rebuilt engine (take the springs to an automotive machine shop for this check).

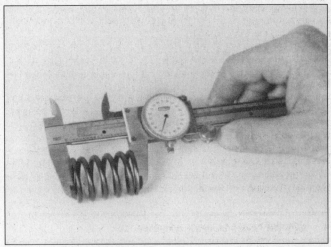

9.17   Measure the free length of each valve spring with a dial or vernier caliper

18   Stand each spring on a flat surface and check it for squareness **(see illustration)**. If any of the springs are distorted or sagged, replace all of them with new parts.

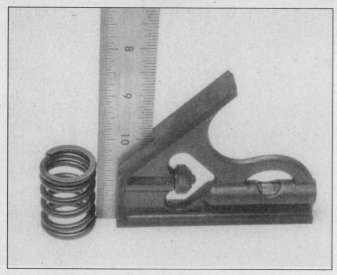

9.18   Check each valve spring for squareness

19   Check the spring retainers and keepers for obvious wear and cracks. Any questionable parts should be replaced with new ones, as extensive damage will occur if they fail during engine operation.

20   Any damaged or excessively worn parts must be replaced with new ones.

21   If the inspection process indicates that the valve components are in generally poor condition and worn beyond the limits specified, which is usually the case in an engine that's being overhauled, reassemble the valves in the cylinder head and refer to valve servicing recommendations (see Section 10).

10   Valves - servicing

1   Because of the complex nature of the job and the special tools and equipment needed, servicing of the valves, the valve seats and the valve guides, commonly known as a valve job, should be done by a professional.

2   The home mechanic can remove and disassemble the head, do the initial cleaning and inspection, then reassemble and deliver it to a dealer service department or an automotive machine shop for the actual service work. Doing the inspection will enable you to see what condition the head and valvetrain components are in and will ensure that you know what work and new parts are required when dealing with an automotive machine shop.

3   The dealer service department, or automotive machine shop, will remove the valves and springs, recondition or replace the valves and valve seats, recondition the valve guides, check and replace the valve springs, spring retainers and keepers (as necessary), replace the valve seals with new ones, reassemble the valve components and make sure the installed spring height is correct. The cylinder head gasket surface will also be resurfaced if it's warped.

4   After the valve job has been performed by a professional, the head will be in like new condition. When the head is returned, be sure to clean it again before installation on the engine to remove any metal particles and abrasive grit that may still be present from the valve service or head resurfacing operations. Use compressed air, if available, to blow out all the oil holes and passages.

11   Cylinder head - reassembly

Refer to illustration 11.3

1   Regardless of whether or not the head was sent to an automotive repair shop for valve servicing, make sure it's clean before beginning reassembly.

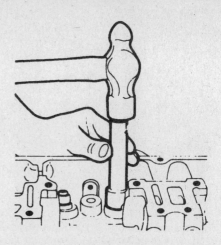

11.3   Gently tap the valve seals into place with a deep socket and hammer1

2   If the head was sent out for valve servicing, the valves and related components will already be in place.3   Install new seals on each of the valve guides. **Note:** *Intake and exhaust valves require different seals - DO NOT mix them up!* Gently tap each intake valve seal into place until it's seated on the guide (see illustration). **Caution:** *Don't hammer on the valve seals once they're seated or you may damage them. Don't twist or cock the seals during installation or they won't seat properly on the valve stems.*

4   Beginning at one end of the head, lubricate and install the first valve. Apply moly-base grease or clean engine oil to the valve stem.

5   Drop the spring seat or shim(s) (if equipped) over the valve guide and set the valve spring and retainer in place.

6   Compress the springs with a valve spring compressor and carefully install the keepers in the upper groove, then slowly release the compressor and make sure the keepers seat properly. Apply a small dab of grease to each keeper to hold it in place if necessary **(see illustration 12.17 in Part A)**.

7   Repeat the procedure for the remaining valves. Be sure to return the components to their original locations - don't mix them up!

12   Pistons/connecting rods - removal

Refer to illustrations 12.1, 12.3, 12.4, and 12.6

Note: *Prior to removing the piston/connecting rod assemblies, remove the cylinder head, the oil pan and the oil pump pick-up tube by referring to the appropriate Sections in Part A.*

1   Use your fingernail to feel if a ridge has formed at the upper limit of ring travel (about 1/4-inch down from the top of each cylinder). If carbon deposits or cylinder wear have produced ridges, they must be completely removed with a special tool **(see illustration)**. Follow the manufacturer's instructions provided with the tool. Failure to remove the ridges before attempting to remove the piston/connecting rod assemblies may result in piston breakage.

2   After the cylinder ridges have been removed, turn the engine upside-down so the crankshaft is facing up.

3   Before the connecting rods are removed, check the endplay with feeler gauges. Slide them between the first connecting rod and the crankshaft throw until the play is removed **(see illustration)**. The endplay is equal to the thickness of the feeler gauge(s). If the endplay exceeds the service limit, new connecting rods will be required. If new rods (or a new crankshaft) are installed, the endplay may fall under the specified minimum (if it does, the rods will have to be machined to restore it - consult an automotive machine shop for advice if necessary). Repeat the procedure for the remaining connecting rods.

4   Check the connecting rods and caps for identification marks. If they aren't plainly marked, use a small center-punch to make the appropriate number of indentations on each rod and cap (1, 2, 3, etc.,

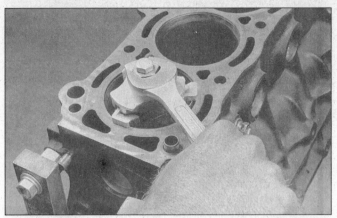

12.1 A ridge reamer is required to remove the ridge from the top of each cylinder - do this before removing the pistons!

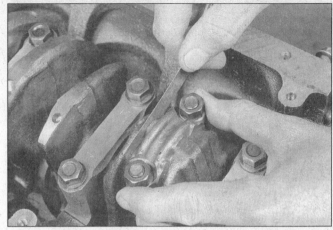

12.3 Check the connecting rod side clearance with a feeler gauge as shown here

12.4 The connecting rods and caps should be marked to indicate which cylinder they're installed in - if they aren't, mark them with a center-punch to avoid confusion during reassembly

12.6 To prevent damage to the crankshaft journals and cylinder walls, slip sections of hose over the rod bolts before removing the pistons

piston is removed **(see illustration)**.

7   Remove the bearing insert and push the connecting rod/piston assembly out through the top of the engine. Use a wooden hammer handle to push on the upper bearing surface in the connecting rod. If resistance is felt, double-check to make sure that all of the ridge was removed from the cylinder.

8   Repeat the procedure for the remaining cylinders.

9   After removal, reassemble the connecting rod caps and bearing inserts in their respective connecting rods and install the cap nuts finger tight. Leaving the old bearing inserts in place until reassembly will help prevent the connecting rod bearing surfaces from being accidentally nicked or gouged.

10   Don't separate the pistons from the connecting rods (see Section 17).

13 Crankshaft - removal

Refer to illustrations 13.1 and 13.3

Note: *The crankshaft can be removed only after the engine has been removed from the vehicle. It's assumed that the flywheel or driveplate, vibration damper, timing belt, oil pan, oil pick-up tube, oil pump and piston/connecting rod assemblies have already been removed. The rear main oil seal retainer must be unbolted and separated from the block before proceeding with crankshaft removal.*

1   Before the crankshaft is removed, check the endplay. Mount a dial indicator with the stem in line with the crankshaft and just touching the crankshaft **(see illustration)**.

13.1 Checking crankshaft endplay with a dial indicator

depending on the engine type and cylinder they're associated with) **(see illustration)**.

5   Loosen each of the connecting rod cap nuts 1/2-turn at a time until they can be removed by hand. Remove the number one connecting rod cap and bearing insert. Don't drop the bearing insert out of the cap.

6   Slip a short length of plastic or rubber hose over each connecting rod cap bolt to protect the crankshaft journal and cylinder wall as the

14.1   Pull the core plugs from the block with pliers

13.3   Checking crankshaft endplay with a feeler gauge

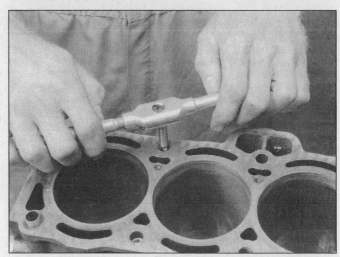

14.8   All bolt holes in the block - particularly the main bearing cap and head bolt holes - should be cleaned and restored with a tap (be sure to remove debris from the holes after this is done)

2   Push the crankshaft all the way to the rear and zero the dial indicator. Next, pry the crankshaft to the front as far as possible and check the reading on the dial indicator. The distance that it moves is the endplay. If it's greater than specified, check the crankshaft thrust surfaces for wear. If no wear is evident, new thrust washers should correct the endplay.

3   If a dial indicator isn't available, feeler gauges can be used. Gently pry or push the crankshaft all the way to the front of the engine. Slip feeler gauges between the crankshaft and the front face of the thrust main bearing to determine the clearance **(see illustration)**. The thrust bearing is number three (center).

4   Check the main bearing caps to see if they're marked to indicate their locations. They should be numbered consecutively from the front of the engine to the rear. If they aren't, mark them with number stamping dies or a center-punch. Main bearing caps generally have a cast-in arrow, which points to the front of the engine. Loosen the main bearing cap bolts 1/4-turn at a time each, starting with the front and rear caps and working toward the center, until they can be removed by hand. Note if any stud bolts are used and make sure they're returned to their original locations when the crankshaft is reinstalled.

5   Gently tap the caps with a soft-face hammer, then separate them from the engine block. If necessary, use the bolts as levers to remove the caps. Try not to drop the bearing inserts if they come out with the caps.

6   Carefully lift the crankshaft out of the engine. It may be a good idea to have an assistant available, since the crankshaft is quite heavy. With the bearing inserts in place in the engine block and main bearing caps or cap assembly, return the caps to their respective locations on the engine block and tighten the bolts finger tight.

14   Engine block - cleaning

Refer to illustrations 14.1, 14.8 and 14.10
Caution: *The core plugs (also known as freeze or soft plugs) may be difficult or impossible to retrieve if they're driven into the block coolant passages.*

1   Remove the core plugs from the engine block. To do this, knock one side of the plugs into the block with a hammer and punch, then grasp them with large pliers and pull them out **(see illustration)**.

2   Using a gasket scraper, remove all traces of gasket material from the engine block. Be very careful not to nick or gouge the gasket sealing surfaces.

3   Remove the main bearing caps or cap assembly and separate the bearing inserts from the caps and the engine block. Tag the bearings, indicating which cylinder they were removed from and whether they were in the cap or the block, then set them aside.

4   Remove all of the threaded oil gallery plugs from the block. The

plugs are usually very tight - they may have to be drilled out and the holes retapped. Use new plugs when the engine is reassembled.

5   If the engine is extremely dirty it should be taken to an automotive machine shop to be steam cleaned or hot tanked.

6   After the block is returned, clean all oil holes and oil galleries one more time. Brushes specifically designed for this purpose are available at most auto parts stores. Flush the passages with warm water until the water runs clear, dry the block thoroughly and wipe all machined surfaces with a light, rust preventive oil. If you have access to compressed air, use it to speed the drying process and to blow out all the oil holes and galleries. **Warning:** *Wear eye protection when using compressed air!*

7   If the block isn't extremely dirty or sludged up, you can do an adequate cleaning job with hot soapy water and a stiff brush. Take plenty of time and do a thorough job. Regardless of the cleaning method used, be sure to clean all oil holes and galleries very thoroughly, dry the block completely and coat all machined surfaces with light oil.

8   The threaded holes in the block must be clean to ensure accurate torque readings during reassembly. Run the proper size tap into each of the holes to remove rust, corrosion, thread sealant or sludge and restore damaged threads **(see illustration)**. If possible, use compressed air to clear the holes of debris produced by this operation. Now is a good time to clean the threads on the head bolts and the main bearing cap bolts as well.

9   Reinstall the main bearing caps and tighten the bolts finger tight.

10   After coating the sealing surfaces of the new core plugs with Permatex no. 2 sealant, install them in the engine block **(see illustration)**. Make sure they're driven in straight and seated properly or leakage could result. Special tools are available for this purpose, but a large

14.10 A large socket on an extension can be used to drive the new core plugs into the bores

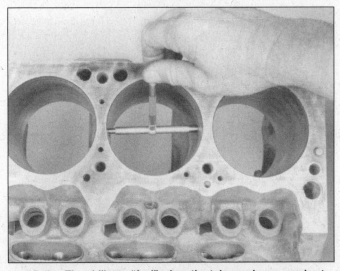

15.4b The ability to "feel" when the telescoping gauge is at the correct point will be developed over time, so work slowly and repeat the check until you're satisfied that the bore measurement is accurate

socket, with an outside diameter that will just slip into the core plug, a 1/2-inch drive extension and a hammer will work just as well.

11 Apply non-hardening sealant (such as Permatex no. 2 or Teflon pipe sealant) to the new oil gallery plugs and thread them into the holes in the block. Make sure they're tightened securely.

12 If the engine isn't going to be reassembled right away, cover it with a large plastic trash bag to keep it clean.

15 Engine block - inspection

Refer to illustrations 15.4a, 15.4b, 15.4c, 15.12a and 15.12b

1 Before the block is inspected, it should be cleaned (see Section 14).

2 Visually check the block for cracks, rust and corrosion. Look for stripped threads in the threaded holes. It's also a good idea to have the block checked for hidden cracks by an automotive machine shop that has the special equipment to do this type of work. If defects are found, have the block repaired, if possible, or replaced.

3 Check the cylinder bores for scuffing and scoring.

4 Measure the diameter of each cylinder at the top (just under the

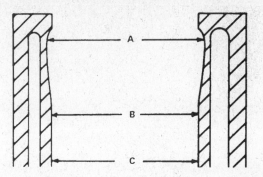

15.4a Measure the diameter of each cylinder just under the wear ridge (A), at the center (B) and at the bottom (C)

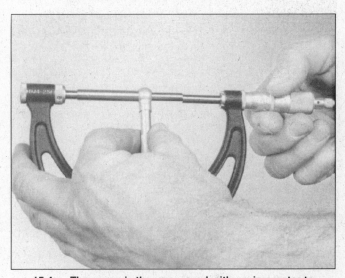

15.4c The gauge is then measured with a micrometer to determine the bore size

ridge area), center and bottom of the cylinder bore, parallel to the crankshaft axis **(see illustrations)**.

5 Next, measure each cylinder's diameter at the same three locations across the crankshaft axis. Compare the results to the Specifications.

6 If the required precision measuring tools aren't available, the piston-to-cylinder clearances can be obtained, though not quite as accurately, using feeler gauge stock. Feeler gauge stock comes in 12-inch lengths and various thicknesses and is generally available at auto parts stores.

7 To check the clearance, select a feeler gauge and slip it into the cylinder along with the matching piston. The piston must be positioned exactly as it normally would be. The feeler gauge must be between the piston and cylinder on one of the thrust faces (90-degrees to the piston pin bore).

8 The piston should slip through the cylinder (with the feeler gauge in place) with moderate pressure.

9 If it falls through or slides through easily, the clearance is excessive and a new piston will be required. If the piston binds at the lower end of the cylinder and is loose toward the top, the cylinder is tapered. If tight spots are encountered as the piston/feeler gauge is rotated in the cylinder, the cylinder is out-of-round.

10 Repeat the procedure for the remaining pistons and cylinders.

11 If the cylinder walls are badly scuffed or scored, or if they're out-of-round or tapered beyond the limits given in the Specifications, have the engine block rebored and honed at an automotive machine shop. If a rebore is done, oversize pistons and rings will be required.

12 Using a precision straightedge and feeler gauge, check the block deck (the surface that mates with the cylinder head) for distortion **(see**

15.12a   Check the block deck for distortion with a precision straightedge and feeler gauges

15.12b   Lay the straightedge across the block, diagonally and from end-to-end when making the check

16.3a   A "bottle brush" hone will produce better results if you have never honed cylinders before

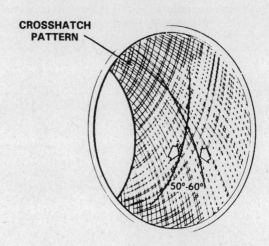

16.3b   The cylinder hone should leave a smooth, crosshatch pattern with the lines intersecting at approximately a 60-degree angle

illustrations). If it's distorted beyond the specified limit, it can be resurfaced by an automotive machine shop.

13   If the cylinders are in reasonably good condition and not worn to the outside of the limits, and if the piston-to-cylinder clearances can be maintained properly, then they don't have to be rebored. Honing is all that's necessary (see Section 16).

16   Cylinder honing

Refer to illustrations 16.3a and 16.3b

1   Prior to engine reassembly, the cylinder bores must be honed so the new piston rings will seat correctly and provide the best possible combustion chamber seal. **Note:** *If you don't have the tools or don't want to tackle the honing operation, most automotive machine shops will do it for a reasonable fee.*

2   Before honing the cylinders, install the main bearing caps (without bearing inserts) and tighten the bolts to the specified torque.

3   Two types of cylinder hones are commonly available - the flex hone or "bottle brush" type and the more traditional surfacing hone with spring-loaded stones. Both will do the job, but for the less experienced mechanic the "bottle brush" hone will probably be easier to use. You'll also need some kerosene or honing oil, rags and an electric drill motor. Proceed as follows:

  a) Mount the hone in the drill motor, compress the stones and slip it into the first cylinder **(see illustration)**. Be sure to wear safety goggles or a face shield!

  b) Lubricate the cylinder with plenty of honing oil, turn on the drill and move the hone up-and-down in the cylinder at a pace that will

produce a fine crosshatch pattern on the cylinder walls. Ideally, the crosshatch lines should intersect at approximately a 60-degrees angle **(see illustration)**. Be sure to use plenty of lubricant and don't take off any more material than is absolutely necessary to produce the desired finish. **Note:** *Piston ring manufacturers may specify a smaller crosshatch angle than the traditional 60-degrees - read and follow any instructions included with the new rings.*

  c) Don't withdraw the hone from the cylinder while it's running. Instead, shut off the drill and continue moving the hone up-and-down in the cylinder until it comes to a complete stop, then compress the stones and withdraw the hone. If you're using a "bottle brush" type hone, stop the drill motor, then turn the chuck in the normal direction of rotation while withdrawing the hone from the cylinder.

  d) Wipe the oil out of the cylinder and repeat the procedure for the remaining cylinders.

4   After the honing job is complete, chamfer the top edges of the cylinder bores with a small file so the rings won't catch when the pistons are installed. Be very careful not to nick the cylinder walls with the end of the file.

5   The entire engine block must be washed again very thoroughly with warm, soapy water to remove all traces of the abrasive grit produced during the honing operation. **Note:** *The bores can be considered clean when a lint-free white cloth - dampened with clean engine oil - used to wipe them out doesn't pick up any more honing residue, which will show up as gray areas on the cloth. Be sure to run a brush through all oil holes and galleries and flush them with running water.*

6   After rinsing, dry the block and apply a coat of light rust preventive oil to all machined surfaces. Wrap the block in a plastic trash bag to keep it clean and set it aside until reassembly.

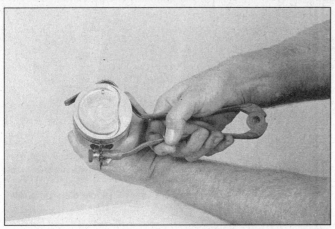

17.4a   The piston ring grooves can be cleaned with a special tool, as shown here, . . .

17.4b   . . . or a section of a broken ring

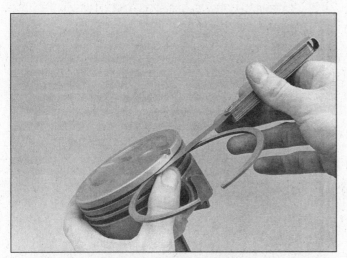

17.10   Check the ring side clearance with a feeler gauge at several points around the groove

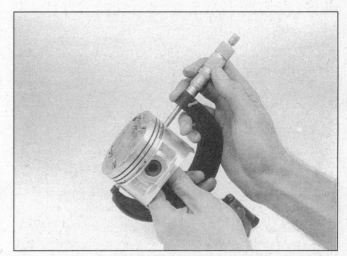

17.11   Measure the piston diameter at a 90-degree angle to the piston pin - depending on the model, the pistons must be measured at a precise point:

17   Pistons/connecting rods - inspection

Refer to illustrations 17.4a, 17.4b, 17.10 and 17.11

1   Before the inspection process can be carried out, the piston/connecting rod assemblies must be cleaned and the original piston rings removed from the pistons. **Note:** *Always use new piston rings when the engine is reassembled.*

2   Using a piston ring installation tool, carefully remove the rings from the pistons. Be careful not to nick or gouge the pistons in the process.

3   Scrape all traces of carbon from the top of the piston. A hand-held wire brush or a piece of fine emery cloth can be used once the majority of the deposits have been scraped away. Do not, under any circumstances, use a wire brush mounted in a drill motor to remove deposits from the pistons. The piston material is soft and may be eroded away by the wire brush.

4   Use a piston ring groove cleaning tool to remove carbon deposits from the ring grooves. If a tool isn't available, a piece broken off the old ring will do the job. Be very careful to remove only the carbon deposits - don't remove any metal and do not nick or scratch the sides of the ring grooves **(see illustrations)**.

5   Once the deposits have been removed, clean the piston/rod assemblies with solvent and dry them with compressed air (if available). Make sure the oil return holes in the back sides of the ring grooves and the oil hole in the lower end of each rod are clear.

6   If the pistons and cylinder walls aren't damaged or worn excessively, and if the engine block is not rebored, new pistons won't be

2S-E engine = 0.59 inch below the centerline of the piston pin hole	*3S-GE engine (1987 and later) = 0.94 inch below the top of the piston*
3S-FE engine = 1.00 inch below the top of the piston	*5S-FE engine = 0.925 inch below the top of the piston*
3S-GE engine (1986) = 0.43 inch above the centerline of the piston pin hole	*4A-FE engine = 0.886 inch below the top of the piston*

necessary. Normal piston wear appears as even vertical wear on the piston thrust surfaces and slight looseness of the top ring in its groove. New piston rings, however, should always be used when an engine is rebuilt.

7   Carefully inspect each piston for cracks around the skirt, at the pin bosses and at the ring lands.

8   Look for scoring and scuffing on the thrust faces of the skirt, holes in the piston crown and burned areas at the edge of the crown. If the skirt is scored or scuffed, the engine may have been suffering from overheating and/or abnormal combustion, which caused excessively high operating temperatures. The cooling and lubrication systems should be checked thoroughly. A hole in the piston crown is an indication that abnormal combustion (preignition) was occurring. Burned areas at the edge of the piston crown are usually evidence of spark knock (detonation). If any of the above problems exist, the causes must be corrected or the damage will occur again. The causes may include intake air leaks, incorrect fuel/air mixture, incorrect ignition timing and EGR system malfunctions.

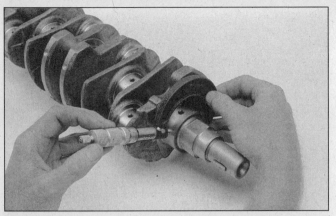

18.6   Measure the diameter of each crankshaft journal at several points to detect taper and out-of-round conditions

9   Corrosion of the piston, in the form of small pits, indicates that coolant is leaking into the combustion chamber and/or the crankcase. Again, the cause must be corrected or the problem may persist in the rebuilt engine.

10   Measure the piston ring side clearance by laying a new piston ring in each ring groove and slipping a feeler gauge in beside it **(see illustration)**. Check the clearance at three or four locations around each groove. Be sure to use the correct ring for each groove - they are different. If the side clearance is greater than specified, new pistons will have to be used.

11   Check the piston-to-bore clearance by measuring the bore (see Section 15) and the piston diameter. Make sure the pistons and bores are correctly matched. Measure the piston across the skirt, at a 90-degree angle to the piston pin, the specified distance down from the top of the piston or the lower edge of the oil ring groove **(see illustration)**. Subtract the piston diameter from the bore diameter to obtain the clearance. If it's greater than specified, the block will have to be re-bored and new pistons and rings installed.

12   Check the piston-to-rod clearance by twisting the piston and rod in opposite directions. Any noticeable play indicates excessive wear, which must be corrected. The piston/connecting rod assemblies should be taken to an automotive machine shop to have the pistons and rods resized and new pins installed.

13   If the pistons must be removed from the connecting rods for any reason, they should be taken to an automotive machine shop. While they are there have the connecting rods checked for bend and twist, since automotive machine shops have special equipment for this purpose. **Note:** *Unless new pistons and/or connecting rods must be installed, do not disassemble the pistons and connecting rods.*

14   If you're working on a 5S-FE engine, see if the nut on each connecting rod bolt can be turned by hand all the way to the end of the threads. If not, measure the outer diameter of the bolt (over the threads) at a point 15 mm from the bolt end. If the bolt diameter is not as specified, use new nuts when the piston/connecting rod assemblies are installed and have an automotive machine shop install new rod bolts.

15   Check the connecting rods for cracks and other damage. Temporarily remove the rod caps, lift out the old bearing inserts, wipe the rod and cap bearing surfaces clean and inspect them for nicks, gouges and scratches. After checking the rods, replace the old bearings, slip the caps into place and tighten the nuts finger tight. **Note:** *If the engine is being rebuilt because of a connecting rod knock, be sure to install new rods.*

18   Crankshaft - inspection

Refer to illustration 18.6

1   Remove all burrs from the crankshaft oil holes with a stone, file or scraper.
2   Clean the crankshaft with solvent and dry it with compressed air

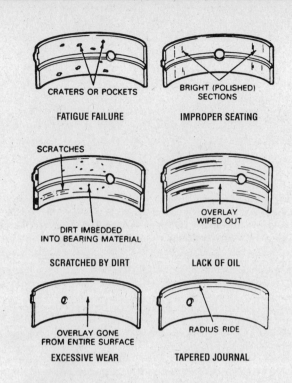

19.1   When inspecting the main and connecting rod bearings, look for these problems

(if available). Be sure to clean the oil holes with a stiff brush and flush them with solvent.

3   Check the main and connecting rod bearing journals for uneven wear, scoring, pits and cracks.

4   Rub a penny across each journal several times. If a journal picks up copper from the penny, it's too rough and must be reground.

5   Check the rest of the crankshaft for cracks and other damage. It should be magnafluxed to reveal hidden cracks - an automotive machine shop will handle the job.

6   Using a micrometer, measure the diameter of the main and connecting rod journals and compare the results to the Specifications **(see illustration)**. By measuring the diameter at a number of points around each journal's circumference, you'll be able to determine whether or not the journal is out-of-round. Take the measurement at each end of the journal, near the crank throws, to determine if the journal is tapered. Crankshaft runout should be checked also, but large V-blocks and a dial indicator are needed to do it correctly. If you don't have the equipment, have a machine shop check the runout.

7   If the crankshaft journals are damaged, tapered, out-of-round or worn beyond the limits given in the Specifications, have the crankshaft reground by an automotive machine shop. Be sure to use the correct size bearing inserts if the crankshaft is reconditioned.

8   Check the oil seal journals at each end of the crankshaft for wear and damage. If the seal has worn a groove in the journal, or if it's nicked or scratched, the new seal may leak when the engine is re-assembled. In some cases, an automotive machine shop may be able to repair the journal by pressing on a thin sleeve. If repair isn't feasible, a new or different crankshaft should be installed.

9   Examine the main and rod bearing inserts (see Section 19).

19   Main and connecting rod bearings - inspection and selection

Inspection

Refer to illustration 19.1

1   Even though the main and connecting rod bearings should be re-

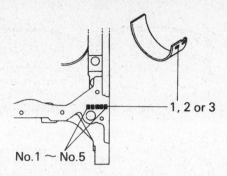

19.10 If the number on the original main bearing is not clear, install a new bearing with a number that matches the number stamped into the block - different journals may require different size bearings (2S-E engine only)

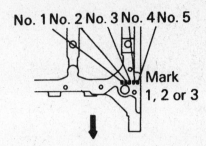

19.11 Main journal grade numbers are stamped into the oil pan mating surface on the block - there are 5 journals, so there are 5 numbers

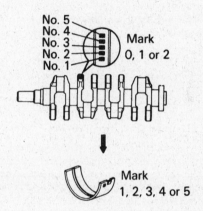

19.12a 3S-FE, 3S-GE, 5S-FE and 4A-FE engine main journal crankshaft grade numbers - most engines have the grade numbers on the edge of one of the crankshaft counter weights, as shown here, but . . .

placed with new ones during the engine overhaul, the old bearings should be retained for close examination, as they may reveal valuable information about the condition of the engine **(see illustration)**.

2 Bearing failure occurs because of lack of lubrication, the presence of dirt or other foreign particles, overloading the engine and corrosion. Regardless of the cause of bearing failure, it must be corrected before the engine is reassembled to prevent it from happening again.

3 When examining the bearings, remove them from the engine block, the main bearing caps, the connecting rods and the rod caps and lay them out on a clean surface in the same general position as their location in the engine. This will enable you to match any bearing problems with the corresponding crankshaft journal.

4 Dirt and other foreign particles get into the engine in a variety of ways. It may be left in the engine during assembly, or it may pass through filters or the PCV system. It may get into the oil, and from there into the bearings. Metal chips from machining operations and normal engine wear are often present. Abrasives are sometimes left in engine components after reconditioning, especially when parts are not thoroughly cleaned using the proper cleaning methods. Whatever the source, these foreign objects often end up embedded in the soft bearing material and are easily recognized. Large particles will not embed in the bearing and will score or gouge the bearing and journal. The best prevention for this cause of bearing failure is to clean all parts thoroughly and keep everything spotlessly clean during engine assembly. Frequent and regular engine oil and filter changes are also recommended.

5 Lack of lubrication (or lubrication breakdown) has a number of interrelated causes. Excessive heat (which thins the oil), overloading (which squeezes the oil from the bearing face) and oil leakage or throw off (from excessive bearing clearances, worn oil pump or high engine speeds) all contribute to lubrication breakdown. Blocked oil passages, which usually are the result of misaligned oil holes in a bearing shell, will also oil starve a bearing and destroy it. When lack of lubrication is the cause of bearing failure, the bearing material is wiped or extruded from the steel backing of the bearing. Temperatures may increase to the point where the steel backing turns blue from overheating.

6 Driving habits can have a definite effect on bearing life. Full throttle, low speed operation (lugging the engine) puts very high loads on bearings, which tends to squeeze out the oil film. These loads cause the bearings to flex, which produces fine cracks in the bearing face (fatigue failure). Eventually the bearing material will loosen in pieces and tear away from the steel backing. Short trip driving leads to corrosion of bearings because insufficient engine heat is produced to drive off the condensed water and corrosive gases. These products collect in the engine oil, forming acid and sludge. As the oil is carried to the engine bearings, the acid attacks and corrodes the bearing material.

7 Incorrect bearing installation during engine assembly will lead to bearing failure as well. Tight fitting bearings leave insufficient bearing oil clearance and will result in oil starvation. Dirt or foreign particles trapped behind a bearing insert result in high spots on the bearing which lead to failure.

Selection

Refer to illustrations 19.10, 19.11, 19.12a, 19.12b, 19.13 and 19.14

8 If the original bearings are worn or damaged, or if the oil clearances are incorrect (see Section 22 or 24), the following procedures should be used to select the correct new bearings for engine reassembly. However, if the crankshaft has been reground, new undersize bearings must be installed - the following procedure should not be used if undersize bearings are required! The automotive machine shop that reconditions the crankshaft will provide or help you select the correct size bearings. Regardless of how the bearing sizes are determined, use the oil clearance, measured with Plastigage, as a guide to ensure the bearings are the right size.

Main bearings

9 If you need to use a STANDARD size main bearing, install one that has the same number as the original bearing (see illustrations 19.10, 19.11 and 19.12 for the bearing number locations).

10 If you're working on a 2S-E engine and the number on the original main bearing has been obscured, install one that has the same number as the number stamped into the block for the corresponding cap location **(see illustration)**.

11 If you're working on any engine except a 2S-E and the number on the original main bearing has been obscured, locate the main journal grade numbers stamped into the oil pan mating surface on the engine block **(see illustration)**.

12 Locate the main journal grade numbers on the crankshaft as well

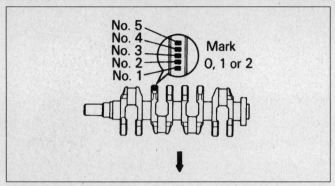

19.12b . . . on some later model engines the grade numbers may be in the locations shown here

	Number marked								
Cylinder block	1			2			3		
Crankshaft	0	1	2	0	1	2	0	1	2
Bearing	1	2	3	2	3	4	3	4	5

EXAMPLE: Cylinder block "2" + Crankshaft "1"
= Bearing "3"

19.13   3S-FE, 3S-GE, 5S-FE and 4A-FE engine main bearing selection chart

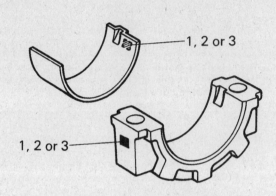

19.14   Connecting rod bearing cap mark location

(see illustrations).

13   Use the accompanying chart to determine the correct bearings for each journal **(see illustration)**.

Connecting rod bearings

14   If you need to use a STANDARD size rod bearing, install one that has the same number as the number stamped into the connecting rod cap **(see illustration)**.

All bearings

15   Remember, the oil clearance is the final judge when selecting new bearing sizes. If you have any questions or are unsure which bearings to use, get help from a Toyota dealer parts or service department.

20   Engine overhaul - reassembly sequence

1   Before beginning engine reassembly, make sure you have all the necessary new parts, gaskets and seals as well as the following items on hand:

  Common hand tools
  A torque wrench
  Piston ring installation tool
  Piston ring compressor
  Short lengths of rubber or plastic hose to fit over connecting rod bolts
  Plastigage
  Feeler gauges
  A fine-tooth file
  New engine oil
  Engine assembly lube or moly-base grease
  Gasket sealant
  Thread locking compound

2   In order to save time and avoid problems, engine reassembly must be done in the following general order:

  Piston rings (Part B)
  Crankshaft and main bearings (Part B)
  Piston/connecting rod assemblies (Part B)
  Rear main (crankshaft) oil seal (Part B)
  Cylinder head and rocker arms or lifters (Part A)
  Camshaft(s) (Part A)
  Oil pump (Part A)
  Oil pick-up (Part A)
  Oil pan (Part A)
  Timing belt and pulleys (Part A)
  Timing belt cover(s) (Part A)
  Valve cover(s) (Part A)
  Intake and exhaust manifolds (Part A)
  Flywheel/driveplate (Part A)

21   Piston rings - installation

Refer to illustrations 21.3, 21.4, 21.9a, 21.9b and 21.12

1   Before installing the new piston rings, the ring end gaps must be checked. It's assumed that the piston ring side clearance has been checked and verified correct (see Section 17).

2   Lay out the piston/connecting rod assemblies and the new ring sets so the ring sets will be matched with the same piston and cylinder during the end gap measurement and engine assembly.

3   Insert the top (number one) ring into the first cylinder and square it up with the cylinder walls by pushing it in with the top of the piston **(see illustration)**. The ring should be near the bottom of the cylinder, at the lower limit of ring travel.

4   To measure the end gap, slip feeler gauges between the ends of the ring until a gauge equal to the gap width is found **(see illustration)**. The feeler gauge should slide between the ring ends with a slight amount of drag. Compare the measurement to the Specifications. If the gap is larger or smaller than specified, double-check to make sure you have the correct rings before proceeding.

5   If the gap is too small, replace the rings - DO NOT file the ends to increase the clearance.

6   Excess end gap isn't critical unless it's greater than 0.040-inch. Again, double-check to make sure you have the correct rings for your engine.

7   Repeat the procedure for each ring that will be installed in the first cylinder and for each ring in the remaining cylinders. Remember to keep rings, pistons and cylinders matched up.

8   Once the ring end gaps have been checked/corrected, the rings can be installed on the pistons.

9   The oil control ring (lowest one on the piston) is usually installed first. It's composed of three separate components. Slip the spacer/expander into the groove **(see illustration)**. If an anti-rotation tang is used, make sure it's inserted into the drilled hole in the ring groove. Next, install the lower side rail. Don't use a piston ring installation tool

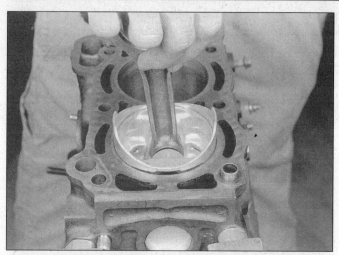

21.3 When checking piston ring end gap, the ring must be square in the cylinder bore (this is done by pushing the ring down with the top of a piston as shown)

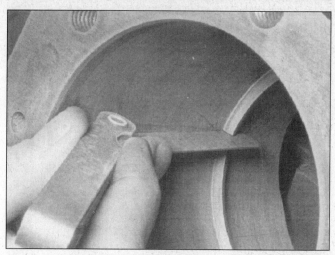

21.4 With the ring square in the cylinder, measure the end gap with a feeler gauge

2B

21.9a Installing the spacer/expander in the oil control ring groove

21.9b DO NOT use a piston ring installation tool when installing the oil ring side rails

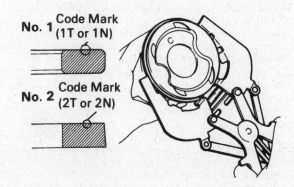

21.12 Install the compression rings with a ring expander - the mark must face up

make sure that both the upper and lower side rails can be turned smoothly in the ring groove.

11   The number two (middle) ring is installed next. It's usually stamped with a mark which must face up, toward the top of the piston. **Note:** *Always follow the instructions printed on the ring package or box - different manufacturers may require different approaches. Do not mix up the top and middle rings, as they have different cross sections.*

12   Use a piston ring installation tool and make sure the identification mark is facing the top of the piston, then slip the ring into the middle groove on the piston **(see illustration)**. Don't expand the ring any more than necessary to slide it over the piston.

13   Install the number one (top) ring in the same manner. Make sure the mark is facing up. Be careful not to confuse the number one and number two rings.

14   Repeat the procedure for the remaining pistons and rings.

---

22   Crankshaft - installation and main bearing oil clearance check

Refer to illustrations 22.10, 22.12, 22.14, 22.19a and 22.19b

1   Crankshaft installation is the first major step in engine reassembly. It's assumed at this point that the engine block and crankshaft have been cleaned, inspected and repaired or reconditioned.

2   Position the engine with the bottom facing up.

on the oil ring side rails, as they may be damaged. Instead, place one end of the side rail into the groove between the spacer/expander and the ring land, hold it firmly in place and slide a finger around the piston while pushing the rail into the groove **(see illustration)**. Next, install the upper side rail in the same manner.

10   After the three oil ring components have been installed, check to

22.10   Lay the Plastigage strips (arrow) on the main bearing journals, parallel to the crankshaft centerline

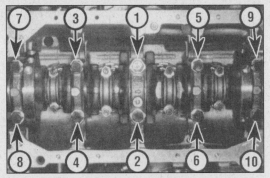

22.12   Main bearing cap bolt tightening sequence

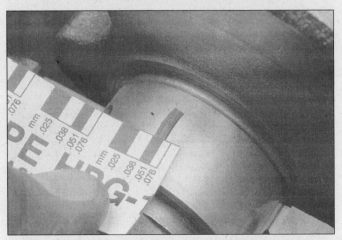

22.14   Compare the width of the crushed Plastigage to the scale on the envelope to determine the main bearing oil clearance (always take the measurement at the widest point of the Plastigage) - be sure to use the correct scale; standard and metric scales are included

3   Remove the main bearing cap bolts and lift out the caps. Lay the caps out in the proper order to ensure correct installation.

4   If they're still in place, remove the old bearing inserts from the block and the main bearing caps. Wipe the main bearing surfaces of the block and caps with a clean, lint-free cloth. They must be kept spotlessly clean!

Main bearing oil clearance check

5   Clean the back sides of the new main bearing inserts and lay the bearing half with the oil groove in each main bearing saddle in the block. Lay the other bearing half from each bearing set in the corresponding main bearing cap. Make sure the tab on each bearing insert fits into the recess in the block or cap. Also, the oil holes in the block must line up with the oil holes in the bearing insert. **Caution:** *Do not hammer the bearings into place and don't nick or gouge the bearing faces. No lubrication should be used at this time.*

6   The thrust bearings (washers) must be installed in the number three (center) cap. The center main bearings on 5S-FE engines are wider than the others. On all engines, the bearings with oil holes go in the block and those without oil holes go in the caps.

7   Clean the faces of the bearings in the block and the crankshaft main bearing journals with a clean, lint-free cloth. Check or clean the oil holes in the crankshaft, as any dirt here can go only one way - straight through the new bearings.

8   Once you're certain the crankshaft is clean, carefully lay it in position in the main bearings.

9   Before the crankshaft can be permanently installed, the main bearing oil clearance must be checked.

10   Trim several pieces of the appropriate size Plastigage (they must be slightly shorter than the width of the main bearings) and place one piece on each crankshaft main bearing journal, parallel with the journal axis **(see illustration)**.

11   Clean the faces of the bearings in the caps and install the caps in their respective positions (don't mix them up) with the arrows pointing toward the front of the engine. Don't disturb the Plastigage. Apply a light coat of oil to the bolt threads and the under sides of bolt heads, then install them.

12   Following the recommended sequence **(see illustration)**, tighten the main bearing cap bolts, in three steps, to the specified torque. Don't rotate the crankshaft at any time during this operation!

13   Remove the bolts and carefully lift off the main bearing caps. Keep them in order. Don't disturb the Plastigage or rotate the crankshaft. If any of the main bearing caps are difficult to remove, tap them gently from side-to-side with a soft-face hammer to loosen them.

14   Compare the width of the crushed Plastigage on each journal to the scale printed on the Plastigage envelope to obtain the main bearing oil clearance **(see illustration)**. Check the Specifications to make sure it's correct.

15   If the clearance is not as specified, the bearing inserts may be the

wrong size which means different ones will be required (see Section 19). Before deciding that different inserts are needed, make sure that no dirt or oil was between the bearing inserts and the caps or block when the clearance was measured. If the Plastigage is noticeably wider at one end than the other, the journal may be tapered (see Section 18).

16   Carefully scrape all traces of the Plastigage material off the main bearing journals and/or the bearing faces. Don't nick or scratch the bearing faces.

Final crankshaft installation

17   Carefully lift the crankshaft out of the engine. Clean the bearing faces in the block, then apply a thin, uniform layer of clean moly-base grease or engine assembly lube to each of the bearing surfaces. Coat the thrust washers as well.

18   Lubricate the crankshaft surfaces that contact the oil seals with moly-base grease, engine assembly lube or clean engine oil.

19   Make sure the crankshaft journals are clean, then lay the crankshaft back in place in the block. Clean the faces of the bearings in the caps or cap assembly, then apply lubricant to them. Install the caps in their respective positions with the arrows pointing toward the front of the engine. **Note:** *Be sure to install the thrust washers* **(see illustrations)**.

20   Apply a light coat of oil to the bolt threads and the under sides of the bolt heads, then install them. Tighten all except the center (number three) cap bolts (the one with the thrust washers) to the specified torque (work from the center out and approach the final torque in three steps). Tighten the center cap bolts to 10-to-12 ft-lbs. Tap the ends of the crankshaft forward and backward with a lead or brass hammer to line up the thrust washer and crankshaft surfaces. Retighten all main

22.19a Rotate the thrust washer into position on the number three crankshaft journal with the oil grooves facing OUT

23.3 After removing the retainer from the block, support it on a couple of wood blocks and drive out the old seal with a punch or screwdriver and hammer

bearing cap bolts to the specified torque, following the recommended sequence.

21   Rotate the crankshaft a number of times by hand to check for any obvious binding.

22   Check the crankshaft endplay with a feeler gauge or a dial indicator (see Section 13). The endplay should be correct if the crankshaft thrust faces aren't worn or damaged and new thrust washers have been installed.

23   Install a new rear main oil seal, then bolt the retainer to the block (see Section 23).

23   Rear main oil seal installation

Refer to illustration 23.3

1   The crankshaft must be installed first and the main bearing caps bolted in place, then the new seal should be installed in the retainer and the retainer bolted to the block.

2   Check the seal contact surface on the crankshaft very carefully for scratches and nicks that could damage the new seal lip and cause oil leaks. If the crankshaft is damaged, the only alternative is a new or different crankshaft.

3   The old seal can be removed from the retainer by driving it out from the back side with a hammer and punch **(see illustration)**. Be sure to note how far it's recessed into the bore before removing it; the new seal will have to be recessed an equal amount. Be very careful not to scratch or otherwise damage the bore in the retainer or oil leaks could develop.

4   Make sure the retainer is clean, then apply a thin coat of engine oil to the outer edge of the new seal. The seal must be pressed squarely into the bore, so hammering it into place isn't recommended.

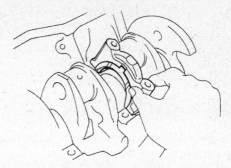

22.19b Install the thrust washer in the number three cap with the oil grooves facing OUT

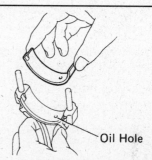

Oil Hole

24.3 Align the oil hole in the bearing with the oil hole in the rod

If you don't have access to a press, sandwich the housing and seal between two smooth pieces of wood and press the seal into place with the jaws of a large vise. The pieces of wood must be thick enough to distribute the force evenly around the entire circumference of the seal. Work slowly and make sure the seal enters the bore squarely.

5   As a last resort, the seal can be tapped into the retainer with a hammer. Use a block of wood to distribute the force evenly and make sure the seal is driven in squarely **(see illustration 17.6 in Part A)**.

6   The seal lips must be lubricated with clean engine oil or moly-based grease before the seal/retainer is slipped over the crankshaft and bolted to the block. Use a new gasket - and sealant - and make sure the dowel pins are in place before installing the retainer.

7   Tighten the bolts a little at a time until they're all at the torque specified in Part A.

24   Pistons/connecting rods - installation and rod bearing oil clearance check

Refer to illustrations 24.3, 24.5, 24.9a, 24.9b, 24.11, 24.13, 24.14 and 24.17

1   Before installing the piston/connecting rod assemblies, the cylinder walls must be perfectly clean, the top edge of each cylinder must be chamfered, and the crankshaft must be in place.

2   Remove the cap from the end of the number one connecting rod (refer to the marks made during removal). Remove the original bearing inserts and wipe the bearing surfaces of the connecting rod and cap with a clean, lint-free cloth. They must be kept spotlessly clean.

Connecting rod bearing oil clearance check

3   Clean the back side of the new upper bearing insert, then lay it in place in the connecting rod. Make sure the tab on the bearing fits into the recess in the rod so the oil holes line up **(see illustration)**. Don't hammer the bearing insert into place and be very careful not to nick or gouge the bearing face. Don't lubricate the bearing at this time.

4   Clean the back side of the other bearing insert and install it in the rod cap. Again, make sure the tab on the bearing fits into the recess in

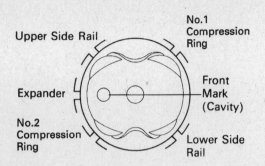

24.5 Stagger the ring end gaps around the piston, as shown, before installing the pistons

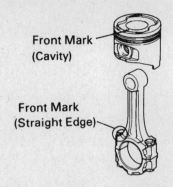

24.9a Check to be sure both the mark on the piston and the mark on the connecting rod are aligned as shown (2S-E engine)

the cap, and don't apply any lubricant. It's critically important that the mating surfaces of the bearing and connecting rod are perfectly clean and oil free when they're assembled.

5   Position the piston ring gaps at staggered intervals around the piston **(see illustration)**.

6   Slip a section of plastic or rubber hose over each connecting rod cap bolt.

7   Lubricate the piston and rings with clean engine oil and attach a piston ring compressor to the piston. Leave the skirt protruding about 1/4-inch to guide the piston into the cylinder. The rings must be compressed until they're flush with the piston.

8   Rotate the crankshaft until the number one connecting rod journal is at BDC (bottom dead center) and apply a coat of engine oil to the cylinder walls.

9   With the dimple on top of the piston **(see illustrations)** facing the front (timing belt end) of the engine, gently insert the piston/connecting rod assembly into the number one cylinder bore and rest the bottom edge of the ring compressor on the engine block.

10   Tap the top edge of the ring compressor to make sure it's contacting the block around its entire circumference.

11   Gently tap on the top of the piston with the end of a wooden hammer handle **(see illustration)** while guiding the end of the connecting rod into place on the crankshaft journal. The piston rings may try to pop out of the ring compressor just before entering the cylinder bore, so keep some pressure on the ring compressor. Work slowly, and if any resistance is felt as the piston enters the cylinder, stop immediately. Find out what's hanging up and fix it before proceeding. Do not, for any reason, force the piston into the cylinder - you might break a ring and/or the piston.

12   Once the piston/connecting rod assembly is installed, the connecting rod bearing oil clearance must be checked before the rod cap is permanently bolted in place.

13   Cut a piece of the appropriate size Plastigage slightly shorter than the width of the connecting rod bearing and lay it in place on the number one connecting rod journal, parallel with the journal axis **(see illustration)**.

14   Clean the connecting rod cap bearing face, remove the protective hoses from the connecting rod bolts and install the rod cap. Make sure the mating mark on the cap is on the same side as the mark on the connecting rod. Check the cap to make sure the front mark is facing the timing belt end of the engine **(see illustration)**.

15   Apply a light coat of oil to the under sides of the nuts, then install and tighten them to the specified torque, working up to it in three steps. Use a thin-wall socket to avoid erroneous torque readings that can result if the socket is wedged between the rod cap and nut. If the socket tends to wedge itself between the nut and the cap, lift up on it slightly until it no longer contacts the cap. Do not rotate the crankshaft at any time during this operation.

16   Remove the nuts and detach the rod cap, being very careful not to disturb the Plastigage.

17   Compare the width of the crushed Plastigage to the scale printed on the Plastigage envelope to obtain the oil clearance **(see illustra-**

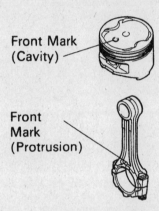

24.9b On 3S-FE, 3S-GE, 5S-FE and 4A-FE engines, both the mark on the piston and the mark on the connecting rod should face the timing belt end of the engine

24.11 The piston can be driven gently into the cylinder bore with the end of a wooden or plastic hammer handle

tion). Compare it to the Specifications to make sure the clearance is correct.

18   If the clearance is not as specified, the bearing inserts may be the wrong size (which means different ones will be required). Before deciding that different inserts are needed, make sure that no dirt or oil was between the bearing inserts and the connecting rod or cap when

24.13   Lay the Plastigage strips on each rod bearing journal, parallel to the crankshaft centerline

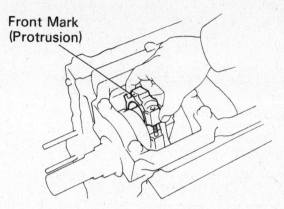

Front Mark (Protrusion)

24.14   Install the connecting rod caps with the front mark facing the timing belt end of the engine

24.17   Measure the width of the crushed Plastigage to determine the rod bearing oil clearance (be sure to use the correct scale - standard and metric scales are included)

2B

the clearance was measured. Also, recheck the journal diameter. If the Plastigage was wider at one end than the other, the journal may be tapered (see Section 18).

Final connecting rod installation

19   Carefully scrape all traces of the Plastigage material off the rod journal and/or bearing face. Be very careful not to scratch the bearing - use your fingernail or the edge of a credit card.

20   Make sure the bearing faces are perfectly clean, then apply a uniform layer of clean moly-base grease or engine assembly lube to both of them. You'll have to push the piston into the cylinder to expose the face of the bearing insert in the connecting rod - be sure to slip the protective hoses over the rod bolts first.

21   Slide the connecting rod back into place on the journal, remove the protective hoses from the rod cap bolts, install the rod cap and tighten the nuts to the specified torque. Again, work up to the torque in three steps.

22   Repeat the entire procedure for the remaining pistons/connecting rods.

23   The important points to remember are:
   a)   Keep the back sides of the bearing inserts and the insides of

the connecting rods and caps perfectly clean when assembling them.
   b)   Make sure you have the correct piston/rod assembly for each cylinder.
   c)   The dimple on the piston must face the front (timing belt end) of the engine.
   d)   Lubricate the cylinder walls with clean oil.
   e)   Lubricate the bearing faces when installing the rod caps after the oil clearance has been checked.

24   After all the piston/connecting rod assemblies have been properly installed, rotate the crankshaft a number of times by hand to check for any obvious binding.

25   As a final step, the connecting rod endplay must be checked (see Section 12).

26   Compare the measured endplay to the Specifications to make sure it's correct. If it was correct before disassembly and the original crankshaft and rods were reinstalled, it should still be right. If new rods or a new crankshaft were installed, the endplay may be inadequate. If so, the rods will have to be removed and taken to an automotive machine shop for resizing.

25   Initial start-up and break-in after overhaul

Warning: *Have a fire extinguisher handy when starting the engine for the first time.*

1   Once the engine has been installed in the vehicle, double-check the engine oil and coolant levels.

2   With the spark plugs out of the engine and the ignition system disabled (see Section 3), crank the engine until oil pressure registers on the gauge or the light goes out.

3   Install the spark plugs, hook up the plug wires and restore the ignition system functions (see Section 3).

4   Start the engine. It may take a few moments for the fuel system to build up pressure, but the engine should start without a great deal of effort.

5   After the engine starts, it should be allowed to warm up to normal operating temperature. While the engine is warming up, make a thorough check for fuel, oil and coolant leaks.

6   Shut the engine off and recheck the engine oil and coolant levels.

7   Drive the vehicle to an area with minimum traffic, accelerate at full throttle from 30 to 50 mph, then allow the vehicle to slow to 30 mph with the throttle closed. Repeat the procedure 10 or 12 times. This will load the piston rings and cause them to seat properly against the cylinder walls. Check again for oil and coolant leaks.

8   Drive the vehicle gently for the first 500 miles (no sustained high speeds) and keep a constant check on the oil level. It is not unusual for

an engine to use oil during the break-in period.

9   At approximately 500 to 600 miles, change the oil and filter.

10   For the next few hundred miles, drive the vehicle normally. Do not pamper it or abuse it.

11   After 2000 miles, change the oil and filter again and consider the engine broken in.

Chapter 3 Cooling, heating and air conditioning systems

Contents

3

Specifications

General

Radiator cap pressure rating	13 psi
Thermostat rating (opening temperature)	180 degrees F
Cooling system capacity	See Chapter 1
Refrigerant capacity	1.3 to 1.9 lbs

Torque specifications

Ft-lbs (unless otherwise indicated)

Thermostat housing nuts	80 In-lbs
Water pump-to-engine block bolts	
4A-FE	11
All others	80 in-lbs
Water pump-to-inlet pipe nuts	80 In-lbs
Water pump-to-inlet pipe nuts (4A-FE)	14

1   General information

Engine cooling system

All vehicles covered by this manual employ a pressurized engine cooling system with thermostatically controlled coolant circulation. An impeller type water pump mounted on the drivebelt end of the block pumps coolant through the engine. The coolant flows around each cylinder and toward the transaxle end of the engine. Cast-in coolant passages direct coolant around the intake and exhaust ports, near the spark plug areas and in close proximity to the exhaust valve guides.

A wax pellet type thermostat is located in a housing near the drivebelt end of the engine. During warm up, the closed thermostat prevents coolant from circulating through the radiator. As the engine nears normal operating temperature, the thermostat opens and allows hot coolant to travel through the radiator, where it's cooled before returning to the engine.

The cooling system is sealed by a pressure type radiator cap, which raises the boiling point of the coolant and increases the cooling efficiency of the radiator. If the system pressure exceeds the cap pressure relief value, the excess pressure in the system forces the spring-loaded valve inside the cap off its seat and allows the coolant to escape through the overflow tube into a coolant reservoir. When the system cools, the excess coolant is automatically drawn from the reservoir back into the radiator.

The coolant reservoir does double duty as both the point at which fresh coolant is added to the cooling system to maintain the proper fluid level and as a holding tank for overheated coolant.

This type of cooling system is known as a closed design because coolant that escapes past the pressure cap is saved and reused.

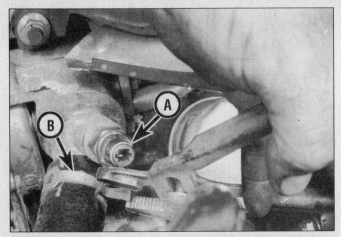

3.8   Disconnect the cooling fan switch (A) and squeeze the hose clamp (B) flanges together to remove the radiator hose

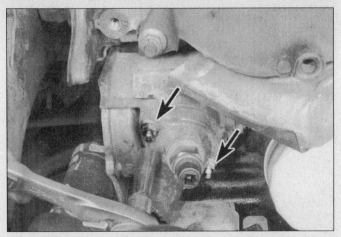

3.10a   Remove the retaining nuts from the housing cover (arrows)

Heating system

The heating system consists of a blower fan and heater core located in the heater box, the hoses connecting the heater core to the engine cooling system and the heater/air conditioning control head on the dashboard. Hot engine coolant is circulated through the heater core. When the heater mode is activated, a flap door opens to expose the heater box to the passenger compartment. A fan switch on the control head activates the blower motor, which forces air through the core, heating the air.

Air conditioning system

The air conditioning system consists of a condenser mounted in front of the radiator, an evaporator mounted adjacent to the heater core, a compressor mounted on the engine, a filter-drier which contains a high pressure relief valve and the plumbing connecting all of the above components.

A blower fan forces the warmer air of the passenger compartment through the evaporator core (sort of a radiator-in-reverse), transferring the heat from the air to the refrigerant. The liquid refrigerant boils off into low pressure vapor, taking the heat with it when it leaves the evaporator.

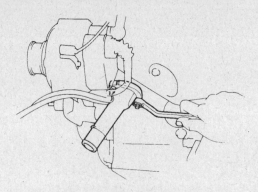

3.10b   On 5S-FE engines the retaining nuts (arrows) are slightly more difficult to reach

auto parts stores to test the coolant. Use antifreeze which meets the vehicle manufacturer's specifications.

2   Antifreeze - general information

Warning: *Do not allow antifreeze to come in contact with your skin or painted surfaces of the vehicle. Rinse off spills immediately with plenty of water. Antifreeze is highly toxic if ingested. Never leave antifreeze lying around in an open container or in puddles on the floor; children and pets are attracted by it's sweet smell and may drink it. Check with local authorities about disposing of used antifreeze. Many communities have collection centers which will see that antifreeze is disposed of safely.*

The cooling system should be filled with a water/ethylene glycol based antifreeze solution, which will prevent freezing down to at least - 20-degrees F, or lower if local climate requires it. It also provides protection against corrosion and increases the coolant boiling point.

The cooling system should be drained, flushed and refilled at the specified intervals (see Chapter 1). Old or contaminated antifreeze solutions are likely to cause damage and encourage the formation of corrosion and scale in the system. Use distilled water with the antifreeze.

Before adding antifreeze, check all hose connections, because antifreeze tends to leak through very minute openings. Engines don't normally consume coolant, so if the level goes down, find the cause and correct it.

The exact mixture of antifreeze-to-water which you should use depends on the relative weather conditions. The mixture should contain at least 50 percent antifreeze, but should never contain more than 70 percent antifreeze. Consult the mixture ratio chart on the antifreeze container before adding coolant. Hydrometers are available at most

3   Thermostat - check and replacement

Warning: *Do not remove the radiator cap, drain the coolant or replace the thermostat until the engine has cooled completely. Do not allow antifreeze to come in contact with your skin or painted surfaces of the vehicle. Rinse off spills immediately with plenty of water. Antifreeze is highly toxic if ingested. Never leave antifreeze lying around in an open container or in puddles on the floor; children and pets are attracted by it's sweet smell and may drink it. Check with local authorities about disposing of used antifreeze. Many communities have collection centers which will see that antifreeze is disposed of safely.*

Check

1   Before assuming the thermostat is to blame for a cooling system problem, check the coolant level, drivebelt tension (see Chapter 1) and temperature gauge operation.

2   If the engine seems to be taking a long time to warm up (based on heater output or temperature gauge operation), the thermostat is probably stuck open. Replace the thermostat with a new one.

3   If the engine runs hot, use your hand to check the temperature of the lower radiator hose. If the hose isn't hot, but the engine is, the thermostat is probably stuck closed, preventing the coolant inside the engine from escaping to the radiator. Replace the thermostat. **Caution:** *Don't drive the vehicle without a thermostat. The computer may stay in open loop causing emissions and fuel economy to suffer.*

4   If the lower radiator hose is hot, it means that the coolant is flowing and the thermostat is open. Consult the *Troubleshooting* section at the front of this manual for cooling system diagnosis.

3.11   Note the position of the air bleed valve (arrow) and how the thermostat is installed

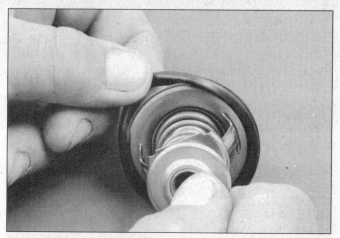

3.12   The thermostat gasket fits over the edge of the thermostat

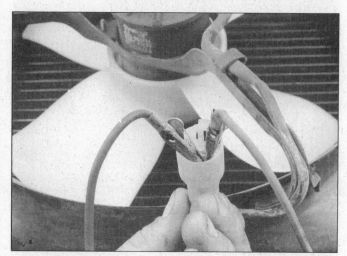

4.3   Disconnect the fan wiring plug and run jumper wires directly to the positive and negative terminals of the battery

Replacement

Refer to illustrations 3.8, 3.10a, 3.10b, 3.11 and 3.12

5   Disconnect the negative battery cable from the battery. **Caution:** *If the stereo in your vehicle is equipped with an anti-theft system, refer to the information on page 0-15 at the front of this manual before detaching the cable.*

6   Drain the cooling system (see Chapter 1). If the coolant is relatively new or in good condition, save it and reuse it.

7   Follow the lower radiator hose to the engine to locate the thermostat housing.

8   . If so equipped, disconnect the cooling fan switch, loosen the hose clamp and detach the hose from the fitting **(see illustration)**. If the hose is stuck, grasp it near the end with a pair of adjustable pliers and twist it to break the seal, then pull it off. If the hose is old or deteriorated, cut it off and install a new one.

9   If the outer surface of the large fitting that mates with the hose is deteriorated (corroded, pitted, etc.) it may be damaged further by hose removal. If it is, the thermostat housing cover will have to be replaced.

10   Remove the bolts/nuts and detach the housing cover **(see illustrations)**. If the cover is stuck, tap it with a soft-face hammer to jar it loose. Be prepared for some coolant to spill as the gasket seal is broken.

11   Note the position of the air bleed valve and how the thermostat is installed (which end is facing up), then remove the thermostat and all traces of old gasket material and sealant from the housing and cover with a gasket scraper. Some engines may not have a housing-to-cover gasket **(see illustration)**.

12   If so equipped, fit a new gasket over the thermostat **(see illustration)**. If a cover-to-housing gasket was removed apply a thin, uniform layer of RTV sealant to both sides of the new gasket and position it on the housing.

13   Install the new thermostat in the housing. Make sure the air bleed faces up and the spring end is directed into the engine **(see illustration 3.11)**.

14   Install the cover and bolts. Tighten the bolts to the torque listed in this Chapter's Specifications.

15   Reattach the hose to the fitting and tighten the hose clamp securely. Reconnect the electrical connector for the cooling fan switch.

16   Refill the cooling system (see Chapter 1).

17   Start the engine and allow it to reach normal operating temperature, then check for leaks and proper thermostat operation (as described in Steps 2 through 4).

---

4   Engine cooling fan(s) - check and replacement

Refer to illustrations 4.3, 4.13a, 4.13b, 4.14, 4.15, 4.19, 4.20 and 4.21

Check

1   The engine cooling fan is controlled by a temperature switch which is mounted (except on 5S-FE engines) on the thermostat cover. On 5S-FE engines the switch is located on the radiator **(see illustration 5.4)**. When the coolant reaches a predetermined temperature, the switch opens the ground return for the fan motor relay, completing the circuit.

2   First, check the fuses (see Chapter 12).

3   To test the fan motor, unplug the electrical connector and use fused jumper wires **(see illustration)** to connect the fan directly to the battery. If the fan still does not work, replace the motor.

4   If the motor tested okay, the fault lies in the coolant temperature switch, the relay or the wiring harness (see Chapter 12).

5   Test the temperature switch by unplugging the connector and with the ignition switch on, ground the connector.

6   If the fan does not operate, check the relay or the wiring (see Chapter 12).

Replacement

Main cooling fan

7   Disconnect the negative battery cable from the battery. **Caution:** *If the stereo in your vehicle is equipped with an anti-theft system, refer to the information on page 0-15 at the front of this manual before detaching the cable.*

8   Raise the front of the vehicle and support it securely on jackstands. Remove the left splash pan.

9   Drain the engine coolant (see Chapter 1).

10   If necessary for access remove the engine relay box.

11   On late model vehicles remove the coolant reservoir **(see Section 6)**.

3

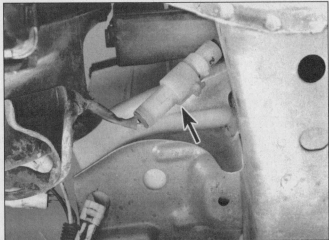

4.13a   Disconnect the electrical connector (arrow) . . .

4.13b   . . . and the fan shroud retention bolts (arrows)

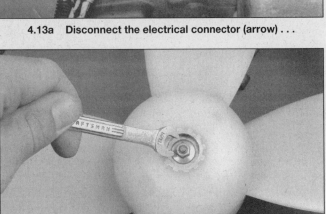

4.14   To replace the fan motor unbolt the fan blade nut . . .

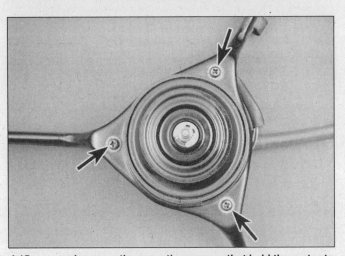

4.15   . . . and remove the mounting screws that hold the motor to the fan bracket (arrows)

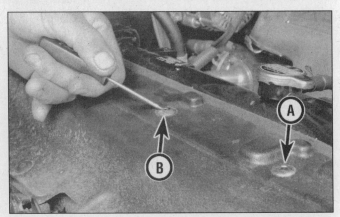

4.19   Remove the plastic pop-rivets by pushing their centers in (A) and then gently prying the rivet out (B) - if this done carefully they can be reused

4.20   Remove the lower retention nut (arrow)

12   Remove the coolant reservoir hose and the upper radiator hose from the radiator (see illustration 5.5).
13   Unplug the cooling fan connector, then unbolt the fan shroud (see illustrations). Be sure to remove the lower shroud bolt.
14   Remove the nut and detach the fan blade assembly from the motor shaft (see illustration).
15   Take out the screws holding the fan motor to the bracket and detach the motor (see illustration).
16   Installation is the reverse of removal. Check the coolant level and the top radiator hose after reassembly - top up the cooling system as necessary (see Chapter 1).

Auxiliary fan - replacement

17   Air conditioned vehicles have an additional fan located in front of the condenser.
18   Disconnect the negative battery cable from the battery. I
19   If so equipped remove the radiator shroud (see illustration).
20   Remove the nut from the lower fan bracket (see illustration).
21   Disconnect the electrical connector, remove the horn if necessary

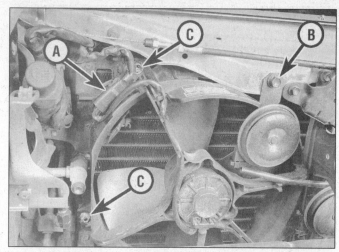

4.21   Disconnect the fan connector (A) and remove the horn (B) if necessary for access. Remove the fan cowl retention bolts (C) and pull the fan free

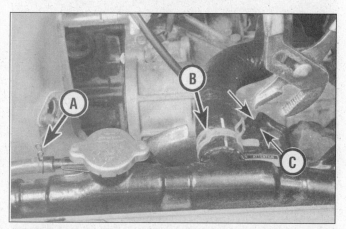

5.5   Remove the coolant reservoir hose (A) and radiator hose (B) by squeezing the clamp protrusions together as illustrated (C)

for access and the remaining top and side fan retention bolts (see illustration). Pull the fan free and follow steps 14 and 15 for the motor removal procedure.
22   Installation is the reverse of the removal procedure.

5   Radiator - removal and installation

Refer to illustrations 5.4, 5.5, 5.8, 5.9, 5.10, 5.11 and 5.14
Warning: *Do not start this procedure until the engine is completely cool. Do not allow antifreeze to come in contact with your skin or painted surfaces of the vehicle. Rinse off spills immediately with plenty of water. Antifreeze is highly toxic if ingested. Never leave antifreeze lying around in an open container or in puddles on the floor; children and pets are attracted by it's sweet smell and may drink it. Check with local authorities about disposing of used antifreeze. Many communities have collection centers which will see that antifreeze is disposed of safely.*

Removal

1   Disconnect the negative battery cable from the battery. **Caution:** *If the stereo in your vehicle is equipped with an anti-theft system, refer to the information on page 0-15 at the front of this manual before detaching the cable.*
2   Raise the front of the vehicle and support it securely on jackstands. Remove the lower splash pans.
3   Drain the cooling system (see Chapter 1). If the coolant is rela-

5.4   On 5S-FE engines disconnect the coolant temperature switch (arrow)

5.8   Disconnect the cooling fan connector (arrow) - late model shown (others similar but may be located under the cooling fan motor, see illustration 4.3)

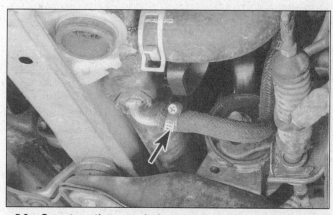

5.9   On automatic transmission models disconnect the cooler lines (arrow), have a drain pan ready to catch spilt fluid

tively new or in good condition, save it and reuse it.
4   On 5S-FE models disconnect the coolant temperature switch connector from the radiator **(see illustration)**.
5   Disconnect the coolant reservoir hose from the radiator and loosen the upper and lower hose clamps, then detach the radiator hoses from the fittings **(see illustration)**. If they're stuck, grasp each hose near the end with a pair of adjustable pliers and twist it to break the seal, then pull it off - be careful not to damage the radiator fittings! If the hoses are old or deteriorated, cut them off and install new ones.
6   Remove the engine relay box and on vehicles with ABS disconnect the ABS relay box from the radiator.
7   Remove the upper radiator cowl **(see illustration 4.19)**.
8   Disconnect the cooling fan connector **(see illustration)**.
9   If the vehicle is equipped with an automatic transaxle, disconnect the cooler lines **(see illustration)** and plug the lines and fittings.

3

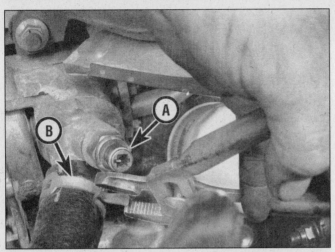

5.10   Remove the radiator mounting bolts (arrow)

5.11   Carefully lift the radiator free, avoid scratching or spilling coolant on the vehicles paint work

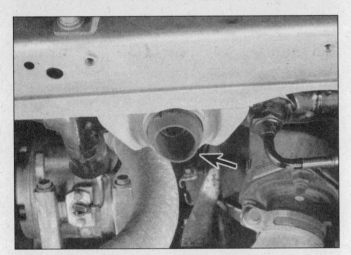

5.14   Ensure that the rubber mountings are securely in place during radiator installation (viewed from below)

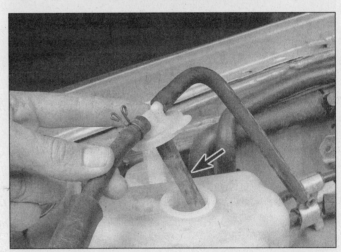

6.1   Remove the coolant reservoir cap and pull the overflow hose from the reservoir (arrow)

10   Remove the radiator mounting bolts (see illustration).
11   Carefully lift out the radiator. Don't spill coolant on the vehicle or scratch the paint (see illustration). Remove the bolts securing the cooling fan to the radiator and pull it free.
12   With the radiator removed, it can be inspected for leaks and damage. If it needs repair, have a radiator shop or dealer service department perform the work as special techniques are required.
13   Bugs and dirt can be removed from the radiator with a garden hose or a soft brush. Don't bend the cooling fins as this is done.

Installation

14   Installation is the reverse of the removal procedure. Be sure the rubber cushions are seated properly at the base of the radiator (see illustration).
15   After installation, fill the cooling system with the proper mixture of antifreeze and water (see Section 2 and Chapter 1).
16   Start the engine and check for leaks. Allow the engine to reach normal operating temperature, indicated by the upper radiator hose becoming hot. Recheck the coolant level and add more if required.
17   If you're working on an automatic transaxle equipped vehicle, check and add fluid as needed (see Chapter 1).

---

6   Coolant reservoir - removal and installation

Refer to illustrations 6.1, 6.5, 6.7a and 6.7b
Warning: *Do not start this procedure until the engine is completely*

cool. Do not allow antifreeze to come in contact with your skin or painted surfaces of the vehicle. Rinse off spills immediately with plenty of water. Antifreeze is highly toxic if ingested. Never leave antifreeze lying around in an open container or in puddles on the floor; children and pets are attracted by it's sweet smell and may drink it. Check with local authorities about disposing of used antifreeze. Many communities have collection centers which will see that antifreeze is disposed of safely.

Early models

1   Lift the cap off the coolant reservoir and withdraw the overflow hose (see illustration).
2   Lift the coolant reservoir straight up to remove it.
3   Pour the coolant into a container. Wash out and inspect the reservoir for cracks and chafing. Replace if damaged.
4   Installation is the reverse of removal.

Late models

5   Remove the battery hold-down bolt and move the bracket aside if necessary for access (see illustration).
6   Lift the cap off the coolant reservoir and withdraw the overflow hose.
7   Some reservoirs lift straight out while others are held in place by bolts which have to be removed before the reservoir can be pulled free (see illustrations).
8   Pour the coolant into a container. Wash out and inspect the reservoir for cracks and chafing. Replace if damaged.
9   Installation is the reverse of removal.

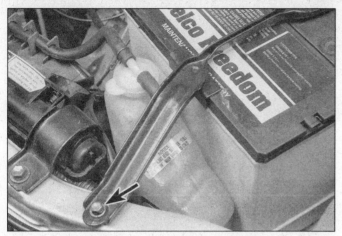

6.5   Remove the battery hold-down bracket (arrow) for access

6.7a   Some late model reservoirs lift off their brackets . . .

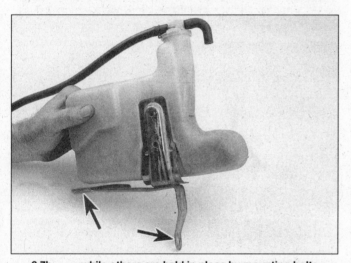

6.7b   . . . while others are held in place by mounting bolts
(reservoir removed to show bolt locations - arrows)

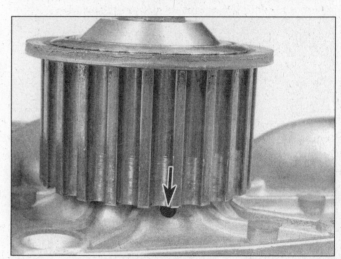

7.4a   If water is leaking from the weep hole (arrow) the water
pump must be replaced

7.4b   Even with the timing belt removed the weep hole is difficult
to see - look for coolant stains on the surface below it (arrow)

7.5   If there is play in the shaft, replace the water pump

7   Water pump - check

Refer to illustrations 7.4a, 7.4b and 7.5

1   A failure in the water pump can cause serious engine damage
due to overheating.

2   There are three ways to check the operation of the water pump
while it's installed on the engine. If the pump is defective, it should be
replaced with a new or rebuilt unit.

3   With the engine running at normal operating temperature,
squeeze the upper radiator hose. If the water pump is working properly, a pressure surge should be felt as the hose is released. **Warning:**
Keep your hands away from the fan blades!

4   Remove the timing belt cover(s) (see Chapter 2A). Water pumps
are equipped with weep or vent holes. If a failure occurs in the pump
seal, coolant will leak from the hole. In most cases you'll need a flashlight to find the hole on the water pump from underneath to check for
leaks **(see illustrations)**.

5   If the water pump shaft bearings fail there may be a howling
sound at the drivebelt end of the engine while it's running. Shaft wear
can be felt if the water pump pulley is rocked up and down **(see illus-**

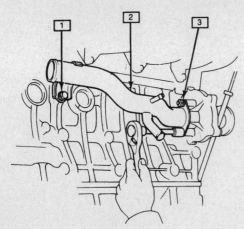

8.5 Disconnect the coolant inlet pipe hoses and its mounting bolt and nuts

1 Mounting bolt *3 Mounting nuts*
2 Coolant inlet pipe

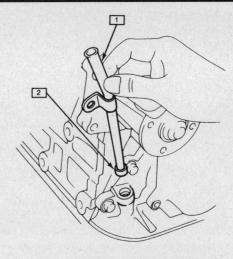

8.6 Unbolt the dipstick and pull it out

1 Oil dipstick tube *2 O-ring*

8.7 Remove the mounting bolts (arrows) and detach the water pump

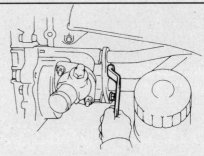

8.20 Although it is not necessary to remove the coolant by-pass pipe to replace the water pump, check it for leaks. If it is leaking remove the two mounting nuts (arrows) and replace the O-ring and gasket

tration). Don't mistake drivebelt slippage, which causes a squealing sound, for water pump bearing failure.

8 Water pump - removal and installation

Warning: *Wait until the engine is completely cool before beginning this procedure. Do not allow antifreeze to come in contact with your skin or painted surfaces of the vehicle. Rinse off spills immediately with plenty of water. Antifreeze is highly toxic if ingested. Never leave antifreeze lying around in an open container or in puddles on the floor; children and pets are attracted by it's sweet smell and may drink it. Check with local authorities about disposing of used antifreeze. Many communities have collection centers which will see that antifreeze is disposed of safely.*

4A-FE engine
Refer to illustrations 8.5, 8.6 and 8.7
Warning: *On all 1990 and later models wait at least 30 seconds after the ignition has been turned off and the battery disconnected before starting work on the water pump or related components.*

1 Disconnect the negative battery cable from the battery. **Caution:** *If the stereo in your vehicle is equipped with an anti-theft system, refer to the information on page 0-15 at the front of this manual detaching the cable.*
2 Drain the cooling system (see Chapter 1). If the coolant is relatively new or in good condition, save it and reuse it.
3 Remove the timing belt covers (see Chapter 2A).
4 Remove the power steering pump adjustment bracket (if equipped) and move the pump aside.
5 Detach the coolant hoses from the coolant inlet pipe and unbolt the pipe **(see illustration)**.

6 Pull the oil dipstick clear of its tube and remove the mounting bolt for the dipstick tube and pull the tube out **(see illustration)**. Plug the hole to prevent dirt or coolant from getting in the oil.
7 Remove the water pump mounting bolts **(see illustration)** and detach the water pump from the engine. If the water pump is stuck gently tap it with a soft faced hammer to break the seal. Note the locations of the various brackets and lengths and different diameters of bolts as they're removed to ensure correct installation.
8 Clean the bolt threads and the threaded holes in the engine to remove corrosion and sealant.
9 Compare the new pump to the old one to make sure they're identical.
10 Remove all traces of old O-rings and gasket material from the sealing surfaces.
11 Install new O-rings on the dipstick tube, in the engine block and behind the water pump. Use a dab of RTV sealant to hold the pump O-rings in place. Wet the dipstick O-ring with engine oil.
12 Carefully mate the pump to the engine. Slip a couple of bolts through the pump mounting holes to hold the O-rings in place.
13 Install the remaining bolts. Tighten them to the torque listed in this Chapter's specifications in 1/4-turn increments. Don't overtighten them or the pump may be damaged.
14 Reinstall all parts removed for access to the pump.
15 Refill the cooling system (see Chapter 1) and check the timing belt tension (see Chapter 2A). Run the engine and check for leaks.

2S-E, 3S-FE, 3S-GE and 5S-FE engines
Refer to illustrations 8.20, 8.21a, 8.21b and 8.23
Warning: *On all 1990 and later models wait at least 30 seconds after the ignition has been turned off and the battery disconnected before*

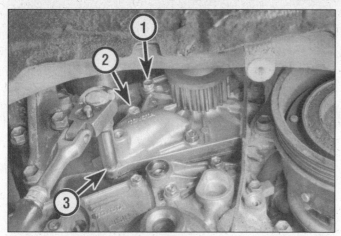

8.21a   Remove the first three water pump mounting bolts in the order shown (arrows) . . .

8.21b   . . . before removing the other mounting bolts (arrows)

8.23   3S-GE water pumps have an recessed mounting hole (arrow) - all pumps look identical in every other respect and although it will fit all other engines the sprocket has fewer teeth

9.3a   On 5S-FE engines the coolant temperature sending unit is located in front of the distributor (arrow - all coolant sending units have only one wire going to them) . . .

starting work on the water pump or related components.

16   Disconnect the negative battery cable from the battery. **Caution:** *If the stereo in your vehicle is equipped with an anti-theft system, refer to the information on page 0-15 at the front of this manual before detaching the cable.*

17   Drain the cooling system (see Chapter 1). If the coolant is relatively new or in good condition, save it and reuse it.

18   Remove the timing belt and pulleys (see Chapter 2A)

19   On all models except 3S-GE engines remove the alternator adjusting bar. Remove the number one alternator and idler pulley brackets on 3S-GE engines.

20   Check the water pump by-pass pipe(s) for leaks. It is not necessary to remove the by-pass pipe(s) for water pump replacement but if it is leaking unbolt the two nuts securing it to the water pump and install a new gasket and O-ring **(see illustration)**.

21   Remove the three bolts on the left of the water pump following the sequence shown and then the remaining bolts **(see illustrations)**. Remove the water pump, if it is stuck gently tap it with a soft faced hammer to break the seal.

22   Clean the bolt threads and the threaded holes in the engine to remove corrosion and sealant.

23   Compare the new pump to the old one to make sure they're identical, if working on a 3S-GE engine ensure that the upper right bolt hole is recessed **(see illustration)**.

24   Remove all traces of old O-rings and gasket material from the sealing surfaces.

25   Install new O-rings, use a dab of RTV sealant to hold the pump O-rings in place.

26   Carefully mate the pump to the engine. Slip a couple of bolts

through the pump mounting holes to hold the O-rings in place.

27   Install the remaining bolts. Tighten them to the torque listed in this Chapter's specifications in 1/4-turn increments. Don't overtighten them or the pump may be damaged.

28   Reinstall all parts removed for access to the pump.

29   Refill the cooling system (see Chapter 1) and check the timing belt tension (see Chapter 2A). Run the engine and check for leaks.

---

9   Coolant temperature sending unit - check and replacement

Refer to illustrations 9.3a through 9.3d
Warning: *The engine must be completely cool before removing the sending unit.*

Check

1   If the coolant temperature gauge is inoperative, check the fuses first (see Chapter 12).

2   If the temperature indicator shows excessive temperature after running awhile, see the *Troubleshooting* section in the front of the manual.

3   If the temperature gauge indicates Hot shortly after the engine is started cold, disconnect the wire at the coolant temperature sending unit **(see illustrations)**. If the gauge reading drops, replace the sending unit. If the reading remains high, the wire to the gauge may be shorted to ground or the gauge is faulty.

4   If the coolant temperature gauge fails to indicate after the engine has been warmed up (approximately 10 minutes) and the fuses checked out okay, shut off the engine. Disconnect the wire at the

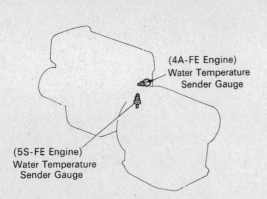

9.3b . . . on 4A-FE engines the unit is mounted above the distributor cap

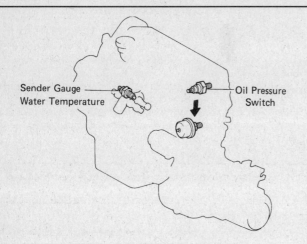

9.3d On 2S-E and 3S-FE engines the coolant temperature unit is located in the same location (arrow)

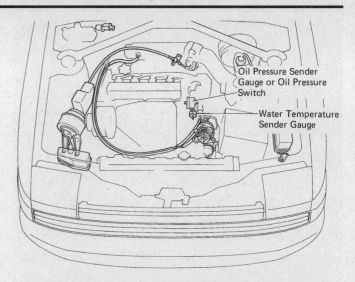

9.3c The coolant temperature unit on 3S-GE engines is located below the oil pressure sender or the oil pressure switch

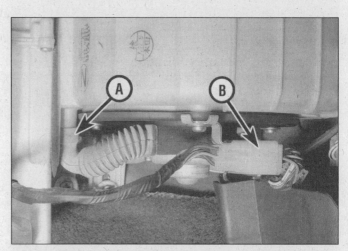

10.3a Working under the blower motor assembly remove the rubber air duct (A), the forward wiring connection (B) , . .

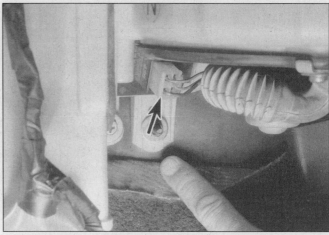

10.3b . . . and the rear wiring connection (arrow)

sending unit and using a jumper wire, connect it to a clean ground on the engine. Turn on the ignition without starting the engine. If the gauge now indicates Hot, replace the sending unit.

5   If the gauge still does not work, the circuit may be open or the gauge may be faulty. See Chapter 12 for additional information.

Replacement

6   With the engine completely cool, remove the cap from the radiator to release any pressure, then reinstall the cap. This reduces coolant loss during sending unit replacement.

7   Disconnect the wiring harness from the sending unit.

8   Prepare the new sending unit for installation by applying a light coat of sealant to the threads.

9   Unscrew the sending unit from the engine and quickly install the new one to prevent coolant loss.

10   Tighten the sending unit securely and connect the wiring harness.

11   Refill the cooling system and run the engine. Check for leaks and proper gauge operation.

10   Blower unit - removal and installation

Refer to illustrations 10.3a, 10.3b and 10.4

1   Disconnect the negative cable from the battery. **Caution:** *If the stereo in your vehicle is equipped with an anti-theft system, refer to the information on page 0-15 at the front of this manual before detaching the cable.*

2   Remove the glove compartment (see Chapter 11).

3   Disconnect the wiring from the blower motor and detach the rubber air duct running between the motor and the evaporator housing **(see illustrations)**.

4   Remove the blower unit retaining screws **(see illustration)** and lower the unit from the housing.

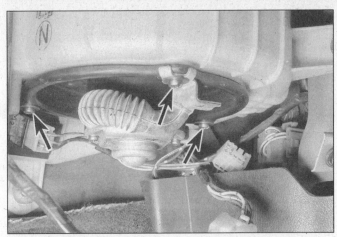

10.4   To replace the motor remove the blower motor retention bolts (arrows) and pull the motor from the assembly

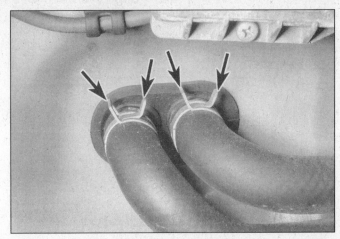

11.3   Disconnect the heater hoses at the firewall by squeezing the hose clamp tags (arrows) together

5   If you are replacing the motor, detach the fan and transfer it to the new motor.
6   Installation is the reverse of removal. Run the blower and check for proper operation.

11   Heater core - removal and installation

Refer to illustrations 11.3 and 11.7

1   Disconnect the negative cable from the battery. **Caution:** *If the stereo in your vehicle is equipped with an anti-theft system, refer to the information on page 0-15 at the front of this manual before detaching the cable.*
2   Drain the cooling system (see Chapter 1).
3   Working in the engine compartment, disconnect the heater hoses where they enter the firewall **(see illustration)**.
4   Remove the center console and center trim panel (see Chapter 11).
5   Remove the heater controls **(see Section 12)**. Be sure to mark the locations of the cable clamps on the cables to ensure correct adjustment upon reinstallation.
6   Label and detach the air ducts, wiring and controls still attached

to the heater housing.
7   Remove the screws and clips and separate the two halves of the heater assembly **(see illustration)**. Take out the old heater core and install the new unit.
8   Reassemble the heater unit and check the operation of the control flaps. If any parts bind, correct the problem before installation.
9   Reinstall the remaining parts in the reverse order of removal.
10   Refill the cooling system, reconnect the battery and run the engine. Check for leaks and proper system operation.

12   Air conditioner and heater control assembly - removal and installation

Refer to illustration 12.4

1   Disconnect the negative cable from the battery. **Caution:** *If the stereo in your vehicle is equipped with an anti-theft system, refer to the information on page 0-15 at the front of this manual before detaching the cable.*
2   Remove the trim panels which surround the radio and heater control assembly (see Chapter 11).

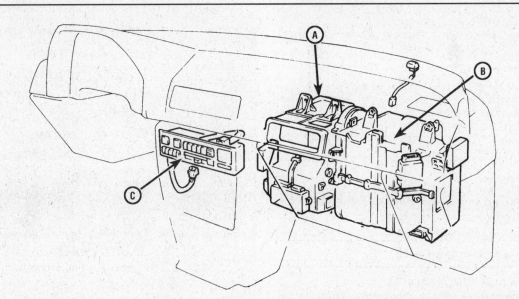

11.7   Remove the various screws and clips from the heater assembly to remove the lower half of the unit

| A | Heater assembly | B | Cooling assembly | C | Heater/air conditioning control assembly |

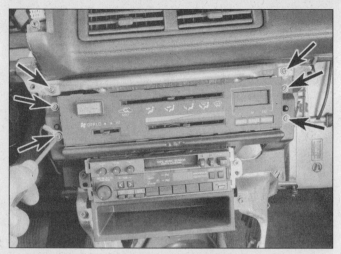

**12.4   Remove the control assembly retaining screws (arrows) -
early model shown, others similar**

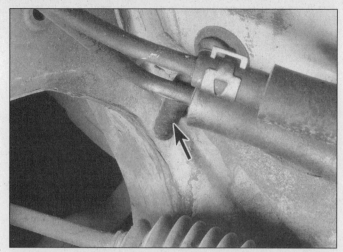

**13.1   The drain tube is located above the right driveaxle boot
(arrow), check that it is not blocked**

3   Remove the glove box and the lower finish panels (see Chapter 11).
4   Remove the control mounting screws **(see illustration)**.
5   Carefully pull and tilt the unit out of the dash, on some models it may be necessary to loosen the trim pad to achieve this.
6   Check the outer sheath of the cables for indentations where the clamps grip them. Mark the cable sheath with paint if no indentation is visible. Remove the clamps and detach the control cables. If necessary, disconnect the control cables at the ends opposite from the control by detaching the cable clamps and separating the cables from the operating levers.
7   Unplug the electrical connectors and lift the control from the vehicle.
8   Installation is the reverse of removal.

---

13   Air conditioning system - check and maintenance

Refer to illustrations 13.1, 13.7 and 13.12
Warning: *The air conditioning system is under high pressure. Do not loosen any fittings or remove any components until after the system has been discharged. Air conditioning refrigerant should be properly discharged into an EPA-approved container at a dealer service department or an automotive air conditioning repair facility. Always wear eye protection when disconnecting air conditioning system fittings.*

Check

1   The following maintenance checks should be performed on a regular basis to ensure that the air conditioner continues to operate at peak efficiency.
  a) Check the compressor drivebelt. If it's worn or deteriorated, replace it (see Chapter 1).
  b) Check the drivebelt tension and, if necessary, adjust it (see Chapter 1).
  c) Check the system hoses. Look for cracks, bubbles, hard spots and deterioration. Inspect the hoses and all fittings for oil bubbles and seepage. If there's any evidence of wear, damage or leaks, replace the hose(s).
  d) Inspect the condenser fins for leaves, bugs and other debris. Use a "fin comb" or compressed air to clean the condenser.
  e) Make sure the system has the correct refrigerant charge.
  f) Check the evaporator housing drain tube for blockage **(see illustration)**
2   It's a good idea to operate the system for about 10 minutes at least once a month, particularly during the winter. Long term non-use can cause hardening, and subsequent failure, of the seals.
3   Because of the complexity of the air conditioning system and the special equipment necessary to service it, in-depth troubleshooting

**13.7   The sight glass (arrow) is mounted in the top of the
receiver-drier**

and repairs are not included in this manual. However, simple checks and component replacement procedures are provided in this Chapter. For more complete information on the air conditioning system, refer to the *Haynes Automotive Heating and Air Conditioning Manual*.
4   The most common cause of poor cooling is simply a low system refrigerant charge. If a noticeable drop in cool air output occurs, one of the following quick checks will help you determine if the refrigerant level is low.
5   Warm the engine up to normal operating temperature.
6   Place the air conditioning temperature selector at the coldest setting and put the blower at the highest setting. Open the doors (to make sure the air conditioning system doesn't cycle off as soon as it cools the passenger compartment).
7   With the compressor engaged - the clutch will make an audible click and the center of the clutch will rotate - inspect the sight glass, if equipped **(see illustration)**. If the refrigerant looks foamy, it's low. Charge the system as described later in this Section.
8   If there's no sight glass, feel the inlet and outlet pipes at the compressor. One side should be cold and one hot. If there's no perceptible difference between the two pipes, there's something wrong with the compressor or the system. It might be a low charge - it might be something else. Take the vehicle to a dealer service department or an automotive air conditioning shop.

Adding refrigerant (all systems)

Note: *At the time this manual was written, the following procedure was still legal. However, new Federal regulations proposed by the Environ-*

13.12   Place the thermometer in the dash vent

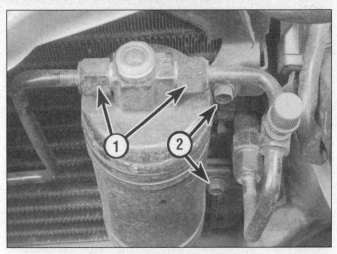

14.3   Once the refrigerant has been discharged detach the refrigerant lines (1) and cap them immediately. Remove the mounting bolts (2) to free the receiver/drier

15.5a   Air conditioning compressor (2S-E, 3S-FE, 3S-GE and 5S-FE engines)   mounting details

1   Mounting bolts
2   Refrigerant lines mounting bolts

mental Protection Agency (EPA) were expected to go into effect soon. Once these new regulations become law, the sale of 14-ounce cans of refrigerant will be prohibited; the only cans available will be the large size (usually 30 pounds). If you decide to add refrigerant from one of these larger cans, you will need a set of manifold gauges, all the necessary fittings, adapters and hoses to hook everything up and a copy of the Haynes Automotive Heating and Air Conditioning Manual.

9   Buy an automotive charging kit at an auto parts store. A charging kit includes a 14-ounce can of refrigerant, a tap valve and a short section of hose that can be attached between the tap valve and the system low side service valve. Because one can of refrigerant may not be sufficient to bring the system charge up to the proper level, it's a good idea to buy a couple of additional cans. Make sure that one of the cans contains red refrigerant dye. If the system is leaking, the red dye will leak out with the refrigerant and help you pinpoint the location of the leak. **Warning:** *Never add more than two cans of refrigerant to the system.*

10   Hook up the charging kit by following the manufacturer's instructions. **Warning:** *DO NOT hook the charging kit hose to the system high side!*

11   Warm up the engine and turn on the air conditioner. Keep the charging kit hose away from the fan and other moving parts.

12   Place a thermometer in the dashboard vent nearest the evaporator **(see illustration)** and add refrigerant until the indicated temperature is around 40 to 45-degrees F.

14   Air conditioning receiver/drier - removal and installation

Refer to illustration 14.3

Warning: *The air conditioning system is under high pressure. Do not loosen any fittings or remove any components until after the system has been discharged. Air conditioning refrigerant should be properly discharged into an EPA-approved container at a dealer service department or an automotive air conditioning repair facility. Always wear eye protection when disconnecting air conditioning system fittings.*

1   Have the refrigerant discharged at a dealer service department or an automotive air conditioning repair facility.

2   The receiver/drier, which acts as a reservoir and filter for the refrigerant, is located in the left front corner of the engine compartment.

3   Detach the two refrigerant lines from the receiver/drier **(see illustration)**.

4   Immediately cap the open fittings to prevent the entry of dirt and moisture.

5   Unbolt the receiver/drier mounting bolts **(see illustration 14.3)** and lift it from the vehicle.

6   Install new O-rings on the lines and lubricate them with clean refrigerant oil.

7   Installation is the reverse of removal. **Note:** *Do not remove the*

sealing caps until you are ready to reconnect the lines. Do not mistake the inlet (marked IN) and the outlet connections.

8   If a new receiver/drier is installed, add 0.7 US fluid ounces (20 cc) of refrigerant oil to the system.

9   Have the system evacuated, charged and leak tested by the shop that discharged it.

15   Air conditioning compressor - removal and installation

Refer to illustrations 15.5a and 15.5b

Warning: *The air conditioning system is under high pressure. Do not loosen any fittings or remove any components until after the system has been discharged. Air conditioning refrigerant should be properly discharged into an EPA-approved container at a dealer service department or an automotive air conditioning repair facility. Always wear eye protection when disconnecting air conditioning system fittings.*

1   Have the refrigerant discharged at a dealer service department or an automotive air conditioning repair facility.

2   Disconnect the negative cable from the battery and remove the battery. **Caution:** *If the stereo in your vehicle is equipped with an anti-theft system, refer to the information on page 0-15 at the front of this*

3

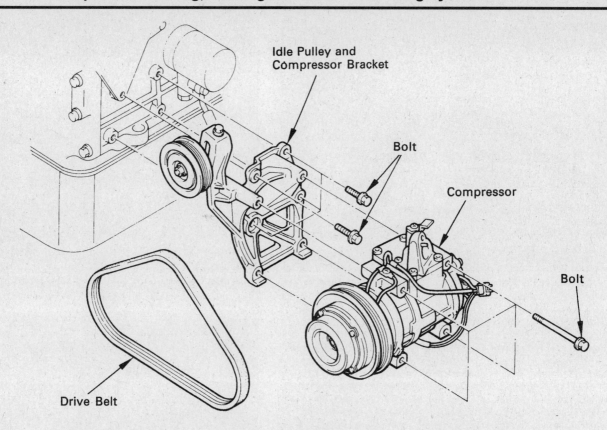

15.5b   Air conditioning compressor mounting details (4A-FE engine) - exploded view

manual detaching the cable.

3   Detach the refrigerant lines from the back of the compressor **(see illustration 15.5a)** and immediately cap the open fittings to prevent the entry of dirt and moisture.

4   Disconnect the clutch wire from the compressor **(see illustration 15.5a)**.

5   Remove the mounting bolts **(see illustrations)** and lower the compressor from the engine compartment. **Note:** *Keep the compressor level during handling and storage. If the compressor seized or you find metal particles in the refrigerant lines, the system must be flushed out by an air conditioning technician and the receiver/drier must be replaced* **(see Section 14)**.

6   Prior to installation, turn the center of the clutch six times to disperse any oil that has collected in the head.

7   Install the compressor in the reverse order of removal.

8   If you are installing a new compressor, refer to the manufacturer's instructions for adding refrigerant oil to the system.

9   Have the system evacuated, charged and leak tested by the shop that discharged it.

16   Air conditioning condenser - removal and installation

Refer to illustrations 16.3 and 16.7

Warning: *The air conditioning system is under high pressure. Do not loosen any fittings or remove any components until after the system has been discharged. Air conditioning refrigerant should be properly discharged into an EPA-approved container at a dealer service department or an automotive air conditioning repair facility. Always wear eye protection when disconnecting air conditioning system fittings.*

1   Have the refrigerant discharged at a dealer service department or an automotive air conditioning repair facility.

2   Remove the grille (see Chapter 11) and the engine under covers.

3   Remove the hood latch and horns **(see illustration)**.

4   Remove the air conditioning fan **(see Section 4)**

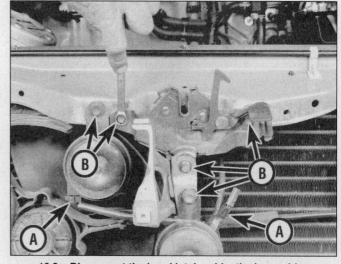

16.3   Disconnect the hood latch cable, the horn wiring connections (A) and the horn and brace mounting bolts (B)

5   Disconnect the refrigerant lines from the condenser. Be sure to use a back-up wrench to avoid twisting the lines (if equipped with two nuts).

6   Immediately cap the open fittings to prevent the entry of dirt and moisture.

7   Unbolt the condenser **(see illustration)** and lift it out of the vehicle. Store it upright to prevent oil loss.

8   Installation is the reverse of removal.

9   If a new condenser was installed, add 1.4 to 1.7 ounces (40 to 50 cc) of refrigerant oil to the system.

10   Have the system evacuated, charged and leak tested by the shop that discharged it.

16.7 Remove the four mounting bolts and pull the condenser free

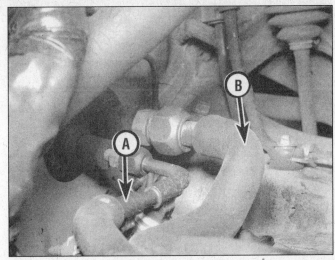

17.3 Using a back-up wrench disconnect the liquid tube (A) and the suction tube (B)

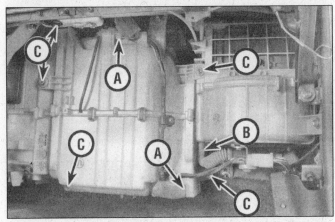

17.6 Disconnect all wiring connections (A) and the air tube (B). Remove the various mounting nuts and bolts (C - not all fasteners are shown)

17 Air conditioning evaporator - removal and installation

Refer to illustrations 17.3, 17.6 and 17.7

Warning: *The air conditioning system is under high pressure. Do not loosen any fittings or remove any components until after the system has been discharged. Air conditioning refrigerant should be properly discharged into an EPA-approved container at a dealer service depart-ment or an automotive air conditioning repair facility. Always wear eye protection when disconnecting air conditioning system fittings.*

1   Have the refrigerant discharged at a dealer service department or an automotive air conditioning repair facility.

2   Disconnect the negative lead from the battery. **Caution:** *If the stereo in your vehicle is equipped with an anti-theft system, refer to the information on page 0-15 at the front of this manual before detaching the cable.*

3   Working in the engine compartment disconnect the suction and liquid tubes, use a back-up wrench to avoid twisting and damaging the lines **(see illustration)**.

4   Immediately cap the open fittings to prevent the entry of dirt and moisture and remove the inlet and outlet grommets.

5   Remove the glove box (see Chapter 11) and the reinforcement bar.

6   Disconnect all electrical connectors and tubing from the assem-bly, remove the mounting nuts and bolts and pull the unit free **(see il-lustration)**.

7   To remove the evaporator disconnect all connectors, unfasten the retaining clips and remove the retaining screws **(see illustration)**.

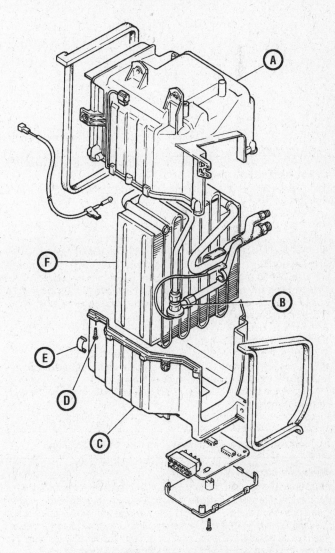

17.7 Cooling unit - exploded view

A Upper cover	*D Retaining screw*
B Expansion valve	*E Retaining clip*
C Lower cover	*F Evaporator*

3

8   Check the evaporator fins for blockage; if they are dirty clean them with compressed air - never use water for this purpose!

9   Check fittings for cracks and signs of wear; replace parts as necessary.

10   Installation is the reverse of the removal procedure. Be sure to replace all O-rings removed during disassembly with new ones.

11   If a new evaporator was installed, add 1.4 to 1.7 ounces (40 to 50 cc) of refrigerant oil to the system.

12   Have the system evacuated, charged and leak tested by the shop that discharged it.

Chapter 4   Fuel and exhaust systems

Contents

Specifications

Fuel pressure

2S-E, 3S-GE engines
    Terminals +B and Fp bridged (engine off)................................. 33 to 38 psi
    Vacuum sensing hose detached (at idle) .... 33 to 38 psi
    Vacuum sensing hose attached (at idle) .... 27 to 31 psi
3S-FE, 5S-FE and 4A-FE engines
    Terminals +B and Fp bridged (engine off)................................. 38 to 44 psi
    Vacuum sensing hose detached (at idle) .... 38 to 44 psi
    Vacuum sensing hose attached (at idle) .... 33 to 37 psi

Fuel injector resistance

2S-E engine .... 1.5 to 3.0 ohms
All others .... 13.8 ohms

Cold start valve resistance

3S-GE engine .... 3 to 5 ohms
All others .... 2 to 4 ohms

Torque specification

Ft-lbs

Throttle body mounting bolts 14

2.1a   Loosen the screw clamp (arrow) and detach the air hose

2.1b   Release the clips, lift the cover/air flow meter off and remove the filter element

1   General information

The fuel system consists of a rear mounted tank, combination metal and rubber fuel hoses, a fuel tank mounted electric pump and an electronic fuel injection system.

The exhaust system is composed of an exhaust manifold, the catalytic converter and a combination muffler and tailpipe assembly.

The emission control systems modify the functions of both the exhaust and fuel systems. There may be some cross-references throughout this Chapter to sections in Chapter 6 because the emissions control systems are integral with the induction and exhaust systems.

Extreme caution should be exercised when dealing with either the fuel or exhaust system. Fuel is a primary element for combustion. Be very careful! The exhaust system is also an area for exercising caution as it operates at very high temperatures. Serious burns can result from even momentary contact with any part of the exhaust system and the fire potential is ever present.

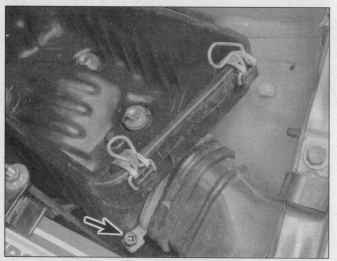

2.2   After loosening the air intake hose screw clamp, detach the hose from the housing

2   Air cleaner assembly - removal and installation

Refer to illustrations 2.1a, 2.1b, 2.2 and 2.3

1   Disconnect the air hose from the air cleaner assembly, detach the clips and remove the cover/air flow meter and the filter element **(see illustrations)**.

2   Disconnect the air intake hose from the housing **(see illustration)**.

3   Remove the three bolts and remove the air cleaner housing from the engine compartment **(see illustration)**.

4   Installation is the reverse of removal.

3   Fuel lines and fittings - inspection and replacement

Warning: *Gasoline is extremely flammable, so take extra precautions when you work on any part of the fuel system. Don't smoke or allow open flames or bare light bulbs near the work area, and don't work in a garage where a natural gas-type appliance (such as a water heater or clothes dryer) with a pilot light is present. If you spill any fuel on your skin, rinse it off immediately with soap and water. When you perform any kind of work on the fuel system, wear safety glasses and have a Class B type fire extinguisher on hand.*

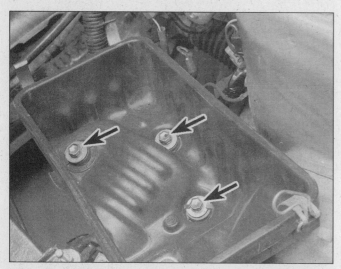

2.3   The air cleaner assembly is held in place by three bolts in the bottom of the housing (arrows)

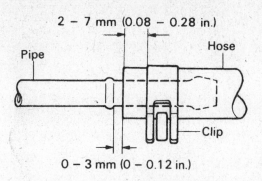

2 – 7 mm (0.08 – 0.28 in.)

Pipe

Hose

Clip

0 – 3 mm (0 – 0.12 in.)

3.6   When attaching a section of rubber hose to metal fuel line, be sure to overlap the hose as shown secure it to the line with a new hose clamp of the proper type

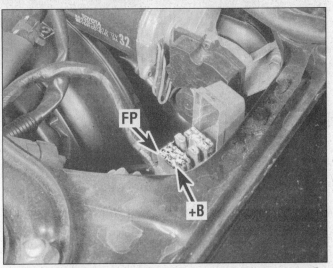

FP

+B

4.2   To check the fuel pump, turn on the ignition switch (but don't start the engine) and bridge the terminal +B and Fp of the service electrical connector

Inspection

1   Once in a while, you will have to raise the vehicle to service or replace some component (an exhaust pipe hanger, for example). Whenever you work under the vehicle, always inspect fuel lines and all fittings and connections for damage or deterioration.
2   Check all hoses and pipes for cracks, kinks, deformation or obstructions.
3   Make sure all hoses and pipe clips attach their associated hoses or pipes securely to the underside of the vehicle.
4   Verify all hose clamps attaching rubber hoses to metal fuel lines or pipes are snug enough to assure a tight fit between the hoses and pipes.

Replacement

Refer to illustration 3.6

5   If you must replace any damaged sections, use original equipment replacement hoses or pipes constructed from exactly the same material as the section you are replacing. Do not install substitutes constructed from inferior or inappropriate material or you could cause a fuel leak or a fire.
6   Always, before detaching or disassembling any part of the fuel line system, note the routing of all hoses and pipes and the orientation of all clamps and clips to assure that replacement sections are installed in exactly the same manner. When attaching hoses to metal lines, overlap them as shown **(see illustration)**.
7   Before detaching any part of the fuel system, be sure to relieve the fuel line and tank pressure by removing the fuel tank cap and disconnecting the battery.Cover the fitting being disconnected with a rag to absorb any fuel that may spray out. **Caution:** *If the stereo in your vehicle is equipped with an anti-theft system, refer to the information on page 0-15 at the front of this manual before detaching the cable.*
8   While you're under the vehicle, it's a good idea to check the condition of the fuel filter - make sure that it's not clogged or damaged (see Chapter 1).

---

4   Fuel pump/fuel pressure - check

Warning: *Gasoline is extremely flammable, so take extra precautions when you work on any part of the fuel system. Don't smoke or allow open flames or bare light bulbs near the work area, and don't work in a garage where a natural gas-type appliance (such as a water heater or clothes dryer) with a pilot light is present. If you spill any fuel on your skin, rinse it off immediately with soap and water. When you perform any kind of work on the fuel system, wear safety glasses and have a Class B type fire extinguisher on hand.*

Fuel pump operation check

Refer to illustrations 4.2 and 4.3

1   Turn on the ignition switch (but do not start the engine).

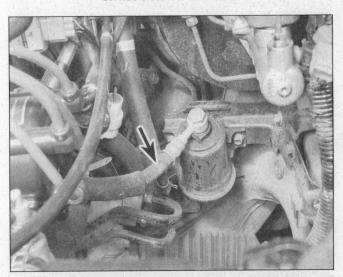

4.3   Listen for fuel return pressure noise from the fuel return hose and verify that there is pressure in the hose from the fuel filter by pinching it at the point shown (arrow)

2   Bridge terminals +B and Fp of the fuel pump check electrical connector with a jumper wire **(see illustration)**.
3   Listen for fuel return noises from the fuel pressure regulator and verify that there is pressure in the hose from the fuel filter **(see illustration)**.
4   Remove the jumper wire. Close the cap on the service electrical connector.
5   Turn the ignition switch off.
6   If there is no pressure, inspect the following components: the EFI 15-amp fuse and the ignition 7.5-amp fuse and/or the EFI main relay (all located in the fuse panel next to the battery); the circuit opening relay, refer to "Electronic Control System" (see Chapter 6); the fuel pump; and the wiring and electrical connectors (see the wiring diagrams at the end of the book).

Fuel pressure check

Refer to illustrations 4.7, 4.12, 4.13a, 4.13b and 4.16

7   A fuel pressure gauge equipped with an 8 mm banjo fitting on the end of the hose (SST 09268-45011) is required for the following procedure. There are a couple of alternatives to buying the special Toyota fuel pressure gauge setup:

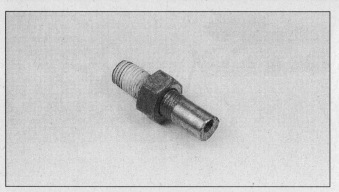

4.7   If you don't have the special Toyota fuel pressure gauge and cannot find the required 8 mm banjo fitting for your own gauge, get an 8 mm bolt, place the bolt in a bench vise, cut the head off, drill out the bolt, add a locknut and wrap teflon tape around the threads

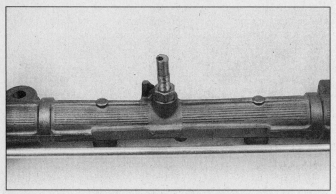

4.13a   If you are using a makeshift adapter bolt, screw it into the fuel rail and tighten the locknut . . .

a) Simply buy an 8 mm banjo fitting and attach it to a fuel pressure gauge hose with a hose clamp.
b) If you can't find the correct size banjo fitting, buy an 8 mm bolt, cut the head off and drill a hole through the center. Add a locknut with the same thread pitch and seal the threads with teflon tape **(see illustration).**
8   Remove the fuel tank cap.
9   Verify that the battery voltage is 12 volts or more (see Chapter 5).
10   Detach the cable from the negative terminal of the battery. **Caution:** *If the stereo in your vehicle is equipped with an anti-theft system, refer to the information on page 0-15 at the front of this manual before detaching the cable.*
11   Detach the electrical connector from the cold start injector.
12   Put a metal container or shop towel under the cold start injector pipe banjo bolt at the fuel rail **(see illustration)**, then remove the banjo bolt and detach the cold start injector pipe from the fuel rail. **Warning:** *Cover the fitting with a rag to absorb any fuel that might spray out.*
13   To attach the fuel pressure gauge to the fuel rail:
a) If you are using the factory setup, or obtained an 8 mm banjo bolt for your pressure gauge kit, use the banjo bolt from the cold start injector pipe to attach the fuel pressure gauge to the fuel rail. Be sure to use crush washers on both sides of the banjo fitting.
b) If you are using a drilled out 8 mm bolt, attach the bolt to the fuel rail, tighten the locknut and attach the fuel pressure gauge hose with a hose clamp **(see illustrations)**.
14   Wipe off any gasoline that has leaked out of the fuel rail and attach the cable to the negative terminal of the battery.
15   Place the transaxle in Neutral (manual) or Park (automatic) and apply the parking brake.
a) Bridge terminals +B and Fp of the check electrical connector **(see illustration 4.2).**
b) Turn the ignition to On.

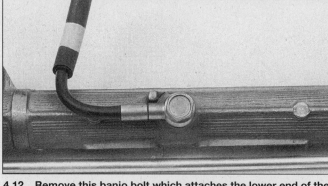

4.12   Remove this banjo bolt which attaches the lower end of the cold start injector pipe to the fuel rail and, using the banjo bolt and two crush washers, attach the banjo fitting of the fuel pressure gauge to the fuel rail (fuel rail removed from the engine for clarity)

4.13b   . . . then attach a fuel pressure gauge hose with a hose clamp (fuel rail removed from the engine for clarity)

4.16   Bridge terminal B+ and Fp of the check electrical connector and measure the fuel pressure at idle

16   Measure the fuel pressure **(see illustration)** and compare it to the fuel pressure listed in this Chapter's Specifications.
a) If the pressure is high, check for a restricted fuel return line. If the line is clear, replace the pressure regulator.
b) If the pressure is low, pinch the fuel return line. If the pressure goes up, replace the fuel pressure regulator. If the pressure does

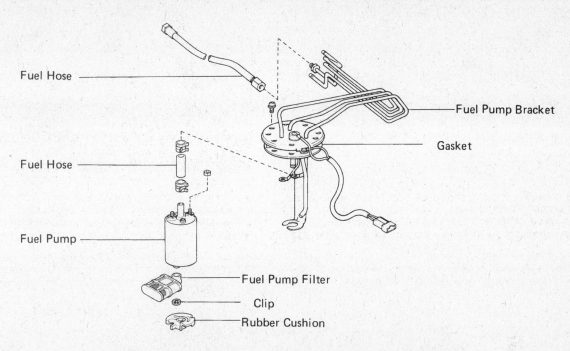

Fuel Hose

Fuel Pump Bracket

Fuel Hose

Gasket

Fuel Pump

Fuel Pump Filter

Clip

Rubber Cushion

5.5   An exploded view of the fuel pump assembly (1989 and earlier models)

not increase, check the fuel feed line, the fuel pump and the fuel filter.

17   Remove the jumper wire from the service electrical connector.

a)   Start the engine.

b)   Detach the vacuum sensing hose from the fuel pressure regulator.

c)   Measure the fuel pressure at idle and compare your reading to the fuel pressure listed in this Chapter's Specifications.

d)   Reattach the vacuum sensing hose to the pressure regulator.

e)   Measure the fuel pressure at idle and compare your reading to the fuel pressure listed in this Chapter's Specifications.

f)   If the pressure is not as specified, check the vacuum sensing hose and fuel pressure regulator.

g)   Stop the engine. Verify that the fuel pressure remains at 21 psi or more for five minutes after the engine is turned off.

18   Detach the cable from the negative terminal of the battery. **Caution:** *If the stereo in your vehicle is equipped with an anti-theft system, refer to the information on page 0-15 at the front of this manual before detaching the cable.*

19   Carefully remove the fuel pressure gauge. Be sure to cover the fitting with a rag before loosening it.

20   Using new crush washers, reattach the cold start injector pipe banjo fitting to the fuel rail.

21   Reattach the electrical connector to the cold start injector. Be sure to wipe up any spilled gasoline.

22   Attach the cable to the negative terminal of the battery.

23   Start the engine and check for leaks.

5   Fuel pump - removal and installation

Warning: *Gasoline is extremely flammable, so take extra precautions when you work on any part of the fuel system. Don't smoke or allow open flames or bare light bulbs near the work area, and don't work in a garage where a natural gas-type appliance (such as a water heater or clothes dryer) with a pilot light is present. If you spill any fuel on your skin, rinse it off immediately with soap and water. When you perform any kind of work on the fuel system, wear safety glasses and have a Class B type fire extinguisher on hand.*

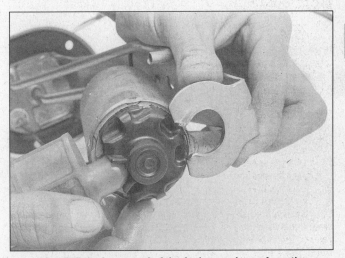

5.7   Pull the lower end of the fuel pump loose from the bracket and remove the rubber cushion that insulates the bottom of the pump

1   Remove the fuel tank cap.

2   Disconnect the cable from the negative terminal of the battery. **Caution:** *If the stereo in your vehicle is equipped with an anti-theft system, refer to the information on page 0-15 at the front of this manual before detaching the cable.*

1989 and earlier models

Refer to illustrations 5.5, 5.7, 5.9 and 5.12

4   Remove the fuel tank (see Section 6) and place it on a workbench.

5   Remove the fuel pump retaining screws **(see illustrations)**.

6   Carefully withdraw the fuel pump/bracket assembly from the fuel tank.

7   Pull the lower end of the fuel pump loose from the bracket **(see illustration)**.

5.9   Pry off the clip that holds the filter to the fuel pump and pull the filter off - replace the clip if it's a loose fit

5.12   Pull the fuel pump loose from the hose far enough to get at the electrical lead near the bracket

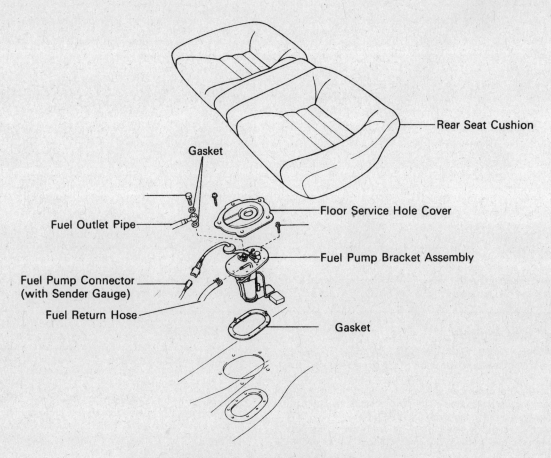

Rear Seat Cushion

Gasket

Fuel Outlet Pipe

Floor Service Hole Cover

Fuel Pump Bracket Assembly

Fuel Pump Connector (with Sender Gauge)

Fuel Return Hose

Gasket

5.15   Fuel pump removal details (1990 and later models)

8   Remove the rubber cushion from the lower end of the fuel pump.

9   Remove the clip securing the filter to the pump **(see illustration)**.

10   Pull out the filter and inspect it for contamination. If it is dirty, replace it.

11   If you are only replacing the fuel pump filter, install the new filter, the clip and the rubber cushion, push the lower end of the pump back into the bracket and install the pump/bracket assembly in the fuel tank.

12   If you are replacing the fuel pump, loosen the hose clamp at the upper end of the pump and disconnect the pump from the hose **(see illustration)**.

13   Disconnect the wires from the pump terminals and remove the pump.

14   Installation is the reverse of removal.

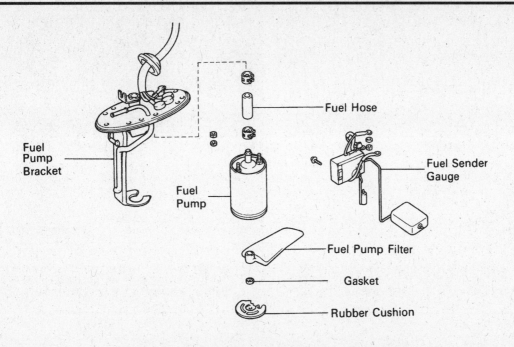

5.16   1990 and later model fuel pump - exploded view

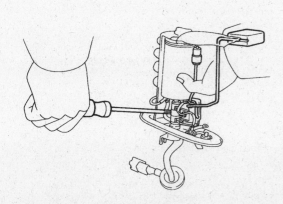

5.17   After disconnecting the wires, remove the two screws and detach the fuel gauge sender from the pump bracket

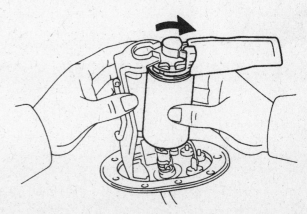

5.18   Pull the lower end of the fuel pump loose from the bracket, disconnect the hose from the bottom and remove the pump

1990 and later models

Refer to illustrations 5.15, 5.16, 5.17, 5.18, 5.20 and 5.23

15   Remove the rear seat cushion and floor service hole cover **(see illustration)**.
16   Remove the fuel union bolt and gaskets, disconnect the outlet pipe then remove the eight retaining bolts and lift the fuel pump and bracket assembly out of the tank **(see illustration)**.
17   Remove the fuel gauge sending unit nut and washer, disconnect the wires, then remove the two screws and detach the sending unit **(see illustration)**.
18   Disconnect the two wires, pull the lower end of the pump out of the bracket, detach the fuel hose and remove the pump from the bracket **(see illustration)**.
19   Remove the rubber cushion from the lower end of the fuel pump.
20   Remove the clip securing the filter to the pump **(see illustration)**.
21   Pull out the filter and inspect it for contamination. If it is dirty, replace it.
22   Install the new filter, the clip and the rubber cushion, push the lower end of the pump back into the bracket and install the pump/bracket assembly in the fuel tank.

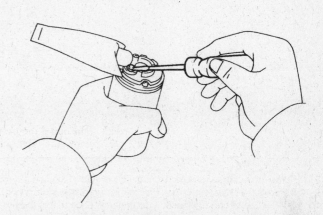

5.20   Use a small screwdriver to detach the clip, then remove the pump filter

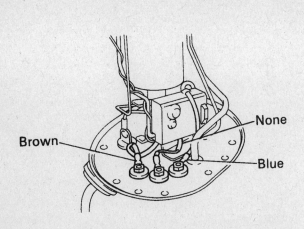

5.23   Fuel pump sending unit-to-bracket connection details

Brown — None — Blue

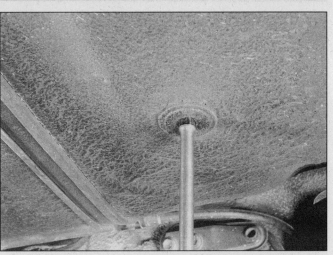

6.1   Remove the fuel filler cap, then use a socket and extension to remove the tank drain plug

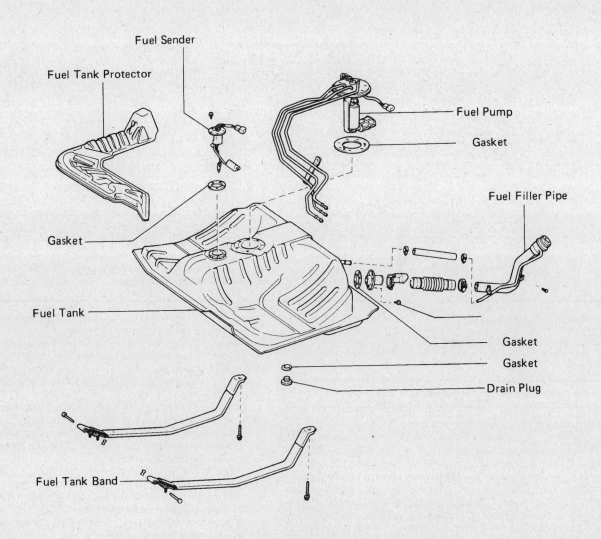

6.6a   Fuel tank and related components (1989 and earlier models)

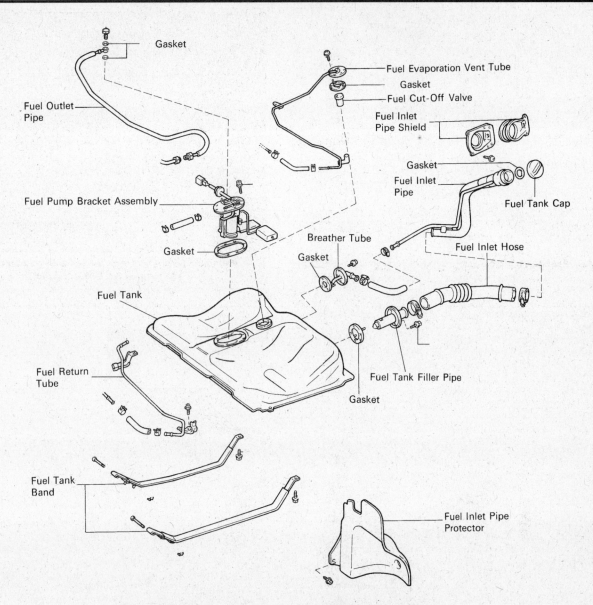

6.6b   Fuel tank and related components (1990 and later models)

23   Install the fuel gauge sending unit to the pump bracket and connect the wires **(see illustration)**. The remainder of installation is the reverse of removal.

6   Fuel tank - removal and installation

Refer to illustrations 6.1, 6.6a, 6.6b and 6.11

Warning: *Gasoline is extremely flammable, so extra precautions must be taken when working on any part of the fuel system. Do not smoke or allow open flames or bare light bulbs near the work area. Also, do not work in a garage if a natural gas-type appliance with a pilot light is present. While performing any work on the fuel tank, wear safety glasses and have a dry chemical (Class B) fire extinguisher on hand. If you spill any fuel on your skin, rinse it off immediately with soap and water.*

1   This procedure is much easier to perform if the fuel tank is empty. These models have a drain plug **(see illustration)** for this purpose. If for some reason the drain plug can't be removed, postpone the job until the tank is empty or siphon the fuel into an approved container using a siphoning kit (available at most auto parts stores). **Warning:** *Do not start the siphoning action by mouth!*

2   Remove the fuel filler cap to relieve fuel tank pressure.

3   Detach the cable from the negative terminal of the battery. **Caution:** *If the stereo in your vehicle is equipped with an anti-theft system, refer to the information on page 0-15 at the front of this manual before detaching the cable.*

4   If the tank is full or nearly full, use a hand-operated pump to remove as much fuel through the filler tube as possible.

5   Raise the vehicle and place it securely on jackstands.

6   Familiarize yourself with the layout of the fuel tank assembly before proceeding **(see illustrations)**.

7   Support the fuel tank with a floor jack. Place a sturdy plank between the jack head and the fuel tank to protect the tank.

8   Detach the fuel line bracket and remove the fuel line or tank protectors **(see illustrations 6.6a and 6.6b)**.

9   Disconnect both fuel tank bands and pivot them down until they are hanging out of the way.

10   Lower the tank enough to disconnect the wires and ground strap from the fuel pump/fuel gauge sending unit, if you have not already done so.

6.11   Loosen the fuel filler and vapor hose clamp screws (arrows) and detach the lines from the fuel tank

11   Disconnect the fuel lines, the vapor return line and the fuel inlet pipe **(see illustration)**. **Note:** *The fuel feed and return lines and the vapor return line are various different diameters, so reattachment is simplified. If you have any doubts, however, clearly label the three lines and their respective inlet or outlet pipes. Be sure to plug the hoses to prevent leakage and contamination of the fuel system.*
12   Remove the tank from the vehicle.
13   Installation is the reverse of removal.

---

7   Fuel tank cleaning and repair - general information

1   Any repairs to the fuel tank or filler neck should be carried out by a professional who has experience in this critical and potentially dangerous work. Even after cleaning and flushing of the fuel system, explosive fumes can remain and ignite during repair of the tank.
2   If the fuel tank is removed from the vehicle, it should not be placed in an area where sparks or open flames could ignite the fumes coming out of the tank. Be especially careful inside garages where a natural gas-type appliance is located, because the pilot light could cause an explosion.

---

8   Accelerator cable - removal, installation and adjustment

Refer to illustration 8.2

Removal

1   Detach the cable from the negative terminal of the battery. **Caution:** *If the stereo in your vehicle is equipped with an anti-theft system, refer to the information on page 0-15 at the front of this manual before detaching the cable.*
2   Unscrew the locknut on the threaded portion of the throttle cable at the throttle body, then grasp the throttle lever arm and rotate it to put some slack in the throttle cable, then slip the cable end out of its slot in the arm **(see illustration)**.
3   Trace the throttle cable to the firewall, detaching it from all brackets.
4   The cable is secured to the firewall with a flange and two mounting bolts that must be removed from inside the vehicle.
6   Detach the throttle cable from the accelerator pedal.
7   From inside the vehicle, pull the cable through the firewall.

Installation and adjustment

8   Installation is the reverse of removal.
9   To adjust the cable, fully depress the accelerator pedal and check that the throttle is fully opened.

8.2   Unscrew the locknut (A) on the threaded portion of the cable, rotate the accelerator arm in the direction shown to provide some slack, then slip the cable end out of the slot (B)

10   If not fully opened, loosen the locknuts, depress accelerator pedal and adjust the cable.
11   Tighten the locknuts and recheck the adjustment. Make sure the throttle closes fully when the pedal isn't depressed.

---

9   Electronic Fuel Injection (EFI) system - general information

Refer to illustrations 9.1a through 9.1d
      These models are equipped with an Electronic Fuel Injection (EFI) system. The EFI system is composed of three basic sub systems: fuel system, air induction system and electronic control system **(see illustrations)**.

Fuel system

      An electric fuel pump located inside the fuel tank supplies fuel under constant pressure to the fuel rail, which distributes fuel evenly to all injectors. From the fuel rail, fuel is injected into the intake ports, just above the intake valves, by four fuel injectors. The amount of fuel supplied by the injectors is precisely controlled by an Electronic Control Unit (ECU). An additional injector, known as the cold start injector, supplies extra fuel into the intake manifold for starting. A pressure regulator controls system pressure in relation to intake manifold vacuum. A fuel filter between the fuel pump and the fuel rail filters fuel to protect the components of the system.

Air induction system

      The air system consists of an air filter housing, an air flow meter (some models) and a throttle body. The air flow meter is an information gathering device for the ECU. A potentiometer measures intake air flow and a temperature sensor measures intake air temperature. This information helps the ECU determine the amount (duration) of fuel to be injected by the injectors. The throttle plate inside the throttle body is controlled by the driver. As the throttle plate opens, the amount of air that can pass through the system increases, so the potentiometer opens further and the ECU signals the injectors to increase the amount of fuel delivered to the intake ports.

Electronic control system

      The Computer Control System controls the EFI and other systems by means of an Electronic Control Unit (ECU), which employs a microcomputer. The ECU receives signals from a number of information sensors which monitor such variables as intake air volume, intake air temperature, coolant temperature, engine rpm, acceleration/deceleration and exhaust oxygen content. These signals help the ECU determine the injection duration necessary for the optimum air/fuel ratio.

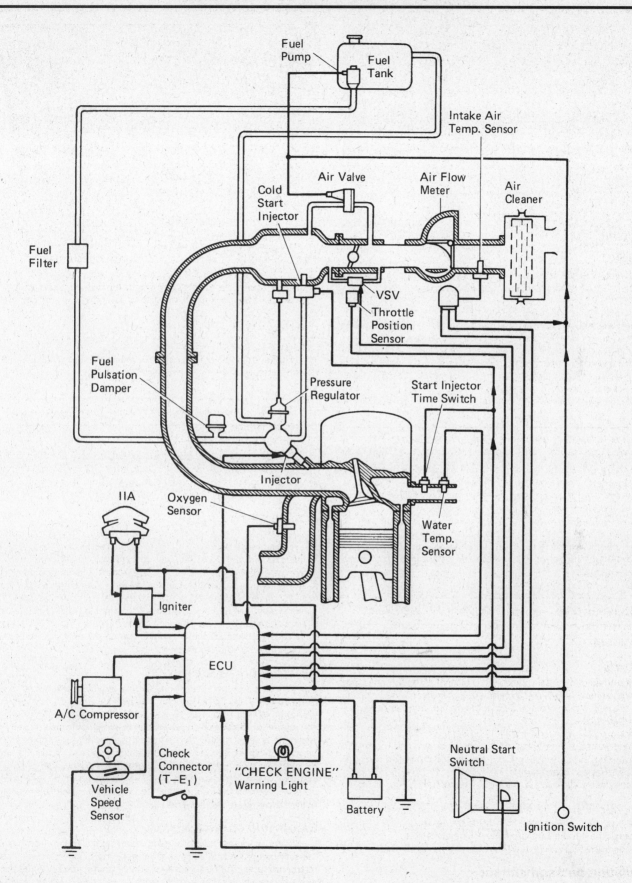

9.1a   The Toyota Computer Control System (TCCS) used on vehicles equipped with 2S-FE engines

4

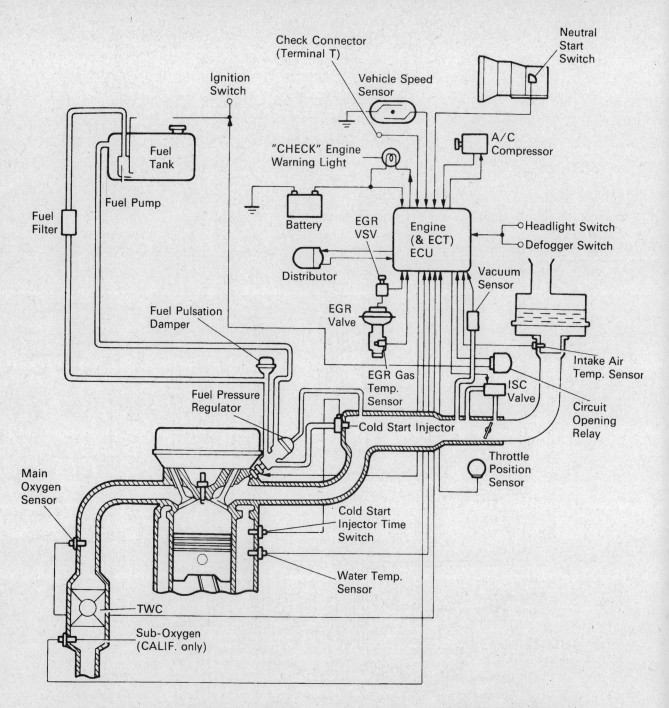

9.1b   The Toyota Computer Control System (TCCS) used on vehicles equipped with 3S-FE and 5S-FE engines

Some of these sensors and their corresponding ECU-controlled relays are not contained within EFI components, but are located throughout the engine compartment. For further information regarding the ECU and its relationship to the engine electrical and ignition system, see Chapter 6.

10   Electronic Fuel Injection (EFI) system - check

Refer to illustrations 10.6a, 10.6b and 10.7
Warning: *Gasoline is extremely flammable, so extra precautions must be taken when working on any part of the fuel system. Do not smoke or*

allow open flames or bare light bulbs near the work area. Also, do not work in a garage if a natural gas-type appliance with a pilot light is present. While performing any work on the fuel system, wear safety glasses and have a dry chemical (Class B) fire extinguisher on hand. If you spill any fuel on your skin, rinse it off immediately with soap and water.

1   Check the ground wire connections for tightness. Check all wiring and electrical connectors that are related to the system. Loose electrical connectors and poor grounds can cause many problems that resemble more serious malfunctions.

2   Check to see that the battery is fully charged, as the control unit and sensors depend on an accurate supply voltage in order to properly meter the fuel.

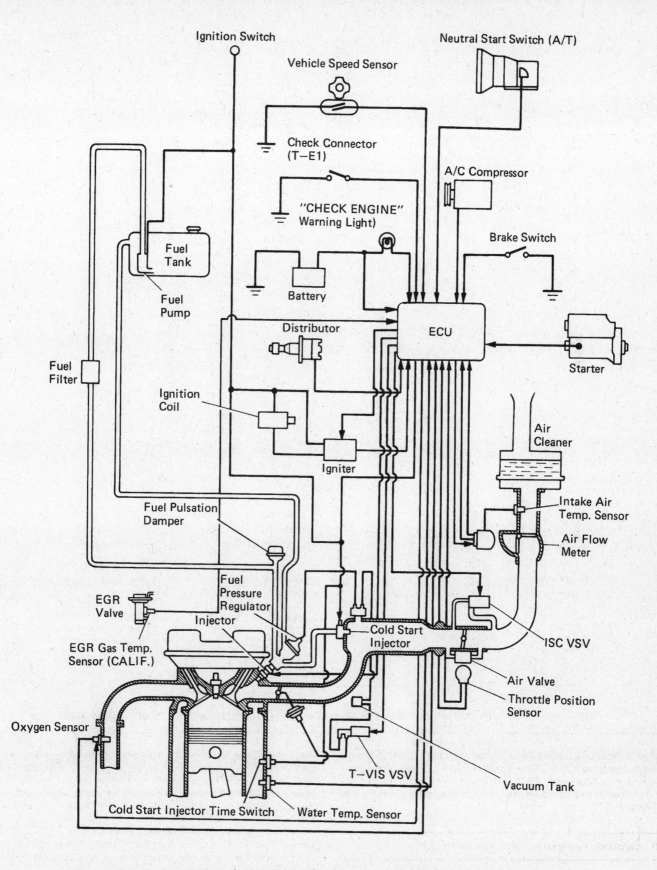

9.1c   The Toyota Computer Control System (TCCS) used on vehicles equipped with the 3S-GE engine

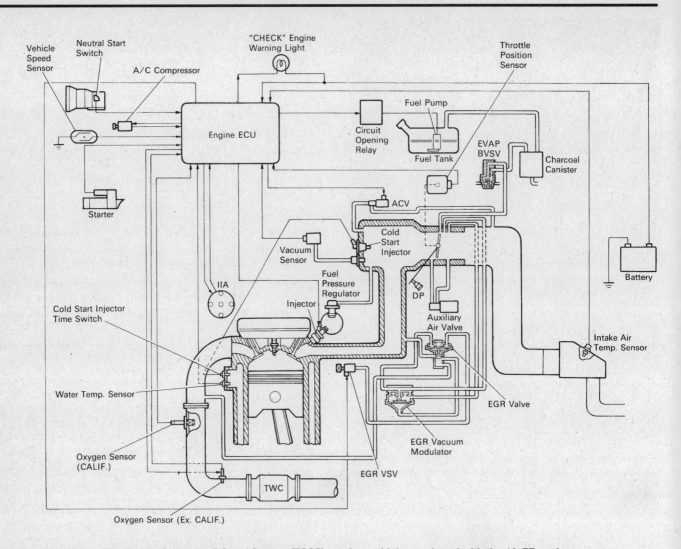

9.1d   The Toyota Computer Control System (TCCS) used on vehicles equipped with the 4A-FE engine

10.6a   This area inside the throttle body near the throttle plate (arrow) usually gets a lot of sludge buildup because the PCV hose vents vapors from the crankcase here

10.6b   With the engine off, use carburetor cleaner (make sure it's safe for use with oxygen sensors and catalytic converters) and a toothbrush to clean the throttle body - open the throttle plate so you can clean behind it

3   Check the air filter element - a dirty or partially blocked filter will severely impede performance and economy (see Chapter 1).

4   If a blown fuse is found, replace it and see if it blows again. If it does, search for a grounded wire in the harness related to the system.

5   Check the air intake duct from the air flow meter to the intake manifold for leaks, which will result in an excessively lean mixture. Also check the condition of the vacuum hoses connected to the intake manifold.

6   Remove the air intake duct from the throttle body and check for dirt, carbon or other residue build-up. If it's dirty, clean with carburetor cleaner (make sure the can says it's safe for use with oxygen sensors and catalytic converters) and a toothbrush **(see illustrations).**

10.7   Use a stethoscope or screwdriver to determine if the injectors are working properly - they should make a steady clicking sound that rises and falls with engine speed changes

7   With the engine running, place a screwdriver or a stethoscope against each injector, one at a time, and listen through the handle for a clicking sound, indicating operation **(see illustration)**.

8   If an injector isn't operating (or sounds different than the others), turn off the engine and unplug the electrical connector from the injector. Check the resistance across the terminals of the injector and compare your reading with the resistance value listed in this Chapter's Specifications. If the resistance isn't as specified, replace the injector with a new one.

9   The remainder of the system checks should be left to a dealer service department or other qualified repair shop, as there is a chance that the control unit may be damaged if not performed properly.

11   Electronic Fuel Injection (EFI) system - component check and replacement

Warning: *Gasoline is extremely flammable, so extra precautions must be taken when working on any part of the fuel system. Do not smoke or allow open flames or bare light bulbs near the work area. Also, do not work in a garage if a natural gas-type appliance with a pilot light is present. While performing any work on the fuel system, wear safety glasses and have a dry chemical (Class B) fire extinguisher on hand. If you spill any fuel on your skin, rinse it off immediately with soap and water.*

Throttle body

Refer to illustrations 11.2 and 11.10

Check

1   Verify that the throttle linkage operates smoothly.

2   Start the engine, detach each vacuum hose and, using your finger, check the vacuum at each port on the throttle body with the engine at idle and above idle, then compare your observations with the vacuum table **(see illustration)**.

Replacement

3   Detach the cable from the negative terminal of the battery. **Caution:** *If the stereo in your vehicle is equipped with an anti-theft system, refer to the information on page 0-15 at the front of this manual before detaching the cable.*

4   Drain the radiator (see Chapter 1).

5   Loosen the hose clamps and remove the air intake duct.

6   Detach the accelerator cable from the throttle lever arm (see Section 8), then detach the throttle cable bracket and set it aside (it's not necessary to detach the throttle cable from the bracket).

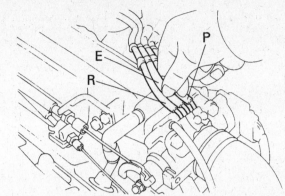

Port name	At idle	Other than idle
P	No vacuum	Vacuum
E	No vacuum	Vacuum
R	No vacuum	No vacuum

11.2   The throttle body vacuum port guide (top) and vacuum table (bottom)

11.10   Remove the four bolts (arrows) to detach the throttle body from the air intake chamber

7   If your vehicle is equipped with an automatic transaxle, detach the throttle valve (TV) cable from the throttle linkage (see Chapter 7B), detach the TV cable brackets from the engine and set the cable and brackets aside.

8   Clearly label, then detach, all vacuum and coolant hoses from the throttle body.

9   Unplug the electrical connector from the throttle position sensor.

10   Remove the throttle body mounting bolts **(see illustration)** and detach the throttle body and gasket from the air intake chamber.

11   Using a soft brush and carburetor cleaner, thoroughly clean the throttle body casting, then blow out all passages with compressed air. **Caution:** *Do not clean the throttle position sensor with anything. Just wipe it off carefully with a clean soft cloth.*

12   Installation of the throttle body is the reverse of removal. Be sure to tighten the throttle body mounting bolts to the torque listed in the Specifications Section at the beginning of this Chapter.

4

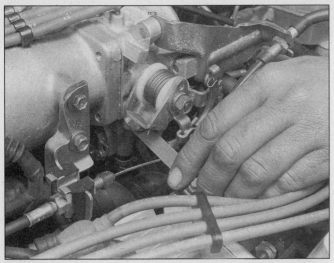

11.14   To check the throttle position sensor, insert a feeler gauge of the specified thickness between the throttle stop screw and the stop lever, then check the continuity between the proper terminals of the sensor

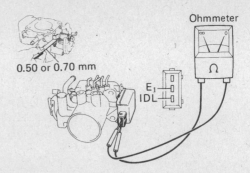

Clearance between lever and stop screw	Continuity IDL-E₁
0.050 mm (0.0197 in)	Continuity
0.90 mm (0.0354 in)	No continuity

11.15a   Throttle position check - terminal guide (top) and continuity table (bottom) for 2S-E engines

Throttle position sensor

Refer to illustrations 11.14, 11.15a, 11.15b, 11.15c and 11.15d

Check

13   Unplug the electrical connector from the throttle position sensor.
14   Insert a feeler gauge of the specified thickness between the throttle stop screw and the stop lever **(see illustration)**.
15   Using an ohmmeter, check the continuity, or measure the resistance, between the indicated terminal pairs **(see illustrations)**.
16   If the resistance is not as specified, loosen the screws and slowly turn the sensor counterclockwise until the ohmmeter needle deflects.
17   Using the feeler gauge, recheck the continuity between the specified terminals.

Replacement

18   If adjustment doesn't bring the sensor within specifications, unplug it, remove the screws and replace it with a new one, then adjust it as described.

Fuel pressure regulator

Check

19   Refer to the fuel pump/fuel pressure check procedure (see Section 4).

Removal

Refer to illustration 11.24

20   Remove the fuel tank cap and detach the cable from the negative terminal of the battery. **Caution:** *If the stereo in your vehicle is equipped with an anti-theft system, refer to the information on page 0-15 at the front of this manual before detaching the cable.*
21   Detach the vacuum sensing hose.
22   Place a metal container or shop towel under the fuel return line banjo fitting. Also cover the banjo bolt with a rag to catch any fuel that may spray out.
23   Slowly loosen the banjo bolt, then remove it along with the crush washers and discard the crush washers or loosen the hose clamp and detach the fuel return hose from the regulator.
24   Remove the pressure regulator mounting bolts **(see illustration)** and detach the pressure regulator from the fuel rail.

Installation

Refer to illustration 11.25

25   Installation is the reverse of removal. Be sure to use new crush

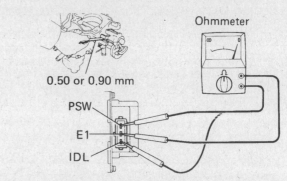

Clearance between lever and stop screw	Continuity between terminals		
	IDL - E1	PSW - E1	IDL - PSW
0.50mm (0.020 in.)	Continuity	No continuity	No continuity
0.90mm (0.035 in.)	No continuity	No continuity	No continuity
Throttle valve fully opened	No continuity	Continuity	No continuity

11.15b   Throttle position check - terminal guide (top) and continuity table (bottom) for 3S-FE and 5S-FE engines

washers and make sure that the pressure regulator is installed properly on the fuel rail **(see illustration)**.
26   The remainder of installation is the reverse of removal.

Cold start injector

Check

Refer to illustration 11.28

27   Unplug the electrical connector from the cold start injector.
28   Using an ohmmeter, measure the resistance between the injector terminals **(see illustration)**. Compare this reading to the one listed in the Specifications Section at the beginning of this Chapter.

a)   If the indicated resistance is within the range listed in the Specifications Section at the beginning of this Chapter, the cold start injector is okay.

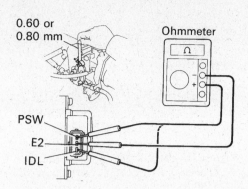

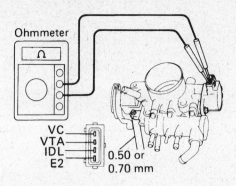

Clearance between lever and stop screw	Continuity between terminals	
	IDL - E2	PSW - E2
0.60 mm (0.024 in.)	Continuity	No continuity
0.80 mm (0.031 in.)	No continuity	No continuity
Throttle valve fully open	No continuity	Continuity

11.15c   Throttle position check - terminal guide (top) and continuity table (bottom) for 4A-FE engines

Clearance between lever and stop screw	Continuity (IDL-E2)
.050 mm (0.020 in)	Continuity
0.70 mm (0.028 in)	No continuity

11.15d   Throttle position check - terminal guide (top) and continuity table (bottom) for 3S-GE engines

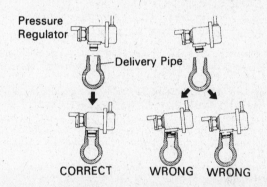

11.25   If the fuel pressure regulator is cocked during installation, it will not seal properly

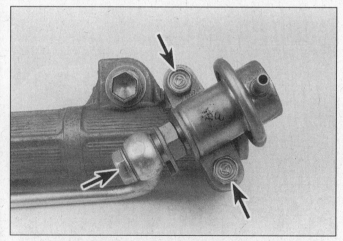

11.24   To detach the fuel pressure regulator from the fuel rail, remove the banjo bolt (arrow) and crush washers, detach the fuel return line, remove the two regulator mounting bolts (arrows), then separate the regulator from the fuel rail (assembly removed from the vehicle for clarity)

b) If the indicated resistance isn't within the specified range, replace the cold start injector.
29   Plug in the cold start injector electrical connector.

Removal

Refer to illustration 11.33

30   Remove the fuel tank cap and detach the cable from the negative terminal of the battery. **Caution:** *If the stereo in your vehicle is equipped with an anti-theft system, refer to the information on page 0-15 at the front of this manual before detaching the cable.*
31   Unplug the cold start injector electrical connector.

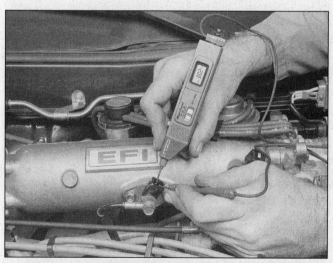

11.28   To check the resistance of the cold start injector, unplug the electrical connector and measure the resistance between the two terminals - check this against those in the Specifications Section

11.33   To replace the cold start injector, unplug the electrical connector, remove the banjo bolt and crush washers, then remove the two mounting bolts (arrows)

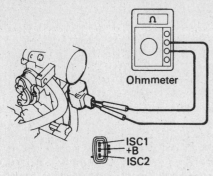

11.41   Check the resistance of the ISC valve between the +B terminal and the other two terminals

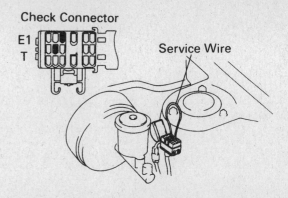

11.37   To check the operation of the ISC valve, warm the engine up to its normal operating temperature and idle speed, bridge terminals T and E1 of the check electrical connector - the idle speed should increase to between 1000 and 1300 rpm and then after five seconds return to idle - if it doesn't, check the ISC valve resistance

11.44   To remove the ISC valve from the throttle body, first remove the throttle body, then remove the four ISC valve retaining screws (arrows) from the underside and detach the valve and gasket

32   Place a metal container or shop towel under the banjo fitting and remove the banjo bolt and crush washers. Discard the washers.
33   Remove the cold start injector mounting bolts, the injector and the gasket **(see illustration)**.

Bench test

34   The cold start injector can be bench tested (for spray pattern) but the test requires special equipment. If you are in any doubt as to the status of the cold start injector, take it to a dealer service department or other repair shop and have it tested.

Installation

35   Installation of the cold start injector is the reverse of removal. Be sure to use new crush washers on each side of the banjo fitting.

Idle speed control (ISC) valve (3S-FE and 5S-FE engines)

Check

Refer to illustrations 11.37, 11.41 and 11.44

36   Start the engine and allow it to reach its normal operating temperature and idle speed (if necessary, adjust the idle speed) and place the transaxle in the Neutral range. Hook up a tachometer in accordance with the manufacturer's instructions.
37   Using a jumper wire, bridge terminals T and E1 of the check electrical connector **(see illustration)**. Engine speed should increase to about 1000 to 1300 rpm.
38   Verify that the engine speed returns to idle speed after it has remained at 1000 to 1300 rpm for five seconds.
   a) If the engine speed changes as described, the ISC valve is okay.
   b) If the engine speed does not change as described, measure the ISC valve resistance.
39   Remove the jumper wire.

40   Unplug the ISC valve electrical connector.
41   Measure the resistance between the terminal +B and each of the other two terminals (ISC1 and ISC2) **(see illustration)**. It should be between 16.0 and 17.0 ohms on 1989 and earlier models or 19.3 and 22.3 ohms on 1990 and later models.
   a) If the resistance is as specified, the ISC valve is okay (but there may be a problem with the wiring or the ECU).
   b) If the resistance is not as specified, replace the valve (see Step 44 below).
42   Plug in the ISC valve electrical connector.

Removal

43   Remove the throttle body.
44   Remove the mounting screws and detach the ISC valve and gasket **(see illustration)**.

Installation

45   Installation of the ISC valve is the reverse of removal for all vehicles. Be sure to use a new gasket when installing the ISC valve.

Fuel rail and fuel injectors

Refer to illustrations 11.52, 11.55, 11.56, 11.58a and 11.58b

Check

46   Refer to the fuel injector checking procedure (see Section 10).

11.52   The injector electrical connectors can be tricky to unplug
- firmly depress the tang (arrow) to unlock each connector

11.55   Carefully remove the fuel rail assembly through the space
between the cam covers and the air intake chamber

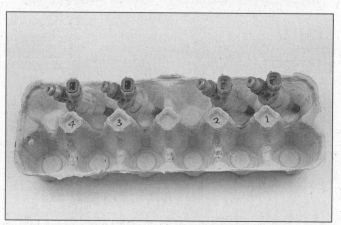

11.56   Unless you are only removing one fuel injector at a time,
it's a good practice to place the injectors in a clearly labeled
container, like an egg carton, to prevent mixing up the injectors
when it's time to install them in the fuel rail

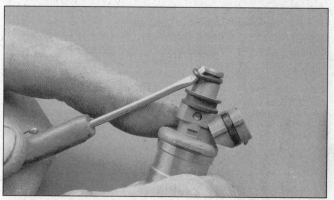

11.58a   Even if you plan to reinstall the same injector(s), be sure
to remove and discard the old O-rings and replace them
with new ones

Replacement

47   Remove the fuel tank cap to relieve the fuel tank pressure.

48   Detach the cable from the negative terminal of the battery. **Caution:** *If the stereo in your vehicle is equipped with an anti-theft system, refer to the information on page 0-15 at the front of this manual before detaching the cable.*

49   Detach the accelerator cable from the throttle linkage and from its bracket on the air intake chamber (see Section 8).

50   Detach the vacuum sensing hose from the fuel pressure regulator.

51   Unplug the cold start injector electrical connector and remove the cold start injector pipe bolt.

52   Unplug the four fuel injector electrical connectors **(see illustration)** and set the injector wire harness aside.

53   Disconnect the fuel lines from the pulsation damper and the fuel rail.

54   Remove the two fuel rail mounting bolts and detach the fuel rail/injector assembly from the cylinder head by pulling on it while wiggling it back and forth.

55   Remove the fuel rail **(see illustration)**.

56   Remove the fuel injectors from the fuel rail and set them aside in a clearly labeled storage container **(see illustration)**.

57   Remove the four fuel rail insulators from the cylinder head and set them aside.

58   If you are replacing the injector(s), discard the old injector, the grommet and the O-ring. If you are simply replacing leaking injector O-

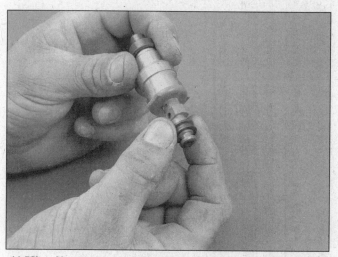

11.58b   Also remove and discard the old grommets and replace
them with new ones

rings and intend to re-use the same injectors, remove the old grommet and O-ring **(see illustrations)** and discard them.

59   Further testing of the injector(s) is beyond the scope of the home mechanic. If you are in doubt as to the status of any injector(s), it can be bench tested for volume and leakage at a dealer service department.

4

60   Installation of the fuel injectors is the reverse of removal. Be sure to use new grommets and O-rings on the injector(s).

12   Exhaust system servicing - general information

Refer to illustration 12.1

Warning: *Inspection and repair of exhaust system components should be done only after enough time has elapsed after driving the vehicle to allow the system components to cool completely. Also, when working under the vehicle, make sure it is securely supported on jackstands.*

1   The exhaust system consists of the exhaust manifold, catalytic converter, the muffler, the tailpipe and all connecting pipes, brackets, hangers and clamps **(see illustration)**. The exhaust system is attached to the body with mounting brackets and rubber hangers. If any of these parts are damaged or deteriorated, excessive noise and vibration will be transmitted to the body.

2   Conduct regular inspections of the exhaust system will keep it safe and quiet. Look for any damaged or bent parts, open seams, holes, loose connections, excessive corrosion or other defects which could allow exhaust fumes to enter the vehicle. Deteriorated exhaust system components should not be repaired - they should be replaced with new parts.

3   If the exhaust system components are extremely corroded or rusted together, they will probably have to be cut from the exhaust system. The convenient way to accomplish this is to have a muffler repair shop remove the corroded sections with a cutting torch. If, however, you want to save money by doing it yourself and you don't have an oxy/acetylene welding outfit with a cutting torch), simply cut off the old components with a hack-saw. If you have compressed air, special pneumatic cutting chisels can also be used. If you do decide to tackle the job at home, be sure to wear eye protection to protect your eyes from metal chips and work gloves to protect your hands.

4   Here are some simple guidelines to apply when repairing the exhaust system:

   a) Work from the back to the front when removing exhaust system components.

12.1   The exhaust pipe is connected to the exhaust system with three nuts - there is a sealing ring under the flange which should be replaced whenever the pipe is unbolted from the manifold

   b) Apply penetrating oil to the exhaust system component fasteners to make them easier to remove.
   c) Use new gaskets, hangers and clamps when installing exhaust system components.
   d) Apply anti-seize compound to the threads of all exhaust system fasteners during reassembly.
   e) Be sure to allow sufficient clearance between newly installed parts and all points on the underbody to avoid overheating the floor pan and possibly damaging the interior carpet and insulation. Pay particularly close attention to the catalytic converter and its heat shield. **Warning:** *The catalytic converter operates at very high temperatures and takes a long time to cool. Wait until it's completely cool before attempting to remove the converter. Failure to do so could result in serious burns.*

Chapter 5 Engine electrical systems

Contents

Specifications

Ignition timing (all models) .... 10-degrees BTDC

Ignition coil
Primary resistance
    2S-E engine .... 0.3 to 0.5 ohms
    3S-GE engine .... 0.4 to 0.5 ohms
    3S-FE engine .... 0.4 to 0.5 ohms
    4A-FE engine .... 1.3 to 1.6 ohms
    5S-FE engine .... 0.4 to 0.5 ohms
Secondary resistance
    2S-E engine .... 7.5 to 10.4 K-ohms
    3S-FE engine .... 10.2 to 13.8 K-ohms
    3S-FE engine .... 7.7 to 10.4 K-ohms
    4A-FE engine .... 10.4 to 14 K-ohms
    5S-FE engine .... 10.0 to 14 K-ohms

Distributor
Air gap (all models) .... 0.008 to 0.016 inch
Pick-up coil resistance
    2S-E, 3S-GE and 3S-FE engines .... 140 to 180 ohms
    4A-FE engine
        1990 and 1991 models .... 140 to 180 ohms
        1992 models .... 185 to 265 ohms
    5S-FE engine
        1990 and 1991 models .... 170 to 210 ohms
        1992 and later models
            G+ and G- terminals .... 185 to 265 ohms
            NE+ and NE- terminals............................... 375 to 530 ohms

Charging system
Charging voltage
    1989 and earlier models.. 13.5 to 15.1 volts
    1990 and later models.. 13.9 to 15.1 volts
Standard amperage
    All lights and accessories turned off .... less than 10 amps
    Headlights (hi-beam) and heater blower motor turned on .... 30 amps or more
Alternator brush length
    Standard .... 0.413 inch
    Minimum .... 0.059 inch

5

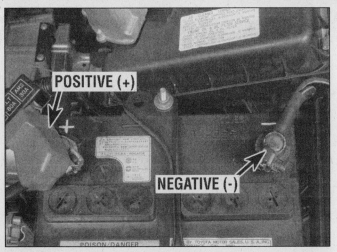

2.1   When detaching the cables from the terminals of the battery, be sure to ALWAYS disconnect the negative cable (the one with the minus sign) first - when reattaching the cables, hook up the positive cable (the one with the plus sign) first

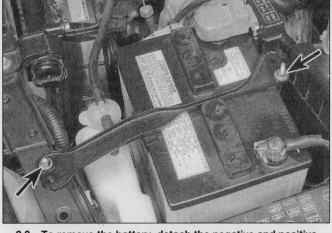

2.2   To remove the battery, detach the negative and positive cables, then remove the hold-down strap bolt (arrow) and nut (arrow) and the strap, then carefully lift the battery out of the engine compartment

1   General information

The engine electrical systems include all ignition, charging and starting components. Because of their engine-related functions, these components are discussed separately from chassis electrical devices such as the lights, the instruments, etc. (which are included in Chapter 12).

Always observe the following precautions when working on the electrical systems:

a) Be extremely careful when servicing engine electrical components. They are easily damaged if checked, connected or handled improperly.

b) Never leave the ignition switch on for long periods of time with the engine off.

c) Don't disconnect the battery cables while the engine is running.

d) Maintain correct polarity when connecting a battery cable from another vehicle during jump starting.

e) Always disconnect the negative cable first and hook it up last or the battery may be shorted by the tool being used to loosen the cable clamps.

It's also a good idea to review the safety-related information regarding the engine electrical systems located in the *Safety first* section near the front of this manual before beginning any operation included in this Chapter.

2   Battery - removal and installation

Refer to illustrations 2.1 and 2.2

1   **Warning:** *Always disconnect the negative cable first and hook it up last or the battery may be shorted by the tool being used to loosen the cable clamps.* Disconnect both cables from the battery terminals **(see illustration). Caution:** *If the stereo in your vehicle is equipped with an anti-theft system, refer to the information on page 0-15 at the front of the manual before detaching the cable.*

2   Remove the battery hold-down clamp **(see illustration)**.

3   Lift out the battery. Be careful - it's heavy.

4   While the battery is out, inspect the carrier (tray) for corrosion (see Chapter 1).

5   If you are replacing the battery, make sure that you get one that's identical, with the same dimensions, amperage rating, cold cranking rating, etc.

6   Installation is the reverse of removal.

3   Battery - emergency jump starting

Refer to the *Booster battery (jump) starting* procedure at the front of this manual.

4   Battery cables - check and replacement

1   Periodically inspect the entire length of each battery cable for damage, cracked or burned insulation and corrosion. Poor battery cable connections can cause starting problems and decreased engine performance.

2   Check the cable-to-terminal connections at the ends of the cables for cracks, loose wire strands and corrosion. The presence of white, fluffy deposits under the insulation at the cable terminal connection is a sign that the cable is corroded and should be replaced. Check the terminals for distortion, missing mounting bolts and corrosion.

3   When removing the cables, always disconnect the negative cable first and hook it up last or the battery may be shorted by the tool used to loosen the cable clamps. **Caution:** *If the stereo in your vehicle is equipped with an anti-theft system, refer to the information on page 0-15 at the front of the manual before detaching the cable.* Even if only the positive cable is being replaced, be sure to disconnect the negative cable from the battery first (see Chapter 1 for further information regarding battery cable removal).

4   Disconnect the old cables from the battery, then trace each of them to their opposite ends and detach them from the starter solenoid and ground terminals. Note the routing of each cable to ensure correct installation.

5   If you are replacing either or both of the old cables, take them with you when buying new cables. It is vitally important that you replace the cables with identical parts. Cables have characteristics that make them easy to identify: positive cables are usually red, larger in cross-section and have a larger diameter battery post clamp; ground cables are usually black, smaller in cross-section and have a slightly smaller diameter clamp for the negative post.

6   Clean the threads of the solenoid or ground connection with a wire brush to remove rust and corrosion. Apply a light coat of battery terminal corrosion inhibitor, or petroleum jelly, to the threads to prevent future corrosion.

7   Attach the cable to the solenoid or ground connection and tighten the mounting nut/bolt securely.

8   Before connecting a new cable to the battery, make sure that it reaches the battery post without having to be stretched.

9   Connect the positive cable first, followed by the negative cable.

6.1 To use a calibrated ignition tester (available at most auto parts stores), simply disconnect a spark plug wire, attach the wire to the tester and clip the tester to a good ground - if there is enough power to fire the plug, sparks will be clearly visible between the electrode tip and the tester body as the engine is turned over

5   Ignition system - general information and precautions

The ignition system includes the ignition switch, the battery, the igniter, the coil, the primary (low voltage) and secondary (high voltage) wiring circuits, the distributor and the spark plugs. The ignition system is controlled by the Electronic Control Unit (ECU). Using data provided by information sensors which monitor various engine functions (such as rpm, intake air volume, engine temperature, etc.), the ECU ensures a perfectly timed spark under all conditions. This system is known as Electronic Spark Advance (ESA).

When working on the ignition system, take the following precautions:

a) Do not keep the ignition switch on for more than 10 seconds if the engine will not start.

b) Always connect a tachometer in accordance with the manufacturer's instructions. Some tachometers may be incompatible with this ignition system. Consult a dealer service department before buying a tachometer for use with this vehicle.

c) Never allow the ignition coil terminals to touch ground. Grounding the coil could result in damage to the igniter and/or the ignition coil.

d) Do not disconnect the battery when the engine is running.

e) Make sure that the igniter is properly grounded.

6   Ignition system - check

Refer to illustration 6.1

Warning: *Because of the high voltage generated by the ignition system, extreme care should be taken whenever an operation is performed involving ignition components. This not only includes the igniter, coil, distributor and spark plug wires, but related components such as plug connectors, tachometer and and other test equipment also.*

1   If the engine turns over but won't start, disconnect the spark plug wire from any spark plug and attach it to a calibrated tester (available at most auto parts stores). Connect the clip on the tester to a bolt or metal bracket on the engine **(see illustration)**. If you're unable to obtain a calibrated ignition tester, remove the wire from one of the spark plugs and using an insulated tool, pull back the boot and hold the end of the wire about 1/4-inch from a good ground.

2   Crank the engine and watch the end of the tester or spark plug wire to see if bright blue, well-defined sparks occur.

If you're not using a calibrated tester, have an assistant crank the engine for you.

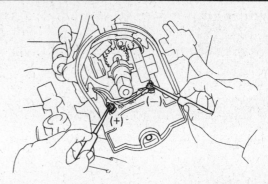

7.3a To check the primary resistance of the coil used on 2S-E, 3S-FE and 5S-FE engine models, measure the resistance between the positive and negative terminals

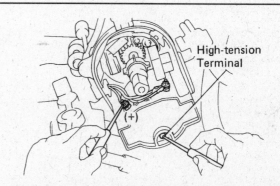

High-tension Terminal

(+)

7.3b To check the secondary resistance of the coil used on 2S-E, 3S-FE and 5S-FE engine models, measure the resistance between the positive terminal and the high tension terminal.

3   If sparks occur, sufficient voltage is reaching the plug to fire it (repeat the check at the remaining plug wires to verify that the distributor cap and rotor are OK). However, the plugs themselves may be fouled, so remove and check them as described in Chapter 1.

4   If no sparks or intermittent sparks occur, remove the distributor cap and check the cap and rotor as described in Chapter 1. If moisture is present, dry out the cap and rotor, then reinstall the cap and repeat the spark test.

5   If there's still no spark, detach the coil secondary wire from the distributor cap and hook it up to the tester (reattach the plug wire to the spark plug), then repeat the spark check. Again, if you don't have a tester, hold the end of the wire about 1/4-inch from a good ground.

6   If sparks now occur, the distributor cap, rotor or plug wire(s) may be defective.

7   If no sparks occur, check the primary wire connections at the coil to make sure they're clean and tight. Check for voltage to the coil. Check the coil (see Section 7). Make any necessary repairs, then repeat the check again.

8   If there's still no spark, the coil-to-cap wire may be bad (check the resistance with an ohmmeter and compare it to the Specifications. If a known good wire doesn't make any difference in the test results, the igniter may be defective.

7   Ignition coil - check and replacement

Refer to illustrations 7.3a through 7.3f

Check

1   Detach the cable from the negative terminal of the battery.

2   Remove the distributor cap (see Chapter 1).

3   Using an ohmmeter, check the coil:

a) Measure the resistance between the positive and negative terminals **(see illustrations)**. Compare your reading with the spec-

5

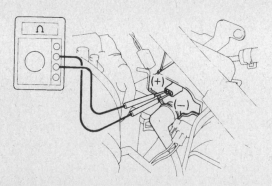

7.3c To check the primary resistance of the coil used on 3S-GE engine models, measure the resistance between the positive and negative terminals

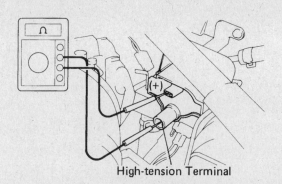

7.3d To check the primary resistance of the coil used on 3S-GE engine models, measure the resistance between the positive and high tension terminals as shown

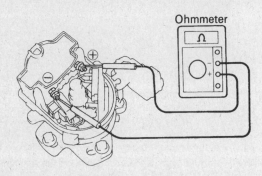

7.3e To check the primary resistance of the coil used on 4A-FE engine models, measure the resistance between the positive and negative terminals

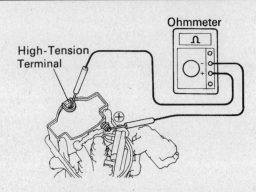

7.3f To check the secondary resistance of the coil used on 4A-FE engine models, measure the resistance between the positive and high tension terminals as shown

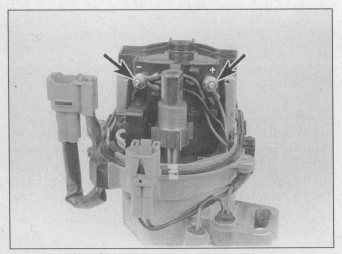

7.8 Label the coil primary wires, remove the negative and positive terminal nuts (arrows) and detach the wires

7.9 Remove the four coil mounting screws to separate the coil from the distributor assembly

ified coil primary resistance listed in the Specifications Section at the beginning of this Chapter.

b) Measure the resistance between the positive terminal and the high tension terminal **(see illustrations)**. Compare your reading with the specified coil secondary resistance listed in the Specifications Section at the beginning of this Chapter.

4   If either of the above tests yield resistance values outside the specified amount, replace the coil.

Replacement

Refer to illustrations 7.8 and 7.9

5   Detach the cable from the negative terminal of the battery. **Caution:** *If the stereo in your vehicle is equipped with an anti-theft system, refer to the information on page 0-15 at the front of the manual before detaching the cable.*

6   Remove the distributor (see Section 8).

8.3   Look for a raised "1" (arrow) on top of the distributor cap to find the number one spark plug terminal (if there is no raised "1" indicating the number one terminal, trace the plug lead from the number one spark plug back to its terminal)

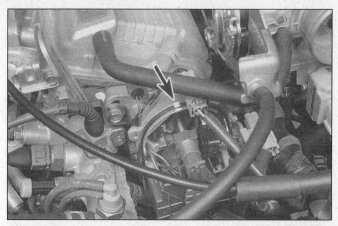

8.5a   Paint or scribe a mark (arrow) on the edge of the distributor housing immediately below the rotor tip to ensure that the rotor is pointing in the same direction when the distributor is reinstalled

8.5b   Paint or scribe another mark across one of the distributor adjustment bolt flanges and the cylinder head (arrow) to ensure that the distributor is aligned correctly when it is reinstalled

7   Remove the coil dust cover.
8   Label and disconnect the electrical wires from the coil terminals **(see illustration)**.
9   Remove the four coil mounting bolts and separate it from the distributor assembly **(see illustration)**.
10   Installation is the reverse of removal.

8   Distributor - removal and installation

Removal

Refer to illustrations 8.3, 8.5a and 8.5b

1   Detach the cable from the negative battery terminal. **Caution:** *If the stereo in your vehicle is equipped with an anti-theft system, refer to the information on page 0-15 at the front of the manual before detaching the cable.*
2   Unplug the electrical connectors from the distributor.
3   Look for a raised "1" on the distributor cap **(see illustration)**. This marks the location for the number one cylinder spark plug wire terminal. If the cap does not have a mark for the number one terminal, locate the number one spark plug and trace the wire back to the terminal on the cap.
4   Remove the distributor cap (1see Chapter 1) and turn the engine over until the rotor is pointing toward the number one spark plug terminal (see locating TDC procedure in Chapter 2).
5   Make a mark on the edge of the distributor base directly below

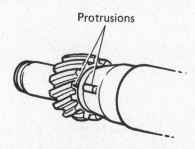

8.8a   On 2S-E engines, align the protrusion on the distributor housing with the one on the spiral gear . . .

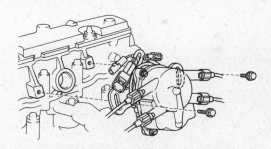

8.8b   . . . then insert the distributor, lining up the center of the flange with the center of the bolt hole on the camshaft housing

the rotor tip and in line with it. Also, mark the distributor base and the engine block to ensure that the distributor is installed correctly **(see illustrations)**.
6   Remove the distributor hold-down bolt(s), then pull the distributor straight out to remove it. **Caution:** *DO NOT turn the crankshaft while the distributor is out of the engine, or the alignment marks will be useless.*

Installation

Refer to illustrations 8.8a, 8.8b, 8.9a, 8,9b and 8.9c
Note: *If the crankshaft has been moved while the distributor is out, locate Top Dead Center (TDC) for the number one piston (see Chapter 2) and position the distributor and the rotor accordingly.*
7   Insert the distributor into the engine in exactly the same relationship to the block that it was in when removed.
8   On models with gear driven distributors, align the dimples on the driven gear and distributor housing **(see illustrations)**. To mesh the

5

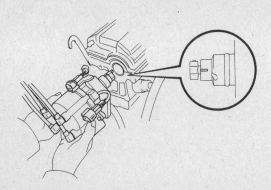

8.9a   On the 3S-FE engine, align the cutout on the coupling with the line on the distributor housing and insert the distributor with the center of the flange aligned with the center of the cylinder head bolt hole

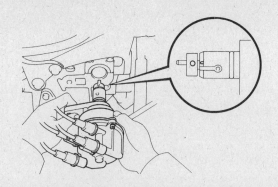

8.9b   On the 3S-GE engine, line up the the drilled mark on the lug with the notch on the distributor housing and insert the distributor with the center of the flange aligned with the center of the cylinder head bolt hole

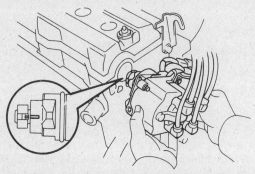

8.9c   On 4A-FE and 5S-FE engine, align the cutout on the coupling with the line on the distributor housing and insert the distributor with the center of the flange aligned with the center of the cylinder head bolt hole

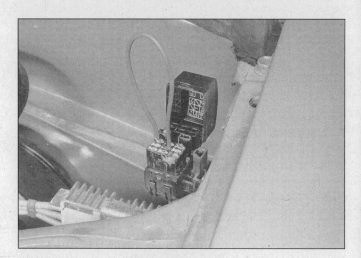

9.3   Use a jumper wire to bridge terminals T and E1 of the check electrical connector

helical gears on the camshaft and the distributor, it may be necessary to turn the rotor slightly.

9   On models with lug-driven distributors, align the distributor match marks **(see illustrations)**.

10   If the distributor does not seat completely, recheck the alignment marks between the distributor base and the block to verify that the distributor is in the same position it was in before removal. Also check the rotor to see if it's aligned with the mark you made on the edge of the distributor base.

11   Loosely install the distributor hold-down bolt(s).

12   Installation is the reverse of removal.

13   Check the ignition timing (see Section 9) and tighten the distributor hold-down bolt securely.

9   Ignition timing - check and adjustment

Refer to illustrations 9.3, 9.4, 9.5a and 9.5b

Note: *The following ignition timing procedure should apply to all vehicles covered by this manual. However, if the procedure specified on the VECI label of your vehicle differs from this one, use the one contained on the VECI label.*

1   Check the engine idle speed and adjust, if necessary (see Chapter 1).

2   With the ignition switch off, connect a timing light in accordance with manufacturers instructions.

3   Locate the diagnostic electrical connector and insert a jumper wire between E1 and T terminals **(see illustration)**.

4   Locate the timing marks on the timing cover and the crankshaft pulley **(see illustration)**.

9.4   Locate the timing notch on the crankshaft pulley (arrow) and the stationary timing marks on the timing cover

9.5a With the engine running, point the timing light at the timing notch and the timing marks and compare your reading with the specified timing

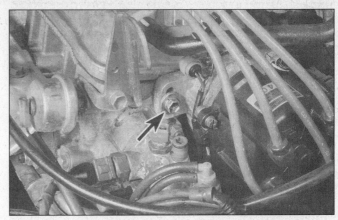

9.5b Loosen the hold-down bolt (arrow) and rotate the distributor to adjust the ignition timing

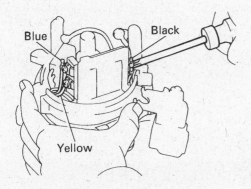

10.4a Label and disconnect the wires

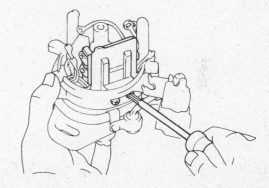

10.4b Remove the mounting screws and detach the igniter

5   Start the engine and aim the timing light at the mark. It should be 10-degrees BTDC **(see illustrations)**. If necessary, loosen the distributor and slowly turn it until the timing marks indicate the specified value. Tighten the hold-down bolt and recheck the timing.
6   Turn the engine off and remove the jumper wire and the timing light.

10   Igniter - replacement

1   Detach the cable from the negative terminal of the battery. **Caution:** *If the stereo in your vehicle is equipped with an anti-theft system, refer to the information on page 0-15 at the front of the manual before detaching the cable.*

Distributor-mounted igniter
Refer to illustrations 10.4a and 10.4b
2   Remove the distributor (see Section 8).
3   Remove the rotor and the igniter dust cover.
4   Label and disconnect the wires from the igniter, then remove the two igniter mounting screws and detach it from the distributor **(see illustrations)**.
5   Installation is the reverse of removal.

Remote-mounted igniter
Refer to illustration 10.6
Note: *See Chapter 6 for component location charts.*
6   Unplug the electrical connector from the igniter **(see illustration)**.
7   Remove the mounting screws from the igniter and detach it from its mounting bracket.
8   Installation is the reverse of removal.

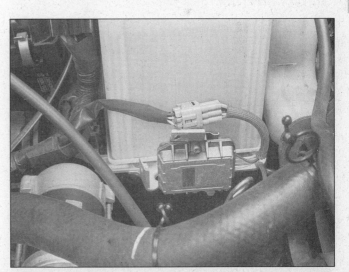

10.6 To detach the igniter, unplug the electrical connector and remove the mounting screws then separate the igniter from the mounting bracket

11   Air gap - check

Refer to illustrations 11.3a, 11.3b and 13.3c
1   Detach the cable from the negative terminal of the battery.
2   Remove the distributor cap (see Chapter 1).
3   Using a feeler gauge, measure the gap between the signal rotor

5

11.3a   Measure the air gap between the signal rotor and the pick-up coil projection - if the gap is not within specification, replace the distributor

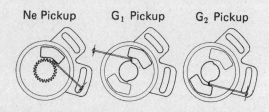

11.3c   Some models have more than one pick-up coil - the gap must be as specified at each one of them

12.1b   When checking the pick-up coil on a 3S-GE engine, the resistance between terminal G- and the other terminals must be 140 to 180 ohms

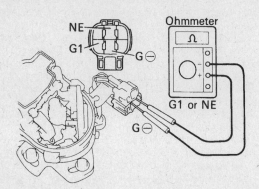

12.1d   On the 4A-FE engine, check the resistance between terminals G1 and G-, then between NE and G-

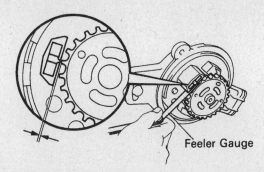

11.3b   Some models may have a signal rotor with gear-like teeth - these are also checked with a feeler gauge to measure the air gap between the signal rotor and the pick-up coil projection - if the gap is not within specification, replace the distributor

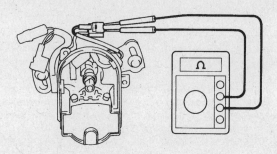

12.1a   When checking the pick-up coil on the 2S-E engine, simply measure the resistance across the two terminals of its electrical connector

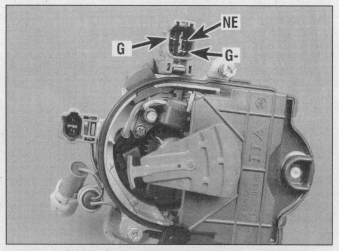

12.1c   Location of the pick-up coil terminals - 3S-FE engine

and the pick-up coil projection **(see illustrations)**. Compare your measurement to the air gap listed in this Chapter's Specifications. If the air gap is not as specified, replace the distributor, as the air gap is not adjustable.

12   Pick-up coil - check

Refer to illustrations 12.1a, through 12.1f

1   Using an ohmmeter, measure the resistance between the pick-up coil terminals **(see illustrations)**.

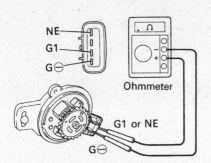

12.1e On 1990 and 1991 5S-FE engines, check the resistance between terminals G- and G1, then between G- and NE

2   Compare the measurements to those listed in the Specifications Section at the beginning of this Chapter. If the resistance is not as specified, replace the distributor.

13   Charging system - general information and precautions

The charging system includes the alternator, an internal voltage regulator, a charge indicator, the battery, a fusible link and the wiring between all the components. The charging system supplies electrical power for the ignition system, the lights, the radio, etc. The alternator is driven by a drivebelt at the front (right end) of the engine.

The purpose of the voltage regulator is to limit the alternator's voltage to a preset value. This prevents power surges, circuit over-loads, etc., during peak voltage output.

The fusible link is a short length of insulated wire integral with the engine compartment wiring harness. The link is several wire gauges smaller in diameter than the circuit it protects. Production fusible links and their identification flags are identified by the flag color. See Chapter 12 for additional information regarding fusible links.

The charging system doesn't ordinarily require periodic maintenance. However, the drivebelt, battery and wires and connections should be inspected at the intervals outlined in Chapter 1.

The dashboard warning light should come on when the ignition key is turned to Start, then should go off immediately. If it remains on, there is a malfunction in the charging system (see Section 14). Some vehicles are also equipped with a voltage gauge. If the voltage gauge indicates abnormally high or low voltage, check the charging system (see Section 14).

Be very careful when making electrical circuit connections to a vehicle equipped with an alternator and note the following:
a) When reconnecting wires to the alternator from the battery, be sure to note the polarity.
b) Before using arc welding equipment to repair any part of the ve-hicle, disconnect the wires from the alternator and the battery terminals.
c) Never start the engine with a battery charger connected.
d) Always disconnect both battery leads before using a battery charger.
e) The alternator is driven by an engine drivebelt which could cause serious injury if your hand, hair or clothes become entan-gled in it with the engine running.
f) Because the alternator is connected directly to the battery, it could arc or cause a fire if overloaded or shorted out.
g) Wrap a plastic bag over the alternator and secure it with rubber bands before steam cleaning the engine.

14   Charging system - check

Refer to illustrations 14.7, 14.8a and 14.8b

1   If a malfunction occurs in the charging circuit, don't automatically

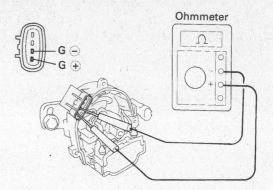

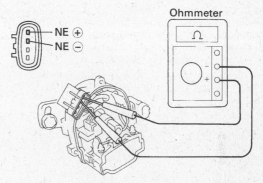

12.1f 1992 5S-FE engine pick-up coil check details - measure the resistance between the indicated terminals

assume that the alternator is causing the problem. First check the fol-lowing items:
a) Check the drivebelt tension and its condition. Replace it if worn or deteriorated.
b) Make sure the alternator mounting and adjustment bolts are tight.
c) Inspect the alternator wiring harness and the electrical connec-tors at the alternator and voltage regulator. They must be in good condition and tight.
d) Check the fusible link (if equipped) located between the starter solenoid and the alternator or the large main fuses in the engine compartment. If it's burned, determine the cause, repair the cir-cuit and replace the link or fuse (the vehicle won't start and/or the accessories won't work if the fusible link or fuse blows).
e) Start the engine and check the alternator for abnormal noises (a shrieking or squealing sound indicates a bad bushing).
f) Check the specific gravity of the battery electrolyte. If it's low, charge the battery (doesn't apply to maintenance free batteries).
g) Make certain that the battery is fully charged (one bad cell in a battery can cause overcharging by the alternator).
h) Disconnect the battery cables (negative first, then positive). In-spect the battery posts and the cable clamps for corrosion. Clean them thoroughly if necessary (see Section 4 and Chap-ter 1). Reconnect the cable to the negative terminal.
i) With the key off, insert a test light between the negative battery post and the disconnected negative cable clamp.
    1) If the test light does not come on, reattach the clamp and proceed to the next step.
    2) If the test light comes on, there is a short in the electrical system of the vehicle. The short must be repaired before the charging system can be checked.
    3) Disconnect the alternator wiring harness.
        (a) If the light goes out, the alternator is bad.
        (b) If the light stays on, pull each fuse until the light goes out (this will tell you which component is shorted).

2   Using a voltmeter, check the battery voltage with the engine off. It should be approximately 12-volts.

14.7   If the alternator is putting out less than standard voltage, ground terminal F, start the engine and check the voltage at terminal B - if the reading is greater than standard voltage, replace the regulator; if the reading is less than standard, check the alternator or have it checked by a dealer

14.8b   An inductive type ammeter like this one, which is available at most auto parts stores, is much cheaper than a professional ammeter, but it's accurate enough for a quick check of the charging system and is quite easy to use: Simply place it on the alternator output lead, start the engine and check charging amperage

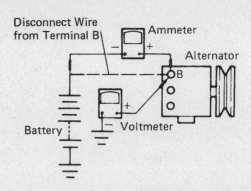

14.8a   Hook up an ammeter as shown to check alternator output

3   Start the engine and check the battery voltage again. It should now be approximately 13.5 to 15.1-volts.
4   Turn on the headlights. The voltage should drop and then come back up, if the charging system is working properly.
5   If the voltage reading is greater than the specified charging voltage, replace the voltage regulator (see Section 16).
6   If the voltmeter reading is less than standard voltage, check the regulator and alternator as follows.
7   Ground terminal F, start the engine, check the voltage at terminal B **(see illustration)** and compare your reading to the standard voltage.
   a) If the voltmeter reading is greater than standard voltage, replace the regulator.
   b) If the voltmeter reading is less than standard voltage, check the alternator (or have it checked by a dealer service department if you do not have an ammeter).
8   If you have an ammeter, hook it up to the charging system as shown **(see illustration)**. If you don't have a professional ammeter, you can also use an inductive-type current indicator **(see illustration)**. This device is inexpensive, readily available at auto parts stores and accurate enough to perform simple amperage checks like the following test.
9   With the engine running at 2000 rpm, check the reading on the ammeter with all accessories and lights off, then again with the high-beam headlights on and the heater blower switch turned to the HI position. Compare your readings to the standard amperage listed in this Chapter's Specifications.
10   If the ammeter reading is less than standard amperage, repair or replace the alternator.

15.2   Before removing the alternator, detach the cable from the negative terminal of the battery, then unplug or disconnect the electrical connectors (arrows) from the alternator - to remove the drivebelt, loosen the adjustment bolts (arrows)

15.3   To remove the alternator, loosen the adjustment bolts shown on other side of adjustment bracket in the previous illustration, then remove the adjustment bolt and pivot bolt (arrows) shown here

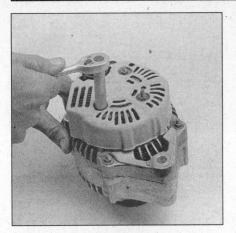

16.2a Remove the three nuts from the rear cover

16.2b Take the nut, washer and insulator off terminal B and remove the alternator end cover

16.3 Once the rear cover is removed, remove the five screws (arrows) that retain the voltage regulator and the brush holder

15 Alternator - removal and installation

Refer to illustrations 15.2 and 15.3

1 Detach the cable from the negative terminal of the battery. **Caution:** *If the stereo in your vehicle is equipped with an anti-theft system, refer to the information on page 0-15 at the front of the manual before detaching the cable.*

2 Detach the electrical connectors from the alternator **(see illustration)**.

3 Loosen the alternator adjustment and pivot bolts **(see illustration)** and detach the drivebelt.

4 Remove the adjustment and pivot bolts and separate the alternator from the engine.

5 If you are replacing the alternator, take the old alternator with you when purchasing a replacement unit. Make sure that the new/rebuilt unit is identical to the old alternator. Look at the terminals - they should be the same in number, size and locations as the terminals on the old alternator. Finally, look at the identification markings - they will be stamped in the housing or printed on a tag or plaque affixed to the housing. Make sure that these numbers are the same on both alternators.

6 Many new/rebuilt alternators do not have a pulley installed, so you may have to switch the pulley from the old unit to the new/rebuilt

one. When buying an alternator, find out the shop's policy regarding installation of pulleys - some shops will perform this service free of charge.

7 Installation is the reverse of removal.

8 After the alternator is installed, adjust the drivebelt tension (see Chapter 1).

9 Check the charging voltage to verify proper operation of the alternator (see Section 14).

16 Voltage regulator and alternator brushes - replacement

Refer to illustrations 16.2a, 16.2b, 16.3, 16.4a, 16.4b, 16.5 and 16.7

1 Remove the alternator (see Section 15) and place it on a clean workbench.

2 Remove the three rear cover nuts, the nut and terminal insulator and the rear cover **(see illustrations)**.

3 Remove the five voltage regulator and brush holder mounting screws **(see illustration)**.

4 Remove the brush holder and the regulator from the rear end frame **(see illustrations)**. If you are only replacing the regulator, proceed to Step 8, install the new unit, reassemble the alternator and install it on the engine (see Section 15). If you are going to replace the brushes, proceed with the next Step.

5

16.4a Remove the brush holder

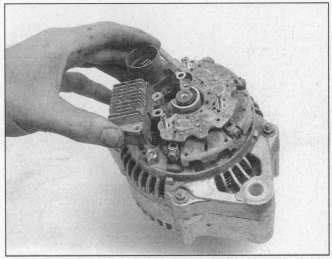

16.4b Remove the regulator

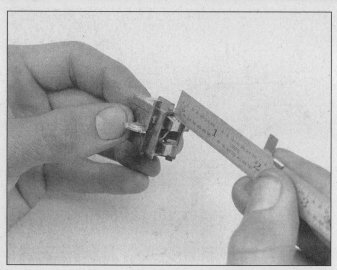

16.5   Measure the exposed length of the brushes and compare your measurements to the specified minimum length to determine whether they should be replaced

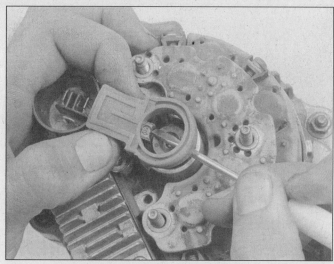

16.7   To facilitate installation of the brush holder, depress each brush with a small screwdriver to clear the shaft

5   Measure the exposed length of each brush **(see illustration)** and compare it to the minimum length listed in this Chapter's Specifications. If the length of either brush is less than the specified minimum, replace the brushes.
6   Make sure that each brush moves smoothly in the brush holder.
7   Install the brush holder by depressing each brush with a small screwdriver to clear the shaft **(see illustration)**.
8   Install the voltage regulator and brush holder screws into the rear frame.
9   Install the rear cover and tighten the three nuts securely.
10   Install the terminal insulator and tighten it with the nut.
11   Install the alternator (see Section 15).

17   Starting system - general information and precautions

The sole function of the starting system is to turn over the engine quickly enough to allow it to start.

The starting system consists of the battery, the starter motor, the starter solenoid and the wires connecting them. The solenoid is mounted directly on the starter motor.

The solenoid/starter motor assembly is installed on the upper part of the engine, next to the transaxle bellhousing.

When the ignition key is turned to the Start position, the starter solenoid is actuated through the starter control circuit. The starter solenoid then connects the battery to the starter. The battery supplies the electrical energy to the starter motor, which does the actual work of cranking the engine.

The starter motor on a vehicle equipped with a manual transaxle can be operated only when the clutch pedal is depressed; the starter on a vehicle equipped with an automatic transaxle can be operated only when the transaxle selector lever is in Park or Neutral.

Always observe the following precautions when working on the starting system:
a)   Excessive cranking of the starter motor can overheat it and cause serious damage. Never operate the starter motor for more than 15 seconds at a time without pausing to allow it to cool for at least two minutes.
b)   The starter is connected directly to the battery and could arc or cause a fire if mishandled, overloaded or shorted out.
c)   \
Always detach the cable from the negative terminal of the battery before working on the starting system. **Caution:** *If the stereo in your vehicle is equipped with an anti-theft system, refer to the information on page 0-15 at the front of the manual before detaching the cable.*

18   Starter motor - testing in vehicle

Note: *Before diagnosing starter problems, make sure that the battery is fully charged.*

1   If the starter motor does not turn at all when the switch is operated, make sure that the shift lever is in Neutral or Park (automatic transaxle) or that the clutch pedal is depressed (manual transaxle).
2   Make sure that the battery is charged and that all cables, both at the battery and starter solenoid terminals, are clean and secure.
3   If the starter motor spins but the engine is not cranking, the over-running clutch in the starter motor is slipping and the starter motor must be replaced.
4   If, when the switch is actuated, the starter motor does not operate at all but the solenoid clicks, then the problem lies with either the battery, the main solenoid contacts or the starter motor itself (or the engine is seized).
5   If the solenoid plunger cannot be heard when the switch is actuated, the battery is bad, the fusible link is burned (the circuit is open) or the solenoid itself is defective.
6   To check the solenoid, connect a jumper lead between the battery (+) and the ignition switch terminal (the small terminal) on the solenoid. If the starter motor now operates, the solenoid is OK and the problem is in the ignition switch, Neutral start switch or in the wiring.
7   If the starter motor still does not operate, remove the starter/solenoid assembly for disassembly, testing and repair.
8   If the starter motor cranks the engine at an abnormally slow speed, first make sure that the battery is charged and that all terminal connections are tight. If the engine is partially seized, or has the wrong viscosity oil in it, it will crank slowly.
9   Run the engine until normal operating temperature is reached, then disconnect the coil wire from the distributor cap and ground it on the engine.
10   Connect a voltmeter positive lead to the battery positive post and connect the negative lead to the negative post.
11   Crank the engine and take the voltmeter readings as soon as a steady figure is indicated. Do not allow the starter motor to turn for more than 15 seconds at a time. A reading of nine volts or more, with the starter motor turning at normal cranking speed, is normal. If the reading is nine volts or more but the cranking speed is slow, the motor is faulty. If the reading is less than nine volts and the cranking speed is slow, the solenoid contacts are probably burned, the starter motor is bad, the battery is discharged or there is a bad connection.

19.3a   To remove the starter motor/solenoid assembly, detach the cable from the negative terminal of the battery, disconnect the electrical connectors and remove the bolts (arrows)

19.3b   Pull the starter motor/solenoid assembly back away from the bellhousing, then lift it straight up out of the engine compartment

20.2   Before disassembling the starter motor, solenoid and gear reduction assembly, scribe or paint an alignment mark across the starter motor and the gear reduction assembly

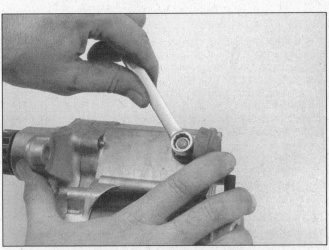

20.3   To disconnect the strap that connects the starter to the solenoid, remove this nut

19   Starter motor - removal and installation

Refer to illustrations 19.3a and 19.3b
1   Detach the cable from the negative terminal of the battery. **Caution:** *If the stereo in your vehicle is equipped with an anti-theft system, refer to the information on page 0-15 at the front of the manual before detaching the cable.*
2   Detach the electrical connectors from the starter/solenoid assembly.
3   Remove the starter motor mounting bolts **(see illustrations)**. Remove the starter.
4   Installation is the reverse of removal.

20   Starter solenoid - removal and installation

Refer to illustrations 20.2, 20.3, 20.4, 20.5, 20.6a and 20.6b
1   Remove the starter motor (see Section 19).
2   Scribe or paint a mark across the starter motor and gear reduction assembly **(see illustration)**.
3   Disconnect the strap from the solenoid to the starter motor termi-

20.4   To detach the solenoid from the starter motor, remove the screws (arrows) which secure the gear reduction assembly to the solenoid . . .

nal **(see illustration)**.
4   Remove the screws **(see illustration)** which secure the gear reduction assembly to the solenoid.

5

20.5 . . . then remove the through-bolts (arrows) which secure the starter motor to the gear reduction assembly

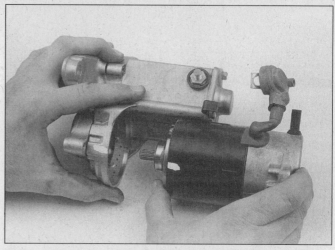

20.6a Separate the starter from the gear reduction assembly, . . .

5   Remove the through-bolts **(see illustration)** which secure the starter motor to the gear reduction assembly.

6   Separate the motor from the gear reduction and solenoid assembly then remove the solenoid from the gear reduction assembly **(see illustrations)**.

7   Installation is the reverse of removal. Be sure to align the paint or scribe mark.

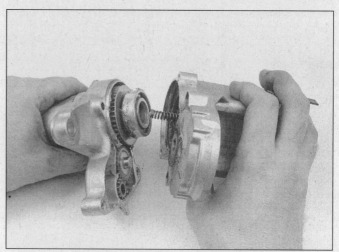

20.6b . . . then separate the solenoid from the gear reduction assembly (note the return spring protruding from the solenoid assembly - make sure that this spring is installed before reassembling the solenoid and the gear reduction assembly)

Chapter 6 Emissions control systems

Contents

1   General information

Refer to illustrations 1.1a through 1.1o, 1.6a and 1.6b

To minimize pollution of the atmosphere from incompletely burned and evaporating gases and to maintain good driveability and fuel economy, a number of emission control systems are used on these vehicles **(see illustrations)**. They include the:

Positive Crankcase Ventilation (PCV) system
Evaporative Emission Control (EVAP) system
Exhaust Gas Recirculation (EGR) system
Catalytic converter
Electronic Fuel Injection (EFI) system (some models)
Dashpot (1990 4A-FE engines only)

The sections in this chapter include general descriptions, checking procedures within the scope of the home mechanic and component replacement procedures (when possible) for each of the systems listed above.

Before assuming an emissions control system is malfunctioning, check the fuel and ignition systems carefully (see Chapters 4 and 5). The diagnosis of some emission control devices requires specialized tools, equipment and training. If checking and servicing become too difficult or if a procedure is beyond the scope of your skills, consult your dealer service department or other repair shop.

This doesn't mean, however, that emission control systems are particularly difficult to maintain and repair. You can quickly and easily perform many checks and do most of the regular maintenance at home with common tune-up and hand tools. **Note:** *The most frequent cause of emissions problems is simply a loose or broken electrical connector or vacuum hose, so always check the electrical connectors and vacuum hoses first.*

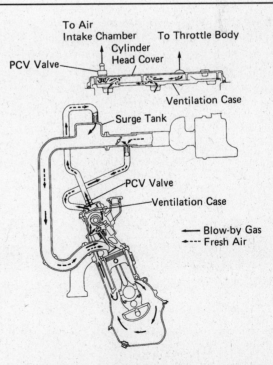

1.1a   Typical emissions control system component locations (1986 2S-E engine)

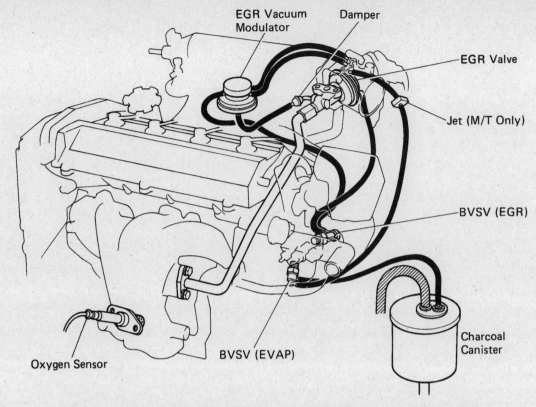

1.1b   Typical emissions control system component locations (1986 and 1987 3S-GE engine)

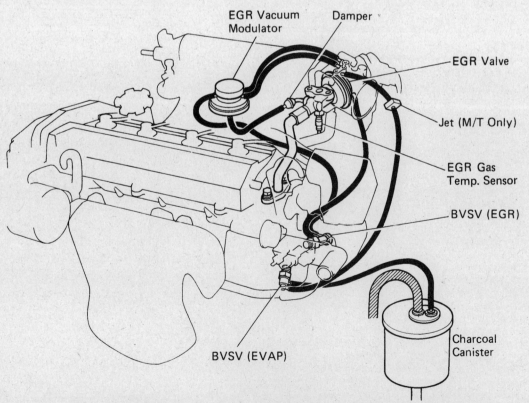

1.1c   Typical emissions control system component locations (1988 and 1989 3S-GE engine)

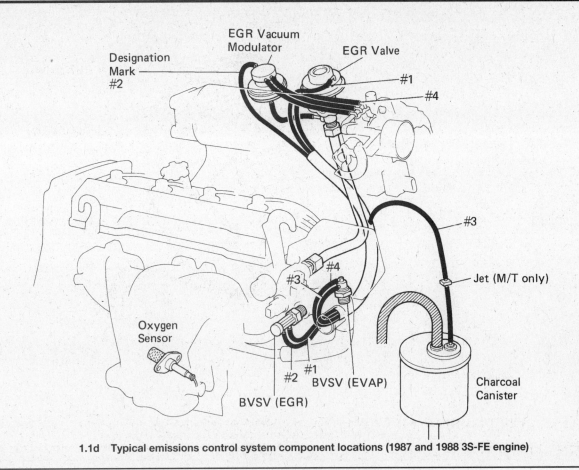

1.1d Typical emissions control system component locations (1987 and 1988 3S-FE engine)

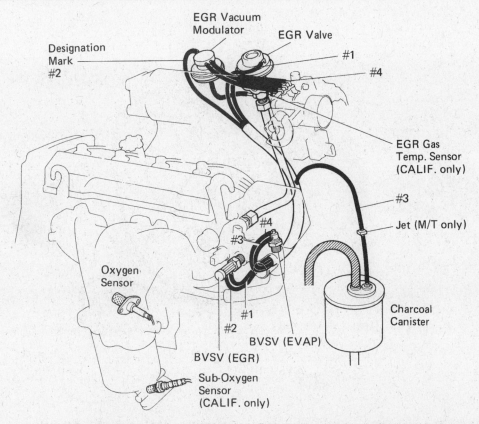

1.1e Typical emissions control system component locations (1989 3S-FE engine)

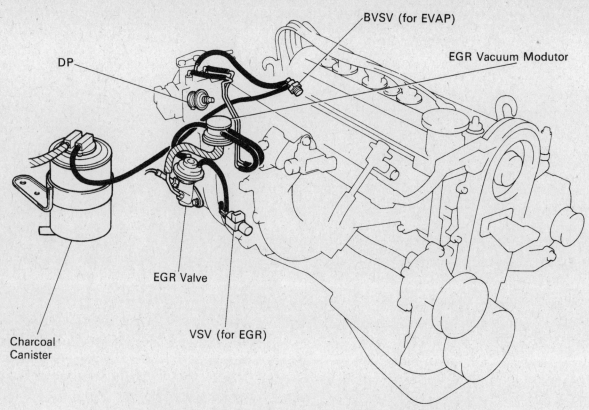

1.1f   Typical emissions control system component locations (1990 4A-FE engine)

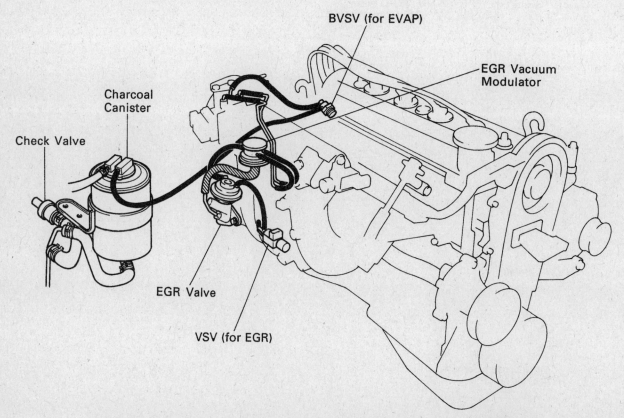

1.1g   Typical emissions control system component locations (1991 and later 4A-FE engine)

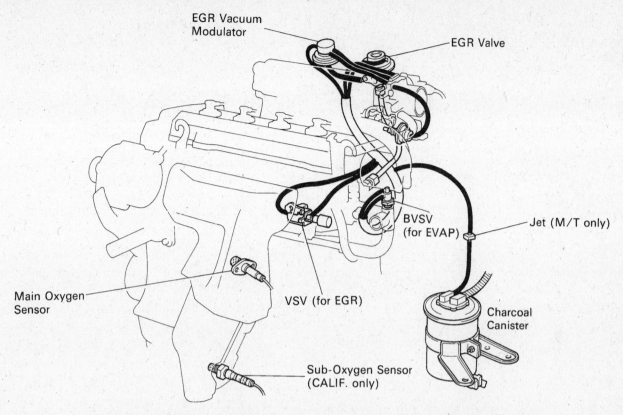

1.1h   Typical emissions control system component locations (1990 and 1991 5S-FE engine)

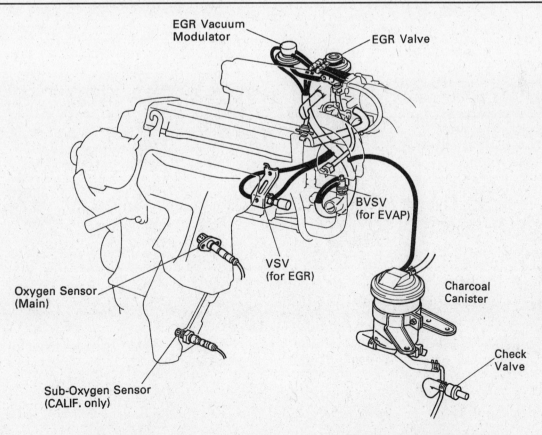

1.1i   Typical emissions control system component locations (1992 and later 5S-FE engine)

6

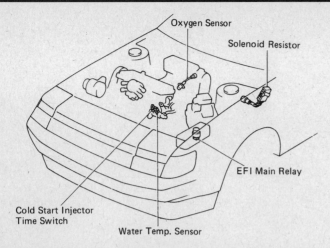

1.1j   Typical fuel system related emissions component locations (2S-E engine)

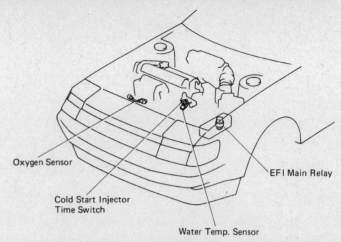

1.1k   Typical fuel system related emissions component locations (3S-GE engine)

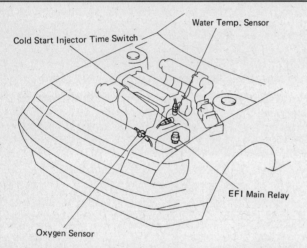

1.1l   Typical fuel system related emissions component locations (3S-FE engine)

Pay close attention to any special precautions outlined in this chapter. It should be noted that the illustrations of the various systems may not exactly match the system installed on your vehicle because of changes made by the manufacturer during production or from year-to-year.

The Vehicle Emissions Control Information (VECI) label and a vacuum hose diagram are located on the hood **(see illustrations)**. These contain important emissions specifications and setting procedures, and a vacuum hose schematic with emissions components identified. When servicing the engine or emissions systems, the VECI label in your particular vehicle should always be checked for up-to-date information.

2   Electronic control system - description and precautions

Description

The Computer Command Control System (CCCS) controls the fuel injection system by means of a microcomputer known as the Electronic Control Module (ECM).

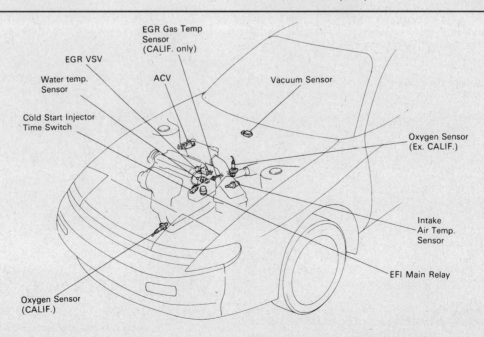

1.1m   Typical fuel system related emissions component locations (4A-FE engine)

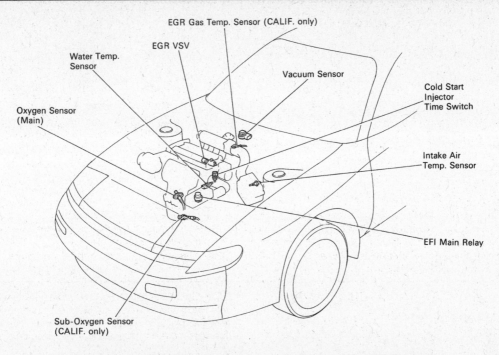

1.1n   Typical fuel system related emissions component locations (5S-FE engine)

The ECM receives signals from various sensors which monitor changing engine operating conditions such as intake air volume, intake air temperature, coolant temperature, engine rpm, acceleration/deceleration, exhaust oxygen content, etc. These signals are utilized by the ECM to determine the correct injection duration.

The system is analogous to the central nervous system in the human body: The sensors (nerve endings) constantly relay signals to the ECM (brain), which processes the data and, if necessary, sends out a command to change the operating parameters of the engine (body).

Here's a specific example of how one portion of this system operates: An oxygen sensor, located in the exhaust manifold, constantly monitors the oxygen content of the exhaust gas. If the percentage of oxygen in the exhaust gas is incorrect, an electrical signal is sent to the ECM. The ECM takes this information, processes it and then sends a command to the fuel injection system telling it to change the air/fuel mixture. This happens in a fraction of a second and it goes on continuously when the engine is running. The end result is an air/fuel mixture ratio which is constantly maintained at a predetermined ratio, regardless of driving conditions.

In the event of a sensor malfunction, a backup circuit will take over to provide driveability until the problem is identified and fixed.

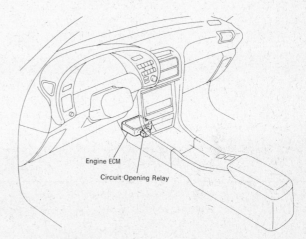

1.1o   The engine ECU and relay are located under the center of the instrument panel

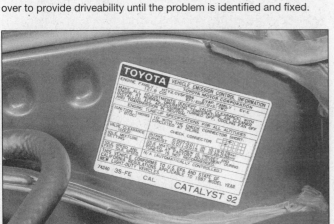

1.6a   The Vehicle Emission Control Information (VECI) label contains tune-up specifications

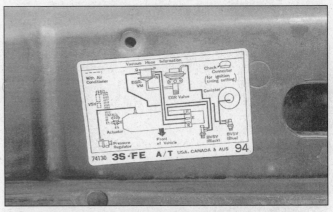

1.6b   The Vacuum Hose information label shows the routing of all emissions related vacuum hose routing and identifies the emissions devices installed on the vehicle

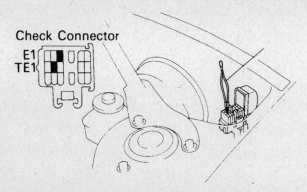

3.3   Display the diagnostic codes by using a jumper wire to bridge terminals TE1 and E1 of the service connector located on the left side of the engine compartment

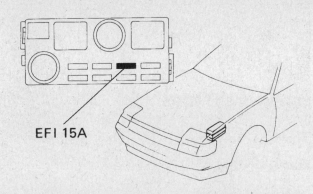

3.7a   The location of the EFI 15A fuse on 1986 through 1989 models equipped with 2S-E and 3S-GE engines

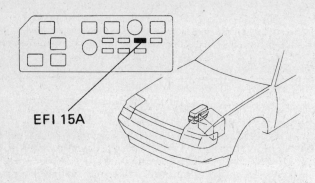

3.7b   1987 through 1989 3S-FE engine EFI 15A fuse location

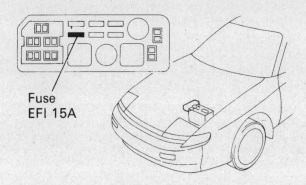

3.7c   Location of the EFI 15A fuse on 1990 and later models

Precautions

a)   Always disconnect the power by either turning off the ignition switch or disconnecting the battery terminals before removing CCCS electrical connectors. **Caution:** *If the stereo in your vehicle is equipped with an anti-theft system, refer to the information on page 0-15 at the front of this manual before detaching the cable.*

b)   When installing a battery, be particularly careful to avoid reversing the positive and negative battery cables.

c)   Do not subject EFI, emissions related components or the ECM to severe impact during removal or installation.

d)   Do not be careless during troubleshooting. Even slight terminal contact can invalidate a testing procedure and damage one of the numerous transistor circuits.

e)   Never attempt to work on the ECM or open the ECM cover. The ECM is protected by a government mandated extended warranty that will be nullified if you tamper with or damage the ECM.

f)   If you are inspecting electronic control system components during rainy weather, make sure that water does not enter any part. When washing the engine compartment, do not spray these parts or their electrical connectors with water.

---

3   Diagnosis system - general information and obtaining code output

General information

The ECM contains a built-in self-diagnosis system which detects and identifies malfunctions occurring in the network. When the ECM detects a problem, three things happen: the Check Engine light comes on, the trouble is identified and a diagnostic code is recorded and stored. The ECM stores the failure code assigned to the specific problem area until the diagnosis system is canceled by removing the stop fuse with the ignition switch off.

The Check Engine warning light, which is located on the instrument panel, comes on when the ignition switch is turned to On and the engine is not running. When the engine is started, the warning light should go out. If the light remains on, the diagnosis system has detected a malfunction in the system.

Obtaining diagnosis code output

Refer to illustration 3.3

1   To obtain an output of diagnostic codes, verify first that the battery voltage is above 11 volts, the throttle is fully closed, the transaxle is in Neutral, the accessory switches are off and the engine is at normal operating temperature. **Caution:** *If the stereo in your vehicle is equipped with an anti-theft system, refer to the information on page 0-15 at the front of this manual before detaching the cable.*

2   Turn the ignition switch to On. Do not start the engine.

3   Use a jumper wire to bridge terminals TE1 and E1 of the service electrical connector **(see illustration).**

4   Read the diagnosis code as indicated by the number of flashes of the "Check Engine" light on the dash (see the accompanying chart). Normal system operation is indicated by Code No. 1 (no malfunctions) for all models. The "Check Engine" light displays a Code No. 1 by blinking once every few seconds.

5   If there are any malfunctions in the system, their corresponding trouble codes are stored in computer memory and the light will blink the requisite number of times for the indicated trouble codes. If there's more than one trouble code in the memory, they'll be displayed in nu-

4.5a   To check the coolant temperature sensor, use an ohmmeter to measure the resistance between the two sensor terminals

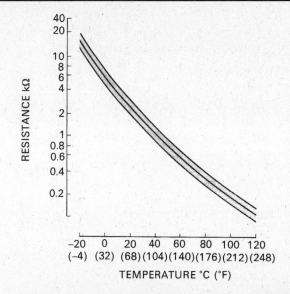

4.5b   Compare the indicated resistance values specified on this graph - note that as the temperature increases (as the engine warms up), resistance decreases

merical order (from lowest to highest) with a pause interval between each one. After the code with the largest number of flashes has been displayed, there will be another pause and then the sequence will begin all over again.

6   To ensure correct interpretation of the blinking "Check Engine" light, watch carefully for the interval between the end of one code and the beginning of the next (otherwise, you will become confused by the apparent number of blinks and misinterpret the display). The length of this interval varies with the model year.

Canceling a diagnostic code

Refer to illustrations 3.7a, 3.7b and 3.7c

7   After the malfunctioning component has been repaired/replaced, the trouble code(s) stored in computer memory must be canceled. To accomplish this, simply remove the 15A EFI fuse for at least ten sec-onds with the ignition switch off (the lower the temperature, the longer the fuse must be left out). The location of this fuse varies with the engine and model year **(see illustrations)**.

8   Cancellation can also be affected by removing the cable from the battery negative terminal, but other memory systems (such as the clock) will also be canceled. **Caution:** *If the stereo in your vehicle is equipped with an anti-theft system, refer to the information on page 0-15 at the front of this manual before detaching the cable.*

9   If the diagnosis code is not canceled it will be stored by the ECM and appear with any new codes in the event of future trouble.

10   Should it become necessary to work on engine components requiring removal of the battery terminal, first check to see if a diagnostic code has been recorded.

6

Code	Circuit or system	Diagnosis	Trouble area
Code 1 1 Flash, Pause, 1 Flash	Normal	This appears when none of the other codes are identified	
Code 12 1 flash, Pause, 2 flashes	RPM signal	*No "Ne" signal to the ECM within several seconds after the engine is cranked. * No "G" signal to the ECM two times in succession when engine speed is between 500 rpm and 4000 rpm.	* Distributor circuit * Distributor * Starter signal circuit * Igniter circuit * Igniter * ECM
Code 13 1 flash, Pause, 3 flashes	RPM signal	No "Ne" signal to the ECM engine speed is above 1500 rpm	* Distributor circuit * Distributor * ECM
Code 14 1 flash, Pause, 4 flashes	Ignition signal	No "IGF" signal to the ECM 4 times in succession	* Igniter circuit * Igniter * ECM
Code 21 2 Flashes, Pause, 1 Flash	Oxygen sensor	Problem in the oxygen sensor circuit	* Oxygen sensor circuit * ECM
Code 22 2 Flashes, Pause, 2 Flashes	Coolant temperature sensor circuit	Open or short in the coolant temperature sensor	* Coolant temperature sensor circuit * Coolant temperature sensor * ECM

Code 24 2 Flashes, Pause, 4 Flashes	Intake air temperature sensor	Open or short in the intake air sensor circuit	* Intake air temperature sensor * Intake air temperature sensor circuit * ECM
Code 25 2 Flashes, Pause, 5 Flashes	Air/fuel ratio lean malfunction	The air/fuel ratio feedback compensation valve or additive control valve continues at the upper (lean) or lower (rich) limit for a certain period of time	* Injector circuit * Injector * Oxygen sensor circuit * Oxygen sensor * ECM * Fuel line pressure * Air leak * Aif flow meter * Air intake system * Ignition system
Code 26 2 Flashes, Pause, 6 Flashes	Air/fuel ratio rich malfunction	The air/fuel ratio is overly rich	* Injector circuit * Injector * Air flow meter * Cold start injector * ECM
Code 27 2 Flashes, Pause, 7 Flashes	Sub-oxygen sensor	Open or shorted circuit	* Sub-oxygen sensor circuit * Sub-oxygen sensor * ECM
Code 31 3 Flashes, Pause, 1 Flash	Vacuum sensor	Open or short circuit	* Vacuum sensor circuit * Vacuum Sensor * No vacuum to sensor
Code 31 or 32 3 Flashes, Pause, 1 or 2 Flashes	Air flow meter	Open or short circuit	* Air flow meter circuit * Air flow meter * ECM
Code 41 4 Flashes, Pause, 1 Flash	Throttle position sensor	Open or short in the throttle position sensor circuit	* Throttle position sensor * Throttle Position * ECM
Code 42 4 Flashes, Pause, 2 Flashes	Vehicle speed sensor	No "SPD" signal for 5 seconds when the engine speed is above 2800 rpm	* Vehicle speed sensor circuit * Vehicle speed sensor * ECM
Code 43 4 Flashes, Pause, 3 Flashes	Starter signal	No "STA" signal to the ECM until engine speed reaches 800 rpm with the vehicle not moving	* Starter signal circuit * Ignition switch * Main relaywitch * ECM
Code 51 5 Flashes, Pause, 1 Flash	A/C switch signal	Air conditioner switch on, idle switch off during diagnosis check	* A/C switch circuit * A/C switch * A/C amplifier * Throttle position sensor circuit * Throttle position sensor * ECM
Code 71 7 Flashes, Pause, 1 Flash	EGR	EGR gas temperature signal is too low	* EGR system (EGR valve, hoses, etc.) * EGR gas temperature sensor circuit * EGR gas temperature sensor * Vacuum switching valve for the EGR circuit * ECM

4   Information sensors

Note: *Most of the components described in this section are protected by a Federally-mandated extended warranty. See your dealer for the details regarding your vehicle. It therefore makes little sense to either check or replace any of these parts yourself as long as they are still under warranty. However, once the warranty has expired, you may wish* to perform some of the component checks and/or replacement procedures in this Chapter to save money.

Oxygen sensor

1   The oxygen sensor is located in the exhaust manifold. It's purpose is to detect the concentration of oxygen in the exhaust gases. On some models, a second oxygen sensor is located in the catalytic converter. This sensor rechecks the emission level after the exhaust gases

4.8   Typical air flow meter installation

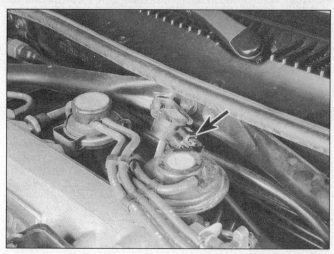

4.9   The vacuum sensor (arrow) is located on the firewall

4.11   The Throttle Position Sensor (arrow) is mounted on the throttle body

pass through the converter and feeds the results back to the main oxygen sensor so the air/fuel ratio is maintained as precisely as possible.

2   An open or shorted oxygen circuit will set a code 21 or 27.

3   See Section 10 for the oxygen sensor replacement procedure.

Coolant temperature sensor

Refer to illustrations 4.5a and 4.5b

4   The coolant temperature sensor is a thermistor (a resistor which varies the value of its voltage output in accordance with temperature changes). A failure in the coolant sensor or circuit will set a code 22. The coolant temperature sensor is located in the thermostat housing or behind the distributor housing.

5   To check the coolant temperature sensor, unplug the electrical connector and use an ohmmeter to measure the resistance between the two terminals **(see illustrations)**.

6   If the indicated resistance is not as specified, replace the sensor. Be sure to use Teflon tape or thread sealant on the threads of the new sensor to prevent leaks.

Intake air temperature sensor

7   The intake air temperature sensor, located in the side of the air cleaner housing, is a thermistor which constantly measures the temperature of the air entering the intake manifold. As air temperature varies, the ECM, by monitoring the sensor, adjusts the amount of fuel according to the air temperature. A failure in the intake air sensor or

circuit will set a code 24. The diagnosis of the intake air sensor should be left to a dealer service department.

Airflow meter

Refer to illustration 4.8

8   The air flow meter, which is located near the air cleaner **(see illustration)**, measures the amount of air which passes through it in a given time. The ECM uses this information to control fuel delivery. A large quantity of air indicates acceleration, while a small quantity indicates deceleration or idle. A failure in the meter or its circuit will set a code 31. Diagnosis of the air flow meter should be left to a dealer service department or other repair shop.

Vacuum sensor (4A-FE and 5S-FE engines)

Refer to illustration 4.9

9   The vacuum sensor **(see illustration)** monitors the intake manifold pressure changes resulting from changes in engine load and speed, then converts the information into a voltage reading. The ECM uses the vacuum sensor to control fuel delivery and ignition timing. A failure in the vacuum sensor or circuit will set a code 31.

10   Other than checking for vacuum, hose connection or electrical connectors the only service possible is unit replacement should diagnosis show the sensor faulty.

Throttle Position Sensor (TPS)

Refer to illustration 4.11

11   The Throttle Position Sensor (TPS) is located on the throttle body **(see illustration)**. By monitoring the output voltage from the TPS, the ECM can determine fuel delivery based on throttle valve angle (driver demand). A failure in the TPS sensor or circuit will set a code 41. If the TPS requires diagnosis or replacement, it should be done by a dealer service department (because of the need for special tools and test equipment).

Park/Neutral switch (automatic transaxle equipped vehicles only)

12   The Park/Neutral switch, located on the automatic transaxle, indicates to the ECM when the transaxle is in park or neutral. The ECM uses this information to control the fuel injectors and the ISC solenoid valve.

Air conditioner (A/C) signal

13   The A/C amplifier supplies a signal to the ECM when the air conditioning is turned on. This signal allows the ECM to adjust engine speed to compensate for the additional load on the engine. A code 51 will set if this signal is not present. Diagnosis should be left to a dealer service department or other repair shop.

6

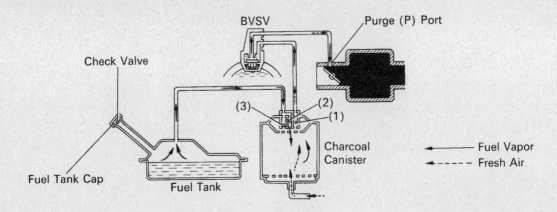

5.2   Typical EVAP system

5.15   After disconnecting the hoses and detaching the bracket clamp, lift the canister out of the engine compartment

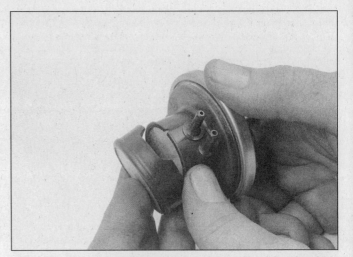

6.7a   To remove the EGR vacuum modulator filters for cleaning, remove the cap...

Vehicle Speed Sensor (VSS)

14   The Vehicle Speed Sensor (VSS) consists of the lead switch and magnet that's built into the speedometer. As the magnet turns with the speedometer cable, its magnetic force causes the lead switch to turn on and off. This pulsing voltage signal is sent to the ECM which is converted into miles per hour. If a failure occurs, a code 42 will be set. Diagnosis and repair should be left to a dealer service department.

Crank angle sensor

15   The crank angle sensor is located in the distributor and consists of a signal generator and signal rotor. As the signal rotor turns, pulsing AC voltage is generated in the pick-up coil. This pulse signal is sent to the ECM where it is used to calculate the engine speed and also as one of the signals to control various devices.

Engine start signal

16   This signal is sent from the engine starter circuit. Receiving it, the ECM detects that the engine is cranking and uses it as one of the signals to control the fuel injectors. A code 43 will be set is this signal is not set or is intermittent.

---

5   Evaporative Emission Control (EVAP) system

General description

Refer to illustration 5.2

1   This system is designed to trap and store fuel that evaporates from the fuel tank, carburetor and intake manifold that would normally enter the atmosphere in the form of hydrocarbon (HC) emissions.

2   The Evaporative Emission Control (EVAP) system consists of a charcoal-filled canister, the lines connecting the canister to the fuel tank and a thermo switch or an ECM-controlled solenoid valve **(see illustration)**.

3   Fuel vapors are transferred from the fuel tank and carburetor to a canister where they're stored when the engine isn't running. When the engine is running, the fuel vapors are purged from the canister by intake air flow and consumed in the normal combustion process.

4   On some models, the ECM operates a solenoid valve which controls vacuum to the purge valve in the charcoal canister. Under cold engine conditions, the solenoid is turned on by the ECM, which closes the valve. The ECM turns off the valve and allows purge when the engine is warm. On some models, a bi-metal thermo switch controls the canister purge.

Checking

5   Poor idle, stalling and poor driveability can be caused by an inoperative purge valve, a damaged canister, split or cracked hoses or hoses connected to the wrong fittings. Check the fuel filler cap for a damaged or deformed gasket (see Chapter 1).

6   Evidence of fuel loss or fuel odor can be caused by liquid fuel leaking from fuel lines, a cracked or damaged canister, an inoperative purge valve, disconnected, misrouted, kinked, deteriorated or damaged vapor or control hoses.

7   Inspect each hose attached to the canister for kinks, leaks and cracks along its entire length. Repair or replace as necessary.

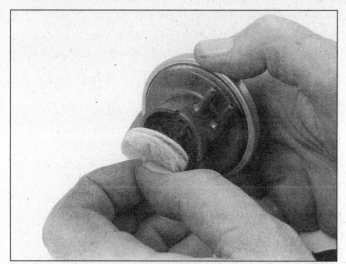

6.7b   ...then pull out the two filters and blow them out with compressed air - be sure the coarse side of the outer filter faces the atmosphere (out) when reinstalling the filters

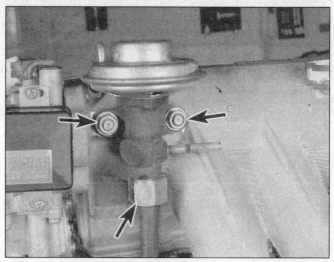

6.10   To remove the EGR valve, unscrew the EGR pipe threaded fitting, remove both mounting bolts and detach the valve from the manifold

8   Inspect the canister. If it's cracked or damaged, replace it.
9   Look for fuel leaking from the bottom of the canister. If fuel is leaking, replace the canister and check the hoses and hose routing.
10   Further testing should be left to a dealer service department.

Charcoal canister replacement
Refer to illustration 5.15
11   Remove the air cleaner assembly (see Chapter 4).
12   Detach the negative cable from the battery. **Caution:** *If the stereo in your vehicle is equipped with an anti-theft system, refer to the information on page 0-15 at the front of this manual before detaching the cable.*
13   Unplug the solenoid electrical connectors, if equipped.
14   Clearly label, then detach the vacuum hoses from the canister.
15   Remove the mounting clamp screw, lift the canister out of the bracket, disconnect the hose and remove it from the vehicle **(see illustration)**.
16   Installation is the reverse of removal.

---

6   Exhaust Gas Recirculation (EGR) system

General description
1   To reduce oxides of nitrogen emissions, some of the exhaust gases are recirculated through the EGR valve to the intake manifold to lower combustion temperatures.
2   The EGR system consists of the EGR valve, the EGR modulator (some models), vacuum switching valve, the Electronic Control Module (ECM) and various sensors. The ECM memory is programmed to produce the ideal EGR valve lift for each operating condition.

Checking
EGR valve
3   Start the engine and allow it to idle.
4   Detach the vacuum hose from the EGR valve and attach a hand vacuum pump in its place.
5   Apply vacuum to the EGR valve. Vacuum should remain steady and the engine should run poorly.
  a) If the vacuum doesn't remain steady and the engine doesn't run poorly, replace the EGR valve and recheck it.
  b) If the vacuum remains steady but the engine doesn't run poorly, remove the EGR valve and check the valve and the intake manifold for blockage. Clean or replace parts as necessary and recheck.

EGR vacuum modulator valve
Refer to illustrations 6.7a and 6.7b
6   Remove the valve (see Step 12 below).
7   Pull the cover off and check the filters **(see illustrations)**.
8   Clean them with compressed air, reinstall the cover and the modulator.

EGR system
9   Any further checking of the EGR systems requires special tools and test equipment. Take the vehicle to a dealer service department for checking.

Component replacement
EGR valve
Refer to illustration 6.10
10   Detach the vacuum hose, disconnect the threaded fitting that attaches the EGR pipe to the EGR valve, remove the two EGR valve mounting bolts, remove the EGR valve from the intake manifold and check it for sticking and heavy carbon deposits **(see illustration)**. If the valve is sticking or clogged with deposits, clean or replace it.
11   Installation is the reverse of removal.

6.12   To remove the EGR vacuum modulator, label and detach the vacuum hoses (arrows) and detach the modulator from the bracket

6

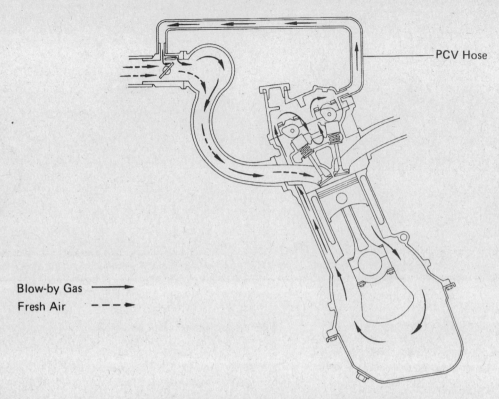

Blow-by Gas   ⟶

Fresh Air   - - - ⟶

7.1a   1989 and earlier PCV system component layout

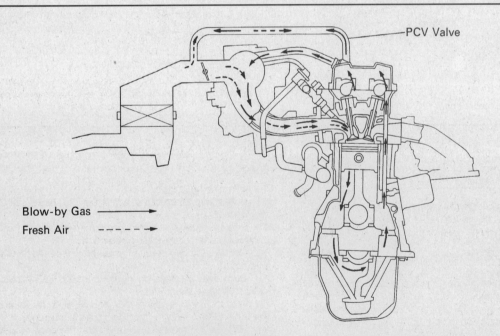

Blow-by Gas   ⟶

Fresh Air   - - - ⟶

7.1b   1990 and later model PCV systems use a PCV valve to regulate the flow of blow-by gasses into the air intake chamber

EGR vacuum modulator valve

Refer to illustration 6.12

12   Label and disconnect the vacuum hoses **(see illustration)** and remove the EGR vacuum modulator from it's bracket.

14   Installation is the reverse of removal.

7   Positive Crankcase Ventilation (PCV) system

Refer to illustrations 7.1a and 7.1b

1   To reduce hydrocarbon (HC) emissions, crankcase blow-by gas is routed to the intake manifold for combustion in the cylinders **(see illustrations)**.

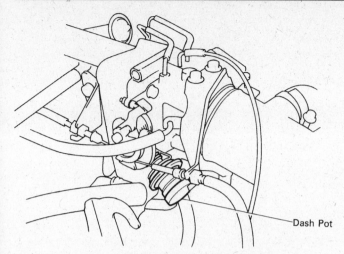

8.1   The dashpot is located on the throttle body

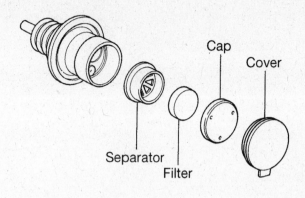

8.5   Dashpot cap, filter and separator details

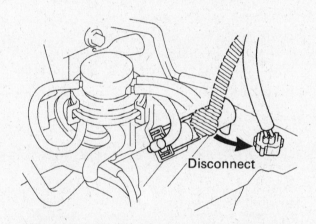

8.6   Unplug the electrical connector from the EGR VSV

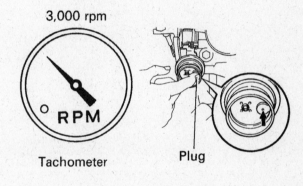

8.7   With the engine at 3000 rpm, plug the VTV hole with your finger and release the throttle - the engine speed should drop to that specified in the text

6

2   On 1989 and earlier models the system consists of a PCV hose between the valve cover and the intake manifold. On 1990 and later models, the main components of the PCV system are the PCV valve, a fresh air filtered inlet and the vacuum hoses connecting these components with the engine.

3   If abnormal operating conditions arise, the system is designed to allow excessive amounts of blow-by gases to flow back through the crankcase vent tube into the air cleaner to be consumed by normal combustion.

4   Checking and replacement of the hoses and (if equipped) PCV valve is covered in Chapter 1.

5   This system directs the blow-by into the throttle body which over time can cause an oily residue build up in that area of the throttle plate. Consequently, it's a good idea to periodically clean this residue from the throttle body. Refer to Chapter 4 for this cleaning procedure.

8   Dashpot (1990 4A-FE engine only)

Refer to illustrations 8.1, 8.5, 8.6, 8.7 and 8.9

Description

1   To reduce hydrocarbon and carbon monoxide emissions, the dashpot opens slightly more during deceleration than it does at idle, promoting a more complete burn of the air/fuel mixture **(see illustration)**.

Check and replacement

Dashpot

2   Warm up the engine.

3   Check and, if necessary, adjust the idle speed (see Chapter 1). It should be 800 rpm.

4   Use a jumper wire to bridge terminals T and E1 of the service electrical connector **(see illustration 3.3)**.

5   Remove the cap, filter and separator **(see illustration)** from the dashpot.

6   Detach the electrical connector from the EGR Vacuum Switching Valve (VSV) **(see illustration)**.

7   With the engine running at 3000 rpm, plug the Vacuum Transmitting Valve (VTV) hole with your finger **(see illustration)**.

8   Release the throttle and verify that the engine speed drops to 1800 rpm (manual transaxle) or 2200 rpm (automatic). If it does, the dashpot is properly adjusted.

9   If engine speed does not drop to the specified rpm, adjust the dashpot adjusting screw and recheck **(see illustration)**.

10   Reinstall the dashpot separator, filter and cap. Make sure that the coarser side of the filter faces out (towards the atmosphere).

Vacuum Transmitting Valve (VTV)

11   With the engine running at 3000 rpm, release the throttle valve and verify that the engine drops to idle in a few seconds. If it doesn't, replace the VTV.

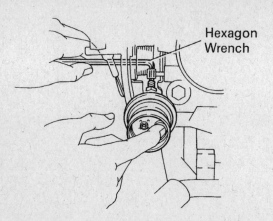

8.9   Hold your finger over the VTV hole while adjusting the dashpot setting

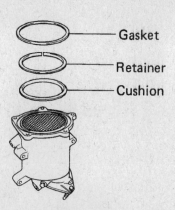

9.2a   On some models the catalytic converter bolts directly to the exhaust manifold

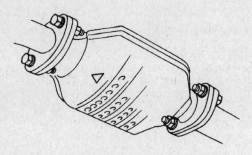

9.2b   The catalytic converter is mounted in the exhaust system on some models

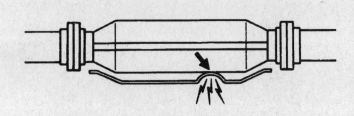

9.4   If the catalytic converter is mounted under the vehicle, periodically inspect the shield for dents and other damage - if a dent is deep enough to touch the surface of the converter, replace the shield

9   Catalytic converter

Refer to illustrations 9.2a, 9.2b, 9.4 and 9.5
Note: *Because of a federally mandated extended warranty which covers emissions-related components such as the catalytic converter, check with a dealer service department before replacing the converter at your own expense.*

General description

1   To reduce hydrocarbon, carbon monoxide and oxides of nitrogen emissions, all vehicles are equipped with a three-way catalyst system which oxidizes and reduces these chemicals, converting them into harmless nitrogen, carbon dioxide and water.
2   On some models the converter is bolted to the exhaust manifold while on others it's mounted in the exhaust system much like a muffler **(see illustrations)**.

Checking

3   Periodically inspect the catalytic converter-to-exhaust pipe mating flanges and bolts. Make sure that there are no loose bolts and no leaks between the flanges.
4   Look for dents in or damage to the catalytic converter protector **(see illustration)**. If any part of the protector is damaged or dented enough to touch the converter, repair or replace it.
5   Inspect the heat insulator for damage. Make sure that there is adequate clearance between the heat insulator and the catalytic converter **(see illustration)**.

Replacement

6   To replace the catalytic converter, refer to Chapter 4.

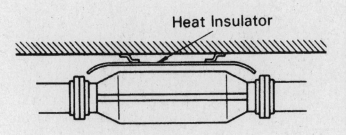

9.5   If the catalytic converter is mounted under the vehicle, periodically inspect the heat insulator to make sure there's adequate clearance between it and the converter

10   Oxygen sensor replacement

Refer to illustrations 10.3a and 10.3b
1   The oxygen sensor is located in the exhaust manifold. Starting at the oxygen sensor, follow the wire back to the electrical connector. Unplug the oxygen sensor wire at the connector.

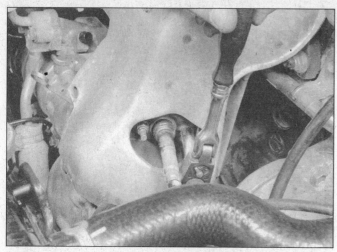

10.3a Use a socket with an extension to remove the oxygen sensor nuts

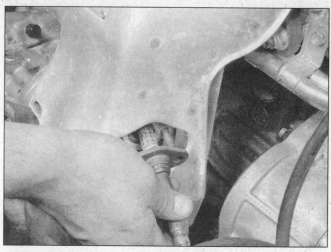

10.3b Withdraw the oxygen sensor from the exhaust manifold

2 Unscrew the oxygen sensor nuts and remove the sensor **(see illustrations)**.

3 Install the new oxygen sensor into the exhaust manifold. Tighten the sensor nuts securely.

4 Plug in the electrical connector.

6

NOTES

Chapter 7 Part A Manual transaxle

Contents

Specifications

General
Shift lever preload.. 0.1 to 0.2 lbs

Torque specifications   **Ft-lbs** (unless otherwise indicated)
Back-up light switch 30
Transaxle mount-to-frame (front and rear)
    1986 through 1989 29
    1990 on 47
Transaxle mount-to-transaxle
    1986 through 1989 29
    1990 on 57
Lower crossmember
    Center bolts
        1986 through 1989 29
        1990 on 38
    Side bolts
        1986 through 1989 154
        1990 on 112
Shifter assembly mount bolts .... 108 in-lbs
Stiffener plate 27
Transaxle case bolts (all) 22
Transaxle case cover bolts
    C-52
        1986 through 1989 22
        1990 on 13
    S-53 (all) 22
Transaxle-to-engine bolts
    10 mm bolts
        1986 29
        1987 on 34
    12 mm bolts (all) 47
Engine mount center member bolt
    1983 through 1986.. 29
    1987 on 45

2.4   Pry out the old oil seal with a screwdriver - don't scratch the seal bore

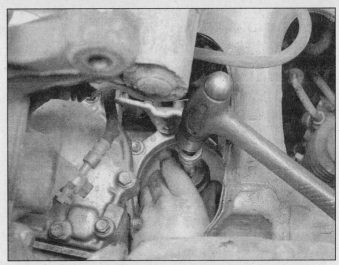

2.6   To install a new oil seal, simply drive it into place with a large socket that has a slightly smaller diameter than the seal

1   General information

The vehicles covered by this manual are equipped with either a 5-speed manual or a 3- or 4-speed automatic transaxle. Information on the manual transaxle is included in this Part of Chapter 7. Service procedures for the automatic transaxle are contained in Chapter 7, Part B.

The manual transaxle is a compact, two-piece, lightweight aluminum alloy housing containing both the transmission and differential assemblies.

Because of the complexity, unavailability of replacement parts and special tools necessary, internal repair procedures for the manual transaxle are not recommended for the home mechanic. For readers who wish to tackle a transaxle rebuild, exploded views and a brief *Manual transaxle overhaul - general information* Section are provided. The bulk of information in this Chapter is devoted to removal and installation procedures.

2   Oil seal replacement

Refer to illustrations 2.4, 2.6, 2.9a, 2.9b and 2.10
1   Oil leaks frequently occur due to wear of the differential side gear shaft seals and/or the speedometer drive gear oil seal and O-rings. Replacement of these seals is relatively easy, since the repairs can usually be performed without removing the transaxle from the vehicle.
2   The differential side gear shaft oil seals are located at the sides of the transaxle, where the side gear shafts are attached. If leakage at the seal is suspected, raise the vehicle and support it securely on jackstands. If the seal is leaking, lubricant will be found on the side of the transaxle.
3   Refer to Chapter 8 and remove the driveaxles and side gear shafts.
4   Using a screwdriver or pry bar, carefully pry the oil seal out of the transaxle bore **(see illustration)**.
5   If the oil seal cannot be removed with a screwdriver or pry bar, a special oil seal removal tool (available at auto parts stores) will be required.
6   Using a large section of pipe or a large deep socket as a drift, install the new oil seal. Drive it into the bore squarely and make sure that it is completely seated **(see illustration)**. Lubricate the lip of the new seal with multi-purpose grease.
7   Install the driveaxle(s) and side gear shaft(s). Be careful not to damage the lip of the new seal.

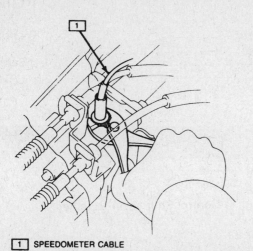

1   SPEEDOMETER CABLE

2.9a   Use a pair of pliers to loosen the speedometer cable fitting

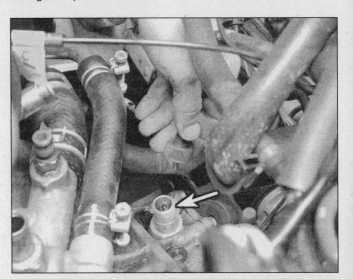

2.9b   Detach the speedometer cable from the speedometer driven gear housing (arrow) on the transaxle

8   The speedometer cable and driven gear housing is located on the transaxle housing. Look for lubricant around the cable housing to determine if the seal and O-ring are leaking.
9   Disconnect the speedometer cable from the transaxle **(see illustrations)**.
10   Using a hook, remove the seal **(see illustration)**.
11   Using a small socket of the appropriate diameter or other similar tool as a drift **(see illustration 2.10)**, install the new seal.
12   Install a new O-ring on the driven gear housing and reinstall the speedometer cable assembly on the housing

3   Shift lever - removal, installation and preload check and adjustment

Refer to illustrations 3.2a, 3.2b and 3.4
1   Remove the center console.
2   Remove the shift and select cable retainers and disconnect both cables from the shift lever. Remove the retaining bolts and detach the shift lever **(see illustrations)**.
3   Installation is the reverse of removal.
4   Prior to installing the console, check the shift lever preload by connecting a spring scale to the top of the shift lever. Pull lightly on the spring scale to make sure the initial pressure required to move the

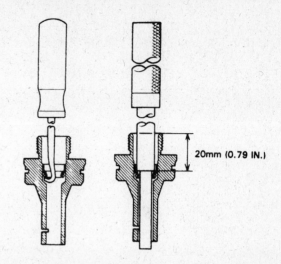

2.10   Use a hooked tool to pull the old speedometer cable seal out of the driven gear housing - use a small hammer and socket to tap the new seal onto place (make sure the seal is recessed the same amount)

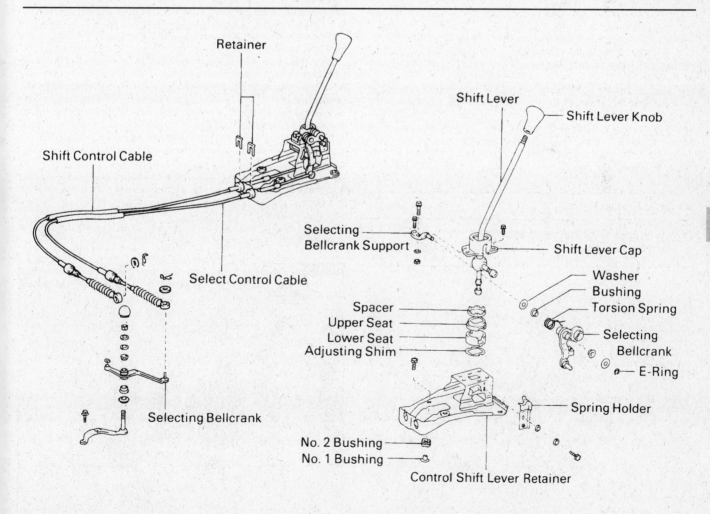

3.2a   Manual transaxle shift lever and mechanism details

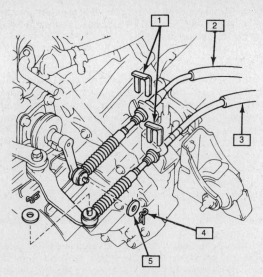

3.2b   Shift cable/linkage details

1 *Cable retainers*
2 *Shift control cable*
3 *Shift select cable*
4 *Retaining clips*
5 *Cable end washer*
6 *Mount bolt shields*

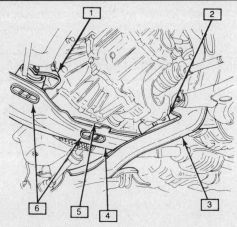

4.3a   Transaxle mount locations

1 *Transaxle front mount*
2 *Transaxle rear mount*
3 *Main crossmember*
4 *Center crossmember*
5 *Transaxle center mount*
6 *Access plugs*

4.3b   Remove the through-bolt (arrow) from the upper transaxle mount

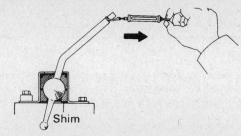

3.4   Use a spring scale to determine the shift lever preload

4.1   Pry on the transaxle mount with a bar or large screwdriver to check for excessive movement

lever is as specified **(see illustration)**.
5   If the preload is not as specified, remove the lever and install the proper adjusting shim (available at a dealer parts department) and recheck the preload.
6   The remainder of installation is the reverse of removal.

4   Transaxle mount - check and replacement

Refer to illustrations 4.1, 4.3a, 4.3b and 4.3c
1   Insert a large screwdriver or prybar between the mount and the transaxle and pry up **(see illustration)**.
2   The transaxle should not move excessively away from the mount. If it does, replace the mount.
3   To replace a mount, support the transaxle with a jack, remove the nuts and bolts and remove the mount **(see illustrations)**. It may be necessary to raise the transaxle slightly to provide enough clearance to remove the mount.
4   Installation is the reverse of removal.

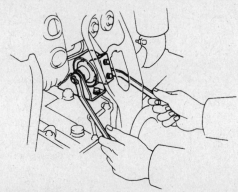

4.3c   Use two wrenches to remove the transaxle mount through-bolt and nut

5   Manual transaxle - removal and installation

Removal

1   Disconnect the negative cable from the battery. **Caution:** *If the stereo in your vehicle is equipped with an anti-theft system, refer to the information on page 0-15 at the front of this manual before detaching the cable.*

2   Raise the vehicle and support it securely on jackstands. Remove the wheels and drain the transaxle fluid (see Chapter 1).

3   Disconnect the shift cables from the transaxle.

4   Disconnect the speedometer cable or speed sensor and all electrical connections from the transaxle.

5   Remove the driveaxles (see Chapter 8).

6   Remove the exhaust system components as necessary for clearance (see Chapter 4).

7   Support the engine. This can be done from above by using an engine hoist, or by placing a jack (with a block of wood as an insulator) under the engine oil pan. The engine should remain supported at all times while the transaxle is out of the vehicle.

8   Support the transaxle with a jack (preferably a special jack made for this purpose). Safety chains will help steady the transaxle on the jack.

9   Remove any chassis or suspension components which will interfere with transaxle removal (see Chapter 10).

10   Remove the transaxle mount bolts/nuts.

11   Remove the bolts securing the transaxle to the engine.

12   Make a final check that all wires and hoses have been disconnected from the transaxle and then move the transaxle and jack toward the side of the vehicle until the transaxle is clear of the engine. Keep the transaxle level as this is done.

13   Once the input shaft is clear, lower the transaxle and remove it from under the vehicle. **Caution:** *Do not depress the clutch pedal while the transaxle is removed from the vehicle.*

14   The clutch components can now be inspected (see Chapter 8). In most cases, new clutch components should be routinely installed whenever the transaxle is removed.

Installation

15   If removed, install the clutch components (see Chapter 8).

16   With the transaxle secured to the jack as on removal, raise it into position and then carefully slide it forward, engaging the input shaft with the clutch splines. Do not use excessive force to install the transaxle - if the input shaft does not slide into place, readjust the angle of the transaxle so it is level and/or turn the input shaft so the splines engage properly with the clutch.

17   Install the transaxle-to-engine bolts. Tighten the bolts to the torque listed in this Chapter's Specifications.

18   Install the transaxle mount nuts and bolts. Tighten all nuts and bolts securely.

19   Install the chassis and suspension components which were removed. Tighten all nuts and bolts securely.

20   Remove the jacks supporting the transaxle and the engine.

21   Install the various items removed previously, referring to Chapter 8 for the installation of the driveaxles and side gear shafts and Chapter 4 for information regarding the exhaust system components.

22   Make a final check that all wires, hoses and the speedometer cable have been connected and that the transaxle has been filled with the specified lubricant to the proper level (see Chapter 1). Lower the vehicle.

23   Working inside the vehicle, connect the shift lever (see Section 3).

24   Connect the negative battery cable. Road test the vehicle to check for proper transaxle operation and check for leakage.

6   Manual transaxle overhaul - general information

Refer to illustrations 6.4a through 6.4f

1   Overhauling a manual transaxle is a difficult job for the do-it-your-

7A

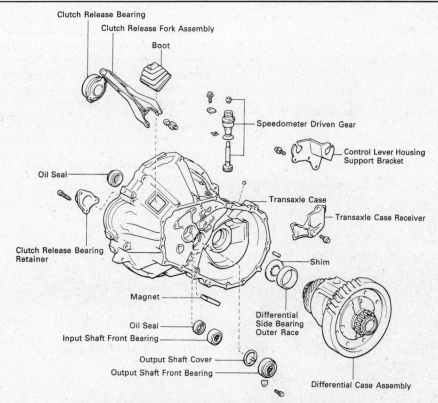

6.4a   C-52 model transaxle case and related components

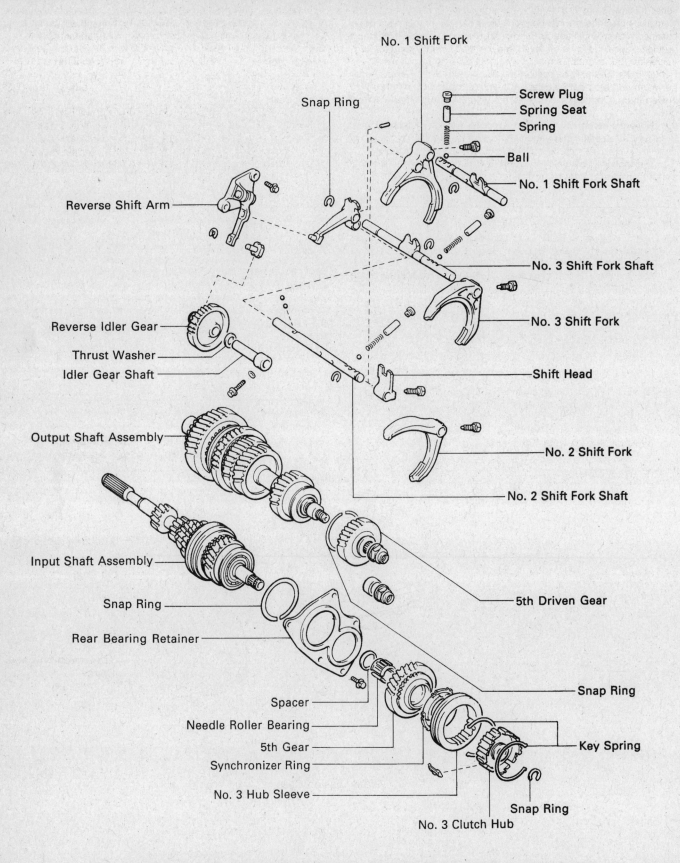

No. 1 Shift Fork

Screw Plug

Spring Seat

Spring

Ball

Snap Ring

No. 1 Shift Fork Shaft

Reverse Shift Arm

No. 3 Shift Fork Shaft

No. 3 Shift Fork

Reverse Idler Gear

Thrust Washer

Idler Gear Shaft

Shift Head

No. 2 Shift Fork

Output Shaft Assembly

No. 2 Shift Fork Shaft

Input Shaft Assembly

5th Driven Gear

Snap Ring

Rear Bearing Retainer

Snap Ring

Spacer

Needle Roller Bearing

Key Spring

5th Gear

Synchronizer Ring

No. 3 Hub Sleeve

Snap Ring

No. 3 Clutch Hub

6.4b   Exploded view of the input and output shafts and shift mechanism components - C-52 transaxle

selfer. It involves the disassembly and reassembly of many small parts. Numerous clearances must be precisely measured and, if necessary, changed with select fit spacers and snap-rings. As a result, if transaxle problems arise, it can be removed and installed by a competent do-it-yourselfer, but overhaul should be left to a transmission repair shop. Rebuilt transaxles may be available - check with your dealer parts department and auto parts stores. At any rate, the time and money involved in an overhaul is almost sure to exceed the cost of a rebuilt unit.

2   Nevertheless, it's not impossible for an inexperienced mechanic to rebuild a transaxle if the special tools are available and the job is done in a deliberate step-by-step manner so nothing is overlooked.

3   The tools necessary for an overhaul include internal and external snap-ring pliers, a bearing puller, a slide hammer, a set of pin punches, a dial indicator and possibly a hydraulic press. In addition, a large, sturdy workbench and a vise or transaxle stand will be required.

4   During disassembly of the transaxle, make careful notes of how each piece comes off, where it fits in relation to other pieces and what holds it in place. Exploded views are included (see illustrations) to show where the parts go - but actually noting how they are installed when you remove the parts will make it much easier to get the transaxle back together.

5   Before taking the transaxle apart for repair, it will help if you have some idea what area of the transaxle is malfunctioning. Certain problems can be closely tied to specific areas in the transaxle, which can make component examination and replacement easier. Refer to the *Troubleshooting* section at the front of this manual for information regarding possible sources of trouble.

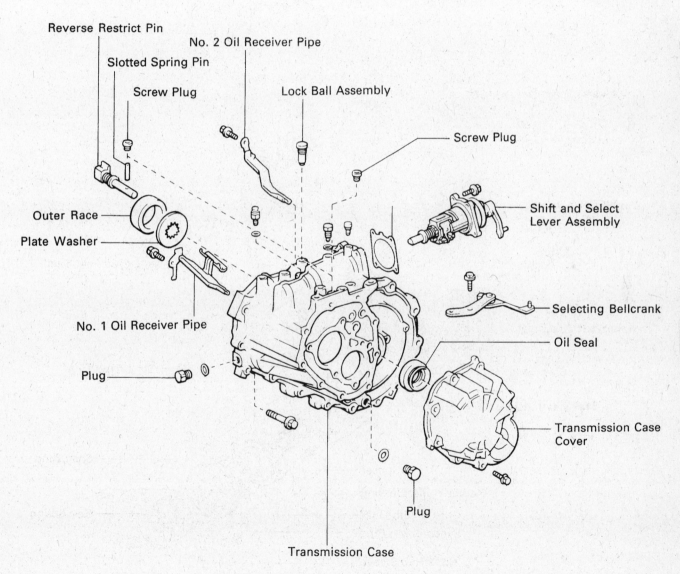

6.4c   C-52 model transaxle case and related components

7A

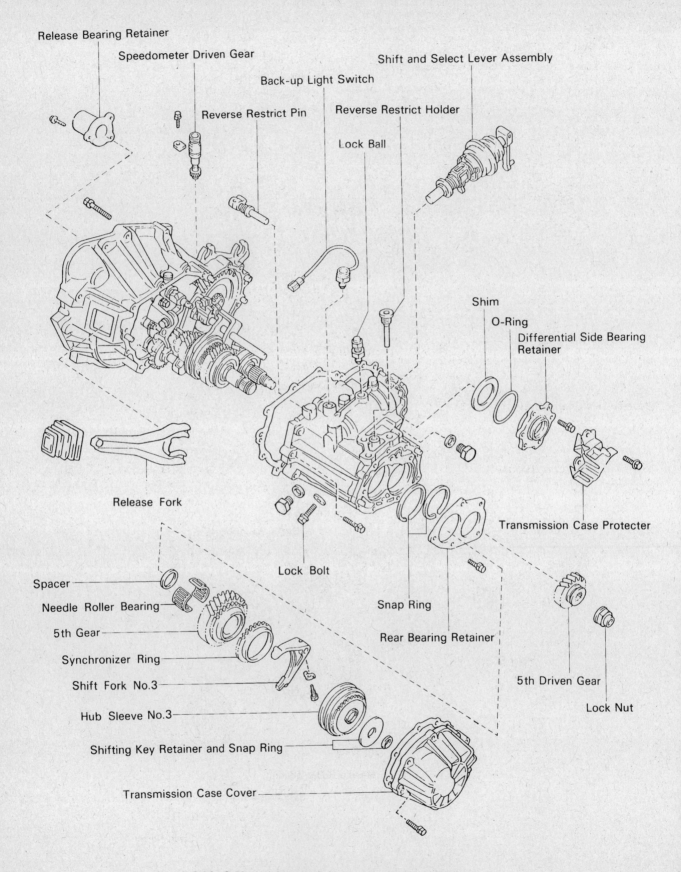

Release Bearing Retainer

Speedometer Driven Gear

Shift and Select Lever Assembly

Back-up Light Switch

Reverse Restrict Pin

Reverse Restrict Holder

Lock Ball

Shim

O-Ring

Differential Side Bearing Retainer

Release Fork

Transmission Case Protecter

Spacer

Needle Roller Bearing

5th Gear

Synchronizer Ring

Shift Fork No.3

Hub Sleeve No.3

Shifting Key Retainer and Snap Ring

Transmission Case Cover

Lock Bolt

Snap Ring

Rear Bearing Retainer

5th Driven Gear

Lock Nut

6.4d   S-53 model transaxle case and related components

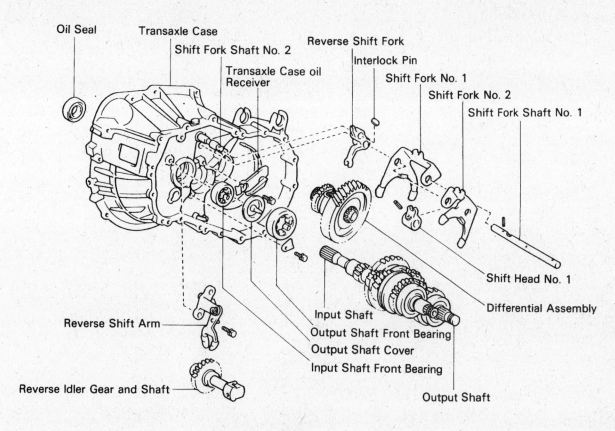

Oil Seal

Transaxle Case

Shift Fork Shaft No. 2

Transaxle Case oil Receiver

Reverse Shift Fork

Interlock Pin

Shift Fork No. 1

Shift Fork No. 2

Shift Fork Shaft No. 1

Shift Head No. 1

Differential Assembly

Reverse Shift Arm

Reverse Idler Gear and Shaft

Input Shaft

Output Shaft Front Bearing

Output Shaft Cover

Input Shaft Front Bearing

Output Shaft

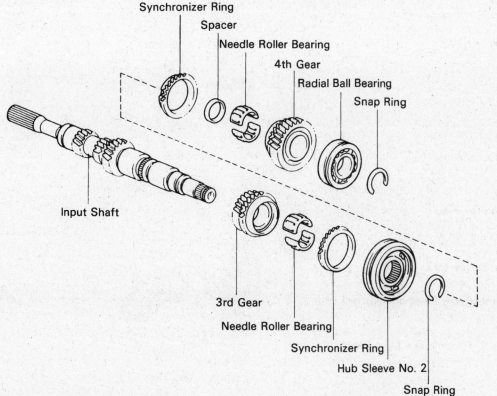

Synchronizer Ring

Spacer

Needle Roller Bearing

4th Gear

Radial Ball Bearing

Snap Ring

Input Shaft

3rd Gear

Needle Roller Bearing

Synchronizer Ring

Hub Sleeve No. 2

Snap Ring

6.4e   S-53 model transaxle input shaft and related components

7A

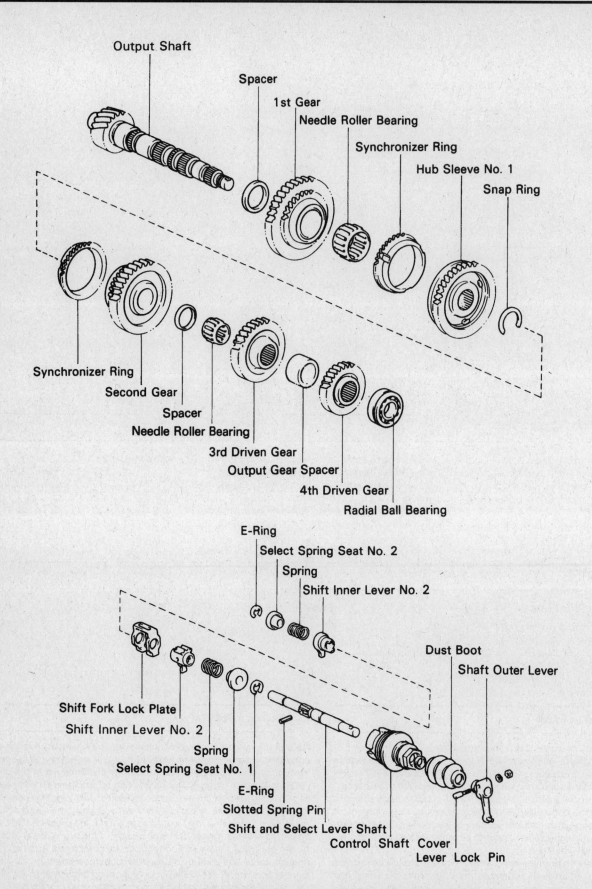

6.4f   S-53 model transaxle output shaft and related components

Chapter 7 Part B Automatic transaxle

Contents

Specifications

Torque specifications

	Ft-lbs
Torque converter to driveplate bolts	20
Transaxle-to-engine mounting bolts	
10 mm	32
12 mm	47

1 General information

All vehicles covered in this manual come equipped with either a 5-speed manual or a 3- or 4-speed automatic transaxle. All information on the automatic transaxle is included in this Part of Chapter 7. Information for the manual transaxle can be found in Part A of this Chapter.

Due to the complexity of the automatic transaxles covered in this manual and to the specialized equipment necessary to perform most service operations, this Chapter contains only those procedures related to general diagnosis, routine maintenance, adjustment and removal and installation.

If the transaxle requires major repair work, it should be left to a dealer service department or an automotive or transmission repair shop. You can, however, remove and install the transaxle yourself and save the expense, even if the repair work is done by a transmission shop.

2 Diagnosis - general

Note: *Automatic transaxle malfunctions may be caused by five general conditions: poor engine performance, improper adjustments, hydraulic malfunctions, mechanical malfunctions or malfunctions in the computer or its signal network. Diagnosis of these problems should always begin with a check of the easily repaired items: fluid level and condition (see Chapter 1), shift linkage adjustment and throttle linkage adjustment. Next, perform a road test to determine if the problem has been corrected or if more diagnosis is necessary. If the problem persists after the preliminary tests and corrections are completed, additional diagnosis should be done by a dealer service department or transmission repair shop. Refer to the Troubleshooting section at the front of this manual for information on symptoms of transaxle problems.*

Preliminary checks

1   Drive the vehicle to warm the transaxle to normal operating temperature.
2   Check the fluid level as described in Chapter 1:
  a) If the fluid level is unusually low, add enough fluid to bring the level within the designated area of the dipstick, then check for external leaks (see below).
  b) If the fluid level is abnormally high, drain off the excess, then check the drained fluid for contamination by coolant. The presence of engine coolant in the automatic transmission fluid indicates that a failure has occurred in the internal radiator walls that separate the coolant from the transmission fluid (see Chapter 3).
  c) If the fluid is foaming, drain it and refill the transaxle, then check for coolant in the fluid, or a high fluid level.
3   Check the engine idle speed. **Note:** *If the engine is malfunctioning, do not proceed with the preliminary checks until it has been repaired and runs normally.*
4   Check the throttle valve cable for freedom of movement. Adjust it if necessary (see Section 4). **Note:** *The throttle cable may function properly when the engine is shut off and cold, but it may malfunction once the engine is hot. Check it cold and at normal engine operating temperature.*
5   Inspect the shift control linkage (see Section 3). Make sure that it's properly adjusted and that the linkage operates smoothly.

Fluid leak diagnosis

6   Most fluid leaks are easy to locate visually. Repair usually consists of replacing a seal or gasket. If a leak is difficult to find, the following procedure may help.
7   Identify the fluid. Make sure it's transmission fluid and not engine oil or brake fluid (automatic transmission fluid is a deep red color).
8   Try to pinpoint the source of the leak. Drive the vehicle several miles, then park it over a large sheet of cardboard. After a minute or two, you should be able to locate the leak by determining the source of the fluid dripping onto the cardboard.
9   Make a careful visual inspection of the suspected component and the area immediately around it. Pay particular attention to gasket mating surfaces. A mirror is often helpful for finding leaks in areas that are hard to see.
10   If the leak still cannot be found, clean the suspected area thoroughly with a degreaser or solvent, then dry it.
11   Drive the vehicle for several miles at normal operating temperature and varying speeds. After driving the vehicle, visually inspect the suspected component again.
12   Once the leak has been located, the cause must be determined before it can be properly repaired. If a gasket is replaced but the sealing flange is bent, the new gasket will not stop the leak. The bent flange must be straightened.
13   Before attempting to repair a leak, check to make sure that the following conditions are corrected or they may cause another leak.

Note: *Some of the following conditions cannot be fixed without highly specialized tools and expertise. Such problems must be referred to a transmission shop or a dealer service department.*

Gasket leaks

14   Check the pan periodically. Make sure the bolts are tight, no bolts are missing, the gasket is in good condition and the pan is flat (dents in the pan may indicate damage to the valve body inside).
15   If the pan gasket is leaking, the fluid level or the fluid pressure may be too high, the vent may be plugged, the pan bolts may be too tight, the pan sealing flange may be warped, the sealing surface of the transaxle housing may be damaged, the gasket may be damaged or the transaxle casting may be cracked or porous. If sealant instead of gasket material has been used to form a seal between the pan and the transaxle housing, it may be the wrong sealant.

Seal leaks

16   If a transaxle seal is leaking, the fluid level or pressure may be too high, the vent may be plugged, the seal bore may be damaged, the seal itself may be damaged or improperly installed, the surface of the shaft protruding through the seal may be damaged or a loose bearing may be causing excessive shaft movement.
17   Make sure the dipstick tube seal is in good condition and the tube is properly seated. Periodically check the area around the speedometer gear or sensor for leakage. If transmission fluid is evident, check the O-ring for damage.

Case leaks

18   If the case itself appears to be leaking, the casting is porous and will have to be repaired or replaced.
19   Make sure the oil cooler hose fittings are tight and in good condition.

Fluid comes out vent pipe or fill tube

20   If this condition occurs, the transaxle is overfilled, there is coolant in the fluid, the case is porous, the dipstick is incorrect, the vent is plugged or the drain-back holes are plugged.

---

3   Shift linkage - adjustment

Refer to illustrations 3.3, 3.4 and 3.6

1   Raise the vehicle and support it securely on jackstands.
2   Remove the left side engine undercover.
3   Loosen the swivel nut on the manual shift lever at the transaxle **(see illustration)**.
4   Push the lever toward the right side of the vehicle and then return it two notches to the Neutral position **(see illustration)**.
5   Move the shift lever inside the vehicle to the Neutral position.
6   While holding the lever with a slight pressure toward the Reverse position, tighten the swivel nut securely **(see illustration)**.
7   Check the operation of the transaxle in each shift lever position

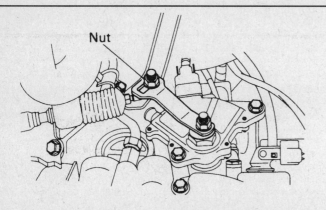

3.3   Loosen the swivel nut on the shift lever

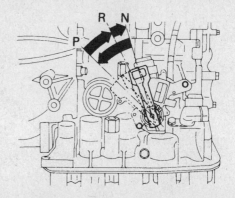

3.4   Push the lever fully toward the right then return the lever two notches to the Neutral position

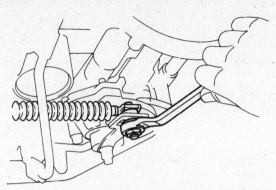

3.6 While pushing the lever lightly toward Reverse, tighten the swivel nut securely

(try to start the engine in each gear - the starter should operate in the Park and Neutral positions only).

4 Throttle valve (TV) cable - check and adjustment

Refer to illustration 4.3

1 Remove the air cleaner duct assembly.

2 Have an assistant hold the throttle pedal down while you watch the TV link in the engine compartment to make sure it opens fully.

3 If the link does not open all the way, have the assistant continue to hold the pedal down, loosen the adjusting nuts and adjust the cable until the mark or stopper is the specified distance from the boot end **(see illustration)**.

4 Tighten the adjusting nuts securely, recheck the clearance and make sure the link opens all the way when the throttle is depressed.

5 Neutral start switch - replacement and adjustment

Replacement

1 Disconnect the negative cable from the battery. **Caution:** If the stereo in your vehicle is equipped with an anti-theft system, refer to the information on page 0-15 at the front of this manual before detaching the cable.

2 Shift the transaxle into Neutral.

3 Remove the nut and lift off the shift lever.

4 Unplug the electrical connector.

5 Remove the attaching bolts and lift the switch off the shift shaft.

6 To install, line up the flats on the shift shaft with the flats in the switch and push the switch onto the shaft.

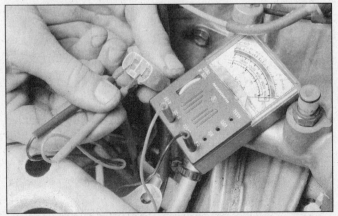

5.9 With the transaxle in Neutral, check continuity with an ohmmeter as shown

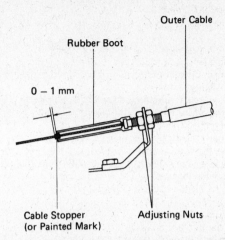

4.3 Loosen the adjusting nuts and adjust the cable housing position until the stopper or painted mark is the specified distance from the boot end

7 Install the bolts, but leave them loose and follow the adjustment procedure below. The remainder of installation is the reverse of removal.

Adjustment

Refer to illustration 5.9 and 5.10

8 There are two ways to adjust the Neutral start switch. One way is to check the continuity of the switch with an ohmmeter. Unplug the electrical connector from the switch and loosen the mounting bolts.

9 Connect an ohmmeter to the switch and rotate the switch until there's continuity between the terminals, indicating that it's now in the Neutral position **(see illustration)**. Tighten the bolts securely.

10 The other way is to rotate the switch until the neutral basic line on the switch housing is lined up with the groove in the shift shaft and tighten the bolts securely **(see illustration)**.

6 Automatic transaxle - removal and installation

Refer to illustrations 6.4, 6.5, 6.10, 6.15 and 6.18

Removal

1 Disconnect the negative cable from the battery. Place the cable out of the way so it cannot accidentally come in contact with the negative terminal of the battery, as this would once again allow power into the electrical system of the vehicle.

2 Raise the vehicle and support it securely on jackstands.

3 Drain the transmission fluid (see Chapter 1).

7B

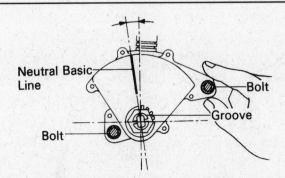

5.10 Align the neutral basic line on the housing with the groove in the shift shaft and tighten the bolts

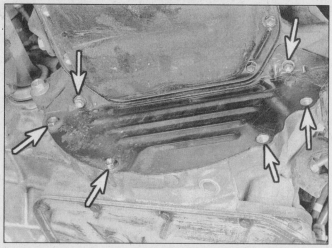

6.4   Torque converter cover bolt locations (arrows)

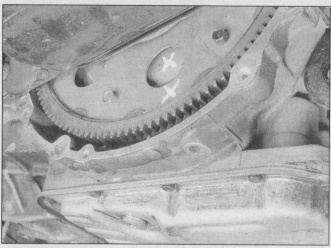

6.5   Mark the relationship of the torque converter to the driveplate so they can be reinstalled in the same relative position

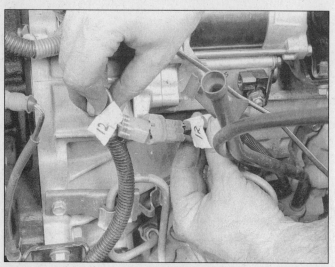

6.10   Tag the electrical connectors with marked pieces of tape before disconnecting them

6.15   If you don't have a regular engine hoist, lay a 4x4 post across the engine compartment like this and support the engine with a heavy chain

4   Remove the torque converter cover (see illustration).
5   Mark the relationship of the torque converter to the driveplate so they can be installed in the same position (see illustration).
6   Remove the six torque converter-to-driveplate bolts. Turn the crankshaft for access to each one in turn.
7   Remove the starter motor (see Chapter 5).
8   Disconnect the driveaxles from the transaxle (see Chapter 8).
9   Disconnect the speedometer cable (see Chapter 7A).
10   Disconnect the electrical connectors from the transaxle (see illustration).
11   On models so equipped, disconnect the vacuum hose(s).
12   Remove any exhaust components which will interfere with transaxle removal (see Chapter 4).
13   Disconnect the TV linkage cable.
14   Disconnect the shift linkage (see Section 3).
15   Support the engine using a hoist from above or a 4x4 wood post across the engine compartment (see illustration), or a jack and a block of wood under the oil pan to spread the load.
16   Support the transaxle with a jack - preferably a special jack made for this purpose. Safety chains will help steady the transaxle on the jack.
17   Remove any chassis or suspension components which will interfere with transaxle removal.
18   Remove the bolts securing the transaxle to the engine (see illus-

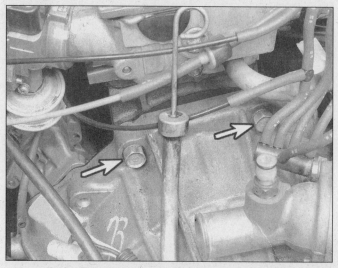

6.18   Remove the upper transaxle bolts (arrows)

tration).

19 Remove the transaxle mount nuts and bolts.
20 Lower the transaxle slightly and disconnect and plug the transaxle cooler lines.
21 Remove the transaxle fluid filler tube.
22 Move the transaxle to the side to disengage it from the engine block dowel pins and make sure the torque converter is detached from the driveplate. Secure the torque converter to the transaxle so that it will not fall out during removal. Lower the transaxle from the vehicle.

Installation

23 Make sure that the torque converter hub is securely engaged in the pump prior to installation.
24 With the transaxle secured to the jack, raise it into position. Be sure to keep it level so the torque converter does not slide forward. Connect the cooler lines.
25 Move the transaxle carefully into place until the dowel pins are engaged and the torque converter is engaged.
26 Turn the torque converter to line up the bolt holes with the holes in the driveplate. The match marks on the torque converter and driveplate, made during step 5, must line up.

27 Install the transaxle-to-engine bolts and nuts. Tighten the bolts and nuts to the torque listed in this Chapter's Specifications.
28 Install the torque converter-to-driveplate bolts. Tighten the bolts to the torque listed in this Chapter's Specifications.
29 Install the transaxle and any suspension and chassis components which were removed. Tighten the bolts and nuts to the torque values listed in the Chapter 10 Specifications section.
30 Remove the jacks supporting the transaxle and the engine.
31 Install the fluid filler tube.
32 Install the starter.
33 Connect the vacuum hose(s) (if equipped).
34 Connect the shift and TV linkage.
35 Plug in the transaxle electrical connectors.
36 Install the torque converter cover.
37 Connect the driveaxles to the transaxle (see Chapter 8).
38 Connect the speedometer.
39 Adjust the shift linkage (see Section 3).
40 Install any exhaust system components which were removed.
41 Lower the vehicle.
42 Fill the transaxle (see Chapter 1). Run the vehicle and check for fluid leaks.

7B

NOTES

Chapter 8 Clutch and driveaxles

Contents

Specifications

Clutch

Fluid type	See Chapter 1
Pedal freeplay	See Chapter 1
Pedal height	See Chapter 1

Driveaxle length (standard)

2S-E, 3S-FE engines	17-1/2 inches
3S-GE engine	
Left	18-5/64 inches
Right	18-3/16 inches
4A-FE engine	
1991 and earlier	
Left...	21-15/64 inches
Right..	33-11/16 inches
1992 on	
Left	
Automatic transaxle...............................	21-15/64 inches
Manual transaxle	21-19/64 inches
Right..	
Automatic transaxle...............................	33-11/16 inches
Manual transaxle	33-31/32 inches
5S-FE engine (all)	
Left	22-inches
Right	33-9/32 inches

Torque specifications

	Ft-lbs (unless otherwise indicated)
Clutch master cylinder mounting nuts	11
Clutch pressure plate-to-flywheel bolts	14
Clutch release cylinder mounting bolts	9
Driveaxle/hub nut	137
Driveaxle inner CV joint-to-differential side gear shaft flange	27
Right driveaxle center bearing bracket bolts	
(models with a 3S-GE, 4A-FE or 5S-FE engine)	47
Wheel lug nuts	See Chapter 1

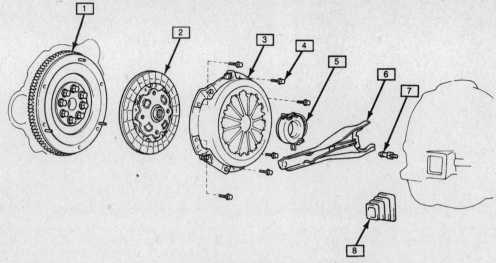

2.1   Clutch components - exploded view

1 *Flywheel*	5 *Release bearing*
2 *Clutch disc*	6 *Release lever*
3 *Pressure plate*	7 *Release lever ball stud*
4 *Pressure plate bolts*	8 *Fork boot*

1   General information

The information in this Chapter deals with the components from the rear of the engine to the front wheels, except for the transaxle, which is dealt with in Chapter 7A and 7B. For the purposes of this Chapter, these components are grouped into two categories: Clutch and driveaxles. Separate Sections within this Chapter offer general descriptions and checking procedures for both groups.

Since nearly all the procedures covered in this Chapter involve working under the vehicle, make sure it's securely supported on sturdy jackstands or a hoist where the vehicle can be easily raised and lowered.

2   Clutch - description and check

Refer to illustration 2.1

1   All vehicles with a manual transaxle use a single dry plate, diaphragm spring type clutch **(see illustration)**. The clutch disc has a splined hub which allows it to slide along the splines of the transaxle input shaft. The clutch and pressure plate are held in contact by spring pressure exerted by the diaphragm in the pressure plate.

2   The clutch release system is operated by hydraulic pressure. The hydraulic release system consists of the clutch pedal, a master cylinder and fluid reservoir, the hydraulic line, a slave cylinder which actuates the clutch release lever and the clutch release (or throw-out) bearing.

3   When pressure is applied to the clutch pedal to release the clutch, hydraulic pressure is exerted against the outer end of the clutch release lever. As the lever pivots, the shaft fingers push against the release bearing. The bearing pushes against the fingers of the diaphragm spring of the pressure plate assembly, which in turn releases the clutch plate.

4   Terminology can be a problem regarding the clutch components because common names have in some cases changed from that used by the manufacturer. For example, the driven plate is also called the clutch plate or disc, the pressure plate assembly is sometimes referred to as the clutch cover, the clutch release bearing is sometimes called a throw-out bearing, and the release cylinder is sometimes called the operating or slave cylinder.

5   Other than replacing components that have obvious damage, some preliminary checks should be performed to diagnose a clutch system failure.

a) The first check should be of the fluid level in the clutch master cylinder (see Chapter 1). If the fluid level is low, add fluid as necessary and inspect the hydraulic clutch system for leaks. If the master cylinder reservoir has run dry, bleed the system (see Section 7) and retest the clutch operation.

b) To check "clutch spin down time," run the engine at normal idle speed with the transaxle in Neutral (clutch pedal up - engaged). Disengage the clutch (pedal down), wait several seconds and shift the transaxle into Reverse. No grinding noise should be heard. A grinding noise would most likely indicate a problem in the pressure plate or the clutch disc.

c) To check for complete clutch release, run the engine (with the parking brake applied to prevent movement) and hold the clutch pedal approximately 1/2-inch from the floor. Shift the transaxle between 1st gear and Reverse several times. If the shift is not smooth, component failure is indicated. Check the release cylinder pushrod travel. With the clutch pedal depressed completely the release cylinder pushrod should extend substantially. If it doesn't, check the fluid level in the clutch master cylinder.

d) Visually inspect the clutch pedal bushing at the top of the clutch pedal to make sure there is no sticking or excessive wear.

e) Under the vehicle, check that the clutch release lever is solidly mounted on the ball stud.

3   Clutch components - removal, inspection and installation

Warning: *Dust produced by clutch wear and deposited on clutch components may contain asbestos, which is hazardous to your health. DO NOT blow it out with compressed air and DO NOT inhale it. DO NOT use gasoline or petroleum based solvents to remove the dust. Brake system cleaner should be used to flush the dust into a drain pan. After the clutch components are wiped clean with a rag, dispose of the contaminated rags and cleaner in a labeled, covered container.*

Removal

Refer to illustration 3.6

1   Access to the clutch components is normally accomplished by

3.6 Mark the relationship of the pressure plate to the flywheel (in case you are going to reuse the same pressure plate)

3.10 Examine the clutch disc for evidence of excessive wear, such as smeared friction material, chewed-up rivets, worn hub splines and distorted damper cushions or springs

removing the transaxle, leaving the engine in the vehicle. If, of course, the engine is being removed for major overhaul, then the opportunity should always be taken to check the clutch for wear and replace worn components as necessary. However, the relatively low cost of the clutch components compared to the time and labor involved in gaining access to them warrants their replacement any time the engine or transaxle is removed, unless they are new or in near-perfect condition. The following procedures assume that the engine will stay in place.

2   Remove the release cylinder (see Section 6). Hang it out of the way with a piece of wire - it's not necessary to disconnect the hose.

3   Remove the transaxle from the vehicle (see Chapter 7A). Support the engine while the transaxle is out. Preferably, an engine hoist should be used to support it from above. However, if a jack is used underneath the engine, make sure a piece of wood is used between the jack and oil pan to spread the load. **Caution:** *The pick-up for the oil pump is very close to the bottom of the oil pan. If the pan is bent or distorted in any way, engine oil starvation could occur.*

4   The release fork and release bearing can remain attached to the transaxle for the time being.

5   To support the clutch disc during removal, install a clutch alignment tool through the clutch disc hub.

6   Carefully inspect the flywheel and pressure plate for indexing marks. The marks are usually an X, an O or a white letter. If they cannot be found, scribe marks yourself so the pressure plate and the flywheel will be in the same alignment during installation **(see illustration)**.

7   Slowly loosen the pressure plate-to-flywheel bolts. Work in a diagonal pattern and loosen each bolt a little at a time until all spring pressure is relieved. Then hold the pressure plate securely and completely remove the bolts, followed by the pressure plate and clutch disc.

Inspection

Refer to illustrations 3.10, 3.12a and 3.12b

8   Ordinarily, when a problem occurs in the clutch, it can be attributed to wear of the clutch driven plate assembly (clutch disc). However, all components should be inspected at this time.

9   Inspect the flywheel for cracks, heat checking, score marks and other damage. If the imperfections are slight, a machine shop can resurface it to make it flat and smooth. Refer to Chapter 2 for the flywheel removal procedure.

10   Inspect the lining on the clutch disc. There should be at least 1/16-inch of lining above the rivet heads. Check for loose rivets, distortion, cracks, broken springs and other obvious damage **(see illustration)**. As mentioned above, ordinarily the clutch disc is replaced as a matter of course, so if in doubt about the condition, replace it with a new one.

11   The release bearing should be replaced along with the clutch disc (see Section 4).

12   Check the machined surface and the diaphragm spring fingers of the pressure plate **(see illustrations)**. If the surface is grooved or oth-

8

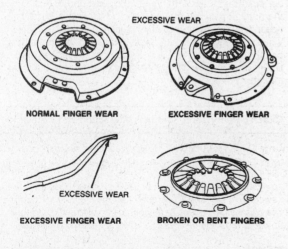

3.12a Replace the pressure plate if any of these conditions are noted

3.12b Examine the pressure plate friction surface for score marks, cracks and evidence of overheating (blue spots)

3.14 Center the clutch disc in the pressure plate with a clutch alignment tool

erwise damaged, replace the pressure plate assembly. Also check for obvious damage, distortion, cracking, etc. Light glazing can be removed with emery cloth or sandpaper. If a new pressure plate is indicated, new or factory rebuilt units are available.

Installation

Refer to illustration 3.14

13   Before installation, carefully wipe the flywheel and pressure plate machined surfaces clean. It's important that no oil or grease is on these surfaces or the lining of the clutch disc. Handle these parts only with clean hands.

14   Position the clutch disc and pressure plate with the clutch held in place with an alignment tool **(see illustration)**. Make sure it's installed properly (most replacement clutch plates will be marked "flywheel side" or something similar - if not marked, install the clutch disc with the damper springs or cushion toward the transaxle).

15   Tighten the pressure plate-to-flywheel bolts only finger tight, working around the pressure plate.

16   Center the clutch disc by ensuring the alignment tool is through the splined hub and into the recess in the crankshaft. Wiggle the tool up, down or side-to-side as needed to bottom the tool. Tighten the pressure plate-to-flywheel bolts a little at a time, working in a criss-cross pattern to prevent distortion of the cover. After all of the bolts are snug, tighten them to the torque listed in this Chapter's Specifications. Remove the alignment tool.

17   Using high-temperature grease, lubricate the inner groove of the release bearing (see Section 4). Also place grease on the release lever contact areas and the transaxle input shaft bearing retainer.

18   Install the clutch release bearing (see Section 4).

19   Install the transaxle, release cylinder and all components removed previously, tightening all fasteners to the proper torque specifications.

---

4   Clutch release bearing and lever - removal, inspection and installation

---

Warning: *Dust produced by clutch wear and deposited on clutch components may contain asbestos, which is hazardous to your health. DO NOT blow it out with compressed air and DO NOT inhale it. DO NOT use gasoline or petroleum-based solvents to remove the dust. Brake system cleaner should be used to flush it into a drain pan. After the clutch components are wiped clean with a rag, dispose of the contaminated rags and cleaner in a labeled, covered container.*

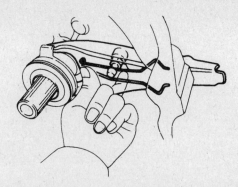

4.3   Reach behind the release lever and disengage the lever from the ball stud by pulling on the retention spring, then remove the lever and bearing

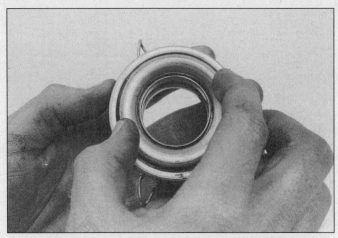

4.4   To check the operation of the bearing, hold it by the outer race and rotate the inner race while applying pressure - the bearing should turn smoothly - if it doesn't, replace it

Removal

Refer to illustration 4.3

1   Disconnect the negative cable from the battery. **Caution:** *If the stereo in your vehicle is equipped with an anti-theft system, refer to the information on page 0-15 at the front of this manual before detaching the cable.*

2   Remove the transaxle (see Chapter 7).

3   Remove the clutch release lever from the ball stud, then remove the bearing from the lever **(see illustration)**.

Inspection

Refer to illustration 4.4

4   Hold the bearing by the outer race and rotate the inner race while applying pressure **(see illustration)**. If the bearing doesn't turn smoothly or if it's noisy, replace the bearing/hub assembly with a new one. Wipe the bearing with a clean rag and inspect it for damage, wear and cracks. Don't immerse the bearing in solvent - it's sealed for life and to do so would ruin it. Also check the release lever for cracks and bends.

Installation

Refer to illustrations 4.5 and 4.6

5   Fill the inner groove of the release bearing with high-temperature grease. Also apply a light coat of the same grease to the transaxle input shaft splines and the front bearing retainer **(see illustration)**.

6   Lubricate the release lever ball socket, lever ends and release .

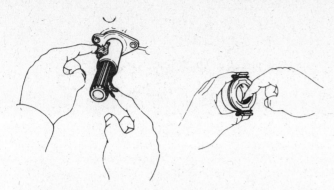

4.5   Apply a light coat of high temperature grease to the transaxle bearing retainer and also fill the release bearing groove

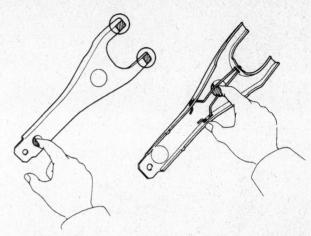

4.6   Apply high temperature grease to the release lever in the areas indicated

cylinder pushrod socket with high-temperature grease **(see illustration)**.

7   Attach the release bearing to the release lever.

8   Slide the release bearing onto the transaxle input shaft front bearing retainer while passing the end of the release lever through the opening in the clutch housing. Push the clutch release lever onto the ball stud until it's firmly seated.

9   Apply a light coat of high-temperature grease to the face of the release bearing where it contacts the pressure plate diaphragm fingers.

10   The remainder of installation is the reverse of the removal procedure.

5   Clutch master cylinder - removal, overhaul and installation

Note: *Before beginning this procedure, contact local parts stores and dealer service departments concerning the purchase of a rebuild kit or a new master cylinder. Availability and cost of the necessary parts may dictate whether the cylinder is rebuilt or replaced with a new one. If it's decided to rebuild the cylinder, inspect the bore as described in Step 12 before purchasing parts.*

Removal

Refer to illustration 5.2

1   Disconnect the negative cable from the battery. **Caution:** *If the*

stereo in your vehicle is equipped with an anti-theft system, refer to the information on page 0-15 at the front of this manual before detaching the cable.*

2   Under the dashboard, disconnect the pushrod from the top of the clutch pedal. It's held in place with a clevis pin **(see illustration)**.

3   Disconnect the hydraulic line at the clutch master cylinder. If available, use a flare-nut wrench on the fitting, which will prevent the fitting from being rounded off. Have rags handy as some fluid will be lost as the line is removed. **Caution:** *Don't allow brake fluid to come into contact with paint, as it will damage the finish.*

4   From under the dash, remove the nut which secures the master cylinder to the engine firewall. Remove the master cylinder, again being careful not to spill any of the fluid.

Overhaul

Refer to illustrations 5.5a, 5.5b, 5.5c, 5.6 and 5.8

5   Remove the reservoir cap and drain all fluid from the master cylinder. On 1989 and earlier models remove the hold-down bolt inside the reservoir, then pull off the reservoir **(see illustrations)**. On 1990 and later models, drive out the spring pin with a hammer and punch, then carefully pry the reservoir off **(see illustration)**.

6   Pull back the dust cover on the pushrod and remove the snap-

5.2   To release the clutch pushrod from the clutch pedal, remove the clip and clevis pin from the clutch pedal

5.5a   On 1989 and earlier models the reservoir tank is attached to the master cylinder with a large nut in the bottom of the tank

8

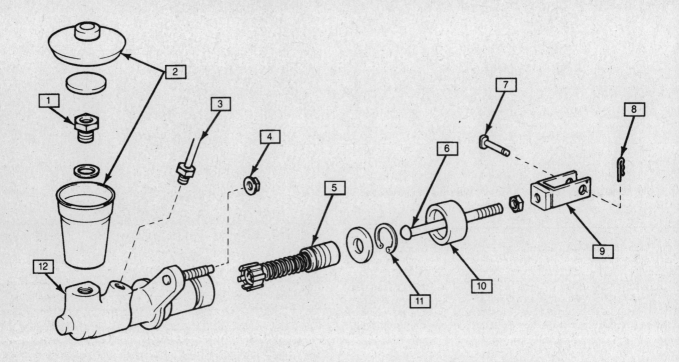

5.5b   Clutch master cylinder - exploded view (1989 and earlier models)

1	Reservoir bolt	5	Piston	9	Clevis
2	Reservoir	6	Pushrod	10	Boot
3	Clutch line	7	Clevis pin	11	Snap-ring
4	Mounting nut	8	Clip	12	Master cylinder

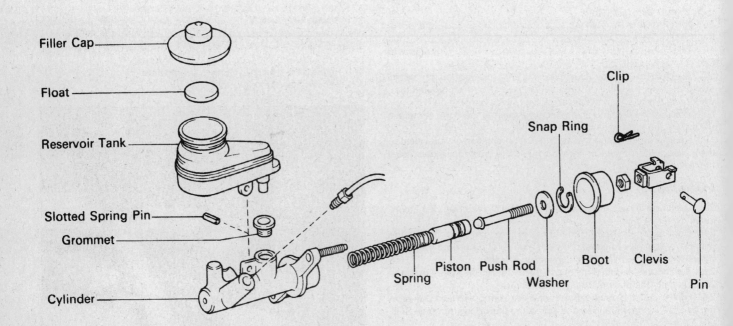

5.5c   Clutch master cylinder - exploded view (1990 and later models)

5.6   Use a small screwdriver to pry the snap-ring from the cylinder bore

ring **(see illustration)**. On some models the snap-ring can be pried-out with a screwdriver. On other models, snap-ring pliers must be used.

7   Remove the retaining washer and the pushrod from the cylinder.

8   Tap the master cylinder on a block of wood to eject the piston assembly from inside the bore **(see illustration)**. **Note:** *If the rebuild kit supplies a complete piston assembly, ignore the Steps which don't apply.*

9   Separate the spring from the piston.

10   Carefully remove the seal from the piston.

11   Wash all parts to be re-used with brake cleaner, denatured alcohol or clean brake fluid. DO NOT use petroleum-based solvents.

12   Inspect the bore of the master cylinder for deep scratches, score marks and ridges. The surface must be smooth to the touch. If the bore isn't perfectly smooth, the master cylinder must be replaced with a new or factory rebuilt unit.

13   If the cylinder will be rebuilt, use the new parts contained in the rebuild kit and follow any specific instructions which may have accompanied the rebuild kit.

14   Attach the seal to the piston. The seal lips must face away from the pushrod end of the piston.

15   Assemble the shim, spring support and spring on the other end of the piston.

16   Lubricate the bore of the cylinder and the seals with plenty of fresh brake fluid (DOT 3).

17   Carefully guide the piston assembly into the bore, being careful not to damage the seals. Make sure the spring end is installed first, with the pushrod end of the piston closest to the opening.

18   Position the pushrod and retaining washer in the bore, compress the spring and install a new snap-ring.

19   Apply a liberal amount of Girling Rubber Grease or equivalent to the inside of the dust cover and attach it to the master cylinder. Install the fluid reservoir

Installation

20   Position the master cylinder on the firewall, installing the mounting nut(s) finger-tight.

21   Connect the hydraulic line to the master cylinder, moving the cylinder slightly as necessary to thread the fitting properly into the bore. Don't cross-thread the fitting as it's installed.

22   Tighten the mounting nut(s) and the hydraulic line fitting securely.

23   Connect the pushrod to the clutch pedal.

24   Fill the clutch master cylinder reservoir with brake fluid conforming to DOT 3 specifications and bleed the clutch system (see Section 7).

25   Check the clutch pedal height and freeplay and adjust if necessary, following the procedure in Chapter 1.

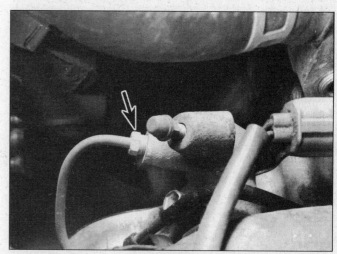

5.8   Invert the cylinder and tap it against a block of wood to eject the piston

6   Clutch release cylinder - removal, overhaul and installation

Note: *Before beginning this procedure, contact local parts stores and dealer service departments concerning the purchase of a rebuild kit or a new release cylinder. Availability and cost of the necessary parts may dictate whether the cylinder is rebuilt or replaced with a new one. If it's decided to rebuild the cylinder, inspect the bore as described in Step 8 before purchasing parts.*

Removal

Refer to illustration 6.3

1   Disconnect the negative cable from the battery. **Caution:** *If the stereo in your vehicle is equipped with an anti-theft system, refer to the information on page 0-15 at the front of this manual before detaching the cable.*

2   Raise the vehicle and support it securely on jackstands.

3   Disconnect the hydraulic line at the release cylinder. If available, use a flare-nut wrench on the fitting, which will prevent the fitting from being rounded off **(see illustration)**. Have a small can and rags handy, as some fluid will be spilled as the line is removed.

4   Remove the release cylinder mounting bolts.

5   Remove the release cylinder.

8

6.3   Use a flare nut wrench when disconnecting the hydraulic fitting to prevent rounding off the corners of the tube nut

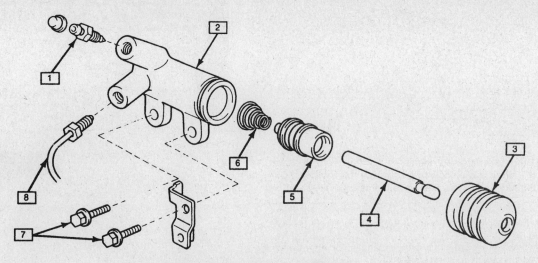

6.6   Clutch release cylinder - exploded view

1 *Bleeder valve*	4 *Pushrod*	7 *Mounting bolts*
2 *Release cylinder body*	5 *Piston/seal assembly*	8 *Hydraulic line*
3 *Boot*	6 *Spring*	

Overhaul

Refer to illustration 6.6

6   Remove the pushrod and the boot **(see illustration)**.

7   Tap the cylinder on a block of wood to eject the piston and seal. Remove the spring from inside the cylinder.

8   Carefully inspect the bore of the cylinder. Check for deep scratches, score marks and ridges. The bore must be smooth to the touch. If any imperfections are found, the release cylinder must be replaced with a new one.

9   Using the new parts in the rebuild kit, assemble the components using plenty of fresh brake fluid for lubrication. Note the installed direction of the spring and the seal.

Installation

10   Install the release cylinder on the clutch housing. Make sure the pushrod is seated in the release fork pocket.

11   Connect the hydraulic line to the release cylinder. Tighten the connection.

12   Fill the clutch master cylinder with brake fluid (conforming to DOT 3 specifications).

13   Bleed the system (see Section 7).

14   Lower the vehicle and connect the negative battery cable.

7   Clutch hydraulic system - bleeding

1   The hydraulic system should be bled of all air whenever any part of the system has been removed or if the fluid level has been allowed to fall so low that air has been drawn into the master cylinder. The procedure is very similar to bleeding a brake system.

2   Fill the master cylinder with new brake fluid conforming to DOT 3 specifications. **Caution:** *Do not re-use any of the fluid coming from the system during the bleeding operation or use fluid which has been inside an open container for an extended period of time.*

3   Raise the vehicle and place it securely on jackstands to gain access to the release cylinder, which is located on the left side of the clutch housing.

4   Remove the dust cap which fits over the bleeder valve and push a length of plastic hose over the valve. Place the other end of the hose into a clear container with about two inches of brake fluid in it. The hose end must be submerged in the fluid.

5   Have an assistant depress the clutch pedal and hold it. Open the

bleeder valve on the release cylinder, allowing fluid to flow through the hose. Close the bleeder valve when fluid stops flowing from the hose. Once closed, have your assistant release the pedal.

6   Continue this process until all air is evacuated from the system, indicated by a full, solid stream of fluid being ejected from the bleeder valve each time and no air bubbles in the hose or container. Keep a close watch on the fluid level inside the clutch master cylinder reservoir; if the level drops too low, air will be sucked back into the system and the process will have to be started all over again.

7   Install the dust cap and lower the vehicle. Check carefully for proper operation before placing the vehicle in normal service.

8   Clutch start switch - check and adjustment

Refer to illustrations 8.4 and 8.5

1   Check the pedal height, pedal freeplay and pushrod play (see Chapter 1).

2   Verify that the engine will not start when the clutch pedal is released.

3   Verify that the engine will start when the clutch pedal is depressed all the way.

4   Measure distance "A" **(see illustration)**. It must be as specified

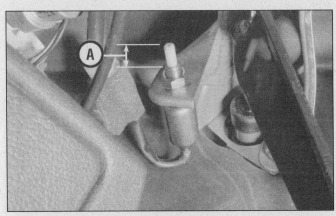

8.4   When the clutch pedal is fully depressed, distance "A" must be greater than 1 mm (0.04 inch). If it isn't, adjust or replace the switch

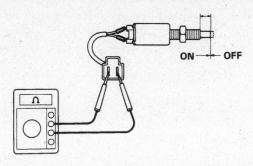

8.5 Using an ohmmeter, check the continuity of the clutch switch - there should be continuity when the switch is On (pushed), but no continuity when it is Off (released)

when the clutch pedal is depressed. If it isn't, adjust or replace the clutch start switch.

5   Verify that there is continuity between the clutch start switch terminals when the switch is On **(see illustration)**.

6   Verify that no continuity exists between the switch terminals when the switch is Off.

7   If the switch fails either of the tests, replace it. This is accomplished by removing the nut nearest the plunger end of the switch and unscrewing the switch. Disconnect the wire harness. Installation is the reverse of removal.

8   To adjust the clutch start switch, depress the clutch pedal completely and turn the switch in or out to achieve the distance shown in illustration 8.4.

9   Verify again that the engine doesn't start when the clutch pedal is released.

9 Driveaxles - general information and inspection

1   Power is transmitted from the transaxle to the wheels through a pair of driveaxles. The inner end of each driveaxle is connected to the transaxle either by a side gear shaft (flanged stub axle) or directly splined to the differential side gears. The side gear shafts (on models so equipped) can be pulled out to replace the oil seals (see Chapter 7A). The outer ends of the driveaxles are splined to the axle hubs and locked in place by a large nut.

2   The inner ends of the driveaxles are equipped with sliding constant velocity joints, which are capable of both angular and axial motion. Each inner joint assembly consists of either a tripod bearing and a joint tulip (housing) or a ball and cage type constant velocity joint in

which the joint is free to slide in-and-out as the driveaxle moves up-and-down with the wheel. The joints can be disassembled and cleaned in the event of a boot failure, but if any parts are damaged, the joints must be replaced as a unit (see Section 12).

3   Each outer joint, which consists of ball bearings running between an inner race and an outer cage, is capable of angular but not axial movement.

4   The boots should be inspected periodically for damage and leaking lubricant. Torn CV joint boots must be replaced immediately or the joints can be damaged. Boot replacement involves removal of the driveaxle (see Section 10). **Note:** *Some auto parts stores carry "split" type replacement boots, which can be installed without removing the driveaxle from the vehicle. This is a convenient alternative; however, the driveaxle should be removed and the CV joint disassembled and cleaned to ensure the joint is free from contaminants such as moisture and dirt which will accelerate CV joint wear.* The most common symptom of worn or damaged CV joints, besides lubricant leaks, is a clicking noise in turns, a clunk when accelerating after coasting and vibration at highway speeds. To check for wear in the CV joints and driveaxle shafts, grasp each axle (one at a time) and rotate it in both directions while holding the CV joint housings, feeling for play indicating worn splines or sloppy CV joints. Also check the driveaxle shafts for cracks, dents and distortion.

10 Driveaxle - removal and installation

Refer to illustrations 10.4, 10.5, 10.6, 10.7, 10.9, 10.10, 10.11, 10.13, 10.14 and 10.15

Note: *Not all of the steps in this procedure apply to all models. Read through the procedure carefully and determine which steps apply to the vehicle being worked on before actually beginning any work.*

Removal

1   Disconnect the cable from the negative terminal of the battery. **Caution:** *If the stereo in your vehicle is equipped with an anti-theft system, refer to the information on page 0-15 at the front of this manual before detaching the cable.*

2   Set the parking brake.

3   Loosen the front wheel lug nuts, raise the vehicle and support it securely on jackstands. Remove the wheel.

4   Remove the cotter pin and the bearing nut lock from the driveaxle hub nut **(see illustration)**.

5   Remove the driveaxle hub nut and washer. To prevent the hub from turning, wedge a prybar between two of the wheel studs and allow the prybar to rest against the ground or the floorpan of the vehicle **(see illustration)**.

8

10.4 Remove the cotter pin and the nut lock

10.5 Use a large prybar to immobilize the hub while loosening the driveaxle hub nut

10.6   Using a hammer and a brass punch, sharply strike the end of the driveaxle - it should move noticeably (don't push it in too far, though; only until it's loose)

10.7   On some models the inner CV joints are attached to the differential side gear shaft (or the center driveshaft) with six nuts

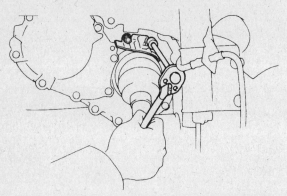

10.9   The transaxle case protector is secured by two bolts

6   To loosen the driveaxle from the hub splines, tap the end of the driveaxle with a soft-faced hammer or a hammer and a brass punch **(see illustration)**. If the driveaxle is stuck in the hub splines and won't move, it may be necessary to remove the brake disc (see Chapter 9) and push it from the hub with a two-jaw puller.

7   On models with flanged inner CV joints, remove the six nuts securing the inner CV joint to the differential side gear shaft or the center driveshaft **(see illustration)**. To prevent the driveaxle from turning, use the same method as described in Step 5.

8   Remove the engine undercover(s). If the vehicle has splined inner CV joints place a drain pan underneath the transaxle just in case lubricant leaks out.

9   If you're removing the left driveaxle on models with splined inner CV joints, remove the transaxle case protector **(see illustration)**.

10   Remove the nuts and bolt securing the balljoint to the control arm, then pry the control arm down to separate the components **(see illustration)**.

11   Pull out on the steering knuckle and detach the driveaxle from the hub **(see illustration)**.

12   If you're working on a model with flanged inner CV joints, the driveaxle can now be removed.

13   If you're removing the left driveaxle on a model with splined inner CV joints, carefully pry the inner CV joint out of the transaxle **(see illustration)**.

14   If you're removing the right driveaxle on a model with a 3S-GE, 4A-FE or 5S-FE engine, remove the two bolts from the center bearing bracket **(see illustration)** and remove the driveaxle and the center driveshaft as an assembly.

15   Should it become necessary to move the vehicle while the driveaxle is out, place a large bolt with two large washers (one on each

10.10   Remove the nuts and bolt then pry the control arm and balljoint apart

10.11   Pull the steering knuckle out and slide the end of the driveaxle out of the hub. There is a sharp ring around the CV joint just behind the stub axle - wrap a rag around it so you don't cut your hand

10.13   When prying the left driveaxle out (splined CV joints only) be careful not to distort the dust shield

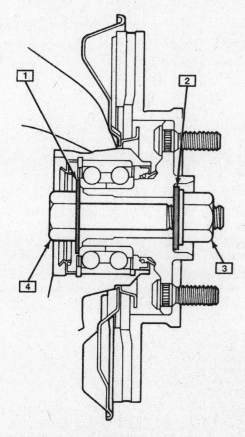

10.15   It isn't a good idea to move the vehicle with a driveaxle removed, but if you must, first install a bolt and   a pair of washers, as shown here, and tighten them securely

1   2-inch (O.D.) washer   3   9/16-inch nut
2   1-3/4 inch (O.D.) washer   4   9/16-inch bolt

side of the hub) through the hub and tighten the nut securely **(see illustration)**.
16   Refer to Chapter 7 for the differential seal replacement procedure. On models with flanged inner CV joints, pull the side gear shaft(s) out with a slide hammer (left side) or remove the center driveshaft (right side - see Section 11) for access to the seals.

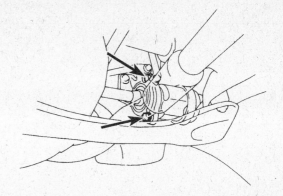

10.14   Remove the two bolts (arrows) from the center bearing bracket and remove the driveaxle and the center driveshaft as an assembly

11.2   Loosen the center driveshaft lock bolt

Installation

17   Installation is the reverse of the removal procedure, but with the following additional points:
  a) Tighten the inner CV joint-to-differential side gear shaft (or center driveshaft) nuts to the torque listed in this Chapter's Specifications (flanged inner CV joints only).
  b) When installing the left driveaxle on models with splined inner CV joints, push the driveaxle sharply inward to seat the retaining ring on the inner CV joint in the groove in the differential side gear.
  c) When installing the right driveaxle/center driveshaft assembly on a model with a 3S-GE, 4A-FE or 5S-FE engine, tighten the center bearing bracket bolts to the torque listed in this Chapter's Specifications.
  d) Tighten the driveaxle hub nut to the torque listed in this Chapter's Specifications, then install the nut lock and a new cotter pin.
  e) Install the wheel and lug nuts, lower the vehicle and tighten the lug nuts to the torque listed in the Chapter 1 Specifications.
  f) Check the transaxle or differential lubricant and add, if necessary, to bring it to the proper level (see Chapter 1).

11   Center driveshaft - removal and installation

Refer to illustrations 11.2, 11.3 and 11.4
1   Remove the right driveaxle (see Section 10).
2   Position a drain pan underneath the transaxle. Loosen the center driveshaft lock bolt **(see illustration)**. Before removing the shaft, check

8

11.3   Use adjustable jaw pliers to squeeze the snap-ring, then move it out of the bearing bracket

11.4   Use a prybar to force the center shaft from the bearing bracket

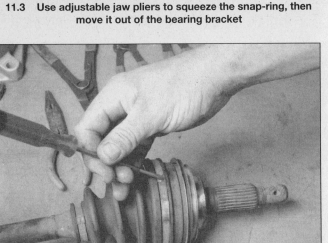

12.3   Lift the tabs on the all the boot clamps with a screwdriver, then open the clamps

12.5   Use a brass bar and a hammer to remove the inner race from the driveaxle, be careful not to hit the cage

the differential side gear shaft seal for evidence of leakage. Refer to Chapter 7A for side gear shaft seal replacement procedure.

3   Remove the snap-ring from the bearing bracket (see illustrations).

4   Use a large screwdriver or prybar to pry the center driveshaft out of the bearing bracket (see illustration), then remove it from the vehicle.

5   Check the center driveshaft bearing for smooth operation. If it feels rough or sticky it should be replaced. Take it to a dealer service department or other repair shop, as special tools are needed to perform this job.

6   Installation is the reverse of removal.

---

12   Driveaxle boot replacement and CV joint overhaul

Note: *If the CV joints must be overhauled (usually due to torn boots), explore all options before beginning the job. Complete rebuilt driveaxles are available on an exchange basis, which eliminates much time and work. Whichever route you choose to take, check on the cost and availability of parts before disassembling the vehicle.*

Outer CV joint

Disassembly
Refer to illustrations 12.3, 12.5, 12.7, 12.8, 12.10 and 12.11

1   Remove the driveaxle (see Section 10).

2   Mount the driveaxle in a vice with wood lined jaws (to prevent damage to the axleshaft). Check the CV joint for excessive play in the radial direction, which indicates worn parts. Check for smooth operation throughout the full range of motion for each CV joint. If a boot is torn, the recommended procedure is to disassemble the joint, clean the components and inspect for damage due to loss of lubrication and possible contamination by foreign matter.

3   Using a small screwdriver, pry the retaining tabs of the clamps up to loosen them and slide them off (see illustration).

4   Use a screwdriver and carefully pry up on the edge of the boot and push it away from the CV joint. Old and worn boots can be cut off.

5   Carefully drive the CV joint off the axleshaft with a brass bar and a hammer (see illustration). Strike the inner race only - be careful not to damage the splines or the cage.

6   Remove the boot.

7   Tilt the inner race and cage assembly (see illustration).

8   Remove the ball bearings one at a time. Pry them out with a dull screwdriver, if necessary (see illustration).

9   Tilt the inner race and cage assembly 90-degrees.

10   Align one of the large windows of the cage with one of the lands of the outer race. Lift the inner race and cage assembly out of the outer race (see illustration).

11   Remove the inner race from the cage by turning the inner race 90-degrees and swinging it out (see illustration).

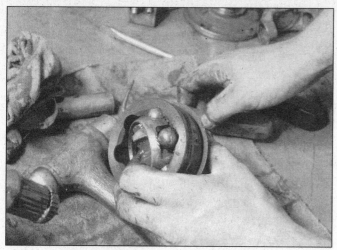

12.7   Tilt the inner race and cage assembly

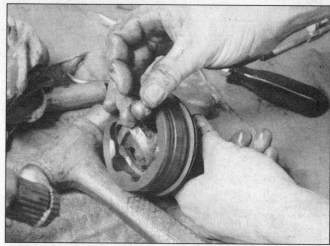

12.8   Remove the ball bearings one at a time - you may have to pry them out with a dull screwdriver (don't scratch any of the components)

12.10   Align a large window of the cage with a land of the outer race

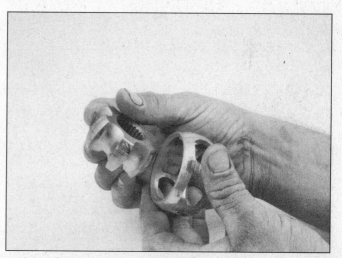

12.11   To remove the inner race from the cage, turn the inner race 90-degrees and place one of the inner race lands into one of the large windows of the cage, then swing the inner race out

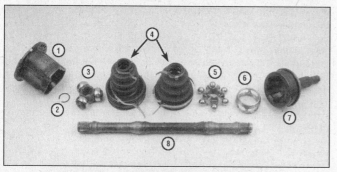

12.12a   The LT hand driveaxle disassembled

1 Tulip
2 Snap-ring
3 Tripod
4 CV joint boots
5 Inner race and ball bearings
6 Cage
7 Outer race
8 Axleshaft

8

Check

Refer to illustrations 12.12a, 12.12b and 12.12c

12   Clean all components with solvent to remove grease. Check for cracks, pitting, scoring and other signs of wear **(see illustrations)**.

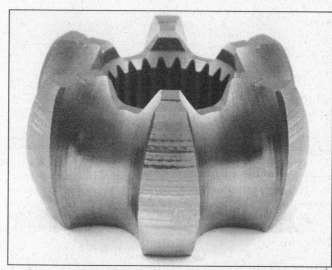

12.12b   Check the inner race lands and grooves for score marks and pitting (also check for damaged splines)

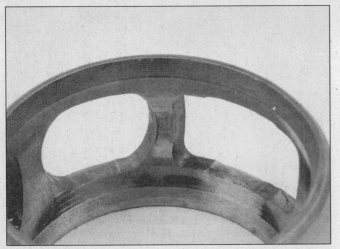

12.12c Check the cage for cracks, pitting and score marks (shiny spots are normal and don't affect operation)

12.13 Place one of the inner race lands into one of the large windows of the cage, then swing the inner race into the cage

12.16 The beveled side of the inner race should be pointing up

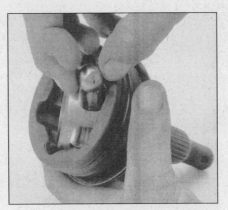

12.17 Tilt the inner race cage assembly to expose the openings in the cage and insert the ball bearings, one at a time, by hand

12.18a Insert grease into the opening for the driveaxle . . .

Reassembly

Refer to illustrations 12.13, 12.16, 12.17, 12.18a and 12.18b

13   Install the inner race into the cage **(see illustration)**.

14   Insert the inner race and cage assembly into the outer race **(see illustration 12.10)**.

15   Rotate the inner race and cage until it's flat within the outer race.

16   The inner race should have a groove and a beveled edge at the splines **(see illustration)**. If the inner race is smooth, flip it over.

17   To install the ball bearings, tilt the inner race and cage assembly to expose the openings **(see illustration)**.

18   Press the ball bearings, in one at a time, turning the inner assembly so that each one can be installed. With all the ball bearings installed, the CV joint can now be packed with grease **(see illustrations)**.

19   Slide the new boot and small clamp onto the axleshaft. Install the CV joint assembly onto the axleshaft and, using a brass hammer, drive the joint onto the shaft until the retaining ring on the shaft engages with the inner race. Pull on the joint to confirm this. Proceed to Step 26.

Inner CV joint

Disassembly

Refer to illustrations 12.20, 12.21, 12.22 and 12.23

20   After removing the boot clamps **(see illustration 12.3)**, pull the boot back from the inner joint and slide the tulip from the tripod **(see illustration)**.

21   Use a center punch to mark the tripod and driveaxle to ensure

12.18b . . . then push the grease down into the joint with your finger or a dowel (this may have to be done a few times until the joint is completely packed)

that they are reassembled properly **(see illustration)**.

22   Remove the tripod joint snap-ring with a pair of snap-ring pliers **(see illustration)**.

23   Use a hammer and a brass punch to drive the tripod joint from the driveaxle **(see illustration)**.

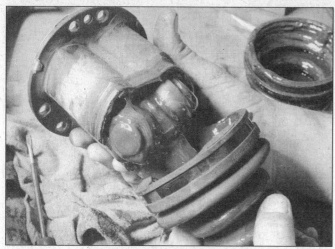

12.20   Remove the boot from the inner CV joint and slide the
tripod from the tulip

12.21   Use a centerpunch to place marks (arrows) on the tripod
and the driveaxle to ensure that they are reassembled properly

12.22   Remove the snap-ring with a pair
of snap-ring pliers

12.23   Drive the tripod joint from the
driveaxle with a brass punch and hammer
(be careful not to damage the bearing
surfaces or the splines on the shaft)

12.25a   Install the tripod with the
recessed portion of the splines facing
the axleshaft

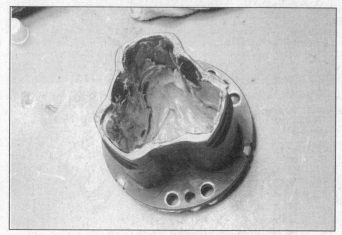

12.25b   Place grease at the bottom of the tulip

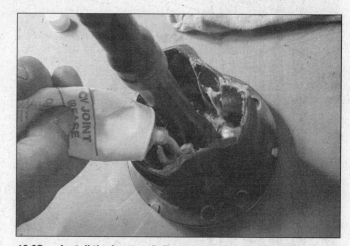

12.25c   Install the boot and clamps onto the axleshaft then insert
the tripod into the tulip, followed by the rest of the grease

8

Check

24   Clean all components with solvent to remove the grease, and
check for cracks, pitting, scoring and other signs of wear.

Reassembly

*Refer to illustrations 12.25a, 12.25b, 12.25c, 12.26, 12.27a, 12.27b
and 12.27c*

25   Slide the clamps and boot onto the axleshaft, place the tripod on
the shaft **(see illustration)** and install the snap-ring. Apply grease to

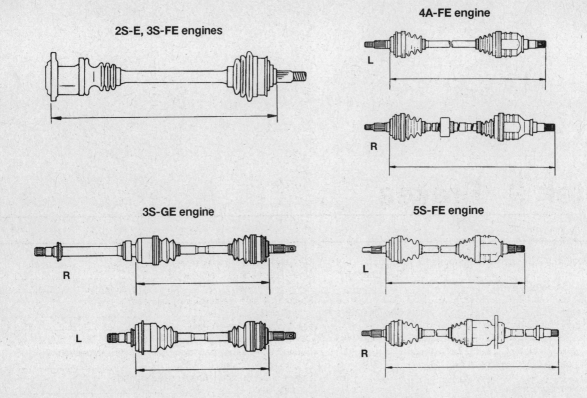

2S-E, 3S-FE engines

4A-FE engine

3S-GE engine

5S-FE engine

12.26   The driveaxle standard length should be set to the dimension listed in this Chapter's Specifications

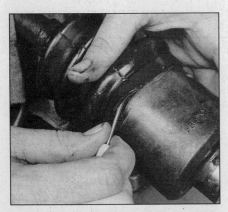

12.27a   Equalize the pressure inside the boot by inserting a small, dull screwdriver between the boot and the outer race

12.27b   To install the new clamps, bend the tang down . . .

12.27c   . . . then tap the tabs over to hold it in place

the tripod assembly and inside the tulip **(see illustrations)**.
26   Slide the boot into place, making sure both ends seat in their grooves. Adjust the length of the driveaxle to the dimension listed in this Chapter's Specifications **(see illustration)**.
27   Equalize the pressure in the boot, then tighten and secure the boot clamps **(see illustrations)**.

Chapter 9 Brakes

Contents

Specifications

General

Brake fluid type..	See Chapter 1
Brake pedal height	
1986 through 1989...............................	6-1/32 to 6-27/64 inches
1990 and later	
Manual transaxle...............................	6-5/8 to 7-1/32 inches
Automatic transaxle	6-39/64 to 7-1/64 inches
Brake pedal freeplay..	1/8 to 1/4 inch
Reserve distance	
1986 through 1988................................	More than 3-5/32 inches
1989	
With rear drum brakes	More than 3-35/64 inches
With rear disc brakes	More than 3-47/64 inches
1990 and later	
Without ABS	More than 3-11/32 inches
With ABS..	More than 3-35/64 inches
Power brake booster pushrod-to-master cylinder	
piston clearance	0.0 inch

Disc brakes

Minimum brake pad thickness	See Chapter 1
Front disc thickness*	
1986 and 1987	
Standard	0.866 inch
Minimum	0.827 inch
1988 and 1989	
All except 3S-GE engine with ABS	
Standard	0.866 inch
Minimum...	0.827 inch
3S-GE engine with ABS	
Standard	0.984 inch
Minimum...	0.945 inch

1990 and 1991	
Standard	0.866 inch
Minimum	0.787 inch
1992 and later	
Standard	0.984 inch
Minimum	0.906 inch
Rear disc thickness (all models with rear disc brakes)*	
Standard	0.394 inch
Minimum	0.354 inch
Disc runout limit (front and rear)	
1986 through 1989	0.006 inch
1990 and later	0.003 inch
Parking brake shoe minimum lining thickness	0.039 inch

Drum brakes

Drum inside diameter*	
Standard	7.874 inch
Maximum	7.913 inch

* **Note:** *If different specifications are cast into the disc or drum, they supersede information printed here.*

Torque specifications

Ft lbs (unless otherwise indicated)

Disc brake caliper mounting bolts	
Front caliper	
1986 through 1988	18
1989	27
1990 and 1991	
13-inch wheel	18
14 and 15-inch wheel	29
1992 and later	29
Rear caliper	14
Front caliper torque plate bolts	
1986 through 1988	69
1989	73
1990 and later	79
Rear caliper torque plate bolts	34
Brake hose-to-caliper banjo fitting bolt	22
Wheel cylinder mounting bolts	84 in-lbs
Master cylinder-to-brake booster nuts	108 in-lbs
Power brake booster mounting nuts	108 in-lbs
Wheel lug nuts	See Chapter 1

1   General information

The vehicles covered by this manual are equipped with hydraulically operated front and rear brake systems. The front brakes are disc type and the rear brakes are either drum or disc type. Both the front and rear brakes are self adjusting. The disc brakes automatically compensate for pad wear, while the drum brakes incorporate an adjustment mechanism which is activated as the parking brake is applied.

Hydraulic system

The hydraulic system consists of two separate circuits. The master cylinder has separate reservoirs for the two circuits, and, in the event of a leak or failure in one hydraulic circuit, the other circuit will remain operative. A dual proportioning valve on the firewall provides brake balance between the front and rear brakes.

Power brake booster

The power brake booster, utilizing engine manifold vacuum and atmospheric pressure to provide assistance to the hydraulically operated brakes, is mounted on the firewall in the engine compartment.

Parking brake

The parking brake operates the rear brakes only, through cable actuation. It's activated by a lever mounted in the center console.

Service

After completing any operation involving disassembly of any part of the brake system, always test drive the vehicle to check for proper braking performance before resuming normal driving. When testing the brakes, perform the tests on a clean, dry, flat surface. Conditions other than these can lead to inaccurate test results.

Test the brakes at various speeds with both light and heavy pedal pressure. The vehicle should stop evenly without pulling to one side or the other. Avoid locking the brakes, because this slides the tires and diminishes braking efficiency and control of the vehicle.

Tires, vehicle load and wheel alignment are factors which also affect braking performance.

2   Anti-lock Brake System (ABS) - general information

The anti-lock brake system was introduced in 1988 and is designed to maintain vehicle steerabilty, directional stability and optimum deceleration under severe braking conditions and on most road surfaces. It does so by monitoring the rotational speed of each wheel and controlling the brake line pressure to each wheel during braking. This prevents the wheel from locking up.

Components

Actuator assembly

Refer to illustrations 2.1a, 2.1b and 2.1c

1   The actuator assembly consists of the master cylinder, an electric hydraulic pump and four solenoid valves **(see illustrations)**.

    a) The electric pump provides hydraulic pressure to charge the reservoirs in the actuator, which supplies pressure to the braking system. The pump and reservoirs are housed in the actuator assembly

    b) The solenoid valves modulate brake line pressure during ABS operation. The body contains four valves - one for each wheel.

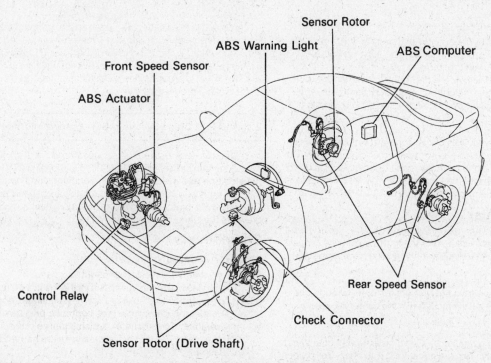

ANTI-LOCK Warning Light

Sensor Rotor

Rear Speed Sensor

A.B.S. Computer

Actuator

Sensor Rotor

Stop Light Switch
Control Relay

Sensor Rotor

Sensor Rotor

Front Speed Sensor

2.1a   Locations of the ABS system components on 1988 and 1989 models

Sensor Rotor

ABS Warning Light

ABS Computer

Front Speed Sensor

ABS Actuator

Rear Speed Sensor

Control Relay

Check Connector

Sensor Rotor (Drive Shaft)

2.1b   Locations of the ABS system components on 1990 and later models

9

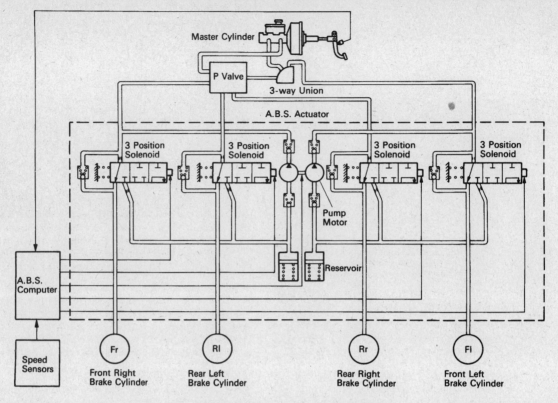

2.1c   A schematic of a typical ABS hydraulic system

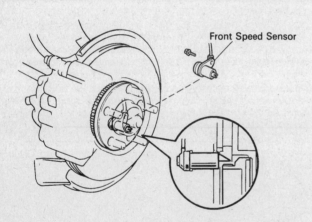

2.3a   On the 1988 and 1989 models, the front speed sensors bolt to the front brake backing plates

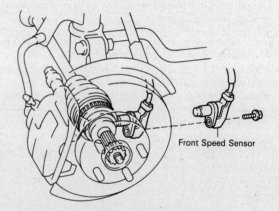

2.3b   On the 1990 and later models, the front speed sensor rings are integral with the outer CV joint

Speed sensors

Refer to illustrations 2.3a, 2.3b, 2.4a and 2.4b

2   These sensors are located at each wheel and generate small electrical pulsations when the toothed sensor rings are turning, sending a signal to the electronic controller indicating wheel rotational speed.

3   On 1988 and 1989 models, the front speed sensors **(see illustration)** are mounted to the front backing plates in close relationship to the toothed sensor rings, which are integral with the front hub assemblies. On 1990 and later models, the sensor rings are integral with the outer Constant Velocity (CV) joint **(see illustration)**.

4   The rear wheel sensors are bolted to the brake backing plates or axle carriers **(see illustrations)**. The sensor rings are integral with the rear hub assemblies.

ABS computer

5   The ABS computer is mounted under the dashboard (1988 and 1989) or in the luggage compartment (1990 and later) and is the "brain" for the ABS system. The function of the computer is to accept and process information received from the wheel speed sensors to control the hydraulic line pressure, avoiding wheel lock up. The computer also constantly monitors the system, even under normal driving conditions, to find faults within the system.

6   If a problem develops within the system, an "ANTI-LOCK" or "ABS" light will glow on the dashboard. A diagnostic code will also be stored in the computer, which, when retrieved by a service technician, will indicate the problem area or component.

Diagnosis and repair

7   If a dashboard warning light comes on and stays on while the ve-

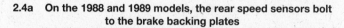

3.5   Using a large C-clamp, push the piston back into the caliper bore - note that one end of the clamp is on the flat area near the brake hose fitting and the other end (screw end) is pressing against the outer brake pad

2.4a   On the 1988 and 1989 models, the rear speed sensors bolt to the brake backing plates

hicle is in operation, the ABS system requires attention. Although a special electronic ABS diagnostic tester is necessary to properly diagnose the system, the home mechanic can perform a few preliminary checks before taking the vehicle to a dealer service department or other repair shop which is equipped with a tester.

a) Check the brake fluid level in the reservoir.
b) Check that all electrical connectors are securely connected.
c) Check the fuses.

8   If the above preliminary checks do not rectify the problem, the vehicle should be diagnosed and repaired by a dealer service department or other repair shop.

3   Disc brake pads - replacement

Refer to illustrations 3.5 and 3.6a through 3.6h
Warning: *Disc brake pads must be replaced on both front or rear*

wheels at the same time - never replace the pads on only one wheel. Also, the dust created by the brake system may contain asbestos, which is harmful to your health. Never blow it out with compressed air and don't inhale any of it. An approved filtering mask should be worn when working on the brakes. Do not, under any circumstances, use petroleum-based solvents to clean brake parts. Use brake cleaner or denatured alcohol only! When servicing the disc brakes, use only high-quality, nationally recognized brand-name pads.
Note: *This procedure applies to both the front and rear disc brakes.*

1   Remove the cap from the brake fluid reservoir.
2   Loosen the wheel lug nuts, raise the front or rear of the vehicle and support it securely on jackstands. Block the wheels at the opposite end.
3   Remove the wheels. Work on one brake assembly at a time, using the assembled brake for reference if necessary.
4   Inspect the brake disc carefully as outlined in Section 5. If machining is necessary, follow the information in that Section to remove the disc, at which time the pads can be removed as well.
5   Push the piston back into its bore to provide room for the new brake pads. A C-clamp can be used to accomplish this **(see illustration)**. As the piston is depressed to the bottom of the caliper bore, the fluid in the master cylinder will rise. Make sure that it doesn't overflow.

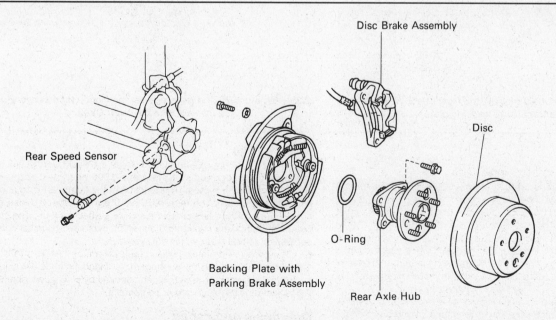

9

2.4b   On the 1990 and later models, the rear speed sensors are bolted to the axle carriers

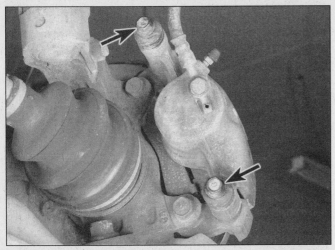

3.6a   Remove the two caliper mounting bolts (arrows) (front brake shown, rear disc brake similar)

3.6b   Pull the caliper straight up and off the disc

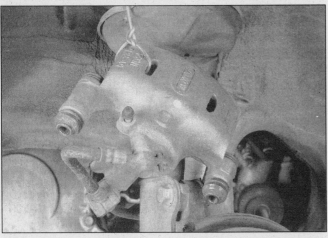

3.6c   Once the caliper is removed from the torque plate, hang it from the coil spring with a piece of wire - DON'T let it hang by the brake hose!

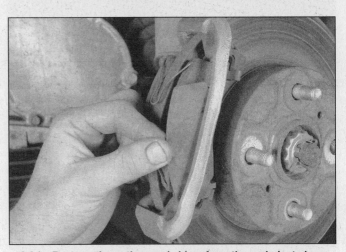

3.6d   Remove the anti-squeal shims from the pads (note how they are positioned - some models have only one shim per pad, others utilize two on the outer pad and one on the inner pad)

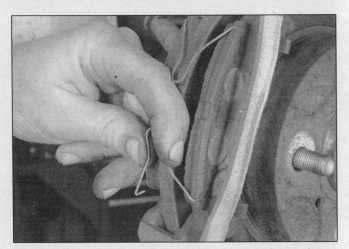

3.6e   Remove the anti-rattle springs, if equipped, from the brake pads

3.6f   To remove the pads, slide them to the side, then straight out of the torque plate

If necessary, siphon off some of the fluid.

6   Follow the accompanying photos, beginning with **illustration 3.6a,** for the actual pad replacement procedure. Be sure to stay in order and read the caption under each illustration.

7   When reinstalling the caliper, be sure to tighten the mounting bolts to the torque listed in this Chapter's Specifications. After the job has been completed, firmly depress the brake pedal a few times to bring the pads into contact with the disc. Check the level of the brake fluid, adding some if necessary. Check the operation of the brakes carefully before placing the vehicle into normal service.

3.6g Remove the pad support plates from the torque plate - they should be replaced with new ones if distorted in any way

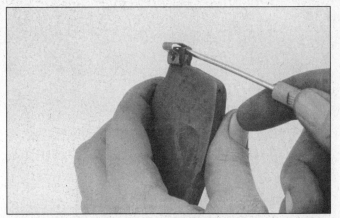

3.6h Pry the wear indicators off the brake pads and transfer them to the new pads - if they are worn or bent, replace them (the remainder of the brake pad replacement procedure is the reverse of removal)

4 Disc brake caliper - removal, overhaul and installation

Refer to illustrations 4.2, 4.4a, 4.4b, 4.4c, 4.5, 4.7, 4.8a and 4.8b

Warning: *Dust created by the brake system may contain asbestos, which is harmful to your health. Never blow it out with compressed air and don't inhale any of it. An approved filtering mask should be worn when working on the brakes. Do not, under any circumstances, use petroleum-based solvents to clean brake parts. Use brake cleaner or denatured alcohol only!*

Note: *If an overhaul is indicated (usually because of fluid leakage), explore all options before beginning the job. New and factory rebuilt calipers are available on an exchange basis, which makes this job quite easy. If it's decided to rebuild the calipers, make sure a rebuild kit is available before proceeding. Always rebuild the calipers in pairs - never rebuild just one of them.*

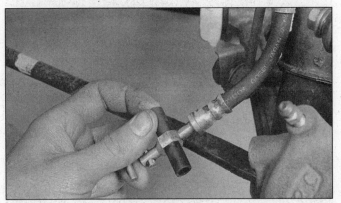

4.2 Using a piece of rubber hose of the appropriate size, plug the brake line

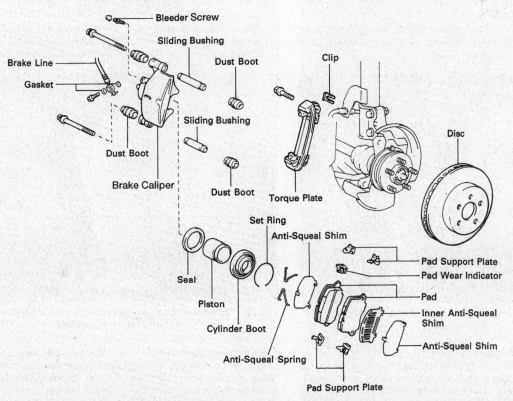

4.4a An exploded view of a typical front caliper assembly (1992 model shown, others similar)

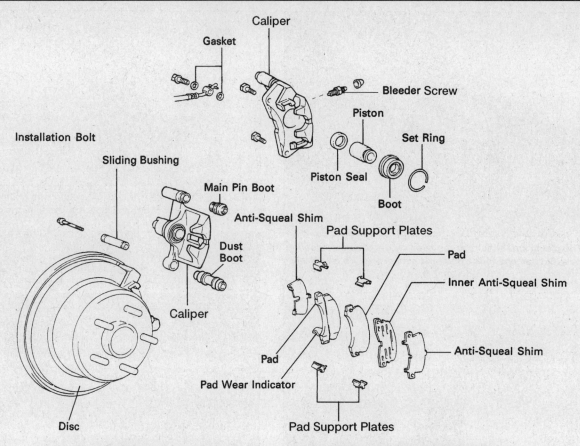

4.4b   An exploded view of a typical rear caliper assembly (1992 model shown, others similar)

4.4c   Using a screwdriver, remove the cylinder boot set ring

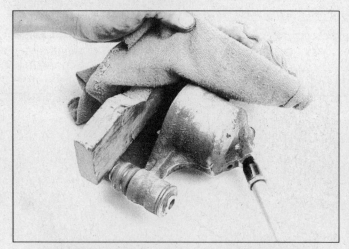

4.5   With the caliper padded to catch the piston, use compressed air to force the piston out of its bore - make sure your hands or fingers are not between the piston and caliper

Removal

1   Loosen the wheel lug nuts, raise the vehicle and support it securely on jackstands. Remove the wheel.

2   Remove the bolt and disconnect the brake hose from the caliper. Plug the brake hose to keep contaminants out of the brake system and to prevent losing any more brake fluid than is necessary **(see illustration)**.

3   Refer to Section 3 for either front or rear caliper removal procedures (it's part of the brake pad replacement procedure).

Overhaul

4   To overhaul the caliper, remove the boot set ring and the boot **(see illustrations)**. Before you remove the piston, place a wood block between the piston and caliper to prevent damage as it is removed.

5   To remove the piston from the caliper, apply compressed air to the brake fluid hose connection on the caliper body **(see illustration)**. Use only enough pressure to ease the piston out of its bore. **Warning:** *Be careful not to place your fingers between the piston and the caliper as the piston may come out with some force.*

6   Inspect the mating surfaces of the piston and caliper bore wall. If there is any scoring, rust, pitting or bright areas, replace the complete caliper unit with a new one.

7   If these components are in good condition, remove the piston seal from the caliper bore using a wooden or plastic tool **(see illustration)**. Metal tools may damage the cylinder bore.

8   Push the sliding bushings out of the caliper ears **(see illustration)** and remove the dust boots from both ends. If equipped, slide the

4.7   The piston seal should be removed with a plastic or wooden tool to avoid damage to the bore and seal groove - a pencil will do the job

4.8b   If equipped, push the bushing sleeve out of the caliper

5.3   The brake pads on this vehicle were obviously neglected, as they wore down to the rivets and cut deep grooves into the disc - wear this severe will require replacement of the disc

bushing sleeves out of the caliper ears **(see illustration)**.
9   Wash all the components in clean brake fluid or brake cleaner.
10   To reassemble the caliper, you should already have the correct rebuild kit for your vehicle.
11   Submerge the new piston seal and the piston in brake fluid and install them into the caliper bore. Do not force the piston into the bore, but make sure that it is squarely in place, then apply firm (but not excessive) pressure to install it.
12   Install the new piston dust boot and set ring.

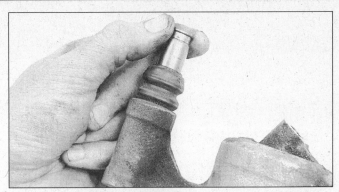

4.8a   Push the sliding bushing on each side of the caliper up through the boot and pull it free, then remove the dust boots

5.2   The torque plate (caliper mounting bracket) is secured to the steering knuckle with two bolts (arrows)

13   Lubricate the sliding bushings and sleeves (if equipped) with silicone-based grease (supplied in the kit) and push them into the caliper ears. Install the dust boots.

Installation

14   Install the caliper by reversing the removal procedure. Remember to replace the copper sealing washers (gaskets) at the brake hose-to-caliper connection (new washers normally come with the rebuild kit).
15   Bleed the brake circuit according to the procedure in Section 10. Make sure there are no leaks from the hose connections. Test the brakes carefully before returning the vehicle to normal service.

---

5   **Brake disc - inspection, removal and installation**

Note: *This procedure applies to both front and rear brake discs.*

Inspection

Refer to illustrations 5.2, 5.3, 5.4a, 5.4b, 5.5a and 5.5b

1   Loosen the wheel lug nuts, raise the vehicle and support it securely on jackstands. Remove the wheel and install two or three lug nuts to hold the disc in place. If the rear brake disc is being worked on, release the parking brake.
2   Remove the brake caliper as outlined in Section 4. It isn't necessary to disconnect the brake hose. After removing the caliper bolts, suspend the caliper out of the way with a piece of wire **(see illustration 3.6c)**. Remove the two torque plate-to-steering knuckle bolts **(see illustration)** and detach the torque plate.
3   Visually inspect the disc surface for score marks and other damage. Light scratches and shallow grooves are normal after use and may not always be detrimental to brake operation, but deep scoring - over 0.039-inch (1.0 mm) - requires disc removal and refinishing by an

9

5.4a   Use a dial indicator to check disc runout - if the reading exceeds the maximum allowable runout limit, the disc will have to be machined or replaced

5.5a   The minimum wear dimension is cast into the back side of the disc

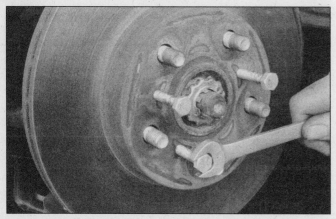

5.6   To help free the disc, thread bolts of the appropriate size into the holes provided in the disc. Alternate between the bolts, turning them a little at a time, until the disc is free

automotive machine shop. Be sure to check both sides of the disc **(see illustration)**. If pulsating has been noticed during application of the brakes, suspect disc runout.

4   To check disc runout, place a dial indicator at a point about 1/2-inch from the outer edge of the disc **(see illustration)**. Set the indicator to zero and turn the disc. The indicator reading should not exceed the specified allowable runout limit. If it does, the disc should be refinished by an automotive machine shop. **Note:** *The discs should be resurfaced regardless of the dial indicator reading, as this will impart a smooth finish and ensure a perfectly flat surface, eliminating any brake pedal pulsation or other undesirable symptoms related to questionable*

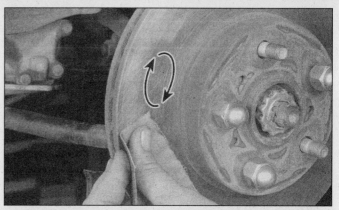

5.4b   Using a swirling motion, remove the glaze from the disc surface with sandpaper or emery cloth

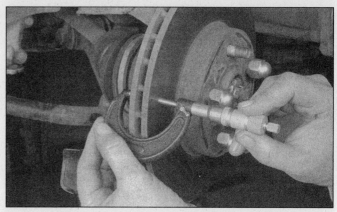

5.5b   Use a micrometer to measure disc thickness

discs. At the very least, if you elect not to have the discs resurfaced, remove the glaze from the surface with emery cloth using a swirling motion **(see illustration)**.

5   It's absolutely critical that the disc not be machined to a thickness under the specified minimum allowable disc refinish thickness. The minimum wear (or discard) thickness is cast into the inside of the disc **(see illustration)**. The disc thickness can be checked with a micrometer **(see illustration)**.

Removal

Refer to illustration 5.6

6   Remove the lug nuts which were put on to hold the disc in place and remove the disc from the hub. If the disc is stuck to the hub and won't come off, thread bolts into the holes provided **(see illustration)** and tighten them. Alternate between the bolts, turning them 1/4-turn at a time, until the disc is free.

Installation

7   Place the disc in position over the threaded studs.

8   Install the torque plate and caliper assembly over the disc and position it on the steering knuckle. Tighten the torque plate bolts to the torque listed in this Chapter's Specifications.

9   Install the wheel, then lower the vehicle to the ground. Tighten the lug nuts to the torque listed in the Chapter 1 Specifications. Depress the brake pedal a few times to bring the brake pads into contact with the disc. Bleeding won't be necessary unless the brake hose was disconnected from the caliper. Check the operation of the brakes carefully before driving the vehicle.

---

6   Drum brake shoes - replacement

Refer to illustrations 6.4a through 6.4x and 6.5

Warning: *Drum brake shoes must be replaced on both wheels at the*

6.4a   Mark the relationship of the drum to the hub, so the balance will be retained

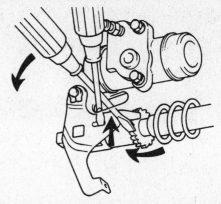

6.4b   If the brake shoes are hanging up on the drum (because of excessive wear), insert two screwdrivers through the hole in the backing plate to push the adjuster lever off the star wheel and turn the star wheel to retract the brake shoes

same time - never replace the shoes on only one wheel. Also, the dust created by the brake system may contain asbestos, which is harmful to your health. Never blow it out with compressed air and don't inhale any of it. An approved filtering mask should be worn when working on the brakes. Do not, under any circumstances, use petroleum-based solvents to clean brake parts. Use brake cleaner or denatured alcohol only!

Caution: *Whenever the brake shoes are replaced, the return and hold-down springs should also be replaced. Due to the continuous heating/cooling cycle the springs are subjected to, they lose tension over a period of time and may allow the shoes to drag on the drum and wear at a much faster rate than normal. When replacing the rear brake shoes, use only high-quality, nationally recognized brand-name parts.*

1   Loosen the wheel lug nuts, raise the rear of the vehicle and support it securely on jackstands. Block the front wheels to keep the vehi-

cle from rolling.
2   Release the parking brake.
3   Remove the wheel. **Note:** *All four rear brake shoes must be replaced at the same time, but to avoid mixing up parts, work on only one brake assembly at a time.*
4   Follow the accompanying illustrations for the brake shoe replacement procedure **(see illustrations 6.4a through 6.4x)**. Be sure to stay in order and read the caption under each illustration. **Note:** *If the brake drum cannot be easily pulled off the axle and shoe assembly, make sure the parking brake is completely released. If the drum still cannot be pulled off, the brake shoes will have to be retracted. This is done by first removing the plug from the backing plate. With the plug removed, push the lever off the adjuster star wheel with a narrow screwdriver*

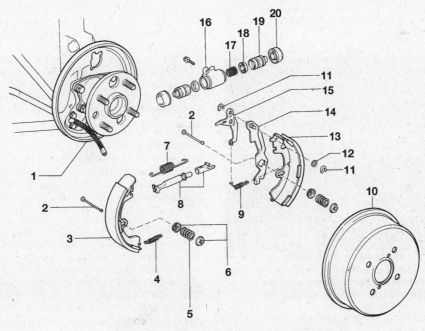

6.4c   An exploded view of the drum brake components

1	Backing plate	8	Adjuster	15	Adjuster lever
2	Hold-down pin	9	Adjuster lever spring	16	Wheel cylinder
3	Front shoe	10	Drum	17	Spring
4	Anchor spring	11	C-Washer	18	Cup
5	Hold-down spring	12	Shim	19	Piston
6	Retainer	13	Rear shoe	20	Boot
7	Return spring	14	Parking brake lever		

9

6.4d   Before removing anything, clean the brake assembly with brake cleaner and allow it to dry - position a drain pan under the brake to catch the fluid and residue - **DO NOT USE COMPRESSED AIR TO BLOW THE DUST FROM THE PARTS!**

6.4e   Unhook the return spring from the front brake shoe. A pair of locking pliers can be used to stretch the spring and pull the end out of the hole in the shoe

6.4f   Depress the hold-down spring and turn the retainer 90-degrees, then release it - a pair of pliers will work, but this special hold-down spring removal tool makes this much easier (they are available at most auto parts stores and aren't very expensive)

6.4g   Remove the front shoe from the backing plate and unhook the anchor spring from the end of the shoe

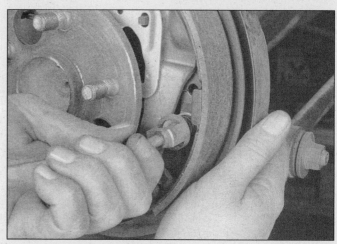

6.4h   Remove the hold-down spring from the rear shoe

6.4i   Remove the rear shoe and adjuster assembly from the backing plate

6.4j   Hold the end of the parking brake cable with a pair of pliers and pull it out of the parking brake lever

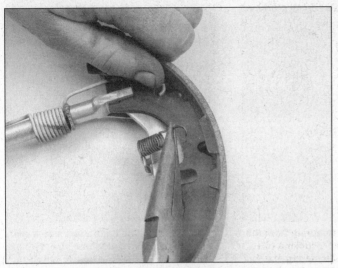

6.4k   Remove the adjusting lever spring

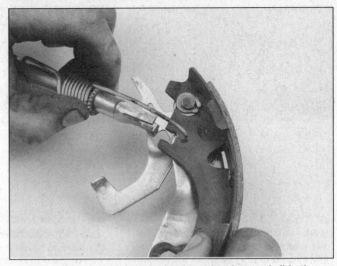

6.4l   Unhook the return spring from the shoe and slide the adjuster and spring off

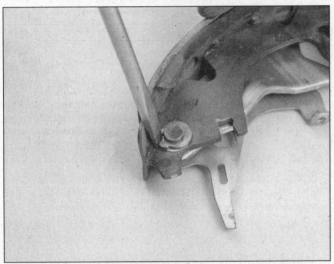

6.4m   Pry the C-washer apart and remove it to separate the parking brake lever and adjuster lever from the rear shoe

6.4n   Assemble the parking brake lever and adjuster lever to the new rear shoe and crimp the C-washer closed with a pair of pliers (always use a new C-washer)

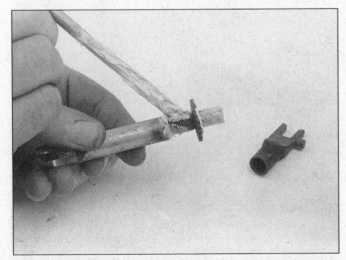

6.4o   Lubricate the moving parts of the adjuster screw with a light coat of high-temperature grease - the screw portion of the adjuster will need to be threaded in further than before to allow the drum to fit over the new shoes

6.4p   Install the adjuster assembly on the rear shoe (make sure the end fits properly into the slot in the shoe and hook the spring into the opening in the shoe)

9

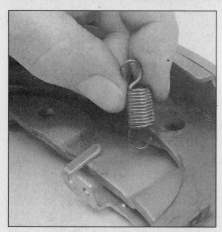

6.4q   Install the adjuster lever spring

6.4r   Lubricate the brake shoe contact area with high-temperature grease

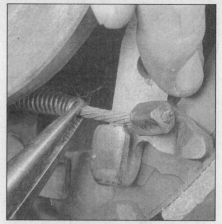

6.4s   Pull the parking brake cable spring back and hold it there with a pair of pliers, then place the cable into the hooked end of the parking brake lever

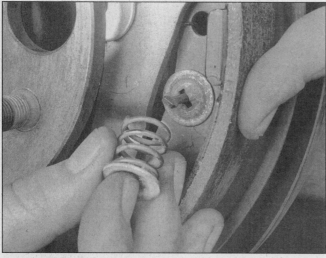

6.4t   Place the rear shoe assembly against the backing plate and push the hold-down spring pin through the shoe. Install the cups (one on each side of the spring) and lock the outer cup to the pin by turning it 90-degrees after the spring has been compressed

6.4u   Connect the anchor spring to the bottom of each shoe and mount the front shoe to the backing plate. Install the hold-down spring and cups

6.4v   Using a screwdriver, stretch the return spring into its hole in the front shoe

6.4w   Pry the parking brake lever forward and check to see that the return spring didn't come unhooked from the rear shoe

6.4x   Wiggle the assembly to make sure it is seated properly
against the backing plate

6.5   The maximum drum diameter is cast into the inside of the
rear drums

faced without exceeding the maximum allowable diameter (stamped into the drum), then new ones will be required **(see illustration)**. At the very least, if you elect not to have the drums resurfaced, remove the glaze from the surface with emery cloth using a swirling motion.

6   Install the brake drum on the axle flange.

7   Mount the wheel, install the lug nuts, then lower the vehicle.

8   Make a number of forward and reverse stops and operate the parking brake to adjust the brakes until satisfactory pedal action is obtained.

9   Check the operation of the brakes carefully before driving the vehicle.

7   Wheel cylinder - removal, overhaul and installation

Note: If an overhaul is indicated (usually because of fluid leaks or sticky operation), explore all options before beginning the job. New wheel cylinders are available, which makes this job quite easy. If it's decided to rebuild the wheel cylinder, make sure a rebuild kit is available before proceeding. Never overhaul only one wheel cylinder - always rebuild both of them at the same time.

Removal
Refer to illustration 7.4

1   Raise the rear of the vehicle and support it securely on jackstands. Block the front wheels to keep the vehicle from rolling.

2   Remove the brake shoe assembly (see Section 6).

3   Remove all dirt and foreign material from around the wheel cylinder.

4   Disconnect the brake line with a flare-nut wrench, if available **(see illustration)**. Don't pull the brake line away from the wheel cylinder.

5   Remove the wheel cylinder mounting bolts.

6   Detach the wheel cylinder from the brake backing plate and place it on a clean workbench. Immediately plug the brake line to prevent fluid loss and contamination.

Overhaul
Refer to illustration 7.7

7   Remove the bleeder screw, cups, pistons, boots and spring assembly from the wheel cylinder body **(see illustration)**.

8   Clean the wheel cylinder with brake fluid, denatured alcohol or brake system cleaner. **Warning:** Do not, under any circumstances, use petroleum-based solvents to clean brake parts!

9   Use compressed air to dry the wheel cylinder and blow out the passages.

10   Check the bore for corrosion and score marks. Crocus cloth can be used to remove light corrosion and stains, but the cylinder must be replaced with a new one if the defects cannot be removed easily, or if

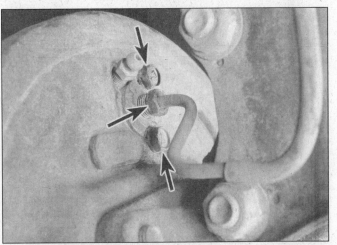

7.4   Disconnect the brake line fitting (arrow), then remove the two wheel cylinder bolts (arrows)

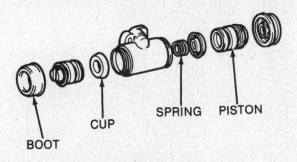

BOOT   CUP   SPRING   PISTON

7.7   An exploded view of the wheel cylinder

while turning the adjuster wheel with another screwdriver, moving the shoes away from the drum **(see illustration 6.4b)**. The drum should now come off.

5   Before reinstalling the drum, it should be checked for cracks, score marks, deep scratches and hard spots, which will appear as small discolored areas. If the hard spots cannot be removed with fine emery cloth or if any of the other conditions listed above exist, the drum must be taken to an automotive machine shop to have it turned. **Note:** Professionals recommend resurfacing the drums each time a brake job is done. Resurfacing will eliminate the possibility of out-of-round drums. If the drums are worn so much that they can't be resur-

9

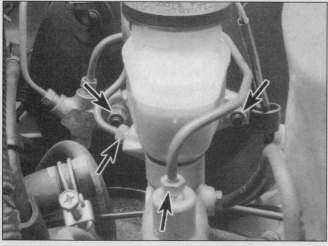

8.4   Completely loosen the brake line fittings (arrows), unplug the electrical connector and remove the mounting nuts (arrows)

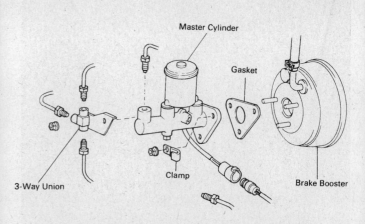

8.6   Typical master cylinder installation details

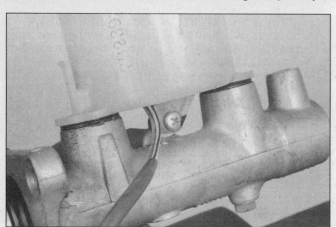

8.8a   The brake fluid reservoir is retained by a set screw

8.8b   After the reservoir has been removed, pull the grommets from the cylinder body. If they are hardened, damaged or appear to have been leaking, replace them

the bore is scored.
11   Lubricate the new cups with brake fluid.
12   Assemble the brake cylinder components **(see illustration 7.7).** Make sure the cup lips face in.

Installation

13   Place the wheel cylinder in position and install the bolts finger tight. Connect the brake line to the cylinder, being careful not to cross-thread the fitting. Tighten the wheel cylinder bolts to the torque listed in this Chapter's Specifications.
14   Tighten the brake line and install the brake shoe assembly.
15   Bleed the brakes (see Section 10).
16   Check the operation of the brakes carefully before driving the vehicle.

---

8   Master cylinder - removal, overhaul and installation

Note: *Before deciding to overhaul the master cylinder, check on the availability and cost of a new or factory rebuilt unit and also the availability of a rebuild kit.*

Removal

Refer to illustrations 8.4 and 8.6

1   The master cylinder is located in the engine compartment, mounted on the power brake booster. If necessary for clearance, remove the following components:
   a) On 1989 and earlier models, remove the suspension upper brace (it bolts to the firewall and the strut tower). Also discon-

nect the connector from the airflow meter and remove the airflow meter with the top of the air cleaner and hose.
   b) On 1990 and later models, remove the air cleaner assembly (see Chapter 5) and the engine wire bracket.
2   Remove as much fluid as possible from the reservoir with a syringe.
3   Place rags under the fittings and prepare caps or plastic bags to cover the ends of the lines once they're disconnected. **Caution:** *Brake fluid will damage paint. Cover all body parts and be careful not to spill fluid during this procedure.*
4   Loosen the fittings at the ends of the brake lines where they enter the master cylinder **(see illustration).** To prevent rounding off the flats, use a flare-nut wrench, which wraps around the fitting hex.
5   Pull the brake lines away from the master cylinder and plug the ends to prevent contamination.
6   Disconnect the electrical connector at the master cylinder, then remove the nuts attaching the master cylinder to the power booster **(see illustration).** Pull the master cylinder off the studs to remove it. Again, be careful not to spill the fluid as this is done.

Overhaul

Refer to illustrations 8.8a, 8.8b, 8.9, 8.10, 8.11a, 8.11b and 8.11c

7   Before attempting the overhaul of the master cylinder, obtain the proper rebuild kit, which will contain the necessary replacement parts and also any instructions which may be specific to your model.
8   Remove the reservoir retaining screw, pull off the reservoir and remove the grommets **(see illustrations).**

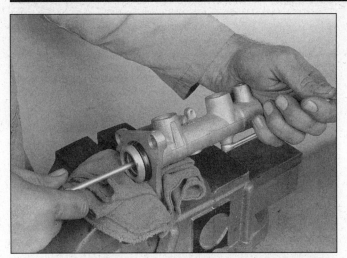

8.9 Using a Phillips screwdriver, depress the pistons, then remove the stopper bolt. Be sure to replace the copper washer (gasket) on the stopper bolt when reassembling

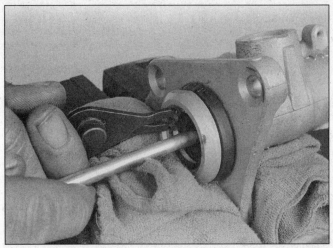

8.10 Depress the pistons again and remove the snap-ring with a pair of snap-ring pliers

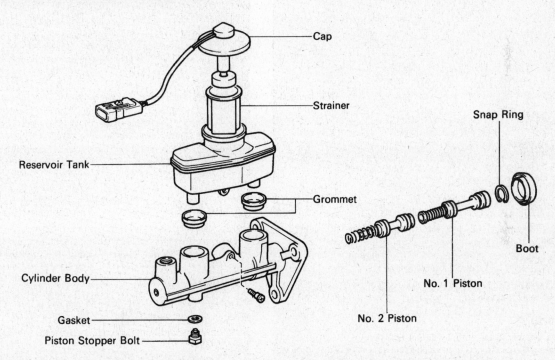

Cap
Strainer
Snap Ring
Reservoir Tank
Grommet
Boot
No. 1 Piston
Cylinder Body
No. 2 Piston
Gasket
Piston Stopper Bolt

8.11a An exploded view of a typical master cylinder - note that the stopper bolt is screwed into the side of some master cylinders

9   Place the cylinder in a vise and use a punch or Phillips screwdriver to depress the pistons until they bottom against the other end of the master cylinder. Hold the pistons in this position and remove the stopper bolt from the master cylinder **(see illustration)**.

10   Carefully remove the snap-ring at the end of the master cylinder **(see illustration)**.

11   The internal components can now be removed from the bore **(see illustrations)**. Make a note of the proper order of the components so they can be returned to their original locations. **Note:** *The two springs are different, so pay particular attention to their installed order.*

12   Carefully inspect the bore of the master cylinder. Any deep score marks or other damage will mean a new master cylinder is required. DO NOT attempt to hone the bore.

13   Replace all parts included in the rebuild kit, following any instructions in the kit. Clean all reused parts with new brake fluid, brake system cleaner or denatured alcohol. **Warning:** *Do not use any petroleum-based solvents. During reassembly, lubricate all parts liberally with* clean brake fluid.

14   Push the assembled components into the bore, bottoming them against the end of the master cylinder, then install the stopper bolt.

15   Install the new snap-ring, making sure it's seated properly in the groove.

16   Install the reservoir grommets, reservoir and screw.

17   Before installing the master cylinder, it should be bench bled. Since you'll have to apply pressure to the master cylinder piston and, at the same time, control flow from the brake line outlets, the master cylinder should be mounted in a vise, with the jaws of the vise clamping on the mounting flange.

18   Insert threaded plugs into the brake line outlet holes and snug them down so no air will leak past them, but not so tight that they can't be easily loosened.

19   Fill the reservoir with brake fluid of the recommended type (see Chapter 1).

20   Remove one plug and push the piston assembly into the bore to

9

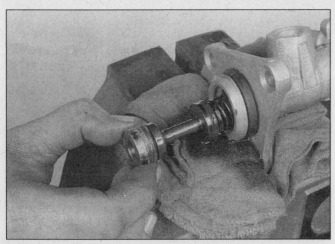

8.11b   After the snap-ring has been removed, the primary (no. 1) piston assembly can be removed

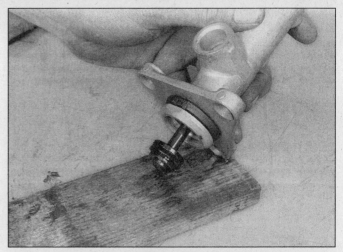

8.11c   Remove the cylinder from the vise and tap it against a block of wood until the secondary (no. 2) piston is exposed. Pull the piston assembly STRAIGHT OUT - if it becomes even slightly cocked, the bore may be damaged

8.27   Have an assistant depress the brake pedal and hold it down, then loosen the fitting nut, allowing the air and fluid to escape. Repeat this procedure on both fittings until the fluid is clear of air bubbles

expel the air from the master cylinder. A large Phillips screwdriver can be used to push on the piston assembly.

21   To prevent air from being drawn back into the master cylinder, the plug must be replaced and snugged down before releasing the pressure on the piston.

22   Repeat the procedure until only brake fluid is expelled from the brake line outlet hole. When only brake fluid is expelled, repeat the procedure at the other outlet hole and plug. Be sure to keep the master cylinder reservoir filled with brake fluid to prevent the introduction of air into the system.

23   Since high pressure isn't involved in the bench bleeding procedure, an alternative to the removal and replacement of the plugs with each stroke of the piston assembly is available. Before pushing in on the piston assembly, remove the plug as described in Step 20. Before releasing the piston, however, instead of replacing the plug, simply put your finger tightly over the hole to keep air from being drawn back into the master cylinder. Wait several seconds for brake fluid to be drawn from the reservoir into the bore, then depress the piston again, removing your finger as brake fluid is expelled. Be sure to put your finger back over the hole each time before releasing the piston, and when the bleeding procedure is complete for that outlet, replace the plug and tighten it before going on to the other port.

Installation

Refer to illustration 8.27

24   Install the master cylinder over the studs on the power brake booster and tighten the nuts only finger-tight at this time.

25   Thread the brake line fittings into the master cylinder. Since the master cylinder is still a bit loose, it can be moved slightly so the fittings thread in easily. Don't strip the threads as the fittings are tightened.

26   Tighten the mounting nuts and the brake line fittings.

27   Fill the master cylinder reservoir with fluid, then bleed the master cylinder (only if hasn't been bench bled) and the brake system (see Section 10). To bleed the master cylinder on the vehicle, have an assistant depress the brake pedal and hold it down. Loosen the fitting to allow air and fluid to escape. Tighten the fitting, then allow your assistant to return the pedal to its rest position. Repeat this procedure on both fittings until the fluid is free of air bubbles **(see illustration)**. Check the operation of the brake system carefully before driving the vehicle.

---

9   Brake hoses and lines - inspection and replacement

Inspection

1   About every six months, with the vehicle raised and supported securely on jackstands, the rubber hoses which connect the steel brake lines with the front and rear brake assemblies should be inspected for cracks, chafing of the outer cover, leaks, blisters and other damage. These are important and vulnerable parts of the brake system and inspection should be complete. A light and mirror will be helpful for a thorough check. If a hose exhibits any of the above conditions, replace it with a new one.

Replacement

Front brake hose

Refer to illustrations 9.3 and 9.4

2   Loosen the wheel lug nuts, raise the vehicle and support it securely on jackstands. Remove the wheel.

3   At the frame bracket, hold the hose fitting with an open-end wrench and unscrew the brake line fitting from the hose **(see illustration)**. Use a flare-nut wrench to prevent rounding off the corners.

4   Remove the U-clip and E-ring, if equipped, from the female fitting at the bracket with a pair of pliers, then pass the hose through the bracket **(see illustration)**.

5   At the caliper end of the hose, remove the banjo fitting bolt, then separate the hose from the caliper. Note that there are two copper sealing washers on either side of the fitting - they should be replaced with new ones during installation.

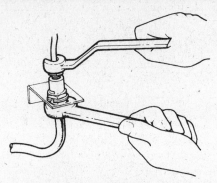

9.3   Hold the hose fitting with a wrench to prevent twisting the line, then loosen the tube nut with a flare-nut wrench to prevent rounding off the corners of the nut

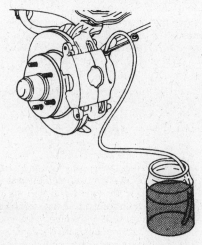

10.8   When bleeding the brakes, a hose is connected to the bleeder valve at the caliper or wheel cylinder and then submerged in brake fluid. Air will be seen as bubbles in the tube and container. All air must be expelled before moving to the next wheel

6   Remove the U-clip from the strut bracket, then feed the hose through the bracket.

7   To install the hose, pass the caliper fitting end through the strut bracket, then connect the fitting to the caliper with the banjo bolt and copper washers. Make sure the locating lug on the fitting is engaged with the hole in the caliper, then tighten the bolt to the torque listed in this Chapter's Specifications.

8   Push the metal support into the strut bracket and install the U-clip. Make sure the hose isn't twisted between the caliper and the strut bracket.

9   Route the hose into the frame bracket, again making sure it isn't twisted, then connect the brake line fitting, starting the threads by hand. Install the clip and E-ring, if equipped, then tighten the fitting securely.

10   Bleed the caliper (see Section 10).

11   Install the wheel and lug nuts, lower the vehicle and tighten the lug nuts to the torque specified in Chapter 1.

Rear brake hose

12   Perform Steps 2, 3 and 4 above, then repeat Steps 3 and 4 at the other end of the hose. Be sure to bleed the wheel cylinder (or caliper) (see Section 10).

Metal brake lines

13   When replacing brake lines, be sure to use the correct parts. Don't use copper tubing for any brake system components. Purchase steel brake lines from a dealer or auto parts store.

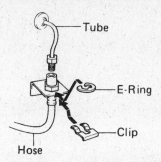

9.4   Once the tube nut has been completely loosened, remove the clip with a pair of pliers - some models may be equipped with an E-ring, as shown here, which can be removed with a screwdriver

14   Prefabricated brake line, with the tube ends already flared and fittings installed, is available at auto parts stores and dealer parts departments. These lines are also bent to the proper shapes.

15   When installing the new line, make sure it's securely supported in the brackets and has plenty of clearance between moving or hot components.

16   After installation, check the master cylinder fluid level and add fluid as necessary. Bleed the brake system (see Section 10) and test the brakes carefully before driving the vehicle in traffic.

10   Brake hydraulic system - bleeding

Refer to illustration 10.8

Warning: *Wear eye protection when bleeding the brake system. If the fluid comes in contact with your eyes, immediately rinse them with water and seek medical attention.*

Note: *Bleeding the hydraulic system is necessary to remove any air that manages to find its way into the system when it's been opened during removal and installation of a hose, line, caliper or master cylinder.*

1   You'll probably have to bleed the system at all four brakes if air has entered it due to low fluid level, or if the brake lines have been disconnected at the master cylinder.

2   If a brake line was disconnected only at a wheel, then only that caliper or wheel cylinder must be bled.

3   If a brake line is disconnected at a fitting located between the master cylinder and any of the brakes, that part of the system served by the disconnected line must be bled.

4   Remove any residual vacuum from the brake power booster by applying the brake several times with the engine off.

5   Remove the master cylinder reservoir cover and fill the reservoir with brake fluid. Reinstall the cover. **Note:** *Check the fluid level often during the bleeding operation and add fluid as necessary to prevent the fluid level from falling low enough to allow air bubbles into the master cylinder.*

6   Have an assistant on hand, as well as a supply of new brake fluid, a clear plastic container partially filled with clean brake fluid, a length of 3/16-inch plastic, rubber or vinyl tubing to fit over the bleeder valve and a wrench to open and close the bleeder valve.

7   Beginning at the right rear wheel, loosen the bleeder valve slightly, then tighten it to a point where it's snug but can still be loosened quickly and easily.

8   Place one end of the tubing over the bleeder valve and submerge the other end in brake fluid in the container **(see illustration).**

9   Have the assistant pump the brakes slowly a few times to get pressure in the system, then hold the pedal down firmly.

10   While the pedal is held down, open the bleeder valve just enough to allow a flow of fluid to leave the valve. Watch for air bubbles to exit the submerged end of the tube. When the fluid flow slows after a couple of seconds, close the valve and have your assistant release the pedal.

11   Repeat Steps 9 and 10 until no more air is seen leaving the tube,

9

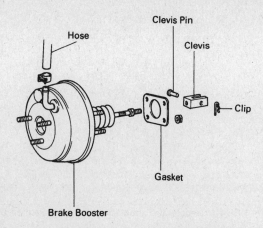

11.7   Power brake booster installation details

then tighten the bleeder valve and proceed to the left front wheel, the left rear wheel and the right front wheel, in that order, and perform the same procedure. Be sure to check the fluid in the master cylinder reservoir frequently.

12   Never use old brake fluid. It contains moisture which will deteriorate the brake system components.

13   Refill the master cylinder with fluid at the end of the operation.

14   Check the operation of the brakes. The pedal should feel solid when depressed, with no sponginess. If necessary, repeat the entire process. **Warning:** *Do not operate the vehicle if you're in doubt about the effectiveness of the brake system.*

---

11   Power brake booster - check, removal and installation

Operating check

1   Depress the brake pedal several times with the engine off and make sure there's no change in the pedal reserve distance.

2   Depress the pedal and start the engine. If the pedal goes down slightly, operation is normal.

Airtightness check

3   Start the engine and turn it off after one or two minutes. Depress the brake pedal slowly several times. If the pedal depresses less each time, the booster is airtight.

4   Depress the brake pedal while the engine is running, then stop the engine with the pedal depressed. If there's no change in the pedal reserve travel after holding the pedal for 30 seconds, the booster is airtight.

Removal

Refer to illustration 11.7

5   Power brake booster units shouldn't be disassembled. They require special tools not normally found in most automotive repair stations or shops. They're fairly complex and, because of their critical relationship to brake performance, should be replaced with a new or rebuilt one.

6   To remove the booster, first remove the brake master cylinder (see Section 8).

7   Remove the left side under-dash panel. Locate the pushrod clevis connecting the booster to the brake pedal **(see illustration)**. It's accessible from inside the vehicle, under the dash on the driver's side.

8   Remove the clevis pin retaining clip with pliers and pull out the pin.

9   Holding the clevis with pliers, unscrew the locknut with a wrench. The clevis is now loose.

10   Disconnect the hose leading from the engine to the booster. Be careful not to damage the hose when removing it from the booster fitting.

11   Remove the four nuts and washers holding the brake booster to

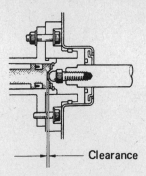

11.14a   There should be no clearance between the booster pushrod and the master cylinder pushrod, but no interference either - if there is interference between the two, the brakes may drag; if there is clearance, there will be excessive brake pedal travel

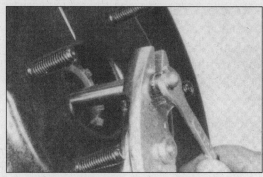

11.14b   To adjust the length of the booster pushrod, hold the serrated portion of the rod with a pair of pliers and turn the adjusting screw in or out, as necessary, to achieve the desired setting

the firewall (you may need a light to see them).

12   Slide the booster straight out from the firewall until the studs clear the holes.

Installation

Refer to illustrations 11.14a and 11.14b

13   Installation procedures are basically the reverse of removal. Tighten the clevis locknut securely and the booster mounting nuts to the torque listed in this Chapter's Specifications.

14   If the power booster unit is being replaced, the clearance between the master cylinder piston and the pushrod in the vacuum booster must be measured and, if necessary, adjusted. Using a depth micrometer or vernier calipers, measure the distance from the seat (recessed area) in the master cylinder to the master cylinder mounting flange. Next, measure the distance from the end of the vacuum booster pushrod to the mounting face of the booster (including gasket) where the master cylinder mounting flange seats. The measurements should be the same **(see illustration)**. If not, turn the adjusting screw on the end of the power booster pushrod until the clearance is within the specified limit **(see illustration)**.

15   After the final installation of the master cylinder and brake hoses and lines, the brake pedal height and freeplay must be adjusted and the system must be bled. See the appropriate Sections of this Chapter for the procedures.

---

12   Parking brake shoes (rear disc brakes only) - inspection and replacement

Refer to illustrations 12.3, 12.4, 12.5, 12.7, 12.8a, 12.8b, 12.10 and 12.15

Warning: *Dust created by the brake system may contain asbestos,*

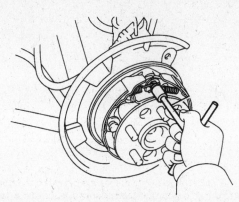

12.3 Unhook the parking brake shoe return springs - a special brake spring tool makes this much easier and is available at most auto parts stores

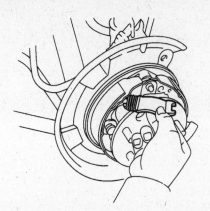

12.4 Remove the shoe strut and spring assembly

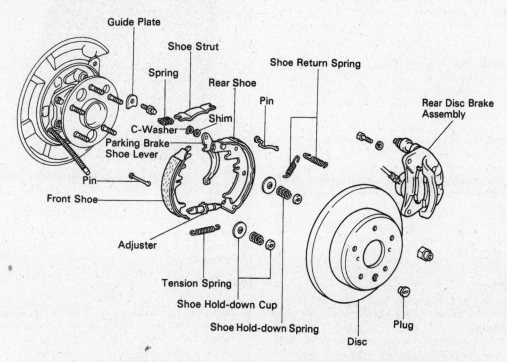

12.5 An exploded view of the parking brake assembly (rear disc brake models only)

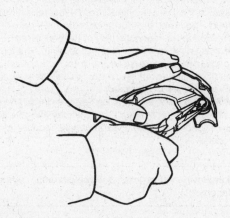

12.7 Use a pair of pliers to crimp the C-washer to the pivot pin

which is hazardous to your health. Never blow it out with compressed air and don't inhale any of it. An approved filtering mask should be worn when working on the brakes. Do not, under any circumstances, use petroleum-based solvents to clean brake parts. Use brake cleaner or denatured alcohol only!

1 Remove the brake disc (see Section 5).
2 Inspect the thickness of the lining material on the shoes. If the lining has worn down to 0.039 inch or less, the shoes must be replaced.
3 Remove the parking brake shoe return springs from the anchor pin **(see illustration)**.
4 Remove the shoe strut from between the shoes **(see illustration)**.
5 Remove the front shoe hold-down spring, then remove the shoe and adjuster **(see illustration)**.
6 Remove the rear shoe hold-down spring, disconnect the parking brake cable from the lever and remove the shoe.
7 Spread the C-washer on the parking brake lever pivot pin with a screwdriver, then remove the lever, shim and pin. Transfer the parts to the new rear shoe and crimp the C-washer to the pin using a pair of pliers **(see illustration)**.

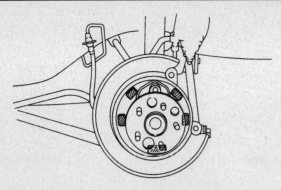

12.8a   Apply a light coat of high-temperature grease to the parking brake shoe contact areas (shaded areas) on the backing plate

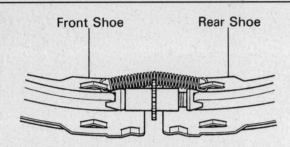

12.10   When assembled, the tension spring and adjuster screw should be arranged as shown

13.3   Loosen the locknut, then turn the adjusting nut until the desired handle travel is obtained

8   Apply a thin coat of high-temperature grease to the shoe contact surfaces of the backing plate and to the threads and sliding portion of the adjuster **(see illustrations)**.

9   Connect the parking brake cable to the lever and mount the rear shoe to the backing plate. Install the hold-down spring.

10   Connect the tension spring to the lower ends of both shoes and install the adjuster **(see illustration)**.

11   Position the front shoe on the plate and install the hold-down spring.

12   Install the parking brake strut, with the spring facing forward, between the two shoes.

13   Install the shoe return springs.

14   Install the brake disc. Temporarily thread three of the wheel lug nuts onto the studs to hold the disc in place.

15   Remove the hole plug from the brake disc. Adjust the parking brake shoe clearance by turning the adjuster star wheel with a brake adjusting tool or screwdriver until the shoes contact the disc and the disc can't be turned **(see illustration)**. Back-off the adjuster eight notches, then install the hole plug.

 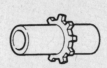

12.8b   Clean the adjuster screw and apply high-temperature grease to the indicated areas (arrows)

12.15   Use a brake adjusting tool or a screwdriver to turn the adjuster star wheel until the disc will not turn, then back off the adjuster eight notches and install the plug (disc removed for clarity)

16   Install the torque plate and brake caliper. Be sure to tighten the bolts to the torque listed in this Chapter's Specifications.

17   Install the wheel and tighten the lug nuts to the torque specified in Chapter 1.

18   Pull up on the parking brake handle and count the number of clicks that it travels. It should be between five and eight clicks - if it's not, adjust the parking brake as described in the next Section.

19   To bed the shoes to the drum, drive the vehicle at approximately 30 mph on a dry, level road. Push in on the parking brake release button and pull up slightly on the lever with about 20 pounds of force. Drive the vehicle for 1/4-mile with the parking brake applied like this.

20   Repeat this procedure two or three times, allowing the brakes to cool between applications.

---

13   Parking brake - adjustment

Refer to illustration 13.3

1   The parking brake lever, when properly adjusted, should travel four to seven clicks when a moderate pulling force is applied. If it travels less than four clicks, there's a chance the parking brake might not be releasing completely and might be dragging on the drum or disc. If the lever can be pulled up more than eight clicks, the parking brake may not hold adequately on an incline, allowing the car to roll.

2   To gain access to the parking brake cable adjuster, remove the center console (see Chapter 11).

3   Loosen the locknut (the upper nut) while holding the adjusting nut (lower nut) with a wrench **(see illustration)**. Tighten the adjusting nut until the desired travel is attained. Tighten the locknut.

4   Install the console.

---

14   Parking brake cables - replacement

Equalizer-to-parking brake cable

Refer to illustrations 14.4, 14.5, 14.6, 14.7 and 14.8

1   Loosen the rear wheel lug nuts, raise the rear of the vehicle and support it securely on jackstands. Block the front wheels. Remove the wheel.

2   Make sure the parking brake is completely released, then remove

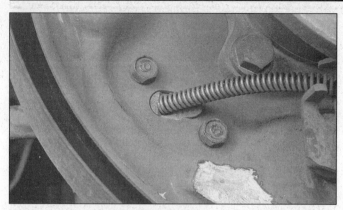

14.4 The parking brake cable casing is bolted to the brake backing plate

14.5 Detach the cable bracket (arrow) from the frame at the forward end of the strut rod

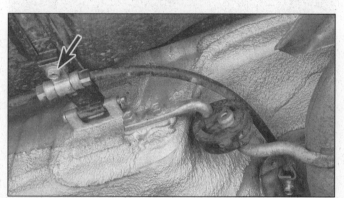

14.6 Detach the cable bracket (arrow) from the forward end of the fuel tank strap

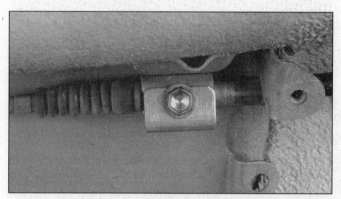

14.7 Loosen this clamp bolt, then slide the cable out of the clamp

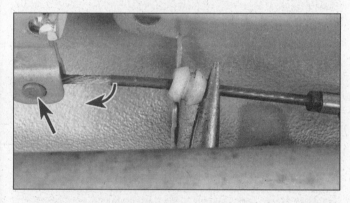

14.8 Pry the cable and grommet out of the guide with a pair of pliers, then rotate the cable end (arrow) clockwise about 90-degrees to align the cable with the slot in the upper half of the lever and detach the cable assembly

14.13 Detach the boot, grasp the cable firmly with a pair of pliers and pull it to the rear, then rotate the cable end 90-degrees

the brake drum (or disc).

3   Remove the brake shoes and disconnect the cable from the parking brake lever (see Section 6 for rear drum brakes or Section 12 for rear disc brakes).

4   Unbolt the cable casing from the backing plate (see illustration).

5   Unbolt the cable bracket from the frame at the forward end of the strut rod (see illustration).

6   Unbolt the cable bracket from the forward end of the fuel tank strap (see illustration).

7   Follow the cable towards the front of the vehicle and locate the cable clamp (see illustration). Loosen the clamp bolt and slide the cable housing out of the clamp.

8   Pry the cable and grommet out of the guide just to the rear of the equalizer (see illustration).

9   Disconnect the cable end from the equalizer by aligning the cable

with the slot in the top of the equalizer. Slide the cable end out of the hole.

10   To install the cable, reverse the removal procedure. Adjust the parking brake as outlined previously (see Section 13).

Equalizer-to-brake lever cable

Refer to illustration 14.13

11   Remove the center console (see Chapter 11).

12   With the lever in the down (off) position, remove the locknut and the adjusting nut (see Section 13) and detach the cable from the lever.

13   Working under the vehicle, pull the cable to the rear, turn it 90-degrees and pass it through the center of the equalizer (see illustration). Pull the cable through the hole in the floorpan.

14   Installation is the reverse of the removal procedure. Apply a light coat of grease to the portion of the cable end that contacts the equalizer. Adjust the parking brake lever as outlined previously (see Section 13).

9

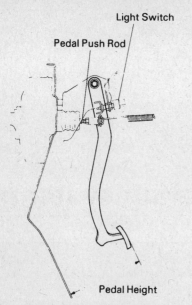
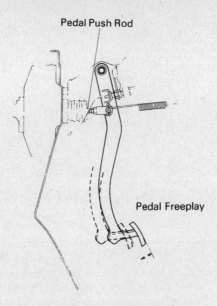
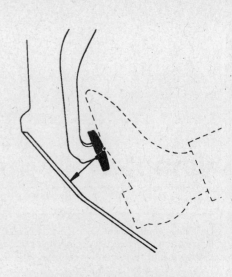

15.6   Measure the distance from the floor to the front of the pedal pad and compare your reading with the Specifications

15.11   The pedal freeplay is the distance the pedal moves before the pushrod contacts the booster air valve

15.13   Measure the pedal reserve distance from the floorboard to the top of the pedal while the pedal is held down

15   Brake pedal - removal, installation and adjustment

Refer to illustrations 15.6, 15.11 and 15.13

Removal and installation

1   Remove the left side under-dash panel.
2   Disconnect the return spring from the outer groove in the pushrod clevis pin.
3   Remove the clip and extract the clevis pin.
4   Unscrew the pivot bolt nut, withdraw the bolt and remove the pedal. Inspect the bushings for wear. Replace them if necessary.
5   Install the brake pedal in the reverse order of removal. Lubricate the pivot with grease.

Adjustment

6   The pedal height is measured from the floor to the top of the pedal. Compare your measurement to the Specifications **(see illustration)**.
7   To adjust the pedal height, block the wheels and release the parking brake lever.
8   Loosen the locknut on the brake light switch and unscrew the switch until it no longer contacts the brake pedal shaft.
9   Depress the pedal a few times to remove any vacuum in the system.
10   Loosen the pushrod locknut and turn the rod in the desired direction to set the pedal.
11   Check the brake pedal freeplay **(see illustration)**. Press on the pedal with your fingers until initial resistance is felt. Compare the measurement to the Specifications.
12   If the freeplay is incorrect, recheck the pedal height and adjust accordingly.
13   Check brake pedal reserve travel **(see illustration)**. Start the engine, depress the brake pedal a few times, then press down hard and hold it.
14   Pedal reserve travel is measured from the floor to the top of the pedal while it's being depressed. Compare the measurement to the Specifications.
15   If the pedal reserve is less than specified, check the adjustment of the rear brake shoes (drum brakes only) and/or the power brake booster pushrod-to-master cylinder piston clearance. If the brake pedal feels spongy, bleed the brake system (see Section 10)
16   Readjust the brake light switch so it's actuated when the pedal is up (not depressed) (see Section 16).

16   Brake light switch - removal, installation and adjustment

Refer to illustration 16.1

Removal and installation

1   The brake light switch is located on a bracket at the top of the brake pedal **(see illustration)**. The switch activates the brake lights at the rear of the vehicle when the pedal is depressed.
2   Disconnect the negative battery cable from the battery. **Caution:** *If the stereo in your vehicle is equipped with an anti-theft system, refer to the information at the front of this manual before detaching the cable.*
3   Disconnect the wiring harness at the brake light switch.
4   Loosen the locknut and unscrew the switch from the pedal bracket.
5   Installation is the reverse of removal.

Adjustment

6   Loosen the locknut, adjust the switch so the threaded portion lightly contacts the pedal stop, then tighten the locknut.
7   Connect the wires at the switch and the battery. Make sure the brake lights are functioning properly.

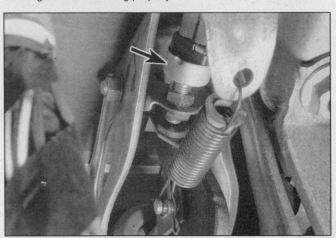

16.1   The brake light switch (arrow) is located on a bracket at the top of the brake pedal arm

Chapter 10 Suspension and steering systems

Contents

Specifications

Torque specifications

Ft-lbs

Front suspension

Strut upper mounting nuts	59
Strut-to-suspension support (damper shaft) nut	34
Strut-to-steering knuckle bolts/nuts	
1986 through 1988	152
1989	188
1990 on	224
Balljoint-to-control arm nuts and bolts	94
Balljoint-to-steering knuckle nut	
1986	93
1987 through 1989	82
1990 and 1991	93
1992 on	76
Control arm U-bracket-to-body bolts	72
Control arm rear nut	
1986 through 1989	76
1990 on	101
Control arm-to-control arm shaft nut	156
Control arm damper plate bolts	101
Control arm shaft-to-body nuts/bolts	
1986 through 1989	154
1990 on	112
Suspension crossmember nuts and bolts	
1986 through 1989	154
1990 on	112

Rear suspension

Strut upper mounting nuts	
1986 and 1987	17
1988 and 1989	23
1990 on	29
Strut-to-suspension support (damper shaft) nut	36

10

Strut-to-axle carrier nuts/bolts
   1986 through 1988 119
   1989 166
   1990 on 188
No.1 rear suspension arm-to-frame nut/bolt
   1986 and 1987 64
   1988 on 83
No.2 rear suspension arm-to-frame nut/bolt
   1986 through 1989 64
   1990 through 1992 and later 83
Rear suspension arm-to-axle carrier nut/bolt
   1986 and 1987 148
   1988 and 1989 134
   1990 on 166
Strut rod bolts/nuts
   1986 and 1987 64
   1988 on 83
Rear hub and bearing assembly-to-axle carrier bolts 59

Steering system
Steering wheel nut 25
Steering gear housing mounting bolts 43
Steering shaft universal joint-to-steering gear 26
Tie-rod end-to-steering knuckle 36
Power steering pump banjo fitting bolt
   1986 through 1988 34
   1989 51
   1990 on 38
Wheel lug nuts .... See Chapter 1

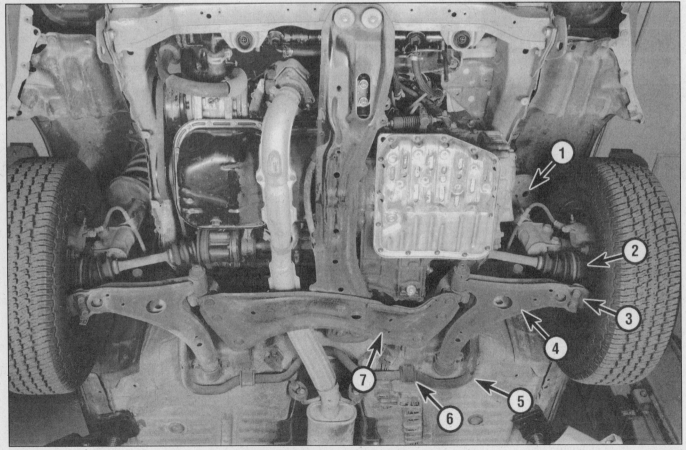

1.1   Underside view of the front suspension components

1   Strut assembly
2   Steering knuckle
3   Balljoint
4   Control arm
5   Stabilizer bar
6   Stabilizer bar bracket
7   Suspension crossmember

1.2   Underside view of the rear suspension (1986 through 1989 model shown, later models similar)

1	Toe adjusting cam	4	Stabilizer bar bracket	7	Strut assembly
2	No. 2 suspension arm	5	Stabilizer bar	8	Rear axle carrier
3	No. 1 suspension arm	6	Stabilizer bar link	9	Strut rod

1   General information

Refer to illustrations 1.1 and 1.2

The front suspension is a Macpherson strut design. The upper end of each strut is attached to the vehicle's body strut support. The lower end of the strut is connected to the upper end of the steering knuckle. The steering knuckle is attached to a balljoint mounted on the outer end of the suspension control arm **(see illustration)**.

The rear suspension also utilizes strut/coil spring assemblies. The upper end of each strut is attached to the vehicle body by a strut support. The lower end of the strut is attached to an axle carrier. The carrier is located by a pair of suspension arms on each side, and a longitudinally mounted strut rod between the body and each knuckle **(see illustration)**.

The rack-and-pinion steering gear is located behind the engine/transaxle assembly on the firewall and actuates the tie-rods, which are attached to the steering knuckles. The steering column is designed to collapse in the event of an accident.

Frequently, when working on the suspension or steering system components, you may come across fasteners which seem impossible to loosen. These fasteners on the underside of the vehicle are continually subjected to water, road grime, mud, etc., and can become rusted or "frozen," making them extremely difficult to remove. In order to unscrew these stubborn fasteners without damaging them (or other components), be sure to use lots of penetrating oil and allow it to soak in for a while. Using a wire brush to clean exposed threads will also ease removal of the nut or bolt and prevent damage to the threads. Sometimes a sharp blow with a hammer and punch will break the bond between a nut and bolt threads, but care must be taken to prevent the punch from slipping off the fastener and ruining the threads. Heating the stuck fastener and surrounding area with a torch sometimes helps too, but isn't recommended because of the obvious dangers associated with fire. Long breaker bars and extension, or "cheater," pipes will increase leverage, but never use an extension pipe on a ratchet - the ratcheting mechanism could be damaged. Sometimes tightening the nut or bolt first will help to break it loose. Fasteners that require drastic measures to remove should always be replaced with new ones.

Since most of the procedures dealt with in this Chapter involve jacking up the vehicle and working underneath it, a good pair of jack-stands will be needed. A hydraulic floor jack is the preferred type of jack to lift the vehicle, and it can also be used to support certain components during various operations. **Warning:** *Never, under any circumstances, rely on a jack to support the vehicle while working on it. Whenever any of the suspension or steering fasteners are loosened or removed they must be inspected and, if necessary, replaced with new ones of the same part number or of original equipment quality and design. Torque specifications must be followed for proper reassembly and component retention. Never attempt to heat or straighten any suspension or steering components. Instead, replace any bent or damaged part with a new one.*

2   Front stabilizer bar and bushings - removal and installation

Refer to illustrations 2.2 and 2.3

Removal

1   Raise the front of the vehicle and support it securely on jackstands. Apply the parking brake and block the rear wheels to keep the vehicle from rolling off the stands.

2   Detach the stabilizer bar links from the control arms **(see illustration)**. **Note:** *If the ballstud turns with the nut, use a 5 mm hex wrench to hold the stud.*

2.2   Unbolt the stabilizer bar links from the control arms

10

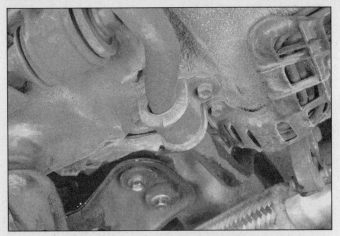

2.3   Remove the bolts and detach the stabilizer bar brackets

3.2   Mark the relationship of the camber adjusting cam to the strut and the steering knuckle (1989 and earlier models only)

3   Detach both stabilizer bar brackets from the vehicle floor pan **(see illustration)**.

4   Disconnect the exhaust pipe from the exhaust manifold (see Chapter 4).

5   Remove the stabilizer bar.

6   While the stabilizer bar is off the vehicle, slide the bracket bushings off and inspect them. If they're cracked, worn or deteriorated, replace them.

7   Clean the bushing area of the stabilizer bar with a stiff wire brush to remove any rust or dirt.

Installation

8   Lubricate the inside and outside of the new bushing with vegetable oil (used in cooking) to simplify reassembly. **Caution:** *Don't use petroleum or mineral-based lubricants or brake fluid - they will lead to deterioration of the bushings.*

9   Installation is the reverse of removal.

---

3   Strut assembly (front) - removal, inspection and installation

---

Refer to illustrations 3.2, 3.4, 3.5a, 3.5b, and 3.6

Removal

1   Loosen the wheel lug nuts, raise the vehicle and support it securely on jackstands. Remove the wheel.

2   If you're working on a 1989 or earlier model, mark the relationship

of the strut to the camber adjuster and steering knuckle and also around the strut-to-steering knuckle nuts **(see illustration)**.

3   Unbolt the brake hose from the caliper (see Chapter 9). Have some rags and a container handy to catch the brake fluid. Unclip the hose from the strut bracket and push it through **(see illustration)**. If the vehicle is equipped with ABS, detach the speed sensor wiring harness from the strut by removing the clamp bracket bolt.

4   Remove the strut-to-knuckle nuts and knock the bolts out with a hammer and punch **(see illustration)**.

5   Separate the strut from the steering knuckle **(see illustrations)**. Be careful not to overextend the inner CV joint.

6   Support the strut and spring assembly with one hand and remove the three strut-to-shock tower nuts **(see illustration)**. Remove the assembly out from the fenderwell.

Inspection

7   Check the strut body for leaking fluid, dents, cracks and other obvious damage which would warrant repair or replacement.

8   Check the coil spring for chips or cracks in the spring coating (this will cause premature spring failure due to corrosion). Inspect the spring seat for cuts, hardness and general deterioration.

9   If any undesirable conditions exist, proceed to the strut disassembly procedure (see Section 4).

Installation

10   Guide the strut assembly up into the fenderwell and insert the three upper mounting studs through the holes in the shock tower.

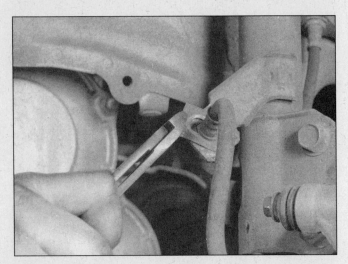

3.3   Remove the brake hose-to-strut bracket clip with a pair of pliers

3.4   Remove the nuts from the steering knuckle-to-strut bolts and drive the bolts out with a hammer and punch

3.5a   Pull the steering knuckle out of the strut bracket - be careful not to pull it out too far or the driveaxle inner CV joint will be over-extended

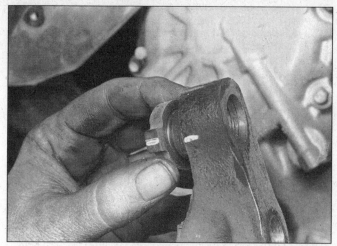

3.5b   The camber adjuster slides into the upper hole in the steering knuckle - don't forget to install it (1989 and earlier models only)

Once the three studs protrude from the shock tower, install the nuts so the strut won't fall back through. This is most easily accomplished with the help of an assistant, as the strut is quite heavy and awkward.

11   Insert the camber adjuster into the upper hole in the steering knuckle, if it fell out (1989 and earlier models only). Slide the steering knuckle into the strut flange and insert the two bolts. Install the nuts, align the previously applied marks (1989 and earlier models only) and tighten them to the torque listed in this Chapter's Specifications.

12   Guide the brake hose through its bracket in the strut, reconnect it to the brake caliper and bleed the brakes (see Chapter 9). Tighten the banjo bolt to the torque listed in the Chapter 9 Specifications Section. If the vehicle is equipped with ABS, install the speed sensor wiring harness bracket.

13   Install the wheel and lug nuts, then lower the vehicle and tighten the lug nuts to the torque listed in the Chapter 1 Specifications.

14   Tighten the three upper mounting nuts to the torque listed in this Chapter's Specifications.

16   Drive the vehicle to an alignment shop to have the front end alignment checked, and if necessary, adjusted.

---

4   Strut/spring assembly - replacement

Refer to illustrations 4.3, 4.4, 4.5, 4.6, 4.7, 4.12, 4.13a and 4.13b

1   If the struts or coil springs exhibit the telltale signs of wear (leaking fluid, loss of damping capability, chipped, sagging or cracked coil springs) explore all options before beginning any work. The strut/shock absorber assemblies are not serviceable and must be replaced if a problem develops. However, strut assemblies complete with springs may be available on an exchange basis, which eliminates much time and work. Whichever route you choose to take, check on the cost and availability of parts before disassembling your vehicle. **Warning:** *Disassembling a strut assembly is a potentially dangerous undertaking and utmost attention must be directed to the job at hand, or serious bodily injury may result. Use only a high quality spring compressor and carefully follow the manufacturer's instructions furnished with the tool. After removing the coil spring from the strut assembly, set it aside in a safe, isolated area (a steel cabinet is preferred).*

Disassembly

2   Remove the strut and spring assembly following the procedure described in the previous Section. Mount the strut assembly in a vise. Line the vise jaws with wood or rags to prevent damage to the unit and don't tighten the vise excessively.

3   Following the tool manufacturer's instructions, install the spring compressor (which can be obtained at most auto parts stores or equipment yards on a daily rental basis) on the spring and compress it sufficiently to relieve all pressure from the upper spring seat **(see illustration)**. This can be verified by wiggling the spring.

3.6   The upper end of the strut assembly is fastened to the shock tower with three nuts

4.3   Install the spring compressor according to the tool manufacturer's instructions and compress the spring until all pressure is relieved from the upper spring seat

10

4.4   Remove the damper shaft nut

4.5   Lift the suspension support off the damper shaft

4.6   Remove the spring seat from the damper shaft

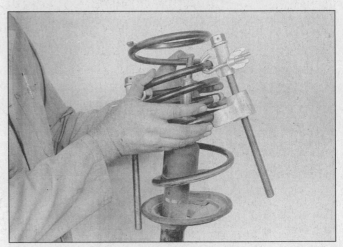

4.7   Remove the compressed spring assembly - keep the ends of the spring pointed away from your body

4   Loosen the damper shaft nut with a socket wrench **(see illustration)**.

5   Remove the nut and suspension support **(see illustration)**. Inspect the bearing in the suspension support for smooth operation. If it doesn't turn smoothly, replace the suspension support. Check the rubber portion of the suspension support for cracking and general deterioration. If there is any separation of the rubber, replace it.

6   Lift the spring seat and upper insulator from the damper shaft **(see illustration)**. Check the rubber spring seat for cracking and hardness, replacing it if necessary.

7   Carefully lift the compressed spring from the assembly **(see illustration)** and set it in a safe place, such as a steel cabinet. **Warning:** *Never place your head near the end of the spring!*

8   Slide the rubber bumper off the damper shaft.

9   Check the lower insulator for wear, cracking and hardness and replace it if necessary.

Reassembly

10   If the lower insulator is being replaced, set it into position with the dropped portion seated in the lowest part of the seat. Extend the damper rod to its full length and install the rubber bumper.

11   Carefully place the coil spring onto the lower insulator, with the end of the spring resting in the lowest part of the insulator **(see illustration)**.

12   Install the upper insulator and spring seat, making sure that the

4.11   When installing the spring, make sure the end fits into the recessed portion of the lower seat (arrow)

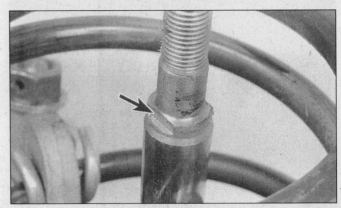

4.12a   The flats on the damper shaft (arrow) must match up with the flats in the spring seat

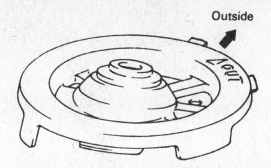

4.12b   The OUT mark on the spring seat must face the strut bracket opening

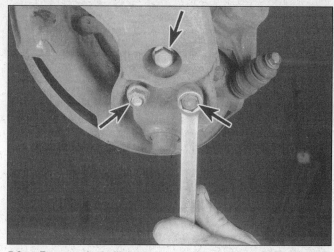

5.2a   Remove the balljoint-to-control arm bolts and nuts (arrows)

5.2b   Use a prybar to separate the balljoint from the control arm

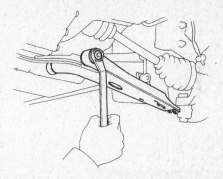

5.4   Remove the nut and washer from the control arm shaft

flats in the hole in the seat match up with the flats on the damper shaft **(see illustrations)**. Also make sure that the "OUT" marking on the spring seat faces toward the lower bracket, where the steering knuckle fits **(see illustration)**.

13   Install the dust seal and suspension support to the damper shaft.

14   Install the nut and tighten it to the torque listed in this Chapter's Specifications.

15   Install the strut/shock absorber and coil spring assembly following the procedure outlined previously (see Section 3).

5   Control arm - removal, inspection and installation

Refer to illustrations 5.2a, 5.2b, 5.4, 5.5, 5.6, 5.7, 5.9 and 5.10

Removal

1   Loosen the wheel lug nuts on the side to be dismantled, raise the front of the vehicle, support it securely on jackstands and remove the wheel.

2   Remove the bolt and two nuts holding the control arm to the steering knuckle. Use a prybar to disconnect the control arm from the steering knuckle **(see illustrations)**. If you're removing the left side control arm on a vehicle equipped with an automatic transmission, remove the suspension crossmember **(see illustration 1.1)**.

3   Remove the nut from the stabilizer bar link and disconnect the link from the control arm **(see illustration 2.2)**.

4   Remove the nut and washer from the control arm shaft (if you're removing the left control arm on a vehicle equipped with an automatic transmission, ignore this step and proceed to the next step) **(see illustration)**.

5   If you're working on a 1990 or later model, unscrew the two bolts and remove the control arm damper plate **(see illustration)**.

6   Remove the two bolts at the rear of the control arm bracket **(see illustration)**.

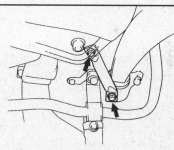

5.5   Remove the damper plate bolts (arrows) and detach the damper plate from the vehicle (1990 and later models only)

5.6   Remove the bracket bolts at the control arm rear pivot

10

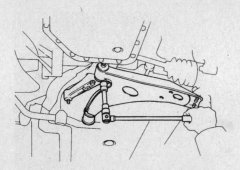
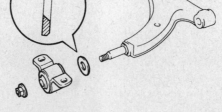
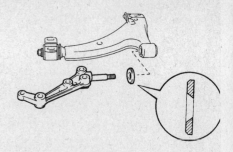

5.7   If you're removing the left control arm on a vehicle equipped with an automatic transmission, the control arm shaft must be removed with the control arm

5.9   Install the new washer on the trailing end of the lower arm with the beveled side facing the front of the vehicle

5.10   Install the forward washer on the shaft, with the beveled side facing the rear of the vehicle

7   The control arm can now be removed, unless you're removing the left control arm on a vehicle equipped with an automatic transmission, in which case the control arm shaft must first be unbolted **(see illustration)**.

Inspection

8   Check the control arm for distortion and the bushings for wear, replacing parts as necessary. Do not attempt to straighten a bent control arm.

Installation

9   Install the new washer at the rear bracket with the beveled side towards the front of the vehicle **(see illustration)**.
10   Install the new washer on the control arm shaft with the beveled side towards the rear of the vehicle **(see illustration)**.
11   The remainder of installation is the reverse of removal. Tighten all of the fasteners to the torque values listed in this Chapter's Specifications.
12   Install the wheel and lug nuts, lower the vehicle and tighten the lug nuts to the torque listed in the Chapter 1 Specifications.
13   It's a good idea to have the front wheel alignment checked, and if necessary, adjusted after this job has been performed.

6   Balljoints - replacement

1   Loosen the wheel lug nuts, raise the vehicle and support it securely on jackstands. Remove the wheel.
2   Remove the cotter pin (if equipped) from the balljoint stud and loosen the nut (but don't remove it yet).
3   Separate the balljoint from the steering knuckle with a picklefork-type balljoint separator. Lubricate the rubber boot with grease and work carefully, so as not to tear the boot. Remove the balljoint stud nut.
4   Remove the bolt and nuts securing the balljoint to the control arm. Separate the balljoint from the control arm with a prybar **(see illustration 5.2b)**.
5   To install the balljoint, position it on the steering knuckle and install the nut, but don't tighten it yet.
6   Attach the balljoint to the control arm and install the bolt and nuts, tightening them to the torque listed in this Chapter's Specifications.
7   Tighten the balljoint stud nut to the torque listed in this Chapter's Specifications and install a new cotter pin. If the cotter pin hole doesn't line up with the slots on the nut, tighten the nut additionally until it does line up - don't loosen the nut to insert the cotter pin.
8   Install the wheel and lug nuts. Lower the vehicle and tighten the lug nuts to the torque listed in the Chapter 1 Specifications.

7   Steering knuckle and hub - removal and installation

Warning: *Dust created by the brake system may contain asbestos, which is harmful to your health. Never blow it out with compressed air and don't inhale any of it. Do not, under any circumstances, use petroleum-based solvents to clean brake parts. Use brake cleaner or denatured alcohol only.*

Removal

1   Loosen the wheel lug nuts, raise the vehicle and support it securely on jackstands. Remove the wheel.
2   Remove the brake caliper and support it with a piece of wire as described in Chapter 9. Remove the caliper mount, separate the brake disc from the hub, then loosen the hub nut (see Chapter 8).
3   If you're working on a 1989 or earlier model, mark the relationship of the strut to the steering knuckle and the camber adjuster **(see illustration 3.2)**. This will simplify reassembly.
4   Loosen, but do not remove the strut-to-steering knuckle bolts **(see illustration 3.4)**.
5   Separate the tie-rod from the steering knuckle arm (see Section 18).
6   Remove the balljoint-to-lower arm bolt and nuts **(see illustration 5.2a and 5.2b)**. The strut-to-knuckle bolts can now be removed.
7   Push the driveaxle from the hub as described in Chapter 8. Support the end of the driveaxle with a piece of wire.
8   Carefully separate the steering knuckle from the strut and lower arm.

Installation

9   Guide the knuckle and hub assembly into position, inserting the driveaxle into the hub.
10   If you're working on a 1989 or earlier model, install the camber adjuster into the knuckle (if removed).
11   Push the knuckle into the strut flange and install the bolts and nuts, but don't tighten them yet.
12   Connect the balljoint to the control arm and install the bolt and nuts (don't tighten them yet).
13   Attach the tie-rod to the steering knuckle arm (see Section 18). Tighten the strut bolt nuts, the balljoint-to-control arm bolt and nuts and the tie-rod nut to the torque values listed in this Chapter's Specifications.
14   Place the brake disc on the hub and install the caliper as outlined in Chapter 9.
15   Install the hub nut and tighten it to the torque listed in the Chapter 8 Specifications.
16   Install the wheel and lug nuts.
17   Lower the vehicle and tighten the lug nuts to the torque listed in the Chapter 1 Specifications.

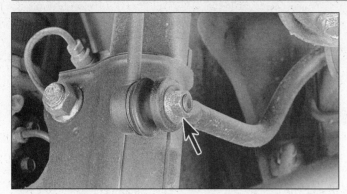

9.2   Remove the nuts from the lower end of the stabilizer bar links

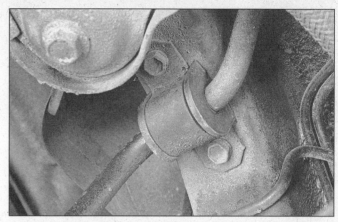

9.3   Each stabilizer bar bracket is retained by two bolts

8   Front hub and bearing assembly - removal and installation

Due to the special tools and expertise required to press the hub and bearing from the steering knuckle, this job should be left to a professional mechanic. However, the steering knuckle and hub may be removed and the assembly taken to a dealer service department or other repair shop. See Section 7 for the steering knuckle and hub removal procedure.

9   Rear stabilizer bar and bushings - removal and installation

Refer to illustrations 9.2 and 9.3

1   Raise the vehicle and support it securely on jackstands.
2   Remove the stabilizer bar link-to-stabilizer bar nuts **(see illustration)**.
3   Unbolt the stabilizer bar brackets from the body **(see illustration)**.
4   Using a floor jack and a block of wood, support the fuel tank and remove the two fuel tank band bolts (see Chapter 4). Allow the bands to hang down and lower the fuel tank about 1-1/2 to 2 inches.
5   The stabilizer bar can now be removed from the vehicle. Pull the U-brackets off the stabilizer bar (if they haven't fallen off already) using

a rocking motion.
6   Check the bushings for wear, hardness, distortion, cracking and other signs of deterioration, replacing them if necessary. Also check the link bushings for these signs.
7   Using a wire brush, clean the areas of the bar where the bushings ride. Installation is the reverse of the removal procedure. If necessary, use a light coat of vegetable oil to ease bushing and U-bracket installation (don't use petroleum based products or brake fluid, as these will damage the rubber).

10   Strut assembly (rear) - removal, inspection and installation

Removal

Refer to illustrations 10.3a, 10.3b, 10.4, 10.6 and 10.7

1   Loosen the wheel lug nuts, raise the vehicle and support it securely on jackstands. Remove the wheel.
2   Unscrew the brake line from the wheel cylinder (or caliper). Use a flare nut wrench to avoid rounding off the corners of the nut.
3   Disconnect the brake line from the flexible hose at the strut bracket **(see illustrations)**. Again, the use of a flare nut wrench is rec-

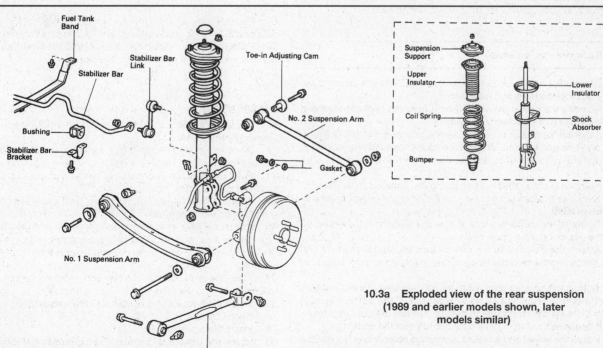

10.3a   Exploded view of the rear suspension (1989 and earlier models shown, later models similar)

10

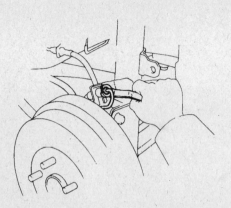

10.3b   Use a flare nut wrench when disconnecting the brake line from the brake hose at the strut bracket

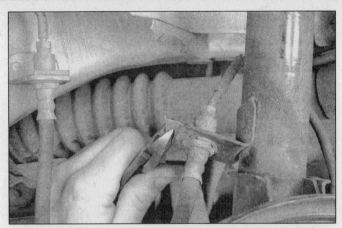

10.4   Use a pair of pliers to remove the retaining clip from the brake hose bracket on the strut, then pull the hose through the bracket

10.6   Remove the strut-to-axle carrier bolts and nuts

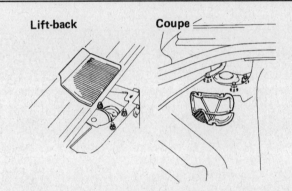

10.7   The speaker grille (liftback models) or access cover (coupe models) must be removed to get at the strut upper mounting nuts

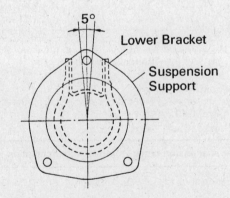

10.10   The bolt hole in the suspension support that is farthest away from the other two must be aligned with the opening in the strut bracket

ommended. Plug the hose end or wrap a plastic bag tightly around the end of the hose to prevent excessive leakage and contamination.

4   Remove the brake hose clip from the strut bracket with a pair of pliers **(see illustration)**, then pull the hose through the bracket. If the vehicle is equipped with ABS, detach the speed sensor wiring harness from the strut.

5   Disconnect the stabilizer bar link from the strut bracket.

6   Support the axle carrier with a floor jack, then remove the two strut-to-axle carrier nuts and bolts **(see illustration)**.

7   On 1989 and earlier models, remove the speaker grille (liftback models) or the access panel in the trunk (coupe models) **(see illustration)**. On 1990 and later models, remove the speaker grille (liftback models) or the panel between the rear seat back and the rear window.

8   Unscrew the three strut upper mounting nuts while an assistant supports the strut so it doesn't fall. Guide the strut out of the fender-well.

Inspection

Refer to illustration 10.10

9   Follow the inspection procedures described in Section 3. If it is determined that the strut assembly must be disassembled for replacement of the strut or the coil spring, refer to Section 4.

10   When reassembling the strut, make sure the suspension support is aligned with the lower bracket (where the axle carrier fits) **(see illustration)**.

Installation

11   Maneuver the assembly up into the fenderwell and insert the mounting studs through the holes in the body. Install the nuts, but don't tighten them yet.

12   Push the axle carrier into the strut lower bracket and install the bolts and nuts, tightening them to the torque listed in this Chapter's Specifications.

13   Connect the stabilizer bar link to the strut bracket.

14   Route the brake hose through its bracket on the strut and connect the brake line, tightening it securely. Connect the other end of the line to the wheel cylinder (or caliper).

15   Install the wheel and lug nuts, lower the vehicle and tighten the lug nuts to the torque listed in the Chapter 1 Specifications.

16   Tighten the three strut upper mounting nuts to the torque listed in

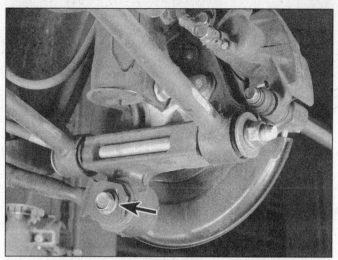

11.2 Remove the strut-to-axle carrier bolt (arrow)

11.3a Remove the nut from the suspension arm-to-rear axle carrier bolt . . .

11.3b . . . then drive the bolt through the axle carrier with a hammer and punch

11.4 Mark the relationship of the toe adjusting cam to the inner mounting bracket of the number two rear suspension arm

this Chapter's Specifications.
17   Bleed the wheel cylinder (or caliper) following the procedure described in Chapter 9.

11   Rear suspension arms - removal and installation

Refer to illustrations 11.2, 11.3a, 11.3b, 11.4, 11.5, 11.6, 11.8a and 11.8b

Removal

1   Raise the rear of the vehicle and support it securely on jackstands. Block the front wheels.
2   Disconnect the strut rod from the axle carrier **(see illustration)**.
3   Remove the suspension arm-to-axle carrier bolt and nut **(see illustrations)**.
4   If one of the number two suspension arms is being removed **(see illustration 1.2)**, mark the relationship of the toe adjuster cam to the suspension arm inner mounting bracket **(see illustration)**. This will ensure the toe adjustment will be returned to the same setting.
5   Using a screwdriver, pry the plastic cover from its hole in the subframe to gain access to the suspension arm inner mounting nuts **(see illustration)**.

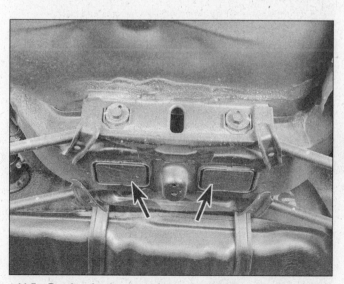

11.5 Pry the plastic covers (arrows) out with a screwdriver . . .

10

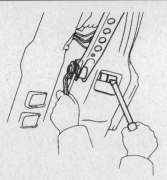

11.6 . . .   then unscrew the inner mounting bolt and nut

6   Remove the inner mounting bolt and nut while supporting the suspension arm **(see illustration)**.
7   Remove the suspension arm from the vehicle.

Installation

8   Position the suspension arm with the slits in the bushings facing the rear. The stamped arms are marked L or R. The tubular arms have a small spot of paint that must be on the wheel end of the arm when installed **(see illustrations)**. Install the inner mounting bolt finger tight.
9   Insert the suspension arm-to-axle carrier bolt through the arms and carrier from the front. Install the nut and washer and tighten the nut hand tight.
10   Connect the strut rod to the axle carrier, tightening the nut hand tight only.
11   Place a jack under the axle carrier and raise it to simulate normal ride height.
12   If you're installing a number two suspension arm, align the previously applied matchmarks on the toe adjuster cam and the inner mounting bracket. Tighten the inner mounting bolt and nut to the torque listed in this Chapter's Specifications. Be sure to align the marks on the toe adjuster and body.
13   Tighten the suspension arm-to-axle carrier bolt/nut to the torque listed in this Chapter's Specifications.
14   Tighten the strut rod bolt to the torque listed in this Chapter's Specifications.
15   Install the wheel and lug nuts, then lower the vehicle to the ground. Tighten the lug nuts to the torque listed in the Chapter 1 Specifications.
16   Have the rear wheel alignment checked by a dealer service department or an alignment shop.

12   Strut rod - removal and installation

Refer to illustration 12.3
1   Loosen the wheel lug nuts, raise the vehicle and support it securely on jackstands. Remove the wheel.
2   Remove the strut rod-to-axle carrier bolt **(see illustration 11.2)**. It isn't necessary to hold the nut with a wrench, because the nut has a tang attached to it to prevent rotation.
3   Remove the strut rod-to-body bracket bolt **(see illustration)** and detach the rod from the vehicle.
4   Installation is the reverse of the removal procedure. Be sure to tighten the bolts to the torque listed in this Chapter's Specifications.

13   Rear hub and bearing assembly - removal and installation

Refer to illustrations 13.3 and 13.5
Warning: *Dust created by the brake system may contain asbestos, which is harmful to your health. Never blow it out with compressed air and don't inhale any of it. Do not, under any circumstances, use petroleum-based solvents to clean brake parts. Use brake cleaner or*

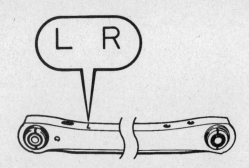

11.8a   The stamped arms are marked as to which side of the vehicle they are installed on - the slits in the bushings also face toward the rear (1989 and earlier models)

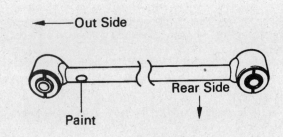

11.8b   The tubular arms have a dot of paint that must be situated on the outer end of the arm - the slits in the bushings also face toward the rear

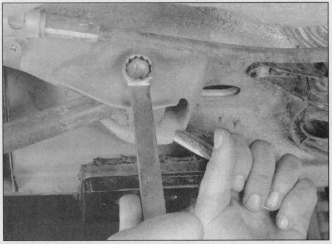

12.3   Remove the strut rod-to-frame bolt and nut

denatured alcohol only.
Note: *Due to the special tools required to replace the bearing, the hub and bearing assembly should not be disassembled by the home mechanic. The assembly can be removed, however, and taken to a dealer service department or other repair shop to have the bearing replaced.*

Removal

1   Loosen the wheel lug nuts, raise the vehicle and support it securely on jackstands. Remove the wheel.
2   Pull the brake drum (or disc) from the hub. If difficulty is encountered, refer to Chapter 9 for the removal procedure.

13.3 The rear hub and bearing assembly is held to the axle carrier with four bolts - turn the hub flange so the hole lines up with each bolt, then remove the bolt with a socket and extension

13.5 Be sure to replace this O-ring on the hub seat

3   Remove the four hub-to-axle carrier bolts, accessible by turning the hub flange so that the large circular cutout exposes each bolt **(see illustration)**.

4   Remove the hub and bearing assembly from its seat, maneuvering it out through the brake assembly.

Installation

5   Remove the old O-ring from the hub seat and install a new one **(see illustration)**.

6   Position the hub and bearing assembly on the axle carrier and align the holes in the backing plate. Install the bolts. A magnet is useful in guiding the bolts through the hub flange and into position. After all four bolts have been installed, tighten them to the torque listed in this Chapter's Specifications.

7   Install the brake drum (or disc) and wheel. Lower the vehicle and tighten the lug nuts to the torque listed in the Chapter 1 Specifications.

---

14 Rear axle carrier - removal and installation

Refer to illustration 14.4

Warning: Dust created by the brake system may contain asbestos, which is harmful to your health. Never blow it out with compressed air and don't inhale any of it. Do not, under any circumstances, use petroleum-based solvents to clean brake parts. Use brake cleaner or denatured alcohol only.

Removal

1   Loosen the wheel lug nuts, raise the vehicle and support it on jackstands. Block the front wheels and remove the rear wheel.

2   Remove the rear brake drum (or disc) (refer to Chapter 9).

3   Disconnect the brake line from the wheel cylinder (or caliper), using a flare nut wrench to prevent rounding off the tube nut corners.

4   Remove the rear hub and bearing assembly following the procedure described in Section 13. Detach the backing plate and rear brake assembly from the axle carrier and suspend it with a piece of wire from the spring (drum brake models only). It isn't necessary to remove the parking brake cable from the backing plate **(see illustration)**.

5   Loosen, but don't remove the strut-to-axle carrier bolts **(see illustration 10.6)**.

6   Remove the suspension arm-to-axle carrier bolt, nut and washers **(see illustrations 11.3b and 11.3b)**.

7   Remove the rear strut-rod bolt **(see illustration 11.2)**.

8   Remove the previously loosened strut-to-axle carrier bolts while supporting the carrier so it doesn't fall.

9   Detach the axle carrier from the strut bracket.

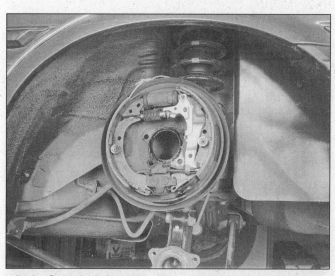

14.4 Once the hub and bearing assembly has been removed, slide the brake backing plate (with the brake shoes still attached) off the axle carrier and hang it from the coil spring with a piece of wire (vehicles with rear drum brakes only)

Installation

10   Inspect the carrier bushing for cracks, deformation and signs of wear. If it is worn out, take the carrier to a dealer service department or other repair shop to have the old one pressed out and a new one pressed in.

11   Push the axle carrier into the strut bracket, aligning the two bolt holes. Insert the two strut-to-carrier bolts and tighten them finger tight.

12   Install the suspension arm-to-axle carrier bolt (from the front), washers and nut. Tighten the nut by hand.

13   Place a jack under the carrier and raise it to simulate normal ride height.

14   Tighten the strut-to-carrier bolts to the torque listed in this Chapter's Specifications.

15   Connect the strut rod and tighten the bolt to the torque listed in this Chapter's Specifications.

16   Tighten the suspension arm bolt/nut to the torque listed in this Chapter's Specifications.

17   Attach the brake backing plate to the axle carrier, install the hub and tighten the four bolts securely.

18   Connect the brake tube to the wheel cylinder. Be careful not to damage the line when bending it back into place.

19   Install the rear brake drum (or disc) (Chapter 9).

10

16.2a   Remove the screws holding the horn pad

20   Install the wheel and lug nuts.
21   Bleed the wheel cylinder or caliper (see Chapter 9).
22   Lower the vehicle and tighten the lug nuts to the torque listed in the Chapter 1 Specifications.

16.2b   Disconnect the horn switch wire (arrow)

16.3   Using a marking pen or a scribe, apply alignment marks from the steering wheel hub to the steering shaft (arrows)

15   Steering system - general information

All models are equipped with rack-and-pinion steering. The steering gear is bolted to the firewall and operates the steering arms via tie-rods. The inner ends of the tie-rods are protected by rubber boots which should be inspected periodically for secure attachment, tears and leaking lubricant.

The power assist system consists of a belt-driven pump and associated lines and hoses. The fluid level in the power steering pump reservoir should be checked periodically (see Chapter 1).

The steering wheel operates the steering shaft, which actuates the steering gear through universal joints. Looseness in the steering can be caused by wear in the steering shaft universal joints, the steering gear, the tie-rod ends and loose retaining bolts.

16   Steering wheel - removal and installation

Refer to illustrations 16.2a, 16.2b, 16.3 and 16.4

Warning: *If the vehicle is equipped with an airbag DO NOT attempt to remove the steering wheel. Have it removed by a dealer service department or other qualified repair shop.*

Removal

1   Disconnect the cable from the negative terminal of the battery. **Caution:** *If the stereo in your vehicle is equipped with an anti-theft system, refer to the information on page 0-15 at the front of this manual before detaching the cable.*
2   Remove the screws from the bottom of the horn pad and pull the pad from the steering wheel **(see illustration)**. Disconnect the wire to the horn switch **(see illustration)**.
3   Remove the steering wheel retaining nut, then mark the relationship of the steering shaft to the hub (if marks don't already exist or don't line up) to simplify installation and ensure steering wheel alignment **(see illustration)**.
4   Use a puller to disconnect the steering wheel from the shaft **(see illustration)**.

Installation

5   To install the wheel, align the mark on the steering wheel hub with the mark on the shaft and slip the wheel onto the shaft. Install the nut and tighten it to the torque listed in this Chapter's Specifications.
6   Connect the horn wire and install the horn pad.
7   Connect the negative battery cable.

16.4   Use a steering wheel puller to separate the steering wheel from the shaft - DON'T attempt to remove the wheel with a hammer

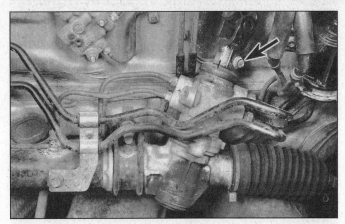

17.3   Mark the relationship of the steering shaft-to-steering gear input shaft, then remove the U-joint bolt (arrow) (engine removed for clarity)

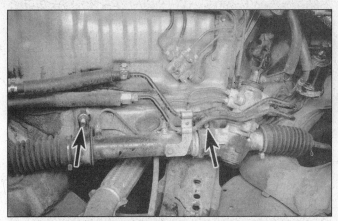

17.7   Location of the steering gear housing bracket bolts (arrows) (engine removed for clarity)

17   Steering gear - removal and installation

Refer to illustrations 17.3 and 17.7

Removal

1   Loosen the front wheel lug nuts, raise the front of the vehicle and support it securely on jackstands. Apply the parking brake and remove the wheels. Remove the engine under covers on models so equipped.

2   Place a drain pan under the steering gear. Detach the power steering pressure and return lines and cap the ends to prevent excessive fluid loss and contamination.

3   Mark the relationship of the lower universal joint to the steering gear input shaft. Remove the lower intermediate shaft pinch bolt **(see illustration)**.

4   Separate the tie-rod ends from the steering knuckle arms (see Section 18).

5   Support the engine with a floor jack and a block of wood, then remove the suspension crossmember and the engine center mounting member (see Section 2). On some models you'll also have to unbolt the engine/transaxle rear mounting bracket from the engine (see Chapter 2).

6   If you're working on a 1989 or earlier model, disconnect the exhaust pipe from the manifold and allow it to hang down (see Chapter 4).

7   Support the steering gear and remove the steering gear bracket-to-firewall mounting bolts **(see illustration)**. Separate the intermediate shaft from the steering gear input shaft, move the unit to the right as far as it will go, then lower it down and pull it out toward the left.

8   Check the steering gear mounting grommets for excessive wear or deterioration, replacing them if necessary.

Installation

9   Raise the steering gear into position and connect the U-joint, aligning the marks.

10   Install the mounting brackets and bolts and tighten them to the torque listed in this Chapter's Specifications.

11   Connect the tie-rod ends to the steering knuckle arms (see Section 18).

12   Install the U-joint pinch bolt and tighten it to the torque listed in this Chapter's Specifications.

13   Connect the power steering pressure and return hoses to the steering gear and fill the power steering pump reservoir with the recommended fluid (see Chapter 1).

14   Install the engine rear mounting bracket, tightening the bolts securely.

15   Install the engine center mounting member and suspension crossmember.

16   Lower the vehicle and bleed the steering system (see Section 21).

18   Tie-rod ends - removal and installation

Refer to illustrations 18.2a, 18.2b and 18.4

Removal

1   Loosen the wheel lug nuts. Raise the front of the vehicle, support it securely on jackstands, block the rear wheels and set the parking brake. Remove the front wheel.

2   Hold the tie-rod with a pair of locking pliers or wrench and loosen the jam nut enough to mark the position of the tie-rod end in relation to the threads **(see illustrations)**.

18.2a   Loosen the jam nut while holding the tie-rod with a wrench (or a pair of locking pliers) on the flat portion of the rod to prevent it from turning

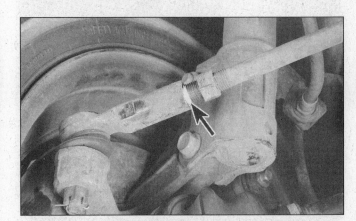

18.2b   Mark the relationship of the tie-rod end to the tie-rod (arrow)

10

18.4   A two-jaw puller works well for separating the tie-rod end from the steering knuckle arm - note that the nut has been loosened, but not removed (it will prevent the two components from separating violently)

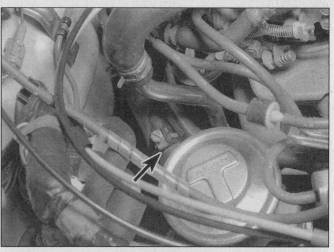

20.4   Loosen the clamp and detach the power steering pump return line (arrow)

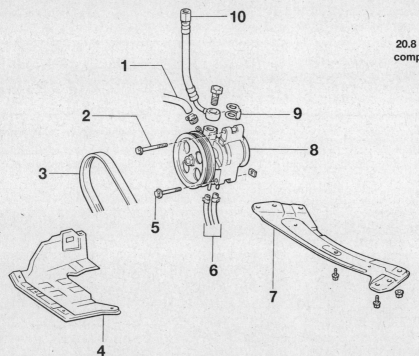

20.8   Power steering pump and related components (1986 through 1988 models)
1   Return hose
2   Bolt
3   Drivebelt
4   Lower engine cover - right side
5   Bolt
6   Vacuum hoses
7   Suspension crossmember
8   Power steering pump
9   Copper gaskets
10   Pressure line\

3   Remove the cotter pin and loosen the nut on the tie-rod end stud.
4   Disconnect the tie-rod from the steering knuckle arm with a puller **(see illustration)**. Remove the nut and separate the tie-rod.
5   Unscrew the tie-rod end from the tie-rod.

Installation

6   Thread the tie-rod end on to the marked position and insert the tie-rod stud into the steering knuckle arm. Tighten the jam nut securely.
7   Install the castellated nut on the stud and tighten it to the torque listed in this Chapter's Specifications. Install a new cotter pin.
8   Install the wheel and lug nuts. Lower the vehicle and tighten the lug nuts to the torque listed in the Chapter 1 Specifications.
9   Have the alignment checked by a dealer service department or an alignment shop.

19   Steering gear boots - replacement

1   Loosen the lug nuts, raise the vehicle and support it securely on jackstands. Remove the wheel.
2   Remove the tie-rod end and jam nut (see Section 18).
3   Remove the steering gear boot clamps and slide the boot off.
4   Before installing the new boot, wrap the threads and serrations on the end of the steering rod with a layer of tape so the small end of the new boot isn't damaged.
5   Slide the new boot into position on the steering gear until it seats in the groove in the steering rod and install new clamps.
6   Remove the tape and install the tie-rod end (see Section 18).
7   Install the wheel and lug nuts. Lower the vehicle and tighten the lug nuts to the torque listed in the Chapter 1 Specifications.

20.9   Power steering pump mounting bolts (arrows)

20   Power steering pump - removal and installation

Removal

Refer to illustration 20.4

1   Disconnect the cable from the negative battery terminal. **Caution:** *If the stereo in your vehicle is equipped with an anti-theft system, refer to the information on page 0-15 at the front of this manual before de-*taching the cable.

2   Using a large syringe or suction gun, suck as much fluid out of the power steering fluid reservoir as possible. Place a drain pan under the vehicle to catch any fluid that spills out when the hoses are disconnected.

3   Loosen the right front wheel lug nuts, raise the vehicle and support it securely on jackstands. Remove the right front wheel.

4   Loosen the clamp and disconnect the fluid return hose from the pump **(see illustration)**.

5   Remove the right lower engine under cover.

1986 through 1988 models

Refer to illustrations 20.8 and 20.9

6   Remove the suspension crossmember **(see illustration 1.1)**.

7   Remove the pressure line-to-pump union bolt and separate the line from the pump. Remove the copper sealing washers on each side of the fitting - these should be replaced when installing the pump.

8   Loosen the pivot and adjuster bolt and remove the drivebelt **(see illustration)**.

9   Remove the pivot, adjuster and upper mounting bolts **(see illustration)**, and lower the pump from the vehicle.

1989 models

Refer to illustration 20.14

10   See steps 1 through 5.

11   Remove the union bolt and disconnect the pressure line from the pump. Unplug the vacuum lines from the switch at the bottom of the pump.

12   Loosen the pivot and adjusting bolts and remove the drivebelt.

13   Disconnect the right side tie-rod end (see Section 18).

14   Remove the pivot, adjusting and upper mounting bolts **(see illustration)**.

15   Remove the power steering pump through the tie-rod end hole.

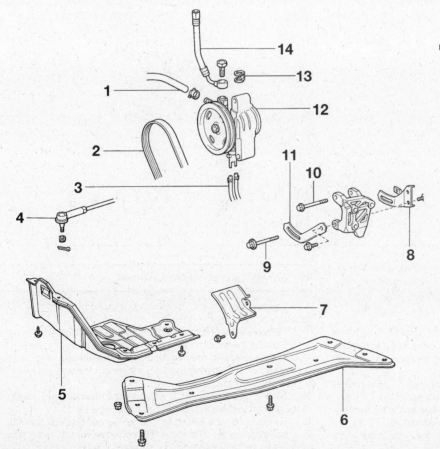

20.14   Power steering pump and related components (1989 models)

1   Return line
2   Drivebelt
3   Vacuum hoses
4   Tie-rod end
5   Lower engine cover (right side)
6   Suspension cross-member
7   Transmission case protector
8   Rear pump bracket
9   Adjuster bolt
10   Pivot bolt
11   Pump adjuster bracket
12   Power steering pump
13   Copper gaskets
14   Pressure hose

10

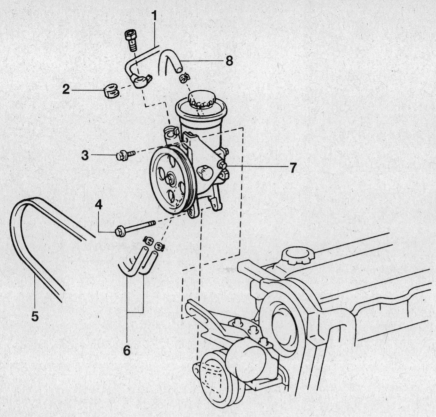

20.20a   Power steering pump and related components (1990 and later models with the 4A-FE engine)

1   Pressure line
2   Copper gaskets
3   Adjuster bolt
4   Pivot bolt
5   Drivebelt
6   Air hose
7   Power steering pump
8   Return hose

20.20b   Power steering pump and related components (1990 and later models with the 5S-FE or 3S-GTE engines)

1   Pressure hose
2   Return hose
3   Bolt
4   Drivebelt
5   Bolt
6   Vacuum hose
7   Lower engine under cover (right side)
8   Suspension crossmember
9   Power steering pump
10   Copper gaskets

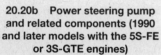
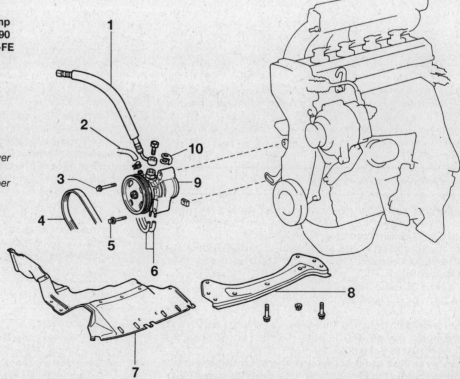

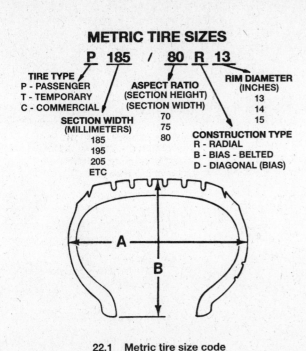

22.1   Metric tire size code

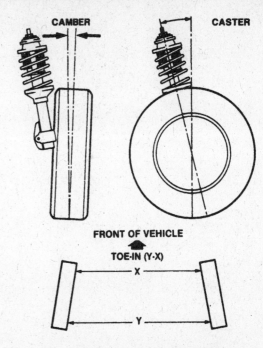

23.1   Camber, caster and toe-in angles

1990 and later models

Refer to illustrations 20.20a and 20.20b

16   See steps 1 through 5.
17   Remove the union bolt and disconnect the pressure line from the pump.
18   Loosen the pivot and adjusting bolts and remove the drivebelt.
19   Remove the pulley nut or bolt and remove the power steering pump pulley.
20   Remove the pivot, adjusting and upper mounting bolts **(see illustrations)**.
21   Remove the power steering pump through the tie-rod end hole.

Installation

22   To install the pump, reverse the removal procedure. Tighten the banjo fitting bolts to the torque listed in this Chapter's Specifications. Adjust the drivebelt tension following the procedure described in Chapter 1.
23   Top up the fluid level in the reservoir (see Chapter 1) and bleed the system (see Section 21).

21   Power steering system - bleeding

1   Following any operation in which the power steering fluid lines have been disconnected, the power steering system must be bled to remove all air and obtain proper steering performance.
2   With the front wheels in the straight ahead position, check the power steering fluid level and, if low, add fluid until it reaches the Cold mark on the dipstick.
3   Start the engine and allow it to run at fast idle. Recheck the fluid level and add more if necessary to reach the Cold mark on the dipstick.
4   Bleed the system by turning the wheels from side to side, without hitting the stops. This will work the air out of the system. Keep the reservoir full of fluid as this is done.
5   When the air is worked out of the system, return the wheels to the straight ahead position and leave the vehicle running for several more minutes before shutting it off.
6   Road test the vehicle to be sure the steering system is function-

ing normally and noise free.
7   Recheck the fluid level to be sure it is up to the Hot mark on the dipstick while the engine is at normal operating temperature. Add fluid if necessary (see Chapter 1).

22   Wheels and tires - general information

Refer to illustration 22.1

1   All vehicles covered by this manual are equipped with metric-sized fiberglass or steel belted radial tires **(see illustration)**. Use of other size or type of tires may affect the ride and handling of the vehicle. Don't mix different types of tires, such as radials and bias belted, on the same vehicle as handling may be seriously affected. It's recommended that tires be replaced in pairs on the same axle, but if only one tire is being replaced, be sure it's the same size, structure and tread design as the other.
2   Because tire pressure has a substantial effect on handling and wear, the pressure on all tires should be checked at least once a month or before any extended trips (see Chapter 1).
3   Wheels must be replaced if they are bent, dented, leak air, have elongated bolt holes, are heavily rusted, out of vertical symmetry or if the lug nuts won't stay tight. Wheel repairs that use welding or peening are not recommended.
4   Tire and wheel balance is important in the overall handling, braking and performance of the vehicle. Unbalanced wheels can adversely affect handling and ride characteristics as well as tire life. Whenever a tire is installed on a wheel, the tire and wheel should be balanced by a shop with the proper equipment.

23   Wheel alignment - general information

Refer to illustration 23.1

A wheel alignment refers to the adjustments made to the wheels so they are in proper angular relationship to the suspension and the ground. Wheels that are out of proper alignment not only affect vehicle control, but also increase tire wear. The front end angles normally measured are camber, caster and toe-in **(see illustration)**. Camber and toe-in are adjustable on 1989 and earlier models. Toe-in is the

10

only adjustable angle on 1990 and later models. The only adjustment possible on the rear is toe-in. The other angles should be measured to check for bent or worn suspension parts.

Getting the proper wheel alignment is a very exacting process, one in which complicated and expensive machines are necessary to perform the job properly. Because of this, you should have a technician with the proper equipment perform these tasks. We will, however, use this space to give you a basic idea of what is involved with a wheel alignment so you can better understand the process and deal intelligently with the shop that does the work.

Toe-in is the turning in of the wheels. The purpose of a toe specification is to ensure parallel rolling of the wheels. In a vehicle with zero toe-in, the distance between the front edges of the wheels will be the same as the distance between the rear edges of the wheels. The actual amount of toe-in is normally only a fraction of an inch. On the front end, toe-in is controlled by the tie-rod end position on the tie-rod. On the rear end, it's controlled by a cam on the inner end of the rear (number two) suspension arm. Incorrect toe-in will cause the tires to wear improperly by making them scrub against the road surface.

Camber is the tilting of the wheels from vertical when viewed from one end of the vehicle. When the wheels tilt out at the top, the camber is said to be positive (+). When the wheels tilt in at the top the camber is negative (-). The amount of tilt is measured in degrees from vertical and this measurement is called the camber angle. This angle affects the amount of tire tread which contacts the road and compensates for changes in the suspension geometry when the vehicle is cornering or traveling over an undulating surface.

Caster is the tilting of the front steering axis from the vertical. A tilt toward the rear is positive caster and a tilt toward the front is negative caster.

Chapter 11 Body

Contents

1 General information

These models feature a "unibody" layout, using a floor pan with front and rear frame side rails which support the body components, front and rear suspension systems and other mechanical components. Certain components are particularly vulnerable to accident damage and can be unbolted and repaired or replaced. Among these parts are the body moldings, bumpers, hood and trunk lids and all glass.

Only general body maintenance practices and body panel repair procedures within the scope of the do-it-yourselfer are included in this Chapter.

2 Body - maintenance

1   The condition of your vehicle's body is very important, because the resale value depends a great deal on it. It's much more difficult to repair a neglected or damaged body than it is to repair mechanical components. The hidden areas of the body, such as the wheel wells, the frame and the engine compartment, are equally important, although they don't require as frequent attention as the rest of the body.

2   Once a year, or every 12,000 miles, it's a good idea to have the underside of the body steam cleaned. All traces of dirt and oil will be removed and the area can then be inspected carefully for rust, damaged brake lines, frayed electrical wires, damaged cables and other problems. The front suspension components should be greased after completion of this job.

3   At the same time, clean the engine and the engine compartment with a steam cleaner or water soluble degreaser.

4   The wheel wells should be given close attention, since undercoating can peel away and stones and dirt thrown up by the tires can cause the paint to chip and flake, allowing rust to set in. If rust is found, clean down to the bare metal and apply an anti-rust paint.

5   The body should be washed about once a week. Wet the vehicle thoroughly to soften the dirt, then wash it down with a soft sponge and plenty of clean soapy water. If the surplus dirt is not washed off very carefully, it can wear down the paint.

6   Spots of tar or asphalt thrown up from the road should be removed with a cloth soaked in solvent.

7   Once every six months, wax the body and chrome trim. If a chrome cleaner is used to remove rust from any of the vehicle's plated parts, remember that the cleaner also removes part of the chrome, so use it sparingly.

11

3   Vinyl trim - maintenance

Don't clean vinyl trim with detergents, caustic soap or petroleum-based cleaners. Plain soap and water works just fine, with a soft brush to clean dirt that may be ingrained. Wash the vinyl as frequently as the rest of the vehicle.

After cleaning, application of a high quality rubber and vinyl protectant will help prevent oxidation and cracks. The protectant can also be applied to weatherstripping, vacuum lines and rubber hoses, which often fail as a result of chemical degradation, and to the tires.

4   Upholstery and carpets - maintenance

1   Every three months remove the carpets or mats and clean the interior of the vehicle (more frequently if necessary). Vacuum the upholstery and carpets to remove loose dirt and dust.
2   Leather upholstery requires special care. Stains should be removed with warm water and a very mild soap solution. Use a clean, damp cloth to remove the soap, then wipe again with a dry cloth. Never use alcohol, gasoline, nail polish remover or thinner to clean leather upholstery.
3   After cleaning, regularly treat leather upholstery with a leather wax. Never use car wax on leather upholstery.
4   In areas where the interior of the vehicle is subject to bright sunlight, cover leather seats with a sheet if the vehicle is to be left out for any length of time.

5   Body repair - minor damage

See photo sequence

Repair of minor scratches

1   If the scratch is superficial and does not penetrate to the metal of the body, repair is very simple. Lightly rub the scratched area with a fine rubbing compound to remove loose paint and built-up wax. Rinse the area with clean water.
2   Apply touch-up paint to the scratch, using a small brush. Continue to apply thin layers of paint until the surface of the paint in the scratch is level with the surrounding paint. Allow the new paint at least two weeks to harden, then blend it into the surrounding paint by rubbing with a very fine rubbing compound. Finally, apply a coat of wax to the scratch area.
3   If the scratch has penetrated the paint and exposed the metal of the body, causing the metal to rust, a different repair technique is required. Remove all loose rust from the bottom of the scratch with a pocket knife, then apply rust inhibiting paint to prevent the formation of rust in the future. Using a rubber or nylon applicator, coat the scratched area with glaze-type filler. If required, the filler can be mixed with thinner to provide a very thin paste, which is ideal for filling narrow scratches. Before the glaze filler in the scratch hardens, wrap a piece of smooth cotton cloth around the tip of a finger. Dip the cloth in thinner and then quickly wipe it along the surface of the scratch. This will ensure that the surface of the filler is slightly hollow. The scratch can now be painted over as described earlier in this section.

Repair of dents

4   When repairing dents, the first job is to pull the dent out until the affected area is as close as possible to its original shape. There is no point in trying to restore the original shape completely as the metal in the damaged area will have stretched on impact and cannot be restored to its original contours. It is better to bring the level of the dent up to a point which is about 1/8-inch below the level of the surrounding metal. In cases where the dent is very shallow, it is not worth trying to pull it out at all.
5   If the back side of the dent is accessible, it can be hammered out gently from behind using a soft-face hammer. While doing this, hold a block of wood firmly against the opposite side of the metal to absorb the hammer blows and prevent the metal from being stretched.

6   If the dent is in a section of the body which has double layers, or some other factor makes it inaccessible from behind, a different technique is required. Drill several small holes through the metal inside the damaged area, particularly in the deeper sections. Screw long, self-tapping screws into the holes just enough for them to get a good grip in the metal. Now the dent can be pulled out by pulling on the protruding heads of the screws with locking pliers.
7   The next stage of repair is the removal of paint from the damaged area and from an inch or so of the surrounding metal. This is done with a wire brush or sanding disk in a drill motor, although it can be done just as effectively by hand with sandpaper. To complete the preparation for filling, score the surface of the bare metal with a screwdriver or the tang of a file, or drill small holes in the affected area. This will provide a good grip for the filler material. To complete the repair, see the subsection on filling and painting later in this Section.

Repair of rust holes or gashes

8   Remove all paint from the affected area and from an inch or so of the surrounding metal using a sanding disk or wire brush mounted in a drill motor. If these are not available, a few sheets of sandpaper will do the job just as effectively.
9   With the paint removed, you will be able to determine the severity of the corrosion and decide whether to replace the whole panel, if possible, or repair the affected area. New body panels are not as expensive as most people think and it is often quicker to install a new panel than to repair large areas of rust.
10   Remove all trim pieces from the affected area except those which will act as a guide to the original shape of the damaged body, such as headlight shells, etc. Using metal snips or a hacksaw blade, remove all loose metal and any other metal that is badly affected by rust. Hammer the edges of the hole in to create a slight depression for the filler material.
11   Wire brush the affected area to remove the powdery rust from the surface of the metal. If the back of the rusted area is accessible, treat it with rust inhibiting paint.
12   Before filling is done, block the hole in some way. This can be done with sheet metal riveted or screwed into place, or by stuffing the hole with wire mesh.
13   Once the hole is blocked off, the affected area can be filled and painted. See the following subsection on filling and painting.

Filling and painting

14   Many types of body fillers are available, but generally speaking, body repair kits which contain filler paste and a tube of resin hardener are best for this type of repair work. A wide, flexible plastic or nylon applicator will be necessary for imparting a smooth and contoured finish to the surface of the filler material. Mix up a small amount of filler on a clean piece of wood or cardboard (use the hardener sparingly). Follow the manufacturer's instructions on the package, otherwise the filler will set incorrectly.
15   Using the applicator, apply the filler paste to the prepared area. Draw the applicator across the surface of the filler to achieve the desired contour and to level the filler surface. As soon as a contour that approximates the original one is achieved, stop working the paste. If you continue, the paste will begin to stick to the applicator. Continue to add thin layers of paste at 20-minute intervals until the level of the filler is just above the surrounding metal.
16   Once the filler has hardened, the excess can be removed with a body file. From then on, progressively finer grades of sandpaper should be used, starting with a 180-grit paper and finishing with 600-grit wet-or-dry paper. Always wrap the sandpaper around a flat rubber or wooden block, otherwise the surface of the filler will not be completely flat. During the sanding of the filler surface, the wet-or-dry paper should be periodically rinsed in water. This will ensure that a very smooth finish is produced in the final stage.
17   At this point, the repair area should be surrounded by a ring of bare metal, which in turn should be encircled by the finely feathered edge of good paint. Rinse the repair area with clean water until all of the dust produced by the sanding operation is gone.
18   Spray the entire area with a light coat of primer. This will reveal any imperfections in the surface of the filler. Repair the imperfections

with fresh filler paste or glaze filler and once more smooth the surface with sandpaper. Repeat this spray-and-repair procedure until you are satisfied that the surface of the filler and the feathered edge of the paint are perfect. Rinse the area with clean water and allow it to dry completely.

19   The repair area is now ready for painting. Spray painting must be carried out in a warm, dry, windless and dust free atmosphere. These conditions can be created if you have access to a large indoor work area, but if you are forced to work in the open, you will have to pick the day very carefully. If you are working indoors, dousing the floor in the work area with water will help settle the dust which would otherwise be in the air. If the repair area is confined to one body panel, mask off the surrounding panels. This will help minimize the effects of a slight mismatch in paint color. Trim pieces such as chrome strips, door handles, etc., will also need to be masked off or removed. Use masking tape and several thicknesses of newspaper for the masking operations.

20   Before spraying, shake the paint can thoroughly, then spray a test area until the spray painting technique is mastered. Cover the repair area with a thick coat of primer. The thickness should be built up using several thin layers of primer rather than one thick one. Using 600-grit wet-or-dry sandpaper, rub down the surface of the primer until it is very smooth. While doing this, the work area should be thoroughly rinsed with water and the wet-or-dry sandpaper periodically rinsed as well. Allow the primer to dry before spraying additional coats.

21   Spray on the top coat, again building up the thickness by using several thin layers of paint. Begin spraying in the center of the repair area and then, using a circular motion, work out until the whole repair area and about two inches of the surrounding original paint is covered. Remove all masking material 10 to 15 minutes after spraying on the final coat of paint. Allow the new paint at least two weeks to harden, then use a very fine rubbing compound to blend the edges of the new paint into the existing paint. Finally, apply a coat of wax.

6   Body repair - major damage

1   Major damage must be repaired by an auto body shop specifically equipped to perform unibody repairs. These shops have the specialized equipment required to do the job properly.

2   If the damage is extensive, the body must be checked for proper alignment or the vehicle's handling characteristics may be adversely affected and other components may wear at an accelerated rate.

3   Due to the fact that all of the major body components (hood, fenders, etc.) are separate and replaceable units, any seriously damaged components should be replaced rather than repaired. Sometimes the components can be found in a wrecking yard that specializes in used vehicle components, often at considerable savings over the cost of new parts.

7   Hinges and locks - maintenance

Once every 3000 miles, or every three months, the hinges and latch assemblies on the doors, hood and trunk should be given a few drops of light oil or lock lubricant. The door latch strikers should also be lubricated with a thin coat of grease to reduce wear and ensure free movement. Lubricate the door and trunk locks with spray-on graphite lubricant.

8   Windshield and fixed glass - replacement

Replacement of the windshield and fixed glass requires the use of special fast-setting adhesive/caulk materials and some specialized tools. It is recommended that these operations be left to a dealer or a shop specializing in glass work.

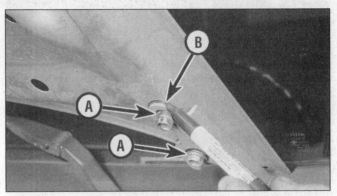

9.1   Before removing the hood make marks around the hinge bolts (A). When adjusting the hood make a mark around the complete hinge plate (B)

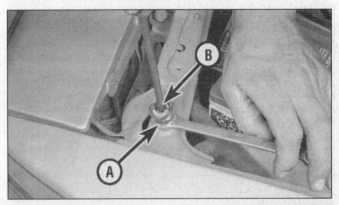

9.11   To adjust the hood bumpers loosen the locking nut (A) and prevent it from tightening while adjusting the screw (B)

9   Hood - removal, installation and adjustment

Refer to illustrations 9.1 and 9.11
Note: *The hood is heavy and somewhat awkward to remove and install - at least two people should perform this procedure.*

Removal and installation

1   Make marks around the bolt heads to ensure proper alignment during installation **(see illustration)**.

2   Use blankets or pads to cover the cowl area of the body and fenders. This will protect the body and paint as the hood is lifted off.

3   Disconnect any cables or wires that will interfere with removal.

4   Have an assistant support the hood. Remove the hinge-to-hood screws or bolts.

5   Lift off the hood.

6   Installation is the reverse of removal.

Adjustment

7   Fore-and-aft and side-to-side adjustment of the hood is done by moving the hinge plate slot after loosening the bolts or nuts.

8   Scribe a line around the entire hinge plate so you can judge the amount of movement **(see illustration 9.1)**

9   Loosen the bolts or nuts and move the hood into correct alignment. Move it only a little at a time. Tighten the hinge bolts or nuts and carefully lower the hood to check the position.

10   If necessary after installation, the entire hood latch assembly can be adjusted up-and-down as well as from side-to-side on the radiator support so the hood closes securely, flush with the fenders. To make the adjustment, scribe a line around the hood latch mounting bolts to provide a reference point, then loosen them and reposition the latch assembly, as necessary. Following adjustment, retighten the mounting bolts.

11

These photos illustrate a method of repairing simple dents. They are intended to supplement *Body repair - minor damage* in this Chapter and should not be used as the sole instructions for body repair on these vehicles.

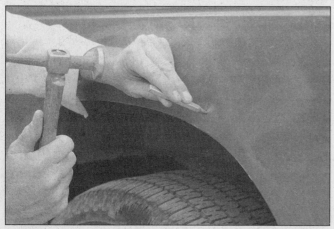

1   If you can't access the backside of the body panel to hammer out the dent, pull it out with a slide-hammer-type dent puller. In the deepest portion of the dent or along the crease line, drill or punch hole(s) at least one inch apart . . .

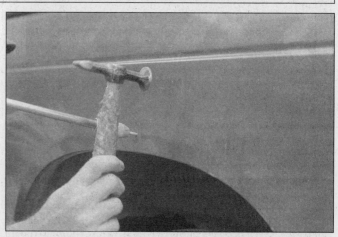

2   . . . then screw the slide-hammer into the hole and operate it. Tap with a hammer near the edge of the dent to help 'pop' the metal back to its original shape. When you're finished, the dent area should be close to its original contour and about 1/8-inch below the surface of the surrounding metal

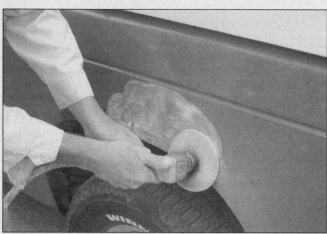

3   Using coarse-grit sandpaper, remove the paint down to the bare metal. Hand sanding works fine, but the disc sander shown here makes the job faster. Use finer (about 320-grit) sandpaper to feather-edge the paint at least one inch around the dent area

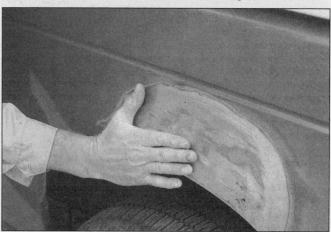

4   When the paint is removed, touch will probably be more helpful than sight for telling if the metal is straight. Hammer down the high spots or raise the low spots as necessary. Clean the repair area with wax/silicone remover

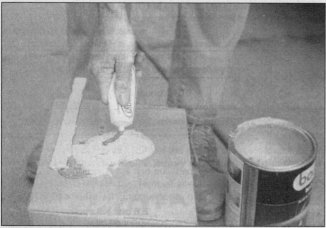

5   Following label instructions, mix up a batch of plastic filler and hardener. The ratio of filler to hardener is critical, and, if you mix it incorrectly, it will either not cure properly or cure too quickly (you won't have time to file and sand it into shape)

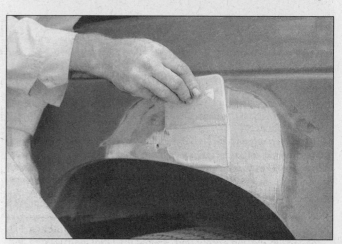

6   Working quickly so the filler doesn't harden, use a plastic applicator to press the body filler firmly into the metal, assuring it bonds completely. Work the filler until it matches the original contour and is slightly above the surrounding metal

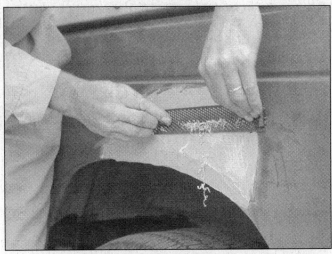

7 Let the filler harden until you can just dent it with your fingernail. Use a body file or Surform tool (shown here) to rough-shape the filler

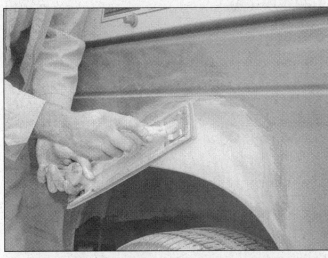

8 Use coarse-grit sandpaper and a sanding board or block to work the filler down until it's smooth and even. Work down to finer grits of sandpaper - always using a board or block - ending up with 360 or 400 grit

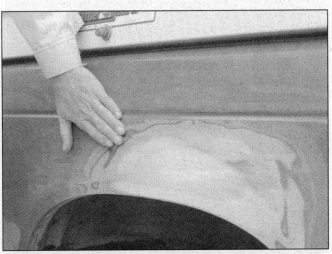

9 You shouldn't be able to feel any ridge at the transition from the filler to the bare metal or from the bare metal to the old paint. As soon as the repair is flat and uniform, remove the dust and mask off the adjacent panels or trim pieces

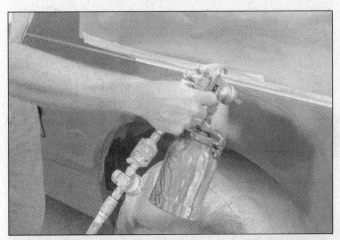

10 Apply several layers of primer to the area. Don't spray the primer on too heavy, so it sags or runs, and make sure each coat is dry before you spray on the next one. A professional-type spray gun is being used here, but aerosol spray primer is available inexpensively from auto parts stores

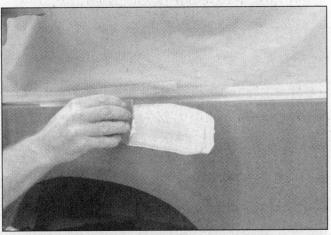

11 The primer will help reveal imperfections or scratches. Fill these with glazing compound. Follow the label instructions and sand it with 360 or 400-grit sandpaper until it's smooth. Repeat the glazing, sanding and respraying until the primer reveals a perfectly smooth surface

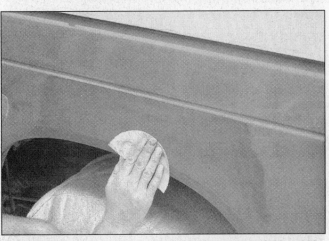

12 Finish sand the primer with very fine sandpaper (400 or 600-grit) to remove the primer overspray. Clean the area with water and allow it to dry. Use a tack rag to remove any dust, then apply the finish coat. Don't attempt to rub out or wax the repair area until the paint has dried completely (at least two weeks)

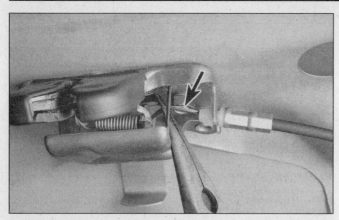

10.2   Push the lock cable out of its groove so the end nipple pops free (arrow). Unclip the cable and any electrical connections that will interfere with removal

11   Finally, adjust the hood bumpers on the radiator support so the hood, when closed, is flush with the fenders **(see illustration)**.

12   The hood latch assembly, as well as the hinges, should be periodically lubricated with white, lithium-base grease to prevent binding and wear.

---

10   Trunk lid/rear liftgate - removal and installation

Refer to illustrations 10.2 and 10.3

Note: *The Trunk lid/rear liftgate is heavy and somewhat awkward to remove and install - at least two people should perform this procedure.*

1   Open the trunk lid and cover the edges of the trunk compartment with pads or cloths to protect the painted surfaces when the lid is removed.

2   Disconnect any cables or wire harness connectors attached to the trunk lid that would interfere with removal **(see illustration)**.

3   Make alignment marks around the hinge bolt mounting flanges **(see illustration)**.

4   Have an assistant support the trunk lid/rear liftgate and detach the support struts (see Section 11).

5   While an assistant supports the lid or liftgate, remove the lid-to-hinge bolts on both sides and lift it off.

6   Installation is the reverse of removal. **Note:** *When reinstalling the trunk lid or liftgate, align the lid-to-hinge bolts with the marks made during removal.*

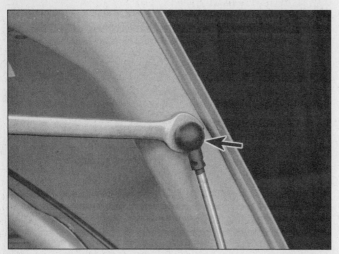

11.1a   With the trunk lid/rear liftgate open loosen the upper retention bolt (arrow) - do not remove it at this stage

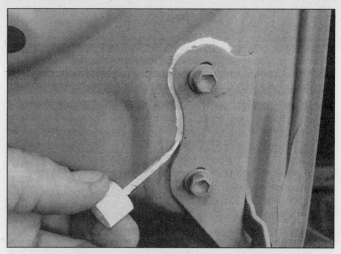

10.3   Scribe a mark around the hinge plate to help with lid/liftgate realignment on installation

7   After installation, close the lid and make sure it's in proper alignment with the surrounding panels. If the lid/liftgate requires adjustment **see Section 12** for the procedure.

---

11   Support strut - replacement

Refer to illustrations 11.1a and 11.1b

Warning: *The support strut is filled with pressurized gas - do not disassemble this component, if it is faulty replace it with a new one.*

Note: *The trunk lid/rear liftgate is heavy and somewhat awkward to hold securely while replacing the struts - at least two people should perform this procedure.*

1   **See illustrations 11.1a and 11.1b** for the removal procedure, be sure to read the accompanying text.

2   Installation is the reverse of the removal procedure.

---

12   Trunk lid/rear liftgate - adjustment

Refer to illustrations 12.1, 12.3a, 12.3b and 12.4

1   Forward-and-backward and side-to-side adjustments are made by loosening the hinge to lid/liftgate bolts and gently moving the lid/liftgate into correct alignment **(see illustration)**.

11.1b   Ensure that the trunk lid/rear liftgate is securely supported and remove the lower retention bolt (arrow). Return to the upper retention bolt, remove the bolt and pull the strut free

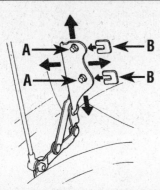

12.1   Loosen the hinge bolts (A) to adjust the lid/liftgate forward-and-backward and side-to-side. Adding or removing shims (B) will alter the vertical alignment of the lid/liftgate

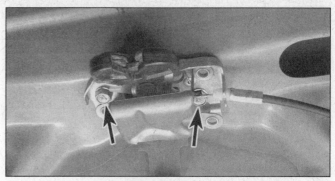

12.3a   Loosen the lock mounting bolts (arrows) to adjust the lock . . .

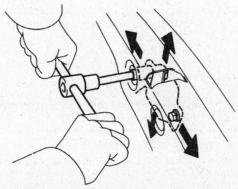

12.3b   . . .on liftgate models the mounting bolts can be reached through the access holes

12.4   Adjust the lock striker by loosening the mounting bolts (arrows) and tapping the striker with a soft-faced hammer

2   Vertical adjustments to the lid /liftgate are made by increasing or decreasing the number of shims used on the hinge **(see illustration 12.1).**
3   On trunk lid models the lock position is altered by loosening the retention bolts securing the lock to the lid. Rear liftgate models have access holes through which the lock retention bolts may be reached **(see illustrations).**
4   Having adjusted the lock the lock striker can be adjusted by loosening the mounting bolts **(see illustration)** and gently tapping it into position with a plastic hammer.

13   Door trim panel - removal and installation

Refer to illustrations 13.3a, 13.3b, 13.3c, 13.4a, 13.4b, 13.4c, 13.4d, 13.4e, 13.6 and 13.7

1   Disconnect the negative cable from the battery. **Caution:** *If the stereo in your vehicle is equipped with an anti-theft system, refer to the information on page 0-15 at the front of this manual before detaching the cable.*
2   Remove the outside mirror bracket cover (see Section 19).
3   On manual window regulator equipped models, remove the window crank by working a cloth back-and-forth behind the handle to dislodge the retainer **(see illustrations).** A special tool is available for this purpose **(see illustration)** but it's not essential. With the retainer removed, pull off the handle.

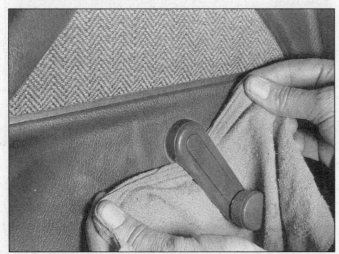

13.3a   Work a cloth up behind the regulator handle and move it back-and-forth . . .

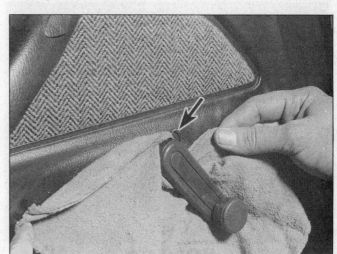

13.3b   . . .until the retainer (arrow) is pushed up so you can remove it

11

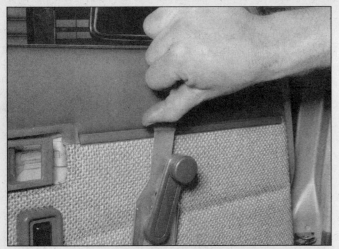

13.3c   If you have access to a special tool like this one, use it to disengage the retainer

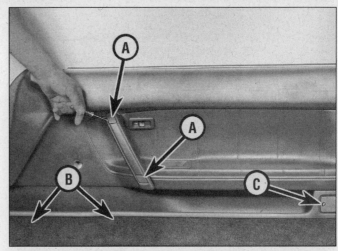

13.4a   To remove the door trim gently pry the armrest screw covers off (A) and remove the screws behind them, remove the lower carpet screws (B) and the door light cover screws (C)

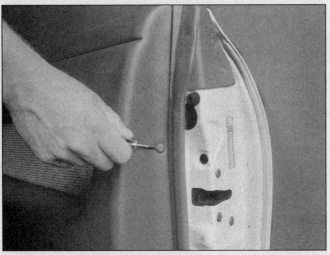

13.4b   Late model vehicles have screws located at the front and back of the trim panel. To remove them gently pry the covers off - notice that the screwdriver tip is wrapped in tape to prevent damaging the trim

13.4c   Disconnect the door light connector and remove the mounting screw (arrow)

13.4d   Remove the door handle screw (arrow) . . .

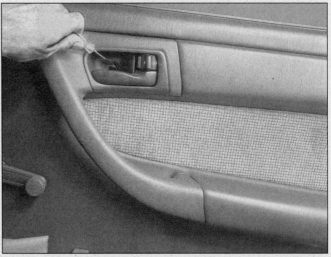

13.4e   . . . on late model vehicles there are two further screws behind the door handle

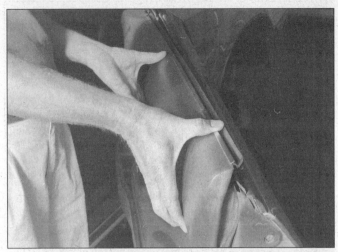

13.6   Pull the door trim up and out to remove it

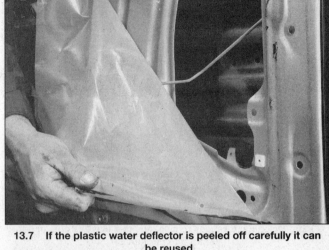

13.7   If the plastic water deflector is peeled off carefully it can be reused

14.2   Use two jackstands padded with rags (to protect the paint) to support the door during the removal and installation procedures

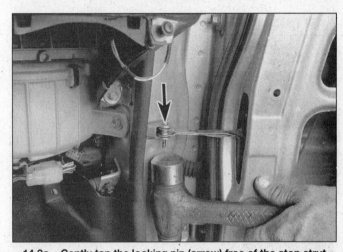

14.3a   Gently tap the locking pin (arrow) free of the stop strut

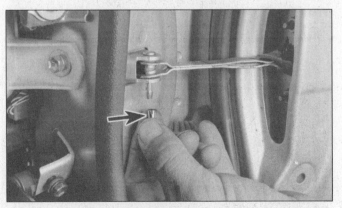

14.3b   Be sure to keep the locking pin retention clip (arrow) for installation

4   Remove any door trim panel retaining screws and door pull/armrest assemblies **(see illustrations)**.

5   Insert a wide putty knife or a thin pry bar between the trim panel and door to disengage the retaining clips. Work around the outer edge until the panel is free.

6   Once all of the clips are disengaged, detach the trim panel, unplug any electrical connectors and remove the trim panel from the vehicle by gently pulling it up and out **(see illustration)**.

7   For access to the inner door, peel back the plastic water deflector, taking care not to tear it **(see illustration)**. To install the trim panel, first press the water deflector into place.

8   Prior to installation of the door panel, be sure to reinstall any clips in the panel which may have come out during the removal procedure and stayed in the door.

9   Plug in any electrical connectors and place the panel in position. Press it into place until the clips are seated and install any retaining screws and armrest/door pulls. Install the manual regulator window crank or power switch assembly.

14   Door - removal, installation and adjustment

Removal and installation

Refer to illustrations 14.2, 14.3a, 14.3b and 14.4

1   Remove the door trim panel (see Section 13) and disconnect any electrical connectors and push them through the door opening so they won't interfere with removal.

2   Position a jack or jackstands under the door or have an assistant on hand to support the door when the hinge bolts are removed **(see illustration)**. **Note:** *If a jack or stand is used, place a rag between it and the door to protect the door's paint.*

3   Remove the door stop strut center pin **(see illustrations)**.

11

14.4   Before loosening or removing them, mark the door bolt locations

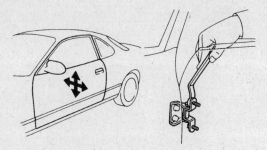

14.6b   Adjust the door up-and-down or in-and-out after loosening the hinge to door bolts

4   Scribe around the door bolts **(see illustration)**.
5   Remove the hinge-to-door bolts and carefully detach the door. Installation is the reverse of removal.

Adjustment

Refer to illustrations 14.6a, 14.6b and 14.6c
6   Following installation, make sure the door is aligned properly. Adjust it if necessary as follows:
  a) Up-and-down and forward-and-backward adjustments are made by loosening the hinge-to-body bolts and moving the door, as necessary. A special offset tool may be required to reach some of the bolts **(see illustration)**.
  b) In-and-out and up-and-down adjustments are made by loosening the door side hinge bolts and moving the door, as necessary. A special offset tool may be required to reach some of the bolts (see illustration).
  c) The door lock striker can also be adjusted both up-and-down and sideways to provide a positive engagement with the locking mechanism. This is done by loosening the screws and moving the striker, as necessary **(see illustration)**.

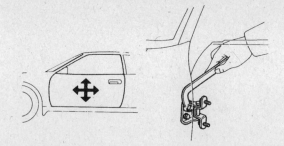

14.6a   When adjusting the door up-and-down or forward-and-backward a special cranked wrench such as this one (SST-09812-00010, available from your dealer) or equivalent will make the job easier

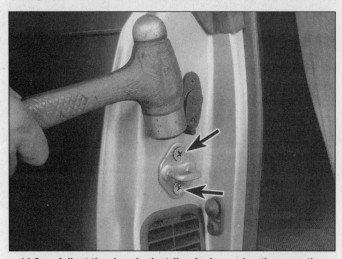

14.6c   Adjust the door lock striker by loosening the mounting screws (arrows) and gently tapping the striker in the desired direction

15   Door latch, lock cylinder and handle - removal and installation

1   Remove the door trim panel and water deflector (Section 13).

Door lock

Refer to illustration 15.2
2   Reach behind the door panel and disconnect the links from the outside handle and the lock cylinder **(see illustration)**.
3   If so equipped disconnect the power door connectors and their bolt. Remove the lock retaining screws from the end of the door and on older models the two retaining bolts **(see illustration 15.2)**.

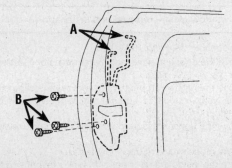

15.2   Disconnect the control links (A) from the outside handle and lock cylinder and remove the mounting bolts (B)

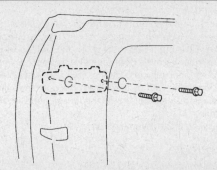

15.7   The outside handle retention bolts can be reached through access holes in the door frame

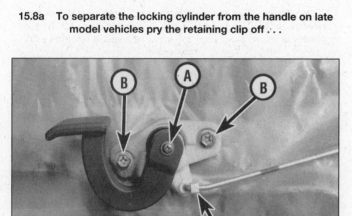

15.8a   To separate the locking cylinder from the handle on late model vehicles pry the retaining clip off . . .

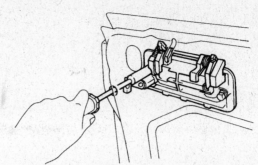

15.8b   . . . on earlier models remove the retention bolt

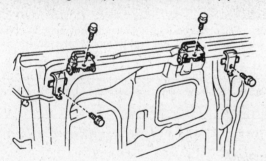

15.10a   On early model handles remove the handle screw (A), the two mounting bolts (B) and the control link (C) . . .

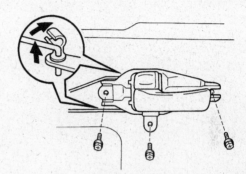

15.10b   . . . late model vehicles have three mounting bolts and two control links

16.4   Typical glass stopper and trim support location

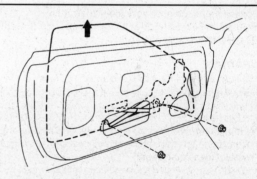

16.6   Remove the two mounting bolts and lift the glass free - place a rag over the glass to help prevent scratching it

4   Detach the door lock and (if equipped) the door lock solenoid.
5   Installation is the reverse of removal.

Lock cylinder and outside handle

Refer to illustration 15.7, 15.8a and 15.8b

6   Disconnect the control link and electrical connector (if equipped) from the lock cylinder and outside handle **(see illustration 15.2)**.
7   Remove the outside handle retention bolts and pull the handle and lock cylinder from the door **(see illustration)**.
8   On late model vehicles use a screwdriver to pry the retaining clip off and remove the lock cylinder from the door **(see illustration)**. On earlier models a single bolt holds the lock cylinder to the handle **(see illustration)**.
9   Installation is the reverse of removal.

Inside handle

Refer to illustration 15.10a and 15.10b

10   Remove the retaining screws **(see illustrations)**.

11   Disconnect the link(s) from the inside handle control **(see illustration 15. 10a and 15.10b)** and pull the handle free.
12   Installation is the reverse of removal.

---

16   Door window glass - removal and installation

Refer to illustrations 16.4 and 16.6

1   Remove the door trim panel and water deflector (Section 13).
2   Lower the window glass.
3   Remove the weatherstrip carefully, remove the clips and screws and pull the weatherstrip free - do not pull strongly as this may damage the weatherstrip.
4   Remove the upper glass stoppers and the trim supports **(see illustration)**.
5   On early models remove the inner stabilizer.
6   Place a rag inside the door panel to help prevent scratching the glass and remove the two glass mounting bolts **(see illustration)**.

11

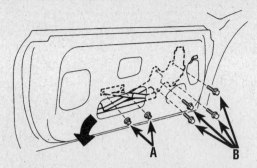

17.4a   Remove the equalizer arm bracket bolts (A) and on late models the four regulator mounting bolts (B) . . .

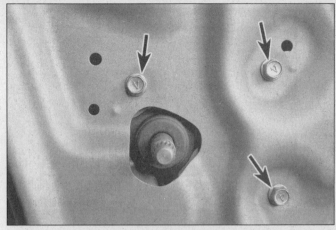

17.4b   . . . early model vehicles have three regulator mounting bolts (arrows)

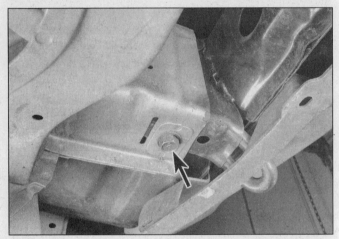

18.3   Remove the bumper retention bolts (viewed from below)

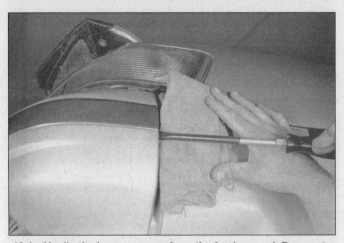

18.4   Unclip the bumper cover from the fender panel. Be sure to protect the fender and bumper cover by using a rag and a taped screwdriver

7   Remove the glass by pulling it up.
8   Installation is the reverse of the removal procedure.

17   Door glass regulator - removal and installation

Refer to illustrations 17.4a and 17.4b

1   Remove the door trim panel and water deflector (see Section 13).
2   Remove the window assembly (see Section 16).
3   If so equipped unclip the power control connector from the panel and disconnect it.
4   Remove the equalizer arm bracket mounting bolts and the regulator mounting bolts **(see illustrations)**
5   Pull the regulator through the service hole to remove it.
6   Installation is the reverse of removal.

18   Front and rear bumper - removal and installation

Front bumper

Refer to illustrations 18.3, 18.4 and 18.5
Warning: *On airbag-equipped models, if the vehicle has been involved in a collision and the airbags discharged, the airbag and sensors should be checked and/or replaced by an authorized dealer. Also, always disconnect the negative battery cable when working in the vicinity of the impact sensors to avoid the possibility of accidental deployment of the airbag, which could cause personal injury.*
Caution: *If the stereo in your vehicle is equipped with an anti-theft system, refer to the information on page 0-15 at the front of this manual before detaching the cable.*

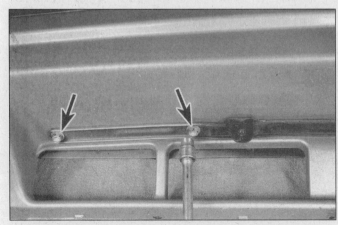

18.5   Remove the upper cover nuts and lower cover bolts (arrows) to free the cover from the bumper

1   Apply the parking brake, block the rear wheels, lift the front of the vehicle and support it securely on jackstands
2   Disconnect the negative battery lead from the battery and disconnect any wiring that would interfere with bumper removal.
3   Pry the bumper cover clips free of the fender, take care to avoid damaging the bumper cover and the fender **(see illustration)**.

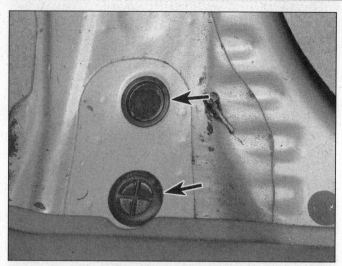

18.7a   Working in the trunk pull the carpet up and pry the rubber grommets out (arrows)

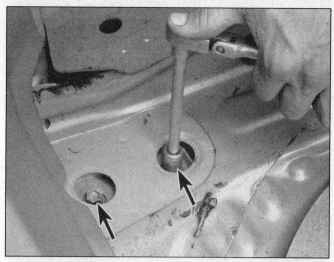

18.7b   Remove the rear bumper retention bolts (arrows)

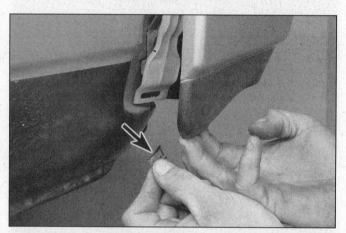

18.7c   Pry the bumper cover from the rear body panel until the upper and lower metal clips are free - lower clip shown (arrow). Pull the complete bumper assembly free

18.7d   To remove the bumper cover unscrew the upper and lower bumper cover nuts/bolts from the bumper (arrows)

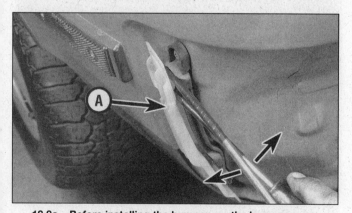
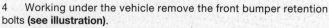

18.8a   Before installing the bumper pry the bumper cover retention strip (A) from the body. Two large screwdrivers covered in tape pushed in opposite directions can be used to pop the strip out

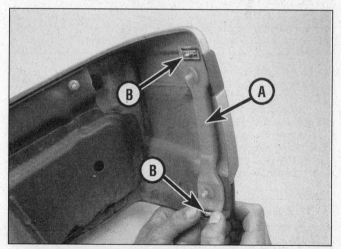

18.8b   Position the retention strip (A) on the corners of the bumper cover and push the retention clips (B) into place. The rest of bumper installation is the reverse of the removal procedure

4   Working under the vehicle remove the front bumper retention bolts **(see illustration)**.
5   Pull the bumper assembly from the vehicle. To remove the bumper cover from the bumper unit remove the upper and lower cover nuts/bolts **(see illustration)**.
6   Installation is the reverse of the removal procedure.

Rear bumper

Refer to illustrations 18.7a, 18.7b, 18.7c, 18.7d, 18.8a and 18.8b
7   For the removal procedure follow **illustrations 18.7a through 18.7d**, taking care to stay in order and to read the accompanying text.
8   Before the bumper is installed reconnect the bumper cover clips **(see illustrations)**. To install the bumper and bumper cover reverse the removal procedure.

11

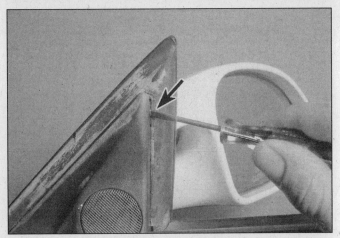

19.1   Gently pry the mirror bracket cover off using a small screwdriver - notice that the screwdriver is wrapped in tape to prevent damaging the trim

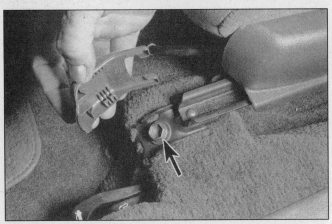

20.1a   Lift off the bolt covers and remove the front (arrow) . . .

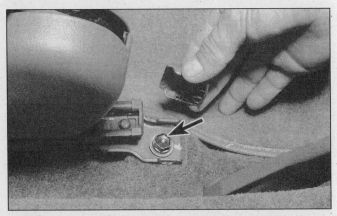

20.1b   . . . and rear retention bolts (arrow) to remove the front seats. Be sure to disconnect any electrical connections

---

19   Outside mirror - removal and installation

Refer to illustrations 19.1, 19.2a and 19.2b

1   Gently pry the mirror bracket cover off using a small screwdriver. Be sure to tape the tip of the screwdriver to prevent damaging the trim **(see illustration)**.

2   Remove the three retaining screws and detach the mirror **(see illustration)**. On models with speakers mounted on the door mirror bracket, remove the two screws securing the speaker to the bracket

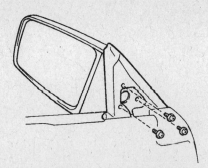

19.2a   Remove the three screws securing the outside mirror to the bracket and lift the mirror free

19.2b   On later models remove the two speaker screws (arrows), move the speaker to one side and remove the screw previously hidden by the speaker

20.3   To release the bottom seat pull the release tab forward (arrow), tilt the front of the seat up and pull free

and the screw behind the speaker **(see illustration)**.

3   Installation is the reverse of removal.

---

20   Seats - removal and installation

Front seats

Refer to illustrations 20.1a and 20.1b

1   Remove the retaining bolts, unplug any electrical connectors and lift the seats from the vehicle **(see illustrations)**.

2   Installation is the reverse of removal.

Rear seats - fixed type

Refer to illustrations 20.3 and 20.4

3   Pull the seat release tabs forward and lift the lower seat cushion up and free **(see illustration)**.

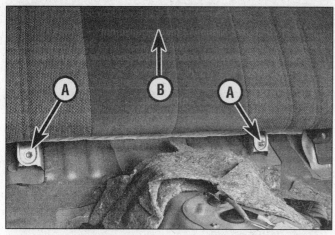

20.4   Remove the mounting bolts (A) and pull the seat up (B)

21.2a   On early models pull the side switches from the panel and disconnect their electrical connections

21.2b   On early models remove the four retention screws (arrows) and pull the panel clear . . .

21.2c   . . . on later models there is a fifth retention screw (arrow) that must be removed before the panel can be pulled clear

4   Remove the mounting bolts from the bottom of the seat back and pull the seat up to free the upper mounting slots (**see illustration**).
5   Installation is the reverse of removal.

Rear seats - split type

6   On split foldable type seats disengage the rear seat back lock.
7   Disengage the seat release tab, tilt the front of the seat up and pull the lower seat free (**see illustration 20.4**).
8   Remove the rear seat hinge bolts and pull the seat clear.

21   Instrument cluster trim panel - removal and installation

Refer to illustrations 21.2a, 21.2b and 21.2c
Warning: *On airbag-equipped models, always disconnect the negative battery cable when working in the vicinity of the impact sensors to avoid the possibility of accidental deployment of the airbag, which could cause personal injury.*
1   Disconnect the negative lead from the battery. **Caution:** *If the stereo in your vehicle is equipped with an anti-theft system, refer to the information on page 0-15 at the front of this manual before detaching the cable.*
2   Follow **illustrations 21.2a through 21.2c** taking care to stay in order and to read the accompanying text.
3   Installation is the reverse of the removal procedure.

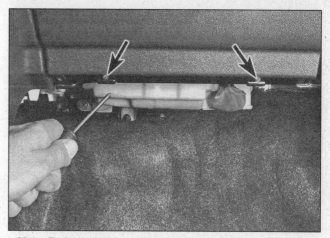

22.1   Early model glove boxes are held in place by two screws (arrows) at the base of the glove box door

22   Glovebox - removal and installation

Refer to illustrations 22.1 and 22.2
1   On early models remove the two screws at the bottom of the glovebox and pull the compartment free (**see illustration**).

11

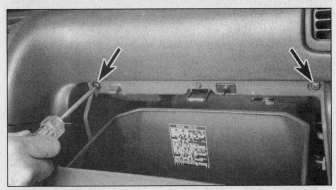

22.2   In addition to the lower screws later models have two screws inside the glove compartment itself (arrows)

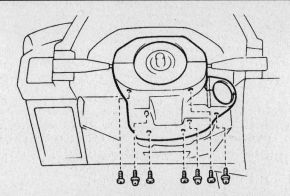

23.1   Remove the lower steering cover screws (early model shown) and pull the cover free

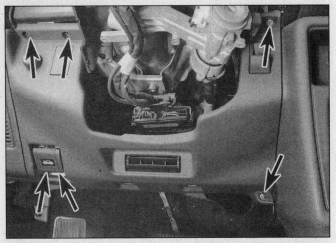

23.2a   Remove the panel screws and the two hood release latch screws (arrows)

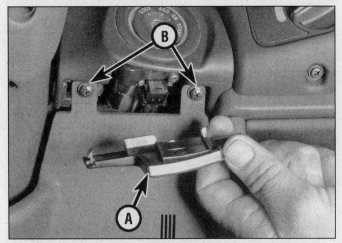

23.2b   On late model vehicles remove the cover plate (A) to gain access to the two panel screws (B) to the right of the steering column

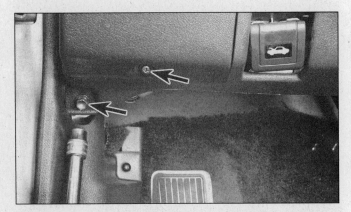

23.3a   On early model vehicles remove the bolt and screw from below the speaker cover

23.3b   Late model vehicles have a single screw in the lower left hand corner of the speaker cover

2   On later models remove the lower screws and then open the glovebox and remove the two upper screws (see illustration).
3   Installation is the reverse of removal.

23   Steering column cover and panel - removal and installation

Refer to illustrations 23.1, 23.2a, 23.2b, 23.3a, 23.3b and 23.4
Warning: *On airbag-equipped models, always disconnect the negative battery cable when working in the vicinity of the impact sensors to avoid the possibility of accidental deployment of the airbag, which could cause personal injury.*

Caution: *If the stereo in your vehicle is equipped with an anti-theft system, refer to the information on page 0-15 at the front of this manual before detaching the cable.*

1   Remove the lower steering cover by removing the retention screws (see illustration).
2   Remove the retention screws from the steering column panel, disengage the hood release latch and remove the two screws securing the latch to the panel (see illustrations).
3   Remove the bolt and/or screw from below the left hand speaker cover (see illustrations).

23.4   Remove the retention screw (arrow) located above the speaker - early model vehicles only

24.1   On early models there are three retention screws on either side of the console (arrows). Late models have two retention screws

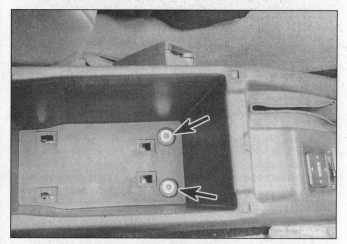

24.2   Remove the console compartment screws (arrows)

24.3   Remove the trim below the handbrake to facilitate console removal

4   On early model vehicles pull the speaker cover off and remove the retention screw located above the speaker (**see illustration**).
5   Disconnect any electrical connections and pull the panel off.
6   Installation is the reverse of the removal procedure.

24   Console and center trim panel - removal and installation

Refer to illustrations 24.1, 24.2, 24.3, 24.5a, 24.5b and 24.6
Warning: *On airbag-equipped models, always disconnect the negative battery cable when working in the vicinity of the impact sensors to avoid the possibility of accidental deployment of the airbag, which could cause personal injury. The center airbag sensor assembly is located under the center console on airbag-equipped models.* **Caution:** *If the stereo in your vehicle is equipped with an anti-theft system, refer to the information on page 0-15 at the front of this manual before detaching the cable.*
1   Disconnect the negative cable from the battery. To remove the console slide the seats fully forward and remove the rear screws - one on either side of the console. Then push the seat fully back and remove the forward retention screw(s) (**see illustrations**).
2   Remove the screws located in the bottom of the console compartment, on late model vehicles pull the tape box out of the console compartment to gain access to the screws (**see illustration**).
3   Pull the hand brake as near to vertical as possible, on early model automatic transaxle equipped vehicles place the gear lever in an up-

24.5a   On early models remove the three panel screws and the strut bolt from either side of the center panel

right position. Remove the trim plate below the handbrake (**see illustrations**).
4   Pull the whole console up and free.
5   Remove the center trim panel side retention bolts (**see illustrations**).

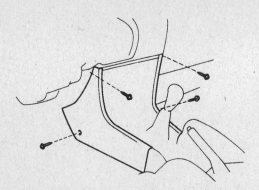

24.5b   On later models remove the four panel screws

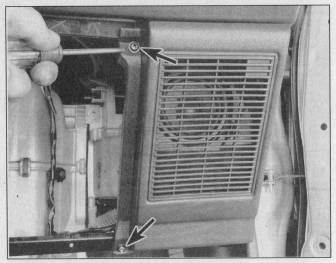

25.3a   Remove the retaining screw (arrows) to the left . . .

6   Pull the ashtray out and remove the front retention screws, pull the gear lever back and pull the trim panel out slightly to allow access to electrical connections (see illustration).
7   Once all electrical connections have been disconnected pull the unit free.
8   Installation is the reverse of the removal procedure.

25   Speaker covers - removal and installation

Refer to illustrations 25.3a, 25.3b and 25.3c
1   Disconnect the negative lead from the battery. Caution: If the stereo in your vehicle is equipped with an anti-theft system, refer to the information on page 0-15 at the front of this manual before detaching the cable.

Front speakers - early models

2.   For the removal of the drivers side speaker cover (see Section 25).
3   Remove the retaining screws (see illustrations) and pull the passenger speaker cover forward to gain access to the electrical connector.

Front speaker - late models

4   Recent models have tweeters mounted in the outside mirror trim panels, to remove them see Section 19.
5   On late model vehicles the right hand speaker cover is part of the glovebox assembly, for the removal procedure see Section 22.

24.6   Remove the two upper screws (arrows - early models only) and having pulled the ashtray from the panel the two lower screws (arrows)

25.3b   . . . and the right (arrows) of the unit

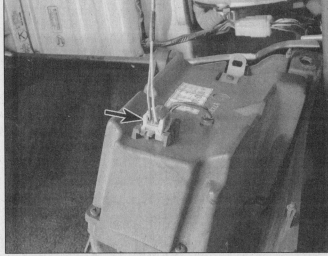

25.3c   Disconnect any electrical connectors and pull the speakers free

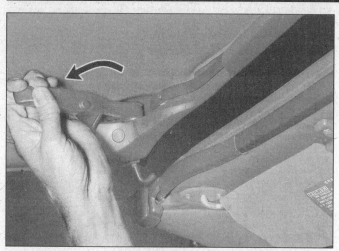

28.10   Release the windshield latch by pulling in the direction indicated . . .

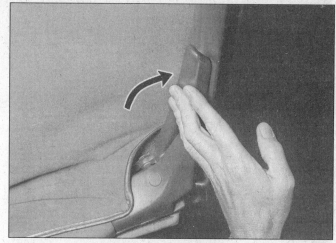

28.11   . . . open the top about seven inches and push the latch back to the locked position. Failure to close the latch may result in damage to the top

6   To remove the drivers side speaker follow the procedure for the removal of the steering column cover (see Section 23).
7   Further speakers are installed in the door panels. To remove them follow the door trim panel removal procedure (see Section 13).

Rear speakers

8   Rear speakers are mounted either on the package shelf or in the rear quarter trim panel.
9   Remove them by gently prying the cover off using a small screwdriver. Be sure to wrap the screwdrivers tip in tape to avoid scratching the trim.
10   Remove any retaining screws, pull the speaker forward and disconnect the electrical connection.
11   Installation is the reverse of the removal procedure.

26   Seat belts - check

1   Check the seat belts, buckles, latch plates and guide loops for any obvious damage or signs of wear.
2   Make sure the seat belt reminder light comes on when the key is turned on.
3   The seat belts are designed to lock up during a sudden stop or impact, yet allow free movement during normal driving. The retractors should hold the belt against your chest while driving and rewind the belt when the buckle is unlatched.
4   If any of the above checks reveal problems with the seat-belt system, replace parts as necessary.

27   Radiator grille - removal and installation

1   If necessary for access remove the radiator shroud cover (see Chapter 3, illustration 4.19).
2   Disengage the grille retaining clips with a pair of needle-nose pliers. On some models, the center of the grille may be retained by two screws instead of clips.
3   Once all of the retaining clips are disengaged, pull the grille out and remove it.
4   To install the grille, press it into place until the clips lock in position].

28   Convertible top - general information

Maintenance

1   Do not run convertible models through automatic car washes, especially those with high pressure water and rotating brushes.
2   Periodically wash the top with mild soap suds, lukewarm water and a sponge. If further cleaning is required a mild foaming cleaner and a soft bristle handbrush may be used.
3   The rear window is made of pliable plastic and care should be taken to avoid scratching it. Wash the window with warm or cold (never hot) water, a mild soap and a soft cloth, do not use solvents or harsh cleaning agents. Clean the cloth frequently and do not rub heavily, rinse the window thoroughly to avoid soap streaks. Never use a scraper or de-icing chemicals to remove ice or snow, instead use warm water.
4   Wait until the top and rear window are completely dry before lowering the top. Lowering the top while damp or wet may result in interior water damage and water stains or mildew forming on the top.

General precautions

5   Keep hands away from the side roof rail hinges when raising or lowering the top and make sure that the top latching handles are in the closed position when lowering the top. Make sure there are no items between the rear seat back and the top stowage area when lowering or raising the top.
6   Do not open the top if the top is damp or wet, or if the rear window is dirty. If the outside temperature is below 41°F (5°C) do not lower or raise the top. To open or close the top in cold weather, warm the interior and the top in a heated garage before operating the top mechanism.
7   Always ensure that the top is either fully closed and latched, or completely open and stowed, never drive the vehicle with the top partially open. Do not sit or place excessive weight on the top at any time.

Opening and closing the top

Refer to illustrations 28.10, 28.11, 28.13 and 28.16
8   Ensure that you are familiar with the precautions listed above before operating the top mechanism.
9   Set the park brake and put the transmission in neutral (manual transmissions) or park (automatic transmissions). Ensure that the ignition is on and lower all side windows and the sun visors.
10   Unhook the tops windshield latches and open the top by pressing the top control switch (see illustration).
11   When the top is about 7 inches (18 cm) from the windshield close the tops windshield latch (see illustration) and continue opening the top until it is all the way down. Failure to close the windshield latches may damage the top.
12   To cover the top when it is fully open, pull the rear seatback forward and remove the top cover from the boot.

11

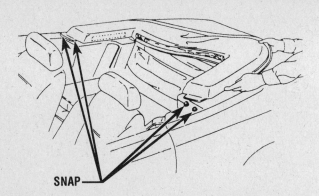

28.13   Snap the retaining clips onto the fasteners (arrows)

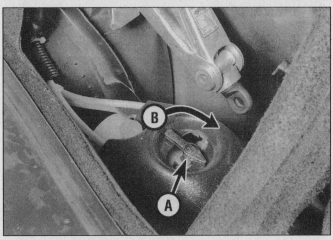

28.16   To operate the top manually twist the release valve switch (A) in the direction of the arrow (B) by 90°

13   Snap the covers forward retention snaps into place **(see illustration)**, secure the rubber retaining strip to the body and return the seatback to the upright position. Ensure the rear seatback has hooked onto the cover and gently rock the seatback to ensure it has locked securely.
14   To return the top to the closed position reverse the opening procedure.
15   If the need arises it is possible to open and close the top manually. Ensure that the car is in neutral (manual transmission) or "P" (au-

tomatic transmission), set the parking brake and lower the side windows and sun visors. If the battery is discharged and it is not possible to lower the windows, open the doors fully.
16   In the trunk behind the right trim panel is a manual release valve **(see illustration)**. Twist the release valve clockwise 90o, and lower or raise the top manually.

Chapter 12 Chassis electrical system

Contents

1 General information

The electrical system is a 12-volt, negative ground type. Power for the lights and all electrical accessories is supplied by a lead/acid-type battery which is charged by the alternator.

This Chapter covers repair and service procedures for the various electrical components not associated with the engine. Information on the battery, alternator, distributor and starter motor can be found in Chapter 5.

It should be noted that when portions of the electrical system are serviced, the cable should be disconnected from the negative battery terminal to prevent electrical shorts and/or fires. **Caution:** *If the stereo in your vehicle is equipped with an anti-theft system, refer to the information on page 0-15 at the front of this manual before detaching the cable.*

2 Electrical troubleshooting - general information

A typical electrical circuit consists of an electrical component, any switches, relays, motors, fuses, fusible links or circuit breakers related to that component and the wiring and electrical connectors that link the component to both the battery and the chassis. To help you pinpoint an electrical circuit problem, wiring diagrams are included at the end of this book.

Before tackling any troublesome electrical circuit, first study the appropriate wiring diagrams to get a complete understanding of what makes up that individual circuit. Trouble spots, for instance, can often be narrowed down by noting if other components related to the circuit are operating properly. If several components or circuits fail at one time, chances are the problem is in a fuse or ground connection, because several circuits are often routed through the same fuse and ground connections.

Electrical problems usually stem from simple causes, such as loose or corroded connections, a blown fuse, a melted fusible link or a bad relay. Visually inspect the condition of all fuses, wires and connections in a problem circuit before troubleshooting it.

If testing instruments are going to be utilized, use the diagrams to plan ahead of time where you will make the necessary connections in order to accurately pinpoint the trouble spot.

The basic tools needed for electrical troubleshooting include a circuit tester or voltmeter (a 12-volt bulb with a set of test leads can also be used), a continuity tester, which includes a bulb, battery and set of test leads, and a jumper wire, preferably with a circuit breaker incorporated, which can be used to bypass electrical components. Before attempting to locate a problem with test instruments, use the wiring diagram(s) to decide where to make the connections.

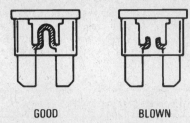

GOOD   BLOWN

3.3   The fuses used in these models can be checked visually to determine if they are blown

Voltage checks

Voltage checks should be performed if a circuit is not functioning properly. Connect one lead of a circuit tester to either the negative battery terminal or a known good ground. Connect the other lead to a electrical connector in the circuit being tested, preferably nearest to the battery or fuse. If the bulb of the tester lights, voltage is present, which means that the part of the circuit between the electrical connector and the battery is problem free. Continue checking the rest of the circuit in the same fashion. When you reach a point at which no voltage is present, the problem lies between that point and the last test point with voltage. Most of the time the problem can be traced to a loose connection. **Note:** *Keep in mind that some circuits receive voltage only when the ignition key is in the Accessory or Run position.*

Finding a short

One method of finding shorts in a circuit is to remove the fuse and connect a test light or voltmeter in its place to the fuse terminals. There should be no voltage present in the circuit. Move the wiring harness from side to side while watching the test light. If the bulb goes on, there is a short to ground somewhere in that area, probably where the insulation has rubbed through. The same test can be performed on each component in the circuit, even a switch.

Ground check

Perform a ground test to check whether a component is properly grounded. Disconnect the battery and connect one lead of a self-powered test light, known as a continuity tester, to a known good ground. **Caution:** *If the stereo in your vehicle is equipped with an anti-theft system, refer to the information on page 0-15 at the front of this manual before detaching the cable.* Connect the other lead to the wire or ground connection being tested. If the bulb goes on, the ground is good. If the bulb does not go on, the ground is not good.

Continuity check

A continuity check is done to determine if there are any breaks in a circuit - if it is passing electricity properly. With the circuit off (no power in the circuit), a self-powered continuity tester can be used to check the circuit. Connect the test leads to both ends of the circuit (or to the "power" end and a good ground), and if the test light comes on the circuit is passing current properly. If the light doesn't come on, there is a break somewhere in the circuit. The same procedure can be used to test a switch, by connecting the continuity tester to the power in and power out sides of the switch. With the switch turned On, the test light should come on.

Finding an open circuit

When diagnosing for possible open circuits, it is often difficult to locate them by sight because oxidation or terminal misalignment are hidden by the electrical connectors. Merely wiggling an electrical connector on a sensor or in the wiring harness may correct the open circuit condition. Remember this when an open circuit is indicated when troubleshooting a circuit. Intermittent problems may also be caused by oxidized or loose connections.

Electrical troubleshooting is simple if you keep in mind that all electrical circuits are basically electricity running from the battery, through the wires, switches, relays, fuses and fusible links to each

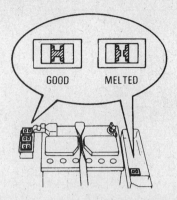

GOOD   MELTED

4.2   Fusible links can be checked visually to determine if they're melted

electrical component (light bulb, motor, etc.) and to ground, from which it is passed back to the battery. Any electrical problem is an interruption in the flow of electricity to and from the battery.

3   Fuses - general information

Refer to illustration 3.3

The electrical circuits of the vehicle are protected by a combination of fuses, circuit breakers and fusible links. The fuse blocks are located under the instrument panel on the left and right sides of the dashboard, and in the engine compartment next to the battery and in front of the ABS actuator **(see illustrations 6.2a and 6.2c)**.

Each of the fuses is designed to protect a specific circuit, and the various circuits are identified on the fuse panel itself.

Miniaturized fuses are employed in the fuse block. These compact fuses, with blade terminal design, allow fingertip removal and replacement. If an electrical component fails, always check the fuse first. A blown fuse is easily identified through the clear plastic body. Visually inspect the element for evidence of damage **(see illustration)**. If a continuity check is called for, the blade terminal tips are exposed in the fuse body.

Be sure to replace blown fuses with the correct type. Fuses of different ratings are physically interchangeable, but only fuses of the proper rating should be used. Replacing a fuse with one of a higher or lower value than specified is not recommended. Each electrical circuit needs a specific amount of protection. The amperage value of each fuse is molded into the fuse body.

If the replacement fuse immediately fails, don't replace it again until the cause of the problem is isolated and corrected. In most cases, this will be a short circuit in the wiring caused by a broken or deteriorated wire.

4   Fusible links - general information

Refer to illustration 4.2

Some circuits are protected by fusible links. The links are used in circuits which are not ordinarily fused, such as the ignition circuit.

The fusible links on these models are similar to fuses in that they can be visually checked to determine if they are melted **(see illustration)**.

To replace a fusible link, first disconnect the negative cable from the battery. **Caution:** *If the stereo in your vehicle is equipped with an anti-theft system, refer to the information on page 0-15 at the front of this manual before detaching the cable.* Unplug the burned-out link and replace it with a new one (available from your dealer or auto parts store). Always determine the cause for the overload which melted the fusible link before installing a new one.

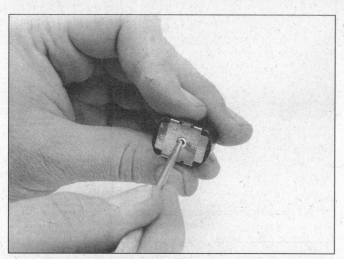

5.3   Insert a pin or paper clip into the circuit breaker reset hole and push it in to reset it

5   Circuit breakers - general information

Refer to illustration 5.3

On early models circuit breakers protect components such as power windows, power door locks and headlights. Some circuit breakers are located in the fuse boxes **(see illustration 6.2c)**.

Because on some models the circuit breaker resets itself automatically, an electrical overload in a circuit breaker protected system will cause the circuit to fail momentarily, then come back on. If the circuit does not come back on, check it immediately. Note, however, that some circuit breakers must be reset manually. Once the condition is corrected, the circuit breaker will resume its normal function.

To reset a manual circuit breaker, first disconnect the cable from the negative battery terminal. **Caution:** *If the stereo in your vehicle is equipped with an anti-theft system, refer to the information on page 0-15 at the front of this manual before detaching the cable.* Remove the circuit breaker, insert a pin into the reset hole and push in **(see illustration)**. Reinstall the circuit breaker.

6   Relays - general information

Refer to illustrations 6.2a, 6.2b, 6.2c, 6.2d and 6.2e

Several electrical accessories in the vehicle use relays to transmit the electrical signal to the component. If the relay is defective, that component will not operate properly.

The various relays are mounted in several locations throughout the vehicle **(see illustrations)**.

If a faulty relay is suspected, it can be removed and tested by a dealer or other qualified shop. Defective relays must be replaced as a unit.

7   Turn signal/hazard flashers - check and replacement

Warning: *On airbag-equipped models, always disconnect the negative battery cable when working in the vicinity of the instrument panel or steering column to avoid the possibility of accidental deployment of the airbag, which could cause personal injury.*
Caution: *If the stereo in your vehicle is equipped with an anti-theft system, refer to the information on page 0-15 at the front of this manual before detaching the cable.*

1   The turn signal/hazard flasher, a small canister shaped unit located behind the left kick panel **(see illustrations 6.2c and 6.2e)**, flashes the turn signals.

2   When the flasher unit is functioning properly, an audible click can be heard during its operation. If the turn signals fail on one side or the

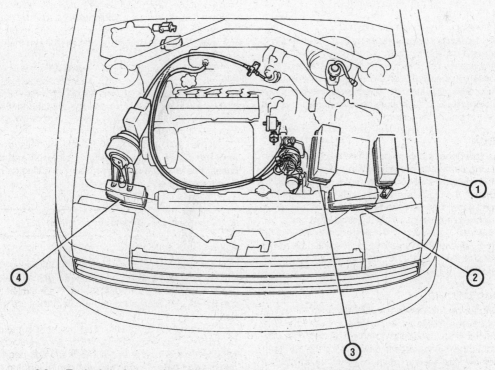

6.2a   Typical engine compartment relay and fuse locations (1986 through 1989 models)

1	No. 2 fuse and relay block (3S-GE & 2S-E engines)	3	No. 2 fuse and relay block (3S-FE engine)
2	No. 5 fuse and relay block (without A.B.S.)	4	No. 5 fuse and relay block (with A.B.S.)

12

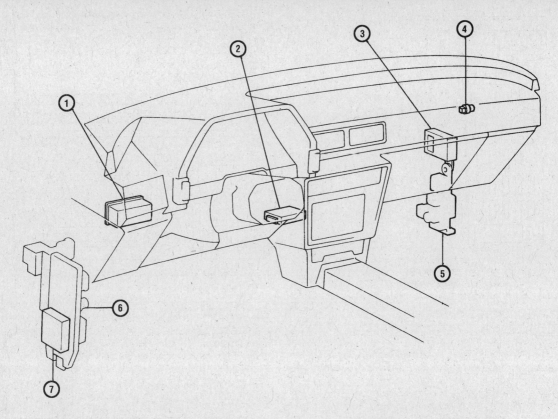

6.2b   Typical passenger compartment relay and fuse locations (1986 through 1989 models)

1	No.3 junction box	5	No.4 Fuse and relay block
2	Light retractor control relay	6	No.1 Fuse and relay block
3	Cruise control computer	7	Integration relay
4	Fog light relay (3S-FE & 3S-GE engines)		

other and the flasher unit does not make its characteristic clicking sound, a faulty turn signal bulb is indicated.

3   If both turn signals fail to blink, the problem may be due to a blown fuse, a faulty flasher unit, a broken switch or a loose or open connection. If a quick check of the fuse box indicates that the turn signal fuse has blown, check the wiring for a short before installing a new fuse.

4   To replace the flasher, simply pull it out of the fuse block or wiring harness.

5   Make sure that the replacement unit is identical to the original. Compare the old one to the new one before installing it.

6   Installation is the reverse of removal.

8   Steering column switches - removal and installation

Combination switch

Refer to illustrations 8.4 and 8.5

Warning: *On airbag-equipped models, always disconnect the negative battery cable when working in the vicinity of the instrument panel or steering column to avoid the possibility of accidental deployment of the airbag, which could cause personal injury.*

Caution: *On all 1990 and later models, wait at least 30 seconds after disconnecting the negative cable from the battery before beginning this procedure.*

1   Disconnect the negative cable at the battery. **Caution:** *If the stereo in your vehicle is equipped with an anti-theft system, refer to the information on page 0-15 at the front of this manual before detaching the cable.*

2   Remove the steering wheel (see Chapter 10).

3   Remove the lower finish panel and steering column cover (see Chapter 11).

4   Remove the combination switch retaining screws **(see illustration)**.

5   Trace the wiring harness down the steering column to the connector. Release the wiring retainer clamps, if equipped **(see illustration)**, unplug the connector and slide the switch up off the column.

6   Installation is the reverse of removal.

Turn signal/headlight control switch

Refer to illustration 8.8, 8.9a and 8.9b

7   Remove the combination switch (see above).

8   Remove the control switch retaining screws **(see illustration)**

9   Disconnect the lever locking tab and push the lever forward and up to free it **(see illustrations)**.

10   Disconnect the switch wiring terminals from the combination switch electrical connector (see Steps 19 through 23).

11   Installation is the reverse of removal.

Cruise control switch

12   Remove the two retaining screws.

13   Detach the electrical connector and the switch and lift it off the combination switch.

14   Disconnect the switch wiring terminals from the combination switch electrical connector (see Steps 19 through 23).

15   Installation is the reverse of removal.

Wiper/washer control switch

Refer to illustrations 8.17a and 8.17b

16   Remove the retention screws from the front of the combination switch **(see illustration 8.8)**.

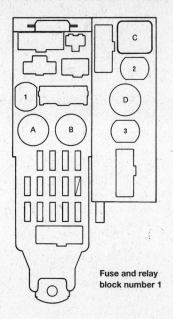

Fuse and relay
block number 1

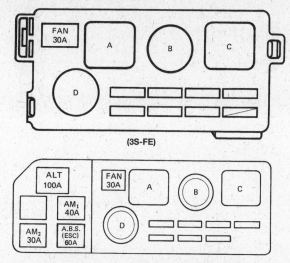

Fuse and relay block number 2 (3S-GE and 2S-FE)

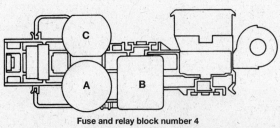

Fuse and relay block number 4

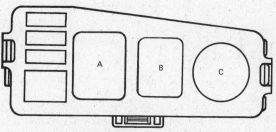

Fuse and relay block number 5

6.2c   Individual relay and circuit breaker locations (1986 through 1989 models)

A/C fan No.2 relay	No.5, A		Fan No.1 relay	No.2, D
A/C magnetic clutch relay	No.5, B		Headlight control relay	No.2, C
A/C fan No.3 relay	No.5, C		Heater circuit breaker	No.4, C
Clutch start relay	No.1, D		Heater relay	No.4, B
Defogger circuit breaker	No.1, 1		Horn relay	No.4, A
Defogger relay	No.1, A		Power window circuit breaker	No.1, 3
Door lock circuit breaker	No.1, 2		Taillight control relay	No.1, B
Engine main relay	No.2, A		Turn signal flasher relay	No.1, C
EFI main relay	No.2, B			

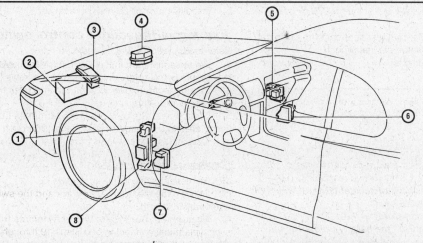

6.2d   Typical fuse and relay locations (1990 and later models)

1	No.1 fuse and relay block		5	No.4 fuse and relay block
2	Battery		6	No.3 relay block
3	No.2 fuse and junction block		7	No.2 relay block
4	No.5 relay block		8	No.1 junction block

12

**Junction block no. 1
and relay block no. 1**

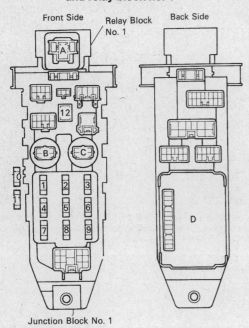

Junction block no. 2

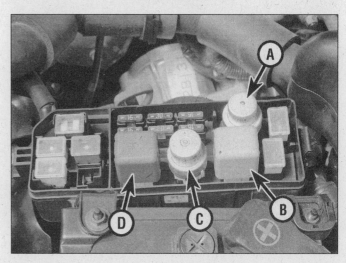

Relay block no. 2   **Relay block no. 3**

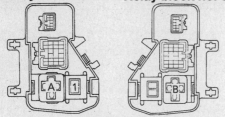

Relay block no. 4

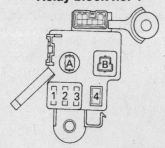

Relay block no. 5

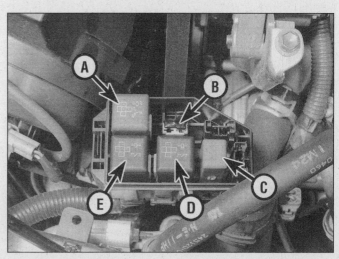

6.2e   Individual relay location (1990 and later models)

Relay	Relay block	Relay	Relay block
A/C fan No.2 relay	No.5 A	Sub fan	No.5 B
A/C fan No.3 relay	No.5 C	Taillight relay	No.1 C
A/C MG	No.5 D	Turn signal flasher relay	No.1 A
Defogger relay	No.1 B	**Relay**	**Junction block**
Front fog light control relay	No.3 B	EFI relay	No.2 C
Heater main relay	No.4 B	Engine main relay	No.2 B
Horn relay	No.5 E	Fan No.1 relay	No.2 A
Power main	No.2 A	Headlight control relay	No.2 D
Starter relay	No.4 A	Integration	No.1 D

17   Remove the four rear retention screws and gently pry the connection free **(see illustrations)**.
18   Disconnect the switch wiring terminals from the combination switch electrical connector (see Steps 19 through 23). Installation is the reverse of removal.

Electrical connectors
Refer to illustrations 8.20, 8.21a, 8.21b and 8.22

19   Trace the wiring harness from the switch be disconnected to the combination switch electrical connector. It may be necessary to de-

8.4   Remove the four combination switch mounting screws (arrows)

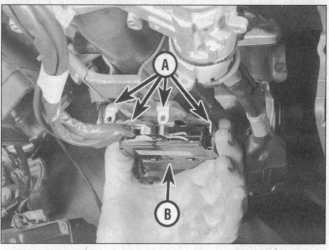

8.5   Unclip the four wiring retainer clamps (A), unplug the connector (B) and slip the combination switch off the steering column

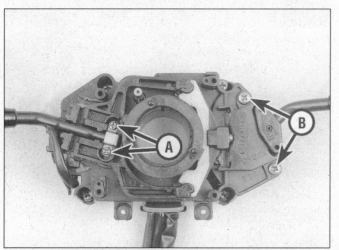

8.8   Both the turn signal/headlight control switch and the wiper/washer control switch have retaining screws at the front of the combination switch

A Turn signal/headlight control switch retention screws
B Wiper/washer control switch retention screws

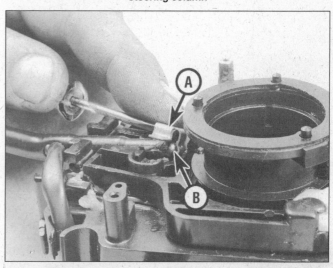

8.9a   Having removed the turn signal/headlight switch retention screws, pry the locking tab (A) up. Take care not to lose the small ball bearing (B)

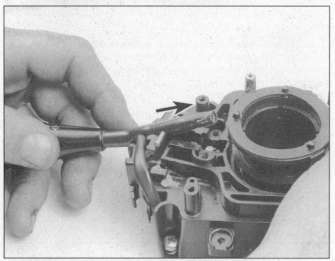

8.9b   To remove the lever push it forward and up (arrow)

8.17a   Remove the retention screws mounted at the rear of the wiper/washer control switch (arrows) . . .

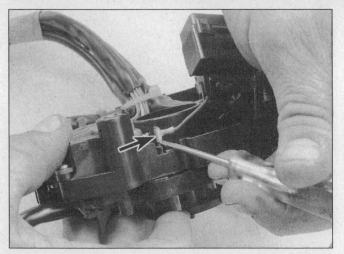

8.17b   . . . and gently pry the connector free

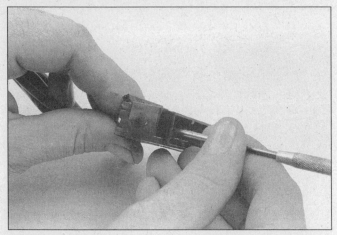

8.21a   Insert a small screwdriver or punch into the connector . . .

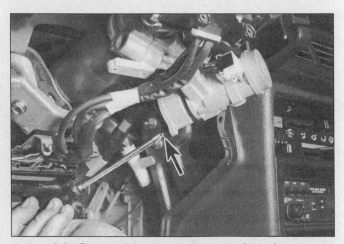

9.4   Remove the rear retention screw (arrow) . . .

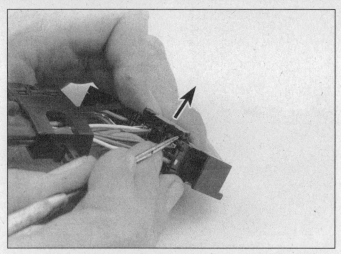

8.20   Use a small screwdriver or punch to push the combination switch connector up (arrow) for access to the terminals

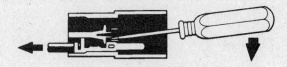

8.21b   . . . and pry the locking lug down so the terminal can be disconnected

8.22   Push in on the connector collar until the connector snaps into place

with a small screwdriver until the locking lug snaps into place **(see illustration)**.
23   Snap the connector cover shut to lock the terminals.

---

9   Ignition switch key lock cylinder - removal and installation

---

Refer to illustrations 9.4, 9.5, 9.6a and 9.6b
Warning: *On airbag-equipped models, always disconnect the negative battery cable when working in the vicinity of the instrument panel or steering column to avoid the possibility of accidental deployment of the airbag, which could cause personal injury.*
Caution: *On all 1990 and later models, wait at least 30 seconds after disconnecting the negative cable from the battery before beginning this procedure.*
1   Disconnect the negative cable at the battery. **Caution:** *If the stereo in your vehicle is equipped with an anti-theft system, refer to the information on page 0-15 at the front of this manual before detaching the cable.*
2   Remove the steering wheel (see Chapter 10).
3   Remove the lower finish panel and the steering column cover (see Chapter 11).
4   Remove the single retaining screw mounted on the rear of the switch **(see illustration)**.
5   Unclip the electrical connector **(see illustration)**.
6   With the key in the Accessory position, insert a pin in the hole in the casting, pull the lock cylinder straight out and remove it from the steering column **(see illustrations)**.
7   Installation is the reverse of removal.

tach or cut some of the wiring ties or straps to separate the wires of a particular switch from the harness. Mark the wires and combination switch terminals with pieces of tape so that only the wires involved with a specific switch are disconnected.
20   Use a small screwdriver or punch to pry the combination switch cover up for access to the terminals **(see illustration)**.
21   Insert a small screwdriver or punch into the connector and pry the locking lug down, disconnect the terminal and then pull it out to remove it **(see illustrations)**.
22   To connect the terminal, insert it into the connector and push in

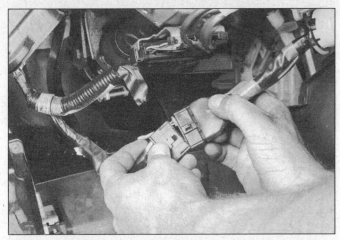

9.5 . . . and disconnect the electrical connector to remove the ignition switch

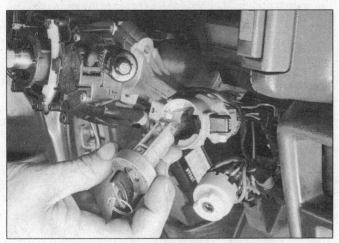

9.6b . . . and pull the cylinder straight out

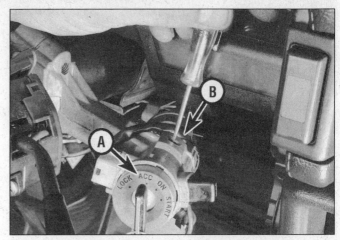

9.6a To remove the ignition lock cylinder place the key in the "ACC" position (A), press on the locking tab (B) . . .

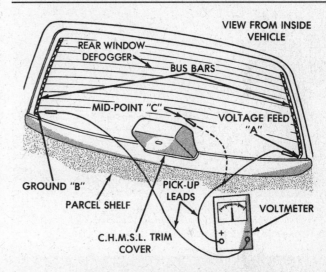

11.4 Rear window defogger test points

10 Rear window defogger switch - removal and installation

Warning: *On airbag-equipped models, always disconnect the negative battery cable when working in the vicinity of the instrument panel or steering column to avoid the possibility of accidental deployment of the airbag, which could cause personal injury.*
Caution: *On all 1990 and later models, wait at least 30 seconds after disconnecting the negative cable from the battery before beginning this procedure.*

1989 and earlier models

1   Detach the cable from the negative battery terminal. **Caution:** *If the stereo in your vehicle is equipped with an anti-theft system, refer to the information on page 0-15 at the front of this manual before detaching the cable.*
2   Squeeze the outside of the switch and pull it gently free.
3   Unplug the electrical connector from the rear window defogger switch.
4   Installation is the reverse of removal.

1990 and later models

5   Detach the cable from the negative battery terminal. **Caution:** *If the stereo in your vehicle is equipped with an anti-theft system, refer to the information on page 0-15 at the front of this manual before detaching the cable.*
6   Remove the steering wheel (see Chapter 10).
7   Remove the screws from the instrument cluster trim panel and remove the trim panel (see Chapter 11).
8   Unplug the electrical connector from the rear window defogger switch.

9   Pop the switch from the instrument cluster trim panel.
10   Installation is the reverse of removal.

11 Rear window defogger - check and repair

Refer to illustrations 11.4 and 11.14

1   The rear window defogger consists of a number of horizontal elements baked onto the glass surface.
2   Small breaks in the element can be repaired without removing the rear window.

Check

3   Turn the ignition switch and defogger system switches On.
4   Ground the negative lead of a voltmeter to terminal B and the positive lead to terminal A **(see illustration)**.
5   The voltmeter should read between 10 and 15 volts. If the reading is lower there is a poor ground connection.
6   Connect the negative lead to a good body ground. The reading should stay the same.
7   Connect the negative lead to terminal B, then touch each grid line at the mid-point with the positive lead.
8   The reading should be approximately six volts. If the reading is 0, there is a break between the mid-point "C" and terminal "A".
9   A 10 to 14 volt reading is an indication of a break between mid-

12

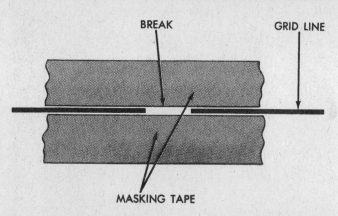

11.14   To repair a broken grid, first apply a strip of masking tape to either side of the grid to mask off the area

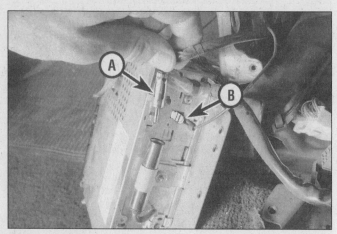

12.4   . . . pull the unit from the mounting bracket, disconnect the antenna (A) and the electrical connector (B)

point "C" and ground B.

10   Move the lead toward the break; the voltage will change when the break is crossed.

Repair

11   Repair the break in the line using a repair kit specifically recommended for this purpose, such as Mopar Repair Kit No. 4267922 (or equivalent). Included in this kit is plastic conductive epoxy.

12   Prior to repairing a break, turn of the system and allow it to de-energize for a few minutes.

13   Lightly buff the element area with fine steel wool, then clean it thoroughly with rubbing alcohol.

14   Use masking tape to mask off the area being repaired **(see illustration)**.

15   Mix the epoxy thoroughly, following the instructions provided with the repair kit.

16   Apply the epoxy material to the slit in the masking tape, overlapping the undamaged area about 3/4-inch on either end.

17   Allow the repair to cure for 24 hours before removing the tape and using the system.

12   Stereo and speakers - removal and installation

Caution: *On all 1990 and later models, wait at least 30 seconds after disconnecting the negative cable from the battery before beginning this procedure.*

1   Disconnect the negative cable at the battery. **Caution:** *If the stereo in your vehicle is equipped with an anti-theft system, refer to the information on page 0-15 at the front of this manual before detaching the cable.*

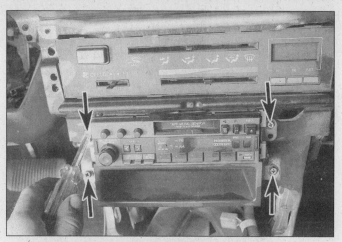

12.3   Remove the mounting screws (arrows) . . .

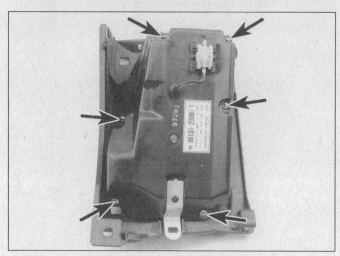

12.8   If equipped with a sound box remove the units retaining screws (arrows) to access the speaker

Radio

Refer to illustrations 12.3 and 12.4, 12.8

2   Remove the center trim panel (see Chapter 11).

3   Remove the radio mounting screws or bolts **(see illustration)**.

4   Pull the radio out, reach behind it, unplug the electrical connector and the antenna lead and lift the radio from the instrument panel **(see illustration)**.

5   Installation is the reverse of removal.

Speakers

6   Remove the speaker covers (see Chapter 11).

7   Remove the speaker retaining screws, pull the speaker forward and unplug the electrical connector to remove the speaker.

8   If so equipped, remove the speaker sound-box screws to access the speaker **(see illustration)**.

9   Installation is the reverse of removal.

13   Headlights - removal and installation

Refer to illustrations 13.4a, 13.4b and 13.5

1   Turn the headlights on, then disconnect the negative cable from the battery and remove the RTR (30A) fuse. **Caution:** *If the stereo in your vehicle is equipped with an anti-theft system, refer to the information on page 0-15 at the front of this manual before detaching the cable. Also,* **Caution:** *On all 1990 and later models, wait at least 30 seconds after disconnecting the negative cable from the battery, before beginning this procedure.*

13.4a Remove the side (arrows) . . .

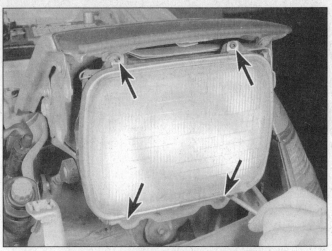

13.4b . . . and front (arrows) retention screws

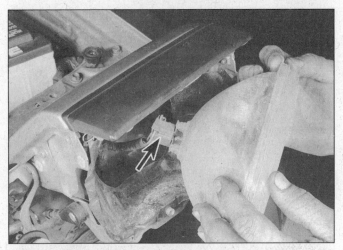

13.5 Pull the headlight forward (if it is a halogen type bulb avoid touching the lens and wear eye protection) and disconnect the electrical connector (arrow)

2   Remove the headlight trim, then remove the headlight retainer screws **(see illustrations)**. Don't disturb the adjustment screws.
3   Pull the headlight out, unplug the electrical connector **(see illustration)** and remove the headlight assembly.
4   Installation is the reverse of removal.

14 Headlights - adjustment

Refer to illustrations 14.1 and 14.2
Note: *It is important that the headlights are aimed correctly. If adjusted incorrectly they could blind the driver of an oncoming vehicle and cause a serious accident or seriously reduce your ability to see the road. The headlights should be checked for proper aim every 12 months and any time a new headlight is installed or front end body work is performed. It should be emphasized that the following procedure is only an interim step which will provide temporary adjustment until the headlights can be adjusted by a properly equipped shop.*
1   Early body style headlights have an adjusting screw on the top controlling up-and-down movement **(see illustration)** and one on the side controlling left-and-right movement **(see illustration 14.2)**.
2   Late models also have two adjustment screws, one to the side controlling left-and-right movement and one below the light for up-and-down movement **(see illustration)**.
3   There are several methods of adjusting the headlights. The simplest method requires a blank wall 25 feet in front of the vehicle and a level floor.

14.1 On early models up-and-down adjustments are controlled by the upper adjustment screw (arrow) . . .

4   Position masking tape vertically on the wall in reference to the vehicle centerline and the centerlines of both headlights.
5   Position a horizontal tape line in reference to the centerline of all the headlights. **Note:** *It may be easier to position the tape on the wall with the vehicle parked only a few inches away.*
6   Adjustment should be made with the vehicle sitting level, the gas tank half-full and no unusually heavy load in the vehicle.
7   Starting with the low beam adjustment, position the high intensity zone so it is two inches below the horizontal line and two inches to the right of the headlight vertical line. Twist the adjustment screws until the desired level has been achieved.
8   With the high beams on, the high intensity zone should be vertically centered with the exact center just below the horizontal line. **Note:** *It may not be possible to position the headlight aim exactly for both high and low beams. If a compromise must be made, keep in mind that the low beams are the most used and have the greatest effect on driver safety.*
9   Have the headlights adjusted by a dealer service department at the earliest opportunity.

15 Bulb replacement

Headlight bulb
Warning: *Some models are equipped with halogen gas filled bulbs which are under pressure and may shatter if the surface is scratched or the bulb is dropped. Wear eye protection and handle the bulbs carefully, grasping only the base whenever possible. Do not touch the surface of the bulb with your fingers because the oil from your skin could cause it to overheat and fail prematurely. If you do touch the bulb sur-*

12

14.2 . . . on later models this function is performed by an adjustment screw (A) under the headlight. On all models right-and-left adjustments are made by an adjusting screw (B) to the side of the light

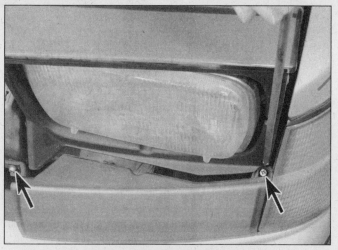

15.2a Remove the lens retaining screws . . .

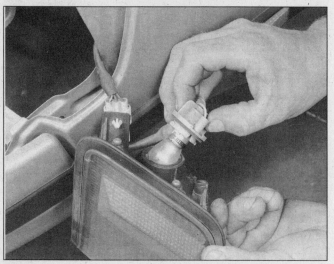

15.2b . . . pull the lens free and twist the bulb counterclockwise to free it

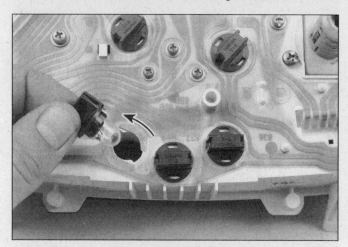

15.4 To remove instrument cluster bulbs twist the bulb holder counterclockwise and pull it free

face, clean it with rubbing alcohol.

1   All headlights on these models are a sealed beam type, therefore, follow the replacement procedure outlined in Section 13.

Miscellaneous bulbs

Refer to illustrations 15.2a, 15.2b, 15.4, 15.5a and 15.5b

2   The lenses of many lights are held in place by screws. To gain access to the bulbs in these assemblies, simply remove the lenses **(see illustrations)**.

3   The lenses of some light assemblies are held in place by clips. You can remove them by unsnapping them or by prying them off with a small screwdriver.

4   Some bulbs can be removed simply by pushing them in and turning them counterclockwise **(see illustration)**.

5   Other bulbs are installed in bulb holders. To release a bulb holder, push it in, turn it counterclockwise and pull it out **(see illustrations)**.

6   Other holders can be unclipped from the terminals or pulled straight out of the socket.

7   To gain access to the instrument cluster illumination lights **(see illustration 15.4)**, the instrument cluster will have to be removed (see Section 17).

---

16   Windshield wiper motor - removal and installation

Refer to illustration 16.4

Warning: *On all 1990 and later models, wait at least 30 seconds after disconnecting the negative cable from the battery before beginning this procedure.*

1   Disconnect the cable from the negative terminal of the battery. **Caution:** *If the stereo in your vehicle is equipped with an anti-theft system, refer to the information on page 0-15 at the front of this manual before detaching the cable.*

2   Following the procedure in Chapter 3, remove the heater core housing.

3   Disconnect the linkage from the wiper motor arm.

4   From inside the engine compartment, unplug the electrical connector and remove the mounting bolts **(see illustration)**. Lift the motor up and tilt it to allow the wiper motor arm to pass through the firewall.

5   Installation is the reverse of removal.

---

17   Instrument cluster - removal and installation

Refer to illustrations 17.3 and 17.4

Warning: *On all 1990 and later models, wait at least 30 seconds after disconnecting the negative cable from the battery before beginning this procedure.*

1   Disconnect the cable from the negative battery. **Caution:** *If the stereo in your vehicle is equipped with an anti-theft system, refer to the*

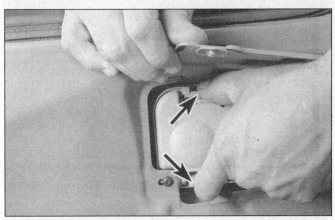

15.5a   To remove tail lights push the clamps (arrows) in and pull the backing free

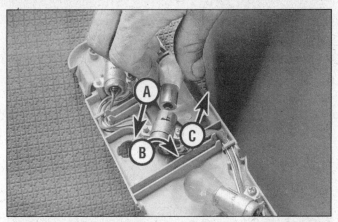

15.5b   Push the bulb in (A), twist it anti-clockwise (B) and pull it free (C)

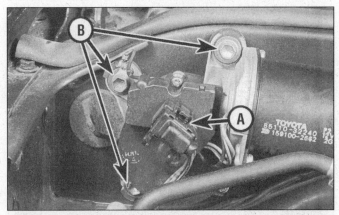

16.4   Unplug the electrical connector (A), remove the bolts (B) and lift the wiper motor off

17.3   Remove the retaining screws (arrows) . . .

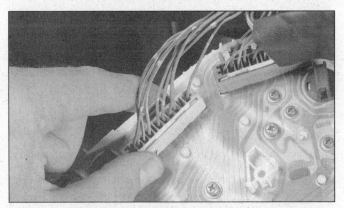

17.4   . . . pull the instrument cluster forward and disconnect all the electrical connectors

information on page 0-15 at the front of this manual before detaching the cable.

2   Remove the instrument cluster trim panel (see Chapter 11).
3   Remove the four retaining screws and pull the cluster forward **(see illustration)**.
4   Pull the connectors from the rear of the instrument cluster **(see illustration)**.
5   Installation is the reverse of the removal procedure.

18   Cruise control system - description and check

The cruise control system maintains vehicle speed by means of a vacuum actuated servo motor located in the engine compartment

which is connected to the throttle linkage by a cable. The system consists of the servo motor, clutch switch, stoplight switch, control switches, a relay and associated vacuum hoses.

Because of the complexity of the cruise control system and the special tools and techniques required for diagnosis and repair, this should be left to a dealer or properly equipped shop. However, it is possible for the home mechanic to make simple checks of the wiring and vacuum connections for minor faults which can be easily repaired. These include:

a) Inspecting the cruise control actuating switches and wiring for broken wires or loose connections.
b) Checking the cruise control fuse.
c) Checking the hoses in the engine compartment for tight connections, cracked hoses and obvious vacuum leaks. The cruise control system is operated by a vacuum so it is critical that all vacuum switches, hoses and connections be secure.

19   Power door lock system - description and check

The power door lock system operates the door lock actuators mounted in each door. The system consists of the switches, actuators and associated wiring. Special tools and techniques are required to fully diagnose this system, and this should be left to a dealer or properly equipped shop. However, it is possible for the home mechanic to make simple checks of the wiring connections and actuators for minor faults which can be easily repaired. These include:

a) Checking the system fuse and/or circuit breaker.
b) Checking the switch wiring for damage or loose connections.
c) Checking the switches for continuity.

12

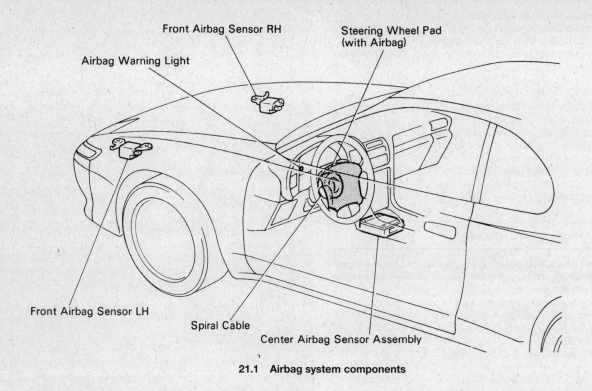

Front Airbag Sensor RH

Steering Wheel Pad
(with Airbag)

Airbag Warning Light

Front Airbag Sensor LH

Spiral Cable

Center Airbag Sensor Assembly

21.1   Airbag system components

d)   Removing the door panel(s) and checking the actuator wiring connections for looseness or damage. Inspect the actuator rods (if equipped) to make sure they are not bent, damaged or binding. The actuator can be checked by applying battery power momentarily. A solid click indicates the solenoid is operating properly.

20   Power window system - description and check

. The power window system operates the electric motors mounted in the doors which lower and raise the windows. The system consists of the control switches, the motors (regulators), glass mechanisms and associated wiring.

Because of the complexity of the power window system and the special tools and techniques required for diagnosis and repair, this should be left to a dealer or properly equipped shop. However, it is possible for the home mechanic to make simple checks of the wiring connections and motors for minor faults which can be easily repaired. These include:

a)   Inspecting the power window actuating switches and wiring for broken wires or loose connections.
b)   Checking the power window fuse and/or circuit breaker.
c)   Removing the door panel(s) and checking the power window motor wiring connections for looseness and damage, and inspecting the glass mechanisms for damage which could cause binding.

21   Airbag - general information

Refer to illustrations 21.1

Later models are equipped with a Supplemental Restraint System (SRS), more commonly known as an airbag. This system is designed to protect the driver from serious injury in the event of a head-on or frontal collision. It consists of an airbag module in the center of the steering wheel, two crash sensors mounted at the front of the vehicle

21.5   When the vehicle is started the "AIRBAG" light should come on for about 6 seconds and then go off. If it fails to go off, have your dealer inspect the vehicle immediately

and a diagnostic module which also contains a crash sensor located inside the passenger compartment **(see illustration)**.

Airbag module

The airbag module contains a housing incorporating the cushion (airbag) and inflator unit. The inflator assembly is mounted on the back of the housing over a hole through which gas is expelled, inflating the bag almost instantaneously when an electrical signal is sent from the system. The specially wound wire that carries this signal to the module is called a spiral cable **(see illustration 21.1)**. The spiral cable is a flat, ribbon like electrically conductive tape which is wound many times so that it can transmit an electrical signal regardless of steering wheel position.

Sensors

The system has three sensors: two crash sensors at the front of the vehicle behind the bumper and above the wheel arches and a safing sensor in the center airbag sensor assembly located under the instrument panel, just in front of the center console.

The front crash sensors are basically pressure sensitive switches that complete an electrical circuit during an impact of sufficient G force. The electrical signal from the crash sensors is sent to the safing sensor in the center airbag sensor assembly, which then completes the circuit and inflates the airbag.

Center Airbag Sensor Assembly (CASA)

The CASA contains the safing sensor and an on-board microprocessor which monitors the operation of the system. It checks this system every time the vehicle is started, causing the "AIRBAG" light to go on **(see illustration)**, then off, if the system is operating properly. If there is a fault in the system, the light will go on and stay on and the CASA will store fault codes indicating the nature of the fault. If the AIRBAG light goes on and stays on, the vehicle should be taken to your dealer immediately for service.

22 Wiring diagrams - general information

Since it isn't possible to include all wiring diagrams for every year covered by this manual, the following diagrams are those that are typical and most commonly needed.

Prior to troubleshooting any circuits, check the fuse and circuit breakers (if equipped) to make sure they are in good condition. Make sure the battery is properly charged and has clean, tight cable connections (see Chapter 1).

When checking the wiring system, make sure that all electrical connectors are clean, with no broken or loose pins. When unplugging an electrical connector, do not pull on the wires, only on the connector housings themselves.

Refer to the accompanying illustration for the wire color codes applicable to your vehicle.

Wiring diagram index

1989 and earlier models

1990 and later models

Wire colors are indicated by an alphabetical code.

B	= Black	L	= Blue	R	= Red
BR	= Brown	LG	= Light Green	V	= Violet
G	= Green	O	= Orange	W	= White
GR	= Gray	P	= Pink	Y	= Yellow

The first letter indicates the basic wire color and the second letter indicates the color of the stripe.

Example: L—Y

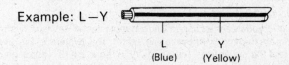

L (Blue)   Y (Yellow)

12

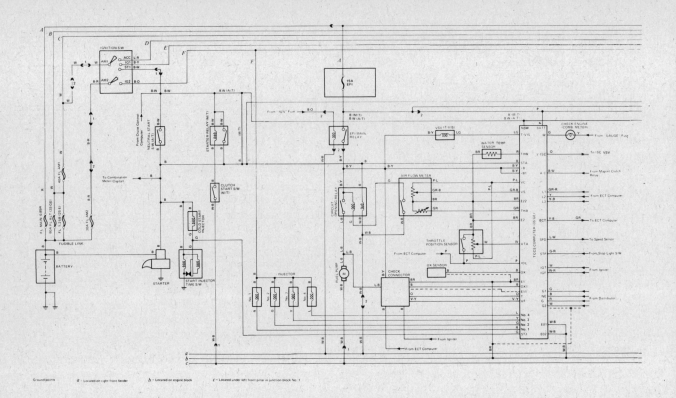

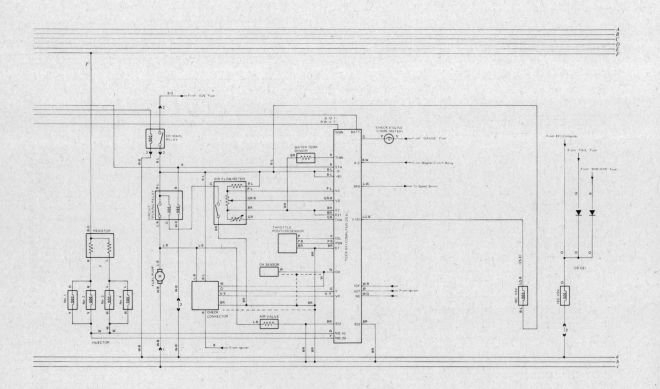

1   Typical early model (2S-E) starting, EFI and idle-up wiring diagram

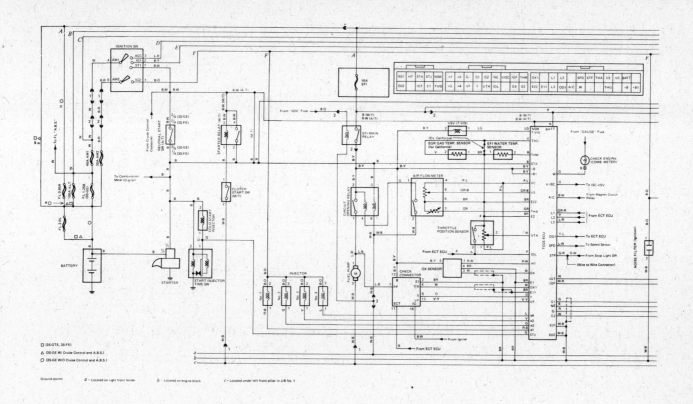

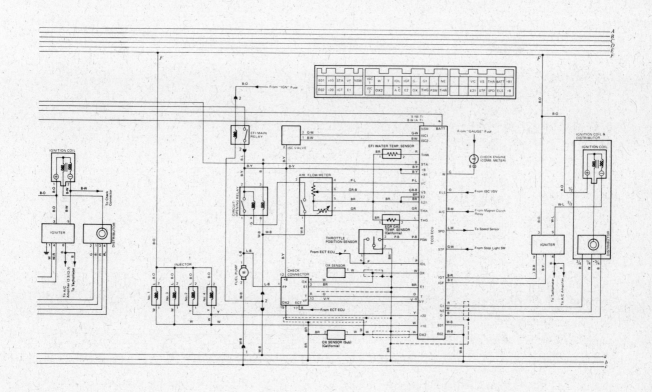

2 Typical early model (3S-FE and 3S-GE) starting and TCCS wiring diagram

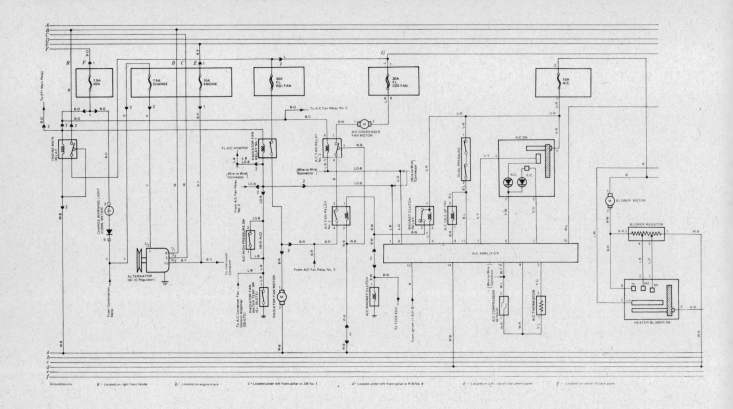

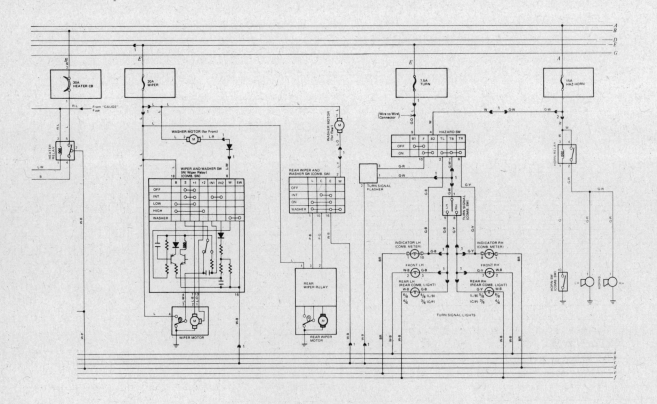

3 Typical early model charging, radiator fan, condenser fan, air conditioning, cooler, heater, wiper and washer, turn signal, hazard and horn wiring diagram

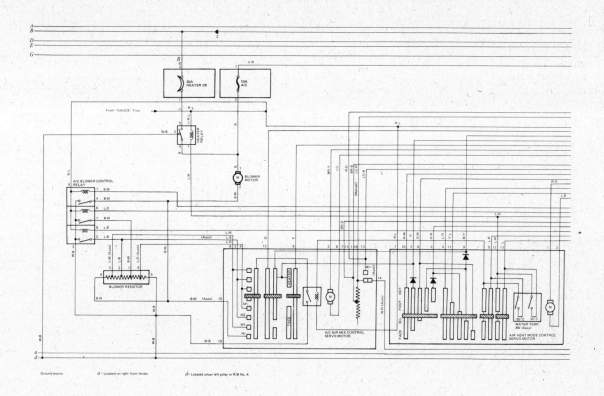

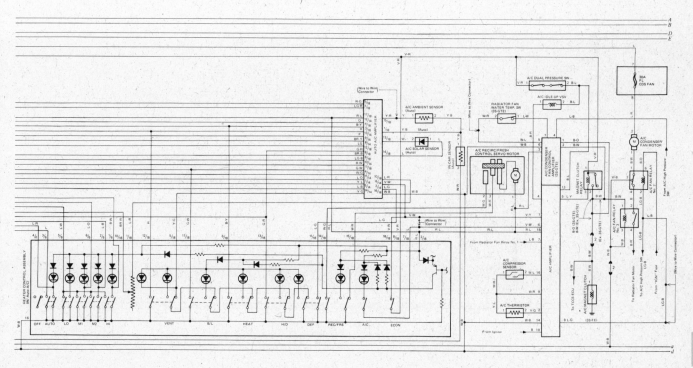

4 Typical early model air conditioning and heater wiring diagram

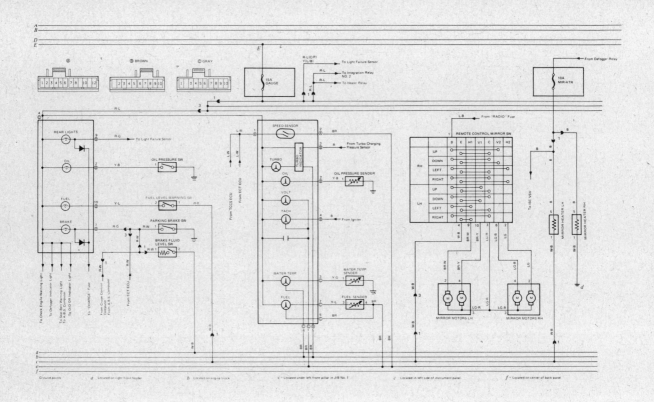

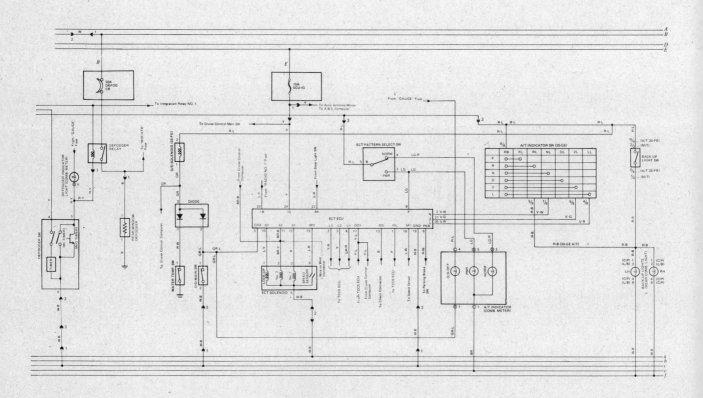

5 Typical early model combination meter, mirror, rear window defogger, overdrive, electronic controlled transmission, automatic transmission indicator and back-up lights wiring diagram

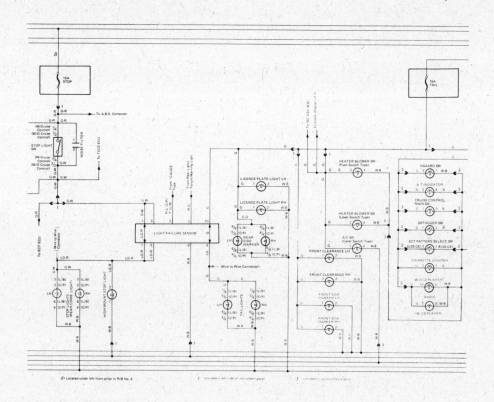

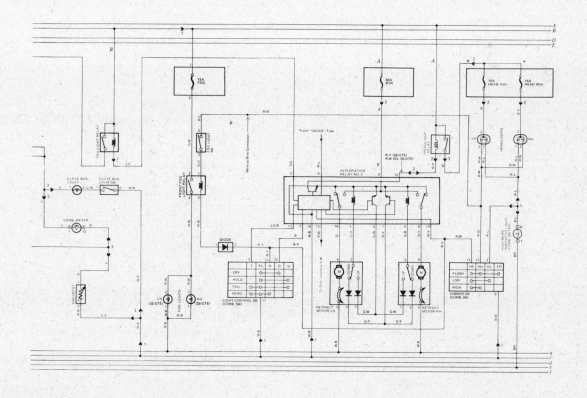

6 Typical early model stop lights, tail lights, illumination, fog lights and headlights wiring diagram

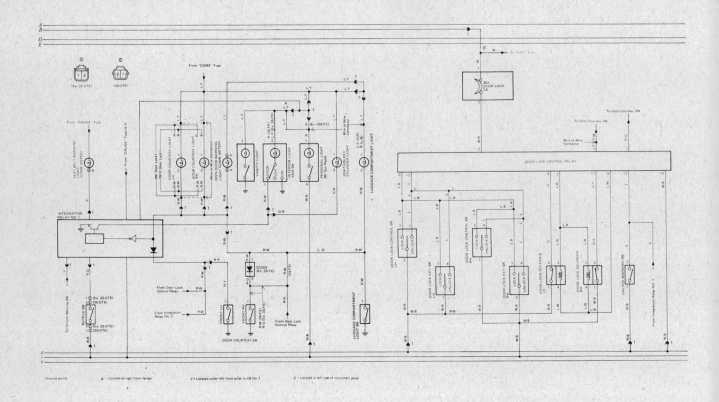

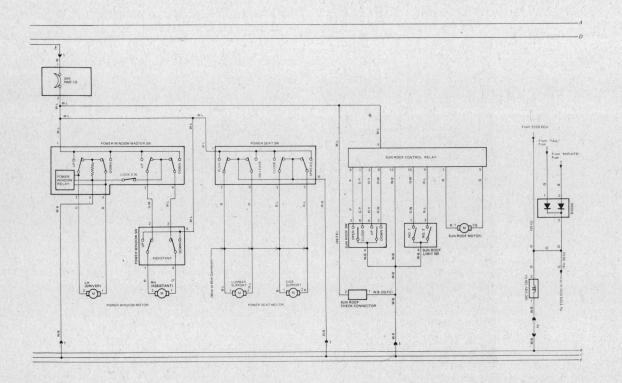

7 Typical early model unlock and seat belt warning, interior lights, door locks, power windows, power seats, sun roof and idle-up wiring diagram

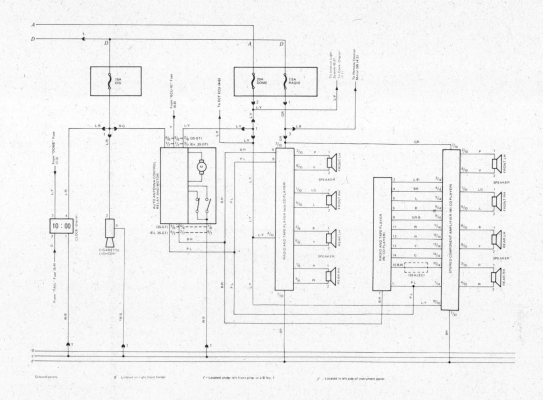

8 Typical early model clock, cigarette lighter, automatic antenna and radio and tape player wiring diagram

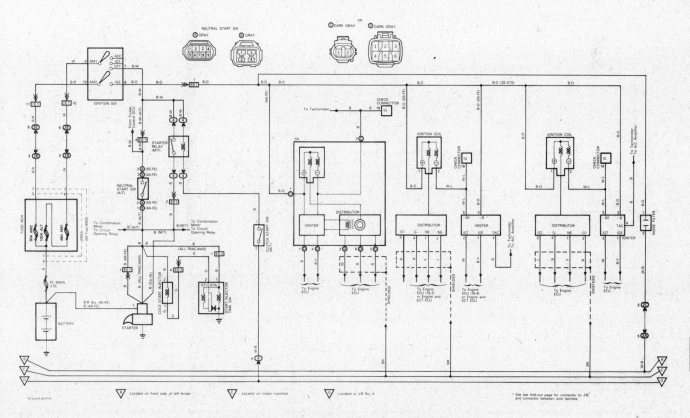

9 Typical late model starting and ignition wiring diagram

12

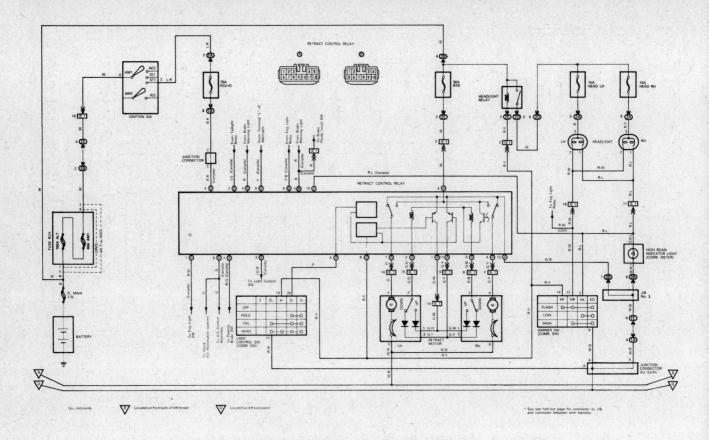

10 Typical late model headlight wiring diagram

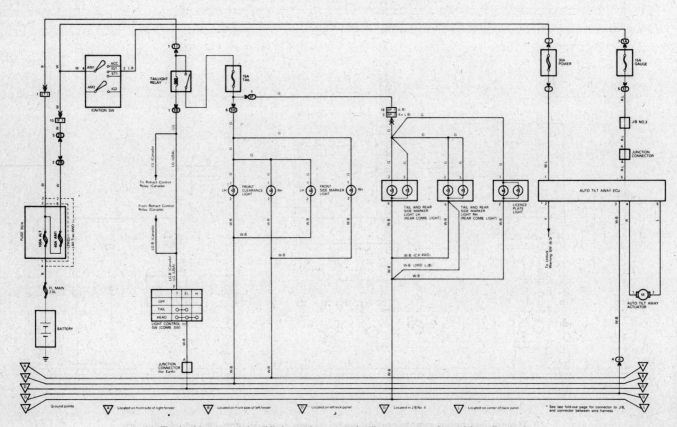

11 Typical late model tail light chand automatic tilt away steering wiring diagram

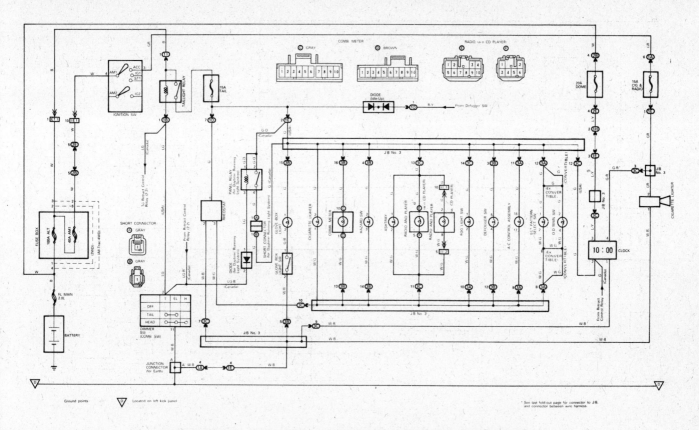

12 Typical late model illumination, clock and cigarette lighter wiring diagram

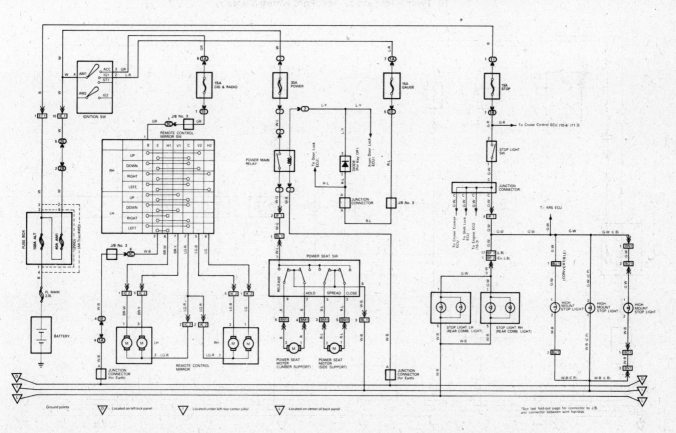

13 Typical late model remote control mirror, power seat and stop light wiring diagram

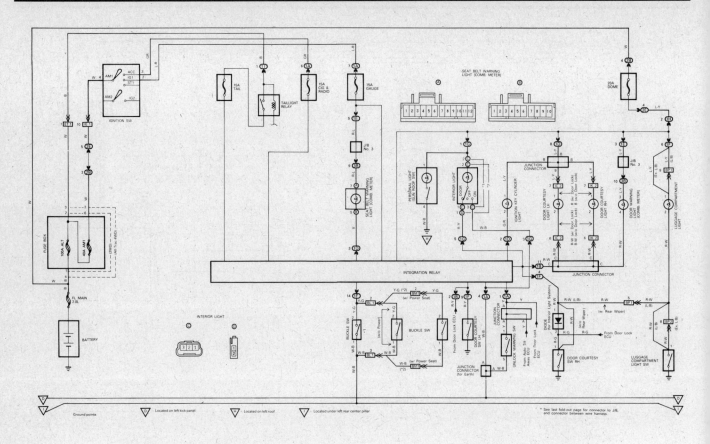

14 Typical late model light reminder, unlock and seat belt warning and interior lights wiring diagram

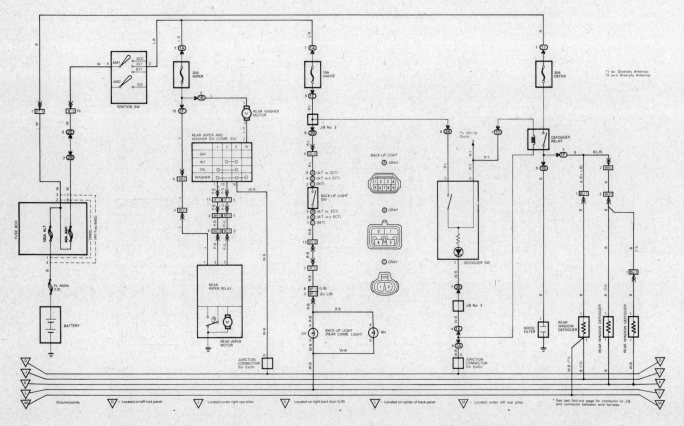

15 Typical late model rear wiper and washer, back-up light and rear window defogger wiring diagram

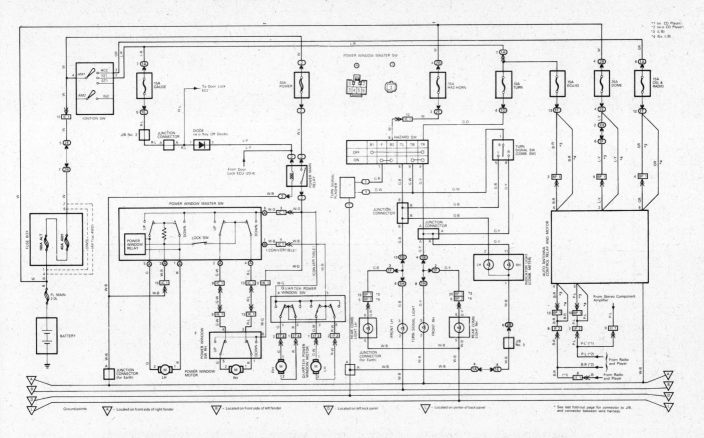

16 Typical late model power window, turn signal, hazard and automatic antenna wiring diagram

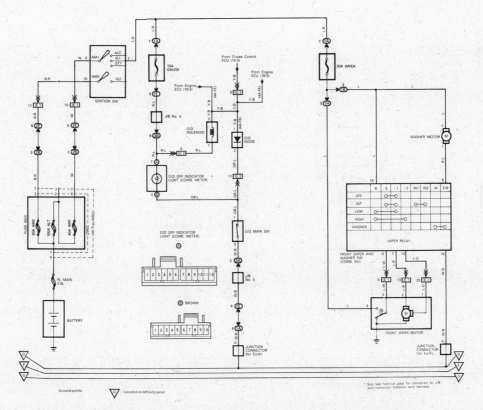

17 Typical late model overdrive, front wiper and front washer wiring diagram

12

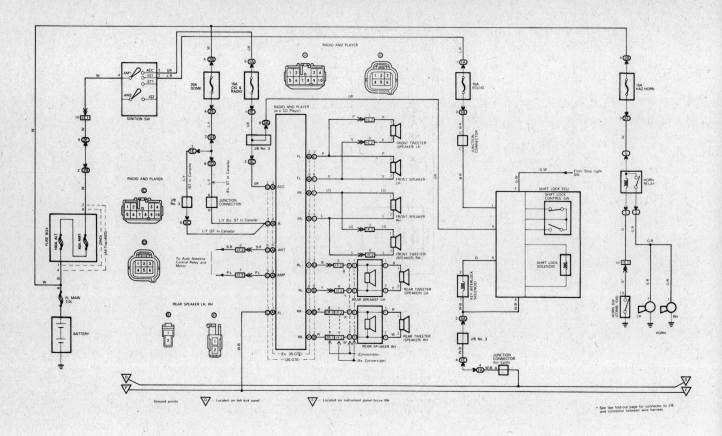

18 Typical late model radio and tape player (w/o CD player), shift lock and horn wiring diagram

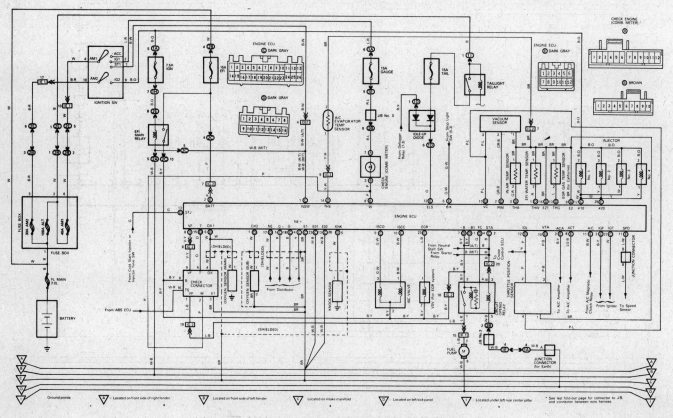

19 Typical late model engine control (5S-FE w/o ECT)

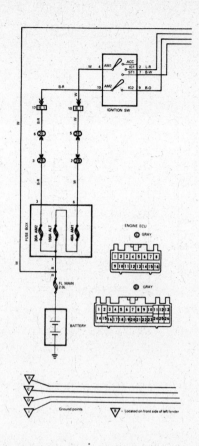

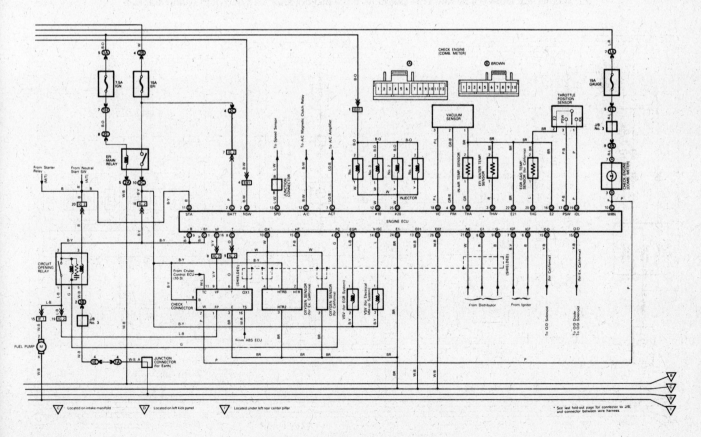

20 Typical late model engine control (4A-FE)

12

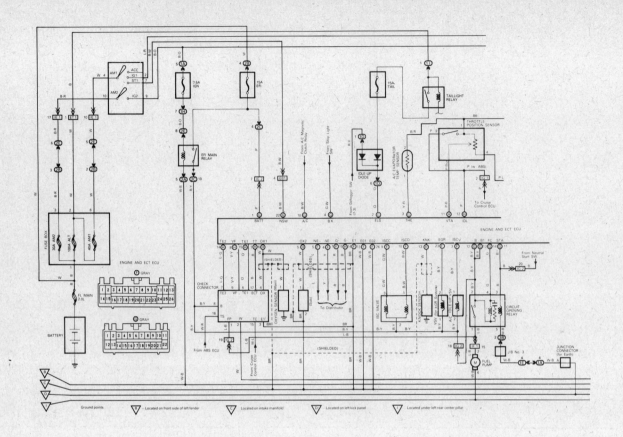

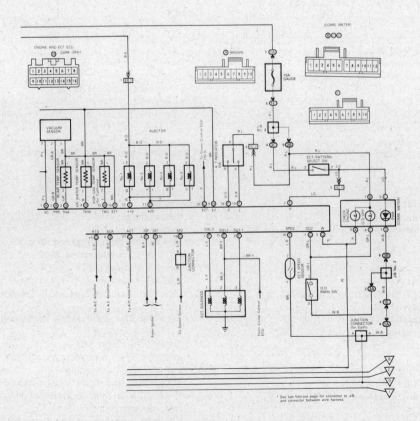

21 Typical late model engine control

Index

Haynes Automotive Manuals

NOTE: New manuals are added to this list on a periodic basis. If you do not see a listing for your vehicle, consult your local Haynes dealer for the latest product information.

ACURA
*1776 **Integra & Legend** all models '86 thru '90

AMC
     Jeep CJ - see JEEP (412)
694 **Mid-size models,** Concord, Hornet, Gremlin & Spirit '70 thru '83
934 **(Renault) Alliance & Encore** all models '83 thru '87

AUDI
615 **4000** all models '80 thru '87
428 **5000** all models '77 thru '83
1117 **5000** all models '84 thru '88

AUSTIN
     Healey Sprite - see MG Midget Roadster (265)

BMW
*2020 **3/5 Series** not including diesel or all-wheel drive models '82 thru '92
276 **320i** all 4 cyl models '75 thru '83
632 **528i & 530i** all models '75 thru '80
240 **1500 thru 2002** all models except Turbo '59 thru '77
348 **2500, 2800, 3.0 & Bavaria** all models '69 thru '76

BUICK
     Century (front wheel drive) - see GENERAL MOTORS (829)
*1627 **Buick, Oldsmobile & Pontiac Full-size (Front wheel drive)** all models '85 thru '95
     Buick Electra, LeSabre and Park Avenue; **Oldsmobile** Delta 88 Royale, Ninety Eight and Regency; **Pontiac** Bonneville
1551 **Buick Oldsmobile & Pontiac Full-size (Rear wheel drive)**
     Buick Estate '70 thru '90, Electra '70 thru '84, LeSabre '70 thru '85, Limited '74 thru '79
     Oldsmobile Custom Cruiser '70 thru '90, Delta 88 '70 thru '85, Ninety-eight '70 thru '84
     Pontiac Bonneville '70 thru '81, Catalina '70 thru '81, Grandville '70 thru '75, Parisienne '83 thru '86
627 **Mid-size Regal & Century** all rear-drive models with V6, V8 and Turbo '74 thru '87
     Regal - see GENERAL MOTORS (1671)
     Skyhawk - see GENERAL MOTORS (766)
     Skylark '80 thru '85 - see GENERAL MOTORS (38020)
     Skylark '86 on - see GENERAL MOTORS (1420)
     Somerset - see GENERAL MOTORS (1420)

CADILLAC
*751 **Cadillac Rear Wheel Drive** all gasoline models '70 thru '93
     Cimarron - see GENERAL MOTORS (766)

CHEVROLET
*1477 **Astro & GMC Safari Mini-vans** '85 thru '93
554 **Camaro V8** all models '70 thru '81
866 **Camaro** all models '82 thru '92
     Cavalier - see GENERAL MOTORS (766)
     Celebrity - see GENERAL MOTORS (829)
625 **Chevelle, Malibu & El Camino** all V6 & V8 models '69 thru '87
449 **Chevette & Pontiac T1000** '76 thru '87
550 **Citation** all models '80 thru '85
*1628 **Corsica/Beretta** all models '87 thru '95
274 **Corvette** all V8 models '68 thru '82
*1336 **Corvette** all models '84 thru '91
1762 **Chevrolet Engine Overhaul Manual**
704 **Full-size Sedans** Caprice, Impala, Biscayne, Bel Air & Wagons '69 thru '90

     Lumina - see GENERAL MOTORS (1671)
     Lumina APV - see GENERAL MOTORS (2035)
319 **Luv Pick-up** all 2WD & 4WD '72 thru '82
626 **Monte Carlo** all models '70 thru '88
241 **Nova** all V8 models '69 thru '79
*1642 **Nova and Geo Prizm** all front wheel drive models, '85 thru '92
420 **Pick-ups '67 thru '87** - Chevrolet & GMC, all V8 & in-line 6 cyl, 2WD & 4WD '67 thru '87; Suburbans, Blazers & Jimmys '67 thru '91
*1664 **Pick-ups '88 thru '95** - Chevrolet & GMC, all full-size pick-ups, '88 thru '95; Blazer & Jimmy '92 thru '94; Suburban '92 thru '95; Tahoe & Yukon '95
*831 **S-10 & GMC S-15 Pick-ups** all models '82 thru '93
*1727 **Sprint & Geo Metro** '85 thru '94
*345 **Vans - Chevrolet & GMC,** V8 & in-line 6 cylinder models '68 thru '95

CHRYSLER
2114 **Chrysler Engine Overhaul Manual**
*2058 **Full-size Front-Wheel Drive** '88 thru '93
     K-Cars - see DODGE Aries (723)
     Laser - see DODGE Daytona (1140)
*1337 **Chrysler & Plymouth Mid-size** front wheel drive '82 thru '93
     Rear-wheel Drive - see Dodge Rear-wheel Drive (2098)

DATSUN
402 **200SX** all models '77 thru '79
647 **200SX** all models '80 thru '83
228 **B - 210** all models '73 thru '78
525 **210** all models '78 thru '82
206 **240Z, 260Z & 280Z** Coupe '70 thru '78
563 **280ZX** Coupe & 2+2 '79 thru '83
     300ZX - see NISSAN (1137)
679 **310** all models '78 thru '82
123 **510 & PL521 Pick-up** '68 thru '73
430 **510** all models '78 thru '81
372 **610** all models '72 thru '76
277 **620 Series Pick-up** all models '73 thru '79
     720 Series Pick-up - see NISSAN (771)
376 **810/Maxima** all gasoline models, '77 thru '84
     Pulsar - see NISSAN (876)
     Sentra - see NISSAN (982)
     Stanza - see NISSAN (981)

DODGE
     400 & 600 - see CHRYSLER Mid-size (1337)
*723 **Aries & Plymouth Reliant** '81 thru '89
1231 **Caravan & Plymouth Voyager Mini-Vans** all models '84 thru '95
699 **Challenger & Plymouth Saporro** all models '78 thru '83
     Challenger '67-'76 - see DODGE Dart (234)
236 **Colt** all models '71 thru '77
610 **Colt & Plymouth Champ** (front wheel drive) all models '78 thru '87
*1668 **Dakota Pick-ups** all models '87 thru '93
234 **Dart, Challenger/Plymouth Barracuda & Valiant** 6 cyl models '67 thru '76
*1140 **Daytona & Chrysler Laser** '84 thru '89
*545 **Omni & Plymouth Horizon** '78 thru '90
*912 **Pick-ups** all full-size models '74 thru '91
*556 **Ram 50/D50 Pick-ups & Raider and Plymouth Arrow Pick-ups** '79 thru '93
2098 **Dodge/Plymouth/Chrysler** rear wheel drive '71 thru '89
*1726 **Shadow & Plymouth Sundance** '87 thru '93
*1779 **Spirit & Plymouth Acclaim** '89 thru '95
*349 **Vans - Dodge & Plymouth** V8 & 6 cyl models '71 thru '91

EAGLE
     Talon - see Mitsubishi Eclipse (2097)

FIAT
094 **124 Sport Coupe & Spider** '68 thru '78
273 **X1/9** all models '74 thru '80

FORD
*1476 **Aerostar Mini-vans** all models '86 thru '94
788 **Bronco and Pick-ups** '73 thru '79
880 **Bronco and Pick-ups** '80 thru '95
268 **Courier Pick-up** all models '72 thru '82
2105 **Crown Victoria & Mercury Grand Marquis** '88 thru '94
1763 **Ford Engine Overhaul Manual**
789 **Escort/Mercury Lynx** all models '81 thru '90
*2046 **Escort/Mercury Tracer** '91 thru '95
*2021 **Explorer & Mazda Navajo** '91 thru '95
560 **Fairmont & Mercury Zephyr** '78 thru '83
334 **Fiesta** all models '77 thru '80
754 **Ford & Mercury Full-size,** Ford LTD & Mercury Marquis ('75 thru '82); Ford Custom 500,Country Squire, Crown Victoria & Mercury Colony Park ('75 thru '87); Ford LTD Crown Victoria & Mercury Gran Marquis ('83 thru '87)
359 **Granada & Mercury Monarch** all in-line, 6 cyl & V8 models '75 thru '80
773 **Ford & Mercury Mid-size,** Ford Thunderbird & Mercury Cougar ('75 thru '82); Ford LTD & Mercury Marquis ('83 thru '86); Ford Torino,Gran Torino, Elite, Ranchero pick-up, LTD II, Mercury Montego, Comet, XR-7 & Lincoln Versailles ('75 thru '86)
*654 **Mustang & Mercury Capri** all models including Turbo. Mustang, '79 thru '93; Capri, '79 thru '86
357 **Mustang V8** all models '64-1/2 thru '73
231 **Mustang II** 4 cyl, V6 & V8 models '74 thru '78
649 **Pinto & Mercury Bobcat** '75 thru '80
1670 **Probe** all models '89 thru '92
*1026 **Ranger/Bronco II** gasoline models '83 thru '93
*1421 **Taurus & Mercury Sable** '86 thru '94
*1418 **Tempo & Mercury Topaz** all gasoline models '84 thru '94
1338 **Thunderbird/Mercury Cougar** '83 thru '88
*1725 **Thunderbird/Mercury Cougar** '89 and '93
344 **Vans** all V8 Econoline models '69 thru '91
*2119 **Vans** full size '92-'95

GENERAL MOTORS
*829 **Buick Century, Chevrolet Celebrity, Oldsmobile Cutlass Ciera & Pontiac 6000** all models '82 thru '93
*1671 **Buick Regal, Chevrolet Lumina, Oldsmobile Cutlass Supreme & Pontiac Grand Prix** all front wheel drive models '88 thru '95
*766 **Buick Skyhawk, Cadillac Cimarron, Chevrolet Cavalier, Oldsmobile Firenza & Pontiac J-2000 & Sunbird** all models '82 thru '94
38020 **Buick Skylark, Chevrolet Citation, Olds Omega, Pontiac Phoenix** '80 thru '85
1420 **Buick Skylark & Somerset, Oldsmobile Achieva & Calais and Pontiac Grand Am** all models '85 thru '95
*2035 **Chevrolet Lumina APV, Oldsmobile Silhouette & Pontiac Trans Sport** all models '90 thru '94
     General Motors Full-size Rear-wheel Drive - see BUICK (1551)

GEO
     Metro - see CHEVROLET Sprint (1727)
     Prizm - see CHEVROLET Nova (1642)
*2039 **Storm** all models '90 thru '93
     Tracker - see SUZUKI Samurai (1626)

GMC
     Safari - see CHEVROLET ASTRO (1477)
     Vans & Pick-ups - see CHEVROLET (420, 831, 345, 1664)

(Continued on other side)

---

* Listings shown with an asterisk (*) indicate model coverage as of this printing. These titles will be periodically updated to include later model years - consult your Haynes dealer for more information.

Haynes North America, Inc., 861 Lawrence Drive, Newbury Park, CA 91320 • (805) 498-6703

Haynes Automotive Manuals (continued)

NOTE: New manuals are added to this list on a periodic basis. If you do not see a listing for your vehicle, consult your local Haynes dealer for the latest product information.

HONDA
351	**Accord CVCC** all models '76 thru '83
1221	**Accord** all models '84 thru '89
2067	**Accord** all models '90 thru '93
42013	**Accord** all models '94 thru '95
160	**Civic 1200** all models '73 thru '79
633	**Civic 1300 & 1500 CVCC** '80 thru '83
297	**Civic 1500 CVCC** all models '75 thru '79
1227	**Civic** all models '84 thru '91
*2118	**Civic & del Sol** '92 thru '95
*601	**Prelude CVCC** all models '79 thru '89

HYUNDAI
*1552	**Excel** all models '86 thru '94

ISUZU
*1641	**Trooper & Pick-up**, all gasoline models Pick-up, '81 thru '93; Trooper, '84 thru '91

JAGUAR
*242	**XJ6** all 6 cyl models '68 thru '86
*478	**XJ12 & XJS** all 12 cyl models '72 thru '85

JEEP
*1553	**Cherokee, Comanche & Wagoneer Limited** all models '84 thru '93
412	**CJ** all models '49 thru '86
50025	**Grand Cherokee** all models '93 thru '95
*1777	**Wrangler** all models '87 thru '94

LINCOLN
2117	**Rear Wheel Drive** all models '70 thru '95

MAZDA
648	**626** Sedan & Coupe (rear wheel drive) all models '79 thru '82
*1082	**626 & MX-6** (front wheel drive) all models '83 thru '91
267	**B Series Pick-ups** '72 thru '93
370	**GLC Hatchback** (rear wheel drive) all models '77 thru '83
757	**GLC** (front wheel drive) '81 thru '85
*2047	**MPV** all models '89 thru '94
	Navajo-see Ford Explorer (2021)
460	**RX-7** all models '79 thru '85
*1419	**RX-7** all models '86 thru '91

MERCEDES-BENZ
*1643	**190 Series** all four-cylinder gasoline models, '84 thru '88
346	**230, 250 & 280** Sedan, Coupe & Roadster all 6 cyl sohc models '68 thru '72
983	**280 123 Series** gasoline models '77 thru '81
698	**350 & 450** Sedan, Coupe & Roadster all models '71 thru '80
697	**Diesel 123 Series** 200D, 220D, 240D, 240TD, 300D, 300CD, 300TD, 4- & 5-cyl incl. Turbo '76 thru '85

MERCURY
See FORD Listing

MG
111	**MGB** Roadster & GT Coupe all models '62 thru '80
265	**MG Midget & Austin Healey Sprite** Roadster '58 thru '80

MITSUBISHI
*1669	**Cordia, Tredia, Galant, Precis & Mirage** '83 thru '93
*2097	**Eclipse, Eagle Talon & Plymouth Laser** '90 thru '94
*2022	**Pick-up & Montero** '83 thru '95

NISSAN
1137	**300ZX** all models including Turbo '84 thru '89
*1341	**Maxima** all models '85 thru '91
*771	**Pick-ups/Pathfinder** gas models '80 thru '95
876	**Pulsar** all models '83 thru '86

*982	**Sentra** all models '82 thru '94
*981	**Stanza** all models '82 thru '90

OLDSMOBILE
	Bravada - see CHEVROLET S-10 (831)
	Calais - see GENERAL MOTORS (1420)
	Custom Cruiser - see BUICK Full-size RWD (1551)
*658	**Cutlass** all standard gasoline V6 & V8 models '74 thru '88
	Cutlass Ciera - see GENERAL MOTORS (829)
	Cutlass Supreme - see GM (1671)
	Delta 88 - see BUICK Full-size RWD (1551)
	Delta 88 Brougham - see BUICK Full-size FWD (1551), RWD (1627)
	Delta 88 Royale - see BUICK Full-size RWD (1551)
	Firenza - see GENERAL MOTORS (766)
	Ninety-eight Regency - see BUICK Full-size RWD (1551), FWD (1627)
	Ninety-eight Regency Brougham - see BUICK Full-size RWD (1551)
	Omega - see GENERAL MOTORS (38020)
	Silhouette - see GENERAL MOTORS (2035)

PEUGEOT
663	**504** all diesel models '74 thru '83

PLYMOUTH
Laser - see MITSUBISHI Eclipse (2097)
For other PLYMOUTH titles, see DODGE listing.

PONTIAC
	T1000 - see CHEVROLET Chevette (449)
	J-2000 - see GENERAL MOTORS (766)
	6000 - see GENERAL MOTORS (829)
	Bonneville - see Buick Full-size FWD (1627), RWD (1551)
	Bonneville Brougham - see Buick (1551)
	Catalina - see Buick Full-size (1551)
1232	**Fiero** all models '84 thru '88
555	**Firebird** V8 models except Turbo '70 thru '81
867	**Firebird** all models '82 thru '92
	Full-size Front Wheel Drive - see BUICK Oldsmobile, Pontiac Full-size FWD (1627)
	Full-size Rear Wheel Drive - see BUICK Oldsmobile, Pontiac Full-size RWD (1551)
	Grand Am - see GENERAL MOTORS (1420)
	Grand Prix - see GENERAL MOTORS (1671)
	Grandville - see BUICK Full-size (1551)
	Parisienne - see BUICK Full-size (1551)
	Phoenix - see GENERAL MOTORS (38020)
	Sunbird - see GENERAL MOTORS (766)
	Trans Sport - see GENERAL MOTORS (2035)

PORSCHE
*264	**911** all Coupe & Targa models except Turbo & Carrera 4 '65 thru '89
239	**914** all 4 cyl models '69 thru '76
397	**924** all models including Turbo '76 thru '82
*1027	**944** all models including Turbo '83 thru '89

RENAULT
141	**5 Le Car** all models '76 thru '83
	Alliance & Encore - see AMC (934)

SAAB
247	**99** all models including Turbo '69 thru '80
*980	**900** all models including Turbo '79 thru '88

SATURN
2083	**Saturn** all models '91 thru '94

SUBARU
237	**1100, 1300, 1400 & 1600** '71 thru '79
*681	**1600 & 1800** 2WD & 4WD '80 thru '89

SUZUKI
*1626	**Samurai/Sidekick and Geo Tracker** all models '86 thru '95

TOYOTA
1023	**Camry** all models '83 thru '91
92006	**Camry** all models '92 thru '95
935	**Celica Rear Wheel Drive** '71 thru '85
*2038	**Celica Front Wheel Drive** '86 thru '92
1139	**Celica Supra** all models '79 thru '92
361	**Corolla** all models '75 thru '79
961	**Corolla** all rear wheel drive models '80 thru '87
*1025	**Corolla** all front wheel drive models '84 thru '92
636	**Corolla Tercel** all models '80 thru '82
360	**Corona** all models '74 thru '82
532	**Cressida** all models '78 thru '82
313	**Land Cruiser** all models '68 thru '82
*1339	**MR2** all models '85 thru '87
304	**Pick-up** all models '69 thru '78
*656	**Pick-up** all models '79 thru '95
*2048	**Previa** all models '91 thru '93
2106	**Tercel** all models '87 thru '94

TRIUMPH
113	**Spitfire** all models '62 thru '81
322	**TR7** all models '75 thru '81

VW
159	**Beetle & Karmann Ghia** all models '54 thru '79
238	**Dasher** all gasoline models '74 thru '81
*884	**Rabbit, Jetta, Scirocco, & Pick-up** gas models '74 thru '91 & Convertible '80 thru '92
451	**Rabbit, Jetta & Pick-up** all diesel models '77 thru '84
082	**Transporter 1600** all models '68 thru '79
226	**Transporter 1700, 1800 & 2000** all models '72 thru '79
084	**Type 3 1500 & 1600** all models '63 thru '73
1029	**Vanagon** all air-cooled models '80 thru '83

VOLVO
203	**120, 130 Series & 1800 Sports** '61 thru '73
129	**140 Series** all models '66 thru '74
*270	**240 Series** all models '76 thru '93
400	**260 Series** all models '75 thru '82
*1550	**740 & 760 Series** all models '82 thru '88

TECHBOOK MANUALS
2108	**Automotive Computer Codes**
1667	**Automotive Emissions Control Manual**
482	**Fuel Injection Manual, 1978 thru 1985**
2111	**Fuel Injection Manual, 1986 thru 1994**
2069	**Holley Carburetor Manual**
2068	**Rochester Carburetor Manual**
10240	**Weber/Zenith/Stromberg/SU Carburetors**
1762	**Chevrolet Engine Overhaul Manual**
2114	**Chrysler Engine Overhaul Manual**
1763	**Ford Engine Overhaul Manual**
1736	**GM and Ford Diesel Engine Repair Manual**
1666	**Small Engine Repair Manual**
10355	**Ford Automatic Transmission Overhaul**
10360	**GM Automatic Transmission Overhaul**
1479	**Automotive Body Repair & Painting**
2112	**Automotive Brake Manual**
2113	**Automotive Detaiing Manual**
1654	**Automotive Eelectrical Manual**
1480	**Automotive Heating & Air Conditioning**
2109	**Automotive Reference Manual & Illustrated Dictionary**
2107	**Automotive Tools Manual**
10440	**Used Car Buying Guide**
2110	**Welding Manual**

SPANISH MANUALS
98905	**Códigos Automotrices de la Computadora**
98915	**Inyección de Combustible 1986 al 1994**
99040	**Chevrolet & GMC Camionetas** '67 al '87 Incluye Suburban, Blazer & Jimmy '67 al '91
99041	**Chevrolet & GMC Camionetas** '88 al '95 Incluye Suburban '92 al '95, Blazer & Jimmy '92 al '94, Tahoe y Yukon '95
99075	**Ford Camionetas y Bronco** '80 al '94
99125	**Toyota Camionetas y 4-Runner** '79 al '95

---

* Listings shown with an asterisk (*) indicate model coverage as of this printing. These titles will be periodically updated to include later model years - consult your Haynes dealer for more information.

Over 100 Haynes motorcycle manuals also available

2-96

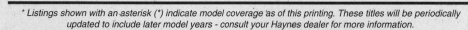

Haynes North America, Inc., 861 Lawrence Drive, Newbury Park, CA 91320 • (805) 498-6703